W9-CEA-572

consumer behaviour

leon g. schiffman
St. John's University

leslie lazar kanuk
City University of New York

mallika das
Mount Saint Vincent University

canadian edition

PEARSON

Prentice
Hall

Toronto

Library and Archives Canada Cataloguing in Publication

Schiffman, Leon G.
    Consumer behaviour / Leon G. Schiffman, Leslie Lazar Kanuk, Mallika Das.—Canadian ed.

Includes bibliographical references and indexes.
ISBN 0-13-146304-7

1. Consumer behaviour—Textbooks. 2. Motivation research (Marketing)—Textbooks. I. Kanuk, Leslie Lazar
II. Das, Mallika, 1950– III. Title.

HF5415.32.S35 2006   658.8'342   C2004-905739-1

Copyright © 2006 Pearson Education Canada Inc., Toronto, Ontario. Original U.S. edition published by Pearson-Prentice Hall Inc., a division of Pearson Education, Upper Saddle River, New Jersey. Copyright © 2004. This edition is authorized for sale only in Canada.

Pearson Prentice Hall. All rights reserved. This publication is protected by copyright, and permission should be obtained from the publisher prior to any prohibited reproduction, storage in a retrieval system, or transmission in any form or by any means, electronic, mechanical, photocopying, recording, or likewise. For information regarding permission, write to the Permissions Department.

For permission to reproduce copyrighted material, the publisher gratefully acknowledges the copyright holders listed on this page and in the sources and credits throughout the text, which are considered an extension of this copyright page.

0-13-146304-7

Vice President, Editorial Director: Michael J. Young
Acquisitions Editor: Laura Forbes
Director of Marketing, Business and Economics: Bill Todd
Developmental Editor: Pamela Voves
Production Editor: Jennifer Handel
Copy Editor: Freya Godard
Proofreader: Dawn Hunter
Production Coordinator: Deborah Starks
Manufacturing Coordinator: Susan Johnson
Page Layout: Carolyn E. Sebestyen
Permissions and Photo Research: Alene McNeil, Karen Taylor, Barb Welling
Art Director: Julia Hall
Interior and Cover Design: The Brookview Group/Gillian Tsintziras
Cover Image: Veer

Statistics Canada information is used with the permission of the Minister of Industry, as Minister responsible for Statistics Canada. Information on the availability of the wide range of data from Statistics Canada can be obtained from Statistics Canada's Regional Offices, its World Wide Web site at http://www.statcan.ca, and its toll-free access number 1-800-263-1136. The Statistics Canada CANSIM II database can be accessed at http://cansim2.statcan.ca/cgi-win/CNSMCGI.EXE.

Chapter-opening photo credits: p. 2: Courtesy of Royal Roads University & Trapeze Communications Inc.; p. 26: Courtesy of Melon. Photo by John Sherlock; p. 70: Courtesy of Acura/Honda Canada Inc.; p. 102: Courtesy of Garnier Fructis; p.142: Courtesy of The Home Depot; p. 180: Courtesy of Ocean Spray International; p. 212: Courtesy of Unilever; p. 242: Courtesy of HSBC Bank Canada. Photography by Richard Pullar; p. 280: © DaimlerChrysler Corporation; p. 312: Courtesy of The New Canadian; p. 342: Acura/Honda Canada Inc.; p. 368: Used with the permission of the David Suzuki Foundation. Design by Alaris Design; p. 410: Courtesy of Colgate Palmolove; p. 456: Courtesy of Pfizer Canada Inc., Pfizer Consumer Healthcare Division: All Rights Reserved; p. 492: Courtesy of Sears Canada.

4 5   10 09

Printed and bound in the United States of America.

To Elaine, Janet, and David Schiffman; Dana and Bradley; Eileen and Alan, Melissa and Rob; and Allison, Noah, and Reid

—L.G.S.

To Jack, Jaqui, and Alan Kanuk; Randi and Van Dauler; and Max and Sarah

—L.L.K.

To my parents, Malathi and Krishna Das, and my husband, Hari, for their love, support, and encouragement

—M.D.

brief contents

contents

INTERNET INSIGHT 8-1 ASSESSING THE EFFECTIVENESS OF WEB-BASED COMMUNICATIONS   271

preface

Welcome to the first Canadian edition of *Consumer Behaviour*. This Canadian edition retains the strengths of the highly popular Schiffman and Kanuk text and builds on them. The Schiffman and Kanuk text has always been known for its strong focus on theory and readability, as well as its emphasis on the marketing strategy implications of consumer behaviour concepts. These aspects have been retained in the first Canadian edition, while every attempt has been made to make it suitable to its Canadian audience.

Practising what is preached in this text, I started out using the key informant method (see Chapter 2) to find out what consumers wanted to see in the first Canadian edition. Instructors who taught consumer behaviour (key informants) using the Schiffman and Kanuk text and its main competitors were polled to find out what they and their students were looking for in a Canadian consumer behaviour text. The following were the main requests:

- Canadian examples and lots of them
- a focus on the unique characteristics of Canadian society in the context of consumer behaviour
- a greater focus on the application of consumer behaviour concepts to marketing strategy
- longer end-of-part cases that relate to more than one chapter, along with short end-of-chapter cases that could be used to illustrate key concepts in each chapter
- more emphasis on consumer decision making
- a strong focus on the impact of the internet on consumer behaviour
- an easy-to-read format

I have attempted to meet all these requests while retaining the structure and strengths of the U.S. edition, which has led to the unique features of this text, discussed below.

UNIQUE FEATURES OF THE CANADIAN EDITION

Canadian examples (local and national in scope) are provided to illustrate key concepts. From Canadian subsidiaries of multinational firms such as Campbell's to small, regional firms like Sabian (which manufactures cymbals), these examples illustrate how several Canadian firms have applied consumer behaviour concepts.

Canadian data on culture, subcultures, and other variables have been added. For example, the chapters on culture and subcultures have been rewritten to highlight Canadian dimensions. There is a section on French Canadians and on some of the other racio-ethnic subcultures that are important parts of the Canadian mosaic. The section on secondary data sources (Chapter 2) now lists the various Canadian sources of secondary information.

A section on marketing strategy implications is incorporated into each and every chapter so that readers can see the relevance of the theoretical concepts covered in the text. The emphasis here is on highlighting how a marketing manager can use the concepts to develop better marketing strategies.

Greater emphasis on the consumer decision-making process has been provided by having two chapters on this topic (rather than the single one in the U.S. edition). Chapter 14 looks at the "process" part of consumer decision making (problem recognition, information search, alternative evaluation, and decision), while Chapter 15 looks at the "outcomes" of this process (purchase and post-purchase evaluation). Although the chapters on decision making appear at the end of the text, the introduction of the model and its key elements in Chapter 1 will give students a framework for studying consumer behaviour and will allow instructors who want to cover consumer decision making earlier to do so.

Internet Insight boxes have been included in each chapter to reflect the increasing impact of the internet on consumer behaviour. Canada is probably the most wired nation in the world, and more than half of all Canadians use the internet on a regular basis. This has influenced the way that they behave as consumers; more and more purchases are being made online, and even those who do not purchase online still use the internet to search for information and comparison-shop. The Internet Insights included in each chapter deal with this new reality; these, and the end-of-chapter **Internet Exercises** help students understand the key role played by the internet in influencing consumer behaviour.

Research Insight boxes have been incorporated into each chapter to provide students with increased understanding of how key consumer behaviour concepts can be researched. This, in combination with the early placement of a chapter on consumer research (Chapter 2), reflects the emphasis placed on consumer research in this text.

End-of-Part Cases have been included in a Case Appendix at the back of the book to provide students with the opportunity to test their understanding of consumer behaviour concepts. These cases are new and entirely Canadian in nature; the questions at the end of each case guide students to think about how they can use the concepts covered in each part while formulating solutions for the problems faced by real-life organizations.

Critical Thinking Questions have been added to each chapter to ensure that students think about the concepts in more depth and learn to apply them to real-life situations.

A simplified layout with clear subtitles, presentation of key information in figures, bulleted lists to emphasize key points, and a simpler presentation of theoretical material should make it easier for students to read and understand the material presented in the text. For example, each chapter begins with a "What is...?" question and goes on to more details on the concept.

The addition of these features makes this a truly Canadian text that meets the needs of its Canadian users without losing any of the strengths of the original and highly successful text by Schiffman and Kanuk.

PLAN OF THIS BOOK

As mentioned earlier, this first Canadian edition maintains the basic structure and format of the U.S. edition of *Consumer Behavior* by Schiffman and Kanuk. The 15 chapters in this text are divided into four parts.

Part 1 consists of two chapters and an appendix, which provide the necessary background for a study of consumer behaviour. Chapter 1, "Introduction to Consumer Behaviour," introduces the reader to the field of consumer behaviour, its development, and the impact of the internet on consumer behaviour. It also introduces the simple model of consumer behaviour used in this text and briefly discusses each part of the model. Chapter 2, "Consumer Research," covers the basic research tools used to study consumer behaviour. The Appendix to Part 1, "Consumer Behaviour and Marketing Strategy," discusses the basic elements of marketing strategy. This topic was moved from Chapter 1 to the Appendix to Part 1 as (1) many reviewers indicated that the concepts covered in it (segmentation, targeting, positioning, and marketing mix variables) would have been covered in an earlier introductory marketing course and, therefore, such an elaborate discussion on marketing strategy was not required; (2) taking this material out of Chapter 1 and placing it in an appendix increased the readability of Chapter 1; and (3) this move also made it possible to cover the model of consumer behaviour in more detail in Chapter 1. Instructors interested in covering this topic in more detail can still do so at the beginning of the term.

Part 2 covers the internal or psychological aspects of consumer behaviour. It begins with a discussion on motivation and involvement (Chapter 3, "Motivation and Involvement") and explores the rational and emotional bases of consumer actions. Chapter 4, "Personality, Self-Image, and Life Style," discusses the impact of personality on consumer behaviour and covers consumer materialism, compulsive consumption behaviour, and fixated behaviour. This chapter also looks at how consumer self-image and life style affect consumer behaviour. Chapter 5, "Consumer Perception," consists of a detailed examination of consumer perception and how it affects consumer behaviour. The topics of product positioning and repositioning are revisited here from the viewpoint of consumer perception. Chapter 6, "Consumer Learning," discusses behavioural and cognitive learning theories; it also deals with consumer information processing. Chapter 7, "Consumer Attitude Formation and Change," deals with consumer attitudes; it discusses how attitudes are formed, their functions, and how they can be changed. Several theories of attitude formation and change are covered in this chapter. Chapter 8, "Communication and Consumer Behaviour," covers the importance of communication, which is the bridge between individuals and the world around them. Instead of covering these issues under different chapters, this chapter brings together various aspects of marketing communication such as media, message strategies, and source credibility under one heading and thus makes it easier for the reader to understand the full impact of communication strategies on consumer behaviour.

Part 3 deals with external (or socio-cultural) influences on consumer behaviour. It starts with culture and its effect on consumer behaviour in Chapter 9, "The Influence of Culture on Consumer Behaviour." This chapter looks at Canadian cultural values and the differences between Canadians and their neighbours to the south in terms of cultural values. Chapter 10, "Subcultures and Consumer Behaviour," covers subcultural influences; this chapter deals with French-Canadian culture, other racio-ethnic subcultures, and other types of subcultures (e.g., age-based, regional, and gender-based). Chapter 11, "Social Class and Consumer Behaviour," deals with social class and discusses its impact on consumer behaviour; Chapter 12, "Reference Groups and Family," covers the impact of reference groups and family on consumer behaviour. The section ends with a look at the diffusion of innovations and examines the impact of personal influence and opinion leadership on an individual's consumption patterns (Chapter 13, "Consumer Influence and the Diffusion of Innovations").

Part 4 revisits the consumer decision-making process and examines it in more detail. In keeping with the increased focus on decision making in this Canadian edition of the text, decision making is covered in two chapters, rather than in just one. Chapter 14, "Consumer Decision Making I: The Process—Problem Recognition, Information Search, and Alternative Evaluation," looks at the "process" part of consumer decision making and examines the steps of problem recognition, information search, alternative evaluation, and choice in depth. Chapter 15, "Consumer Decision Making II: The Outcomes—Purchase, Post-purchase," covers the "outcomes" of these processes—consumer purchase and post-purchase behaviours.

The decision to leave consumer decision making to the end of the text was not an easy one. The majority of the reviewers felt that students would be in a better position to understand and apply the difficult concepts in this part after they have covered the internal and external influences on consumer behaviour. This led to the decision to cover consumer decision making at the end of the text. However, the modular format used in this text and the introduction of the model in Chapter 1 (along with a brief discussion on decision making) makes it possible for instructors to modify the sequencing of coverage and deal with consumer decision making earlier if they want to do so.

To summarize, the basic structure of the U.S. edition of Schiffman and Kanuk has been maintained with two major exceptions: marketing strategy is covered in an appendix (rather than in Chapter 1), and the coverage of consumer decision making has been expanded significantly (from one chapter to two).

PEDAGOGICAL FEATURES

Once again, the focus of this Canadian edition has been on maintaining the key pedagogical features of the original U.S. version and adding to it according to the feedback received from reviewers. The key pedagogical features of this edition are as follows:

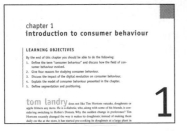

Chapter Overview
Each chapter opens with a brief overview of the chapter, which provides the student with an idea of what is covered in the chapter.

Learning Objectives
A list of learning objectives highlighting the key concepts covered in the chapter is provided at the beginning of each chapter.

Advertisements
Ads that illustrate key concepts are included to enhance students' understanding of these concepts.

Figures
Each chapter contains figures that provide insights into the topics covered in it. Summaries of theories and concepts are also provided as needed to make it easier for students to learn the material.

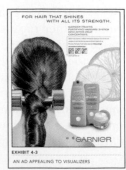

EXHIBIT 4-3

AN AD APPEALING TO VISUALIZERS

Research Insights

Every chapter has a Research Insight box that provides additional information on one key concept or measurement issue covered in the chapter.

Internet Insights

Each chapter also has an Internet Insight box that focuses on how a concept can be used while marketing online.

Chapter Review

All key points in each chapter are provided in an easy-to-read, bulleted format at the end of the chapter.

Key Terms

To highlight the key concepts that students have to understand, a list of key terms is provided in each chapter. The definitions of these are provided as marginalia within the chapters and reproduced in the glossary.

Discussion Questions

Questions that take the students through the main concepts covered in each chapter are provided at the end of each chapter.

Critical Thinking Questions

These questions (provided at the end of each chapter) are designed to make students think in more depth about the key concepts dealt with in the text; they also lead students to apply the concepts that they have learned.

Internet Exercises

As part of the increased focus on the impact of the internet on marketing, each chapter provides at least three questions that will enable students to examine how the internet has affected marketing.

Appendix to Part 1

Although most students enrol for a course on consumer behaviour after taking at least one introductory course on marketing, a review of the basics of marketing strategy is provided in the Appendix to Part 1, which follows Chapter 2. This can serve as a refresher for students who took their introductory marketing course a few years ago.

INSTRUCTOR RESOURCES

The following resources are available to aid instructors:

Instructor's Resource CD-ROM

Instructor's Resource Manual

The Instructor's Resource Manual provides answers to Discussion and Critical Thinking Questions, suggestions for teaching key concepts covered in each chapter, teaching notes for the cases in the Case Appendix in the text, and video cases and video guide for the *Consumer Behaviour* Video Library. The Instructor's Resource Manual also provides Self-Training and Reinforcement (S.T.A.R) projects. These are divided into three types: ethical issues, small group projects, and additional internet exercises. These are classroom-tested projects that students can have fun with and that instructors can assign as class projects.

Pearson TestGen

This special computerized test item file enables instructors to view and edit the existing questions, add questions, generate tests, and print the tests in a variety of formats. Powerful search and sort functions make it easy to locate questions and arrange them in any order desired. TestGen also enables instructors to administer tests on a local area network, have the tests graded electronically, and have the results prepared in electronic or printed reports. The Pearson TestGen is compatible with IBM or Macintosh systems.

PowerPoint Slides

The PowerPoint slides, which provide key points covered in each chapter, are included to aid instructors in the presentation of text material.

Image Gallery

Selected four-colour ads published in the text are available for viewing in the Image Gallery included on this CD.

Consumer Behaviour Video Library

Videos developed specifically for the U.S. edition are available in VHS format and can also be accessed through the Companion Website. Although the cases are based on American companies, they are firms that most Canadians are familiar with and the cases should be of interest to students. Accompanying video cases and a video guide are provided in the Instructor's Resource Manual.

Companion Website

A Companion Website at **www.pearsoned.ca/schiffman** provides an online study guide and additional learning aids for students. The Instructor's Resource Manual is also available for downloading in a protected area for instructors.

ACKNOWLEDGMENTS

I would like to thank the following people for the help and assistance that they provided me with during the writing of this text. To begin with, I would like to thank Kelly Torrance, Senior Acquisitions Editor, for her faith in my ability to Canadianize the highly successful Schiffman and Kanuk text on consumer behaviour. Special thanks are also due to two people: Pamela Voves, the Developmental Editor for this project, and Jennifer Handel, the Production Editor. Their prompt feedback and constant support were invaluable, and their gentle nudging kept me on track—thank you Pam and Jen! Other members of the Pearson Education Canada team—especially Freya Godard, Copy Editor; Dawn Hunter, Proofreader; Lu Cormier, Cold Reader; and Deborah Starks, Production Coordinator—also helped in the production phase of this text.

Many people were involved in reviewing this text. Their comments helped me restructure several parts of this text, and I feel that the text is much stronger thanks to their input. Several of the reviews were done over the Christmas break and during April, the busiest months of the year for those in academia. I would like to thank the following reviewers for so generously giving their time and providing me with thoughtful comments:

Harj Dhaliwal, Kwantlen Univeristy College
A. Jane Dunnett, University of New Brunswick
Webb Dussome, University of Alberta
Jordan L. Le Bel, John Molson School of Business

David MacLeod, NBCC Moncton
Kalyani Menon, Wilfrid Laurier University
Sanjay Putrevu, Brock University
Jim Sherritt, University of Northern British Columbia
Jim Swaffield, University of Alberta

 I would also like to thank my husband, Hari; but for his encouragement, I would not have taken on this task. He and our daughter, Nitya, made me feel that I could handle this challenge. For that, I am grateful.

—Mallika Das

A Great Way to Learn and Instruct Online

The Pearson Education Canada Companion Website is easy to navigate and is organized to correspond to the chapters in this textbook. Whether you are a student in the classroom or a distance learner you will discover helpful resources for in-depth study and research that empower you in your quest for greater knowledge and maximize your potential for success in the course.

Companion
Website

[www.pearsoned.ca/schiffman]

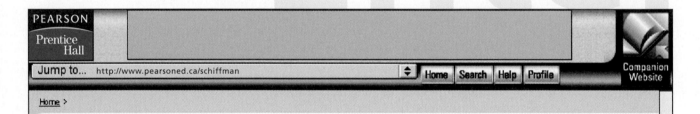

PEARSON
Prentice
Hall

Jump to...   http://www.pearsoned.ca/schiffman   ⬍   Home Search Help Profile

Companion
Website

Home >

PH Companion Website

Consumer Behaviour, Canadian Edition, by Schiffman, Kanuk, and Das

Student Resources

The modules in this section provide students with tools for learning course material. These modules include:

- Chapter Overview
- Destinations
- Quizzes
- Internet Exercises
- PowerPoint Presentations
- Glossary
- *Consumer Behaviour* Video Library

In the quiz modules students can send answers to the grader and receive instant feedback on their progress through the Results Reporter. Coaching comments and references to the textbook may be available to ensure that students take advantage of all available resources to enhance their learning experience.

Instructor Resources

A link to this book on the Pearson online catalogue (www.pearsoned.ca) provides instructors with additional teaching tools. Downloadable PowerPoint Presentations and an Instructor's Resource Manual are just some of the materials that may be available. The catalogue is password protected. To get a password, simply contact your Pearson Education Canada Representative or call Faculty Sales and Services at 1-800-850-5813.

part one
introduction to consumer behaviour

Part 1 provides the background and the tools for a strong and comprehensive understanding of consumer behaviour.

Chapter 1 introduces the reader to the study of consumer behaviour, its diversity, and its development, and to the importance of consumer research. It introduces a simple model of consumer decision making and demonstrates how consumer-behaviour variables provide both a conceptual framework and a strategic direction to marketers. Chapter 2 examines the role of consumer research in understanding consumer behaviour and discusses qualitative and quantitative research techniques used to study consumer behaviour. Appendix 2A provides an overview of the fundamentals of marketing strategy; for students who have completed a course in basic marketing, this can serve as a refresher.

1

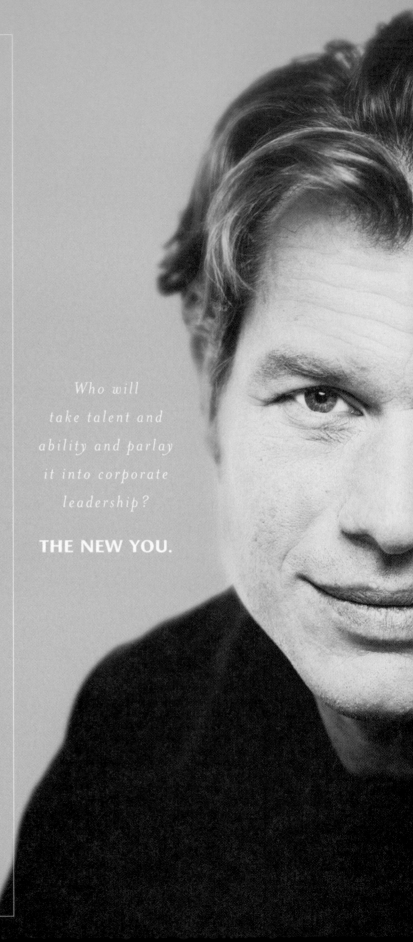

Getting an MBA can change your life. From taking up the challenges you feel most passionate about, to leading change within an organization — you with an MBA may just be a whole new you.

Royal Roads University offers one of the most innovative and comprehensive MBA programs in Canada, with unique specializations in growth careers. We help you get there by offering a combination of internet learning and short residencies, making your commitment to further education manageable.

MBA Programs in:

> **Executive Management**
> **Public Relations**
> **Digital Technologies**
> **Human Resources**
> **Leadership**
> **Educational Administration**
> **Global Aviation Management**
> **Management Consulting**

Royal Roads University is located in Victoria, British Columbia. Visit us on our web site at **www.royalroads.ca** for more information or call us at **1-877-775-7272**.

Royal Roads University specializes in post-secondary education for working professionals. Our programs are designed to prepare you for tomorrow's careers and the challenges that face our world.

ROYAL ROADS UNIVERSITY

You can get there from here

Who will take talent and ability and parlay it into corporate leadership?

THE NEW YOU.

chapter 1
introduction to consumer behaviour

LEARNING OBJECTIVES

By the end of this chapter you should be able to:

1. Define the term "consumer behaviour" and discuss how the field of consumer behaviour evolved.
2. Give four reasons for studying consumer behaviour.
3. Discuss the impact of the digital revolution on consumer behaviour.
4. Explain the model of consumer behaviour presented in the chapter.
5. Define segmentation and positioning.

tom landry does not like Tim Hortons oatcakes, doughnuts, or apple fritters any more. He is a diabetic, who, along with some of his friends, is considering switching to Robin's Donuts. Why the sudden change in preference? Tim Hortons recently changed the way it makes its doughnuts; instead of making them daily at the store, it has started pre-cooking its doughnuts at a large plant in Markham, Ontario, and shipping them to stores across the country, where the cooking is completed. The chain says this enables individual stores to put smaller batches of doughnuts in the oven more often, and hence they are fresher than before, when most stores baked only once or twice a day. However, the customers were not convinced; Landry says, "I don't like any of them now. There's no flavour."[1] Another customer, who agreed with Landry, thought the texture of Tim Hortons products had changed and that "they bounce back on your teeth.... It's almost like they are stale."[2]

Harry had always wanted to buy a Mercedes, but on his income as a high school teacher in Toronto, he knew that he would probably never be able to. And then, one day he saw it! An ad in the paper for a Mercedes for only $15 000! He made up his mind to be one of the first to buy the car in Toronto. He loved the looks of the car—a 2.5 metre two-seater—and its 40-horsepower diesel engine that used only 3.5 litres of fuel for every 100 kilometres travelled. He also liked the fact that it could be personalized—the interchangeable door panels allowed owners to change the colours whenever they wanted. But most of all, he liked the fact that it was a Mercedes.

Michelle Macumber, a native of Bridgewater, Nova Scotia, was delighted to hear that her boyfriend, Steve Cook, was one of the three men shortlisted to win the title of the Most Romantic Man in America on the *Oprah Winfrey Show*. Steve Cook beat several thousands of other candidates to win a spot on the show, and what was surprising to many was the fact that he was kilometres away from Michelle for long periods of time. But as one of her co-workers said, he sent her roses, cards, and special presents for their monthly anniversaries and special days just to let her know he was thinking of her. How did Steve do this? As he said, he knew he was going to have some difficulties keeping the flame alive while he was on duty in Iraq and Afghanistan; so before he left for duty each time, he went online, ordered and paid for the presents, and arranged for them to be delivered on specific dates. He shopped online to find the most romantic gifts that would be delivered on the right day to the right place.

As the above examples show, consumer behaviour covers a range of different kinds of behaviour, from buying a doughnut to buying a big-ticket item like a car to sending roses to your sweetheart on that special day. What do these examples tell us about consumers and their behaviour? They show us how some personal and interpersonal variables affect consumers and the radical changes that have swept our purchasing behaviour with the advent of internet shopping. We shall examine each one of these situations in more detail in the next few paragraphs.

Let's face it, Canadians love doughnuts! So when Tim Hortons decided to change the way it made its doughnuts, it was big news in many parts of Canada. What is interesting in the above example is that the company was sure its customers would not taste a difference between a doughnut that was freshly baked on the premises and one that was pre-baked thousands of kilometres away. In fact, a spokesperson for the company said that people who had been eating them for a week only started complaining when the change became big news. But as the saying goes, "perception is reality"; the knowledge that the doughnuts were made elsewhere and shipped to the neighbourhood Tim Hortons led to Landry's *perception* that they are of lower quality, which, in turn, led to a negative *attitude* about them; this was perhaps compounded by the decision by his co-workers who are his *reference group members* to switch to Robin's Donuts. The end result was a decision to stick to tea from Tim's and buy his doughnuts at another store.

www.timhortons.ca

Harry's admiration for and interest in Mercedes shows us the importance of brand names to consumers. Owning a Mercedes is also a symbol of *social class* and status in our society. In fact, Mercedes decided to introduce the "Smart"—the two-seater Mercedes that we discussed earlier—to appeal to people like Harry who were not part of the original *target market* for the company's products. Canadians, unlike Americans, prefer compact and subcompact cars, probably because of a difference in *cultural values*. The fact that the cars could be personalized probably attracted Harry with his fun-loving, adventurous *personality*.

Now to the most romantic man in America. Steve won not only his lady's heart but also those of millions of viewers by his thoughtfulness and romantic actions such as sending Michelle flowers, cards, and special gifts though he was far, far away. Unlike many men who buy their Valentine presents in a hurry, Steve went through a long search process; he spent several hours on the internet looking at stores and possible gifts because his special circumstances (being away from his girlfriend) increased the importance of the decision to him and his *involvement* in the decision itself. As we shall learn later, Steve's *decision-making process* was probably different from that of most men and so was his *search* process. The presents that he sent Michelle to mark their anniversaries also reflect the influence of his *culture*; giving flowers is valued in Canada and the United States. Of course, Steve would have had difficulty delivering his gifts from thousands of kilometres away if it hadn't been for the digital revolution. The internet made his search and his decision a lot easier.

These examples show us the multitude of factors that affect consumer behaviour. It is a challenging field; at the same time, it is an enjoyable and exciting field of study that has a great influence on marketing and hence on society. This book covers the various topics that these examples touch upon (e.g., perception, attitudes, and culture) and several others and shows their relevance to a marketing manager; in other words, you not only will learn about the theoretical concepts that affect consumers and their purchase patterns, but you will also learn to use this knowledge to develop effective marketing strategies.

The next two sections deal with what the field of consumer behaviour covers and how a study of consumer behaviour can help you to develop marketing strategies. Then, we examine how the digital revolution has changed consumer behaviour and marketing. The chapter ends with a model of consumer behaviour that is expanded upon in later chapters.

CHAPTER OVERVIEW

In this chapter, which introduces the field of consumer behaviour, we will look at how the study of consumer behaviour came into being and the reasons for studying consumer behaviour and will then go on to a simplified model of consumer decision making. This will be followed by a plan of the book that shows how the various topics and chapters fit into this model. The chapter ends with a look at the basic elements of marketing strategy—segmentation and targeting, positioning and developing a marketing mix—which reviews the concepts presented in many marketing courses.

WHAT IS CONSUMER BEHAVIOUR?

One of the most important constants among all of us, despite our differences, is that above all we are consumers. We regularly use or consume food, clothing, shelter, transportation, education, equipment, vacations, necessities, luxuries, services, and even ideas. As consumers, we play a vital role in the health of the economy—local, national, and international. The purchasing decisions we make affect the demand for basic raw materials, for transportation, for production, and for banking services; they affect the employment of workers and the deployment of resources, the success of some industries and the failure of others. In order to succeed in any business, and especially in today's dynamic and rapidly evolving marketplace, marketers need to know everything they can about consumers—what they want, what they think, how they work, and how they spend their spare time. Marketers need to understand the personal and group influences that affect consumer decisions and how these decisions are made.

Consumer behaviour is defined as the behaviour that consumers display in *searching for, purchasing, using, evaluating, and disposing of products and services that they expect will satisfy their needs*. This definition highlights some crucial points about consumer behaviour as a discipline:

- Consumer behaviour focuses on *how* individuals make decisions to spend their available resources (time, money, and effort) on products and services. In other words, it examines the mental and physical processes that precede the actual behaviour of consumers.

- Consumer behaviour is applicable to the purchase, use, and disposal of services as well as products.

- Consumer behaviour is applicable to any behaviour related to the purchase and use of products and services. It is just as applicable to companies that market a

Consumer behaviour:
The behaviour that consumers display in searching for, purchasing, using, evaluating, and disposing of products and services that they expect will satisfy their needs.

service like insurance as it is to those who market physical goods like toothpaste or canned soup.

■ The primary reason for studying consumer behaviour is to understand how and why products and services satisfy consumers' needs.

The term *consumer behaviour* can refer to the behaviour of two different kinds of consuming entities: the personal consumer and the organizational consumer. The *personal consumer* buys goods and services for his or her own use, for the use of the household, or as gifts. In each of these situations, the products are bought for final use by individuals, who are referred to as *end users* or ultimate consumers. The second category of consumer—the *organizational consumer*—comprises both for-profit and not-for-profit businesses, government agencies (local, provincial or territorial, and federal), and institutions (e.g., schools, hospitals and prisons), all of which must buy products, equipment, and services in order to run their organizations. Despite the importance of both categories of consumers—individuals and organizations—this book concentrates on the individual consumer, who makes purchases for his or her own personal use or for household use. End-use consumption is perhaps the most pervasive of all types of consumer behaviour, for it involves every individual, of every age and background, as a buyer or user or both.

It should also be noted that several variables—some that are internal or psychological, others that are external or socio-cultural—affect all aspects of consumer behaviour. The next two sections of this book are concerned with internal (or psychological) and external (or socio-cultural) factors and their influence on consumer behaviour.

DEVELOPMENT OF THE MARKETING CONCEPT AND THE DISCIPLINE OF CONSUMER BEHAVIOUR

The study of consumer behaviour is rooted in the marketing concept, a business orientation that evolved in the 1950s through several alternative approaches toward doing business, which are referred to, respectively, as the *production concept,* the *product concept,* and the *selling concept.*

Production concept:
The assumption that consumers are mostly interested in product availability at low prices.

The production concept: The production concept assumes that consumers are mostly interested in product availability at low prices; its implicit marketing objectives are cheap, efficient production and intensive distribution. This orientation makes sense when consumers are more interested in obtaining the product than they are in specific features and will buy what is available rather than wait for what they really want. Today this orientation makes sense in developing countries or in other situations in which the main objective is to expand the market.

No product has affected North Americans more than the private car. And the business leader who gave us the affordable car and the business approach called the *production concept* was Henry Ford. In the early 1900s, Henry Ford became consumed with the idea of producing cars that average Americans could afford. In 1908, Ford began selling the sturdy and reliable Model T for $850—a low price for that day. Soon he found that he could not meet the overwhelming consumer demand for his cars and, in 1913, he introduced the assembly line. The new production method enabled Ford to produce good-quality cars more quickly and much less expensively. By 1916, Ford was selling Model Ts for $360, and he sold more than 100 times as many cars that year as he had sold in 1908.[3]

Product concept:
The assumption that consumers will buy the product that offers them the highest quality, the best performance, and the most features.

The product concept: The product concept assumes that consumers will buy the product that offers them the highest quality, the best performance, and the most features. A product orientation leads a company to strive constantly to improve the quality of its product and to add new features without finding out first whether or not the consumers really want these features. A product orientation often leads to "marketing myopia," that is, a focus on the product rather than on the consumer needs it presumes to satisfy. Marketing myopia may cause a company to ignore crucial changes in the marketplace because it causes marketers to look in the mirror rather than through the window.

Canadian railways today are a far less significant economic force than they were some 50 years ago because their management was convinced that travellers wanted trains and overlooked the competition for transportation from cars, airlines, buses, and trucks. These railway executives focused on the product (i.e., trains) rather than the need that it satisfies (transportation).[4]

The selling concept: A natural evolution from both the production concept and the product concept is the *selling concept,* in which a marketer's primary goal is to sell the product or products that it has unilaterally decided to produce. The assumption of the selling concept is that consumers are unlikely to buy the product unless they are aggressively persuaded to do so—mostly through the "hard sell" approach. The problem with this approach is that it fails to consider customer satisfaction. When consumers are induced to buy products they do not want or need, they will not buy them again. They are also likely to convey any dissatisfaction with the product through word of mouth, and this dissuades other people from making similar purchases. Today the selling concept is used by marketers of unsought goods (such as life insurance), by political parties that "sell" their candidates aggressively to apathetic voters, and by firms that have excess inventory.

The marketing concept: Instead of trying to persuade customers to buy what the firm had already produced, marketing oriented firms found that it was much easier to produce only products that they knew, from market research, the consumers wanted. Consumer needs and wants became the firm's primary emphasis. This consumer-oriented marketing philosophy came to be known as the marketing concept.

The assumption underlying the marketing concept is that, to be successful, a company must determine the needs and wants of specific target markets and deliver the desired satisfaction better than the competition. The marketing concept is based on the premise that a marketer should make what it can sell, instead of trying to sell what it has made. Whereas the selling concept concentrates on the needs of the *sellers* and on existing products, the marketing concept focuses on the needs of the *buyer.* The selling concept strives for profits through sales volume; the marketing concept strives for profits by satisfying the customers.

It is interesting to note that even before the evolution of the marketing concept, an intuitive understanding of consumer behaviour was the key to the growth of companies that remained highly successful. Apparently, companies that understand their customers are the ones that continue to grow and remain leaders in their industries in spite of increased competition and changing business environments. Three anecdotes describing three business leaders who led such companies are presented in Figure 1-1.

The marketing concept as we know it—meeting the needs of target audiences—is not always applicable. This is particularly true when the means of satisfying a need or the product or service that will fulfill the customer's "needs" may be harmful to the individual or to society (as in the case of drugs or tobacco) or may damage the natural environment. A reassessment of the marketing concept gave rise to the societal marketing concept.

Selling concept: The assumption that a marketer's primary goal should be to sell the product(s) that it has unilaterally decided to produce.

Marketing concept: A consumer-oriented marketing philosophy that states that, to be successful, a company must determine the needs and wants of specific target markets and deliver the desired satisfaction better than the competition.

FIGURE 1-1	Three Business Leaders Who Understood Consumer Behaviour Long before the Development of the Marketing Concept

1. In 1923, as the automobile market was growing rapidly thanks to Henry Ford's mass production, *Alfred P. Sloan* became president and chairman of General Motors. He inherited a company that was built through takeovers of small car companies and therefore produced many ill-assorted models, unguided by clear business objectives. Sloan reorganized the company and in 1924 articulated the company's product strategy as "a car for every purse and purpose." While Ford continued to produce the Model T until 1927, GM offered a variety of affordable mass-produced models—from the aristocratic Cadillac to the proletarian Chevrolet—and took over a large portion of Ford's market share. About 30 years before the birth of the marketing concept, Alfred Sloan realized that not all consumers are alike and the importance of *market segmentation.*[a]

2. In the 1930s, *Colonel Sanders,* America's Chicken King, opened a roadside restaurant where he developed the recipes and cooking methods that are the key to KFC's successes even today. As the restaurant grew in popularity, Sanders enlarged it and also opened a roadside motel. At that time, motels had a bad reputation, and "nice" people driving long distances generally stayed at downtown hotels. Sanders decided to try and overcome this image by putting a sample room of his clean and comfortable motel in the middle of his successful restaurant, and he even put the entrance to the restaurant's ladies' room in that room. Sanders understood the importance of image and of turning an offering into a success by *repositioning,* long before this idea was articulated as a business objective. Later on, Sanders came up with the idea of franchising his cooking methods and chicken recipe, while keeping the ingredients of the recipe a secret, and founded KFC and a businees model that has since been adopted by many other fast food chains.[b]

3. In the 1950s, *Ray Kroc* met the brothers McDonald, who pioneered the idea of fast food as we know it today in a single outlet in California, and became their partner. Ray Kroc envisioned thousands of McDonald's outlets across the country. Trying to pinpoint the best locations for the new restaurants, Kroc used to fly over towns and look for church steeples. He believed that where there were churches, there were good American families—the kind of people he wanted as customers. Intuitively, Kroc understood and practised *market targeting.* In 1961, Kroc opened Hamburger University as a training centre for the company's franchisees and their employees, and pioneered the idea of centralized training as a key to delivering standardized products across a large number of geographically spread-out outlets.[c]

[a] www.gm.com/company/corp_info/history.
[b] *Colonel Sanders, America's Chicken King,* VHS Tape, A&E Television Networks, 1998.
[c] *Ray Kroc, Fast Food McMillionaire,* VHS Tape, A&E Television Networks, 1998.

Societal marketing concept:
A philosophy of marketing that requires all marketers to adhere to principles of social responsibility in the marketing of their goods and services.

The **societal marketing concept** requires that all marketers adhere to principles of social responsibility in the marketing of their goods and services; that is, they should endeavour to satisfy the needs and wants of their target markets in ways that preserve and enhance the well-being of consumers and society as a whole. Thus, a revised definition of the marketing concept calls on marketers to *fulfill the needs of the target audience in ways that improve society as a whole, while attaining the objectives of the organization.*

www.heartandstroke.
org

One in two Canadian adults is overweight; one in seven is obese. Fat has been called "the new tobacco"[5] by leading heart experts. Whereas fewer Canadians are smoking (one in five, or fewer than 50 percent of the number who smoked 30 years ago), Dr. Graham, a cardiologist and spokesperson for the Heart and Stroke Foundation of Canada, says of the rate of obesity, "This is profound, this is anomalous and, above all, it's scary."[6] The Heart and Stroke Foundation has called on the food industry to take a series of corrective measures including (1) banning the advertising of fast food and junk food to children, (2) reducing the amount of saturated fats and transfats in processed foods, and (3) providing nutritional information on restaurant menus. Although such measures may not be attractive to the fast food industry in the short term, by incorporating such changes, the industry is likely to benefit in the long term through increased customer satisfaction and continued customer loyalty.

The societal marketing concept

- takes a long-term outlook that recognizes that all companies would be better off in a stronger, healthier society (as opposed to a short-term emphasis on profits and market share); and

- believes that companies that are ethical and socially responsible in all their business dealings will attract and maintain the loyalty of their customers over the long term.

As a result, many trade associations have developed industry-wide *codes of ethics,* because they recognize that industry-wide self-regulation is in every member's best interests in that it deters governments from imposing their own regulations on the industry. A number of companies have incorporated specific social goals into their mission statements and include programs in support of these goals as integral components of their strategic planning. They believe that **marketing ethics** and social responsibility are important components of organizational effectiveness. Most companies recognize that socially responsible activities improve their image among consumers, shareholders, the financial community, and other relevant publics and that they lead, ultimately, to increased sales. In other words, ethical and socially responsible practices are simply good business. The converse is also true: perceptions of a company's lack of social responsibility or unethical marketing strategies negatively affect consumer purchase decisions.

The widespread adoption of the marketing concept by businesses provided the impetus for the study of consumer behaviour. The marketing concept underscored the importance of consumer research and laid the groundwork for the application of consumer behaviour principles to marketing strategy. The strategic tools that are used to implement the marketing concept include *segmentation, targeting, positioning,* and the *marketing mix,* which form the foundation of modern marketing.

www.the-cma.org/ consumer/ethics.cfm

Marketing ethics: Designing marketing mixes and programs in such a way that negative consequences to consumers, employees, and society in general are avoided.

Consumer Behaviour and Decision Making Are Interdisciplinary

Although the popularity of the marketing concept led to increased interest in consumer behaviour as a field of study, it had no history or body of research of its own; for that reason, marketing theorists and consumer researchers borrowed heavily from other scientific disciplines, such as *psychology* (the study of the individual), *sociology* (the study of groups), *social psychology* (the study of how an individual operates in groups), *anthropology* (the influence of society on the individual) and *economics,* to form the basis of this new marketing discipline. Many early theories concerning consumer behaviour were based on the economic theory that individuals act rationally to maximize their benefits (satisfaction) in the purchase of goods and services. Later research, however, discovered that consumers are just as likely to purchase impulsively and to be influenced not only by their family, friends, advertisers, and role models but also by mood, situation, and emotion. All these factors combine to form a comprehensive model of consumer behaviour that recognizes both the cognitive and the emotional aspects of consumer decision making.

WHY STUDY CONSUMER BEHAVIOUR?

As explained above, consumer behaviour grew as a field of study as marketers recognized the importance of the marketing concept and as the prevalence of marketing in modern society began to grow. However, a study of consumers and their behaviour can be of benefit to many people in many ways. Here are some reasons why you (and others) should enter this exciting field of study:

Understanding consumer behaviour will make you a better marketer: If you are planning to enter the field of marketing, a study of consumer behaviour will be of great benefit since the application of the marketing concept requires an understanding of consumers. More specifically, studying consumer behaviour

- will help you understand and use research tools developed by consumer researchers to identify unsatisfied consumer needs; this is the first step in applying the marketing concept.
- will provide you with the knowledge to cater to the needs and priorities of different consumers by grouping them together into segments.
- will help you design new products and marketing strategies that will fulfill consumer needs.
- will help you not just to *attract* customers but to *keep* them by helping you build better relationships with your customers.

Understanding consumer behaviour will help you develop marketing programs in not-for-profit settings: It is also important to remember that these marketing tools are of relevance not just to the private sector, but also to public sector and not-for-profit organizations. Whereas the private sector has been quick to adopt the marketing concept, the public and not-for-profit sectors have only recently realized its importance to them. However, we now see a wide range of organizations, including universities, charities, and government organizations, following the marketing concept in order to reach their audiences and convince them of the need for their products and services.

www.royalroads.ca

Royal Roads University, located in Victoria, B.C., has differentiated itself from other Canadian universities by targeting working professionals and focusing on four themes: entrepreneurship and management, leadership, environmental sustainability, and conflict resolution. Through shorter residency requirements and internet learning, it offers students the chance to keep on working while attending university. It further differentiates itself by offering primarily master's programs and a few innovative undergraduate programs. Exhibit 1-1 shows an advertisement from Royal Roads University.

Understanding consumer behaviour will help you in developing public policy: Consumer behaviour is the study of individuals, their behaviour, and all that precedes it—in other words, it pertains not only to their purchasing behaviour (in relation to physical products and services) but also to other kinds of behaviour, such as exercising, recycling, and so on; it also examines the reasons behind the behaviour (e.g., the motivation behind recycling, why people begin smoking, why so many young adults do not vote). Thus, an understanding of consumer behaviour is essential for policy makers, for it will enable them to market public policy initiatives and information programs more effectively.

As mentioned earlier, Canadians are increasingly becoming a nation of overweight and obese people, and the costs of this to our nation will be significant. According to some researchers, being obese reduces a person's life expectancy by 10 years, and deaths directly associated with obesity have doubled in the past 15 years (from 2514 in 1985 to 4321 in 2000). Treating the medical conditions that arise from being overweight (e.g., cardiovascular disease and diabetes) costs our health system at least $2 billion annually in direct health-care costs.[7] How can policy makers deal with this problem? Any effective solution or public policy would have to be based on how and why people gain weight. Although it is well known that a poor diet and lack of physical activity are the main culprits, public policy makers need to understand why people resist changing their diet and what would encourage them to be more physically active.

Understanding consumer behaviour may help you understand your own behaviour: As you go through this book, you will learn about a wide variety of issues and topics: what motivates people, how others affect you, how your attitudes (and those of others) are formed, and other related topics. By studying these topics, you may understand why you behave in certain ways and why certain products and advertisements appeal to you. Thus, studying consumer behaviour will help you understand your own behaviour better.

THE IMPACT OF THE DIGITAL REVOLUTION ON CONSUMER BEHAVIOUR

In the futuristic thriller movie *Minority Report*, which takes place in 2054, the hero, played by Tom Cruise, experiences the ultimate one-to-one marketing. As he passes a billboard featuring the American Express card, the billboard becomes a hologram, presumably visible only to him, portraying his picture and personal data and urging him to use the card. He then enters a Gap store, where customers are met by voices greeting them by name, asking them how they liked their previous purchases and suggesting items that they may like on the basis of their past purchases. Indeed, as portrayed in this film, the year 2054 will be a marketer's paradise.

In many ways futuristic marketing is already here: shoppers in many supermarkets receive, at the checkout, personalized coupons based on their purchases; many newspapers allow online readers to create personalized editions in which customized ads are featured; and consumers can now purchase highly personalized versions of many products.

As we marvel at these new marketing technologies, we must also put them in perspective. In principle, they are extensions of the salesperson in a local shoe store who recognizes the customers by name and by preferences, or the neighbourhood grocer who remembers each customer's routine purchases and puts them on the counter before the customer even asks for them, or the small-town jeweller who keeps track of customers' special occasions and prepares a selection of suitable gifts for them to buy as anniversaries and birthdays approach. All these businesspeople were engaging in one-to-one marketing long before the term was coined

EXHIBIT 1-1

ROYAL ROADS DIFFERENTIATES ITSELF BY CATERING TO WORKING PROFESSIONALS

Courtesy of Royal Roads University & Trapeze Communications Inc.

and many decades before personalized digital communication became available. And the goals of the shoe salesperson, the grocer, and the jeweller were the same then as those of large companies today: to obtain customers, keep good customers, sell them more products, and make a profit.

Today, the *digital revolution* of the marketplace allows much greater customization of products, services, and promotional messages than did older marketing tools. By doing so, it enables marketers to build and maintain relationships with customers—just like the salesperson, grocer, and jeweller have done for many decades—but on a much greater and more efficient scale. Digital technologies also enable marketers to collect and analyze increasingly complex data on consumers' buying patterns and personal characteristics. However, the same technologies enable consumers to find more information about products and services, including prices, more easily and efficiently and, for the most part, from the comfort of their own homes.

Over a decade or so, the digital revolution has introduced several dramatic changes into the business environment:

Consumers have more power than ever before. They can use search engines, special websites, and so on, to find the best prices for products or services, bid on various marketing offerings, bypass distribution outlets and intermediaries, and shop for goods around the globe and around the clock from the convenience of their homes.

Canadians, who are one of the world's most electronically connected consumers, use the internet to search for information more than their U.S. neighbours do. A majority of Canadians now have internet access, and more than half of them have high-speed internet connections. Internet Insight 1-1 provides more details on Canadians' use of the internet.

Consumers have access to more information than ever before. They can easily find reviews of products they are considering buying that have been posted by previous buyers, click a button to compare the features of different product models at the sites of online retailers, and subscribe to "virtual communities" of persons who share their interests.

Marketers can offer more services and products than ever before. The digitization of information enables sellers to *customize* their products and services and still sell them at reasonable prices. It also allows marketers to customize the promotional messages directed at many customers.

www.amazon.ca

Amazon.ca sends personalized emails to previous book purchasers announcing newly published books; these suggestions are based on a determination of the interests of the targeted consumers derived from their past purchases. Similarly, an online drugstore may vary the initial display seen by returning buyers when they revisit its website. Buyers whose past purchases indicate that they tend to buy national brands will see a display arranged by brand. Past purchasers who bought mostly store brands or products that were on sale see a display categorized by price and discounted products.

The exchange between marketers and customers is increasingly interactive and instantaneous. Traditional advertising is a one-way street where marketers pay large sums of money to reach a large number of potential buyers via a mass medium. Then, on the basis of market studies and sales, marketers assess whether the message was effective. Conversely, digital communication makes a two-way interactive exchange possible: consumers can instantly react to the marketer's message by, say, clicking on links on a website or even by leaving the site. Thus, marketers can quickly gauge the effectiveness of their online communication rather than rely on delayed information from sales figures or surveys of attitudinal change.

Marketers can gather more information about consumers more quickly and easily. Marketers can track consumers' online behaviour and also gather informa-

INTERNET INSIGHT 1-1
HOW CONNECTED ARE CANADIANS?

Canadians are perhaps the world's most connected people. More than 52 percent of the Canadian population (or more than 17 million people) are online, and the number is increasing steadily. Of these, 57.3 percent had high-speed internet access (in 2003), compared with only 34.1 percent of the U.S. online population. Here are some other interesting facts about Canadians and their use of the internet:

Age group spending the most time on the internet (as a percentage of total internet time): 35–54

Time spent by 35–54-year-olds as a percentage of the total minutes: 40.2 percent

Proportion of the online population with high-speed internet access: 57.3 percent

Canadians who have a computer and a TV in the same room: 50 percent

Percentage of the above Canadians who use the internet while watching television: 80 percent

Proportion of total advertising (by all Canadian firms) spent on internet advertising: 1.5 percent[a]

Proportion of total advertising (by all U.S. firms) spent on internet advertising: 3.3 percent[b]

Industry sector spending the most on internet advertising: retail ($12 500 000+ in 2003 third quarter)

Breakdown of visitors to retail internet sites by total number of minutes:

- Males—55.9 percent; females—44.1 percent
- Household income 60K+: 43.9 percent
- Households without children: 51.9 percent
- Region spending most minutes: Ontario—36.3 percent

Average number of searches per month by Canadian internet users: 40

Average number of searches per month by U.S. internet users: 35

Proportion of Canadian online users who did at least one search in the past month: 85 percent

Proportion of U.S. online users who did at least one search in the past month: 73 percent

Total Canadian household spending online in 2003: slightly over $3 billion[c]

Items bought online most often: reading materials (30 percent of users bought books, magazines, etc.) followed by travel (22 percent made travel arrangements online)[c]

[a] IAB Canada estimate.
[b] Pricewaterhouse Cooper Internet Ad Revenue Report.
[c] "E-Commerce: Household Shopping on the Internet," *The Daily*, September 23, 2004, Statistics Canada.

Sources: Various press releases, www.newswire.ca/en; and comScore MediaMatrix, www.comscore.com, various articles.

---

tion by requiring visitors to websites to register and provide some information about themselves,. Thus, marketers can construct and update their consumer databases efficiently and inexpensively.

www.statcan.ca

Impact reaches beyond the PC-based connection to the web. At present, most of the digital communication between consumers and marketers takes place from a PC connected to the web with a phone line, a cable modem, or another high-speed connection. But the digital revolution also gave us PDAs (personal digital assistants), which are rapidly becoming connected to the web, often wirelessly, and combined with cell phones. In addition, many Canadian homes now have TV cable boxes that make two-way communication with broadcasters possible. As we switch to high-definition TV, all cable subscribers will have such boxes. Many experts also predict that TV and the PC will merge into a single device that will provide households with hundreds of cable channels, the ability to interact with broadcasters, and high-speed, wireless access to the web. Two of the many additional products made possible by recently developed technologies are supermarket scanners that keep track of households' purchases and instantly issue personalized coupons at the checkout counter and telephone devices that enable us to identify telemarketers automatically.

Difficulties Presented by the Digital Revolution

The digital revolution of the marketplace and its influence on consumer behaviour present many difficulties for today's marketers:

Consumer segmentation strategies may have to be revamped: Technology has changed consumers' buying patterns to such an extent that new ways of segmenting consumers and positioning products may be necessary. This, of course, does not mean that traditional bases for segmentation are not valid for online marketers; it does mean that some of these may have to be altered or modified to suit the new marketplace. For example, Netpoll provides a psycho-demographic segmentation of web users based on age, access to the internet, and other factors into six categories. Research Insight 1-1 provides more details of Netpoll's segmentation of web users.

In addition, marketers need to realize that people use the internet in different ways and for different purposes. For example, some people may use the internet to search for product information but do not purchase online. Others search online for information, which they use to make a decision but go to a traditional brick-and-mortar retailer to make the purchase. Although the number of online purchases in most product categories is increasing, many customers are still reluctant to make the actual purchase online in some product categories. Research shows that consumers who window-shop online but are reluctant to make a purchase have more doubts about the security of making a financial transaction on the internet than do those who actually buy online. In fact, misgivings about the security of online financial transactions and about privacy are the main reasons that most Canadians do not purchase online.[8] Surprisingly, the number of Canadians who say they are more concerned about the security of online transactions has been increasing rather than decreasing (from 2001 to 2004). Perhaps this is because nearly one in three Canadian internet users has experienced breach of personal information submitted online.[9] Marketers may need to use different strategies to attract the segments of the population that are reluctant to buy online.

Promotional budgets and methods may have to be re-evaluated: Traditional forms of promotion may no longer be adequate or effective. TiVo digital recorder allows viewers to control what they watch on television, when they watch it, and whether or not to watch the commercials for which marketers spend billions of dollars every year. The TiVo recorder downloads program information and allows users to record many hours of television programs onto a hard drive without the inconvenience of videocassettes. Users can program the recorder by topic or keyword, easily play back selected segments, and to the delight of many viewers, hit a single button to skip strings of commercials.

Should marketers begin reducing their advertising expenditures on the major networks' television programs in anticipation of the growth of products such as TiVo? How can the internet be used in an effective way to promote a company's products? Or should marketers invest in technologies that embed electronic tags of ads visible only to digital video recorder users, as some advertisers are already doing?[10]

Better integration of online and off-line marketing efforts are necessary: The internet not only offers marketers a new promotional tool, but it also makes it necessary for them to coordinate all their marketing efforts to a greater extent. Both online and off-line efforts have to be synchronized and have to complement each other.

RESEARCH INSIGHT 1-1
PSYCHO-DEMOGRAPHIC SEGMENTATION OF WEB USERS

Netpoll, a company that specializes in providing information for emarketers, classifies web users into six categories according to age, access to the internet, and selected AIO (activities, interests, and opinions) items. Though based on the British market, this segmentation of internet users is of interest to anyone involved in web-based marketing.

The GameBoy: Age: 15 years; male; accesses the internet mainly from home but at times from school or a cybercafe. Primarily uses the internet for playing online games and participating in MUDs (Multiple User Dungeons). Considers himself to be net savvy and hip. Interested in football.

The CyberLad: Age: 23 years; male; accesses the internet at work and at home; considers himself to be a skilled internet user; interests include sex and sport; into emailing and visiting pornographic sites.

The CyberSec: Age: 31 years; female; competent, well-dressed, works as an assistant to a manager in a small or medium-sized firm; accesses the internet primarily at work for official purposes; likes to shop; is beginning to use the web for her own interests.

The InfoJunky: Age: 40 years; equally likely to be a man or woman; married with two children; probably working for the government as a middle-level manager; likes the sense of control that the internet gives; probably wastes a lot of office time on the internet by using it inefficiently; avid reader of newspapers and magazines.

The Hit 'n' Runner: Age: 38: equally likely to be a male or a female; successful professional; career-minded; yet to start a family; accesses the internet at work and primarily for gathering information; impatient with slow or inefficient sites; banks online; uses the internet for researching vacation spots.

The CyberMum: Age: 42; female with kids at home; works in a "caring" profession like nursing; overweight and always on a diet; primarily uses the internet for emailing relatives; may be interested in shopping online once she is comfortable with it.

Source: Netpoll (**www.netpoll.net**); quoted in D. Chaffey, R. Mayer, K. Johnston, and F. Ellis-Chadwick, *Internet Marketing*, 2nd ed. (Prentice Hall, 2000), 68–69.

QUESTIONS:
1. Which one of the above profiles best describes you?

Scotiabank publishes a monthly email newsletter, called *The Vault*, that contains personal banking advice and is tied into current off-line promotions or mass advertising. For example, an issue of *The Vault* that went out at the RRSP season dovetailed with Scotia's off-line RSP advertising. Michael Seaton, director of one-to-one marketing at Scotiabank says, "We're making sure it's a singular brand voice that the customer has in their in-box, on their TV set or in their mail box at the end of the day. It's really been a successful strategy, because it makes sense to a customer the more they see a new product or a new solution we have to offer."[11]

Distribution systems may have to be revamped: The increasing willingness on the part of consumers to use the internet to place orders (and not just to get information) may lead to a re-evaluation of the methods of distribution that a company uses. Several firms are finding it increasingly attractive to go directly to the consumer and avoid retailers (or at least decrease their dependence on them).

When you are planning a trip, do you look at the websites of various airlines? Research shows that only 36 percent of potential travellers buy their tickets through a travel agent; 44 percent buy through a travel site and the rest use the airline's website or toll-free number.[12] In fact, Air Canada, WestJet, and other airlines—Canadian and International—are offering consumers incentives to buy directly from them instead of going through a travel agent. Air Canada has reduced

www.netpoll.net

the discounts that it gives travel agents for booking tickets, with the result that travel agents are passing on more of their costs to their customers. Airlines offer other benefits for booking online; Air Canada, for example, offers extra Aeroplan miles. These, combined with webspecials, have increased online bookings

Increased need to provide custom-made alternatives to consumers: The two-way interactive nature of the internet has made it possible, and at times necessary, to offer customized products. Companies that rely totally on direct marketing have been doing this for several years now; for example, one of Dell's competitive advantages has always been its ability to put together a computer that is custom-made to meet consumers' needs. The popularity of online buying has made it necessary and possible for other companies to offer the same benefits to consumers. At Nike's website, buyers can now choose among many styles of sneakers in different price ranges and customize the shoe by choosing several colours and features (e.g., some models even allow buyers to choose the colours of the Nike Swoosh and the laces) and put a personal ID on each shoe. Still on the website, consumers can pay for the shoes and have them shipped directly to them.

A careful evaluation of pricing strategies may be necessary: Some suggest that because virtual competition eliminates distance and location-based benefits (such as a desirable store location) and because it is increasingly dominated by intelligent merchant-brokerage agents that steer consumers toward the lowest possible price for a product, online competition is likely to resemble perfect competition. In such a marketplace, sellers will compete almost exclusively on the basis of price, and any other differentiation features—such as a strong brand name and reputation—will matter less. Does this mean that branding and competitive differentiation—two key features of modern marketing—will become meaningless in the virtual market-place? What do you think?

New research methods may have to be developed to study the behaviour of internet buyers: Although traditional forms of consumer research (e.g., focus groups and surveys) are still effective, the increased use of the internet has led to some interesting questions and challenges for marketers. For example, measuring the effectiveness of online advertising poses some unique problems for marketers. Should an ad be considered effective if enough people "visit" the page, or should other measures of effectiveness be used? Are the participants in internet panels representative of the general population given the fact that the participants have to have special software installed on their computers? Can online surveys take the place of the typical telephone or mail survey? Is it as effective to test a product by providing a product concept online as it is to have consumers read a description and discuss it in a focus group?

Most marketers agree that although the digital revolution may have changed the way a company can and should market itself, many of the fundamental principles of marketing still apply in today's world. The next section looks at four models of consumer behaviour, describes a simplified overall model of consumer behaviour, and gives an overview of the chapters to follow.

MODELS OF CONSUMERS

Before presenting an overview model of how consumers make decisions, we will consider several schools of thought that depict consumer decision making in distinctly different ways. The term *models of consumers* refers to a general view or perspective of how (and why) individuals behave as they do. Specifically, we will examine models of consumers from four views: (1) an *economic view,* (2) a *passive view,* (3) a *cognitive view,* and (4) an *emotional view.*

An Economic View

In the field of theoretical economics, which portrays a world of perfect competition, the consumer has often been characterized as making rational decisions. This model, called the *economic man* theory, has been criticized by consumer researchers for a number of reasons. To behave rationally in the economic sense, a consumer would have to

- be aware of all available products;
- be capable of correctly ranking each product according to its benefits and disadvantages; and
- be able to identify the one best choice.

Realistically, however, consumers rarely have all the information or accurate enough information or even enough involvement or motivation to make the so-called "perfect" decision.

It has been argued that the classical economic model of an all-rational consumer is unrealistic for the following reasons: (1) people are limited by their skills, habits, and reflexes; (2) people are limited by their values and goals; and (3) people are limited by the extent of their knowledge.[13] Consumers operate in an imperfect world in which they do not maximize their decisions in terms of economic considerations, such as price-quantity relationships, marginal utility, or indifference curves. Indeed, the consumer is generally unwilling to engage in extensive decision making and will settle, instead, for a "satisfactory" decision, one that is "good enough."[14] For this reason, the economic model is often rejected as too idealistic and simplistic. For example, recent research has found that consumers' primary motivation for haggling about a price, which was long thought to be the desire to obtain a better price (i.e., better dollar value for the purchase), may instead be related to the need for achievement, affiliation, and dominance.[15]

A Passive View

Quite opposite to the rational economic view of consumers is the *passive* view that depicts the consumer as basically submissive to the self-serving interests and promotional efforts of marketers. In the passive view, consumers are perceived as impulsive and irrational purchasers, ready to yield to the aims of—and into the arms of—marketers. At least to some degree, the passive model of the consumer was subscribed to by the hard-driving super-salespeople of old, who were trained to regard the consumer as an object to be manipulated.

The principal limitation of the passive model is that it fails to recognize that the consumer plays an equal, if not dominant, role in many buying situations—sometimes by seeking information about alternative products and choosing the product that appears to offer the greatest satisfaction and at other times by impulsively choosing a product that satisfies the mood or emotion of the moment. All that we will study about motivation (Chapter 3), selective perception (Chapter 5), learning (Chapter 6), attitudes (Chapter 7), communication (Chapter 8), and opinion leadership (Chapter 13) will support the proposition that consumers are rarely objects of manipulation. Therefore, this simple and single-minded view should also be rejected as unrealistic.

A Cognitive View

The third model portrays consumers as *thinking problem solvers*, receptive to or actively searching for products and services that meet their needs and enrich their lives. The cognitive model focuses on the processes by which consumers seek and evaluate information about selected brands and retail outlets.

The cognitive model views consumers as information processors. Information processing leads to the formation of preferences and, ultimately, to purchase intentions. The cognitive view also recognizes that the consumer is unlikely even to try to obtain all available information about every choice. Instead, consumers are likely to cease their information-seeking efforts when they perceive that they have enough information about some of the alternatives to make a "satisfactory" decision. As this information-processing viewpoint suggests, consumers often develop shortcut decision rules (called *heuristics*) to facilitate their decisions (see Chapter 14). They also use decision rules to cope with too much information (i.e., *information overload*).

The cognitive, or problem-solving, view describes a consumer who falls somewhere between the extremes of the economic and passive views, who does not (or cannot) have total knowledge about the products available and, therefore, cannot make *perfect* decisions, but who nonetheless actively seeks information and tries to make *satisfactory* decisions.

Consistent with the problem-solving view is the notion that a great deal of consumer behaviour is goal-directed. For example, a person might buy a computer in order to manage his or her finances or look for a laundry detergent that will be gentle on fabrics. Setting goals is especially important when it comes to the adoption of new products, because the newer they are, the more difficult it would be for the consumer to evaluate the product and relate it to his or her need (because of a lack of experience with the product).[16]

Although the cognitive view may be the most suitable one for analyzing major consumer decisions (e.g., the purchase of a car or a computer), it may not be applicable in the case of inexpensive items and impulse purchases (e.g., buying candy at the checkout counter). In such cases, an emotional view of consumer behaviour might provide better insights for marketing strategy.

An Emotional View

Although long aware of the *emotional* or *impulsive* model of consumer decision making, marketers often prefer to think of consumers in terms of either economic or passive models. In reality, however, each of us is likely to associate deep feelings or emotions, such as joy, fear, love, hope, sexuality, fantasy, and even a little "magic," with certain purchases or possessions. These feelings or emotions are likely to be highly involving. For instance, a person who misplaces a favourite fountain pen might go to great lengths to look for it, despite the fact that he or she has six others at hand.

Possessions may also preserve a sense of the past and act as familiar transitional objects when a person is confronted with an uncertain future. For example, members of the armed forces invariably carry photographs of "the girl (or guy) back home," their families, and their lives in earlier times. These memorabilia frequently serve as hopeful reminders that normal life will someday resume.

If we were to reflect on the nature of our recent purchases, we might be surprised to realize just how impulsive some of them were. Rather than carefully searching, deliberating, and evaluating the alternatives before buying, we are just as likely to have made many of these purchases on impulse, on a whim, or because we were emotionally driven. However, not all of our purchases are impulse- or emotion-driven. Thus, this view will apply only to some of our purchases.

A SIMPLIFIED MODEL OF CONSUMER DECISION MAKING

Consumer decision making can be viewed as two distinct but interlocking stages: the *process* stage and the *outcome* stage. Both of these are affected by certain factors or inputs: the firm's marketing efforts (the product itself, its price, its promotion, and

Consumer decision making:

Two distinct but interlocking stages: the process (recognition of problem, pre-purchase search, and evaluation of alternatives) and its outcomes (purchase and post-purchase evaluation). Both stages are influenced by factors internal and external to the consumer.

where it is sold), external sociological influences on the consumer (family, friends, neighbours, other informal and non-commercial sources, social class, and membership in a culture or subculture), and the psychological factors inherent in each individual (motivation, perception, learning, personality, and attitudes) that affect the way a consumer interprets and reacts to the sources of information. These stages are depicted in the simplified model of consumer decision making in Figure 1-2.

This section presents an overview model of consumer decision making that represents the *cognitive* (or *problem-solving*) consumer and, to some degree, the *emotional consumer.* The model is designed to tie together many of the ideas on consumer decision making and consumption behaviour discussed throughout the book. It does not presume to give an exhaustive picture of the complexities of consumer decision making. Rather, it is designed to synthesize and coordinate relevant concepts into a significant whole. The model, presented in Figure 1-2, has two main parts: inputs (a firm's marketing efforts, socio-cultural variables, and psychological factors) and the consumer's decision-making process.

Inputs

Consumer decision making is affected by three types of inputs: the *marketing-mix activities* of organizations that attempt to communicate the benefits of their products

FIGURE 1-2   A Simplified Model of Consumer Behaviour

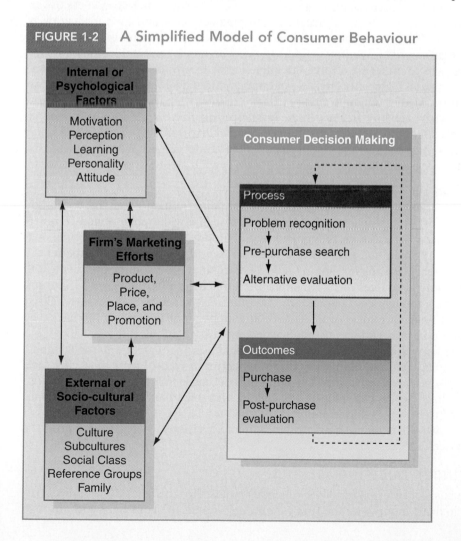

and services to potential consumers, the consumer's internal or *psychological influences,* and the non-marketing *socio-cultural influences,* which, when internalized, affect the consumer's purchase decisions. Let us examine these in more detail.

Marketing Inputs

The firm's marketing activities are a direct attempt to reach, inform, and persuade consumers to buy and use its products. These inputs to the consumer's decision making take the form of specific marketing-mix strategies that consist of the product itself (including its package, size, and guarantees); mass-media advertising, direct marketing, personal selling, and other promotional efforts; pricing policy; and the selection of distribution channels to move the product from the manufacturer to the consumer.

Ultimately, the success of a firm's marketing efforts in large measure is governed by the consumer's perception of these efforts. Thus, marketers should remain diligently alert to consumer perceptions by sponsoring consumer research, rather than rely on the *intended* impact of their marketing messages.

Internal or Psychological Factors

To understand the consumer's decision making, we must consider the influence of the psychological concepts examined in Part 2. The *psychological field* represents the internal influences (motivation, perception, learning, personality, and attitudes) that affect consumers' decision making (what they need or want, their awareness of various product choices, their information-gathering activities, and their evaluation of alternatives). These internal factors have a significant influence on how a consumer views a firm's marketing efforts and on the way he or she makes decisions.

The firm's marketing efforts, the influence of family, friends, subcultures, and society's current code of behaviour, and the psychological factors that are internal to the consumer are all inputs that are likely to affect what consumers buy and how they use what they buy. Because these influences may be directed to the individual or actively sought by the individual, a two-headed arrow is used to link these *inputs* to the consumer decision-making segment of the model (Figure 1-2). To indicate the interaction between the inputs themselves, two-headed arrows are used to link them.

External or Socio-cultural Factors

The *socio-cultural environment* also exerts a major influence on the consumer. Socio-cultural inputs (examined in Part 3) consist of a wide range of non-commercial influences. For example, the comments of a friend, an editorial in the newspaper, use by a family member, an article in *Consumer Reports,* or the views of experienced consumers participating in a special-interest discussion group on the internet are all non-commercial sources of information. The influences of social class, culture, and subculture, although less tangible, are important input factors that are internalized and affect how consumers evaluate and ultimately adopt (or reject) products. The unwritten codes of conduct communicated by culture subtly indicate which consumption behaviour should be considered "right" or "wrong" at a particular time. For example, Japanese mothers maintain much more control over their children's consumption than North American mothers do, because in North America, children are socialized to be individualistic (*to stand out*), whereas in Japan children are socialized to be integrated with others (*to stand in*).[17]

Next, we will examine how consumers make decisions when choosing products and services.

Consumer Decision Making

On the basis of external (or environmental) inputs, the consumer's own internal (or psychological) inputs, and the firm's marketing inputs, the consumer goes through a decision-making process that results in certain outputs. The process of decision making includes the recognition of a need, a pre-purchase search for information, and an evaluation of various alternatives. This decision process leads to two outcomes: purchase and post-purchase processes. The experience gained from the decision-making process and its outcomes could, in turn, affect the consumer's view of the inputs. Let us examine these in more detail.

Process

The *process* component of the model is concerned with how consumers make decisions. As pictured in the *process* component of the model (Figure 1-2), the act of making a consumer decision consists of three stages: (1) recognition of need, (2) pre-purchase search, and (3) evaluation of alternatives..

Recognition of Need The *recognition of a need* is likely to occur when a consumer is faced with a "problem." Problem or need recognition happens when there is a discrepancy between the actual and the desired states of a consumer.

Pre-purchase Search The *pre-purchase search* begins when a consumer perceives a need that might be satisfied by the purchase and consumption of a product. The recollection of past experiences (drawn from his or her long-term memory) might give the consumer enough information to make the present choice. However, when the consumer has had no prior experience, he or she may have to engage in an extensive search of the outside environment for useful information on which to base a choice.

The consumer usually searches his or her memory (the *psychological field* depicted in the model) before seeking external sources of information regarding a given consumption-related need. Past experience is considered an internal source of information. The greater the relevant past experience, the less external information the consumer is likely to need to reach a decision. Many consumer decisions are based on a combination of past experience (internal sources) and marketing and non-commercial information (external sources). The degree of the apparent risk can also influence this stage of the decision process (see Chapter 6).

Once they have collected information (on the criteria to base their choice on and the alternatives—or brands—available), consumers move to the next stage: the evaluation of alternatives.

Evaluation of Alternatives Equipped with the information that they have collected, consumers start evaluating various alternative products (or services).

When evaluating alternatives, consumers tend to use two types of information: (1) a "list" of brands (or models) from which they plan to make their selection (the evoked set) and (2) the criteria they will use to evaluate each brand (or model). Making a selection from a *sample* of all possible brands (or models) is a human characteristic that helps simplify the decision.

The criteria consumers use to evaluate the alternative products are the important attributes of the product, such as price, quality, and size.

Consumer decision rules, often referred to as *heuristics, decision strategies*, and *information-processing strategies,* are procedures used by consumers to facilitate brand (or other consumption-related) choices. These rules reduce the burden of making complex decisions by providing guidelines or routines that make the process less taxing. These will be discussed in more detail in Chapter 14.

Outcomes

The result of this process or the *outcome* stage of the consumer decision-making model consists of two closely related post-decision activities: purchase behaviour and post-purchase evaluation.

Purchase Behaviour Purchase behaviour for a low-cost, non-durable product (e.g., a new shampoo) may be influenced by a manufacturer's coupon and may actually be a trial purchase; if the consumer is satisfied, he or she may repeat the purchase. The trial is the exploratory phase of purchase behaviour, in which the consumer evaluates the product through direct use. A repeat purchase usually signifies adoption of the product. For a relatively durable product such as a laptop, the purchase is more likely to signify adoption.

Post-purchase Evaluation As consumers use a product, especially during a trial purchase, they evaluate its performance in light of their own expectations. There are three possible outcomes of these evaluations: (1) actual performance matches expectations, leading to a neutral feeling; (2) performance exceeds expectations, causing what is known as *positive disconfirmation of expectations* (which leads to satisfaction); and (3) performance is below expectations, causing *negative disconfirmation of expectations* and dissatisfaction.[18] Depending on the outcome of these evaluations, a consumer's future behaviour as far as the particular product is concerned would be affected. This post-purchase evaluation (or experience) would also influence a consumer's perception of various inputs.

This chapter ends with a look at the plan of the book and an explanation of how the various chapters fit into the model of consumer behaviour presented above.

PLAN OF THE BOOK

In an effort to build a useful conceptual framework that both enhances understanding and permits a practical application of consumer behaviour principles to marketing strategy, this book is divided into four parts. Part 1 introduces the study of consumer behaviour and the consumer behaviour model used in the text (Chapter 1); it also has a chapter on consumer research that provides an overview of the various research methods used to study consumer behaviour. Included in this part is an appendix that takes a brief look at the fundamentals of marketing strategy and can serve as a review for students who have already taken a basic course in marketing. Part 2 discusses the consumer as an individual (i.e., the psychological or internal factors). Part 3 examines consumers in their social and cultural settings (or the external factors). Consumer decision making is covered in two chapters in Part 4.

Chapter 1 introduces the reader to the study of consumer behaviour and describes the reasons for the development and study of consumer behaviour as an academic discipline and an applied science. It covers the influence of the digital revolution on consumer behaviour and introduces the simplified model of consumer decision making that forms the framework of this book. Given the emphasis on consumer research in this text, Chapter 2 examines the consumer research process and the qualitative and quantitative consumer research methods.

Part 2 is concerned with the internal or psychological characteristics of the consumer. Chapter 3 discusses how individuals are motivated, Chapter 4 examines the influence of individual personality characteristics on consumer behaviour, Chapter 5 explores consumer perception, Chapter 6 examines how consumers learn, Chapter 7 discusses consumer attitudes, and Chapter 8 concludes Part 2 with an examination of the communications process and its impact on consumer attitudes and perception.

Part 3 looks at consumers as members of society whose buying behaviour is subject to varying external influences. We begin with the broader or more general influences on consumers such as culture and cultural values (Chapter 9), subcultures that a consumer might be part of (Chapter 10), and the social class or stratum that a consumer might belong to (Chapter 11). Then we move on to the external influences that are closer to a consumer, that is, his or her immediate reference groups and family (Chapter 12). The final chapter in this part (Chapter 13) discusses opinion leadership and the consumer's reactions to innovation and change and describes the process by which new products are adopted and spread throughout society.

We will revisit consumer decision making in Part 4 and will examine both the process of decision making that a consumer goes through (Chapter 14) and the outcomes of this process (Chapter 15) in more detail.

SUMMARY

- The study of consumer behaviour enables marketers to understand and predict how consumers will behave in the marketplace; it is concerned not only with what consumers buy but also with why, when, where, how, and how often they buy it.

- Consumer behaviour is interdisciplinary; that is, it is based on concepts and theories about people that have been developed by scientists in such diverse disciplines as psychology, sociology, social psychology, cultural anthropology, and economics.

- Studying consumer behaviour will help you to become a better marketer, design effective public policies and, perhaps, understand your own purchase behaviour better.

- Consumer decision making is seen as being influenced by internal (or psychological) factors such as motivation and learning, and by external (or environmental) factors such as culture and social class. Besides these, consumer decisions are also affected by marketing inputs, primarily the marketing-mix variables (product, price, place, and promotion) that a firm uses to attract consumers.

- Consumer decision making consists of two parts: the process (recognition of need, pre-purchase search, and evaluation of alternatives); and its outcomes (purchase and post-purchase evaluation). The feedback from post-purchase evaluation, in turn, affects the way a consumer views the external inputs, the firm's marketing efforts, and his or her own internal processes.

- The digital revolution has changed consumer behaviour in many ways; for example, consumers have more power than before, and the exchange between marketers and customers is increasingly interactive and instantaneous.

DISCUSSION QUESTIONS

1. Discuss the influence of the social and behavioural sciences in the development of the consumer decision-making model.

2. Why should a marketer study consumer behaviour? How can it enable him or her to devise better marketing strategies?

3. Explain the production, product, selling, marketing, and societal marketing concepts. What are the advantages (to a firm) of following the marketing concept?

4. Describe the economic, passive, cognitive, and emotional models of consumer behaviour. Can you find examples from your experience to fit each one of these models?

5. Describe the basic consumer behaviour model presented in the chapter.

CRITICAL THINKING QUESTIONS

1. Assume that you are marketing the following products:

    MP3 players   Summer clothing
    Insurance   University textbooks

    Which model of consumer behaviour presented in this chapter (economic, passive, cognitive, or emotional would be best suited to your needs? Why?

2. Think about a recent major purchase that you made (e.g., computer, MP3 player, house, condo, decision to attend university). Using the model presented in this chapter, discuss the external and internal inputs that affected your decision.

INTERNET EXERCISES

1. Visit the website of Ford Motor Company of Canada (www.ford.ca). Is the site interactive? What makes it interactive?

2. Look at a few ads from Scotiabank and go to Scotiabank's website (www.scotiabank.com). How are the two integrated? What information could a person interested in Scotiabank's services get from the website that would help him or her prepare for a meeting with a bank officer to apply for a mortgage?

3. Frequently asked questions, or FAQs, are used by companies to divert routine questions from off-line customer service representatives to the online mode and thus to save money. Visit the website of your local power company (e.g., Ontario Hydro or Nova Scotia Power) and your telephone company and go to the FAQ section. What kinds of routine questions are handled there? Would these resolve your typical customer-service problems?

4. Visit the website of two Canadian magazines and look at their online subscription offers. Are these different from those offered to their regular subscribers? Is this a fair marketing practice? Why or why not?

KEY TERMS

- Consumer behaviour *(p. 5)*
- Consumer decision making *(p. 18)*
- Marketing concept *(p. 7)*
- Product concept *(p. 6)*
- Production concept *(p. 6)*
- Selling concept *(p. 7)*
- Societal marketing concept *(p. 8)*
- Marketing ethics *(p. 9)*

CASE 1-1: THE GROWTH OF "PERSONAL TV"

The digital revolution has had a profound impact on consumer behaviour and on marketing. One area in which technology is rapidly changing long-established behaviour is TV viewing. For example, the TiVo digital recorder and service allow viewers to control what they watch on TV, when they watch it, and whether or not they watch the commercials for which marketers spend billions of dollars a year. The TiVo recorder downloads program information and allows users to record many hours of TV programs onto a hard drive. Users can program the recorder by topic or by a keyword and easily play back selected segments. In addition, they can "pause live TV" when they want to take a short break from watching a live broadcast and then resume watching at the same place, and use "thumbs up" and "thumbs down" buttons to indicate how much they liked or disliked what they were watching. TiVo records these preferences and then suggests programs that these viewers may want to watch. Users can hit a single button for pre-set quick skips of strings of commercials.

ReplayTV, which is similar to TiVo, allows viewers to skip commercials when they watch recorded programs. It has no "thumbs up/down" buttons, but its "quick skip" feature is a little more advanced than TiVo's. Unlike TiVo, ReplayTV also allows viewers to share programs with others over the internet. However, sending a high-quality video by internet, even over a high-speed connection, takes a very long time and as yet is impractical for most consumers. ReplayTV 4000 also allows a recorded program to be stored on a VHS tape that can be shared with others, a feature that is similar to recording a program on a standard VCR. In 2002, SonicBlue—the manufacturer of ReplayTV 4000—was in the middle of a lawsuit. The legal action, brought by numerous media companies representing TV networks and movie studios, alleged that ReplayTV contributed to copyright infringement.

DISCUSSION QUESTIONS

1. Because TiVo and ReplayTV are shifting the power over viewing behaviour from the broadcaster to the viewer, should broadcasters develop their own TiVo-like systems?

2. Should broadcasters try to block the sales of such devices legally on the grounds that they contribute to copyright infringement? Or should they develop business models centred on viewers who pay for content? In your answer, be sure to describe the threats and opportunities that the new recording devices and services represent for the TV networks and advertisers.

NOTES

1   Davene Jeffrey, "Tim's New Plan Hard to Swallow," Halifax *Mail-Star*, February 12, 2004, p. A3.

2   Ibid.

3   Davis Hounshell, *From the American System to Mass Production, 1800–1932* (Baltimore: John Hopkins University Press, 1984), 224.

4   Theodore Levitt, "Marketing Myopia," *Harvard Business Review*, July–August 1960, 45–56.

5   Andre Picard, "Fat 'the New Tobacco,' Heart Group Warns," *Globe and Mail*, February 11, 2004, p. A5.

6   Ibid.

7   Ibid.

8   Statistics Canada, "E-commerce: Household Spending on the Internet," *The Daily*, October 23, 2001.

9   "Canadian Internet Users More Concerned about Internet Security," *Canadian Interactive Reid Report*, June 27, 2003.

10 Paul-Mark Rendon, "Sweet Marketing Harmony," *Digital Marketing*, March 1, 2004.

11 John MacIntyre, "Good News, Bad News—Order a Pizza," Halifax *Mail-Star*, February 14, 2004, p. C2.

12 Steve Mossop and Chris Ferneyhough, "More Canadians Look to the Internet to Book Travel Plans," Ipsos Reid Report, August 28, 2003.

13 Herbert A. Simon, *Administrative Behavior*, 2nd ed. (New York: Free Press, 1965), 40.

14 James G. March and Herbert A. Simon, *Organizations* (New York: Wiley, 1958), 140–241.

15 Michael A. Jones, Philip J. Trocchia, and David L. Mothersbaugh, "Noneconomic Motivations for Price Haggling: An Exploratory Study," in *Advances in Consumer Research*, 24, eds. Merrie Brucks and Deborah J. MacInnis (Provo, UT: Association for Consumer Research, 1997), 388–391.

16 Richard P. Bagozzi and Utpal Dholakia, "Goal Setting and Goal Striving in Consumer Behavior," *Journal of Marketing*, 63 (1999), 19–32.

17 Gregory M. Rose, "Consumer Socialization, Parental Style, and Developmental Timetables in the United States and Japan," *Journal of Marketing*, 63, 3 (July 1999), 105–119.

18 Ernest R. Cadotte, Robert B. Woodruff, and Roger L. Jenkins, "Expectations and Norms in Models of Consumer Satisfaction," *Journal of Marketing Research*, 24 (August 1987), 305–314.

MEL**O**N

GRAPHIC DESIGN
ADVERTISING
INTERIOR DESIGN

been inside? www.melon.bz

photo: john sherlock

chapter 2
consumer research

LEARNING OBJECTIVES

By the end of this chapter, you should be able to:

1. Define consumer research and explain the two major consumer-research paradigms of positivism and interpretivism.
2. List and explain the various steps in the consumer research process.
3. Explain four qualitative and quantitative consumer research methods and their pros and cons.
4. Define probability and non-probability samples and discuss at least three of each in detail.
5. Discuss how marketers can assess consumer satisfaction.

are you an avid user of online banking services? If you are, you are among the trend setters in this category in Canada. In 2002, 34 percent of Canadians were using online banking services. Online banking was more popular among people in the 18- to 34-year age category and least popular among people 55 years of age or older. Online banking was used by 45 percent of 18- to 34-year-olds, but only 21 percent of people 55 and over.

Why are older Canadians less willing to embrace this new technology? One of the main reasons may be the feeling of older generations that an advanced understanding of technology is needed for online banking. This, combined with their perception that they do not have an adequate understanding of technology, may be the reason for the lower use of online banking among people 55 years or older.

How did the Canadian Bankers' Association identify these issues? They surveyed 1200 Canadians, 18 years and older, by telephone in a one-month period. Almost all the questions were closed-ended (i.e., the respondents had to choose from a list of alternatives given); the survey is considered accurate within plus or minus 2.9 percentage points, 19 times out of 20.[1]

Banks are not the only organizations interested in finding out what their customers feel about the services and products that they offer. Almost all organizations are interested in finding out consumer attitudes, usage patterns, and satisfaction levels with their products and services. This chapter examines the field of consumer research and outlines the steps in conducting research on consumers. The chapter also covers major research methods employed in consumer research. More details of these will be found in later chapters and in the Research Insight boxes provided throughout the text.

CHAPTER OVERVIEW

This chapter gives an overview of consumer research, including the major types of consumer research, paradigms (positivism and interpretivism), the steps involved in consumer research, and the main methods of data collection. Additional information on these will be provided in later chapters (when relevant); the Research Insight boxes in each chapter will also provide more information on consumer research methodologies.

WHAT IS CONSUMER RESEARCH?

Consumer research:
Methodology used to study consumer behaviour.

Consumer research developed as an extension of marketing research. Like the findings of marketing research, the findings of consumer research were used to improve managerial decisions. Studying consumer behaviour enables marketers to predict how consumers will react to promotional messages and to understand why they make the purchase decisions they do. Marketers realize that if they know more about the consumer decision-making process, they can design marketing strategies and promotional messages that will influence consumers more effectively. Recently marketers have begun to realize that customer research is a unique subset of marketing research and that it needs specialized research methods that collect customer data and also enhance the company's relationship with its customers.

Consumer Research Paradigms

The early consumer researchers gave little thought to the effect of mood, emotion, or situation on consumer decisions. They believed that marketing was simply applied economics and that consumers were rational decision makers who objectively evaluated the goods and services available to them and selected those that gave them the highest utility (satisfaction) at the lowest cost.

Motivational research:
Qualitative research aimed at uncovering consumers' subconscious or hidden motivations.

Very soon, however, researchers realized that consumers were not always conscious of why they made the decisions they did. Even when they were, they were not always willing to reveal those reasons. In 1939, a Viennese psychoanalyst named Ernest Dichter began to use Freudian psychoanalytic techniques to uncover the hidden motivations of consumers. By the late 1950s, his research methodology (called **motivational research**), which was essentially qualitative in approach, was widely adopted by consumer researchers. As a result of Dichter's work and subsequent research designed to search deep within the consumer's psyche, consumer researchers today use two different research methods to study consumer behaviour—**quantitative research** and **qualitative research.**

Quantitative research:
Research methods (surveys, observation, and experiments) that are empirical and descriptive, and that describe consumer behaviour, explain the effects of marketing inputs on consumer behaviour, or predict consumer behaviour.

Quantitative Research

Quantitative research is descriptive and empirical; it is used by researchers to understand the effects of various marketing inputs on the consumer, thus enabling marketers to "predict" consumer behaviour. This research approach is known as **positivism,** and consumer researchers primarily concerned with predicting consumer behaviour are known as *positivists*. The research methods used in positivist research are borrowed primarily from the natural sciences; they consist of experiments, survey techniques, and observation.

Qualitative research:
Research methods (interviews, focus groups, projective techniques, etc.) that are more subjective and that try to explain the act of consumption and hidden motivations for consumption.

Quantitative techniques—regardless of the exact method used—share these characteristics:

■ The findings are descriptive and empirical.

Positivism:
A research approach that regards consumer behaviour as an applied science and focuses primarily on consumer decision making.

■ If the data are collected randomly (i.e., from a probability sample), they lead to findings that can be generalized to larger populations.

■ Because the data collected are quantitative, they lend themselves to sophisticated statistical analysis.

Research Insight 2-1 describes data mining, a data analytical technique that is being used more frequently by companies now.

RESEARCH INSIGHT 2-1
DATA MINING: MAKING THE MOST OF YOUR RESOURCES

Do you need to find out how you can keep your customers? Or who your best customers are? Or reduce the number of delinquent accounts? Or perhaps you want to tailor your promotional campaigns in such a way that they reach your best customers at the right time. Regardless of your goal, one technique that may be of use is data mining. Although there is no one accepted definition of data mining (in fact, it is more often defined by what it is not than by what it is), here is one simple definition: "applications that look for hidden patterns in a group of data that can be used to predict future behavior."[a] Another source defines it as "an information extraction activity whose goal is to discover hidden facts contained in databases. Using a combination of machine learning, statistical analysis, modeling techniques and database technology, data mining finds patterns and subtle relationships in data and infers rules that allow the prediction of future results...."[b] Most definitions emphasize the following points:

■ Data mining aims to discover hidden patterns; if the goal is just to understand patterns, it is a *descriptive data mining project*.
■ Data mining uses several quantitative methods, such as modelling, machine learning, and statistical analysis.
■ Data mining requires a sound knowledge of database technology.
■ Data mining generally tries to predict the future through the use of information that has already been collected—data mining of that kind is *predictive*.

In other words, data mining goes beyond usual statistical analyses such as regression, cluster analysis, or factor analysis to discover hidden patterns in data; the goal is always to predict some future behaviour.

Any data-mining task requires four steps: classification (the labelling of records—e.g., delinquent or non-delinquent customer, buyer or non-buyer), estimation (filling in missing values in incoming records), segmentation (dividing the population into relevant subgroups with similarity in behaviour), and description (giving a clear picture of the types of behaviour through visual or text displays).

Let us look at an actual example of data mining.[c] A retailer wanted to improve its customer retention rates through improved relationship marketing efforts while keeping marketing costs to a minimum. The retailer had several business units, ranging from household appliances to clothing to automotive parts. The company had a return on investment target of 10 to 1 for the data-mining project. The data mining started with a detailed look at the company's customer database. This showed that there were several contact points and that many relationship marketing efforts were being made by the company. For example, its credit department contacted the customer five times a year, and these contacts included bimonthly statements, holiday planners in December, and a follow-up (in January); its mail order department sent eight direct-mail pieces, one 10-percent-off coupon, and one holiday gift notice and made two telemarketing calls. Its customer service department contacted customers every month with telemarketing calls, maintenance agreements, or special mailers. Often, customers received more than one call or mailer a month from the company, and some were contacted 100 times a year or more.

Another issue was the data entry being made when customers purchased something from the company. The company tracked individual customers rather than households, which meant that if two people from one household bought products from the company, they would be considered different customers; this resulted in an increase in marketing efforts.

Next, the company looked at the revenue stream from each customer and found that after approximately 45 contacts, there was no additional return from sending out more materials. Finally, the company analysed customer loyalty and found that its customers could be classified into four categories according to the total amount spent and number of purchases made each year. Ten percent of its customers fell into the first group, the most loyal customers; they were consistent in their purchase patterns and tended to buy certain types of products. The company also found that it lost many of these customers after a few years. The second group also bought several product categories and were fairly regular customers, but they were not as consistent in their patterns as the first group. The third group (40 percent of its customers) made fewer visits and bought fewer categories of products, but they had the most potential. The final group were occasional or one-time shoppers who visited the store to buy a particular item that was on sale.

Using that information, the company took the following actions:

- It designated each household, rather than each individual, as a data point. Some criteria had to be set for this purpose to avoid roommates being considered one household. The company decided to use mailing address and last name (from three different business units) for the purpose and assigned a unique ID to each household.

- It created a calendar of marketing activities that enabled it to coordinate the marketing activities of various subunits. This reduced the number of duplicate mailings and prevented the same customer from being contacted several times each month.

- The customer-loyalty detection procedure also helped the company identify life-cycle stages and the peaks and troughs in purchase that followed changes in life-cycle stages. The company used this information to tailor its promotional messages and packages. For example, if a customer's purchase pattern suggested that the person had just had a baby, the company started sending information on toddler products and toys after a few months; if the couple had a toddler, the company, after waiting for a certain time, started mailing out information on swings, bicycles, and so on.

- It concentrated on keeping its loyal customers and attempted to increase purchases by its third-level loyalists.

[a] www.webopedia.com/TERM/D/data_mining.html.

[b] www.twocrows.com/glossary.htm.

[c] Christopher Westphal and Teresa Blaxton, *Data Mining Solutions* (John Wiley, 1998), 501–512.

Qualitative Research

Qualitative research methods consist of depth interviews, focus groups, metaphor analysis, collage research, and projective techniques (discussed later in the chapter). These techniques are administered by a highly trained interviewer-analyst who also analyzes the findings; thus, the findings tend to be somewhat subjective.

Qualitative research techniques such as depth interviews, projective techniques, and other methods are also being used increasingly by some consumer behaviour researchers to study the act of *consumption* (i.e., decision making) rather than the act of *buying*. These researchers view consumer behaviour as a subset of human behaviour and greater understanding as a key to reducing the negative aspects of consumer behaviour (the so-called dark side of consumer behaviour), such as drug addiction, shoplifting, alcoholism, and compulsive buying. Interest in understanding consumer experiences has led to the term **interpretivism,** and the researchers who adopt this paradigm are known as *interpretivists*. Besides the usual qualitative techniques, these researchers have used other methods borrowed from

Interpretivism:
A postmodernist approach to the study of consumer behaviour that focuses on the act of consuming rather than on the act of buying.

cultural anthropology, such as *ethnography*, to study the meanings of cultural practices and symbols.

All qualitative techniques have two characteristics in common:

■ Their samples are small.
■ Their findings are not generalizable to larger populations (owing to the small sample sizes).

In spite of these limitations, qualitative research nevertheless has an important place in managerial decision making. Figure 2-1 compares the purposes and assumptions of positivist research and interpretivist research.

FIGURE 2-1	Comparisons between Positivism and Interpretivism

	POSITIVISM	**INTERPRETIVISM**
Purpose	Prediction of consumer actions	Understanding consumption practices
Other descriptive terms	Positivism is also known as modernism, logical empiricism, operationalism, and objectivism	Interpretivists are also known as experientialists and postmodernists; interpretivism is also known as naturalism, humanism, and postpositivism
Methodology and research tools	*Quantitative* research: surveys, experiments, and observations	*Qualitative research:* depth interviews and projective techniques
		Ethnography: a technique borrowed from cultural anthropology in which the researchers place themselves (participate) in the society under study in an effort to absorb the meaning of various cultural practices
		Semiotics: the study of symbols and the meanings they convey
Assumptions	• Rationality: consumers make decisions after weighing alternatives	• There is no single objective truth
	• The causes and effects of behaviour can be identified and isolated	• Reality is subjective
	• Individuals are problem solvers who engage in information processing	
	• A single reality exists	
	• Events can be objectively measured	• Each consumption experience is unique
		• Researcher-respondent interactions affect research findings
	• Causes of behaviour can be identified; by manipulating causes (i.e., inputs), the marketer can influence behaviour (i.e., outcomes)	• Often findings are not generalizable to larger populations
	• Findings can be generalized to larger populations	

Note: Not all researchers agree that interpretive research enhances traditional quantitative and qualitative market research. There is also disagreement regarding the alternative terms used to describe each research approach. The following sources illustrate the various conceptualizations of positivism and interpretivism.

Sources: Richard Lutz, "Positivism, Naturalism, and Pluralism in Consumer Research: Paradigms in Paradise," *Advances in Consumer Research*, 16 (Provo, UT: Association for Consumer Research, 1989), 17; John Sherry, "Postmodern Alternatives: The Interpretive Turn in Consumer Research," in *Handbook of Consumer Behavior,* eds. H. Kassarjian and T. Robertson (Upper Saddle River, NJ: Prentice Hall, 1991); Morris B. Holbrook and John O'Shaughnessy, "On the Scientific Status of Consumer Research and the Need for an Interpretive Approach to Studying Consumption Behavior," *Journal of Consumer Research*, 15, December 1988, 398–402; and Morris Holbrook and Elizabeth C. Hirschman, "The Experimental Aspects of Consumption: Consumer Fantasies, Feelings, and Fun," *Journal of Consumer Research*, 9, 2 (1982): 132–134.

Combining Qualitative and Quantitative Research Findings

Marketers often use a combination of quantitative and qualitative research to help them make strategic marketing decisions. For example, they use qualitative research findings to discover new ideas and develop promotional strategy, and they use quantitative research findings to predict consumer reactions to various promotional inputs. Frequently, ideas stemming from qualitative research are tested empirically and become the basis for the design of quantitative studies.

Marketers have discovered that these two research paradigms are really complementary. Together, the predictions made possible by quantitative (positivist) research and the understanding provided by qualitative (interpretivist) research produce a richer and more robust profile of consumer behaviour than either research approach used alone. The combined findings enable marketers to design more meaningful and effective marketing strategies.

THE CONSUMER RESEARCH PROCESS

The major steps in the consumer research process are the following: (1) defining the objectives of the research, (2) collecting and evaluating secondary data, (3) designing a primary research study, (4) collecting primary data, (5) analysing the data, and (6) preparing a report on the findings. Figure 2-2 shows a model of the consumer research process.

FIGURE 2-2 The Consumer Research Process

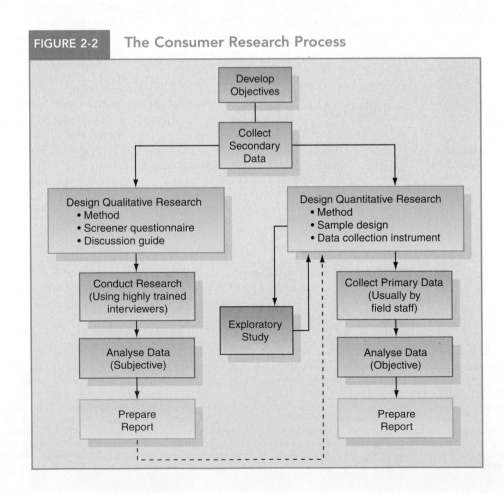

Developing Research Objectives

The first step in consumer research is to define carefully the *objectives* of the study. Is it to segment the market for plasma television sets? To find out consumer attitudes about online shopping? To determine what percentage of households use email? It is important for the marketing manager and the researcher to agree at the outset on the purposes and objectives of the study to ensure that the research design is suitable. A carefully thought-out statement of objectives helps to define the type and level of information needed.

For example, if the purpose of the study is to find new ideas for products or promotional campaigns, then a qualitative study is usually undertaken, in which respondents spend a significant amount of time face to face with a highly trained professional interviewer-analyst, who also does the analysis. Because of the high cost of each interview, a fairly small sample of respondents is studied; thus, the findings are not projectable to the marketplace. If the purpose of the study is to find out what percentage of the population uses certain products and how often, then a quantitative study that can be analysed by computer is undertaken. Sometimes, in designing a quantitative study, the researcher may not know what questions to ask. In such cases, before undertaking a full-scale study, the researcher is likely to conduct a small-scale **exploratory study** to identify the critical issues to include in the data-collection instrument (e.g., a questionnaire).

Collecting Secondary Data

A search for **secondary data** generally follows the statement of objectives. Secondary data are any data originally generated for some purpose other than that of the present research. They include findings based on research done by outside organizations, data generated in-house for earlier studies, and even customer information collected by the firm's sales or credit departments. Finding secondary data is called **secondary research**. (Original research that is done to meet specific objectives where **primary data** is collected is called **primary research**.) Starting with secondary research has several benefits:

- The findings from secondary research sometimes provide sufficient insight into the problem at hand to eliminate the need for primary research.
- Often it provides clues and direction for the design of primary research.
- It is less expensive than primary research.

The sources of secondary market data include government agencies, private population data firms, marketing research companies, and advertising agencies. For example, Statistics Canada collects data on the age, education, occupation, and income of Canadian residents by province and territory and region and also makes projections about the future growth or decline of various demographic segments. Additional information on rents, places of work, car ownership, and patterns of migration is provided in studies of census tracts in major metropolitan areas. Canada Post provides profiles of consumers by postal code. Any firm operating globally may find statistics about any country in the world in the CIA's electronic *World Factbook* published on the web. Figure 2-3 lists some major sources of secondary data.

If more detailed information on purchasing patterns or product usage is needed, or if psychological or socio-cultural consumer information is sought, primary data must be collected. Research to obtain such information costs more and takes more time than secondary research, but it is likely to yield a more accurate picture than studies based on secondary data alone.

Exploratory study:
A small-scale study carried out to identify the critical issues that need to be examined in further detail.

Secondary data:
Data collected for purposes other than problems under study.

Secondary research:
Research aimed at locating secondary data.

Primary data:
Data collected specifically for the purposes of a particular research study.

Primary research:
Original research aimed at collecting primary data.

www.cia.gov/cia/
publications/
factbook

| FIGURE 2-3 | Secondary Data Sources |

A. Internal Sources

Company profit and loss statements, balance sheets, sales figures, sales-call reports, invoices, inventory records, and prior research reports.

B. Government Sources

- Statistics Canada, various publications
- *Canada Year Book* (annual summary data)
- *Market Research Handbook* (summary data)
- Statistics Canada *Daily* (provides highlights of newly released data)
- *Infomat* (a weekly review of Canadian economic and social trends)
- *Canadian Social Trends* (online quarterly version and hard copy)
- Industry Canada
- Business Development Bank of Canada

C. Periodicals and Books

- Business Periodicals Index
- Standard and Poor's Industry
- *Moody's* manuals
- Encyclopedia of Associations
- Marketing journals, including *Journal of Marketing, Journal of Marketing Research,* and *Journal of Consumer Research*
- Trade magazines, including *Marketing Magazine, Advertising Age, Canadian Banker, Canadian Business, Progressive Grocer, Sales and Marketing Management,* and *Canadian Consumer*
- General business magazines, including *Business Week, Canadian Business, Report on Business, Atlantic Business, Fortune, Forbes, The Economist, Harvard Business Review,* and *Canadian Journal of Administrative Sciences*

D. Commercial Data

- Nielsen Company: Data on products and brands sold through retail outlets (Retail Index Services), supermarket scanner data (Scantrack), data on television audiences (Media Research Services), magazine circulation data (Neodata Services, Inc.), and others
- Consumer Panel of Canada

E. Professional Associations, Research Bureaus

- Conference Board of Canada
- Retail Council of Canada
- Interactive Advertising Bureau

F. Online Sources

- CBCA: Canadian Business and Current Affairs (**www.micromedia.ca/Products_Services/NEWS.htm**)
- Canadian Corporate Newsnet (**www.cdn-news.com**)
- Canada Newswire (**www.newswire.ca**)

Syndicated Data

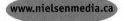

Because it is often very expensive to collect primary data, many companies routinely buy syndicated data about consumption patterns. Syndicated data are data that are of interest to a large number of users and that are collected periodically, compiled and analysed according to a standard procedure, and then sold to interested buyers. Nielsen Media Research, for example, by means of computerized units with modems connected to each television set in the households sampled, compiles reports on the number of Canadian households tuned to national television broadcasts. By means of "people meters" (devices that enable members of the sampled households to record their individual viewing patterns), it determines who *is watching* national television programs. And by means of diaries in which samples of viewers record the programs they watched, it collects information about the viewing of local television programs. Reports containing that information are sold to companies and advertising agencies and are used to set advertising rates; that is, the larger the audience that a program delivers, the more the commercial time in that program is worth to advertisers.

Internal Data

The widely cited "80/20 rule" states that, generally, a relatively small percentage of a company's customers (e.g., 20 percent) accounts for a disproportionately large part of the company's sales and profits (e.g., 80 percent). With the increased emphasis on building and maintaining long-term relationships with customers, many companies are now developing systems that will identify highly profitable customers as quickly as possible and target these customers with special offers to encourage them to buy even more of the company's products and services. Such systems stem from the collection and analysis of *internal* secondary data, such as

- past customer transactions,
- letters from customers,
- sales-call reports, and
- warranty cards.

Using these data, savvy marketers draw up **customer lifetime value (CLV)** profiles for various categories of customers. The CLV can be computed from customer acquisition costs (the resources needed to establish a relationship with the customer), the profits generated from individual sales to each customer, the cost of handling customers and their orders (some customers may place more complex and variable orders that cost more to handle), and the expected duration of the relationship.

Customer lifetime value (CLV): Profiles of customers drawn from internal data that show the net value of customers to the firm.

The next step—designing primary research—depends on the purposes of the study. If descriptive information is needed, a quantitative study is likely to be undertaken; if the purpose is to get new ideas (e.g., for repositioning a product), a qualitative study is undertaken.

Conducting Primary Research—Quantitative Research Methods

A quantitative research study involves choosing a research design, identifying data collection methods and instruments to be used, and choosing a sample design.

Quantitative Research Method

Three basic designs are used in quantitative research: observation, experimentation (in a laboratory or in the field, such as in a retail store), and surveys (i.e., questioning people).

Observational Research Observational research is an important method of consumer research because marketers recognize that the best way to gain an in-depth understanding of the relationship between people and products is to watch them in the process of buying and using products. Many large corporations and advertising agencies use trained researchers and observers to watch, note, and sometimes videotape consumers in stores, malls, or their own homes.

For example, in studying responses to a new mint-flavoured Listerine, the Warner Lambert Company hired a research firm that paid 37 New York City families to let it install cameras in their bathrooms to videotape the way they used mouthwash. The study found that consumers who used Scope gave the product a swish and spat it out. Conversely, users of the new Listerine kept the mouthwash in their mouths for much longer (one subject even kept it in his mouth as he left home and got into the car, and spat it out only after driving a couple of blocks).[2]

By watching people interact with products, observational researchers gain a better understanding of what the product symbolizes to a consumer and greater insight into the bond between people and products that is the essence of brand loyalty.

Mechanical Observation Mechanical observation uses a mechanical or electronic device to record customer behaviour or response to a particular marketing stimulus. For example, a retailer may use a traffic counter to determine the business viability of a new store location, government planners may use data collected from electronic devices in passenger cars, such as EZ Pass, to decide which roads should be widened, and banks can use security cameras to observe problems that customers may have in using ATMs.

Consumers are using more and more technological devices for making purchases because such devices generally reduce consumers' reliance on cash or sales assistance and often provide rewards for using the devices. People who use supermarket frequency shopping cards, for example, often receive offers for promotional discounts tailored specifically for them, on the basis of their purchases, at checkout counters. Moviegoers who order tickets online can pick them up at ATM-like devices at movie theatres and avoid waiting in line at the box office. Of course, as consumers use more and more highly convenient technologies, such as credit and ATM cards, EZ Passes, frequency cards, automated phone systems, and online shopping, there are more and more electronic records of their consumption patterns. These records are not anonymous, and sophisticated marketers are beginning to collect these data and use them, sometimes almost instantly, to influence consumption behaviour.

The ethical and privacy issues stemming from collecting data that are not anonymous with technological devices are receiving more and more public debate.

Gambling casinos have been in the forefront of developing systems that track individual customer data collected during the various stages of a customer's visit and matching them with data (including amounts spent) collected on previous visits by that customer. The casinos use these data to classify visitors according to their "loyalty levels" and design corresponding rewards that are given almost immediately.

For example, most casinos use magnetic "frequent-player cards." Sophisticated electronic network systems monitor the gaming patterns, eating habits, and room preferences of all visitors. When a player sits at a table, within seconds the casino's manager can read, on the screen, the guest's history, including alcoholic beverages preferred and gaming habits. Because there are electronic tags in the chips issued to each player, when a player leaves the table, his or her record is updated instantly and made available at any contact point for that customer throughout the entire casino complex. Thus, the casino can instantly reward customers who are good for business by giving them free meals and room upgrades and inviting them to gamble in designated VIP lounges.[3]

Marketers also use physiological observation devices that monitor respondents' patterns of information processing. For example, an electronic eye camera may be used to monitor the eye movements of subjects looking at a series of product advertisements, and electronic sensors placed on the subjects' heads can monitor the brain activity and attentiveness involved in viewing each ad.

Experimentation It is possible to test the relative sales appeal of many types of variables, such as package design, price, promotional offers, or advertising themes,

www.ernex.com

through experiments designed to identify cause and effect. In such experiments (called *causal research*), only some variables are manipulated (the *independent variables*), while all other elements are kept constant. A **controlled experiment** of this type ensures that any difference in the outcome (the *dependent variable*) is due to different treatments of the variable under study and not to extraneous factors.

One study, for example, tested the effectiveness of using an attractive versus unattractive endorser in promoting two types of products: products that are used to enhance attractiveness (e.g., a men's cologne) and products that are not (e.g., a pen). The photograph depicting the attractive endorser was a scanned image of an attractive athletic man, whereas the picture depicting the unattractive endorser was the same image graphically modified to make the man less attractive. The subjects viewed each endorser-product combination for 15 seconds (simulating the viewing of an actual print ad) and then filled out a questionnaire that measured their attitudes and purchase intentions toward the products advertised. Here, the combinations of the product (i.e., used or not used to enhance attractiveness) and the endorser's attractiveness (i.e., attractive or unattractive endorser) were the *manipulated treatments* (i.e., the independent variables) and the combination of the attitudes toward the product and purchase intentions was the *dependent variable*. Results indicated that the attractive endorser was more effective in promoting both types of product.[4]

A major application of causal research is test marketing, in which, before a new product is launched, elements such as package, price, and promotion are manipulated in a controlled setting in order to predict sales or gauge the possible responses to the product. Today some researchers employ *virtual reality methods*.

For example, in a market test, respondents can view supermarket shelves stocked with many products, including different versions of the same product, on computer screens, "pick up" an item by touching the image, examine it by rotating the image with a track ball, and place it in a shopping cart if they decide to buy it. The researchers observe how long the respondents spend in looking at the product, the time spent in examining each side of the package, the products purchased, and the order of the purchases.[5]

Surveys If researchers want to ask consumers about their purchase preferences and consumption experiences they can do so in person, by telephone, by mail, or online. Each of these survey methods has advantages and disadvantages that the researcher must weigh when selecting the method of contact (see Figure 2-4).

> **Controlled experiment:** A causal research study in which some variables (independent variables) are manipulated in one group but not in another to ensure that any difference in the outcome (the dependent variable) is due to different treatments of the variable under study and not to extraneous factors.

| FIGURE 2-4 | Comparative Advantages and Disadvantages of Personal Interview, Telephone, Mail, and Online Surveys |

	PERSONAL INTERVIEW	TELEPHONE	MAIL	ONLINE SURVEY
Cost	High	Moderate	Low	Low
Speed	Slow	Immediate	Slow	Fast
Response rate	High	Moderate	Low	Self-selected
Geographic flexibility	Difficult	Good	Excellent	Excellent
Interviewer bias	Problematic	Moderate	N/A	N/A
Interviewer supervision	Difficult	Easy	N/A	N/A
Quality of response	Excellent	Limited	Limited	Excellent

Personal interview surveys most often take place in the home or in retail shopping areas. The latter, referred to as *mall intercepts,* are used more frequently than home interviews because so many people are at work during the day and because many people today are reluctant to allow strangers into their homes.

Telephone surveys are also used to collect consumer data; however, evenings and weekends are often the only times to reach telephone respondents, who tend to be less responsive—even hostile—to calls that interrupt them when they are having dinner, watching television, or simply relaxing. The difficulties of reaching people with unlisted telephone numbers have been solved through random-digit dialling, and the costs of a widespread telephone survey are often minimized by using toll-free telephone lines. Other problems arise, however, from the increased use of answering machines and call-display services to screen calls. Some market research companies have tried to automate telephone surveys, but many respondents are even less willing to talk to an electronic voice than to a live interviewer.

Mail surveys are conducted by sending questionnaires directly to individuals at their homes. One of the chief problems of mail questionnaires is a low response rate, but researchers have developed a number of techniques to increase returns, such as enclosing a stamped, self-addressed envelope, using a provocative questionnaire, and sending prenotification letters as well as follow-up letters. A number of commercial research firms that specialize in consumer surveys have set up panels of consumers who, for a token fee, agree to complete the research company's mail questionnaires regularly. Sometimes panel members are also asked to keep diaries of their purchases.

Online surveys are sometimes conducted on the internet. Respondents are directed to the marketer's (or researcher's) website by computer ads or home pages; thus, the samples are self-selected and the results, therefore, cannot be projected to the larger population. Most computer polls ask respondents to complete a profile consisting of demographic questions that enable the researchers to classify the responses to the product or service questions.

Researchers who conduct computer polling believe that the anonymity of the internet encourages people to be more forthright and honest than if they were asked the same questions in person or by mail; others believe that the data collected may be suspect because some respondents may create new online personalities that do not reflect their own beliefs or behaviour. Some survey organizations cite the inherent advantages of wide reach and affordability in online polling. Internet Insight 2-1 describes some ways in which marketers can make their online surveys more effective.

Data-Collection Instruments for Quantitative Research

Data collection instruments are developed as part of the total research design of a study in order to systematize the collection of data and to ensure that all respondents are asked the same questions in the same order. Data collection instruments include questionnaires, personal inventories, attitude scales, and, for qualitative data, discussion guides. Data collection instruments are usually pretested and "debugged" to ensure that the study possesses two crucial qualities: validity and reliability.

Validity:
The degree to which a measurement instrument accurately measures what it claims to measure.

■ **Validity** refers to the degree to which a measurement instrument accurately measures what it claims to measure, or whether or not the data needed to answer the questions or objectives stated in the first (objectives) stage of the research process have been collected.

INTERNET INSIGHT 2-1
MAKING ONLINE SURVEYS MORE EFFECTIVE

Online surveys are popping up everywhere. There is hardly a site now that does not have some form of online survey. For example, the website of *Marketing Magazine* has a web poll that changes with each issue of the magazine. Why are web surveys so popular? As mentioned earlier, they are cheaper than off-line surveys, are less intrusive, and can reach specifically targeted populations.

There are three types of online surveys.

Email surveys: Respondents are first sent an email inviting them to participate in a survey. The names of potential participants may be drawn from the company's email list or through a large internet-based panel.

Pop-up surveys: Unlike email surveys, pop-up surveys choose respondents randomly from visitors to the website. The random selection process makes it better suited to customer-satisfaction surveys and to testing new product ideas.

Tracking surveys: A variation of the pop-up method, tracking surveys randomly select respondents from visitors to the website, but once a person agrees to take part in the survey, the person's behaviour as he or she navigates the site and the time spent on the site are tracked (with his or her permission). As visitors leave the site, they are then surveyed on various aspects of the website and their online experience with the firm. For example, Surveysite, a Toronto company, has its own tracking survey system called SiteTrax.

There are several ways to make these surveys more useful:

1. Give special incentives for participating in surveys.
2. Let consumers know why the company is conducting the survey and assure them that the information will not be used for other purposes.
3. Assure consumers that the information they give will remain confidential.
4. Keep the questionnaire short and simple.
5. Have easy and interesting questions near the beginning.

QUESTIONS:

1. Visit the websites of an auto maker and a magazine that have online surveys. Evaluate the effectiveness of the surveys.
2. Are people who are likely to answer these surveys different from the typical consumer? If so, in what ways would they be different?

Reliability is the degree to which a measurement instrument is consistent in what it measures, or whether the same questions, asked of a similar sample, would produce the same findings. Often a sample is systematically divided in two, and each half is given the same questionnaire to complete. If the results from each half are similar, the questionnaire is said to have *split-half reliability*.

Reliability:
The degree to which a measurement instrument is consistent in what it measures.

www.marketingmag.ca

www.surveysite.com

Questionnaires For quantitative research, the primary data-collection instrument is the questionnaire, which can be sent through the mail to selected respondents for self-administration or can be administered by field interviewers in person or by telephone. In order to motivate people to respond to surveys, researchers have found that questionnaires must be interesting, objective, unambiguous, easy to complete and generally not burdensome. To enhance the analysis and facilitate the classification of responses into meaningful categories, questionnaires include both substantive questions that are relevant to the purposes of the study and pertinent demographic questions.

Questionnaires can be classified in two ways:

- *Disguised versus undisguised:* When the purpose of a study is not divulged, the questionnaire is considered to be a disguised questionnaire. A disguised questionnaire sometimes yields more truthful answers and prevents respondents from giving the answers they think are expected or looked for.

- *Closed-ended versus open-ended:* Open-ended questionnaires require answers in the respondent's own words, whereas in closed-ended ones, the respondent merely chooses an answer from a list of options.

Open-ended questions are

- more difficult to code and analyse (closed-ended are simple to code);
- likely to yield more insightful information since, unlike with closed-end questions, the answers are not limited to those provided.

The format of the questionnaire and the wording and order of the questions affect the validity of the responses and, in the case of mail questionnaires, the number of responses received. Hence, regardless of the type of questionnaire used, some general guidelines should be followed:

- Great care must be taken in wording each question to avoid biasing the responses.

- The order of the questions is also important: the opening questions must be interesting enough to persuade the respondent to take part, and the questions must proceed in a logical order.

- Demographic (classification) questions should be at the end, where they are more likely to be answered.

- Respondents should be offered confidentiality or anonymity to encourage honest, open answers and to dispel any reluctance about self-disclosure.

Attitude Scales Researchers often present respondents with a list of products or product attributes for which they are asked to indicate their relative feelings or evaluations. The instruments most often used to capture this evaluative data are called attitude scales. The most common attitude scales are Likert scales, semantic differential scales, behaviour intention scales, and rank-order scales.

Likert scale: The Likert scale is the most popular form of attitude scale because it is easy for researchers to prepare and interpret and simple to answer. The respondent checks or writes the number corresponding to his or her "agreement" or "disagreement" with each of a series of statements that describes the attitude object under investigation. The scale consists of an equal number of agreement or disagreement choices on either side of a neutral choice. A principal advantage of the Likert scale is that it gives the researcher the option of considering the responses to each statement separately or combining the responses to produce an overall score.

Semantic differential scale: Like the Likert scale, this is relatively easy to construct and administer. The scale usually consists of a series of bipolar adjectives (such as good/bad, hot/cold, like/dislike, or expensive/inexpensive), one of each pair being placed at one end of an odd-numbered (e.g., five- or seven-point) continuum. Respondents are asked to evaluate a concept or a product or company on the basis of each attribute by checking the point on the continuum that best expresses their feelings or beliefs. Care must be taken to vary the location of positive and negative terms from the left side of the continuum to the right side to avoid biasing the answers. Sometimes an even-numbered scale is used to eliminate the option of a neutral answer. An important feature of the semantic differential scale is that it can be used to develop consumer profiles of the concept under study. Semantic differential profiles are also used to compare consumer perceptions of competitive products and to indicate areas for product improvement when perceptions of the existing product are measured against perceptions of the "ideal" product.

Behaviour intention scale: This scale measures the likelihood that consumers will act in a certain way in the future, such as buying the product again or recommending it to a friend. These scales are easy to construct, and consumers are asked to make subjective judgments regarding their future behaviour.

Rank-order scale: Subjects are asked to rank items, such as products or retail stores or websites, in order of preference in terms of some criterion, such as overall quality or value for the money. Rank-order scaling provides important competitive information and enables marketers to identify areas of product design and product positioning that need improving. Figure 2-5 shows examples of the attitude scales that are often used in consumer research.

Conducting Primary Research—Qualitative Research

Unlike quantitative research, qualitative studies are often based on small samples and emphasize qualitative data (as opposed to large amounts of data). The purpose is often to get more in-depth information from a smaller number of people.

Qualitative Research Designs

In selecting the research format for a qualitative study, the researcher has to take into consideration the purpose of the study and the types of data needed. Although the research methods used may differ in composition, they all have roots in psychoanalytic and clinical aspects of psychology, and they stress open-ended and free-response types of questions to stimulate respondents to reveal their innermost thoughts and beliefs.

The principal data collection techniques for qualitative studies are depth interviews, focus groups, projective techniques, and metaphor analysis. These techniques are regularly used in the early stages of attitude research to pinpoint relevant product-related beliefs or attributes and to develop an initial picture of consumer attitudes (especially the beliefs and attributes they associate with particular products and services).

Depth Interviews A **depth interview** is a long (generally 30 minutes to an hour), unstructured interview between a respondent and a highly trained interviewer, who minimizes his or her own participation in the discussion after establishing the general subject to be discussed. (However, as noted earlier, interpretative researchers often take a more active part in the discussion.) Respondents are encouraged to talk freely about their activities, attitudes, and interests in addition to the product category or brand under study. Transcripts, videotapes, or audiotape recordings of interviews are then carefully studied, together with reports of respondents' moods and any gestures or "body language" they may have used to convey attitudes or motives. Such studies give marketers valuable ideas about product design or redesign and offer insights for positioning or repositioning the product. For purposes of copy testing, respondents might be asked to describe in depth various ads they are shown. Other techniques include *auto-driving,* in which the researcher shows the respondents photos, videos, and audiotapes of their own shopping behaviour and asks them to comment specifically on their consumption actions.[6]

Depth interview:
A long (generally 30 minutes to an hour), unstructured interview between a respondent and a highly trained interviewer.

FIGURE 2-5   Attitude Scales

LIKERT SCALE

For each of the following statements, please check the response that best describes the extent to which you agree or disagree with each statement.

	Strongly agree	Somewhat agree	Neither agree nor disagree	Somewhat disagree	Strongly disagree
It's fun to shop online.					
I am afraid to give my credit card number online.					

Two widely used applications of the Likert scale to measure consumer attitudes are:

SATISFACTION MEASURES

Overall, how satisfied are you with Bank X's online banking?

Very satisfied	Somewhat satisfied	Neither satisfied nor dissatisfied	Somewhat dissatisfied	Very dissatisfied

IMPORTANCE SCALES

The following features are associated with shopping on the internet. For each feature, please check the one alternative that best expresses how important or unimportant that feature is to you.

	Extremely important	Somewhat important	Neither important nor unimportant	Somewhat unimportant	Not at all important
Speed of downloading the order form					
Being able to register with the site					

SEMANTIC DIFFERENTIAL SCALE

For each of the following features, please check one alternative that best expresses your impression of how that feature applies to **online banking:**

Competitive rates ├─┼─┼─┼─┼─┼─┼─┤ Non-competitive rates

Reliable ├─┼─┼─┼─┼─┼─┼─┤ Unreliable

Note: The same semantic differential scale can be applied to two competitive offerings, such as online banking and regular banking, and a graphic representation of the profiles of the two alternatives, along with the bipolar adjectives included in the scale, can be easily constructed.

BEHAVIOUR INTENTION SCALES

How likely are you to continue using Bank X's online banking for the next six months?

Definitely will continue	Probably will continue	Might or might not continue	Probably will not continue	Definitely will not continue

How likely are you to recommend Bank X's online banking to a friend?

Definitely will recommend	Probably will recommend	Might or might not recommend	Probably will not recommend	Definitely will not recommend

RANK ORDER SCALE

We would like to find out about your preferences regarding banking methods. Please rank the following banking methods by placing a "1" in front of the method that you prefer most, a "2" next to your second preference, and continuing until you have ranked all of the methods.

_____ Inside the bank   _____ Online banking   _____ Banking by telephone

_____ ATM   _____ Banking by mail

Focus Groups A **focus group** consists of 8 to 10 respondents who meet with a moderator-analyst for a group discussion "focused" on a particular product or product category (or any other subject of research interest). Respondents are encouraged to discuss their interests, attitudes, reactions, motives, life styles, and feelings about the product or product category, their experience of using it, and so forth.

Focus group:
A focused discussion of a product or any other subject of interest with a group of 8 to 10 respondents, moderated by a trained researcher.

Because a focus group takes about two hours, a researcher can easily conduct two or three (with a total of 30 respondents) in one day, whereas it might take that same researcher five or six days to conduct 30 individual depth interviews. Analysis of responses in both depth interviews and focus groups requires a great deal of skill on the part of the researcher. Focus groups are invariably taped, and sometimes videotaped, to assist in the analysis. Interviews are usually held in specially designed conference rooms with one-way mirrors that enable marketers and advertising agency staff to observe the sessions without disrupting or inhibiting the responses.

Respondents are recruited on the basis of a carefully drawn consumer profile (called a screener questionnaire) based on specifications defined by marketing management, and they are usually paid a fee for participating. Sometimes users of the company's brands are clustered in one or more groups, and their responses are compared with those of non-users interviewed in other groups.

Some marketers prefer focus groups to individual depth interviews because it takes less time to conduct the study, and they think that the freewheeling group discussions and group dynamics tend to yield a greater number of new ideas and insights than do depth interviews. Other marketers prefer individual depth interviews because they believe that respondents, being free of group pressure, are less likely to give socially acceptable (and not necessarily truthful) responses, are more likely to remain attentive during the entire interview, and—because of the greater individual attention they receive—are more likely to reveal their private thoughts. Figure 2-6 presents a portion of a discussion guide that might be used in a focus-group session to gain insights into the attitudes of consumers toward various providers of cellular telephone service. The findings would be equally relevant to the positioning of a new service provider or the repositioning of an existing provider.

Projective Techniques **Projective techniques** are designed to tap the underlying motives of individuals despite their unconscious rationalizations or conscious efforts at concealment. The techniques consist of a variety of disguised "tests" that contain ambiguous stimuli, such as incomplete sentences, untitled pictures or cartoons, ink blots, word-association tests, and other-person characterizations. Projective techniques are sometimes administered as part of a focus group, but

Projective techniques:
Motivational research methods designed to tap the underlying (and often unconscious) motives of individuals.

FIGURE 2-6   Selected Portions of a Discussion Guide

1. Why did you decide to use your current cellular company? (Probe)
2. How long have you used your current cellular company? (Probe)
3. Have you ever switched services? When? What caused the change? (Probe)
4. What do you think of the overall quality of your current service? (Probe)
5. What are the important criteria in selecting a cellular service? (Probe)

Examples of probe questions:
    a. Tell me more about that . . .
    b. Share your thinking on this . . .
    c. Does anyone see it differently . . .

more often they are used during depth interviews. Because projective methods are closely associated with researching consumer needs and motivation, they are discussed more fully in Chapter 3.

Metaphor analysis:
The use of one form of expression (e.g., pictures collages) to describe or represent feelings about a product or service.

www.olsonzaltman.com

Metaphor Analysis In the 1990s, a branch of consumer research emerged that suggested most communication is non-verbal and that people do not think in words but in images. If consumers' thought processes consist of series of images, or pictures in their mind, then it is likely that many respondents cannot adequately express their feelings and attitudes about the research subject (such as a product or brand) in words alone. Therefore, it is important to enable consumers to represent their images in an alternative, non-verbal form—through the use, say, of sounds, music, drawings, or pictures. The use of one form of expression to describe or represent feelings about another is called a *metaphor*. A number of consumer theorists have come to believe that people use metaphors as the most basic method of thought and communication.

The Zaltman Metaphor Elicitation Technique (ZMET)—the first patented marketing research tool in the United States—relies on visual images to assess consumers' deep and subconscious thoughts about products, services, and marketing strategies. In one study about consumer perceptions of advertising, pre-screened respondents were asked to take to a depth interview pictures that illustrated their opinions of the value of advertising. They were asked to bring pictures from magazines, newspapers, artwork, or photos they took especially for the study or from existing collections but not actual print advertisements. (The average number pictures taken to the interview was 13.) Each respondent took part in a two-hour videotaped interview, which used several methods that are part of the ZMET technique to elicit key metaphors and the relationships among them from the respondents. The interviews were then analysed by qualified researchers according to the ZMET criteria. The findings revealed that the *ambivalent* respondents had both favourable and unfavourable impressions of advertising (e.g., it has value as information and entertainment but can also be a misrepresentation of reality); *skeptics* had mostly negative, but some positive, impressions of advertising; and *hostile* respondents viewed advertising as an all-negative force.[7] Another application of ZMET is to get consumers' reactions to movie scripts.[8]

Sampling and Data Collection

An integral component of a research design is the sampling plan. Specifically, the sampling plan must answer three questions: whom to survey (the sampling unit), how many to survey (the sample size), and how to select the respondents (the sampling procedure). Deciding whom to survey requires an explicit definition of the *universe* or boundaries of the market from which data are sought so that a suitable sample can be chosen (such as working mothers). Interviewing the correct target market or potential target market is fundamental to the validity of the study.

The size of the sample depends on both the size of the budget and the degree of confidence that the marketer wants to place in the findings. The larger the sample, the more likely the responses will be representative of the total universe under study. It is interesting to note, however, that a small sample can often provide highly reliable findings, depending on the sampling procedure adopted. (The exact number needed to achieve a specific level of confidence in the accuracy of the findings can be computed with a mathematical formula that is beyond the scope of this discussion.)

Samples can be broadly classified into one of two types:

- **Probability samples** are samples in which respondents are chosen by some probability technique. This enables the researcher to get findings that are projectable to the total population.
- **Non-probability samples** are samples based on some criterion other than randomness (or probability).

Figure 2-7 summarizes the features of various types of probability and non-probability designs.

As indicated earlier, qualitative studies usually require the data to be collected by highly trained social scientists. A quantitative study generally uses a field staff that is either recruited and trained directly by the researcher or contracted from a company that specializes in conducting field interviews. In either case, it is often necessary to verify whether the interviews have, in fact, taken place. This is sometimes done by a postcard mailing to respondents asking them to verify that they participated in an interview on a particular date. Completed questionnaires are examined regularly as the research study progresses to ensure that the answers recorded are clear, complete, and legible.

Data Analysis and Reporting of Research Findings

In qualitative research, the moderator or test administrator usually analyses the responses received. In quantitative research, the researcher supervises the analysis. Open-ended responses are first coded and quantified (i.e., converted into numerical scores); then all the responses are tabulated and analysed by sophisticated

Probability samples: Samples in which respondents are chosen by some probability technique that leads to findings that are projectable to the entire population.

Non-probability samples: Samples that are chosen by non-probability methods that lead to findings that may not be projectable to the entire population.

FIGURE 2-7	Sampling

PROBABILITY SAMPLE	
Simple random sample	Every member of the population has a known and equal chance of being selected.
Systematic random sample	A member of the population is selected at random and then every "nth" person is selected.
Stratified random sample	The population is divided into mutually exclusive groups (such as age groups), and random samples are drawn from each group.
Cluster (area) sample	The population is divided into mutually exclusive groups (such as blocks), and the researcher draws a sample of the groups to interview.
NON-PROBABILITY SAMPLE	
Convenience sample	The researcher selects the most accessible population members from whom to obtain information (e.g., students in a classroom).
Judgment sample	The researcher uses his or her judgment to select population members who are good sources for accurate information (e.g., experts in the relevant field of study).
Quota sample	The researcher interviews a prescribed number of people in each of several categories (e.g., 50 men and 50 women).

analytical programs that correlate the data by selected variables and cluster the data by selected demographic characteristics.

In both qualitative and quantitative research, the research report includes a brief executive summary of the findings. Depending on the assignment from marketing management, the research report may or may not include recommendations for marketing action. The body of the report includes a full description of the method used and, for quantitative research, tables and graphs showing the findings. The questionnaire is usually included in the appendix to enable management to evaluate the objectivity of the findings.

One of the main areas of primary consumer research is the measurement of consumer satisfaction; that is the subject of the following section.

Customer Satisfaction Measurement

Customer satisfaction measurement:
Quantitative or qualitative studies aimed at gauging customer satisfaction and its determinants.

Gauging customer satisfaction and its determinants is crucial for every company. Marketers can use such data to retain customers, sell more products and services, improve the quality and value of their offerings, and operate more effectively and efficiently. **Customer satisfaction measurement** includes quantitative and qualitative measures, as well as a variety of contact methods with customers. These methods and instruments and examples of their application to business situations are detailed in Figure 2-8.

Organizations have to recognize that customer satisfaction has a great influence on customer loyalty. Customers who are dissatisfied are not only more likely to complain about the product or service (thus creating negative word-of-mouth communication), but may also switch to competitors' products. Establishing a good complaint system will encourage customers to make their complaints to the company and, if these are handled well, lead to retention of customers, increased loyalty, and positive word-of-mouth communications. A good complaint system should

■ encourage customers to complain and make suggestions for improvements by having adequate forms (with enough space for comments) and mechanisms beyond the routine "how was everything?" questions. A good approach is to include examples on the forms of how past comments by customers have helped improve service.

■ establish "listening posts" (e.g., in a hotel lobby or in checkout lines) where specially designated employees either listen to customers' comments or actively solicit suggestions from them.

■ create a system to categorize and analyse complaints because each complaint, by itself, provides little information.

■ use software to speed up the handling and analysis of complaints. eBay uses software on its website to track customers' opinions, record complaints, and follow up on them very quickly. The company says it has reduced customer dissatisfaction by nearly 30 percent after one year of using this tool.[9]

CONDUCTING A RESEARCH STUDY

In designing a research study, researchers adapt the research process described in the previous sections to the special needs of the study. If a researcher is told, for example, that the purpose of the study is to develop a segmentation strategy for a new online dating service, he or she would first collect secondary data, such as population statistics (e.g., the number of men and women online in selected metropolitan

FIGURE 2-8	Methods of Customer Satisfaction Research	

METHOD	EXPLANATION	MARKETING STRATEGY IMPLICATIONS
Customer satisfaction surveys	Important attributes of product (e.g., warrantee, performance) or service (friendliness, efficiency) are identified Likert or semantic differential scales are used to judge satisfaction Generally 5-point scales are used	Need to focus on attributes that the company scored lower on Need to strive for more than "satisfied" since research indicates that customers who are "very satisfied" are more profitable and loyal[a] Comparison with previous years' data needed to see trends in customer satisfaction levels
Customer expectations versus their opinion of the product or service	Satisfaction is seen as the result of differences between actual and expected performance Can use both "adequate" and "desired" service levels to gauge consumer expectations[b] Semantic differential or Likert-type scales used to measure both actual and expected levels	More sophisticated than general satisfaction surveys Can identify levels of an attribute needed or expected by consumers (e.g., the delivery time that consumers find adequate or desirable); therefore, better corrective actions are possible
Mystery shoppers	Employment of professional observers who pose as customers and provide an unbiased evaluation of the firm's operation Focus is on the service provided by the firm	Very useful for service-oriented firms Can identify weakness in service
Critical incident method	Consumers are asked to think back and describe interactions with employees in a particular firm or in the industry in general	Can be used to identify actual or potential areas of dissatisfaction Consumers may or may not remember critical incidents Better used in association with another method than by itself[c]
Analysing consumer complaints	Consumers have a way to complain (e.g., suggestion boxes, feedback forms, customer service numbers, or email address)	Need to categorize complaints into groups and analyse frequency and trends Develop procedure for dealing with complaints and empower front-line employees to handle complaints
Analysing customer defections	Interviews with customers who are at the point of switching or those who have switched to other products or service providers	Interviews might provide information on drawbacks of the product or service; measures to correct these have to be taken Easier to keep a customer than to get a new one; hence, all possible measures to prevent customers from switching or to win back lost customers should be taken[a]

[a] Thomas O. Jones and W. Earl Sasser, Jr., "Why Satisfied Customers Defect," *Harvard Business Review,* November–December 1995, 88–99.
[b] A. Parasuraman, Valarie A. Zeithaml, and Leonard L. Berry, "Moving Forward in Service Quality Research: Measuring Different Customer-Expectation Levels, Comparing Alternative Scales, and Examining the Performance-Behavioral Intentions Link," Report No. 94–114, Marketing Science Institute, 1994.
[c] Bo Edvardsson and Tore Strandvik, "Is a Critical Incident Critical for a Customer Relationship?" *Managing Service Quality,* 2000, 82–91.

areas within a certain age range, their marital status, and occupations). Then, together with the marketing manager, the researcher would specify the parameters (i.e., define the sampling unit) of the population to be studied (e.g., single, college-educated men and women between the ages of 18 and 45 who live or work in the Montreal metropolitan area). A qualitative study (e.g., focus groups) might be undertaken first to gather information about the target population's attitudes about meeting people online, their special interests, the specific services they would like an online dating service to provide, and the precautions the service should take to protect their privacy. This phase of the research should result in tentative generalizations about the specific age group or groups to target and the services to offer.

The marketing manager might then instruct the researcher to conduct a quantitative study to confirm and attach "hard" numbers (percentages) to the findings that emerged from the focus groups. The first-phase study should have provided enough insights to enable the researcher to develop a research design and to launch directly into a large-scale survey. If, however, there is still doubt about any element of the research design, such as wording or format of the questions, it might be decided first to do a small-scale exploratory study. Then, after refining the questionnaire and, if necessary, other elements of the research design, the company would launch a full-scale quantitative survey, using a probability sample that would allow it to project the findings to the total population of singles (as originally defined). The analysis should cluster prospective consumers of the online dating service into segments based on relevant socio-cultural or life-style characteristics and on media habits, attitudes, perceptions, and geodemographic characteristics.

SUMMARY

- The field of consumer research developed as an extension of the field of marketing research to enable marketers to predict how consumers would react in the marketplace and to understand why they made the purchase decisions they did.

- Consumer research can be classified as positivistic or interpretivistic. Positivist research is quantitative and empirical and tries to identify cause-and-effect relationships in buying situations. It is often supplemented with qualitative research. Interpretivism, a qualitative research perspective, is generally more concerned with understanding the act of consuming (consumer decision making) rather than the act of buying.

- The consumer research process—whether quantitative or qualitative—generally consists of six steps: defining objectives, collecting secondary data, developing a research design, collecting primary data, analysing the data, and preparing a report of the findings.

- Major quantitative research methods are surveys, experiments, and observation; major qualitative research methods are focus groups, in-depth interviews, projective techniques, and metaphor analysis.

- There are two major sampling methods for choosing respondents: probability and non-probability techniques. Probability samples (simple random, systematic, stratified, or cluster samples) are chosen by some random technique to identify individual respondents. The data collected from probability samples can be subject to rigorous statistical analysis, and the results can be generalized to the entire population. Non-probability samples (e.g., convenience, judgment, quota) are smaller and since the respondents are not chosen by a random method, do not lead to results that can be generalized to the entire population.

DISCUSSION QUESTIONS

1. What is the difference between primary and secondary research? Under what circumstances might the availability of secondary data make primary research unnecessary? What are some important sources of secondary data?

2. Explain the various types of surveys and the advantages and disadvantages of each.

3. What are probability and non-probability samples? Explain two probability sampling methods and two non-probability sampling methods.

4. What are attitude scales? Explain three types of attitude scales.

5. What are focus groups? What are the advantages and disadvantages of focus groups compared to depth interviews?

6. Discuss three main ways in which customer satisfaction can be measured.

CRITICAL THINKING QUESTIONS

1. Identify a purchase you have made that was motivated primarily by your desire to obtain a special "feeling" or an "experience." Would the positivist or interpretivist research paradigm be a more suitable way to study your consumption behaviour? Explain your answer.

2. A manufacturer of powdered fruit drinks would like to investigate the effects of food colour and label information on consumers' perceptions of flavour and their product preferences. Would you advise the manufacturer to use observational research, experimentation, or a survey? Explain your choice.

3. Why is customer-satisfaction measurement an important part of marketing research? If you had to measure your fellow students' satisfaction with the services provided by the registrar's office at your university or college, which method would you choose? Why?

4. Assume that you had to conduct a survey to find out the attitudes of the students at your university toward tuition increases. Explain which sampling method you would use to choose respondents for the study (a) if you had to submit a report in one day to your professor, (b) if you had to submit a report to the board of governors of the university by the end of the day that would be taken as representative of the student population's opinion, and (c) if you had the time to conduct a study that would lead to results that were projectable to the entire student population.

5. Neutrogena is a manufacturer of personal-care products for young adults. The company would like to extend its line of facial-cleansers. Create (1) a qualitative and (2) a quantitative research design for the company.

INTERNET EXERCISES

1. Visit the websites of A.C. Nielsen Research. Which of Nielsen's syndicated data services would you use to develop a customer lifetime value and profitability analysis for a product or service of your choice?

2. Assume that you are marketing cell phones to families with teenage children. Visit the website of Statistics Canada (**www.statscan.ca**) and calculate the size of the target market in your city and province or territory.

3. Visit the website of the Canadian Bankers' Association (**www.cba.ca**) and go through one of the research studies that are posted on the site. What type of survey method, sample, and research instruments were used in the study?

Do you think they are suitable for the purposes of the research?

4. Visit the website of the *Globe and Mail* (**www.globeandmail.ca**) and check the online poll. Would this poll result in findings that are projectable to the entire Canadian population? Why or why not?

5. Visit the website of Surveysite (**www.surveysite.com**) and examine the qualitative research studies that they offer. How would these compare with their off-line counterparts?

KEY TERMS

Consumer research   *(p. 28)*
Controlled experiment   *(p. 37)*
Customer lifetime value   *(p. 35)*
Customer satisfaction measurement   *(p. 46)*
Depth interview   *(p. 41)*
Exploratory study   *(p. 33)*
Focus group   *(p. 43)*

Interpretivism   *(p. 30)*
Metaphor analysis   *(p. 44)*
Motivational research   *(p. 28)*
Non-probability sample   *(p. 45)*
Positivism   *(p. 28)*
Primary data   *(p. 33)*
Primary research   *(p. 33)*
Probability sample   *(p. 45)*

Projective techniques   *(p. 43)*
Qualitative research   *(p. 28)*
Quantitative research   *(p. 28)*
Reliability   *(p. 39)*
Secondary data   *(p. 33)*
Secondary research   *(p. 33)*
Validity   *(p. 38)*

CASE 2-1: USING SECONDARY DATA IN TARGETING CONSUMERS

The importance and strategic value of secondary data are discussed in the text. Today, thanks to technology, high-quality secondary marketing data are readily available to marketing students and educators. Mediamark Research Inc., for example, is a well-known provider of specialized, syndicated secondary data describing the audiences of selected media. The company also provides online access to some of its data through its MRI1 service.

In this hands-on case, we would like you to use some of Mediamark's secondary data. First, in order to use the data, you must register (free) with Mediamark at **www.mriplus.com**.

After you register and your user status is activated, sign in and go to "Create Reports." Then, under "Pocketpieces," select "MRI—Magazine Pocketpiece." Check all the data categories in the "Select Data to Display" window. Then select up to five magazines that you read or are familiar with and generate Pocketpiece Reports for them. You can download these reports as Excel files.

Then obtain recent copies of the magazines for which you selected the MRI reports and make a list of all the products and brands featured in full-page ads in these publications. You now have the two sets of data needed to complete this case study.

QUESTIONS

1. In general, are the products that are advertised prominently in each magazine consistent or inconsistent with the magazine's MRI audience profile? Explain your answers.

2. Rather than relying on MRI's data, should the marketers of the products you selected collect their own data about the audiences of magazines in which they want to advertise? Why or why not? Be sure to describe the advantages and disadvantages of relying on secondary research data in making strategic marketing decisions.

NOTES

1   Canadian Bankers' Association, "Technology and Banking: A Survey of Consumer Attitudes," 2002.

2   Leslie Kaufman, "Enough Talk," *Newsweek,* August 19, 1997, 48–49.

3   Kim S. Nash, "Casinos Hit Jackpot with Customer Data," *Computer World,* July 2, 2001, 16–17; *Modern Marvels: Casino Technology,* VHS tape, 1999, A&E Television Networks.

4   Brian D. Till and Michael Busler, "The Match-Up Hypothesis: Physical Attractiveness, Expertise, and the Role of Fit on Brand Attitude, Purchase Intent and Brand Beliefs," *Journal of Advertising,* Fall 2000, 1–13.

5   Joseph F. Hair, Robert P. Bush, and David J. Ortinau, *Marketing Research,* 2nd ed. (New York: McGraw Hill Irwin, 2003), Chapter 10.

6   Deborah D. Heisley and Sidney J. Levy, "Autodriving: A Photoelicitation Technique," *Journal of Consumer Research,* December 1991, 257–272.

7   Robin A. Coutler, Gerald Zaltman, and Keith S. Coutler, "Interpreting Consumer Perceptions of Advertising: An Application of the Zaltman Metaphor Elicitation Technique," *Journal of Advertising,* Winter 2001, 1–21.

8   Emily Eakin, "Penetrating the Mind by Metaphor," *New York Times,* February 23, 2002, B9, B11.

9   L. Biff Motley, "Speeding Up Handling of Satisfaction Problems," *Bank Marketing,* September 2001, 35.

Appendix to Part 1
CONSUMER BEHAVIOUR AND MARKETING STRATEGY

As explained in Chapter 1, marketing strategy involves (1) segmenting consumers into distinct subgroups with similar needs and choosing a segment on which to focus the firm's marketing efforts, (2) finding a unique position for the product in these consumers' minds, (3) developing a marketing mix that will cater to the target market, and (4) finding ways of building relationships with consumers that will lead to high levels of customer satisfaction and retention. Let's look at each one of these steps in more detail.

STEPS IN DEVELOPING A MARKETING STRATEGY

Segmenting the Market and Targeting the Right Customers

Market segmentation:
The process of dividing a market into distinct subsets of consumers with common needs or characteristics.

Targeting:
The selection of one or more segments to focus on with a distinct marketing mix.

www.toyota.ca

www.sodexho.com

www.gap.ca

www.bananarepublic.ca

www.oldnavy.ca

Positioning:
Developing a distinct image for the product or service in the mind of the consumer in order to differentiate the offering from those of competitors.

The first step in developing a marketing strategy is to segment the market. **Market segmentation** can be defined as the process of dividing a market into distinct subsets of consumers with common needs or characteristics; the next step, which is **targeting**, is the selection of one or more segments to focus on with a distinct marketing mix.

Toyota targets its Celica with its sporty styling, minimal back seat, and small trunk to young singles; it targets its Avalon, a much larger vehicle, at the family-car buyer who needs a roomier vehicle.

Another example is the market segmentation frequently carried out by food service companies operating on university campuses. Sodexho has developed a segmentation program called Lifestyling that allows the company to segment the student body into six segments, each with its own life-style characteristics, which determine the type of menu items various students prefer, the brands they prefer, the times they prefer to eat, and how best to reach them.[1] Figure A-1 presents a closer look at two of these six segments.

Market segmentation also has been adopted by retailers. A great example is Gap, which targets different age, income, and life-style segments in a diversity of retail outlets. Gap and Super Gap stores are designed to attract a wide age range of consumers who are looking for a casual and relaxed style of dress. Gap targets upscale consumers through its Banana Republic stores and somewhat downscale customers with its Old Navy Clothing Company stores. It targets young parents (who are also likely to be Gap or Banana Republic shoppers) with its Baby Gap and Gap Kids stores.[2] Gap takes pains to cater to the needs of specific market components and to acknowledge their unique or particular buying patterns.

Market segmentation is covered in more detail later in this appendix, but let us first take a brief look at the other steps in developing a marketing strategy.

Positioning the Product

Once a target market has been identified, a firm has to decide on a basic positioning strategy to convey the benefits of it product to the target market. **Positioning** is

FIGURE A-1	Campus Dining

STAR GAZERS SEGMENT	FUN EXPRESS SEGMENT
Light and healthy foods	Variety, taste, and nutrition
Breakfast: bagel, muffin, cereal	Breakfast: Belgian waffles, omelets, fruit
Lunch: Italian, deli, wraps, expensive options	Lunch: Italian, Mexican, meat/potato/ veggie, grilled/fried chicken sandwich
Late night: frozen yogurt, ice cream	Late night: bakery, cereal, fruit
Price-insensitive	Price-conscious, like to buy on sale
Brand-conscious, follow fashion	Like counterculture brands that change
Work full-time over summer	Work part-time over summer
Active, outgoing, social	Value leisure time
Parents' household income: $100,000+	Parents' household income: $30 000–$60 000
Impulsive shopper	

Source: From "You Are What You Eat," David J. Lipke, *American Demographics,* October 2000. Copyright © 2000 Media Central Inc., a Primedia Company. All rights reserved. Reprinted by permission.

the creation of a distinct image for the product or service in the mind of the consumer, an image that will differentiate the offering from competing ones and tell consumers clearly that the particular product or service will meet their needs better than competing brands. Successful positioning centres on two principles. The first is to communicate the *benefits* that the product will provide rather than the features of the product. Second, because there are many similar products in almost any marketplace, an effective positioning strategy must develop and communicate a "unique selling proposition"—a distinct benefit or point of difference—for the product or service. In fact, most of the new products introduced by marketers (including new forms of existing products such as new flavours, sizes, etc.) fail to capture a significant market share and are discontinued because they are seen by consumers as "me too" products lacking a unique image or benefit. In Chapter 5, the concepts and tools of positioning are explored further.

Developing the Marketing Mix

The **marketing mix** consists of a company's services or products that it offers to consumers and the methods and tools by which it sells them. The marketing mix has four elements: (1) the *product* or *service* (i.e., the features, designs, brands, and packaging, along with post-purchase benefits such as warranties and return policies); (2) the *price* (the list price, including discounts, allowances, and payment methods); (3) the *place* (specific store and non-store outlets where the product or service is distributed); and (4) *promotion* (the advertising, sales promotion, public relations, and sales efforts designed to build awareness of and demand for the product or service).

Marketing mix:
The combination of product, price, promotion, and place (or distribution) that a company offers.

Finding Ways to Satisfy and Retain Customers

Although identifying a good target market, positioning the product well, and developing an effective marketing mix may attract consumers to the brand, a company should also find ways of keeping these customers. This requires developing brand loyalty and commitment and finding ways of reducing consumer dissatisfaction. Consumers who are dissatisfied with a company' s offerings are likely to talk about their negative experiences with the product. Hence, for a firm to be successful in the long term, it is perhaps as important to find ways of reducing such negative word-of-mouth communication as it is to find ways of creating positive word-of-mouth advertising. These topics are covered in more detail in Chapter 13.

The rest of this appendix deals with market segmentation in more detail.

MARKET SEGMENTATION AND TARGET MARKET SELECTION

If all consumers were alike—if they all had the same needs, wants, and desires and the same background, education, and experience—mass (undifferentiated) marketing would be a logical strategy. The primary advantage of mass marketing is that it costs less: only one advertising campaign is needed, only one marketing strategy is developed, and usually only one standardized product is offered. Some companies, mainly those that deal in agricultural products or very basic manufactured goods, can follow a mass-marketing strategy successfully. Other marketers, however, see major drawbacks in undifferentiated marketing. When trying to sell the same product to every prospective customer with a single advertising campaign, the marketer must portray the product as a means for satisfying a common or generic need and, therefore, often ends up appealing to no one. A hot water heater may fulfill a widespread need for hot water in the home for bathing, washing dishes, and washing clothes, but a standard-sized hot water heater may be too big for a grandmother who lives alone and too small for a family of six. Without market differentiation, both the grandmother and the family of six would have to make do with the same model, and, as we all know, "making do" is a far cry from being satisfied.

The strategy of segmentation allows producers to avoid head-on competition in the marketplace by differentiating their offerings, not only on the basis of price, but also through styling, packaging, promotional appeal, method of distribution, and superior service. Marketers have found that the costs of consumer-segmentation research, shorter production runs, and differentiated promotional campaigns are usually more than offset by increased sales. In most cases, consumers readily accept the passed-through cost increases for products that more closely satisfy their specific needs.

Bases for Segmentation

The first step in developing a segmentation strategy is to choose the most suitable basis (or bases) on which to segment the market. The most popular bases consist of nine major categories of consumer characteristics. They are geographic factors, demographic factors, psychological factors, psychographic (life-style) characteristics, socio-cultural variables, use-related characteristics, use-situation factors, benefits

Hybrid segmentation: Combining several segmentation variables to divide the market.

sought, and forms of **hybrid segmentation** that use a combination of several segmentation bases (e.g., demographic-psychographic profiles and geodemographic factors). Figure A-2 lists the nine segmentation bases, divided into specific variables with examples of each. The following section briefly discusses each of the nine segmentation bases. These are discussed in more detail in later chapters. (Various psychological and life-style segmentation variables are examined in greater depth in Chapter 4 and demographic segmentation in Chapters 10 and 11.) This appendix offers a bird's-eye view of various segmentation bases and serves as a review of a topic that is covered in many introductory marketing courses.

FIGURE A-2	Market Segmentation Categories and Selected Variables

SEGMENTATION BASE	SELECTED SEGMENTATION VARIABLES
Geographic Segmentation	
Region	Atlantic, Quebec, Ontario, Prairies, British Columbia, the North
City size	Major metropolitan areas, small cities, towns
Density of area	Urban, suburban, rural
Demographic Segmentation	
Age	Under 12, 12–17, 18–34, 35–49, 50–64, 65–74, 75–99, 100+
Sex	Male, female
Marital status	Single, married, divorced, living together, widowed
Income	Under $25 000, $25 000–$34 999, $35 000–$49 999, $50 000–$74 999, $75 000–$99 999, $100 000 and over
Education	Some high school, high school graduate, some university, university graduate, post-graduate
Occupation	Professional, blue-collar, white-collar, agricultural
Psychological Segmentation	
Needs-motivation	Shelter, safety, security, affection, sense of self-worth
Personality	Extroverts, novelty seekers, aggressives, low dogmatics
Perception	Low-risk, moderate-risk, high-risk
Learning involvement	Low-involvement, high-involvement
Attitudes	Positive attitude, negative attitude
Psychographic Segmentation	
Life style	Economy-minded, couch potatoes, outdoors enthusiasts, status seekers
Socio-cultural Segmentation	
Subcultures (based on race and ethnicity)	Aboriginal, Black,[a] Chinese, French-Canadian, South Asian
Religion	Catholic, Protestant, Jewish, Moslem, Hindu, other
Social class	Lower, middle, upper
Family life cycle	Bachelors, young marrieds, full nesters, empty nesters
Use-Related Segmentation	
Usage rate	Heavy users, medium users, light users, non-users
Awareness status	Unaware, aware, interested, enthusiastic
Brand loyalty	None, some, strong
Use-Situation Segmentation	
Time	Leisure, work, rush, morning, night
Objective	Personal use, gift
Location	Home, work, friend's home, in-store
Person	Self, family members, friends, boss, peers
Benefit Segmentation	Convenience, social acceptance, long lasting, economy, value-for-the-money
Hybrid Segmentation	
Demographic-psychographic	Combination of demographic and psychographic profiles of consumer segments
SRI VALS[b]	Actualizer, Fulfilled, Believer, Achiever, Striver, Experiencer, Maker, Struggler

[a] This is the term used by Statistics Canada; an alternative term sometimes used is "African Canadian."

[b] VALS™ is an example of a demographic-psychographic profile.

Geographic Segmentation

Geographic
segmentation:
Dividing the market or consumers by location.

In **geographic segmentation**, the market is divided by location. The theory behind this strategy is that people who live in the same area share some similar needs and wants and that these needs and wants differ from those of people living in other areas. For example, certain foods sell better in one region than in others.

Some marketing scholars have argued that direct-mail merchandise catalogues, national toll-free telephone numbers, satellite television transmission, global communication networks, and especially the internet have erased all regional boundaries and that geographic segmentation should be replaced by a single global marketing strategy. Obviously, any company that decides to put its catalogue on the internet makes it easy for people all over the world to browse and become customers. And for the consumers who shop on the internet, it often makes little difference if online retailers are around the corner or halfway around the world—the only factor that differs is the shipping charge.

www.campbellsoup.com

Other marketers have, for a number of years, been moving in the opposite direction and developing highly regionalized marketing strategies. Campbell's Soup, for example, segments its North American market into more than 20 regions, each with its own advertising and promotion budget. Within each region, Campbell's sales managers have the authority to develop specific advertising and promotional campaigns geared to local market needs and conditions, using local media, ranging from newspapers to church bulletins. They work closely with local retailers on displays and promotions, and they report that their **micromarketing** strategies have won strong consumer support.

Micromarketing:
Highly regionalized mar-
keting strategies that use
promotional campaigns
geared to local market needs.

In summary, geographic segmentation is a useful strategy for many marketers. It is relatively easy to find geographically based differences for many products. In addition, geographic segments can be reached easily through the local media, including newspapers, TV, radio, and regional editions of magazines.

Demographic Segmentation

The most common basis for market segmentation is demographic characteristics, such as age, sex, marital status, income, occupation, and education. Demography refers to the vital and measurable statistics of a population. Demographics help to *locate* a target market, whereas psychological and socio-cultural characteristics help to *describe* how its members *think* and how they *feel*. Using demographic information is often the easiest and most cost-effective way to identify a target market. Indeed, most secondary data, including census data, are expressed in demographic terms. Demographics are easier to measure than other segmentation variables; they are invariably included in psychographic and socio-cultural studies because they add meaning to the findings. Every month *Canadian Social Trends* publishes research dealing with demographic issues, and a number of its articles relate demographic variables to other segmentation bases.

Demographic variables reveal trends that signal business opportunities, such as shifts in age, gender, and income distribution. For example, the growing importance of the "tween" market has led several marketers to design products to cater to this target market.

www.minutemaid.com

Although children often drink boxed juice drinks, Minute Maid Company offers single-serve drinks in pouches, rather than in boxes, in order to appeal better to the "tween" market.[3] And Heinz has introduced EZ Squirt ketchup (which includes green and purple versions) to appeal more to tweens.[4]

Figures A-3 and A-4 present samples of segmentation by various demographic variables. As mentioned earlier, these will be covered in more detail in Chapters 10 and 11.

FIGURE A-3	Segmentation by Seven Life Development Stages

MAJOR PHASE	AGE	LIFE DEVELOPMENT STAGE	MAJOR TASK
Provisional Adulthood	18–29	Pulling Up Roots	Detaching from family, searching for identity, choosing a career
First Adulthood	30–49	Reaching Out (30–35)	Selecting a mate, working on career
		Questions (36–44)	Searching for personal values, re-evaluating relationships
		Midlife Explosion (45–49)	Searching for meaning, reassessing marriage, relating to teenage children with depression being common in this stage
Second Adulthood	50–85+	Settling Down (50–55)	Adjusting to realities of work, adjusting to an empty nest, being active in community
		Mellowing (56–64)	Adjusting to health problems, approaching retirement
		Retirement (65+)	Adjusting to retirement, reassessing finances, being concerned with health

Source: Adapted from Linda Morton, "Segmenting Publics by Life Development Stages," *Public Relations Quarterly,* Spring 1999, 46; as based on Gail Sheehy, *New Passages: Mapping Your Life Across Time* (New York: Ballantine Books, 1995).

FIGURE A-4	Six American Adult Cohorts

NAME	BIRTH DATES	CHARACTERISTICS	MARKETING EXAMPLE
Depression Cohort	1912–1921	Defined by the Great Depression. Greatly concerned with financial security; values economic security and frugality.	A West Coast savings and loan association used Groucho Marx's *You Bet Your Life* TV sidekick to assure potential depositors hat their money twas "safe."
World War II Cohort	1922–1927	Defined by World War II. Faced a common enemy, left loved ones behind, deferred marriage, children, and careers.	To attract women in this age group who value independence, a major clothing retailer markets clothing that is stylish and easy to put on, like its line of clothing with Velcro fasteners (instead of buttons), bigger armholes, and other features that make it possible for women to get dressed without assistance.
Postwar Cohort	1928–1945	Benefited from a long period of economic growth and social calm. Act conservatively and prefer the familiar, the secure, and the comfortable.	The Vermont Country Store, a marketer of nostalgic products, includes pictures from the 1950s and cohort-appropriate copy in its catalogues.

(continued)

FIGURE A-4	Six American Adult Cohorts (continued)		
Boomers I Cohort	1946–1954	Came of age during the Post–World War II era. Value individualism, self-indulgence, and stimulation. Grew up in economic good times and spend heavily because they expect the good times to continue. Very cause-oriented.	Baby Boomers' parents, not Baby Boomers, relate to prunes, but research by the California Prune Board found that prunes contain ingredients that allow aging Baby Boomers to hold onto their sexual vitality.
Boomers II Cohort	1956–1965	Came of age as Vietnam War ended, in the early 1970s during a period of low economic gains. Have little faith in institutions but have a narcissistic preoccupation that leads to self-help activities and self-deprecation. Spend like Boomers I because they feel they can always get a loan, a second mortgage, or another credit card.	A finance company advertises to Boomers II with a radio commercial that says, "Everyone else has a BMW or a new set of golf clubs, and they're not any better than you are."
Generation X Cohort	1966–1976	Often called "slackers" "whiners," and/or "a generation of aging Bart Simpsons." Have little to hang on to and are often the children of divorce and daycare. Feel alienated and believe that they have little hope of being able to have their parents' lifestyle. This cohort has no "defining moment."	Can be reached with irreverent, rebellious, self-mocking portrayals, such as the *Simpsons, South Park,* and *Married with Children* TV programs.

Source: Adapted from Charles Schewe, Geoffrey Meredith, and Stephanie Noble, "Defining Moments: Segmenting by Cohorts," *MM,* Fall 2000, 48–53.

Psychological Segmentation

Psychological segmentation:
Segmenting the market by means of intrinsic or inner qualities (e.g., motivation, personality) of consumers.

Psychological characteristics refer to the inner or intrinsic qualities of the individual consumer. Consumer segmentation strategies are often based on specific psychological variables. For instance, consumers may be segmented according to their *motivations, personality, perceptions, learning,* and *attitudes.* (Part 2 of this book examines in detail the wide range of psychological variables that influence consumer decision making and consumption behaviour.)

Psychographic Segmentation

Psychographic segmentation:
Segmenting consumers on the basis of their activities, interests, and opinions.

Marketing practitioners have heartily embraced psychographic research, which is closely aligned with psychological research, especially personality and attitude measurement. This form of applied consumer research (commonly referred to as life-style analysis) has proved to be a valuable marketing tool that helps identify promising consumer segments that are likely to be responsive to specific marketing messages.

The psychographic profile of a consumer segment can be thought of as a composite of consumers' measured activities, interests, and opinions (AIOs). As an approach to constructing consumer psychographic profiles, AIO research collects consumers' responses to a large number of statements that measure their activities (how the consumer or family spends time, e.g., golfing, volunteering at a local blood bank, or gardening); interests (the consumer's or family's preferences and priorities, e.g., home, fashion, or food); and their opinions (about a wide variety of events and

---

INTERNET INSIGHT A-1
DO MEN AND WOMEN USE THE INTERNET DIFFERENTLY?

MALE AND FEMALE SEGMENTS OF INTERNET USERS
Key Usage Situation—Favourite Internet Materials

Female Segments

Social Sally	Making friends	Chat and personal webpage
New Age Crusader	Fighting for causes	Books and government information
Cautious Mom	Nurturing children	Cooking and medical facts
Playful Pretender	Role playing	Chat and games
Master Producer	Job productivity	White pages and government information

Male Segments

Bits and Bytes	Computers and hobbies	Investments, discovery, software
Practical Pete	Personal productivity	Investments, company listings
Viking Gamer	Competing and winning	Games, chat, software
Sensitive Sam	Helping family and friends	Investments, government information
World Citizen	Connecting with world	Discovery, software, investments

Source: Scott Smith and David Whitlark, "Men and Women Online: What Makes Them Click," *Marketing Research*, Summer 2001, 22.

FIGURE A-5	A Portion of an AIO Inventory Used to Identify Techno-Road-Warriors

Instructions: *Please read each statement and place an "x" in the box that **best** indicates how strongly you **"agree"** or **"disagree"** with the statement.*

	AGREE COMPLETELY						DISAGREE COMPLETELY
I feel that my life is moving faster and faster, sometimes just too fast.	[1]	[2]	[3]	[4]	[5]	[6]	[7]
If I could consider the "pluses" and "minuses," technology has been good for me.	[1]	[2]	[3]	[4]	[5]	[6]	[7]
I find that I have to pull myself away from email.	[1]	[2]	[3]	[4]	[5]	[6]	[7]
Given my life style, I have more of a shortage of time than money.	[1]	[2]	[3]	[4]	[5]	[6]	[7]
I like the benefits of the internet, but I often don't have the time to take advantage of them.	[1]	[2]	[3]	[4]	[5]	[6]	[7]
I am generally open to considering new practices and new technology.	[1]	[2]	[3]	[4]	[5]	[6]	[7]

political issues, social issues, and the state of the economy or the environment). In their most common form, AIO-psychographic studies use a battery of statements (called a psychographic inventory) to identify relevant aspects of a consumer's personality, buying motives, interests, attitudes, beliefs, and values. Figure A-5 presents a portion of a psychographic inventory designed to gauge "techno-road-warriors," that is, businesspeople who spend a high percentage of their work week on the road, equipped with laptop computers, pagers, cellular telephones, and electronic organizers. Figure A-6 presents a hypothetical psychographic profile of a techno-road-warrior. The appeal of psychographic research lies in the frequently vivid and practical profiles of consumer segments that it can produce (which will be illustrated later in this appendix).

The results of psychographic segmentation efforts are frequently reflected in firms' marketing messages. For instance, Centrum Performance vitamins (see Exhibit A-1) are targeted to individuals who would prefer to spend their lunch hour working out rather than eating out. Psychographic segmentation is also discussed later in the appendix, where we consider strategies for hybrid segmentation that combine psychographic and demographic variables to create rich descriptive profiles of consumer segments.

EXHIBIT A-1

CENTRUM PERFORMANCE TARGETS A "WORKING OUT" LIFE STYLE.

© Wyeth and used with permission.

 Socio-cultural segmentation:

Using group and cultural variables to segment consumers.

Socio-cultural Segmentation

Sociological (group) and *anthropological* (cultural) variables—that is, socio-cultural variables—are further bases for market segmentation. For example, consumer markets have been successfully subdivided into segments on the basis of stage in the family life cycle, social class, core cultural values, subcultural membership, and cross-cultural affiliation. Several companies have benefited from the use of socio-cultural segmentation.

Part 3 (Chapters 9 to 13) examines these variables and their influence on consumer behaviour in greater detail.

FIGURE A-6   A Hypothetical Psychographic Profile of the Techno-Road-Warrior

- Goes on the internet more than six times a week
- Sends and/or receives 15 or more email messages a week
- Regularly visits websites to gather information and/or to comparison shop
- Often buys personal items via 800 numbers and/or over the internet
- May trade stocks and/or make travel reservations over the internet
- Earns $100 000 or more a year
- Belongs to several rewards programs (e.g., frequent flyer programs, hotel programs, rent-a-car programs)

Use-Related Segmentation

An extremely popular and effective form of segmentation categorizes consumers according to product, service, or brand usage characteristics, such as level of usage, level of awareness, and degree of brand loyalty.

Rate of usage segmentation differentiates among heavy users, medium users, light users, and non-users of a specific product, service, or brand. For example, research has consistently found that between 25 percent and 35 percent of beer drinkers account for more than 70 percent of all beer that is drunk. For this reason, most marketers prefer to target their advertising campaigns to heavy users rather than spend considerably more money trying to attract light users.

Recent studies have found that heavy soup users were more socially active, creative, optimistic, witty, and less stubborn than light users and non-users, and they were also less likely to read entertainment and sports magazines and more likely to read family and home magazines. Likewise, heavy users of travel agents in Singapore were more involved with and more enthusiastic about vacation travel, more innovative with regard to their selection of vacation travel products, more likely to travel for pleasure, and more widely exposed to travel information from the mass media.[5]

Marketers of a host of other products have also found that a relatively small group of heavy users accounts for a disproportionately large percentage of product usage; targeting these heavy users has become the basis of their marketing strategies. Other marketers, who have noticed the gaps in market coverage for light and medium users, have profitably targeted those segments.

Use-Situation Segmentation

Marketers recognize that the occasion or situation often determines what consumers will buy or use. For this reason, they sometimes focus on the use situation as a segmentation variable.

The following three statements reveal the potential of situation segmentation: "Whenever our daughter Jamie gets a raise or a promotion, we always take her out to dinner." "When I'm away on business for a week or more, I try to stay at a Suites hotel." "I always buy my wife flowers on Valentine's Day." Under other circumstances, in other situations, and on other occasions, the same consumer might make other choices. Some situational factors that might influence a purchase or consumption choice are whether it is a weekday or weekend (e.g., going to a movie); whether there is enough time (e.g., use of regular mail or express mail); whether it is a present for a girlfriend, a parent, or oneself (a reward to oneself).

Many products are promoted for special occasions. The greeting card industry, for example, stresses special cards for a variety of occasions that seem to be increasing almost daily (Grandparents' Day, Secretaries' Day, etc.). The florist and candy industries promote their products for Valentine's Day and Mother's Day, the diamond industry promotes diamond rings as an engagement symbol, and the wristwatch industry promotes its products as graduation gifts. The Godiva chocolate ad in Exhibit A-2 is an example of situational, special-usage segmentation. It appeared in magazines a week before Valentine's Day; it suggests that a box of Godiva chocolate "will make her heart skip a beat."

Benefit Segmentation

Marketing and advertising executives constantly try to identify the one benefit of their product or service that will be most meaningful to consumers. Some commonly used benefits are *financial security* (Prudential Financial), *data protection* (iomega), *good health* (Wheaties), *fresh breath* (Eclipse gum), and *peace of mind* (Hefty One Zip bags).

EXHIBIT A-2

GODIVA USES AN OCCASION-SPECIFIC AD FOR VALENTINE'S DAY

Courtesy of Margeotes/Fertitta & Partners and Godiva. Image © Kenro Izu.

In a recent article about brand strategies in India, the point is made that "nothing is as effective as segmentation based on the benefits a group of customers seek from your brand." To illustrate, the article points out that in India Dettol soap is targeted to the hygiene-conscious consumer—the person seeking protection from germs and contamination—rather than the consumer looking for beauty, fragrance, freshness, or economy.[6]

Changes in life styles also help to determine the product benefits that are important to consumers and provide marketers with opportunities for new products and services. The microwave oven, for example was the perfect answer to the needs of two-income households, where neither the husband nor the wife has much time to spend preparing meals. Food marketers offer busy families the *benefit* of breakfast products that take only seconds to prepare.

Benefit segmentation can be used to position various brands within the same product category.[7] The classic case of successful benefit segmentation is the market for toothpaste. A recent article suggested that if consumers are socially active, they want a toothpaste that can give them white teeth and fresh breath; if they smoke, they want a toothpaste to fight stains; if disease prevention is their main concern, they want a toothpaste that will fight germs; and if they have children, they want to lower their dental bills.[8] Exhibit A-3 suggests that the primary benefits derived from using Crest Whitening Plus Scope toothpaste are whiter teeth and fresh breath.

Hybrid Segmentation

Benefit segmentation: Segmenting consumers according to the benefits of the product or service that is meaningful to them.

Marketers commonly segment markets by combining several segmentation variables rather than relying on a single basis for segmentation. This section examines two kinds of hybrid segmentation that provide marketers with richer and more accurately defined consumer segments than can be derived from using a single segmentation variable. These include psychographic-demographic profiles, geodemographics, VALS, and Yankelovich's Mindbase Segmentation.

Psychographic-Demographic Profiles Psychographic and demographic profiles are highly complementary approaches that work best when used together. By combining the knowledge gained from both demographic and psychographic studies, marketers can obtain powerful information about their target markets.

Demographic-psychographic profiling has been widely used in the development of advertising campaigns to answer three questions: "Whom should we target?" "What should we say?" "Where should we say it?" To help advertisers answer the third question, many advertising media vehicles sponsor demographic-psychographic research on which they base very detailed *audience profiles*. Figure A-7 presents a selected demographic and psychographic profile of a *Maclean's* subscriber. By offering media buyers

www.macleans.ca

such carefully defined dual profiles of their audiences, mass-media publishers and broadcasters make it possible for advertisers to select media whose audiences most closely resemble their target markets.

Finally, advertisers are increasingly designing ads that depict in words and/or pictures the essence of a particular target-market life style or segment that they want to reach. In this spirit, Aqua Cat Cruises appeals to people with specific active and outdoor life styles (see Exhibit A-4).

Geodemographic Segmentation This type of hybrid segmentation scheme is based on the notion—similar to the old adage "Birds of a feather flock together"—that people who live close to one another are likely to have similar financial means, tastes, preferences, life styles, and consumption habits. Marketers use the cluster data for direct-mail campaigns, to select retail sites and merchandise mixes, to locate banks and restaurants, and to design marketing strategies for specific market segments. For example, Eddie Bauer has employed Claritas demographics to evaluate locations for new retail stores; and Duke Energy Corporation, as part of its customer-retention program, has profiled its residential and small business customers with Claritas's databases.[9]

Over the past 25 years, as the firm that started the clustering phenomenon, Claritas has increased the number of segments in American society from the 40 segments used in the 1970s and 1980s to the 62 segments it uses today. The Claritas search engine will pick the top five life-style clusters for each zip code. Environics, a Canadian market research company, has developed similar segments for the Canadian market.

Geodemographic segmentation is most useful when the market segment targeted by an advertiser or marketer (in terms of consumer personalities, goals, and interests) can be isolated according to where they live. However, for products and services used by a broad cross-section of the public, other segmentation schemes may be more productive.

Several other hybrid-segmentation methods have been developed by companies such as SRI Consulting Business Intelligence and Environics Group. These are covered in more detail in Chapter 4.

EXHIBIT A-3

CREST OFFERS CONSUMERS THE COMBINED BENEFITS OF WHITER TEETH AND FRESH BREATH

Courtesy of The Procter & Gamble Company. Used by permission.

> **Geodemographic segmentation:** A type of hybrid segmentation that uses geographic variables (e.g., postal codes or neighbourhoods) and demographic variables to segment markets.

www.claritas.com

Criteria for Effective Targeting of Market Segments

The previous sections have described various bases on which consumers can be clustered into homogeneous market segments. The next challenge for the marketer is to select one or more segments to target. To be a useful target, a market segment should be (1) identifiable, (2) large enough, (3) stable or growing, and (4) accessible (reachable) in terms of both media and cost.

Identification

To divide the market into separate segments on the basis of a series of *common* or *shared* needs or characteristics that are relevant to the product or service, a marketer must be able to identify these relevant characteristics. Some segmentation variables, such as *geography* (location) or *demographics* (age, gender, occupation, race), are relatively easy to identify or can even be observed. Others, such as *education, income,* or *marital status,* can be determined through questionnaires. However, other characteristics, such as *benefits sought* or *life style,* are more difficult to identify. A knowledge of consumer behaviour is especially useful to marketers, who use such intangible consumer characteristics as the basis for market segmentation.

Sufficiency

For a market segment to be a worthwhile target, it must consist of enough people to warrant tailoring a product or promotional campaign to its specific needs or interests. To estimate the size of each segment under consideration, marketers often use secondary demographic data, such as those provided by Statistics Canada (available at many libraries and on the internet), or they undertake a probability

| FIGURE A-7 | Selected Demographic-Psychographic Profile of a *Maclean's* Subscriber |

Total Readers	**2 910 000**
Median age	43
Male readers	1 506 000 (52%)
Female readers	1 405 000 (48%)
Average household income	$72 310 (15% above national average)
Technology Use	**% Reach**
Cell phone	16%
Use computer daily	17%
Access internet daily	17%
Own electronic organizer	19%
Purchased home theatre system in the past 2 years	18%
Education and Occupation	
Post-graduates	23%
Senior executive/Manager	21%
MOPEs (manager, owner, professional)	18%
Household income of $125 000 or more	23%
Personal income of $100 000 or more	26%
Investment Profile	
Holds mutual funds	18%
Owns self-directed RRSPs	17%
Holds stocks/bonds	17%
Travel	
2+ business trips within Canada in the past year	22%
7+ business trips by air in the past year	35%
25+ nights away from home in the past year	21%

Source: PMB 2004: English Canada 18+. Audiences are based on single-issue reach. Courtesy Maclean's Magazine.

Aqua Cat at anchor in the Exuma Cays
Land and Sea Park, Bahamas

AQUA CAT
CRUISES

diving, snorkeling, sea-kayaking, fishing, birding, beaching, sunning, snoozing...

...102 feet of liveaboard luxury leaving weekly from Nassau to the Exumas.
O.P.O. Box 661658 Miami, FL 33266
Tel: 1-888-327-9600 • 305-888-3002   Fax: 305-885-3323
email: sd@aquacatcruises.com   www.aquacatcruises.com
© 2001 Rick Frehsee/Aqua Cat Cruises

EXHIBIT A-4

AQUA CAT CRUISES TARGETS AN OUTDOOR ACTIVE LIFE STYLE

© 2001 Rickerschsee/Aqua Cat Cruises.

survey whose findings can be projected to the total market. (Consumer research methodology is covered in Chapter 2.)

Stability

Most marketers prefer to target consumer segments that are relatively stable in terms of demographic and psychological factors and needs and that are likely to grow larger. They prefer to avoid "fickle" segments that are unpredictable and tend to embrace new fads. For example, teens are a sizeable and easily identifiable market segment, eager to buy, able to spend, and easily reached. Yet, by the time a marketer produces merchandise for a popular teenage fad, interest in it may have waned.

Accessibility

A fourth requirement for effective targeting is accessibility, which means that marketers must be able to reach the market segments they want to target in an economical way. Despite the wide availability of special-interest magazines and cable TV programs, marketers are constantly looking for new media that will enable them to reach their target markets with minimum waste of circulation and competition. One way this can be done is on the internet. Upon the request of the consumer, a growing number of websites periodically send email messages concerning a subject of special interest to the computer user. For example, a resident of Halifax who likes to take short vacation trips might have Air Canada email her the coming weekend's special airfare, hotel, and car-rental deals through its weekly *Web Saver* newsletter.

Implementing Segmentation Strategies

Firms that use market segmentation can pursue one of two strategies—concentrated marketing or differentiated marketing.

Concentrated Marketing

Concentrated marketing is the targeting of just one segment with a unique marketing mix. Concentrated marketing is suitable for companies that are small or new to the field, for it gives them a chance to survive and prosper by filling a niche not occupied by stronger companies.

Differentiated Marketing

Differentiated marketing involves targeting several segments with individual marketing mixes. Differentiated marketing is a highly effective segmentation strategy for financially strong companies that are well-established in a product category and competitive with other firms that are also strong in the category (e.g., soft drinks, cars, or detergents).

Nissan Canada Inc. posted a 7 percent sales gain in Canada in 2003 thanks to the strategy of its parent company, Nissan Motor Company Ltd.—entering new segments with new vehicles. In the words of Brad Bradshaw, president of Nissan Canada, most of the company's growth in the last few years came from "entering segments where we weren't really present"; the company has introduced several new products in the past few years. Besides its range of cars, the company has several new entrants in the market—the Titan, aimed at the pickup market; the Quest, which caters to buyers who want a minivan; and the Altima, which caters to the family-sedan market. Even in the SUV market, the company has several entrants: the Pathfinder Armada, which is aimed at consumers who want a full-sized SUV; the X-trail, aimed at the compact SUV market; and, soon to be released, the redesigned version of the Pathfinder aimed at the mid-sized SUV market. Besides all these products, Nissan also has the Infiniti line, which caters to the luxury-car market and which has outsold major competitors like Toyota's Lexus, Cadillac, and Lincoln.[10]

Sometimes companies find that they must reconsider the extent to which they are segmenting their markets. They might find that some segments have gradually contracted to the point that they do not warrant an individually designed marketing program. In such cases, the company looks for a more generic or common need or consumer characteristic that would apply to the members of two or more segments and recombines those segments into a larger single segment that could be targeted with an individually tailored product or promotional campaign. This is called a **counter-segmentation** strategy.

The *Mail-Star* and the *Chronicle-Herald*, two Nova Scotia papers owned and operated by the Dennis family, traditionally catered to different segments. The *Mail-Star* was the evening edition of the *Halifax Herald*, a staunch supporter of the Conservative Party; the *Chronicle* was a left-wing paper that supported the Liberals. When the *Chronicle* and the *Herald* merged (to form the *Chronicle-Herald*), the *Mail-Star* became a late-afternoon paper and it concentrated on local

Concentrated marketing:
Targeting just one segment with a unique marketing mix.

Differentiated marketing:
Targeting several segments with individual marketing mixes.

www.herald.ns.ca

Counter-segmentation:
Recombining two or more segments into a larger single segment that could be targeted with an individually tailored product or promotional campaign.

news in Halifax County. Over a period, however, the papers began to share a common editorial, and the *Mail-Star* even started reprinting entire articles.

After investing in a state-of-the art printing press, the owners began to wonder if two separate papers were necessary—the readership had changed, and the old political affiliations were disappearing. Consumer research revealed that the readers of the *Mail-Star* and the *Chronicle-Herald* wanted the same things: more local news and a better-organized paper. The result? The owners decided to go the counter-segmentation route and introduced one paper (to be distributed at the usual times). To maintain the loyalty of the readers of the *Mail-Star*, they made the *Mail-Star* into a section of the main paper that concentrated on the news in Halifax Metro; a new section, "The Province," was added to cover provincial news.[11]

As explained above, segmentation and identifying the needs of various segment are a crucial function of marketing managers. Marketers need to understand consumer behaviour well in order to be able to identify consumer needs and develop suitable marketing strategies.

KEY TERMS

Benefit segmentation   *(p. 62)*
Concentrated marketing   *(p. 66)*
Counter-segmentation   *(p. 66)*
Differentiated marketing   *(p. 66)*
Geodemographic segmentation
   (p. 63)
Geographic segmentation   *(p. 56)*

Hybrid segmentation   *(p. 54)*
Market segmentation   *(p. 52)*
Marketing mix   *(p. 53)*
Micromarketing   *(p. 56)*
Positioning   *(p. 52)*
Psychographic segmentation
   (p. 58)

Psychological segmentation
   (p. 58)
Socio-cultural segmentation
   (p. 60)
Targeting   *(p. 52)*

NOTES

1   David J. Lipke, "You Are What You Eat," *American Demographics,* October 2000, 42–46.

2   Nina Munk, "Gap Gets It," *Fortune,* August 3, 1998, 68–82.

3   Stephanie Thompson, "Minute Maid Line Takes Cooler Tack to Attract Tweens," *Advertising Age,* August 14, 2000, 43.

4   "Superstars of Spending," *Advertising Age,* February 12, 2001, S1, S10.

5   Brian Wansink and Sea Bum Park, "Methods and Measures That Profile Heavy Users," *Journal of Advertising Research,* July–August 2000, 61–72; Ronald E. Goldsmith and Stephen W. Litvin, "Heavy Users of Travel Agents: A Segmentation Analysis of Vacation Travelers," *Journal of Travel Research,* November 1999, 127–133.

6   "India: Mantras to Work Brand Magic," *Businessline,* April 26, 2001, 1–4.

7   Russell Haley, "Benefit Segmentation: A Decision-Oriented Research Tool," *Marketing Management,* 4, Summer 1995, 59–62; Dianne Cermak, Karen Maru File, and Russ Alan Prince, "A Benefit

Segmentation of the Major Donor Market," *Journal of Business Research,* February 1994, 121–130; Elisabeth Kastenholz, Duane Davis, and Gordon Paul, "Segmenting Tourism in Rural Areas: The Case of North and Central Portugal," *Journal of Travel Research,* 37, May 1999, 353–363

8   William Trombetta, "A Strategic Overview," *Pharmaceutical Executive Supplement,* May 2001, 8–16.

9   **www.claritas.com**; Patricia Lloyd Williams, "Energy Marketing: What Do Customers Want?" *Fortnightly's Energy Customer Management,* Fall 2000, 36–41.

10 Greg Keenan, "New, Redesigned Vehicles Fuel Nissan's Performance," *Globe and Mail,* February 9, 2004, p. B1, B3.

11 Graham W. Dennis, "New Role for Mail-Star in Redesigned Newspaper," *Mail-Star,* February 14, 2004, p. A 1; John Gillis, "The Mail-Star to Hold Special Spot in New Herald," *Mail-Star,* February 14, 2004, p. A6.

part two
internal influences on consumer behaviour

Part 2 discusses internal influences on consumer behaviour.

Consumer behaviour is influenced by several internal (or psychological) factors. In Part 2, we will examine the role these factors play in consumer decision making. We will begin with a discussion of motivation and involvement (Chapter 3); next, we will examine the role of personality and self-concept in consumer decision making (Chapter 4). Chapter 5 will deal with perception, while Chapter 6 will examine how consumers learn about products and product attributes. Consumer attitude formation and attitude change will be covered in Chapter 7. The final chapter in this part (Chapter 8) will deal with communication and how marketers can communicate effectively with consumers.

Midway through the curve the balance of power shifts. G-force smiles. It's business as usual. Without batting an eye, the 300-horse RL orders all of its rear axle torque to the outside, pushing back into the turn with magnetic-like force. Your laws of physics are no good here, Mr. Newton. This car has something you've never seen before. **Super Handling All-Wheel Drive.**

acura.ca

DO AWAY WITH THOSE MINOR INCONVENIENCES OF THE ROAD

LIKE GRAVITATIONAL PULL

chapter 3
motivation and involvement

LEARNING OBJECTIVES

By the end of this chapter, you should be able to:

1. Define motivation and describe the various types of needs and goals.
2. Name at least five factors that make motivation a dynamic process.
3. Explain three motivational theories.
4. Describe the major motivational research methods and the problems with each one.
5. Summarize how marketers can use motivational concepts while developing marketing strategy.
6. Define involvement and discuss the factors that lead to high involvement.
7. Explain the impact of involvement on marketing strategy

when john goes to Montreal, he prefers to stay at Hotel Le Germain, and when he is in Vancouver for a meeting with his Asian clients from Hong Kong, he stays at the Listel Vancouver. These are not hotels that the average person is familiar with. What is so special about these hotels?

Both the Listel and Le Germain are part of a new trend in the hotel industry—boutique hotels. What is a boutique hotel? As Christiane Germain, president of the Quebec City-based Groupe Germain, operator of three boutique hotels in Quebec says, "there are as many definitions of a boutique hotel as there are boutique hotels owners." The general consensus is that boutique hotels are small (with no more than 150 rooms), have a unique identity of their own (as opposed to even the high-end big-box or chain hotels like the Marriott or the Sheraton), and offer highly personalized service. Of course, they are also expensive—prices range from $159 to $495 a night—but they are no more expensive than the high-end hotel chains.

What makes people like John choose a boutique hotel over similarly priced chain hotels like the Sheraton or Four Seasons? The general manager of the Listel Vancouver, Mr. Mockford, says, "Boutique hotels offer their guests an experience that's unique to that property."[1] The Listel Vancouver which has partnerships with local museums and art galleries, has two Gallery Floors where each guest room features original and limited-edition works by international and regional artists. Its Museum Floor rooms (formed in partnership with the University of British Columbia's Museum of Anthropology) have contemporary furniture made of hemlock and cedar and Northwest Coast art to match its theme—"all things British Columbian."

These features, and the personalized care that these hotels offer, seem to meet certain needs in people. Christopher Ashby, general manager of Ottawa's ARCthe.hotel notes, "Our lives are bombarded with so much all the time. When we can, we want to slow it down. We want people to know who we are, to pay attention to our personal needs, and not lump us into the cookie-cutter approach." To others, staying at a boutique hotel may simply satisfy their ego needs. Ashby says many of their guests are consultants, experts at what they do, and "just as unique as they are... they've chosen a hotel that is equally unique."

CHAPTER OVERVIEW

In this chapter, we will look at the concept of motivation, or the drive that leads people to action. We will examine the factors that make motivation a dynamic concept, something that is not easy for marketers to understand and use. We will examine some basic theories of motivation and motivational research methods.

Whereas motivation is the force that drives people to action, it is the related concept of involvement that explains the variation in the extent of time and effort that people spend in their search for a product. Hence, the last part of this chapter deals with involvement and its influence on marketing.

MOTIVATION

Human needs—consumer needs—are the basis of all modern marketing. Needs are the essence of the marketing concept. The key to a company's survival, profitability, and growth in a highly competitive marketplace is its ability to identify and satisfy unfulfilled consumer needs better and sooner than the competition. Organizations such as ARCthe.hotel and the Listel Vancouver are examples of companies that have identified consumer needs—in this instance the need for personalized care rather than just clean accommodation—and found ways of satisfying them well.

www.arcthehotel.com

www.listel-vancouver.
com

Marketers do not create needs, though in some instances they may make consumers more keenly aware of unfelt needs. Successful marketers define their markets in terms of the needs they presume to satisfy, not of the products they sell. A marketing orientation focuses on the needs of the buyer; a production orientation focuses on the needs of the seller. The marketing concept implies that the manufacturer will make only what it knows people will buy; a production orientation implies that the manufacturer will try to sell whatever it decides to make.

This chapter discusses basic needs that operate in most people to motivate their behaviour. It examines the influence that such needs have on consumption behaviour. Later chapters in Part 2 explain why and how these basic human needs, or motives, are expressed in so many diverse ways. This chapter also deals with consumer involvement—a concept that explains why people with similar motives have entirely different levels of interest in a purchase.

What Is Motivation?

Motivation:
The driving force within individuals that impels them to action.

Motivation is the driving force in individuals that impels them to action. This driving force is produced by a state of tension that results from of an unfulfilled need. Individuals strive both consciously and subconsciously to reduce this tension through behaviour that they anticipate will fulfill their needs and thus relieve them of the stress they feel. Figure 3-1 presents a model of the motivational process. It portrays motivation as a state of need-induced tension that "drives" the individual to engage in behaviour that he or she believes will satisfy the need and thus reduce the tension. Whether gratification is actually achieved depends on the course of action pursued. The specific goals individuals select and the patterns of action they undertake to achieve their goals are the results of individual thinking and learning. Therefore, marketers must view motivation as the force that induces consumption and, through consumption experiences, the process of consumer learning (discussed in Chapter 6).

Before we proceed further, let us examine needs and goals in more detail.

Needs

Every individual has needs: some are innate, others are acquired. **Physiological (or biogenic) needs** are *innate* needs; they include the needs for food, water, air, clothing, shelter, and sex. Because they are needed to sustain biological life, the biogenic needs are considered *primary needs* or motives.

Psychological (or psychogenic) needs, conversely, are considered *secondary needs*, and since the way we satisfy them is learned in response to our culture or environment, these are sometimes called acquired needs. These may include needs for self-esteem, prestige, affection, power, and learning. They result from the individual's subjective psychological state and from relationships with others.

All individuals need shelter from the elements; thus, finding a place to live fulfills an important primary need for a newly transferred executive. However, the kind of home she rents or buys may be the result of secondary needs. She may seek a place in which she and her husband can entertain large groups of people (and fulfill social needs) or she may want to live in an exclusive community to impress her

Physiological (or biogenic) needs:
Innate or biogenic needs, such as the need for food.

Psychological (or psychogenic) needs:
Acquired needs learned in response to our cultural environment.

FIGURE 3-1   Model of the Motivation Process

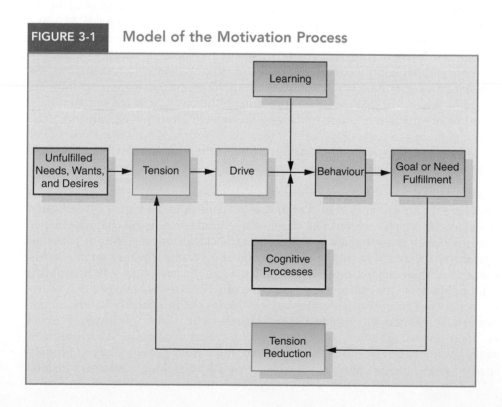

friends and family (and fulfill ego needs). The place where an individual ultimately chooses to live may therefore serve to fulfill both primary and secondary needs.

Some consumer behaviourists distinguish between so-called **rational motives** and **emotional motives**. They use the term *rationality* in the traditional economic sense, which assumes that consumers behave rationally by carefully considering all alternatives and choosing those that give them the greatest utility. In a marketing context, the term *rationality* implies that consumers select goals according to totally objective criteria, such as size, weight, price, or kilometres per litre. Emotional motives imply the selection of goals according to personal or subjective criteria (e.g., pride, fear, affection, or status). It is worth noting that whereas everyone would consider physiological needs to be rational, some psychological needs (or at least the way a person chooses to satisfy them) would be considered emotional motives.

The assumption underlying this distinction is that subjective or emotional criteria do not maximize utility or satisfaction. However, the assessment of satisfaction is a very personal process, which is based on the individual's own need structure, as well as on past behavioural and social (or learned) experiences. What may appear irrational to an outside observer may be perfectly rational in the context of the consumer's own psychological state. For example, a person who has extensive plastic surgery in order to appear younger is spending a significant amount of money on the surgery, is losing time while recovering, is putting up with a good deal of inconvenience, and is running the risk that something may go wrong. But to that person, the pursuit of the goal of looking younger and the use of the resources involved are perfectly rational choices. However, to many other people in the same culture who are less concerned with aging, and certainly to people from other cultures that are not as preoccupied with personal appearance as Westerners are, these choices appear completely irrational.

Finally, motives can be classified as latent or manifest. **Latent motives** are those that the consumer is either unaware of or is unwilling to recognize. **Manifest motives** are those that the consumer is aware of and willing to express. It is important for marketers to recognize that latent needs are harder to identify but may be far more influential in a consumer's decision making than manifest motives. For example, a woman may say she bought an SUV because it is more suitable for Canadian winters or that she needs it to drive to her cottage in the summer; these would be her manifest motives for buying the vehicle. However, equally important to her might be the sense of power that the vehicle provides, but she may be unwilling to admit to or unaware of this latent motive. Often, latent motives can be identified only through qualitative research.

Goals

Goals are the sought-after results of motivated behaviour. As Figure 3-1 indicated, all behaviour is goal-oriented. Our discussion of motivation in this chapter is in part concerned with **generic goals**, that is, the general classes or categories of goals that consumers see as a way to fulfill their needs. If a person tells his parents that he wants to get a graduate degree, he has stated a generic goal. If he says he wants to get an MBA in marketing from the Rotman School of Management of the University of Toronto, he has expressed a product-specific goal. Marketers are particularly concerned with **product-specific goals**, that is, the specifically branded products and services that consumers select for goal fulfillment. Marketing managers are interested in getting consumers to move from generic goals to product-specific goals. In fact, most advertising is aimed at making consumers become

Rational motives: Goals chosen according to totally objective criteria, such as quantity or price.

Emotional motives: Goals chosen according to personal or subjective criteria such as desire for social status.

Latent motives: Motives that the consumer is either unaware of or unwilling to recognize.

Manifest motives: Motives that the consumer is aware of and willing to recognize.

Goals: The sought-after results of motivated behaviour.

Generic goals: Product categories or classes that a consumer seeks in order to fulfill his or her needs.

Product-specific goals: Specific brands that a consumer seeks in order to fulfill his or her needs.

brand-loyal and move toward product-specific goals. For example, Heinz spends a considerable amount on advertising to make consumers ask for Heinz by name and not just for ketchup by saying, "There are no other kindz."

Motivation can be **positive or negative** in direction. We may feel a driving force *toward* some object or condition or a driving force *away* from some object or condition. For example, a person may be impelled toward a restaurant to fulfill a need to eat, and away from a motorcycle as a means of transportation to fulfill a safety need. When motivation is positive, the goal or object toward which behaviour is directed is often referred to as an **approach object**. A negative goal is one from which behaviour is directed away; it is referred to as an **avoidance object**. The product featured in the first ad of Exhibit 3-1 offers users a positive goal and approach object, whereas the second ad in Exhibit 3-1 depicts an avoidance object.

The Dynamic Nature of Motivation

Motivation is a highly dynamic construct that is constantly changing in reaction to life experiences. Needs and goals change and grow in response to an individual's physical condition, environment, interactions with others, and experiences. As individuals attain their goals, they develop new ones. If they do not attain their goals, they continue to strive for old goals or they develop substitute goals. There are various reasons why need-driven human activity never ceases.

Needs Are Never Fully Satisfied

Most human needs are never fully or permanently satisfied. For example, at fairly regular intervals throughout the day everyone experiences a need for food that must be satisfied. Most people regularly seek companionship and approval from others to satisfy their social needs. Even more complex psychological needs are rarely fully satisfied. For example, Rina may satisfy her ego needs by buying a Mercedes, but this may just whet her need for status and recognition; thus she may

Positive motivation: A motive that drives a person toward an object.

Negative motivation: A motive that drives a person away from an object.

Approach object: An object that the consumer is directed toward.

Avoidance object: An object that the consumer is directed away from.

EXHIBIT 3-1

POSITIVE VERSUS NEGATIVE MOTIVATION

Courtesy of Johnson & Johnson Inc.

end up buying a sports model of another expensive brand of car or a yacht to satisfy further her need for higher status.

New Needs Emerge as Old Needs Are Satisfied

Some motivational theorists believe that a hierarchy of needs exists and that new, higher-order needs emerge as lower-order needs are fulfilled. For example, a man who has largely satisfied his basic physiological needs (for food, shelter, etc.) may turn his efforts to achieving acceptance among his new neighbours by joining their political clubs and supporting their candidates. Once he is confident that he has achieved acceptance, he then may seek recognition by giving lavish parties or building a larger house.

Marketers must be attuned to changing needs. The Mercedes-Benz ad shown in Exhibit 3-2 portrays three different car models corresponding to an individual's needs as he or she matures.

A Given Need May Lead to Totally Different Goals

For any given need, there are many different and appropriate goals. The goals chosen by individuals depend on their personal experiences, physical capacity, the prevailing cultural norms and values, and the attainability in the physical and social environment. For example, a young woman may want to get a deep and even tan and may envisage spending time in the sun as a way to achieve her goal. However, if her dermatologist advises her to avoid direct exposure to the sun, she may settle for a self-tanning product instead. The goal object has to be both socially acceptable and physically attainable. If cosmetic companies did not offer effective alternatives to tanning in the sun, our young woman would either have to ignore the advice of her dermatologist or choose a substitute goal, such as untanned (but undamaged) youthful-looking skin.

EXHIBIT 3-2

PRODUCT ALTERNATIVES FOR CHANGING CONSUMER NEEDS

Courtesy of Mercedes-Benz. Image © Jake Chessum.

Consumers Are More Aware of Their Goals Than of Their Needs

Needs and goals are interdependent; neither exists without the other. However, people are often not as aware of their needs as they are of their goals. A teenager may not be consciously aware of his social needs, but he may join a photography club to make new friends. A local politician may not consciously be aware of a need for power but may regularly run for public office. A university student may not consciously recognize her need for achievement but may strive to obtain an A in every course.

Individuals are usually somewhat more aware of their *physiological* needs than they are of their *psychological* needs. Most people know when they are hungry, thirsty, or cold, and they take steps to satisfy these needs. The same people, however, may not be aware of their needs for acceptance, self-esteem, or status. They may, however, subconsciously engage in behaviour that satisfies their psychological (i.e., acquired) needs.

EXHIBIT 3-3

DIFFERENT APPEALS FOR THE SAME GOAL OBJECT

Courtesy of Illuminating Experiences. Agency is BrandStreet Advertising LLC. Copy by Ed Shankman, art by Dave Frank, and design by Joe Gwgliuzza.

Goals Are Influenced by a Consumer's Values, Personality, and Self-Concept

Individuals set goals on the basis of their personal values, and they choose the means (or actions) that they believe will help them achieve their goals. To understand the complex process of goal setting, marketers use a technique called laddering (refer to Research Insight 3-1), which attempts to trace the underlying needs and goals of consumers and the values associated with them. An individual's own view of himself or herself also influences the specific goals selected. A product that is thought to match a consumer's self-image is more likely to be chosen than one that is not.

Exhibit 3-3 presents a series of advertisements for Illuminating Experiences that recognizes that individuals with different needs and interests still have the same need for appropriate lighting. Each ad in the series symbolically represents a specific personality and self-image with which viewers can identify, while providing an effective goal object to satisfy the need for good lighting.

RESEARCH INSIGHT 3-1
UNCOVERING CONSUMER NEEDS AND UNDERLYING VALUES USING LADDERING

As mentioned earlier, consumers have multiple needs and goals, which are often complex and difficult to identify. One of the techniques used to uncover the underlying needs of consumers is called laddering. Laddering is done through in-depth personal interviews.

- First, the researcher asks the participant to identify the key attributes (or qualities) of a product that are important to him or her.
- Next, the interviewer asks, "Why is that important to you?"
- The interviewer keeps on questioning the participant until the underlying needs are uncovered.

This results in a means-end chain, or hierarchy, that helps marketers understand why a consumer buys a product.

Let us look at an example. Most of us have, at one time or another, embarked upon an exercise program—many of us have taken the formal, structured route of joining a health club or an exercise class. If we are using laddering to uncover the underlying motives that drive a consumer to join an exercise class, we will have to start by asking the consumer what she values in an exercise program. Some of the decisive attributes might be small classes, other participants who are at the same level of fitness, a knowledgeable instructor, low cost, and closeness to work or home. If we asked the consumer why she values each one, we might end up with a variety of answers.

Let us just take two attributes as examples—small classes and closeness to work or home. If asked why she values small class sizes, the consumer might say she likes them because they will help her feel more comfortable; when she is questioned further ("Why do they make you comfortable?"), she might say that in small classes, she may get to know the other participants; questioned still further ("why do you want to get to know the other participants?"), she might say she likes their company and sees this as a way of meeting friends. So one of the underlying motives is her need for affiliation or belonging.

A similar probing about the second attribute ("closeness to work or home") may result in the following means-end chain—"will help me keep up my exercise schedule," "keeping up a regular schedule will lead to losing weight," "weight loss will lead to my feeling and looking good," and "looking and feeling good will boost my self-confidence and self-esteem." So another underlying motive is the need to maintain one's self-esteem.

Often, means-end chains have four levels—attributes, functional consequences, psychological consequences, and underlying motives or values. The attributes of the exercise program discussed above have the following functional and psychological consequences and underlying motives:

ATTRIBUTE	FUNCTIONAL CONSEQUENCES	PSYCHOLOGICAL CONSEQUENCES	UNDERLYING NEED
Closeness to work	Will help me keep up my exercise schedule, which will lead to weight loss	Will look and feel good	Self-confidence, self-esteem
Small classes	Will get to know other participants	Can make new friends	Belonging

Marketers can use the knowledge that they gain through laddering in many ways.

- First of all, it lets them understand what consumers mean when they say they want a certain attribute and the underlying reasons for the importance they place on a particular attribute.
- Secondly, since it identifies underlying (and often latent) needs, they can incorporate these needs into their promotional messages.
- Finally, since the exercise leads to the identification of functional consequences that consumers are seeking, companies can work backward and incorporate attributes that lead to that functional consequence. For example, if getting to know other participants (and the friendships that this can lead to) are important to consumers, companies can find other ways (e.g., theme nights, group rates for a company) that can lead to the same result.

QUESTION:

1. Assume you are the marketing manager of a company producing laundry detergent. What would be some attributes that consumers are looking for when buying a laundry detergent? What are some functional and psychological consequences of these attributes? What are some underlying values and needs that these consequences will satisfy?

Success and Failure Influence Goals

A number of researchers have studied the nature of the goals that individuals set for themselves. Broadly speaking, they have concluded that people who achieve their goals usually set new and higher goals; that is, they raise their *level of aspiration*. This may be due to the fact that their success in reaching lower goals makes them more confident of their ability to reach higher goals. Conversely, those who do not reach their goals sometimes lower their aspirations.[2] Thus, goal selection is often a function of success and failure. For example, an undergraduate student who is not accepted into medical school may try instead to become a dentist or a podiatrist.

When an individual cannot reach a specific goal or type of goal that he or she thinks will satisfy certain needs, one of two things may occur: either the behaviour may be directed to a *substitute goal*, or the person may become *frustrated*. Although the substitute goal may not be as satisfactory as the primary goal, it may be sufficient to dispel uncomfortable tension. Continued deprivation of a primary goal may result in the substitute goal assuming primary-goal status. For example, a woman who has stopped drinking whole milk because she is dieting may actually begin to prefer skimmed milk. A man who cannot afford a BMW may convince himself that a Mazda Miata has an image he clearly prefers.

Some individuals who are less adaptive may regard their inability to achieve a goal as a personal failure. Such people are likely to adopt a **defence mechanism** in order to protect their egos from feelings of inadequacy. A young woman may yearn for a European vacation she cannot afford. The coping individual may select a less expensive vacation to Disneyland or to a national park. The person who cannot cope may react with anger toward her boss for not paying her enough that she can afford the vacation she prefers, or she may persuade herself that Europe is unseasonably warm this year. These last two possibilities are examples, respectively, of aggression and rationalization, just two of many defence mechanisms that people sometimes adopt to protect their egos from feelings of failure when they do not reach their goals. Marketers should consider consumers' defence mechanisms while developing advertising appeals and construct advertisements that portray a person resolving a particular frustration through the use of the advertised product.

Defence mechanisms: Methods of coping with the frustration that results when a person fails to achieve a goal.

Multiplicity of Needs

A consumer's behaviour often fulfills more than one need. In fact, it is likely that specific goals are chosen because they meet several needs. We buy clothing for protection from the cold and for a certain degree of modesty; in addition, our clothing fulfills a wide range of personal and social needs, such as acceptance or ego needs. Usually, however, there is one overriding (prepotent) need that initiates behaviour. For example, a woman may consider joining a health club because she has nothing special to do most evenings, she wants to wear midriff-revealing clothes, and she wants to meet men in a place other than a bar. If the cumulative amount of tension produced by these three reasons is sufficiently strong, she will probably join a health club. However, just one of the reasons (e.g., the desire to meet new men) may serve as the triggering mechanism; that would be the **prepotent need.**

Prepotent need: The need or motive that serves as the triggering mechanism that moves a consumer to action.

Motives Are Difficult to Infer from Behaviour

One cannot accurately infer motives from behaviour. People with different needs may seek fulfillment by choosing the same goal; people with the same needs may choose different goals. Consider the following examples. Five people who are active in a consumer-advocacy organization may each belong for a different reason. The first may be genuinely concerned with protecting consumer interests; the second may be concerned about an increase in counterfeit merchandise; the third may be looking for social contacts at meetings of the organization; the fourth may enjoy the power of directing a large group; and the fifth may enjoy the status of belonging to a well-known organization.

Similarly, five people may be driven by the same need (e.g., an ego need) to seek fulfillment in different ways. The first may look for advancement and recognition through a professional career; the second may become active in a political organization; the third may run in regional marathons; the fourth may take professional dance lessons; and the fifth may seek attention by monopolizing classroom discussions.

Motives May Sometimes Be in Conflict with Each Other

Motivational conflict: Conflict between two motives.

As we have seen, consumers are drawn toward a positive goal or object (i.e., an approach object) and drawn away from a negative goal or object (i.e., an avoidance object). What would happen if an object has both positive and negative aspects? Or what if a consumer is drawn toward two different positive or approach objects at the same time? In situations such as these, a consumer is said to be facing **motivational conflict.**

There are three types of motivational conflict. Let us examine three different situations in which motivational conflict exists:

- Marsha is a university student with a small budget. She has the money to buy either a nice winter coat or a good-quality multi-function printer (i.e., one that can print, scan, fax, and copy).

- Steve loves movies and wants to buy a large-screen projection television to watch his favourite films on. However, the price tag (approximately $3000) is making him wonder if he should make the purchase.

- John's car failed to start this morning—just as it had a couple of times in the last one month. John knew he should buy a new battery, but he hated the thought of having to spend money on a maintenance item like that.

The above three situations illustrate three different types of motivational conflict. In the first situation, the consumer is torn between two positive goals or objects—a coat and a printer. Since she likes both of them and is drawn toward both of these approach objects, she is facing *approach-approach conflict*. In the second case, the consumer is torn between positive and negative aspects in the goal object (or is both drawn toward and away from this object) and hence is facing *approach-avoidance conflict*. In the final situation, the consumer does not want to spend money on the car battery (hence it is an avoidance object), but if he does not buy it, the consequences will also be unpleasant (and hence are to be avoided); so he is facing *avoidance-avoidance conflict*. The marketing implications of these types of conflict are provided later on in the chapter.

Motives Can Be Aroused in Many Ways

Most of an individual's specific needs are dormant much of the time. The arousal of any particular set of needs at a specific moment may be caused by internal stimuli found in the individual's physiological condition, by emotional or cognitive processes, or by stimuli in the outside environment. Since physiological conditions are beyond the marketer's control, we will discuss only the other means of arousing motives.

Emotional Arousal Sometimes daydreaming results in the arousal or stimulation of latent needs. People who are bored or who are frustrated in trying to achieve their goals often engage in daydreaming (autistic thinking), in which they imagine themselves in all sorts of desirable situations. These thoughts tend to arouse dormant needs, which may produce uncomfortable tensions that drive them into goal-oriented behaviour. A man who daydreams of a torrid romance may spend his free time in internet singles' chat rooms; a young woman who dreams of being a famous novelist may enroll in a writing workshop.

Cognitive Arousal Sometimes random thoughts can lead to a cognitive awareness of needs. An advertisement that reminds us of home might trigger an instant yearning to speak to our parents. This is the basis for many long-distance telephone company campaigns that stress the low cost of international phone calls.

Environmental Arousal The set of needs that an individual experiences at a particular time are often activated by specific cues in the environment. Without these cues, the needs might remain dormant. For example, the 6 o'clock news, the sight or smell of bakery goods, fast food commercials on television, the end of the school day—all of these may arouse the "need" for food. A most potent form of situational cue is the product itself. A woman may experience an overwhelming need for a new television set when she sees her neighbour's new high-definition home theatre; a man may suddenly feel a "need" for a new car when passing a dealer's display window.

It is important to recognize that one type of arousal may lead quickly to another. For example, day dreaming may lead to emotional arousal, which may lead to a visit to the chat room; the next time that the consumer is in a totally different chat room, she my remember the pleasant experience that she had in the first chat room and may revisit it. Often the only question is how the initial arousal is accomplished.

Theories of Motivation

For many years, psychologists and others interested in human behaviour have attempted to develop exhaustive lists of human needs. Such lists tend to vary both in content and in length. Although there is little disagreement about specific physiological needs, there is considerable disagreement about specific psychological (i.e., psychogenic) needs.

In 1938, psychologist Henry Murray drew up a detailed list of 28 psychogenic needs. His research was probably the first systematic approach to the understanding of non-biological human needs. Murray believed that everyone has the same basic set of needs but that individuals differ in how they rank these needs. Murray's basic needs include many motives that are assumed to play an important role in consumer behaviour. Since his original classification of human motives, other researchers have followed with their own theories of motivation. Two such broad theories will be discussed here; these will be followed by four mid-range theories (or theories that attempt to explain the motives that lead to some, but not all, human behaviour).

Maslow's Hierarchy of Needs

Dr. Abraham Maslow, a clinical psychologist, formulated a widely accepted theory of human motivation based on the notion of a universal hierarchy of human needs. Maslow's theory identifies five basic levels of human needs, which are ranked in order of importance from lower-level (biogenic) needs to higher-level (psychogenic) needs.

The theory postulates that

- Individuals seek to satisfy lower-level needs before higher-level needs emerge.
- The lowest level of chronically unsatisfied need that an individual experiences serves to motivate his or her behaviour.

■ When that need is "fairly well" satisfied, a new (and higher) need emerges that the individual is motivated to fulfill. When this need is satisfied, a new (and still higher) need emerges, and so on.

■ If a person again experiences a lower-level need, such as thirst, that is not satisfied, that need may temporarily become dominant again.

Maslow's hierarchy of needs:

A theory of motivation that states that people move through five levels of needs—from physiological to self-actualization.

Figure 3-2 presents a diagram of **Maslow's hierarchy of needs.** For clarity, the levels are depicted as mutually exclusive. According to the theory, however, there is some overlap between each level, since no need is ever completely satisfied. For this reason, although all levels of need below the level that is currently dominant continue to motivate behaviour to some extent, the prime motivator—the major driving force in the individual—is the lowest level of need that remains largely unsatisfied.

Physiological Needs In the hierarchy-of-needs theory, physiological needs are the first and most basic level of human needs. According to Maslow, physiological needs are dominant when they are chronically unsatisfied: "For the man who is extremely and dangerously hungry, no other interest exists but food. He dreams food, he remembers food, he thinks about food, he emotes only about food, he perceives only food, and he wants only food."[3] These needs, which are required to sustain biological life, include food, water, air, shelter, clothing, sex—all the biogenic needs, in fact, that were listed as primary needs above.

Safety Needs After the first level of need is satisfied, safety and security needs become the driving force behind an individual's behaviour. These needs are concerned not only with physical safety but also with order, stability, routine, familiarity, and control over one's life and environment. Health and the availability of health care are important safety concerns. Savings accounts, insurance policies, education, and vocational training are all means by which individuals satisfy the need for security.

FIGURE 3-2   Maslow's Hierarchy of Needs

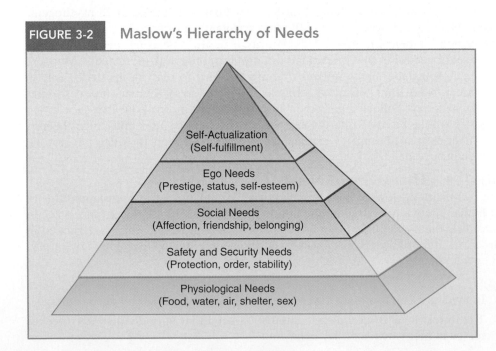

www.skillsontario.com

Gail Smyth, the executive director of Skills Canada-Ontario, recognizes the importance of catering to the safety needs of young Canadians. Her organization, which aims to encourage more young people to choose an occupation in the skilled trades, recently ran a television campaign that showed young tradespeople driving around in luxury cars. "We wanted to show the money factor; that's why they are driving nice cars,"[4] says Smyth; most young people don't realize that it is possible for a skilled tradesperson to have a six-figure income.

Social Needs The third level of Maslow's hierarchy consists of such needs as love, affection, belonging, and acceptance. People seek warm and satisfying human relationships with other people and are motivated by love for their families. Because of the importance of social motives in our society, advertisers of many product categories emphasize this appeal in their advertisements.

Egoistic Needs When social needs are more or less satisfied, the fourth level of Maslow's hierarchy becomes operative. This level is concerned with egoistic needs. These needs can take either an inward or an outward orientation, or both. Inwardly directed ego needs reflect an individual's need for self-acceptance, self-esteem, success, independence, and personal satisfaction with a job well done. Outwardly directed ego needs include the needs for prestige, reputation, status, and recognition from others. The presumed desire to "show off" success and achievement through material possessions is a reflection of an outwardly oriented ego need. (See Exhibit 3-4.)

EXHIBIT 3-4

APPEAL TO EGOISTIC NEEDS

Courtesy of DaimlerChrysler Corporation.

The boutique hotels that were discussed in the opening vignette aim to satisfy their customers' need for prestige and status, besides satisfying their need for a comfortable place to rest.

Need for Self-Actualization According to Maslow, most people never satisfy their ego needs sufficiently to move to the fifth level—the need for self-actualization (self-fulfillment). This need refers to an individual's desire to fulfill his or her potential—to become everything he or she is capable of becoming. In Maslow's words, "what a man can be, he must be."[5] This need is expressed in different ways by different people. A young man may desire to be an Olympic star and work single-mindedly for years to become the best in his sport. An artist may need to express herself on canvas; a research scientist may strive to find a new drug that eradicates cancer. Maslow noted that the self-actualization need is not necessarily a creative urge but that it is likely to take that form in people with some capacity for creativity. Some of our largest companies use motivation-based promotion to encourage their highly paid employees to look beyond their paycheques to find gratification and self-fulfillment in the workplace—to view their jobs as the way to become "all they can be." Exhibit 3-5 shows an ad for athletic shoes based on a self-actualization appeal (note that the shoes themselves are not shown).

To summarize, Maslow's hierarchy-of-needs theory postulates a five-level hierarchy of prepotent human needs. Higher-order needs become the driving force behind human behaviour as lower-level needs are satisfied. The theory says, in effect, that behaviour is motivated, not by satisfaction, but by dissatisfaction.

The need hierarchy has received wide acceptance in many social disciplines because it appears to explain the assumed or inferred motivations of many people in our society. The five levels of need postulated by the hierarchy are sufficiently general to encompass most lists of individual needs. The main problem with the theory is that it cannot be tested empirically; there is no way to measure precisely how satisfied one level of need must be before the next higher need becomes operative. The need hierarchy also appears to be very closely bound to our contemporary North American culture (i.e., it appears to be both culture- and time-bound). Despite these limitations, the hierarchy offers a highly useful framework for marketers trying to develop advertising appeals for their products.

McClelland's Trio of Needs

McClelland proposed a trio of basic needs: the need for power, for affiliation, and for achievement. These needs can each be subsumed within Maslow's need hierarchy (e.g, the need for affiliation is similar to Maslow's social needs); considered individually, however, each has a unique relevance to consumer motivation.

Power The need for power is related to an individual's desire to control his or her environment. It

shine.

EXHIBIT 3-5

APPEAL TO SELF-ACTUALIZATION
Courtesy of Converse.

EXHIBIT 3-6

ADS APPEALING TO THE POWER NEED

Courtesy of Acura/Honda Canada Inc. Courtesy of General Motors of Canada.

includes the need to control other persons and various objects. This need appears to be closely related to the ego need, in that many individuals experience increased self-esteem when they exercise power over objects or people. (Two examples of an appeal to the power need are shown in Exhibit 3-6A and 3-6B).

Affiliation Affiliation is a well-known and well-researched social motive that has a far-reaching influence on consumer behaviour. The need for affiliation suggests that behaviour is strongly influenced by the desire for friendship, acceptance, and belonging. People with high affiliation needs tend to be socially dependent on others. They often choose goods that they feel will meet with the approval of friends. Teenagers who hang out at malls or techies who congregate at computer shows often do so more for the satisfaction of being with others than for making a purchase. An appeal to the affiliation needs of young adults is shown in Exhibit 3-7. The affiliation need is very similar to Maslow's social need.

Achievement A considerable number of research studies have focused on the achievement need.[6] Individuals with a strong need for achievement often regard personal accomplishment as an end in itself. The achievement need is closely related to both the egoistic need and the self-actualization need. People with a high need for achievement tend to be self-confident, enjoy taking calculated risks, actively research their environments, and value feedback about their performance. Monetary rewards provide an important type of feedback as to how they are doing. People with high achievement needs prefer situations in which they can take personal responsibility for finding solutions. The promise of high achievement is a useful promotional strategy for many products and services targeted to educated and affluent consumers. Exhibit 3-8 depicts a car ad appealing to female high achievers.

Nothing should get in the way of being close.

With Head & Shoulders Dry Scalp Care Shampoo and Conditioner, dandruff definitely won't. Its gentle ingredients protect your scalp's natural moisture balance to give you hair that's beautiful and virtually flake free.

www.headandshoulders.com

EXHIBIT 3-7

AN AD APPEALING TO THE AFFILIATION NEED

Courtesy of Procter & Gamble.

Psychological reactance:
Motivational arousal due to a threat to behavioural freedom.

Opponent process theory:
A theory that states that an extreme positive (or negative) initial reaction will be followed by an extreme negative (or positive) reaction.

Priming:
The desire for more of a stimulus (or product) that occurs when a person is exposed to small amounts of it.

Hedonic consumption:
The need to obtain pleasure through the senses.

Mid-range Theories of Motivation

Whereas the above theories attempt to explain a wide range of (if not all) human behaviour, others attempt to explain only one (or a few) type of behaviour. Such theories are called mid-range theories of motivation. The following are a few examples of mid-range motivational theories:

Psychological Reactance Sometimes people become motivationally aroused by a threat to or the loss of a behavioural freedom, such as the freedom to make a product choice. This motivational state is called **psychological reactance.** A classic example occurred in 1985 when the Coca-Cola Company changed its traditional formula and introduced "New Coke." Many people reacted negatively to the notion that their "freedom to choose" had been taken away, and they refused to buy New Coke. Company management responded to this unexpected psychological reaction by reintroducing the original formula as Classic Coke and gradually developing additional versions of Coke.

A recent example of psychological reactance occurred when Molson Canada redesigned its **iam.ca** website and took away the chat (Pub Chat) function in it since not many people were using it. "We took it away without asking users or telling them.... There was an outcry. Molson was flooded with e-mails, and the discussion board, The Wall, was flooded with postings by loyal users of the website. They wanted it back, and kicked and screamed and stomped until we gave it back to them,"[7] says Michael Sutton, an account executive in charge of the Molson account.

Opponent Process Theory Under certain circumstances, when a person experiences a stimulus that leads to an extreme positive (or negative) emotional reaction, this is followed by the opposite—and extreme negative (or positive) reaction. Called the **opponent process theory**, this explains certain human reactions, such as the pleasure we feel when we buy something on credit, which is often followed by negative feelings (or guilt) for having spent too much money.

A related concept called priming explains why people are drawn to certain activities when they are exposed to them in small quantities. **Priming** states that when a person is exposed to small amounts of a certain stimulus, he or she will desire more of it; however, too much exposure to the same stimulus will lead to a negative reaction or withdrawal. This theory explains behaviours such as video game playing and even consumer reactions to sampling in grocery stores. In both instances, exposure to small quantities can lead to an increased desire to buy more of the products.

Hedonic Consumption Human beings seem to have a need to experience a wide variety of stimuli (through our senses), to create fantasies, and to experience emotional arousal. This need for gaining pleasure through the senses is termed the need for **hedonic consumption**. It explains our attraction to rides such as roller coasters, movies, rock concerts, and other such entertainment. It also helps us understand why we get involved in most of our leisure activities.

The recent increase in singles vacation spots is an example of the growing need of Canadians for fun, excitement, and a little romantic adventure. Although traditionally the term "sex tourist" has conjured up images of a bald, middle-aged American man, the female segment of the market is growing at a fast pace. Leah McLaren writes, "For the female sex tourist, as with the male, desire is the same. What differs is the method and the approach."[8] They, like the men, seek sexual adventure, but the women are looking for "a bit of discreet and temporary love." One of the hot spots for single women is actually called Hedonism II; its website encourages its guests to let loose. "While you are here, you'll find yourself doing things you never thought you would... or could. Things you wouldn't tell your mother about."[9]

Optimum Stimulation Level People seem to have a strong desire to maintain an **optimum stimulation level.** The level of stimulation that is considered optimal will vary from one individual to another; some seem to prefer high levels of stimulation, while others are satisfied with much lower levels. Marketing examples include brand-switching and other ways of looking for variety.

In summary, individuals with specific psychological needs tend to be receptive to advertising appeals directed at those needs. They also tend to be receptive to certain kinds of products. Thus, a knowledge of motivational theory provides marketers with a crucial means of segmenting markets and developing promotional strategies.

EXHIBIT 3-8

AN AD APPEALING TO THE ACHIEVEMENT NEED

Courtesy of Canon.

Optimum stimulation level:

The level of stimulation that an individual considers to be ideal.

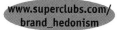
www.superclubs.com/ brand_hedonism

Motivational Research

How are motives identified? How are they measured? How do researchers know which motives are responsible for certain kinds of behaviour? These are difficult questions because motives are abstract constructs—that is, they cannot be seen or touched, handled, smelled, or otherwise tangibly observed. For this reason, no single measurement method can be considered a reliable index. Instead, researchers usually rely on a combination of various quantitative and qualitative research techniques to try to establish the presence or the strength of various motives.

Some psychologists are concerned that many quantitative measurement techniques may not identify latent motives or even all manifest motives. This has led to the popularity of qualitative measures of consumer motives. Many consumer researchers feel confident that they are achieving more valid insights into consumer motivations when they use a combination of techniques (called *triangulation*) than they would by using any one technique alone. Hence, they use more than one method for researching consumer motivation: behavioural data (observation), subjective data (self-reports), and qualitative data (projective tests, collage research, etc.). The next section looks at the development of motivational research and the most commonly used qualitative research methods.

The Development of Motivational Research The term **motivational research,** which should logically include all types of research into human motives, has become a "term of art" used to refer to qualitative research designed to uncover the consumer's subconscious or hidden motivations. Motivational research, which is based on the premise that consumers are not always aware of the reasons for their actions, tries to discover underlying feelings, attitudes, and emotions concerning product, service, or brand.

Sigmund Freud's psychoanalytic theory of personality (discussed in Chapter 4) was the foundation for the development of motivational research. This theory was built on the premise that unconscious needs or drives—especially biological and sexual drives—are at the heart of human motivation and personality. Freud's psychoanalytical techniques were adapted to the study of consumer buying habits by Dr. Ernest Dichter, a Viennese psychoanalyst. Dichter used qualitative research methods to find out *why* people bought what they did. Marketers were quickly fascinated by the glib, entertaining, and usually surprising explanations offered for consumer behaviour, especially since many of these explanations were based on sex. Four product profiles developed by Dichter and their applications to contemporary products are presented in Figure 3-3. Figure 3-4 describes some frequently used projective techniques used to tap into consumers' hidden (or latent) motivations. In addition, there are a number of associated qualitative research techniques that are used to delve into the consumer's unconscious or hidden motivations. These include collage research, metaphor analysis, and laddering (see Chapter 2 and Figure 3-4).

Despite the criticisms of motivational research (e.g., small sample sizes, low generalizability, subjectivity in analysis that led to inconsistent interpretations), it is still regarded as an important tool by marketers who want to gain deeper insight into the *reasons* for consumer behaviour than conventional marketing research techniques can yield. Since motivational research often reveals unsuspected consumer motivations for product or brand usage, its principal use today is in the development of new ideas for promotional campaigns, ideas that can penetrate the consumer's conscious awareness by appealing to unrecognized needs.

For example, in trying to discover why women bought traditional roach sprays rather than a brand packaged in little plastic trays, researchers asked women to draw pictures of roaches and write stories about their sketches. They found that, for many of their respondents, roaches symbolized men who had left them feeling poor and powerless. The women reported that spraying the roaches and "watching them squirm and die" allowed them to express their hostility toward men and gave them feelings of greater control.[10]

Motivation and Marketing Strategy

Marketers can incorporate their knowledge and understanding of motivational concepts in many ways. The following are some of the most important implications of the concepts discussed so far:

The greatest needs and goals of the target market can be determined: Since marketers can succeed only when they develop products that meet consumers' needs, it is important that a marketing program begin with the identification of the needs and goals of consumers. The use of quantitative and qualitative methods can lead to the identification of latent and manifest motives.

Motivational research: Qualitative research aimed at uncovering consumers' subconscious or hidden motivations.

www.cinstmarketing.ca/ publications/v2i3/ v2i3focus.htm

FIGURE 3-3	Dichter's Research: Selected Product Personality Profiles and Current Applications

BAKING

Dichter described *baking* as an expression of femininity and motherhood, evoking nostalgic memories of delicious odours pervading the house when the mother was baking. He said that when baking a cake, a woman is subconsciously and symbolically going through the act of giving birth, and the most fertile moment occurs when the baked product is pulled from the oven. Dichter also maintained that when a woman bakes a cake for a man, she is offering him a symbol of fertility.[a] The Betty Crocker image was based on this profile.

AUTOMOBILES

According to Dichter, the car allows consumers to convert their subconscious urges to destroy and their fear of death—two key forces in the human psyche—into reality. For example, the expression "step on it" stems from the desire to feel power, and the phrase "I just missed that car by inches" reflects the desire to play with danger. Based on this view, Dichter advised Esso to tap into consumers' aggressive motives for driving cars in promoting the superiority of its gasoline product. The slogan "Put a tiger in your tank" was developed as a result of his advice.[b]

Dichter also maintained that cars have personalities and that people become attached to their cars and view them as companions rather than objects. This notion stands behind his views that a man views a convertible as a mistress and a sedan as his wife.

DOLLS

Dolls play an important part in the socialization of children and are universally accepted as an essential toy for girls. Parents choose dolls that have the kind of characteristics they want their children to have, and the doll is an object for both the parents and the children to enjoy. When Mattel introduced Barbie in 1959, the company hired Dichter as a consultant. His research indicated that although girls liked the doll, their mothers detested the doll's perfect bodily proportions and Teutonic appearance. Dichter advised Mattel to market the doll as a teenage fashion model, reflecting the mother's desire for a daughter's proper and fashionable appearance. The advertising themes used subtly told mothers that it is better for their daughters to appear attractive to men rather than nondescript.[c]

ICE CREAM

Dichter described ice cream as an effortless food that does not have to be chewed and that melts in your mouth, a sign of abundance, an almost orgiastic kind of food that people eat as if they want it to run down their chins. Accordingly, he recommended that ice cream packaging should be round, with illustrations that run around the box panel, suggesting unlimited quantity.

[a]Ernest Dichter, *Handbook of Consumer Motivations* (New York: McGraw-Hill Book Company, 1964); Jack Hitt, "Does the Smell of Coffee Brewing Remind You of Your Mother?" *New York Times Magazine*, May 7, 2000, 6, 71.
[b]Phil Patton, "Car Shrinks," *Fortune*, March 18, 2002, 6.
[c]Barbara Lippert, "B-Ball Barbie," *Adweek*, November 9, 1998, 39.

A knowledge of needs can be used to segment the target market and position the product: For example, Maslow's need hierarchy is readily adaptable to market segmentation and the development of advertising appeals, because there are consumer goods designed to satisfy each of the need levels and because most needs are shared by large segments of consumers. For example, people buy health foods, medicines, and low-fat and diet products to satisfy physiological needs. They buy insurance, preventive medical services, and home security systems to satisfy safety and security needs. Almost all personal care and grooming products (e.g., cosmetics, mouthwash, and shaving cream), as well as most clothes, are bought to satisfy social needs. High-tech products such as computers or sound systems and luxury products such as furs, big cars, or expensive furniture are often bought to fulfill ego and esteem needs. Post-graduate education, hobby-related products, exotic, and physically demanding adventure trips are sold as ways of achieving self-fulfillment.

www.imperialoil.ca

| FIGURE 3-4 | Projective Techniques Used in Motivational Research |

TECHNIQUE	EXPLANATION AND EXAMPLE
Metaphor analysis	Using images or metaphors to represent feelings about a product *Using ZMET technique, Coca-Cola asked consumers to compose collages of pictures to represent their thoughts about the brand. It was found that Coke invoked feelings of calm, solitude, and relaxation, not invigoration or sociability.*
Story telling	Asking consumers to tell stories about their use of the product under study *Kimberly-Clark discovered that parents viewed diapers as clothing related to a particular stage in the child's development. Hence, if their children wore diapers too long, parents became distressed and embarrassed at what they viewed as their own failure as parents. Using this information, the company created Huggies Pull Ups "training pants."*
Picture drawing	Asking respondents to draw pictures of typical users of a brand *Pillsbury asked respondents to draw pictures of the typical Pillsbury and Duncan Hines cake-mix users. The Pillsbury users were depicted as old-fashioned, chubby women wearing frilly aprons, while the Duncan Hines user was a slim, "with it" woman wearing heels and a miniskirt. Pillsbury used this information to update and reposition its product.*
Photo sorts	Asking respondents to sort photos to depict a brand or even themselves *Playtex gave consumers stacks of photos and asked them to select the ones portraying their own self-images. Even though the respondents were overweight, full-breasted, and old-fashioned in appearance, they selected photos showing physically fit, well-dressed, and independent women. As a result, Playtex stopped stressing the comfort of its bras and started promoting them as "the fit that makes the fashion," using sexy, thin, and big-bosomed models.*
Thematic apperception test	Developed by Henry A. Murray, the TAT consists of showing individuals pictures and asking respondents to tell a story about each picture *Clearasil showed the image of a girl looking at herself in a mirror under the caption "Here is a teenager looking into the mirror and seeing pimples." The TAT tests showed that teenagers saw their lives as fast-paced and socially active, and a pimple as something that disrupted it. Clearasil developed an ad in which a teenager walking down a busy street discovers a pimple on his face while looking in a store window and the action around him stops. He applies Clearsil, the pimple disappears, and life resumes its pace.*
Word association	Presenting respondents with words (or brand names), one at a time, and asking them to utter the first word that comes to mind *Ganong, the Atlantic Canadian chocolate maker, asked consumers to say the words that came to mind when different brands of chocolate were mentioned. They found that Black Magic was considered "an older man, tall, mysterious, safe and trustworthy," Pot of Gold was "middle-aged, overweight, drives a van," and Ganong elicited words such as "Frenchness, suave, elegant, exotic and romantic."*[11]
Sentence completion	Similar to word association, except that it involves giving respondents a sentence to complete (e.g., "People who drive convertibles are...")
Third-person technique	Similar to story telling, except it involves asking for the stories about someone else *If persons who are afraid of flying are asked to tell a story about why a person would be afraid to fly (but not directly about their fear of flying), they are likely to project their own apprehensions and anxieties regarding flying onto a third person.*

Marketers may use their understanding of consumer needs for *positioning* their products—that is, deciding how the product should be seen by prospective consumers. The key to positioning is to find a niche—an unsatisfied need—that is not occupied by a competing product or brand. Maslow's need hierarchy is a very versatile tool for developing positioning strategies because different appeals for the same product can be based on different needs included in this framework. Many ads for soft drinks stress social appeal by showing a group of young people enjoying themselves and the drink being advertised. Ads for nutritional drinks stress refreshment (a physiological need); still others may focus on low caloric content (thus indirectly appealing to the ego need).

What needs do you think reading a Harlequin novel satisfies? Is it just the need for romance? How can a publisher of romantic novels motivate readers to visit its website? Internet Insight 3-1 provides details of how Harlequin uses its website to motivate its readers.

www.eharlequin.com

INTERNET INSIGHT 3-1
THE NEED FOR ROMANCE?

Did you know that Harlequin Enterprises is Canada's largest and most global publisher? With sales in 131 international markets (in 25 languages), Harlequin sells about 200 million books each year under a variety of brand names. Besides the classic Harlequin romances that most of us associate the company with (which are aimed at women who are about 40 years old), the company also publishes books for younger women who are not looking for a romantic novel that ends in marriage (the Red Dress Ink series), for readers who want romantic suspense (the Intrigue series), and finally one aimed at those who seek adventure—those who read a book and say, "I want this to happen to me" (the Blaze series).

Besides understanding the motivations of its various target markets, Harlequin has succeeded in part because of its effective use of its website to attract new readers. Since it was created a few years ago, the website has drawn a membership of more than a million readers. What makes the Harlequin website such a success? A visit to the website will show that it uses a number of motivational concepts to attract readers to the site repeatedly.

- It has several chat rooms, each serving the need to belong and the need for affiliation in slightly different ways. The Community chat room lets you talk to other romantic fiction enthusiasts, and the message boards in Reader-to-Reader enable you to talk about what is going on in your lives and meet your needs for belonging (or affiliation) in other ways.

- You can read free samples of the latest novels, which will lead to priming (based on opponent-process theory) and hence increase your motivation to read the novels.

- It has an ongoing writing competition, called Writing Round Robin, which lets you try your hand at writing a romance novel. If your entry is chosen, your photo will appear on the website with your biographical information (along with your story, of course). Since a lot of people consider themselves budding authors, this can provide a chance for them to satisfy their ego and perhaps even their self-actualization needs.

- Finally, as Marsha Zinberg notes in her column on the website, romance novels allow the reader to escape from day-to-day pressures and live life vicariously. They provide pleasurable experiences—and hence may fulfill our need for hedonistic consumption. The website further satisfies this need through its various components.

Source: http://www.eharlequin.com/cms/learntowrite/ltwArticle.jhtml?pageID=021101wc01002 ("The Appeal of Romance," Marsha Zinberg, August 20, 2003). Courtesy of Harlequin Enterprises Limited.

Although the examples given above deal with Maslow's hierarchy of needs, it is important to note that other motivational theories may also be used to segment and position products.

An understanding of consumer needs can be used to develop promotional strategies: Once a target market has been identified and a basic positioning strategy has been developed, marketers can use their understanding of the needs and goals of their target consumers to develop their promotional strategy.

For example, the Ford Taurus has been designed and advertised as a family car (a social appeal). Ads for the Mustang stress power (egoistic) needs, as do the car ad shown in Exhibit 3-6, which suggests that driving the car advertised will impress other drivers. An ad for a very expensive sports car may use a self-actualization appeal, such as "you deserve the very best." Volvo, on the other hand, targets more traditional buyers and its ads stress the safety appeal.

Again, it is important to appeal to a consumer's manifest and latent motives in promotional strategies. The other characteristics of consumer motivation discussed earlier can also help in the development of advertising appeals. For example, since consumers often attempt to satisfy multiple needs through their purchases, it is important for an ad to show how the product can meet a consumer's multiple needs.

A marketer can resolve any motivational conflict that the consumer may have: As we saw earlier, sometimes consumers face situations of motivational conflict. Understanding these conflicts can help a marketer reduce or resolve them, and in turn, the consumer may actually buy the company's product. There are several kinds of motivational conflicts that a marketer can help to resolve.

Approach-approach conflict: Make buying one of the options (i.e., the company's product) desirable through special offers or easier payment terms or simply by offering a better product.

Approach-avoidance conflict: Make the product attractive to the consumer by removing or reducing the negative aspects, such as offering a "buy now, pay later" option or a low-calorie version of desserts.

Avoidance-avoidance conflict: Make the consumer realize that the cost of delaying the purchase is going to be greater than the cost of purchasing the product; make the ads for these grudge items (i.e., products that people do not like buying) interesting and engaging to achieve high levels of top-of-mind awareness for the brand (so that when consumer is finally ready to buy, your brand wins out).

Recently, Target Marketing and Communications of St. John's, Newfoundland, ran a series of ads for furnaces sold by Irving Oil Ltd. Since the target audience comprised homeowners in the 50-plus age category, the ads featured popular 1970s products like the Ford Pinto and eight-track stereos to remind the target market about how old their furnace was. Each ad had a bold, amusing headline (e.g., "My furnace is older than my car. And my car's a Pinto.") while the copy highlighted the economic benefits of replacing their existing furnace with an Irving product.[12]

CONSUMER INVOLVEMENT

Although theories of motivation may help us understand consumer needs and thus what drives them to action, they still do not explain why with the same basic need, some consumers are willing to spend a lot of time on buying a product while others are unwilling to do so. The difference, often, is due to the level of involvement. In this section, we will look at what involvement is (including types of involvement), the factors that lead to high involvement, how we can measure involvement, and the impact of involvement on marketing strategy.

What Is Involvement?

Let us look at the following two consumers, both with the same need but with entirely different purchasing processes:

John and Tim are first-year university students. Before they entered university, both decided to buy a computer as they knew that having one would help them considerably during their years at university. After two weeks of searching, which involved asking friends, visiting local computer retailers, looking on the internet, reading *Consumer Reports,* and visiting the university's computer store, John finally made a decision. He bought a custom-made Dell laptop because he thought he could get the best value for his money with a custom-made computer from a well-known computer manufacturer.

www.consumerreports.org

Tim, conversely, made the decision in a day. He went to the university's computer store and looked at the two brands that the store carried. Then he asked his sister, who was at the same university, whether she had heard anything about the brands that the store sold. His sister had bought one of these brands and was happy with her purchase, and so Tim decided to buy the same brand.

Obviously not all of us are willing to spend the same effort in buying a product, even one that we know we need. This difference in the effort that consumers spend in processing information, searching for alternatives, and making the purchase itself is related to their involvement level. Whereas motivation theories deal with the basic needs that move a consumer to action, **involvement** is the degree of interest a consumer has in a product or purchase, and that is often related to the level of personal relevance that she sees in a product.

Involvement:
The level of personal relevance that a consumer sees in a product.

Involvement theory developed from a branch of research called *hemispheral lateralization*, or split-brain theory. The basic premise of *split-brain theory* is that the right and left hemispheres of the brain each "specialize" in processing certain kinds of information. The left hemisphere is primarily responsible for cognitive activities, such as reading, speaking, and processing attributional information. Individuals who are exposed to verbal information analyse the information cognitively through left brain processing and form mental images. Unlike the left hemisphere, the right hemisphere of the brain is concerned with non-verbal, timeless, pictorial, and holistic information. Put another way, the left side of the brain is rational, active, and realistic; the right side is emotional, metaphoric, impulsive, and intuitive.[13]

Building on this notion of split-brain theory, Krugman, a pioneer consumer researcher, theorized that a person's brain sometimes processes and stores information—especially non-verbal information—without much active involvement of the individual.[14] In other words, repeated visual presentation of a message can cause a person to learn without actually trying to. This led to the idea of television as low-involvement media and print as high-involvement media. Very soon, this led to the examination of why consumers are likely to be passive learners in some situations and active learners in other situations. It was briefly hypothesized that there are high- and low-involvement consumers, and then, that there are high- and low-involvement purchases.

These two approaches led to the notion that a consumer's level of involvement depends on how personally relevant the product is for that consumer. Under this definition, high-involvement purchases are those that are very important to the consumer (e.g., in terms of perceived risk) and thus provoke extensive problem solving (information processing). A car and a dandruff shampoo both may represent high-involvement purchases under this scenario—the car because of high financial risk, the shampoo because of high social risk. Low-involvement purchases are purchases that are not very important to the consumer, hold little relevance, and have little perceived risk, and thus provoke very little information processing. Highly involved consumers find fewer brands acceptable (they are called *narrow categorizers*); uninvolved consumers are likely to be receptive to a greater number of advertising messages regarding the purchase and will consider more brands (they are *broad categorizers*).

Thus, the extent to which a consumer is involved in purchase greatly influences that person's decision making. Under high-involvement conditions, the consumer will go through all (or most) of the steps in the decision-making process, whereas in low-involvement situations, the consumer might go from problem recognition to decision (or purchase) with very little time spent on searching for information or evaluating alternatives.

Types of Involvement

Enduring involvement: Involvement that is long-lasting; arises out of a sense of high personal relevance.

Situational involvement: Short-term involvement in a product or purchase of low personal relevance.

Consumer involvement can be at different levels and with different aspects of a consumer's decision making. For example, are you a person who collects and processes information about computers and computer accessories? If so, you have **enduring involvement** in computers. Conversely, if you look at computer ads and gather information about computers only when you are in the market for one, then you have **situational involvement** in the product. Consider the following examples:

- Mary is a freelance photographer who specializes in nature photography. She is always on the lookout for better cameras and related products such as lenses and filters. Recently, she had to upgrade her wide-angle lens and spent a week searching for the right kind.

- John does not usually drink wine. However, he has been invited to a party at a colleague's house and wants to take a good wine as a gift. Being a newcomer to the company, he wants to make a good impression by choosing a good wine. So John makes a trip to the liquor store and asks one of the employees to suggest a few good-quality wines, from which he chooses one that is within his budget.

While Mary has high and enduring involvement (as shown by her continuous interest in cameras and her willingness to spend time searching for the right product), John has only short-term, situational involvement, brought on by the nature of the purchase situation (i.e., a gift purchase). Although this involvement may be high at the point of decision making, it is short-lived; consumers with such short-term involvement are unlikely to be open to information at other times.

Cognitive involvement: Involvement at a rational level in products that are seen as major purchases.

Affective involvement: Involvement in products at an emotional level.

Finally, involvement can be at a **cognitive** (i.e., rational) level or at an **affective** (i.e., emotional) level. Products such as cars, houses, and major appliances are examples of high-cognitive-involvement purchases, while perfumes, clothing, and jewellery are high-affective-involvement purchases. In general, food is a low-cognitive-involvement purchase, while candy, magazines, and several other impulse purchases are low-affective-involvement purchases.

What Leads to High Involvement?

Since the level of involvement a consumer has in a purchase depends on the relevance of the product to her, anything that increases the product's relevance to her will lead to higher levels of involvement. In general, the following factors affect consumer involvement:

- the level of perceived risk (social, financial, or physical risk)
- the level of personal interest in a product category

- the probability of making a mistake (i.e., buying a bad product)
- the amount of pleasure in buying and using a product
- the number and similarity of competitive brands available

Measures of Involvement

In examining the evolution of involvement theory, it is not surprising to find that there is great variation in the conceptualization and measurement of involvement itself. Involvement theory evolved from the notion of high- and low-involvement media, to high- and low-involvement consumers, to high- and low-involvement products and purchases, to methods of persuasion in situations of high and low product relevance. Researchers have defined and thought of involvement in a variety of ways, including ego involvement, commitment, communication involvement, purchase importance, and extent of information search.[15] Some studies have tried to differentiate between brand involvement and product involvement.[16] Others differentiate among situational, enduring, and response involvement.[17]

The lack of a clear definition of the essential components of involvement poses some measurement problems. Researchers who regard involvement as a cognitive state are concerned with the measurement of ego involvement, risk perception, and purchase importance. Researchers who focus on the behavioural aspects of involvement measure such factors as the search for and evaluation of product information. Others argue that involvement should be measured by the degree of importance the product has to the buyer.

Because of the many different dimensions and conceptualizations of involvement, many researchers agree that it makes more sense to develop an *involvement profile* than to measure a single involvement level. The suggested profile would include interest in the product category, the rewarding nature (perceived pleasure) of the product, its perceived ability to reflect the purchaser's personality, and the perceived risk associated with the purchase.[18] This view is consistent with the notion that involvement should be measured on a continuum rather than as a dichotomy consisting of two mutually exclusive categories of "high" and "low" involvement.[19] Figure 3-5 presents a semantic differential scale designed to measure involvement. Figure 3-6 shows a personal involvement inventory developed to measure a consumer's "enduring involvement" with a product.

Involvement and Marketing Strategy

Involvement theory has a number of strategic applications for the marketer. Involvement affects the way a consumer processes information and learns about products.

Choose media based on consumer's involvement level: The left-brain (cognitive processing)/right-brain (passive processing) paradigm seems to have strong implications for the content, length, and presentation of both print and television advertisements. There is evidence that people process information extensively when the purchase is of high personal relevance and engage in limited information processing when the purchase is of low personal relevance. Hence high-involvement products can be advertised in print media and the messages can be more complex, whereas low-involvement products are better promoted through television advertisements and simpler messages.

| FIGURE 3-5 | Measuring Involvement on a Semantic Differential Scale |

TO ME, [INSERT PRODUCT OR PRODUCT CATEGORY] IS:

	1	2	3	4	5	6	7	
1. Important	—	—	—	—	—	—	—	Unimportant
2. Interesting	—	—	—	—	—	—	—	Boring
3. Relevant	—	—	—	—	—	—	—	Irrelevant
4. Exciting	—	—	—	—	—	—	—	Unexciting
5. Meaningful	—	—	—	—	—	—	—	Meaningless
6. Appealing	—	—	—	—	—	—	—	Unappealing
7. Fascinating	—	—	—	—	—	—	—	Ordinary
8. Priceless	—	—	—	—	—	—	—	Worthless
9. Involving	—	—	—	—	—	—	—	Uninvolving
10. Necessary	—	—	—	—	—	—	—	Unnecessary

Source: Adapted from Judith Lynne Zaichowsky, "The Personal Involvement Inventory: Reduction, Revision, and Application to Advertising," *Journal of Advertising*, 23, 4, December 1994: 59–70. Reprinted by permission.

| FIGURE 3-6 | Product Involvement Inventory Measuring Consumers' Enduring Involvement with Products |

1. I would be interested in reading about this product.
2. I would read a *Consumer Reports* article about this product.
3. I have compared product characteristics among brands.
4. I usually pay attention to ads for this product.
5. I usually talk about this product with other people.
6. I usually seek advice from other people prior to purchasing this product.
7. I usually take many factors into account before purchasing this product.
8. I usually spend a lot of time choosing what kind to buy.

Source: Edward F. McQuarrie and J. Michael Munson, "A Revised Product Involvement Inventory: Improved Usability and Validity," *Diversity in Consumer Behavior: Advances in Consumer Research*, vol. 19 (Provo, UT: Association for Consumer Research, 1992), 108–15. Reprinted by permission.

Choose messages that are appropriate for the level of consumer involvement: Besides the complexity of the message, other elements of the message also need to be modified to suit the level of involvement. Uninvolved consumers appear to be susceptible to different kinds of persuasion than are highly involved consumers. One study found that comparative ads (see Chapter 8) are more likely to be processed centrally (purposeful processing of message arguments), whereas noncomparative ads are commonly processed peripherally (with little message elaboration and a response derived from other executional elements in the ad).[20] Another study found that the use of metaphors and other figures of speech that deviate from the expected in print ads places added processing demands on the readers and make the ad more persuasive and memorable. The metaphors examined in this study were such slogans as "It forced other car makers into the copier business" (Mercury Sable) and "In the Caribbean, there's no such thing as a party of one" (Malibu Caribbean Rum).[21]

Find ways to raise the level of consumer involvement: By understanding the nature of low-involvement information processing, marketers can take steps to make customers more involved with their ads. For example, advertisers can use sensory appeals, unusual stimuli, and celebrity endorsers to attract more attention to their messages. Marketers should also focus on increasing customer involvement levels by creating bonds with their customers.[22] Of course, the best strategy for increasing the personal relevance of products to consumers is the same as the core of modern marketing itself: provide benefits that are important and relevant to customers, improve the product and add benefits as competition intensifies, and forge *bonds* and *relationships* with customers rather than just engage in *transactions*.

SUMMARY

- Motivation is the driving force within individuals that impels them to action; it is produced by a state of uncomfortable tension, which exists as the result of an unsatisfied need.

- Goals are the sought-after results of motivated behaviour. There are two types of goals: generic (or product-category) goals and product-specific (or brand-specific) goals.

- Needs can be classified into physiological, or those an individual is born with (e.g., food, water, clothing, shelter, sex, and physical safety) and psychogenic, or those that an individual develops after birth (e.g., love, acceptance, esteem, and self-fulfillment). Needs can also be classified into latent (or hidden) and manifest (or known and expressed).

- Motivation is a dynamic concept since individuals have multiple needs and goals. These are complex and they change over time, vary with individual and cultural factors, and are hard to predict from a person's behaviour.

- There are several theories of motivation. Murray identified 28 psychogenic needs (besides the usual physiological needs). Maslow's hierarchy-of-needs theory proposes five levels of prepotent human needs: physiological needs, safety needs, social needs, egoistic needs, and self-actualization needs. McClelland classified psychological needs into the need for power, for affiliation, and for achievement. There are several mid-range theories of motivation that explain some kinds of consumer behaviour, but not all of them.

- There are three commonly used methods for identifying and "measuring" human motives: observation and inference, subjective reports, and qualitative research (including projective techniques). Researchers often use a combination of two or three techniques to assess the presence or strength of consumer motives.

- Once consumer needs are identified, they can be used to segment and position a product and to help the development of promotional messages. Finally, marketers need to find ways of reducing motivational conflict.

- Involvement is the level of personal relevance a product has for a consumer. The higher the involvement, the more willing a consumer would be to process information and the higher the likelihood of brand loyalty.

- Involvement can be classified as either enduring (i.e., ongoing) or situational (i.e., short term), and as either cognitive or emotional.

- Involvement depends on the level of perceived risk, the probability of failure, personal interest in the product category, the pleasure in the purchase, and the similarity of alternatives.

- The media and the message strategy used for advertisements should match the consumer's level of involvement in the product.

- Marketers can increase the level of involvement in the product by using sensory appeals, unusual stimuli, and celebrity endorsers.

DISCUSSION QUESTIONS

1. Consumers have both innate and acquired needs. Give examples of each kind of need, and show how the same purchase can serve to meet either or both kinds of needs.

2. Why are consumers' needs and goals constantly changing? What factors influence the formation of new goals?

3. (a) How do researchers identify and measure human motives? Give examples.

   (b) What are the strengths and weaknesses of motivational research?

4. Explain briefly the needs for power, affiliation, and achievement. Find three advertisements that are designed to appeal to these needs.

5. What is involvement? What factors cause high involvement?

6. Discuss how a marketer can use the concept of involvement while developing marketing strategies.

CRITICAL THINKING QUESTIONS

1. You are a member of an advertising team assembled to develop a promotional campaign for a new digital camera. (a) Develop a mean-end chain for this product. (b) Develop three headlines for this campaign based on the underlying need and its level in Maslow's hierarchy.

2. Consider the products given below and (a) specify both latent and manifest needs that would be useful bases for developing promotional strategies for these products; (b) discuss whether they are high- or low-involvement products; and (c) develop a marketing strategy for each, incorporating the motivational and involvement concepts that were covered in this chapter.

   ▪ global positioning systems
   ▪ Harley-Davidson motorcycles
   ▪ recruiting fourth-year university students to work in the public service (federal or provincial or territorial)

3. Assume that you are the marketing manager of a funeral home that provides traditional funeral services. Consider the level of involvement of this product and whether its purchase would generate any type of motivational conflict. Using your responses to these issues, develop an ad that would help in the marketing of these services.

4. For each of the situations listed in question 2, select one level from Maslow's hierarchy of human needs that can be used to segment the market and position the product (or the organization). Explain your choices. What are the advantages and disadvantages of using Maslow's need hierarchy for segmentation and positioning applications?

INTERNET EXERCISES

1. Visit the websites of some soft drink and beer marketers. Can you see any applications of Maslow's hierarchy of needs or McLelland's trio of needs in these websites?

2. Visit websites of several household products (e.g., Proctor & Gamble, General Mills, Colgate-Palmolive) and find examples of mid-range theories of motivation being used.

3. Look at the pop-up ads that appear on your computer while you are accessing various websites. Are the marketers of these companies using any techniques to increase your involvement in the product? If so, give examples of the techniques used.

4. Visit the websites of two companies in the furniture industry and two in the automobile

industry, and give examples of techniques used to reduce motivational conflict. Choose products that are positive (approach objects) and negative (avoidance objects) so that you can give examples of all three types of motivational conflicts.

KEY TERMS

Affective involvement   *(p. 94)*
Approach object   *(p. 75)*
Avoidance object   *(p. 75)*
Cognitive involvement   *(p. 94)*
Defence mechanisms   *(p. 79)*
Emotional motives   *(p. 74)*
Enduring involvement   *(p. 94)*
Generic goals   *(p. 74)*
Goals   *(p. 74)*
Hedonic consumption   *(p. 86)*

Involvement   *(p. 93)*
Latent motives   *(p. 74)*
Manifest motives   *(p. 74)*
Maslow's hierarchy of needs   *(p. 82)*
Motivation   *(p. 72)*
Motivational conflict   *(p. 80)*
Motivational research   *(p. 88)*
Negative motivation   *(p. 75)*
Opponent process theory   *(p. 86)*
Optimum stimulation level   *(p. 87)*

Physiological needs   *(p. 73)*
Positive motivation   *(p. 75)*
Priming   *(p. 86)*
Prepotent need   *(p. 79)*
Product-specific goals   *(p. 74)*
Psychological (or psychogenic) needs   *(p. 73)*
Psychological reactance   *(p. 86)*
Rational motives   *(p. 74)*
Situational involvement   *(p. 94)*

CASE 3-1: THE PRODUCT COLLECTION AT NEW PRODUCT WORKS

The essence of the marketing concept is understanding consumer needs and developing products that meet these needs effectively. And yet, every year scores of new products are withdrawn from the market after being introduced; many other products also "fail" when their sales fall short of the revenues needed to cover their development costs and also generate profits. Clearly, understanding consumer needs is a complex matter.

Most of the new products introduced, including failed products, fall within the product categories sold in supermarkets—including categories such as food, beverages, household maintenance, personal care, baby care. In an effort to pinpoint

causes of product failures in these areas, an organization named New Product Works maintains a vast collection of food, beverage, household, and personal-care products that were introduced and subsequently withdrawn from the marketplace (see **www.newproductworks.com)**.

The purpose of New Product Works is to provide grounded-in-the-marketplace assistance to companies developing new products. The organization's product collection also offers insights into how a misunderstanding of consumer needs can lead to the development and introduction of costly but unsuccessful products.

QUESTIONS

1. Visit the online product collection at New Product Works. Go to the "Poll: Hits or Misses?" link. Rate three of the new products featured on this link, and compare your ratings with those of previous respondents. Explain your ratings in the context of the chapter's discussion of consumer needs and motivation.

2. Now go to the "Hits & Misses" section (located in the "Poll" section). Scroll down to "Favorite Failures." Select three of the products featured there and explain, with reference to consumer needs and motivation, why they failed.

NOTES

1   Rebecca Harris, "Different by Design," *Hotelier*, January–February, 2003, 63–65. All quotes in this opening vignette are taken from this article.

2   A number of studies have examined human levels of aspiration. See, for example, Kurt Lewin et al., "Level of Aspiration," in *Personality and Behavior Disorders,* ed. J. McV. Hunt (New York: Ronald Press, 1944); Howard Garland, "Goal Levels and Task Performance: A Compelling Replication of Some Compelling Results," *Journal of Applied Psychology,* 67 (1982), 245–248; Edwin A. Locke, Elizabeth Frederick, Cynthia Lee, and Philip Bobko, "Effect of Self Efficacy, Goals and Task Strategies on Task Performance," *Journal of Applied Psychology,* 69, 2 (1984): 241–251; Edwin A. Locke, Elizabeth Frederick, Elizabeth Buckner, and Philip Bobko, "Effect of Previously Assigned Goals on Self Set Goals and Performance," *Journal of Applied Psychology,* 72, 2 (1987): 204–211; and John R. Hollenbeck and Howard J. Klein, "Goal Commitment and the Goal Setting Process: Problems, Prospects and Proposals for Future Research," *Journal of Applied Psychology* 2 (1987): 212–220.

3   H. Maslow Abraham, "A Theory of Human Motivation," *Psychological Review*, 50, 1943, 380.

4   Katherine Harding, "Trading Spaces," *Globe and Mail*, August 27, 2003, p. C2.

5   Abraham, H. Maslow, op. cit.

6   See, for example, David C. McClelland, *Studies in Motivation* (New York: Appleton Century Crofts, 1955); David C. McClelland, "Business Drive and National Achievement," *Harvard Business Review,* July–August 1962; "Achievement Motivation Can Be Developed," *Harvard Business Review*, 5, 24 (November–December 1965); and Abraham K. Korman, *The Psychology of Motivation* (Upper Saddle River, NJ: Prentice Hall, 1974).

7   C. Daniels, "From I AM," *Digital Marketing*, July 2002, 12.

8   Leah McLaren, "Women Who Travel for Sex," *Globe and Mail*, August 30, 2003, T2.

9   Ibid., T5

10   Andre Venoit, "Her Name on the Box," *Progress*, January–February, 2003, 39-43.

11   Daniel Goleman, "New View of Mind Gives Unconscious an Expanded Role," *New York Times,* February 7, 1984, C1–2.

12   Chilton, D., "Not Just Pretty Pictures," *Profit*, March 2003, 34.

13   Flemming Hansen, "Hemispheral Lateralization: Implications for Understanding Consumer Behavior," *Journal of Consumer Research*, 8 (June 1981), 23–36; Peter H. Lindzay and Donald Norman, *Human Information Processing* (New York: Academic Press, 1977); and Merlin C. Wittrock, *The Human Brain* (Upper Saddle River, NJ: Prentice Hall, 1977).

14   Herbert E. Krugman, "The Impact of Television Advertising: Learning without Involvement," *Public Opinion Quarterly*, 29 (Fall, 1965), 349–56; "Brain Wave Measures of Media Involvement," *Journal of Advertising Research*, 11 (February, 1971), 3–10.

15   Theo B.C. Poiesz and J.P.M. de Bont, "Do We Need Involvement to Understand Consumer Behavior?" *Advances in Consumer Research,* 22, 1995, 448–452; Judith L. Zaichkowsky, "Conceptualizing Involvement," *Journal of Advertising,* 15, 2, 1986, 4–34. See also the following articles in *Advances in Consumer Research,* 11, ed. Thomas C. Kinnear (Provo, UT: Association for Consumer Research, 1984): James A. Muncy and Shelby D. Hunt, "Consumer Involvement: Definitional Issues and Research Directions," 193–196; John H. Antil, "Conceptualization and Operationalization of Involvement," 203–209; and Michael L. Rothschild, "Perspectives on Involvement: Current Problems and Future Directions," 216–217.

16   Banwari Mittal and Myung Soo Lee, "Separating Brand Choice Involvement from Product Involvement via Consumer Involvement Profiles," in *Advances in Consumer Research,* vol. 15, ed. Michael Houston (Provo, UT: Association for Consumer Research, 1988), 43–49.

17   See Marsha L. Richins, Peter H. Bloch, and Edward F. McQuarrie, "How Enduring and Situational Involvement Combine to Create Involvement Responses," *Journal of Consumer Psychology,* 1, 2, 1992, 143–153.

18   Gilles Laurent and Jean Noel Kapferer, "Measuring Consumer Involvement Profiles," *Journal of Marketing Research,* 22, February 1985, 41–53; Jean Noel Kapferer and Gilles Laurent, "Consumer Involvement Profiles: A New Practical Approach to Consumer Involvement," *Journal of Advertising Research,* 25, 6, December 1985–January 1986, 48–56.

19   Kenneth Schneider and William Rodgers, "An 'Importance' Subscale for the Consumer Involvement Profile," *Advances in Consumer Research,* vol. 23, ed. Kim Corfman and John Lynch (Provo, UT: Association for Consumer Research, 1996), 249–254.

20   Sanjay Putrevu and Kenneth R. Lord, "Comparative and Noncomparative Advertising:

Attitudinal Effects Under Cognitive and Affective Involvement Conditions" Journal of Advertising, 23, 2, June 1994, 77–91.

21   Mark Toncar and James Munch, "Consumer Responses to Tropes in Print Advertising," *Journal of Advertising*, Spring 2001, 55–65.

22   Simon Walls and David W. Schumann, "Measuring the Customer's Perception of the Bond between the Customer and the Company," American Marketing Association Educators' Conference Proceedings, 12, 2001, 388400.

FOR HAIR THAT SHINES
WITH ALL ITS STRENGTH

GARNIER FRUCTIS FORTIFYING HAIRCARE SYSTEM WITH ACTIVE FRUIT CONCENTRATE.

Garnier Fructis shampoo, conditioner and treatment nourish your hair from the root strengthen the hair fibre from deep inside and smooth it right to the tip.

It's proven: The Garnier Fructis system makes hair **5 times stronger and smoother for brilliant shine.***

www.garnier.ca

* Garnier shampoo, conditioner and treatment compared to an ordinary shampoo.

GARNIER

chapter 4
personality, self-image, and life style

LEARNING OBJECTIVES

By the end of this chapter, you should be able to:

1. Define personality and discuss its key characteristics.
2. Summarize Freudian, neo-Freudian, and cognitive theories and discuss three single-trait theories of personality.
3. Define brand personality and state how marketers can develop a brand's personality.
4. Explain how an understanding of personality theories can help marketers develop better marketing strategies.
5. Define the concept of self-image and discuss the various types of self-image.
6. Explain how marketers can use the concept of self-image while developing marketing strategies.
7. Explain what is meant by consumer life style and psychographics; discuss three consumer life-style classification systems.
8. Explain how marketers can use the concept of life style while developing marketing strategies.

4

what is your self-image? If you are like 99 percent of Canadian women, you probably do not consider yourself to be beautiful. Would the average Canadian woman then react well to ads that feature beautiful women with perfect figures? Until recently, marketers have worked on the assumption that portraying an "ideal" woman would make the average Canadian woman buy a product in the hope that it might make her closer to the "ideal" image of beauty portrayed in the ad. However, research indicates that 68 percent of women around the world agree that ads portray an ideal image of beauty that they find unattainable. Dove has decided to deal with this issue by showing women that beauty is within their reach by launching its "Campaign for Real Beauty," which features a bald fitness trainer, a 95-year-old wrinkled woman, and a freckled redhead. Similar campaigns that aim to boost consumer self-image by making them comfortable with—and even proud of—their bodies were also run by Kellogg's ("Look Good on Your Own Terms") and Addition Elle ("Make a Statement").[1]

CHAPTER OVERVIEW

This chapter examines the nature of personality, reviews several major personality theories, and describes how marketers can apply these theories while marketing products and services. The chapter also considers the important topics of *brand personality*. Next, the chapter examines the related concepts of *self* and *self-image* and their influence on consumer attitudes and behaviour. The final section of the chapter covers consumer life styles, which often reflect their personality and self-image.

Why are these concepts dealt with in one chapter? A consumer's personality and self-concept affect his or her life style; moreover, consumers often buy products that either reflect or bolster their personalities and self-concepts. Thus, these concepts are highly interrelated, and their marketing implications are interlinked.

WHAT IS PERSONALITY?

Personality:
Those inner psychological characteristics that both determine and reflect how a person responds to his or her environment.

The study of **personality** has been approached by theorists in a variety of ways. Some have emphasized the dual influence of heredity and early childhood experiences on personality development; others have stressed broader social and environmental influences and the fact that personalities are developing continuously. Some theorists prefer to view personality as a unified whole; others focus on specific traits. The wide variation in viewpoints makes it difficult to arrive at a single definition. However, we propose that personality be defined as *those inner psychological characteristics that both determine and reflect how a person responds to his or her environment.*

The emphasis in this definition is on *inner characteristics*—those specific qualities, attributes, traits, factors, and mannerisms that distinguish one individual from another. The deeply ingrained characteristics that we call personality (which are discussed later in the chapter) are likely to influence the individual's product choices: they may also affect the way consumers respond to marketers' promotional efforts and when, where, and how they buy particular products or services. Therefore, the identification of specific personality characteristics associated with consumer behaviour has proved to be highly useful in the development of a firm's market segmentation strategies.

In the study of personality, three distinct factors are of central importance: (1) *Personality reflects individual differences.* (2) *Personality is consistent and enduring.* (3) *Personality can change.*

Personality Reflects Individual Differences

Because the inner characteristics that constitute an individual's personality are a unique combination of factors, no two individuals are exactly alike. Nevertheless, many individuals may be similar in terms of a single personality characteristic but not in terms of others. For instance, some people can be described as "high" in *venturesomeness* (e.g., willing to accept the risk of doing something new or different, such as skydiving or mountain climbing), whereas others can be described as "low" in *venturesomeness* (e.g., afraid to buy a really new product). Personality is a useful concept because it enables us to categorize consumers into different groups on the basis of one or even several traits. If all the personality traits of every person were different, it would be impossible to group consumers into segments, and there would be little reason for marketers to develop products and promotional campaigns targeted to particular segments.

Personality Is Consistent and Enduring

An individual's personality tends to be both consistent and enduring. Indeed, the mother who comments that her child "has been impulsive from the day he was born" is supporting the contention that personality has both consistency and endurance. Both qualities are essential if marketers are to explain or predict consumer behaviour in terms of personality.

Although marketers cannot change consumers' personalities to conform to their products, if they know which personality characteristics influence specific consumer responses, they can attempt to appeal to the relevant traits inherent in their target group of consumers.

Even though consumers' personalities may be consistent, their consumption behaviour often varies considerably because of the various psychological, sociocultural, environmental, and situational factors that affect behaviour. For instance, although an individual's personality may be relatively stable, specific needs or motives, attitudes, reactions to group pressures, and even responses to new brands may cause a change in the person's behaviour. Personality is only one of a combination of factors that influence how a consumer behaves.

Personality Can Change

Under certain circumstances personalities change. A person's personality may be altered by major life events, such as the birth of a child, the death of a loved one, a divorce, or a significant career promotion. Personality can also change as part of a gradual maturing process—"He's growing up; he is much calmer," says an aunt after not seeing her nephew for five years.

There is also evidence that personality stereotypes may change over time. More specifically, although it is thought that the male personality has generally remained relatively constant over the past 50 years, the female personality seems to have become more masculine and will probably continue to do so over the next 50 years. This prediction indicates a *convergence* in the personality characteristics of men and women.[2] The reason for this shift is that women have been moving into occupations that have traditionally been dominated by men and, therefore, have been associated with masculine personality attributes.

THEORIES OF PERSONALITY

This section briefly summarizes four major theories of personality: (1) Freudian theory, (2) neo-Freudian theory, (3) cognitive theory, and (4) trait theory. These theories have been chosen for discussion from among many theories of personality because each has been prominent in the study of the relationship between consumer behaviour and personality.

Freudian Theory

Sigmund Freud's **psychoanalytic theory of personality** is a cornerstone of modern psychology. This theory was built on the premise that *unconscious needs or drives*, especially sexual drives and other biological drives, are at the heart of human motivation and personality. Freud constructed his theory on the basis of patients' recollections of early childhood experiences, on his analysis of their dreams, and on the specific nature of their mental and physical adjustment problems.

Psychoanalytic theory: A theory of personality built on the premise that unconscious needs or drives, especially sexual and other biological drives, are at the heart of human motivation.

Id, Superego, and Ego

On the basis of his analyses, Freud proposed that the human personality consists of three interacting systems:

The *id* is a "warehouse" of primitive and impulsive drives—basic physiological needs such as thirst, hunger, and sex—for which the individual seeks immediate

EXHIBIT 4-1

AN AD PORTRAYING THE "FORCES" OF THE ID

Courtesy of MISTIC, a registered trademark of Mistic Brands, Inc. Reprinted by permission.

satisfaction without concern for the specific means of satisfaction. The ad for Mistic juice drinks (see Exhibit 4-1) captures the exciting "forces" associated with the primitive drives of the *id* when it declares, "Give in to the juice." The positioning and appearance of the model add to this sense of excitement.

The *superego* is conceptualized as the individual's internal expression of society's moral and ethical codes of conduct. The task of the superego is to see that the individual satisfies needs in a socially acceptable fashion. Thus, the superego is a kind of "brake" that restrains or inhibits the impulsive forces of the id.

The *ego* is the individual's conscious control. It functions as an internal monitor that attempts to balance the impulsive demands of the id and the socio-cultural constraints of the superego. Figure 4-1 represents the relationships among the three interacting systems.

Freudian Theory and "Product Personality"

Researchers who apply Freud's psychoanalytic theory to the study of consumer personality believe that human drives are largely *unconscious* and that consumers are primarily unaware of their true reasons for buying what they buy. These researchers tend to see consumer purchases and consumption situations as a reflection and an extension of the consumer's own personality. In other words, they consider the consumer's appearance and possessions—grooming, clothing, jewellery, and so forth—as reflections of the individual's personality. Figure 4-2 presents the results of a study of 19 000 consumers that examines the link between snack food perceptions and selected personality traits.[3] The findings of the research, for example, reveal that potato chips are associated with being ambitious, successful, a high achiever, and impatient with less than the best, whereas popcorn seems to be related to a personality that takes charge, pitches in often, is modest and self-confident but not a show-off. (The related topics of *brand personality* and the self and *self-images* are considered later in the chapter.)

Neo-Freudian Personality Theories

Neo-Freudian personality theories: A school of personality theory that stresses that social relationships are fundamental to the formation and development of personality.

Several of Freud's colleagues disagreed with his contention that personality is primarily instinctual and sexual. Instead, these neo-Freudians believed that *social relationships* are fundamental to the formation and development of personality.

Karen Horney, one of the well-known neo-Freudian theorists, emphasized the influence of child-parent relationships and the individual's desire to conquer feelings of anxiety. Horney proposed that individuals be classified into three personality groups: *compliant, aggressive,* and *detached.*[4]

1. Compliant individuals are those who move toward others (they desire to be loved, wanted, and appreciated).

2. Aggressive individuals are those who move against others (they desire to excel and win admiration).

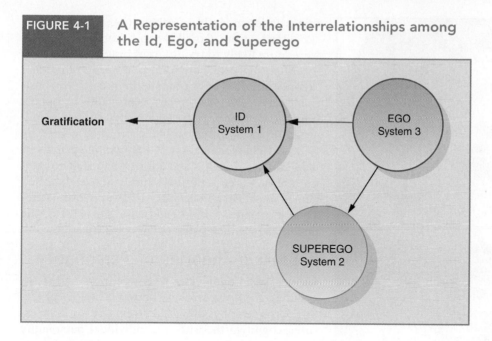

FIGURE 4-1 A Representation of the Interrelationships among the Id, Ego, and Superego

FIGURE 4-2 Snack Foods and Personality Traits

SNACK FOOD	PERSONALITY TRAITS
Potato chips	Ambitious, successful, high achiever, impatient with less than the best.
Tortilla chips	Perfectionist, high expectations, punctual, conservative, responsible.
Pretzels	Lively, easily bored with same old routine, flirtatious, intuitive, may overcommit to projects.
Snack crackers	Rational, logical, contemplative, shy, prefers time alone.
Cheese curls	Conscientious, principled, proper, fair, may appear rigid but has great integrity, plans ahead, loves order.
Nuts	Easygoing, empathetic, understanding, calm, even-tempered.
Popcorn	Takes charge, pitches in often, modest, self-confident but not a show-off.
Meat snacks	Gregarious, generous, trustworthy, tends to be overly trusting.

Source: Alan Hirsch, MD, *What Flavor is Your Personality? Discover Who You Are by Looking at What You Eat* (Naperville, Il: Sourcebooks, 2001).

3. Detached individuals are those who move away from others (they desire independence, self-reliance, self-sufficiency, and individualism or freedom from obligations).

A personality test based on Horney's theory (the CAD) has been developed and tested in relation to consumer behaviour.[5] The first CAD research uncovered a number of tentative relationships between college students' scores and their choice of products and brands. Highly *compliant* students, for example, were found to prefer name-brand products such as Bayer Aspirin; students classified as *aggressive* showed a preference for Old Spice deodorant over other brands (seemingly because of its masculine appeal); and highly *detached* students proved to be heavy tea drinkers (possibly reflecting their desire not to conform). More recent research has found that children who scored high in self-reliance—who preferred to do

www.karenhorney center.org

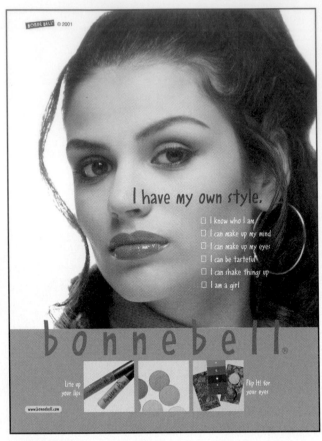

EXHIBIT 4-2

AN AD APPLYING HORNEY'S DETACHED
PERSONALITY

Courtesy of Bonne Bell.

Cognitive theories of personality:
A school of personality theories that see individual personality differences as differences in cognitive process, that is, in how consumers process and react to information.

Need for cognition:
The personality trait that measures a person's craving for or enjoyment of thinking.

Visualizers:
Consumers who prefer visual information.

Verbalizers:
Consumers who prefer written or verbal information.

things independently of others (i.e., *detached* personalities)—were *less* likely to be brand-loyal and were *more* likely to try different brands.[6]

Many marketers use some of these neo-Freudian theories intuitively. For example, marketers who position their products or services as providing an opportunity to belong or to be appreciated by others in a group or social setting would seem to be guided by Horney's characterization of the *compliant* individual. Exhibit 4-2 shows an ad for Bonne Bell cosmetics that captures a positive image of the detached person. Its headline declares: "I have my own style." Then it includes a short (and cute) checklist of the underlying characteristics of "my own style."

Cognitive Theories of Personality

Unlike psychoanalysts, who see personality as resulting from the struggle between biological factors (or inner physiological drives) and social pressures, cognitive theorists see individual personality differences as differences in cognitive process – that is, in how consumers process and react to information. Two popular **cognitive theories of personality** are discussed in the following sections.

Need for Cognition

A promising cognitive personality characteristic is the **need for cognition (NC)**. It expresses a person's craving for or enjoyment of *thinking*. Available research indicates that consumers who are *high* in NC are more likely to

- be responsive to the part of an ad that is rich in product-related information or description; consumers who are relatively *low* in NC are more likely to be attracted to the background or peripheral aspects of an ad, such as an attractive model or well-known celebrity.[7]

- respond more favourably to written messages than to cartoon messages.[8]

- be less affected by message framing, that is, whether a message is phrased positively or negatively.[9]

- spend more time processing print advertisements, which results in a superior ability to remember brands and ad claims.[10]

- enjoy using the internet to obtain product information, current events, and news, and for learning and education—all activities that incorporate a cognitive element.[11]

Such research insights provide advertisers with valuable guidelines for creating advertising messages (including supporting art) that appeal to a particular target audience grouping's *need for cognition*.

Visualizers versus Verbalizers

It is fairly well established that some people seem to be more open to and prefer the written word as a way of securing information, whereas others are more likely to respond to and prefer visual images or messages as sources of information. Thus, cognitive personality research classifies consumers into two groups:

- **visualizers** (consumers who prefer visual information and products that stress the visual, such as membership in a videotape club)
- **verbalizers** (consumers who prefer written or verbal information and products, such as membership in book clubs or audiotape clubs)

Some marketers stress strong visual elements in order to attract visualizers (see Exhibit 4-3); others ask a question and provide the answer, or feature a detailed description or point-by-point explanation to attract verbalizers (see Exhibit 4-4).

Trait Theory

Trait theory, like cognitive theories, is a major departure from the *qualitative* measures that typify the Freudian and neo-Freudian movements (e.g., personal observation, self-reported experiences, dream analysis, and projective techniques).

The orientation of trait theory is primarily quantitative or empirical; it focuses on the measurement of personality in terms of specific psychological characteristics, called traits. A *trait* is defined as "any distinguishing, relatively enduring way in which one individual differs from another."[12] Trait theorists are concerned with the construction of personality tests (or inventories) that enable them to pinpoint individual differences in terms of specific traits.

Trait theories can be classified into two categories: single-trait theories, which measure just one trait (e.g., self-confidence) and multi-trait theories, which use several traits in combination to capture the main elements of an individual's personality. Selected *single-trait personality* tests are often developed specifically for consumer behaviour studies. These tailor-made personality tests measure such traits as **consumer innovativeness** (how receptive a person is to new experiences), **consumer materialism** (the consumer's attachment to worldly possessions), and **consumer ethnocentrism** (the consumer's likelihood of accepting or rejecting foreign-made products). These are discussed in more detail in the next section.

Although single-trait theories emphasize one particular trait that may be relevant to understanding a particular behaviour, multiple-trait (or multitrait) theories attempt to combine a group of traits that, together, explain a wide range of behaviours. One such theory is the Five-Factor Model, which incorporates five personality traits—extroversion, instability, agreeableness, openness to experience, and conscientiousness (see Figure 4-3). This model has been used by marketers to understand behaviours such as compulsive shopping[13] and complaining about products or services.[14]

Trait researchers have found that it is generally more realistic to expect personality to be linked to how consumers *make their choices* and to the purchase or consumption of *a broad product*

Trait theory:
A theory of personality that focuses on the measurement of specific psychological characteristics.

Consumer innovativeness:
The degree to which a consumer is receptive to new products, services, or practices.

Consumer materialism:
A personality-like trait that distinguishes between individuals who regard possessions as essential to their identities and their lives and those for whom possessions are secondary.

Consumer ethnocentrism:
A consumer's predisposition to accept or reject foreign-made products.

EXHIBIT 4-3

AN AD APPEALING TO VISUALIZERS

Courtesy of Garnier Fructis.

EXHIBIT 4-4

AN AD APPEALING TO VERBALIZERS

Courtesy of Pfizer Consumer Group, Pfizer, Inc.

Consumer innovators: People who are likely to be the first to try new products, services, or practices.

category rather than the purchase of a specific brand. For example, there is more likely to be a relationship between a personality trait and whether or not an individual owns a convertible sports car than between a personality trait and the model of convertible sports car the person bought.

Consumer Innovativeness

Marketing practitioners try to learn all they can about **consumer innovators**—those who are likely to be the first to try new products, services, or practices—for the market response of such innovators is often a critical indication of the eventual success or failure of a new product or service.

Consumer researchers have tried to develop measurement instruments to gauge the level of consumer innovativeness, because such measures provide important insights into the nature and boundaries of a consumer's willingness to innovate.[15] Figure 4-4 presents a six-item measure of consumer innovativeness that has been designed to be adaptable to various domains; that is, it can be used to study a broad product category (e.g., personal computers), a subproduct category (e.g., notebook computers), or a product type (e.g., six-kilogram mini-notebook computers).

Recent consumer research points to a positive relationship between innovative use of the internet and buying online.[16] Still further, other research into the association between personality traits and innovative internet behaviour has reported that internet shoppers tend to see themselves as being able to control their own future, using the internet to seek out information, enjoying change, and not being afraid of uncertainty.[17]

Other personality traits that have been useful in differentiating between consumer innovators and non-innovators include dogmatism, social character, need for uniqueness, optimum stimulation level, sensation-seeking, and variety- or novelty-seeking. These are discussed in further detail in Figure 4-5.

Consumer Materialism

Consumer materialism is a topic frequently discussed in newspapers, in magazines, and on television (e.g., "North Americans are very materialistic") and in everyday

FIGURE 4-3	The Five Factor Model
TRAIT	**CHARACTERISTICS OF PERSONS WITH THE TRAIT**
Extroversion	Talkative, enjoys being in large groups and hates being alone
Instability	Moody, touchy, and temperamental
Agreeableness	Sympathetic, polite, and kind to others
Openness to experience	Innovative, finds new solutions to problems, loves art, and is imaginative
Conscientiousness	Careful, efficient, and precise

Source: Adapted from Table 10.3, page 369 of *Consumer Behavior: Implications for Marketing Strategy* by D. Hawkins, et al. © McGraw Hill Companies, Inc.

FIGURE 4-4	A Consumer Innovativeness Scale

In general, I am among the last in my circle of friends to buy a new (rock album[a]) when it appears.[b]

If I heard that a (new rock album) was available in the store, I would be interested enough to buy it.

Compared to my friends, I own few (rock albums).[b]

In general, I am the last in my circle of friends to know the (titles of the latest rock albums).[b]

I will buy a new (rock album), even if I haven't heard it yet.

I know the names of (new rock acts) before other people do.

Note: Measured on a 5-point "agreement" scale.
[a]The product category and related wording are altered to fit the purpose of the researcher.
[b]Items with a ([b]) are negatively worded and are scored inversely.

Source: Ronald E. Goldsmith and Charles F. Hofacker, "Measuring Consumer Innovativeness," *Journal of the Academy of Marketing Science,* 19, 1991, 212. Copyright © 1991 Academy of Marketing Science. Reprinted by permission.

FIGURE 4-5	Personality Traits Related to Consumer Innovativenss

PERSONALITY TRAIT	DESCRIPTION	CONNECTION TO CONSUMER INNOVATIVENESS
Dogmatism	A measure of the degree of rigidity (versus openness) that individuals display toward the unfamiliar and toward information that is contrary to their own established beliefs.[18]	Consumers who are low in dogmatism are more likely to be innovators than those high in dogmatism.
Social character: inner- versus other-directed	Inner-directed consumers (unlike other-directed consumers) tend to rely on their own inner values or standards.	Inner-directed consumers are more likely to be consumer innovators.
Need for uniqueness	The need to be different from others.	Consumers with a high need for uniqueness (NFU) are more likely to be innovators, especially when they are asked to explain their choices, but are not concerned about being criticized by others.[19]
Optimum stimulation level	Variation in individual need for stimulation.	High *optimum stimulation levels* (OSL) are linked with greater willingness to take risks, to try new products, to be innovative, to seek purchase-related information, and to accept new retail facilities than low OSLs.
Sensation-seeking	A trait characterized by the need for varied, novel, and complex sensations and experiences, and the willingness to take physical and social risks for the sake of such experiences.	High sensation seekers (SS) are more likely to engage in innovative behaviour. Research shows that teenage boys with higher SS scores are more likely than other teenagers to like listening to heavy metal music and to engage in reckless or even dangerous behaviour.[20]
Variety- or novelty-seeking	The need to have variety or novel experiences.	A person scoring high in variety-seeking is likely to be more innovative and attracted to brands with more novel features than is a consumer with a lower variety-seeking score.

conversations ("He's so materialistic!"). The term materialistic in reference to personalities describes individuals who regard possessions as essential to their identities and their lives as opposed to those for whom possessions are secondary.[21] Researchers have found some general support for the following characteristics of materialistic people:

- They especially value acquiring possessions and showing them off.
- They are particularly self-centred and selfish.
- They seek life styles full of possessions (e.g., they want to have lots of "things," rather than a simple, uncluttered life).
- Their many possessions do not give them greater satisfaction (i.e., their possessions do not lead to greater happiness).[22]

Figure 4-6 presents sample items from a materialism scale.

Materialism has often been linked to advertising, and researchers have suggested that in the developed world the print media have reflected an increase in materialism. It is important to remember, though, that the extent of consumer materialism can vary from country to country (e.g., consumer materialism is less developed in Mexico than in Canada) and, therefore, marketers must be careful when trying to export a successful Canadian marketing mix to another country.[23] Exhibit 4-5 shows an ad appealing to consumers' materialism.

Consumer Ethnocentrism: Responses to Foreign-Made Products

In an effort to distinguish between consumer segments that are likely to be receptive to foreign products and those that are not, researchers have developed and tested the consumer ethnocentrism scale, called CETSCALE (see Figure 4-7).[24] The

---

FIGURE 4-6   Sample Items from a Materialism Scale

SUCCESS

The things I own say a lot about how well I'm doing in life.
I don't place much emphasis on the amount of material objects people own as a sign of success.[a]
I like to own things that impress people.

CENTRALITY

I enjoy spending money on things that aren't practical.
I try to keep my life simple, as far as possessions are concerned.[a]
Buying things gives me a lot of pleasure.

HAPPINESS

I'd be happier if I could afford to buy more things.
I have all the things I really need to enjoy life.[a]
It sometimes bothers me quite a bit that I can't afford to buy all the things I'd like.

Note: Measured on a 5-point "agreement" scale.
[a]Items with an ([a]) are negatively worded and are scored inversely.

Source: Marsha L. Richins and Scott Dawson, "A Consumer Values Orientation for Materialism and Its Measurement: Scale Development and Validation," *Journal of Consumer Research*, 19, December 1992, 310. Reprinted by permission of The University of Chicago Press as publisher.

CETSCALE has been successful in identifying consumers with a predisposition to accept (or reject) foreign products. Consumers who are highly ethnocentric are likely to feel that it is wrong to buy foreign products because of the resulting harm to the domestic economy, whereas non-ethnocentric consumers tend to evaluate foreign products—ostensibly more objectively—for their intrinsic characteristics (e.g., "How good are they?"). A proportion of the consumers who would score low on an ethnocentric scale are actually likely to be quite receptive to products made in foreign countries.

Ethnocentrism has been found to vary by country and product. Mexican consumers, for example, are more ethnocentric than their French and American counterparts; and Malaysian consumers prefer slacks, shirts, undergarments, and belts that are manufactured locally but want to buy imported sunglasses and watches.[25]

Marketers can successfully target ethnocentric consumers in any national market by stressing a nationalistic theme in their promotional appeals (e.g., "Made in Canada" or "Made in France") because this segment is predisposed to buy products made in their own country. Exhibit 4-6 shows effective use of Canadians' ethnocentrism. Figure 4-8 presents a marketing mix strategy that can be used to manage country-of-origin effects. Specifically, if marketers determine that the potential customers in a particular country have a *positive* image of products

EXHIBIT 4-5

AN AD APPEALING TO MATERIALISM

Courtesy of Infiniti and O'Regan's Infiniti, Halifax.

FIGURE 4-7	The Consumer Ethnocentrism Scale—CETSCALE

1. _____ people should always buy _____-made products instead of imports.
2. Only those products that are unavailable in _____ should be imported.
3. Buy _____-made products. Keep _____ working.
4. _____ products, first, last, and foremost.
5. Purchasing foreign-made products is un-_____.
6. It is not right to purchase foreign products, because it puts _____ out of jobs.
7. A real _____ should always buy _____-made products.
8. We should purchase products manufactured in _____ instead of letting other countries get rich off us.
9. It is always best to purchase _____ products.
10. There should be very little trading or purchasing of goods from other countries unless out of necessity.
11. _____ should not buy foreign products, because this hurts _____ business and causes unemployment.
12. Curbs should be put on all imports.
13. It may cost me in the long run but I prefer to support _____ products.
14. Foreigners should not be allowed to put their products on our markets.
15. Foreign products should be taxed heavily to reduce their entry into _____.
16. We should buy from foreign countries only those products that we cannot obtain within our own country.
17. _____ consumers who purchase products made in other countries are responsible for putting their fellow _____ out of work.

Notes: Response format is a 7-point Likert-type scale (strongly agree = 7, strongly disagree = 1). Range of scores is from 17 to 119. Calculated from confirmatory factor analysis of data from 4-area study; fill in the blanks with the appropriate country information.

Source: Terence A. Shimp and Subhash Sharma, "Consumer Ethnocentrism: Construction and Validation of the CETSCALE," *Journal of Marketing Research,* 24, August 1987, 282. Reprinted by permission.

FIGURE 4-8   Strategies for Managing Country-of-Origin Effects

MARKETING MIX	COUNTRY IMAGE	
	Positive	Negative
Product	Emphasize "Made in"	Emphasize brand name
Price	Premium price	Low price to attract value conscious
Place (channel of distribution)	Exclusive locations	Establish supply chain partners
Promotion	Country image nation sponsored	Brand image manufacturer sponsored

Source: Osman Mohamad, Zafar U. Ahmed, Earl D. Honeycutt, Jr., and Taizoon Hyder Tyebkhan, "Does 'Made In...' Matter to Consumers? A Malaysian Study of Country of Origin Effect," *Multinational Business Review*, Fall 2000, 73.

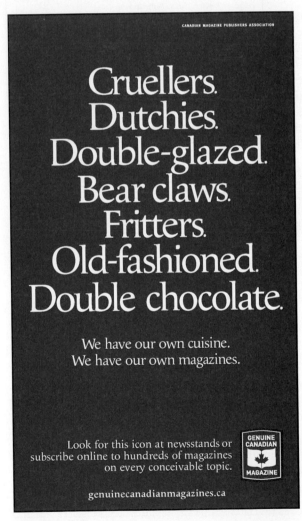

EXHIBIT 4-6

AN AD APPEALING TO ETHNOCENTRISM

Courtesy of Canadian Magazine Publishers Association.

made in the country in which their products originate, the marketers may be able to create a marketing mix strategy that follows options in the "Positive" column of Figure 4-8. In contrast, if marketers determine that the potential customers in a particular country have a *negative* image of products made in the country in which their products originate, the marketers might be wise to elect a marketing mix strategy that follows options in the "Negative" column.

There are several other personality-trait-like characteristics that are of interest to marketers. Two of these are discussed in Research Insight 4-1. A summary of all the personality theories covered so far is provided in Figure 4-9.

BRAND PERSONALITY

Early in this chapter, as part of our discussion of Freudian theory, we introduced the notion of *product personality*. Consumers also subscribe to the notion of *brand personality;* that is, they attribute various descriptive personality-like traits or characteristics to different brands in a wide variety of product categories. For instance, with some help from frequent advertising, consumers tend to see Volvo as representing safety, Nike as the athlete in all of us, and BMW as performance-driven.[26] In a similar fashion, the brand personality for Levi's 501 jeans is "dependable and rugged," "real and authentic," and "American and Western." Such personality-like images of brands reflect consumers' visions of the inner core of many strong brands of consumer products. As these examples reveal, a brand's personality can either be functional ("provides safety") or sym-

FIGURE 4-9	Summary of Personality Theories	
PERSONALITY TRAIT OR THEORY	**EXPLANATION**	**MARKETING APPLICATION**
Freudian theory	Personality consists of three related parts—id, ego, and superego. Unconscious needs or drives, especially sexual or biological ones, are at the heart of human motivation and personality.	Marketers can cater to the id, ego, or superego. Consumers may not be conscious of the reasons for their purchases. Qualitative research methods may be needed to uncover hidden motives.
Horney's neo-Freudian theory	Individuals can be classified into three personality groups: compliant, aggressive, and detached (CAD).	Consumers' propensity to buy brand-name products rather than private labels may be related to CAD; choice of individual brands may also be related to CAD personality types.
Cognitive theories: Need for cognition	People with a high need for cognition enjoy thinking or even have a craving for thinking.	Need for cognition affects type of media preferred, type of message that might appeal to a consumer, and internet usage for product information, news, etc.
Cognitive theories: Verbalizer versus visualizers	A classification based on the type of information (visual as opposed to verbal) that consumers prefer.	Visualizers need strong visual cues in ads; verbalizers prefer written or verbal information.
Trait theories: Consumer innovativeness	Innovativeness leads to early trial of new products and services; is related to other personality traits, such as dogmatism, variety-seeking, etc.	Early marketing efforts have to be aimed at innovators; innovators are open to new ideas, will seek variety and novelty in products.
Trait theories: Consumer materialism	Materialists regard possessions as essential to their identities and lives.	Materialists value acquiring and showing off possessions; shopping is pleasurable; ads could focus on how product ownership can impress others.
Trait theories: Consumer ethnocentrism	Ethnocentric people are predisposed to reject foreign ideas and products.	"Made in Canada" appeals needed; patriotic appeals would work. Country of origin—if not favourable has to be compensated for by other appeals.

RESEARCH INSIGHT 4-1
ARE YOU A COMPULSIVE SHOPPER?

Answer the following questions:[a]

1. When I have money, I cannot help but spend part or the whole of it.
2. I am often impulsive in my buying behaviour.
3. As soon as I enter a shopping centre, I have an irresistible urge to go into a store to buy something.

4. I am one of those people who often responds to direct-mail offers (e.g., for books or compact discs).
5. I have often bought a product that I did not need, while knowing I had very little money left.

If you answered Yes to these five questions, you may be a compulsive buyer! Compulsive buying and fixated consumption behaviour are two interesting personality traits that are often discussed in the literature. Let us look at fixated consumption behaviour first.

Fixated Consumption

Unlike a materialistic person who views products as essential to his or her identity and life, a fixated consumer has enduring involvement in some objects (but not all) and collects these objects in an ardent way. Two characteristics that separate a fixated consumer from others are: (1) a willingness to go to considerable lengths to secure additional examples of the object or product category of interest, and (2) the dedication of a considerable amount of time and money to searching out the object or product.[b] This profile of the fixated consumer describes many collectors (e.g., collectors of coins, stamps, antiques, vintage wristwatches, or fountain pens). Research into the dynamics of the fixated consumer (in this case, coin collectors) revealed that there is not only an enduring involvement in the object category itself but also a considerable amount of involvement in acquiring the object (sometimes referred to as the "hunt").[c]

Like materialism, *fixated consumption behaviour* is in the realm of normal and socially acceptable behaviour. Fixated consumers do not keep their objects or purchases of interest a secret; rather, they frequently display them, and their involvement is openly shared with others who have a similar interest. However, compulsive consumption goes beyond what is considered to be socially acceptable.

Compulsive Consumption Behaviour

Unlike materialism and fixated consumption, *compulsive consumption* is in the realm of abnormal behaviour—an example of the dark side of consumption. Consumers who are compulsive have an *addiction*; in some respects they are out of control, and their actions may have damaging consequences to them and to those around them. Examples of compulsive consumption problems are uncontrollable shopping, gambling, drug addiction, alcoholism, and various food and eating disorders.[d] For instance, there are many women and a small number of men who are *chocoholics*—they have an intense craving (also termed an addiction) for chocolate.[e] From the perspective of marketing and consumer behaviour, *compulsive buying* can also be included in any list of compulsive activities. To control or possibly eliminate such compulsive problems generally requires some type of therapy or clinical treatment.

There have been some research efforts to develop a screener inventory to pinpoint compulsive buying behaviour. The questions provided at the beginning of this Research Insight are samples from such inventories. Evidence suggests that some consumers use "self-gifting," impulse buying, and compulsive buying as a way to influence their mood; that is, the act of purchasing may convert a negative mood to a more positive one ("I'm depressed—I'll go out shopping and I'll feel better").[f]

[a] These five questions are from the Valence, D'Astous, and Fortier Compulsive Buying Scale. *Source:* Gilles Valence, Alain d'Astous, and Louis Fortier, "Compulsive Buying: Concept and Measurement," *Journal of Consumer Policy*, 11, (1988), 419–433.
[b] Ronald J. Faber and Thomas C. O'Guinn, "A Clinical Screener for Compulsive Buying," *Journal of Consumer Research*, 19, December 1992, 459–469.
[c] Ibid.
[d] Elizabeth C. Hirschman, "The Consciousness of Addiction: Toward a General Theory of Compulsive Consumption," *Journal of Consumer Research*, 19, September 1992, 155–179; Seung-Hee Lee, Sharron J. Lennon, and Nancy A. Rudd, "Compulsive Consumption Tendencies Among Television Shoppers," *Family and Consumer Sciences Research Journal*, 28, no. 4, June 2000, 463–488; and Booth Moore, "Shopping for a Defense—Consumer-Driven Culture Spills over into the Courtroom," *Houston Chronicle*, July 11, 2001, 8.
[e] Kristen Bruinsma and Douglas L. Taren, "Chocolate: Food or Drug?" *Journal of the American Dietetic Association*, 99, no. 10, October 1999, 1249–1256.
[f] Ronald J. Faber and Gary A. Christenson, "Can You Buy Happiness?: A Comparison of the Antecedent and Concurrent Moods Associated with the Shopping of Compulsive and Non-Compulsive Buyers," in *1995 Winter Educator's Conference*, 6, eds. David W. Stewart and Naufel J. Vilcassin (Chicago: American Marketing Association, 1995), 378–379.

bolic ("the athlete in all of us").[27] There is common sense and research evidence to conclude that any brand personality, as long as it is *strong* and *favourable*, will strengthen a brand.[28] It is not clear, however, how many consumers would be willing, for example, to pay a 10 percent to 15 percent premium for a brand-name diamond.[29]

Two of the fast food chains that many readers of this textbook may patronize with some frequency, Wendy's and McDonald's, are examples of companies that have built distinctive brand personalities for themselves. The Wendy's brand personality has been built around Dave Thomas, the chain's founder, who represented the "clumsy guy next door in search of good fast food." In contrast, the McDonald's brand personality, through Ronald McDonald and other cartoon characters, has always been associated with fun.[30]

In other cases, marketers have provided an instant personality or heritage for a new product by employing a symbolic or fictional historical branding strategy. When Brown Forman entered the micro-brewery beer market in 1996, it used the brand name "1886" for its new beer, which is the year that one of its other products, Jack Daniel's bourbon, was first distilled.[31] Creating a brand personality takes a long time. A brand personality is created through consistent advertising that stresses special attributes of a brand, the use of brand personification (the use of human-like characters to represent a brand), the brand logo and slogan, and the linking of a brand to a particular sex, colour, or geographic location. More details on these are provided in the following sections.

Brand Personification

Some marketers find it useful to create a **brand personification**, which tries to recast consumers' perception of the attributes of a product or service into a human-like character. For instance, in focus group research, well-known brands of dish detergent have been likened to "demanding task masters" or "high-energy people." Many consumers express their inner feelings about products or brands in terms of their association with known personalities. Identifying consumers' current brand-personality links and creating personality links for new products are important marketing tasks.

Brand personification: The ascription of specific personality-type traits or characteristics to brands.

The M&M "people" are a current "fun" example of brand personification. It is based on the line of questioning that might ask, "If an M&M (or a variety of chocolate-coated peanut) were a person, what kind of person would it be?" Additional questioning would be likely to explore how the colour of the coating affects consumers' view of the personality for the "M& M people." There are many examples of brand personification.

www.m-ms.com

To personify and humanize its model consumer, Celestial Seasonings, Inc., the leading specialty tea maker in North America, refers in its advertising to "Tracy Jones." And just who is Tracy Jones? According to Celestial Seasonings, she is "female, upscale, well educated, and highly involved in life in every way."[32]

www.celestial seasonings.com

Mr. Coffee, a popular brand of automatic-drip coffee makers, unexpectedly found in its focus group research that consumers were referring to Mr. Coffee as if the product were a person (e.g., "he makes good coffee" and "he's got a lot of different models and prices").[33] After careful consideration, the marketers decided to explore the possibility of creating a *brand personification*. Initial consumer research indicated that Mr. Coffee was seen as being "dependable," "friendly," "efficient," "intelligent," and "smart."

www.mrcoffee.com

As part of its relaunch of the brand, John Wiley & Sons, Canada launched the Dummies man to help create a personality for its *Dummies* book series. The mascot appeared in book stores in Winnipeg, Vancouver, and Edmonton and gave out bookmarks and key chains at stores.[34]

Figure 4-10 presents a *brand personality framework* that reflects extensive consumer research designed to pinpoint the structure and nature of a brand's personality. The framework suggests that there are five defining *dimensions* of a brand's personality ("sincerity," "excitement," "competence," "sophistication," and "ruggedness"), and 15 *facets* of personality that flow from the five dimensions (e.g., "down-to-earth," "daring," "reliable," "upper class," and "outdoors").[35] If we examine these brand personality dimensions and facets, it appears that this framework tends to accommodate the brand personalities pursued by many consumer products.

Steam Whistle, a small brewery based in southern Ontario, has been successful in developing a unique personality for itself. Its image of an honest, down-to-earth and wholesome product is created through a range of things—the name ("Steam Whistle"), the nostalgic logo (a steam whistle), the slogan ("The good beer folks"), and the location of the brewery (an old railway roundhouse)—that create a simpler, old-fashioned goodness image. And the old-style bottle—cast from a custom-designed mould, which is heavier than standard beer bottles and which is a distinctive green that is similar to imports such as Stella Artois and Heineken (as opposed to the usual brown bottles)—conveys the impression of a sophisticated and unique beer.[36]

Brand Personality and Gender

A brand personality, or persona, frequently endows the brand with a gender. For instance, Celestial Seasonings gave Tracy Jones a feminine persona, whereas Mr. Coffee was given a masculine personality. The assigning of gender as part of a product's personality description is fully consistent with the marketplace reality that products and services, in general, are viewed by consumers as having gender.

Ganong, the Atlantic Canadian chocolate manufacturer found (through focus groups) that the ideal chocolate was considered "female, outgoing, beautiful, out-

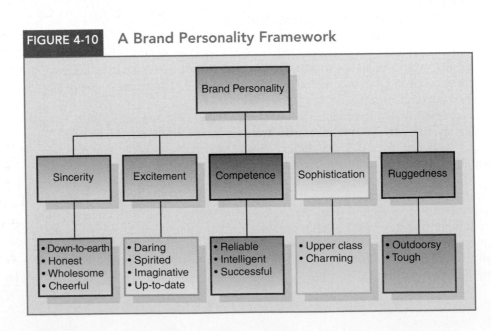

FIGURE 4-10   A Brand Personality Framework

doorsy, contemporary, stylish." Different brands had different images too. Black Magic was "an older man, tall, mysterious, safe and trustworthy," and the word Ganong elicited responses such as "French, suave, elegant, exotic and romantic"—all positive terms, but still not in line with consumer preferences. To update its image and bring it in line with consumer preferences, Ganong introduced a new line: the New Ganong Collection with a stylized "G" signed by Bryana Ganong, the 29-year-old brand development manager and third-generation Ganong. She was chosen by focus group participants who saw her photo (even before the respondents knew who she was) and gave her the same attributes that the ideal box of chocolate was supposed to possess.[37]

www.ganong.com

Armed with knowledge of the perceived sex of a product or a specific brand, marketers are in a better position to select visuals and text for various marketing messages.

Brand Personality and Geography

Marketers learned long ago that certain products, in the minds of consumers, possess a strong geographical association (e.g., a New York bagel). Consequently, by using geography in the product's name, the manufacturer creates a geographic personality for the product. Such a geographic personality can lead to geographic equity for the brand, meaning that in the consumer's memory the knowledge of the brand reflects a strong geographic association.

Interestingly, geographic brand names can be familiar, unfamiliar, or even fictitious. Philadelphia cream cheese is, in fact, manufactured in Illinois. But more important than whether the name is real or fictitious is whether the location and its image add to the product's brand equity.[38] The Old El Paso brand of salsa capitalizes on the Mexican influence in the Southwest. The product may be made in Minneapolis, but a brand of salsa named Twin Cities Salsa (i.e., Minneapolis/ St. Paul) just doesn't have the same cachet.

Brand Personality and Colour

Consumers not only ascribe personality traits to products and services, but they also tend to associate personality factors with specific colours. Coca-Cola is associated with red, which connotes excitement. Blue bottles are often used to sell wine because blue appeals particularly to female consumers and most wine is bought by women.[39] Yellow is associated with novelty, and black frequently connotes sophistication.[40] For this reason, brands wanting to create a sophisticated persona (such as Minute Maid) or an upscale or premium image (e.g., Black Magic Chocolates) use labelling or packaging that is primarily black. A combination of black and white suggests that a product is carefully engineered, high-tech, and sophisticated in design. IBM has consistently used an all-black case with a few red buttons and bars to house its very successful line of ThinkPad laptops. Nike has used black, white, and a touch of red for selected models of its sport shoes. This colour combination seems to imply advanced-performance sports shoes.

Recently, M&M/Mars has exploited the folklore that its green M&Ms are aphrodisiacs by creating a green female M&M character that it has featured in some of its ads.[41] A recent print and outdoor advertising campaign for LifeSavers, based on consumer research into flavours and colours, characterizes *cherry* as "Ms. Popularity," *lime* as "The Outsider," and *sour apple and cherry* (targeted to teens) as "The Troublemaker."[42] And although we all know that ketchup is red, Heinz developed its green ketchup after doing research with more than 1000 children, who helped decide on the product's green colour and its packaging (e.g., the bottle is designed to fit small hands).[43] As mentioned earlier, Steam Whistle chose green for its beer bottles so that its beer would stand out from domestic brands that use brown bottles and would compete with imports like Stella Artois and Heineken that use green bottles.[44]

Many fast food restaurants use combinations of bright colours, like red, yellow, and blue, for their roadside signs and interior designs. These colours have come to be associated with fast service and inexpensive food. In contrast, fine-dining restaurants tend to use sophisticated colours like grey, white, tan, or other soft, pale, or muted colours to express the feeling of good, leisurely service.

Figure 4-11 presents a list of various colours, their personality-like meanings, and associated marketing insights. It is important to note that the meanings associated with colours are not the same in every culture or even in every market segment. In Canada, white signifies purity and innocence, but in India it is the colour of sorrow and death. In fact, until a few decades ago, widows in India were required to wear white to show they were in mourning, just as widows in the Western world wore black. Similarly, while pink might be seen as a good, "fun" colour by young girls, an older woman may view it differently. Hence marketers have to be careful that the colours they choose fit their target market.

PERSONALITY AND MARKETING STRATEGY

Marketers can use personality theories in several ways when they are developing marketing strategies.

| FIGURE 4-11 | Colours and Their Associations |

COLOUR	ASSOCIATION AND MARKETING APPLICATION
Blue	Commands respect, authority Men seek products packaged in blue
Yellow	Caution, novelty, temporary, warmth Registers fast; may be seen as weak
Green	Secure, natural, relaxed, or easygoing; living things Suits vegetable-based food items; colour of TD Canada Trust
Red	Human, exciting, hot, passionate, strong Makes products seem "rich"; women prefer bluish red while men prefer yellowish red
Brown	Informal, relaxed, masculine, related to nature Men prefer products packaged in brown
White	Goodness, purity, chastity, cleanliness Suggests low in calories; pure and wholesome; feminine
Black	Sophistication, power, authority, mystery Good for high-tech electronics; provides a sense of class
Silver, gold, platinum	Regal, wealthy, stately Suggests premium price

Source: From Bernice Kanner, "Color Schemes," *New York* magazine, April 3, 1989, 22–23. Copyright 1996, *New York* Magazine. Distributed by Los Angeles Times. Reprinted with permission. Courtesy of *New York* Magazine.

Identify relevant personality traits: One of the first things that a marketer needs to do is identify the personality traits that are relevant for the marketing of a product. In other words, what type of consumer does the product appeal to? For example, an innovative product is likely to appeal to consumers who are high in innovativeness; these consumers are also likely to possess personality traits such as dogmatism, need for uniqueness, desire for novelty, and inner-directedness. For an existing product, marketers could examine the personality traits of current users and heavy users to understand the personality traits of their customers and compare these with those of their competitors' customers.

Find ways to target customers with the relevant personality traits: It should be noted that one of the major problems that marketers have is how to identify and target consumers with specific personality traits. For example, how can a marketer identify and target people who have a high need for cognition? Do such people have a certain personality profile? If so, what is it? The need to identify the demographic profile is often tied to the need to find ways to target specific consumers. In the case of most personality traits, it is difficult for marketers to determine who has certain personality traits.

One way for marketers to use personality-related information might be to find out the activities and interests of people with specific personality traits. For example, people who are variety seekers may be interested in watching television shows on travel or food shows that feature unusual cuisines and new products; people who are ethnocentric are unlikely to watch such shows. Similar connections may exist between other personality traits and consumer interests and activities. Marketers should attempt to identify these and use the information to target their consumers effectively.

Develop promotional messages that appeal to consumers with the identified personality traits: Once the key personality traits of potential buyers of a product are identified, marketers should use them when developing an advertising message. Ads for innovative products should emphasize how buying and using the product would reflect these traits. If the target market for a product is likely to be ethnocentric, it may be effective to use a patriotic appeal by emphasizing that the product is made in Canada.

Take steps to develop the brand's personality: As pointed out earlier, a brand's personality can be developed in many ways through the use of cartoons, celebrities, and attribution of human traits to a brand; the use of colour; and associating the brand with a certain sex and geographical location. A firm's marketing mix variables also have an impact on a brand's personality. Frequent price reductions can lead to the brand being perceived as cheap; very frequent changes in promotional themes can lead to an impression that the brand is fickle.

SELF AND SELF-IMAGE

Consumers have a variety of enduring images of themselves. These self-images, or perceptions of self, are very closely associated with personality in that individuals tend to buy products and services and patronize retailers whose images or personalities are related in some meaningful way to their own self-images. In essence, consumers seek to depict themselves in their brand choices—they tend to approach products with images that could enhance their self-concept and to avoid those products that do not.[45] In this section, we examine the issue of *one* or *multiple* selves, the makeup of the self-image, the notion of *extended self*, and the possibilities or options of *altering the self-image*.

One or Multiple Selves

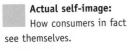

Multiple selves:
The different images that consumers have of themselves in response to different situations and different people that may cause them to react differently.

Historically, individuals have been thought to have a single self-image and to be interested, as consumers, in products and services that satisfy that single self. However, it is more accurate to think of consumers as having **multiple selves**.[46] This change in thinking is due to the realization that a single consumer is likely to act quite differently with different people and in different situations. A person is likely to behave in different ways with his or her parents, at school, at work, at a museum opening, or with friends at a nightclub. The healthy or normal person is likely to display a somewhat different personality in each of these different situations or social *roles*. In fact, acting exactly the same way in all situations or roles and not adapting to the situation at hand may be considered a sign of an abnormal or unhealthy person.

In reference to consumer behaviour, the idea that an individual embodies a number of different "selves" (i.e., has multiple self-images) suggests that marketers should target their products and services to *a particular "self"* and, in certain cases, by offering a choice of different products for different *selves*. (The notion of a consumer having multiple selves or playing multiple roles supports the application of usage situation as a segmentation base discussed in Chapter 1.)

The Makeup of the Self-Image

In keeping with the idea of multiple self-images, each individual has an image of him- or herself as a certain kind of person, with certain traits, skills, habits, possessions, relationships, and ways of behaving. Like other types of images and personality, the individual's self-image is unique, the outgrowth of that person's background and experience. Individuals develop their self-images through interactions with other people—first their parents and then other individuals or groups with whom they relate over the years.

Products and brands have symbolic value for individuals, who evaluate products on the basis of their consistency (congruence) with the consumers' personal pictures or images of themselves. Some products seem to match one or more of an individual's self-images; others seem totally alien. It is generally believed that consumers attempt to preserve or enhance their self-images by choosing products and brands with "images" or "personalities" that they believe are congruent with their own self-images and by avoiding products that are not.[47] This seems to be especially true for women; research reveals that more women than men (77 percent versus 64 percent) feel that the brands that they select reflect their personalities.[48] Given this relationship between brand preference and consumers' self-images, it is natural that consumers use brands to help them define themselves. Research shows that consumers who have strong links to particular brands—a positive self-brand connection—see such brands *as representing an aspect of themselves*. For marketers, such connections are certainly an important step in the formation of consumer loyalty and a positive relationship with consumers.[49]

A variety of different self-images have been recognized in the consumer behaviour literature for a long time. In particular, many researchers have depicted some or all of the following kinds of self-image:

Actual self-image:
How consumers in fact see themselves.

Ideal self-image:
How consumers would like to see themselves.

Social self-image:
How consumers feel others see them.

Ideal social self-image:
How consumers would like others to see them.

- **actual self-image** (how consumers in fact see themselves),
- **ideal self-image** (how consumers would like to see themselves),
- **social self-image** (how consumers feel others see them), and
- **ideal social self-image** (how consumers would like others to see them).

It also seems useful to think of two other types of self-images—*expected self* and the *ought-to self*.

■ The **expected self-image** (how consumers expect to see themselves at some specified future time) is somewhere between the *actual* and *ideal* self-images. It is a future-oriented combination of what is (the actual self-image) and what consumers would like to be (the ideal self-image).

■ The **"ought-to" self** consists of traits or characteristics that an individual believes it is his or her duty or obligation to possess.[50] Examples of this form of self-image might be striving to achieve a deeper religious understanding or seeking a fair and just solution to a challenging ethical problem. Because the expected self and the ought-to self give consumers a realistic opportunity to change the self, they are both likely to be more valuable to marketers than the actual or ideal self-image as a guide for designing and promoting products.

Expected self-image: How consumers expect to see themselves at some specified future time.

"Ought-to" self: Consists of traits or characteristics that an individual believes it is his or her duty or obligation to possess.

The Extended Self

The relationship between consumers' self-images and their possessions (i.e., objects they call their own) is an exciting topic. Specifically, consumers' possessions can be seen to confirm or extend their self-images. For instance, acquiring a much-desired or sought-after pair of "vintage" Nike sneakers (often one of the previous year's hard-to-get styles) might expand or enrich a Japanese teenager's image of self, and she might now see herself as more desirable, more fashionable, and more successful. Similarly, if the bracelet that a university student (let's call her Eleanor) was given by her aunt was stolen, Eleanor is likely to feel diminished in some way. Indeed, the loss of a prized possession may lead Eleanor to grieve and to experience a variety of emotions, such as frustration, loss of control, the feeling of being violated, and even the loss of magical protection. Exhibit 4-7 shows an ad that asks consumers to contemplate their self-image.

Extended self: Consumers' use of possessions to confirm or extend their self-images.

Figure 4-12 presents sample items from a measurement instrument designed to show how particular possessions (e.g., a mountain bike) might become part of a person's **extended self**.

The previous examples suggest that much human emotion can be connected to valued possessions. In such cases, possessions are considered extensions of the self. It has been proposed that possessions can extend the self in a number of ways:

(1) *actually,* by allowing the person to do things that otherwise would be very difficult or impossible (e.g., solving problems by using a computer);

(2) *symbolically,* by making the person feel better or "bigger" (e.g., receiving an employee award for excellence);

(3) by *conferring status or rank* (e.g., among collectors of rare works of art because of the ownership of a particular masterpiece);

EXHIBIT 4-7

PATEK PHILIPPE ASKS CONSUMERS TO CONTEMPLATE THEIR SELF-IMAGE
Courtesy of Patek Philippe.

(4) by *bestowing feelings of immortality* by leaving valued possessions to young family members (this also has the potential of extending the recipients' selves); and

(5) by *endowing with magical powers* (e.g., a pocket watch inherited from one's grandfather might be considered a magic amulet that bestows good luck when it is worn).[51]

The following example shows how possessions can become extremely important to people and can even become part of their extended selves:

T. Dana Boutillier had a dream from the time he was 12 years old—to own a Ford Mustang. His dream came true 23 years later—in 1999 when he saw an ad for a 1967 lime-green and gold Mustang. When Boutillier went to buy it, the owner told him that he was unwilling to sell it until he found the right buyer—not someone who could offer him the price he wanted, but someone who really loved the car! Boutillier's enthusiasm and fascination with the car won the owner over and Boutillier drove away in his dream. He loves the stylish design, rumbling engine and speed, and though he owns other sports cars, the Mustang is special to him. "Everyone has a Boxster... but not everyone has a Mustang Fastback," says Boutillier. He is already imagining the day his daughters will drive it to their high school proms. He has spent more than four times the amount he paid for the car ($5900) on bodywork, paint jobs, and parts. It is obvious that to him, the car is more than just a car—"You don't get mad at her if she needs some work, you just get her fixed," says Boutillier and adds, "My Mustang is like my third child. She has my unconditional love."[52]

Altering the Self

Sometimes consumers want to change themselves to become a different or improved self. Clothing, grooming aids or cosmetics, and all kinds of accessories (such as sunglasses, jewellery, tattoos, or even coloured contact lenses) offer consumers the opportunity to modify their appearance and thereby to alter their "selves." In using *self-altering products,* consumers are frequently attempting to express their individualism or uniqueness by creating a new self, maintaining the existing self (or preventing its loss), and extending the self (modifying or changing the self). Sometimes consumers use self-altering products or services to conform to or take

---

| FIGURE 4-12 | Sample Items from an Extended Self-Survey |

My _____ holds a special place in my life.

My _____ is central to my identity.

I feel emotionally attached to my _____ .

My _____ helps me narrow the gap between what I am and try to be.

If my _____ was stolen from me, I would feel as if part of me is missing.

I would be a different person without my _____ .

I take good care of my _____ .

I trust my _____ .

A 6-point agree–disagree scale was used.

Source: Kimberly J. Dodson, "Peak Experiences and Mountain Biking: Incorporating the Bike in the Extended Self," *Advances in Consumer Research,* 1996. Reprinted by permission.

on the appearance of a particular type of person (such as a soldier, a doctor, a business executive, or a university professor).

Closely related to both self-image and alterations of the self is the idea of *personal vanity*. As a descriptor of people, vanity is often associated with behaviour that is self-important or self-interested, or with admiration for one's own appearance or achievements. Using a "vanity scale" (Figure 4-13), researchers have investigated both *physical vanity* (an excessive concern for, or a positive—or inflated—view of, one's physical appearance) and *achievement vanity* (an excessive concern for, or a positive or inflated view of, one's personal achievements). They have found both these ideas are related to materialism, use of cosmetics, concern with clothing, and membership in country clubs.[53]

Altering the self, particularly our appearance or our body, can be done by using cosmetics, restyling or colouring hair, getting a tattoo, switching from eyeglasses to contact lenses (or the reverse), or undergoing cosmetic surgery (see Exhibit 4-8).

The widespread use of internet chat rooms has led to the concept of a virtual self. People often use totally different names and project very different images of themselves in these chat rooms. Internet Insight 4-1 takes a look at the notion of a virtual personality.

SELF-CONCEPT AND MARKETING STRATEGY

Use self-concept for segmentation and positioning purposes: Marketers can segment their markets on the basis of relevant consumer self-images and then position their products or services as symbols of such self-images. Such a strategy is fully

---

FIGURE 4-13	Sample Items from a Vanity Scale

PHYSICAL-CONCERN ITEMS

1. The way I look is extremely important to me.
2. I am very concerned with my appearance.
3. It is important that I always look good.

PHYSICAL-VIEW ITEMS

1. People notice how attractive I am.
2. People are envious of my good looks.
3. My body is sexually appealing.

ACHIEVEMENT-CONCERN ITEMS

1. Professional achievements are an obsession with me.
2. Achieving greater success than my peers is important to me.
3. I want my achievements to be recognized by others.

ACHIEVEMENT-VIEW ITEMS

1. My achievements are highly regarded by others.
2. I am a good example of professional success.
3. Others wish they were as successful as me.

Source: Richard G. Netemeyer, Scot Burton, and Donald R. Lichtenstein, "Trait Aspects of Vanity: Measurement and Relevance to Consumer Behavior," *Journal of Consumer Research*, 21, March 1995, 624. Reprinted by permission of The University of Chicago Press as publisher.

EXHIBIT 4-8

SALON SELECTIVES SUGGESTS THAT CONSUMERS ALTER THEMSELVES

Courtesy of Unilever.

consistent with the marketing concept in that the marketer first assesses the needs of a consumer segment (with respect to both the product category and a symbol of self-image) and then proceeds to develop and market a product or service that meets both criteria.

It is essential that once a product position is identified, marketers spend time and effort on developing a strong brand image. Brand equity theory, which examines the value inherent in a brand name, states that the power of a brand resides in the consumer's mind from both lived experiences (purchase and use) and mediated experiences (advertising and promotion). Hence without promotional efforts, consumers may not be able to identify with a brand's image.[54]

Use the idea of actual and ideal self-concepts effectively while promoting products: In different situations or with respect to different products, consumers might select a different self-image to guide their attitudes or behaviour. With some everyday household products, they might be guided by their actual self-image, whereas for some socially enhancing or socially conspicuous products, they might be guided by their social self-image. When it comes to a so-called fantasy product, they might be guided by either their ideal self-image or ideal social self-image.

Promote products as ways of extending and altering one's self-image: By understanding the relationship between consumers' self-images and their possessions, marketers can position products as ways of extending a person's self-image. A car can be positioned not just as transportation but also as a part of a consumer's persona and a reflection of his or her self-image.

The idea that products reflect the personality and self-image of their owners fits with one of the segmentation variables that was covered in the Appendix to Part 1—psychographic segmentation and related hybrid segmentation techniques. These segmentation methods are based on the idea that a person's life style reflects (and perhaps is a product of) several variables, including his or her activities, interests, and opinions; these in turn, affect the person's purchases and consumption patterns. In the next section, we will examine consumer life styles and the different methods of segmenting life styles.

CONSUMER LIFE STYLE AND PSYCHOGRAPHICS

The term *life style* refers to the shared values and behaviour of a group; life styles are important to marketers because they affect (or are reflected in) a person's consumption patterns. Early efforts at life-style segmentation were based on psychographic research, which is closely aligned with psychological research, especially personality and attitude measurement. This form of applied consumer research

INTERNET INSIGHT 4-1
VIRTUAL PERSONALITY OR SELF

With the widespread interest in the internet as a form of entertainment and as a social vehicle for meeting new people with similar interests, there has been a tremendous growth in the use of online chat rooms. People who visit chat rooms are able to carry on real-time conversations about themselves and topics of mutual interest with people from all over the world. Because at the present time most chats are actually text conversations rather than live video broadcasts, the participants usually never see each other. This creates an opportunity for chat room participants to try out new identities or to change their identities while online. For instance, a person can change from male to female (known as "gender swapping"), from old to young, or from married to single; from white-collar professional to blue-collar worker, or from grossly overweight to svelte. A person can change his or her personality from mild-mannered to aggressive, or from introvert to extrovert.

The notion of a *virtual personality* or *virtual self* enables a person to try on different personalities or different identities, similar to going to a mall and trying on different outfits in a department or specialty store. If the identity fits or the personality can be enhanced, the individual may decide to keep the new personality in preference to his or her old personality. From a consumer behaviour point of view, it is likely that such opportunities to try out a new personality or alter the self may result in changes in some forms of purchase behaviour. This may in turn offer marketers new opportunities to target various "online selves."

Do you want to find out about your personality online? One website, Tickle, offers internet users an online exam called "The Ultimate Personality Test," which takes perhaps 10 minutes and categorizes the test taker into one of 13 personality types. Give it a try.[55]

(commonly referred to as life-style analysis) has proved to be a valuable marketing tool that helps identify promising consumer segments that are likely to be responsive to specific marketing messages.

The psychographic profile of a consumer segment can be thought of as a composite of consumers' measured activities, interests, and opinions (AIOs). As an approach to constructing consumer psychographic profiles, AIO research seeks consumers' responses to a large number of statements that measure their activities (how the consumer or family spends time, e.g., golfing, volunteering at a local blood bank, or gardening), interests (the consumer's or family's preferences and priorities, e.g., concerning home, fashion, and food), and opinions (how the consumer feels about a wide variety of events and political issues, social issues, the state of the economy, and the environment). In their most common form, AIO-psychographic studies use a battery of statements (a *psychographic inventory*) designed to identify relevant aspects of a consumer's personality, buying motives, interests, attitudes, beliefs, and values.

The results of **psychographic segmentation** efforts are often seen in firms' marketing messages. For instance, a recent Absolut Vodka ad is targeted to individuals who are interested in mobile technology and consider themselves to be the first to buy technologically advanced products.

The increase in internet shopping has also led to concentrated efforts by marketers to understand the online buyer. A number of different research organizations have devised their own schemes to segment internet users. Internet Insight 4-2 presents a segmentation system, developed by Harris Interactive, that defines six internet shopper segments and is intended to provide etailers with a peek at the rich combination of spending habits and motivational factors underlying specific segments of internet buyers.[56]

http://web.tickle.com

Psychographic segmentation: Segmenting of consumers on the basis of their activities, interests, and opinions.

www.harrisinteractive.com

INTERNET INSIGHT 4-2
WHO SHOPS ON THE INTERNET?

Harris Interactive, a firm that tracks internet shopping, has identified six types of internet shoppers:

E-bivalent newbies—Representing just 5 percent of the online shopping population, this group is the newest to the internet, is somewhat older, likes shopping online the least, and spends the least online.

Time-sensitive materialists—At 17 percent of all cybershoppers, these individuals are most interested in convenience and saving time and less likely to read product reviews, compare prices, or use coupons.

Clicks & mortar—At 23 percent of the e-commerce community, this group tends to shop online but prefers to buy offline, is more likely to be female homemakers, has privacy and security concerns about buying online, and visits real shopping malls the most often.

Hooked, online, and single—Representing 16 percent of the online shopping population, these individuals are likely to be young, single men with high incomes, to have been on the internet the longest of any group, and to play games, download software, bank, invest, and shop online the most often.

Hunter-gatherers—At 20 percent of the cybershopping set, members of this group are usually aged 30–49 with two children, and most often go to sites that provide analysis and comparison of products and prices.

Brand loyalists—At 19 percent of the online purchasing community, these individuals are the most likely to go directly to the site address of a merchant they know, are the most satisfied with shopping online, and spend the most online.

Source: www.harrisinteractive.com

Today, marketers use psychographics in conjunction with demographic variables to develop consumer profiles. Such methods, which are called hybrid segmentation, include psychographic-demographic profiles, **geodemographics**, VALS, and Yankelovich's Mindbase Segmentation.

Geodemographic segmentation:
Dividing the market or consumers by location. (See next page.)

Psychographic-Demographic Profiles

Psychographic and demographic profiles are highly complementary approaches that work best when used together. By combining the knowledge gained from both demographic and psychographic studies, marketers obtain powerful information about their target markets.

Demographic-psychographic profiling has been widely used in the development of advertising campaigns to answer three questions: "Whom should we target?" "What should we say?" "Where should we say it?" To help advertisers answer the third question, many advertising media vehicles sponsor demographic-psychographic research, on which they base very detailed *audience profiles*. Figure 4-14 presents a short profile of a *Canadian Geographic* subscriber, with comparisons with subscribers of two news magazines (*Maclean's* and *Time*). By offering media buyers such carefully defined dual profiles of their audiences, mass media publishers and broadcasters make it possible for advertisers to select media whose audiences most closely resemble their target markets.

www.cangeo.ca/mediazone

Finally, advertisers are increasingly designing ads that depict in words and/or pictures the essence of a particular target-market life style or segment that they want to reach. In this spirit, the Prince Edward Island Tourism ad shown in Exhibit 4-10 appeals to people with specific active and outdoor lifestyles.

Geodemographic Segmentation

This type of hybrid segmentation scheme is based on the notion that people who live close to one another are likely to have similar financial means, tastes, preferences, life styles, and consumption habits (i.e., "birds of a feather flock together"). This segmentation approach uses computers to generate geodemographic market clusters of like consumers. Specifically, computer software clusters the nation's neighbourhoods into life-style groupings based on postal codes. Clusters are based on consumer life styles, and a specific cluster includes postal codes that comprise people with similar life styles widely scattered throughout the country. Marketers use the cluster data for direct-mail campaigns, to select retail sites and merchandise mixes, to locate banks and restaurants, and to design marketing strategies for specific market segments. For instance, *Men's Fitness* magazine (see Exhibit 4-9) is targeted toward men who are interested in having a muscular body and emphasizes how the magazine would help them achieve their goals.[57]

Geodemographic segmentation is most useful when an advertiser's or a marketer's best prospects (in terms of consumer personalities, goals, and interests) can be isolated according to where they live. However, for products and services used by a broad cross-section of the public, other segmentation schemes may be more productive.

EXHIBIT 4-9

ACHIEVING GOALS BY SUBSCRIBING TO A MAGAZINE

www.mensfitness.com

FIGURE 4-14	Profiles of Subscribers to Three Canadian Magazines		
DEMOGRAPHIC AND LIFESTYLE CHARACTERISTICS	*CANADIAN GEOGRAPHIC*	*MACLEAN'S*	*TIME*
Principal grocery shoppers	2 358 000[a] (18.3%)[b]	1 860 000 (14.5%)	n/a
Have a self-directed RRSP	718 000 (19.5%)	658 000 (17.8%)	557 000 (15.6%)
Bought a PC in the past two years	1 361 000 (20.9%)	1 044 000 (16.1%)	945 000 (14.5%)
Have one or more new vehicles in household	833 000 (18.0%)	819 000 (17.7%)	628 000 (13.6%)
Own a luxury vehicle	100 000 (16.1%)	99 000 (15.8%)	108 000 (17.3%)
Own SUV/Jeep-type vehicle	251 000 (20.6%)	184 000 (15.1%)	141 000 (11.5%)
Went downhill skiing in past year	363 000 (26.1%)	273 000 (19.6%)	n/a
Business travel by air in past year	267 000 (21.8%)	284 000 (23.3%)	213 000 (17.4%)
1+ vacation travel by air in past year	1 168 000 (21.0%)	943 000 (17.0%)	818 000 (14.7%)
Attended museums in past year	677 000 (25.5%)	500 000 (18.9%)	402 000 (15.1%)
Drank liquor in past 30 days	715 000 (21.0%)	576 000 (16.9%)	n/a

[a] Number of subscribers involved in activity; English Canadians 18+ only.
[b] Percentages within category

Source: Canadian Geographic, **www.cangeo.ca/mediazone**, November 9, 2003. Courtesy of *Canadian Geographic.*

EXHIBIT 4-10

PEI TARGETS AN ACTIVE OUTDOOR LIFE STYLE

Courtesy Tourism Prince Edward Island.

www.sri.com

SRI Consulting's Values and Life Style System

Drawing on Maslow's need hierarchy (see Chapter 3) and the concept of social character, researchers at SRI Consulting in the late 1970s developed a generalized segmentation scheme of the American population known as the values and life style system (VALS) (Figure 4-15). This original system was designed to explain the dynamics of societal change and was quickly adapted as a marketing tool.

In 1989 SRIC revised the VALS system to explain consumer purchase behaviour more explicitly. The current VALS typology classifies the American population into eight distinctive subgroups (segments) based on consumers' responses to 35 attitudinal and four demographic questions.[58] Figure 4-15 depicts the VALS classification scheme and offers a brief profile of the consumer traits of each of the VALS segments. The major groups (from left to right in Figure 4-15) are defined in terms of three major *self-orientations* and (from top to bottom) a new definition of resources: the *principle-oriented* (consumers whose choices are motivated by their beliefs rather than by desires for approval), the *status-oriented* (consumers whose choices are guided by the actions, approval, and opinions of others), and the *action-oriented* (consumers who are motivated by a desire for social or physical activity, variety, and risk). Each of these three major self-orientations represents distinct attitudes, life styles, and decision-making styles. Resources (from most to least) are the range of psychological, physical, demographic, and material means and capacities consumers have to draw upon, including education, income, self-confidence, health, eagerness to buy, and energy. For example, research indicates that *actualizers, experiencers,* and *achievers* are more likely than are other segments to take part in thrill-oriented sports.[59]

In terms of consumer characteristics, the eight VALS segments differ in some important ways. For instance, *believers* tend to buy products made in their own country and are slow to alter their consumption-related habits, whereas *actualizers* are drawn to top-of-the-line and new products, especially innovative technologies. Therefore, it is not surprising that marketers of intelligent technologies for cars (such as global positioning devices) must first target the *actualizers,* because they are early adopters of new products.[60]

Another popular hybrid segmentation approach is the Yankelovich Mindbase segmentation and PRIZM, developed by Claritas.

The Environics Segments

Environics, a Canadian research firm with headquarters in Toronto, has developed a classification system somewhat similar to the VALS scheme. The Environics clus-

FIGURE 4-15   SRI VALS™ Segments

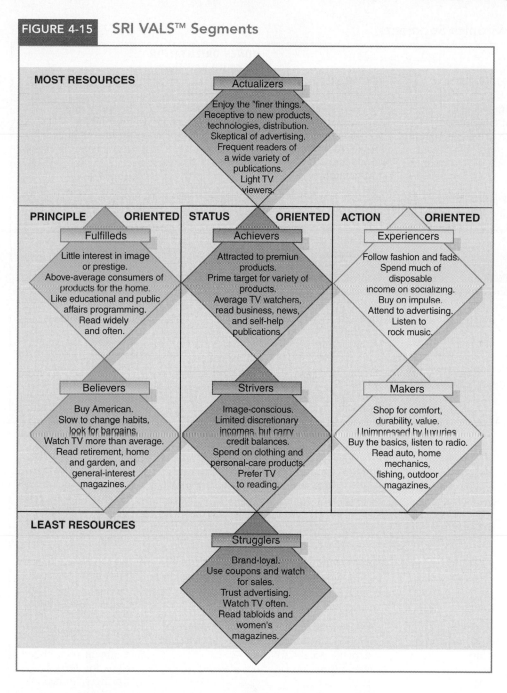

MOST RESOURCES

Actualizers

Enjoy the "finer things."
Receptive to new products,
technologies, distribution.
Skeptical of advertising.
Frequent readers of
a wide variety of
publications.
Light TV
viewers.

PRINCIPLE   ORIENTED   STATUS   ORIENTED   ACTION   ORIENTED

Fulfilleds

Little interest in image
or prestige.
Above-average consumers of
products for the home.
Like educational and public
affairs programming.
Read widely
and often.

Achievers

Attracted to premium
products.
Prime target for variety of
products.
Average TV watchers,
read business, news,
and self-help
publications.

Experiencers

Follow fashion and fads.
Spend much of
disposable
income on socializing.
Buy on impulse.
Attend to advertising.
Listen to
rock music.

Believers

Buy American.
Slow to change habits,
look for bargains.
Watch TV more than average.
Read retirement, home
and garden, and
general-interest
magazines.

Strivers

Image-conscious.
Limited discretionary
incomes, but carry
credit balances.
Spend on clothing and
personal-care products.
Prefer TV
to reading.

Makers

Shop for comfort,
durability, value.
Unimpressed by luxuries.
Buy the basics, listen to radio.
Read auto, home
mechanics,
fishing, outdoor
magazines.

LEAST RESOURCES

Strugglers

Brand-loyal.
Use coupons and watch
for sales.
Trust advertising.
Watch TV often.
Read tabloids and
women's
magazines.

ters are based on two dimensions: a person's level of *traditionalism* (i.e., whether a person is traditional or modern in outlook) and *individualism* (i.e., whether a person is social or individual in orientation). Environics uses a two-stage method to classify Canadians; first, a person is classified according to his or her age group into one of three categories (pre-boomer, boomer, or Generation X) and then according to several psychographic variables. Details of the Environics segments are provided in Figure 4-16.

www.environics.ca

FIGURE 4-16 The Environics Segments

SEGMENT	FUNDAMENTAL MOTIVATIONS	KEY VALUES	MONEY ORIENTATION (TOWARD SAVING MONEY)	ICONS
Pre-boomers: Rational Traditionalist	Financial independence, security, and stability	Risk aversion, rationality, respect for historical tradition, respect for authority, duty, deferred gratification	A penny saved is a penny earned	Former Ontario Premier Mike Harris, businessman and politician C.D. Howe
Pre-boomers: Extroverted Traditionalists	Traditional communities, institutions, and social status	Religiosity, family, respect for historical tradition and institutions, duty, deferred gratification	Wait till the neighbours see this	Prime minister Jean Chrétien, former Quebec premier Maurice Duplessis
Pre-boomers: Cosmopolitan Modernists	Personal autonomy and experience-seeking	Control of destiny, global world view, respect for education, desire for innovation, community involvement	Do I need it? Will it really make me happy?	Author Pierre Berton, Maurice Strong, columnist Dalton Camp
Boomers: Autonomous Rebels	Personal autonomy and self-fulfillment	Skepticism toward traditional institutions, suspicion of authority, freedom, individuality	Gotta risk some to make some; I know what I'm doing	Governor General Adrienne Clarkson, philosopher and critic Mark Kingwell, talk-show host Pamela Wallin, environmentalist David Suzuki
Boomers: Anxious Communitarians	Traditional communities, institutions, and social status	Consumerism, deference to authority, need for respect	I leave it to the experts; I don't want to do anything rash or foolish	Comedian Tim Allen, household guru Martha Stewart, talk-show host Oprah Winfrey, Princess Diana
Boomers: Connected Enthusiasts	Self-exploration and experience-seeking	Self-exploration, community, experimentation, hedonism	I need my money now; I can't risk it in the short term	Pop star Madonna, Film-maker Denys Arcand, Celine Dion, Shirley MacLaine
Generation X: Aimless Dependants	Financial independence, security and stability	Ostentatious consumption, desire for independence, fatalism, nihilism	It's my money; I'd better not lose any	WWF star "The Rock," rap artist Eminem, metal band Slipknot, Jerry Springer, Stone Cold Steve Austin
Generation X: Thrill-Seeking Materialists	Traditional communities, social status, and experience-seeking	Desire for money and material possessions, desire for recognition, respect, admiration, aesthetics	Already? What for?	Former basketball superstar Michael Jordan, singer/actress Jennifer Lopez, singer Shania Twain, actress Pamela Lee Anderson, rap star Jay-Z

(continued)

FIGURE 4-16	The Environics Segments (continued)			
Generation X: New Aquarians	Social justice and experience-seeking	Adaptability, concern for the less fortunate, concern for the environment, respect for education, contempt for traditional authorities, hedonism	I'm not saving much now, but when I do I'll call the shots	Singer Sarah McLachlan, author Naomi Klein, singer/activist Jello Biafra, rap-metal group Rage Against the Machine
Generation X: Autonomous Postmaterialists	Personal autonomy and self-fulfillment	Freedom, spontaneity	I'm testing the market so I can make my own decisions when the time comes	Dot-com millionaires (any of them), computer hacker Mafiaboy, editor Richard Martineau, animated character Bart Simpson, Steve Jobs, tennis player Venus Williams
Generation X: Social Hedonists	Hedonism and new communities	Risk-taking, aesthetics, sexual permissiveness, immediate gratification	I'll start saving when fashion stands still	Race car driver Jacques Villeneuve, extreme sports athletes, pop-punk band Blink 182, pop star Ricky Martin, movie character Austin Powers
Generation X: Security-Seeking Ascetics	Family, security and stability	Security, simplicity, deferred gratification	Save doggedly	Their own parents and grandparents, Russell Crowe in the film *The Gladiator*, any mother protecting her kids, talk-show host Rosie O'Donnell, Paul Martin

Source: The Environics Group; http://3sc.environics.net/surveys. Courtesy of Environics Group.

Life Styles and Marketing Strategy

Life-style analysis is an extremely beneficial tool for marketers.

Segmentation and positioning: Life-style analysis and related segmentation schemes can help a company segment the market for its products and position its offerings effectively. For example, a financial institution targeting the Environics segment of "security-seeking ascetics" would do well to position its savings and investment schemes as safe rather than as yielding high returns.

These segmentation methods are likely to be even more beneficial if the segments (or clusters, as they are usually called) are developed for specific product categories; in other words, rather than find the segments (using AIO items, life styles, and demographics) of the population as a whole, marketers should develop segments within users of each product category. For example, the Print Marketing Bureau has developed both general societal attitude clusters of Canadians and clusters specific to certain product categories. One of them is the "I love my wheels" automotive cluster.

www.pmb.ca

RESEARCH INSIGHT 4-2
IDENTIFYING GENERAL AND PRODUCT-RELATED PSYCHOGRAPHIC CLUSTERS

The Print Measurement Bureau, which is a non-profit organization, has been measuring the circulation of newspapers and magazines and exposure to non-print media in Canada for 25 years. It represents almost all the major Canadian publishers, more than 60 advertising agencies, and more than 185 advertisers. The PMB also examines Canadians' product usage in a wide variety of categories and collects life-style and psychographic information.

PMB has been measuring print readership in Canada since 1973. Its annual surveys of a nationally representative sample of 24 000 people examines the readership of more than 100 publications and the use of more than 2500 products and brands. Let's look at how the PMB goes about collecting these data.

Sample selection: The PMB uses a randomly selected sample of 2000 enumeration areas out of a total of approximately 47 000 such areas across the country. Ten households are chosen in each enumeration area, and one person from each household is surveyed. The total sample is distributed among the provinces and regions as follows: Atlantic 1003, Quebec 5279, Ontario 6117, Prairies 2555, and British Columbia 2667.

The Readership Survey: The surveys are conducted year-round through personal interviews. Readership is measured with a "recent reading" measure, which works as follows:

1. Respondents are shown a card bearing the logo of one publication.
2. They are asked if they have read any issue of that publication in the past 12 months.
3. Those saying "yes" or "not sure" are asked if they can remember when they looked into that publication.
4. Depending on the frequency of the publication, respondents are considered "qualified readers" if they have read the publication within a certain period—for example, in the past seven days for a weekly publication, in the past 30 days for a monthly publication, and so on.
5. The process is repeated for each magazine.

The PMB also collects data on the frequency of reading, the number of reading occasions, the time spent reading, how and where the respondent got the magazine, and how interested he or she is in the magazine.

Life style and psychographic information: The PMB also collects information about life events that the respondent has experienced (e.g., marriage, quitting smoking, buying a home or car, changing jobs), leisure activities, education, sports activities, and attendance at sports events.

The organization collects general AIO information, but it also collects specific information on interests and opinions in nine different product categories. One of the product categories is "snacks/candy." These are some of the questions for this catgory:

I feel guilty when I eat "junk food."
I like to have a wide variety of snacks.
I look for low calorie/light snacks.
I often buy snacks with just myself in mind.
I often reward myself by having a snack.

Such information, when combined with the demographic data that is collected during the survey, enables the PMB to provide psychographic clusters for each product category. These are the clusters for "snacks/candy."

Snack Happy

This is a young, even teenaged, group. They agree that they eat a lot of junk food. They buy snacks for the flavour rather than nutritional value, and they tend to be self-indulgent with snacks, agreeing with the statement "I often buy snacks with just myself in mind."

Closet Snackers

Closet snackers will reward themselves by snacking, but they will eat their snacks alone, and they feel guilty about eating what they consider to be junk food. They often eat snacks instead of regular meals (shown by their consumption of meal replacement bars and nutritional drinks). They are aware of nutritional issues, and their guilt at snacking is shown in their consumption of artificial sweeteners, sugarless gum, and rice cakes.

Anti-snackers

This group tends to reject the concept of snacks and snacking. They don't indulge in snacks; and they steer clear of junk food. They don't substitute snacks for regular meals and don't even eat low-calorie snacks.

Low-cal Snackers

This group feels extremely guilty about eating junk food, even though they claim to eat it very rarely. They eat light, low-calorie, and nutritious snacks.

Relaxed Nibblers

This group appears to have few guilt feelings about eating junk food. Although they don't buy snacks just for themselves, they enjoy a variety of snacks at home.

Other media exposure: Besides print readership, PMB surveys also collect information on television and radio exposure, use of transit, trips to shopping malls, and use of the Yellow Pages.

QUESTIONS:

1. Which one of the above "snack/candy" clusters do you fall into?
2. How can a marketer use the above information to develop a marketing strategy for a new kind of snack?

Source: The Print Measurement Bureau's website, **www.pmb.ca**. Accessed on November 11, 2003.

"I love my wheels" expresses this group's infatuation with all things automotive, including performance, looks, colour, accessories, and even car maintenance. They think that a car tells a lot about the person who owns it.[61]

Such individuals are likely to be a good targets for sports cars, which are positioned unique products that are extensions of the persons themselves.

Research Insight 4-2 looks at how the Print Marketing Bureau of Canada develops psychographic clusters of the Canadian population for specific product categories.

Planning effective media campaigns: Life-style analysis and related segmentation methods can give marketers a more accurate picture of their target markets. This, in turn, can help them develop more effective communication strategies, including choosing the right media and developing suitable messages. For example, while catering to the "security-seeking ascetics" in Figure 4-16, a financial institution may need to choose women's magazines and television shows that cater to women because a majority of security-seeking ascetics are women; the promotions should emphasize the simplicity of their investment schemes, how these investments are protected by the Canada Deposit and Insurance Corporation (CDIC), and how they would enable the consumer to protect her children's future.

SUMMARY

- Personality can be described as the psychological characteristics that both determine and reflect how a person responds to his or her environment. Although personality tends to be consistent and enduring, it may change abruptly in response to major life events, as well as gradually.

- Four theories of personality are prominent in the study of consumer behaviour: psychoanalytic theory, neo-Freudian theory, cognitive theory, and trait theory.

- Freud's psychoanalytic theory operates on the premise that human drives are largely unconscious and serve to motivate many consumer actions, whereas neo-Freudian theory tends to emphasize the fundamental role of social relationships in the formation and development of personality.

- Cognitive and trait theories are major departures from the qualitative (or subjective) approach to personality measurement. Cognitive theory looks at the differences in the way people process and store information; trait theory states that individuals possess innate psychological traits (e.g., innovativeness, desire for novelty, need for cognition, materialism) to a greater or lesser degree, and that these traits can be measured by specially designed scales or inventories.

- Product and brand personalities represent real opportunities for marketers to take advantage of consumers' connections to the various brands they offer. Brands often have personalities—some include "human-like" traits and even a sex.

These brand personalities help shape consumer responses, preferences, and loyalties.

- Each individual has a self-image (or multiple self-images) as a certain kind of person with certain traits, habits, possessions, relationships, and ways of behaving.

- Consumers often try to preserve, enhance, alter, or extend their self-images by buying products or services and shopping at stores that they think are consistent with their relevant self-image(s) and by avoiding products and stores that they think are not.

- With the growth of the internet, virtual selves or virtual personalities seem to be emerging. Consumer experiences with chat rooms sometimes provide an opportunity to explore new or alternative identities.

- An individual's consumption patterns and life style are also affected by psychographic and demographic variables. While psychographic segmentation is based on a person's activities, interests, and opinions alone, the newer hybrid segmentation methods include demographic or geographic variables to psychographics to get a richer profile of consumers. These segmentation methods can be used to discover product usage patterns, to segment and position products, and to develop promotional campaigns.

DISCUSSION QUESTIONS

1. Contrast the major characteristics of the following personality theories: (a) Freudian theory, (b) neo-Freudian theory. Illustrate how each theory is applied to the understanding of consumer behaviour.

2. Compare cognitive and trait theories of personality. Illustrate how each theory is applied to the understanding of consumer behaviour.

3. Explain the following personality traits and discuss their relevance to marketers: (a) consumer innovativeness, (b) consumer materialism, and (c) consumer ethnocentrism.

4. Describe the four types of consumer self-image and explain their relevance to marketers.

5. How can a marketer of cameras use the research finding that a target market consists primarily of inner-directed or other-directed consumers? Of consumers who are high (or low) on innovativeness?

6. Explain the concept of brand personality. Discuss three ways in which a company can develop a personality for its products.

CRITICAL THINKING QUESTIONS

1. Assume that you are in charge of marketing a digital video camera and that you have to develop a promotional message for the following market segments. What would your promotional message to each segment be?
    (a) highly dogmatic consumers
    (b) inner-directed consumers
    (c) highly innovative consumers
    (d) consumers with a high need for recognition
    (e) consumers who are visualizers versus consumers who are verbalizers

2. Consider how your clothing preferences differ from those of two of your friends. What personality traits might explain why your preferences are different from those of your friends?

3. Assume that you are the marketing manager in charge of the products listed below. In each case, state whether you would promote your product to cater to your target consumers' actual self, ideal self, social self, or ideal social self-image.
    (a) a soft drink
    (b) jeans
    (c) a watch
    (d) health food

4. Name two products that are part of (or could become part of) your extended self-image (you can complete the sample items from the Extended Self Survey provided in this chapter to do so). What do these products have in common? How can a marketer make products part of the extended self-image of someone your age?

INTERNET EXERCISES

1. Visit several company websites and find one that appeals to the following personality traits:

    Need for cognition
    Consumer materialism
    Consumer ethnocentrism
    Consumer innovativeness

2. Visit the websites of companies in the cosmetic industry (e.g., Revlon, Avon), and those that manufacture perfumes. What part of a consumer's self-image are they appealing to? Do you see differences in the appeals made by the various firms?

3. Visit the websites of high-end car manufacturers and find examples of appeals to specific personality traits and/or self-image.

4. Visit one of the following sites and take the survey. Which one provides a better picture of your life style and values?

    - Environics website (**http://erg.environics.net/surveys**)
    - SRIC-BI's VALS website (**www.sric-bi.com/VALS**) and the VALS survey.

KEY TERMS

Actual self-image *(p. 122)*
Brand personification *(p. 117)*
Cognitive theories of personality *(p. 108)*
Consumer ethnocentrism *(p. 109)*
Consumer innovativeness *(p. 109)*
Consumer innovators *(p. 110)*
Consumer materialism *(p. 109)*
Expected self-image *(p. 123)*
Extended self *(p. 123)*
Geodemographic segmentation *(p. 128)*
Ideal self-image *(p. 122)*
Ideal social self-image *(p. 122)*
Multiple selves *(p. 122)*
Need for cognition *(p. 108)*
Neo-Freudian personality theories *(p. 106)*
"Ought-to" self *(p. 123)*
Personality *(p. 104)*
Psychoanalytic theory *(p. 105)*
Psychographic segmentation *(p. 127)*
Social self-image *(p. 122)*
Trait theory *(p. 109)*
Verbalizers *(p. 108)*
Visualizers *(p. 108)*

CASE 4-1: FOUR-ON-THE-FLOOR

At one time, the typical purchaser of a car with a manual transmission was a person who wanted to save money (an automatic transmission can sometimes add more than $1000 to the price of a car) or wanted better gasoline mileage (manual transmissions usually offer slightly better gas mileage). Today, though, the buyer of a manual-transmission vehicle is most likely to be an affluent, university-educated man at least 45 years of age. It has been written that "driving a stick shift reflects a preoccupation with authenticity and the unrefined... that provides its own cachet in our plastic, materi-alistic society." The driver of a manual-transmission car is also saying to the world, "I would rather drive the car than have the car drive me."

Research results also reveal that owners of cars with manual transmissions are more likely than the average consumer to cook from scratch, do their own financial planning, and engage in "solo" leisure activities, such as jogging and skiing. They also like to make their own bread and pasta and prefer buying foods that require more work (e.g., they brew their coffee rather than spoon out instant coffee).

QUESTION

1. Considering the discussion of trait theory in Chapter 4, which traits do you believe owners of manual-transmission vehicles might score higher or lower on than would the general Canadian population?

Source: Michael J. Weiss, "Feel of the Road," *American Demographics,* March 2001, 72–73.

NOTES

1   Rebecca Harris, "Keeping It Real," *Marketing Magazine,* November 8, 2004, 10.

2   Amanda B. Diekman and Alice H. Eagly, "Stereotypes as Dynamic Constructs: Women and Men of the Past, Present, and Future," *Personality and Social Psychology Bulletin,* 26, no. 10, October 2000, 1171–1188.

3   Ellen Creager, "Do Snack Foods Such as Nuts and Popcorn Affect Romance?" *Patriot-News,* Harrisburg, PA, February 14, 2001, E11.

4   For example, see Karen Horney, *The Neurotic Personality of Our Time* (New York: Norton, 1937).

5   Joel B. Cohen, "An Interpersonal Orientation to the Study of Consumer Behavior," *Journal of Marketing Research,* 6, August 1967, 270–278; Arch G. Woodside and Ruth Andress, "CAD Eight Years Later," *Journal of the Academy of Marketing Science,* 3, Summer–Fall 1975, 309–313; see also Jon P. Noerager, "An Assessment of CAD: A Personality Instrument Developed Specifically for Marketing Research," *Journal of Marketing Research,* 16, February 1979, 53–59; and Pradeep K. Tyagi, "Validation of the CAD Instrument: A Replication," in *Advances in Consumer Research,* 10, eds. Richard P. Bogazzio and Alice M. Tybout (Ann Arbor, MI: Association for Consumer Research, 1983), 112–114.

6   Morton I. Jaffe, "Brand-Loyalty/Variety-Seeking and the Consumer's Personality: Comparing Children and Young Adults," in *Proceedings of the Society for Consumer Psychology,* eds. Scott B. MacKenzie and Douglas M. Stayman (La Jolla, CA: American Psychological Association, 1995), 144–151.

7   Richard Petty et al., "Personality and Ad Effectiveness: Exploring the Utility of Need for Cognition," in *Advances in Consumer Research,* 15, ed. Michael Houston (Ann Arbor, MI: Association for Consumer Research, 1988), 209–212; and Susan Powell Mantel and Frank R. Kardes, "The Role of Direction of Comparison, Attribute-Based Processing, and Attitude-Based Processing in Consumer Preference," *Journal of Consumer Research,* 25, March 1999, 335–352.

8   Arnold B. Bakker, "Persuasive Communication About AIDS Prevention: Need for Cognition Determines the Impact of Message Format," *AIDS Education and Prevention,* 11, no. 2), 1999, 150–162.

9   Yong Zhang and Richard Buda, "Moderating Effects of Need for Cognition on Responses to

Positively versus Negatively Framed Advertising Messages," *Journal of Advertising,* 28, no. 2, Summer 1999, 1–15.

10   Ayn E. Crowley and Wayne D. Hoyer, "The Relationship between Need for Cognition and Other Individual Difference Variables: A Two-Dimensional Framework," in *Advances in Consumer Research,* 16, ed. Thomas K. Srull (Provo, UT: Association for Consumer Research, 1989), 37–43; and James W. Peltier and John A. Schibrowsky, "Need for Cognition, Advertisement Viewing Time and Memory for Advertising Stimuli," *Advances in Consumer Research,* 21, 1994: 244–250.

11   Tracy L. Tuten and Michael Bosnjak, "Understanding Differences in Web Usage: The Role of Need for Cognition and the Five Factor Model of Personality," *Social Behavior and Personality,* 29, no. 4, 2001, 391–398.

12   J.P. Guilford, *Personality* (New York: McGraw-Hill, 1959), 6.

13   J.C. Mowen and N. Spears, "Understanding Compulsive Buying among College Students," *Journal of Consumer Psychology*, 8, no. 4 1999, 407–430

14   E.G. Harris and J.C. Mowen, "The Influence of Cardinal-Central and Surface-Level Personality Traits on Consumers' Bargaining and Complaint Behaviors," *Psychology and Marketing,* November 2001, 1155–1185.

15   Ronald E. Goldsmith and Charles F. Hofacker, "Measuring Consumer Innovativeness," *Journal of the Academy of Marketing Science,* 19 (1991): 209–221; Suresh Subramanian and Robert A. Mittelstaedt, "Conceptualizing Innovativeness as a Consumer Trait: Consequences and Alternatives," in *1991 AMA Educators' Proceedings,* eds. Mary C. Gilly and F. Robert Dwyer et al. (Chicago: American Marketing Association, 1991), 352–360; and "Reconceptualizing and Measuring Consumer Innovativeness," in *1992 AMA Educators' Proceedings,* eds. Robert P. Leone and V. Kumor, et al. (Chicago: American Marketing Association, 1992), 300–307.

16   Alka Varma Citrin, David E. Sprott, Steven N. Silverman, and Donald E. Stem, Jr., "From Internet Use to Internet Adoption: Is General Innovativeness Enough?" in *1999 AMA Winter Educators' Conference,* 10, eds. Anil Menon and Arun Sharma (Chicago: American Marketing Association, 1999), 232–233.

17   Angela D'Auria Stanton and Wilbur W. Stanton, "To Click or Not to Click: Personality Characteristics of Internet versus Non-Internet Purchasers," in *2001 AMA Winter Educators'*

Conference, 12, eds. Ram Krishnan and Madhu Viswanathan (Chicago: American Marketing Association, 2001), 161–162.

18   Milton Rokeach, *The Open and Closed Mind* (New York: Basic Books, 1960).

19   Itamar Simonson and Stephen M. Nowlis, "The Role of Explanations and Need for Uniqueness in Consumer Decision Making: Unconventional Choices Based on Reasons," *Journal of Consumer Research,* 27, June 2000, 49–68.

20   Linda McNamara and Mary E. Ballard, "Resting Arousal, Sensation Seeking, and Music Preference," *Genetic, Social, and General Psychology Monographs,* 125, no. 3, 1999, 229–250.

21   Russell W. Belk, "Three Scales to Measure Constructs Related to Materialism" and "Materialism: Trit Aspects of Living in the Material World," *Journal of Consumer Research*, 12, December 1985, 265–280.

22   Marsha L. Richins and Scott Dawson, "A Consumer Values Orientation for Materialism and Its Measurement: Scale Development and Validation," *Journal of Consumer Research,* 19, December 1992, 303–316; and Jeff Tanner and Jim Roberts, "Materialism Cometh," *Baylor Business Review,* Fall 2000, 8–9.

23   Reto Felix, Roberto Hernandez, and Wolfgang Hinck, "An Empirical Investigation of Materialism in Mexico," in *2000 AMA Educators' Proceedings,* 11, eds. Gregory T. Gundlach and Patrick E. Murphy (Chicago: American Marketing Association, 2000), 279–286.

24   Terrance Shimp and Subhash Sharma, "Consumer Ethnocentrism: Construction and Validation of the CETSCALE," *Journal of Marketing Research*, 24, UFUAR 1987, 280–289.

25   Osman Mohamad, Zafar U. Ahmed, Earl D. Honeycutt, Jr., and Taizoon Hyder Tyebkhan, "Does 'Made In' Matter to Consumers? A Malyalasian Study of Country of Origin Effect," Multinational Business Review, Fall 2000, 69–73; and Irwin Clarke, Mahesh N. Shankarmahesh, and John B. Ford, "Consumer Ethnocentrism, Materializm and Values: A Four Country Study," in *2000 AMA Winter Educators' Conference,* 11, eds. John P. Workman and William D. Perreault (Chicago: American Marketing Association, 200), 102–103.

26   David Martin, "Branding: Finding That 'One Thing,'" *Brandweek,* February 16, 1998, 18.

27   Subodh Bhat and Srinivas K. Reddy, "Symbolic and Functional Positioning of Brands," *Journal of Consumer Marketing,* 15 (1998), 32–43.

28   Traci L. Haigood, "The Brand Personality Effect: An Empirical Investigation," in *1999 AMA Winter*

Educators' Conference, 10, eds. Anil Menon and Arun Sharma (Chicago: American Marketing Association, 1999), 149–150; and Traci L. Haigood, "Deconstructing Brand Personality," in *2001 AMA Educators' Proceedings,* 12, eds. Greg W. Marshall and Stephen J. Grove (Chicago: American Marketing Association, 2001), 327–328.

29　Lauren Weber, "The Diamond Game: Shedding Its Mystery," *New York Times,* April 8, 2001, P1.

30　Judy A. Siguaw, Anna Mattila, and Jon R. Austin, "The Brand-Personality Scale," *Hotel and Restaurant Administration Quarterly,* June 1999, 48–55.

31　Janice S. Griffiths, Mary Zimmer, and Sheniqua K. Little, "The Effect of Reality Engineering on Consumers' Brand Perceptions Using a Fictional Historical Branding Strategy," *American Marketing Association,* Winter 1999, 250–258.

32　Tim Triplett, "When Tracy Speaks, Celestial Listens," *Marketing News,* October 24, 1994, 14.

33　David M. Morawski and Lacey J. Zachary, "Making Mr. Coffee," *Quirk's Marketing Research Review,* 6 (March 1992), 6–7, 29–33.

34　Sarah Dobson, "Publisher Gives *Dummies* a Push," *Marketing Magazine*, March 3, 2003, 3.

35　Jennifer L. Aaker, "Dimension of Brand Personality," *Journal of Marketing Research,* 35, August 1997, 351–352.

36　Kali Pearson, "Beer Story," *Profit*, March 2003, 39–45.

37　Andre Veniot, "Her Name on the Box," *Progress,* January–February, 2003, 29–43.

38　Max Blackston, "Observations: Building Brand Equity by Managing the Brand's Relationships," *Journal of Advertising Research,* November/December 2000, 101–105.

39　Elizabeth Jensen, "Blue Bottles, Gimmicky Labels Sell Wine," *Wall Street Journal,* July 7, 1997, B1.

40　Pamela S. Schindler, "Color and Contrast in Magazine Advertising," *Psychology & Marketing,* 3 (1986), 69–78.

41　Sally Goll Beatty, "Mars Inc. Dips into Sex to Lure Consumers into Arms of M&Ms," *Wall Street Journal,* January 23, 1997, 9.

42　Stephanie Thompson, "LifeSavers Effort Gets Personality," *Advertising Age,* January 21, 2002, 42. See also Lawrence L. Garber, Jr., Eva M. Hyatt, and Richard G. Starr, Jr., "The Effects of Food Color on Perceived Flavor," *Journal of Marketing Theory and Practice,* Fall 2000, 59–72.

43　"Heinz EZ Squirt™ Hits Store Shelves; Industry Watches Unusual Food Phenomenon Unfold," *PR Newswire,* October 17, 2000, 1.

44　Kali Pearson, "Beer Story," *Profit*, March 2003, 39–45.

45　Kiran Karande, George M. Zinkhan, and Alyssa Baird Lum, "Brand Personality and Self Concept: A Replication and Extension," *AMA Summer 1997 Conference,* 165–171.

46　Hazel Markus and Paula Nurius, "Possible Selves," *American Psychologist,* 1986, 954–969.

47　For a detailed discussion of self-images and congruence, see M. Joseph Sirgy, "Self-Concept in Consumer Behavior: A Critical Review," *Journal of Consumer Research,* 9 (December 1992), 287–300; C.B. Claiborne and M. Joseph Sirgy, "Self-Image Congruence as a Model of Consumer Attitude Formation and Behavior: A Conceptual Review and Guide for Future Research," in *Developments in Marketing Science,* 13, ed. B.J. Dunlap (Cullowhee, NC: Academy of Marketing Science, 1990), 1–7; and J.S. Johar and M. Joseph Sirgy, "Value-Expressive versus Utilitarian Advertising Appeals: When and Why to Use Which Appeal," *Journal of Advertising,* 20, September 1991, 23–33.

48　"Sex Appeal," *Brandweek,* April 20, 1998, 26.

49　Susan Fournier, "Consumers and Their Brands: Developing Relationship Theory in Consumer Research," *Journal of Consumer Research,* 24, March 1998; and Kimberly J. Dodson, "Peak Experiences and Mountain Biking: Incorporating the Bike in the Extended Self," in *Advances in Consumer Research,* incomplete vol. 23, eds. Kim P. Cofman and John G. Lynch, Jr. (Provo, UT: Association for Consumer Research 1996), 317–322.

50　Marlene M. Moretti and E. Tory Higgens, "Internal Representations of Others in Self-Regulation: A New Look at a Classic Issue," *Social Cognition,* 17, no. 2, 1999, 186–208.

51　Russell W. Belk, "Possessions and the Extended Self," *Journal of Consumer Research,* 15, September 1988, 139–168; and Amy J. Morgan, "The Evolving Self in Consumer Behavior: Exploring Possible Selves," in *Advances in Consumer Research,* 20, eds. Leigh McAlister and Michael L. Rothschild (Provo, UT: Association for Consumer Research, 1992), 429–432.

52　Jennifer Stewart, "Me and My Baby," *Progress,* April, 2003, p. 66.

53　Richard G. Netemeyer, Scot Burton, and Donald R. Lichtenstein, "Trait Aspects of Vanity: Measurement and Relevance to Consumer Behavior," *Journal of Consumer Research,* 21, March 1995, 613.

54　Robert Underwood, Edward Bond, and Robert Baer, "Building Service Brands via Social Identity: Lessons from the Sports Marketplace," *Journal of Marketing Theory and Practice,* Winter 2001, 1–13.

55　"Finding Out about Yourself Has Never Been This Fun! Emode's New Ultimate Personality Test

Connects People Online," *PR Newswire*, October 24, 2000, 1.

56   Michael J. Weiss, "Online America," *American Demographics,* March 2001, 53–60.

57   **www.claritas.com**; Patricia Lloyd Williams, "Energy Marketing: What Do Customers Want?" *Fortnightly's Energy Customer Management,* Fall 2000, 36–41.

58   "Mediamark Research Inc. Enhances Data with Segmentation Analysis from VALS™ and Forrester," *PR Newswire,* August 22, 2001, 1; Linda P. Morton, "Segmenting Publics by

Lifestyles," *Public Relations Quarterly,* Fall 1999, 46–47.

59   Rebecca Piirto Heath, "You Can Buy a Thrill: Chasing the Ultimate Rush," *American Demographics*, June 1997, 48.

60   "Who Will Buy Intelligent In-Vehicle Products? New Report Assesses Consumer Perceptions and Acceptance of Intelligent Transportation Systems Products," *Business Wire,* November 2, 1999, 1.

61   Print Marketing Bureau; **http://www.pmb.ca/public/e/index.htm**.

© 1998, HOMER TLC, Inc. Available in U.S. only.

The Gift Registry

Okay, it's not as traditional as china or silver. But for practical gifts you'll actually use for years to come, nothing beats Home Depot's Gift Registry. Tools, gas grills, lawn mowers. If you need it, your local Home Depot makes it easy for friends and family across the entire country to purchase it for you. In fact, it's a piece of cake.

chapter 5
consumer perception

LEARNING OBJECTIVES

By the end of this chapter, you should be able to:

1. Define perception and discuss three key elements of the perceptual process.
2. Explain the dynamics of perception by discussing factors affecting perceptual selection, perceptual organization, and perceptual interpretation.
3. Discuss any five factors that affect consumer imagery of products.
4. Explain how marketers can use their knowledge of the perceptual process to develop more effective marketing strategies.

it seems as if bad carbs are everywhere these days! Every magazine, most talk shows, television newscasts, and other media—all seem to suddenly be focusing on the negative effects of carbohydrates, especially the "bad carbs." Of course all this is bad news for manufacturers of pasta, bread, beer, and other carbohydrate-rich foods, all of which have been scrambling to deal with the "low-carb" craze. Labatt is no exception; the company has just introduced Labatt Sterling, a beer with just 2.5 grams of carbs (compared with the usual 11 to 17 grams found in most Canadian beers).

Interestingly enough, beer is not very high in carbohydrates—even at 11 to 17 grams per bottle, the amount of carbohydrates found in beer is not the main problem or the cause of beer bellies; the reason for the gain in weight and the beer belly are the snacks that are eaten along with beer (e.g., trail mix). The problem is consumers' perception of beer—most Canadians see beer as a calorie- and carb-rich food. For example, a recent survey of boomers (people 40–59 years of age) found that most of them overestimated the number of calories in a typical bottle of beer by as much as 300 percent! Although the actual number of calories in a bottle of beer is about 140, the average Canadian boomer thought it had 447 calories.[1] Obviously, no new "low-carb" beer can succeed unless this misconception about the calories and carbohydrates in beer is dealt with. For beer companies (as well as manufacturers of pasta, bread, and other carb-rich products), the problem is more complex, because if they emphasize that their new products are low in carbs, they might damage the sales of their other, carb-rich offerings.

Labatt decided to correct consumer misconceptions about beer through a good PR program. But it did not just promote Labatt Sterling as a low-carb product or say, "Carbs are bad, so here is a low-carb product." Instead, the company used its launch of Sterling to tell consumers that beer is not high in carbohydrates. Once this lead message was conveyed, the ads pitched Sterling as the brand of beer to choose if a consumer wants to virtually eliminate carbs from his or her diet. Luckily for Labatt, its campaign coincided with the Brewers Association of Canada's PR initiative, which also had dieticians on news programs like *Canada AM* pointing out that beer is not a high-carb drink and has fewer carbs than a glass of orange juice.

www.labatt.ca

Was Labatt successful in changing consumer perceptions of beer? Although it is too early to say for sure, the campaign registered 20 million media impressions, and nearly 85 000 six-packs of beer were sold in the first week. Labatt Sterling gained a 1 percent share of the market, which is impressive for a niche product.[2]

CHAPTER OVERVIEW

This chapter examines the psychological and physiological bases of human perception and discusses the principles that influence our perception and interpretation of the world we see. Knowledge of these principles enables astute marketers to develop advertisements that have a better-than-average chance of being seen and remembered by their target consumers.

WHAT IS PERCEPTION?

Individuals act and react on the basis of their perceptions, not on the basis of objective reality. For each individual, *reality* is a totally personal phenomenon, based on that person's needs, wants, values, and personal experiences. Thus, to the marketer, consumers' perceptions are much more important than their knowledge of objective reality. For it's not what actually *is* so, but what consumers *think* is so, that affects their actions, their buying habits, their leisure habits, and so forth. And if marketers are to know what makes people buy, it is important that they understand the whole notion of perception and its related concepts. This often necessitates changing advertising campaigns and revamping a brand's image, as Labatt attempted to do with its new advertising campaign.

Perception:
The process by which an individual selects, organizes, and interprets stimuli into a meaningful and coherent picture of the world.

Perception is defined as the process by which an individual selects, organizes, and interprets stimuli into a meaningful and coherent picture of the world. It can be described as "how we see the world around us." Two individuals may be exposed to the same stimuli under the same apparent conditions, but how each person recognizes, selects, organizes, and interprets these stimuli is a highly individual process based on each person's own needs, values, and expectations. The influence that each of these variables has on the perceptual process and its relevance to marketing will be explored later in the chapter. First, however, we will examine some of the basic concepts that underlie the perceptual process. These will be discussed within the framework of consumer behaviour.

Sensation:
The immediate and direct response of the sensory organs to stimuli.

Sensory receptors:
The human organs (the eyes, ears, nose, mouth, and skin) that receive sensory inputs.

Sensation

Sensation is the immediate and direct response of the sensory organs to stimuli. A *stimulus* is any unit of input to any of the senses. Examples of stimuli (i.e., sensory input) are products, packages, brand names, advertisements, and commercials. **Sensory receptors** are the human organs (the eyes, ears, nose, mouth, and skin) that receive sensory inputs. Their sensory functions are to see, hear, smell, taste, and feel. All of these functions are called into play, either singly or in combination, in the evaluation and use of most consumer products. Human sensitivity refers to the experience of sensation. Sensitivity to stimuli varies with the quality of an individual's sensory receptors (e.g., eyesight or hearing) and the amount (or *intensity*) of the stimuli to which he or she is exposed. For example, a blind person may have a more highly developed sense of hearing than the average sighted person does and may be able to hear sounds that the average person cannot.

Sensation itself depends on energy change within the environment where the perception occurs (i.e., on differentiation of input). A perfectly unchanging environment, regardless of the strength of the sensory input, provides little or no sensation at all. Thus, a person who lives on a busy street in downtown Toronto would probably receive little or no sensation from such noisy stimuli as horns honking, tires screeching, and fire engine sirens screaming, because such sounds are so commonplace in big cities. In situations in which there is a great deal of sensory input, the senses do not detect small changes or differences in input. Thus, one honking horn more or less would never be noticed on a street with heavy traffic.

As sensory input *decreases,* however, our ability to detect changes in input or intensity *increases,* to the point that we attain maximum sensitivity under conditions of minimal stimulation. This accounts for the statement "It was so quiet I could hear a pin drop." The ability of the human organism to accommodate itself to varying levels of stimuli as external conditions vary not only provides more sensitivity when it is needed but also protects us from damaging, disruptive, or irrelevant bombardment when the input level is high.

The Absolute Threshold

The lowest level at which an individual can experience a sensation is called the **absolute threshold**. The point at which a person can detect a difference between "something" and "nothing" is that person's absolute threshold for that stimulus. To illustrate, the distance at which a driver can note a specific billboard on a highway is that individual's absolute threshold. Two people riding together may first spot the billboard at different times (i.e., at different distances); thus, they appear to have different absolute thresholds. Under conditions of constant stimulation, such as driving through a "corridor" of billboards, the absolute threshold increases (i.e., the senses tend to become increasingly dulled). After an hour of driving through billboards, it is doubtful that any one billboard will make an impression. Hence, we often speak of "getting used to" a hot bath, a cold shower, or the bright sun. As our exposure to the stimulus increases, we notice it less. In the field of perception, the term *adaptation* is the process of getting used to certain sensations, that is, becoming accommodated to a certain level of stimulation.

Sensory adaptation is a problem that concerns many national advertisers, which is why they try to change their advertising campaigns regularly. They are concerned that consumers will get so used to their current print ads and television commercials that they will no longer "see" them; that is, the ads will no longer provide sufficient sensory input to be noticed.

In an effort to cut through the advertising clutter and ensure that consumers note their ads, some marketers try to *increase* sensory input. Apple Computer once bought all the advertising space in an issue of *Newsweek* magazine to ensure that the readers would notice its ads. From time to time, various advertisers have taken all of the bus cards on certain bus routes to advertise their products, ensuring that wherever a rider sits, he or she will be exposed to the ad. Other advertisers try to attract attention by *decreasing* sensory input. For example, some print ads include a lot of empty space (see Exhibit 5-1) in order to accentuate the brand name or

Absolute threshold: The lowest level at which an individual can experience a sensation.

Sensory adaptation: Getting used to certain sensations or becoming accommodated to a certain level of stimulation.

EXHIBIT 5-1

AD SHOWING EFFECTIVE USE OF EMPTY SPACE

Courtesy of Berkshire Blanket.

Differential threshold, or j.n.d:

The minimal difference that can be detected between two similar stimuli.

Weber's law:

A law that states that the the j.n.d. between two stimuli depends on the intensity of the first stimulus.

product illustration, and some television ads use silence, the absence of sound, to attract attention. Exhibit 5-2 depicts the use of increased sensory input to support the product's advertising claim.

Some marketers seek unusual or technological media in which to place their advertisements in an effort to gain attention. Examples of such media include small monitors attached to shopping carts that feature actual brands in television shows and in movies, individual television screens on the back of each seat on airplanes, and monitors integrated into the above-the-door floor indicators on elevators. Perfume marketers often include samples of perfume in sealed inserts in their direct-mail and magazine advertisements. Researchers have reported that the use of an ambient scent in a retail environment enhances the shopping experience for consumers and makes the time they spend examining merchandise, waiting in line, and waiting for help seem shorter than it actually is.[3] Some marketers have invested in the development of specially engineered scents to enhance their products and entice consumers to buy. Package designers try to determine consumers' absolute thresholds to make sure that their new-product designs will stand out from competitors' packages on retailers' shelves.

The Differential Threshold

The minimal difference that can be detected between two similar stimuli is called the **differential threshold**, or the **just noticeable difference** (the j.n.d.). A nineteenth-century German scientist named Ernst Weber discovered that the j.n.d. between two stimuli was not an absolute amount, but an amount relative to the intensity of the first stimulus. **Weber's law,** as it has come to be known, states that the stronger the initial stimulus, the greater the additional intensity needed for the second stimulus to be perceived as different. For example, if the price of a large container of premium, freshly squeezed orange juice is \$5.50, most consumers will probably not notice an increase of 25 cents (i.e., the increment would fall below the j.n.d.), and it may take an increase of 50 cents or more before a differential in price would be noticed. However, a similar 25-cent increase in the price of gasoline would be noticed very quickly because it is a significant percentage of the initial (base) cost of the gasoline.

According to Weber's law, an additional level of stimulus equivalent to the j.n.d. must be added for the majority of people to perceive a difference between the resulting stimulus and the initial stimulus.

Harvey's recently introduced its mega burger "Big Harv"— a six-ounce burger that is 50 percent bigger than most large burgers sold by other chains. Is this a good move by the chain? That depends on what increase in the size of the patty is needed for consumers to notice the difference. If the j.n.d. is less than two ounces, then Harvey's has increased the size of the patty to beyond what would capture

EXHIBIT 5-2

INCREASED SENSORY INPUT
Courtesy New Brunswick Department of Tourism and Parks.

consumers' attention; if the j.n.d. is over two ounces, then the increase in the size of Harvey's burger would go unnoticed. The best scenario for the hamburger chain would be if the j.n.d. for an increase in the size of a burger is exactly two ounces, for then, the company's product change would be noticed by consumers without it having spent more money than required in increased material costs.

The marketing implications of j.n.d are provided in Figure 5-1.

Subliminal Perception

In Chapter 3 we spoke of people being *motivated* below their level of conscious awareness. People are also *stimulated* below their level of conscious awareness; that is, they can perceive stimuli without being consciously aware that they are doing so. Stimuli that are too weak or too brief to be consciously seen or heard may nevertheless be strong enough to be perceived by one or more receptor cells. This process is called **subliminal perception** because the stimulus is beneath the threshold, or "limen," of conscious awareness, though obviously not beneath the absolute threshold of the receptors involved. (Perception of stimuli that are above the level of conscious awareness is technically called *supraliminal perception*, though it is usually referred to simply as perception.)

Subliminal perception: Unconscious awareness of weak stimuli.

FIGURE 5-1	Marketing Applications of the J.N.D.

NATURE OF THE CHANGE STRATEGY

Negative changes (e.g., increases in price, decreases in quantity)	Identify the j.n.d. for the change and keep the change *below* the j.n.d. For example, when the cost of raw materials goes up, either increase the price of the finished product just below the j.n.d., or keep the price constant and decrease the quantity slightly.
	Kimberley-Clarke, the manufacturer of Huggies, reduced the number of diapers in a package from 240 to 228 (and continued pricing it at $31.99).
	PepsiCo reduced the weight of one snack food bag from 14.5 ounces to 13.5 ounces (and maintained the price at $3.29).
	Poland Spring reduced its water-cooler-sized bottle from 6 to 5 gallons (and maintained the price at $9.25).
Positive changes (e.g., increases in quality or size; decreases in price)	Identify the j.n.d. and make sure the change is *above* the j.n.d.
	Harvey's, the Canadian hamburger chain, recently introduced its mega burger—made with a solid 6 ounces of ground beef. It is the biggest burger in Canada, and the increase in quantity (from 4 to 6 ounces) is probably well above the j.n.d.
Neutral changes (e.g., changes in brand name, packaging, logo)	Make a number of small changes, each carefully designed to fall below the j.n.d., so that consumers will notice only a very slight difference, if any, between succeeding versions.
	Betty Crocker, the General Mills symbol, was updated seven times from 1936 to 1996 (see Figure 5-2).
	Lexmark officials conducted a four-stage campaign for emphasizing the Lexmark name on products. As Figure 5-3 indicates, Stage 1 carried only the IBM name, Stage 2 featured the IBM name and downplayed Lexmark, Stage 3 featured the Lexmark name and downplayed IBM, and Stage 4 features only the Lexmark name. Ivory soap, which was introduced in 1879, has gone through several subtle packaging changes. Each change was small enough not to be noticed.

Since the 1950s, there have been sporadic reports of marketers using subliminal messages in their efforts to influence consumption behaviour. At times, it has been difficult to separate truth from fiction regarding such alleged manipulations. When some of the subliminal methods were tested methodically with scientific research procedures, the research results did not support the notion that subliminal messages can persuade consumers to act in a given manner. The most widely publicized uses (or alleged uses) of subliminal messages and the corresponding research findings are described in Figure 5-4.

FIGURE 5-2   Sequential Changes in the Betty Crocker Symbol Fall below the J.N.D.

FIGURE 5-3   Gradual Changes in Brand Name below the J.N.D.

FIGURE 5-4	Subliminal Perception: History and Research Findings

A DRIVE-IN MOVIE THEATRE IN NEW JERSEY (1957)

The effectiveness of so-called subliminal advertising was reportedly tested at a drive-in movie in New Jersey in 1957, where the words "Eat popcorn" and "Drink Coca-Cola" were flashed on the screen during the movie. Exposure times were so short that viewers were unaware of seeing a message. It was reported that during the six-week test period, popcorn sales increased 58 percent and Coca-Cola sales increased 18 percent.[a] The public frenzy was further fuelled by the publication of a book on motivational research entitled *The Hidden Persuaders,* which examined and further pursued the same kind of unconscious motives that were outlined in Dichter's research (see Chapter 3).[b] A series of highly imaginative laboratory experiments gave some support to the notion that individuals could perceive below the level of their conscious awareness but found no evidence that they could be persuaded to act in response to such subliminal stimulation. For example, one researcher found that although the simple subliminal stimulus COKE served to arouse thirst in subjects, the subliminal command DRINK COKE did not have a greater effect, nor did it have any behavioural consequences.[c]

THE PUBLICATION OF *SUBLIMINAL SEDUCTION* (1974)

Public indignation at the possibility of subliminal manipulation surfaced again in 1974 following the publication of a book entitled *Subliminal Seduction.*[d] The book charged that advertisers were using subliminal embeds in their print ads to persuade consumers to buy their advertised brands. It was alleged, for example, that liquor advertisers were trying to increase the subconscious appeal of their products by embedding sexually suggestive symbols in ice cubes floating in a pictured drink. As consumers increasingly complained about alleged subliminal messages on TV, even the U.S. Federal Communications Commission (FCC) studied the subject.[a] Research findings indicate that sexually oriented embeds do not influence consumer preferences.[e] Several experiments into the effectiveness of subliminal messages in television commercials concluded that it would be very difficult to use the technique on television, but that even if subliminal messages were to have "some influence," they would be much less effective than overt advertising messages and would likely interfere with consumers' memory for brand names.[f]

THE ALLEGATIONS AGAINST DISNEY (1990s)

There have been a number of allegations made about movies and videos produced by the Walt Disney Studios. For example:

1. *Aladdin:* Allegations that the hero whispers "good teenagers, take off your clothes" in a sub-audible voice.
2. *The Little Mermaid:* Allegations that one of the castle's spires on the video's cover resembles a penis; also that the minister officiating at a wedding ceremony in the movie displays an erection.
3. *The Lion King:* The letters "S-E-X" are formed in a cloud of dust.
4. *The Rescuers:* A very speedy image of a topless female appears in one scene.

As a result of these allegations, which Disney denied, Disney's products were boycotted by some consumer groups. However, it was later discovered that the nude image that appeared in the movie *The Rescuers* was apparently inserted as a prank in the movie's master in 1997, and Disney recalled copies of the movie in 1999.[g]

Sources: [a] sbe.d.umn.edu/subliminal/index.html. [b] Vance Packard, *The Hidden Persuaders* (New York: Pocket Books, 1957). [c] Sharon E. Beatty and Del I. Hawkins, "Subliminal Stimulation: Some New Data and Interpretation," *Journal of Advertising,* 18, 1989, 4–8. [d] Wilson Bryan Key, *Subliminal Seduction* (New York: New American Library, 1973). [e] Myron Gable, Henry T. Wilkens, Lynn Harris, and Richard Feinberg, "An Evaluation of Subliminally Embedded Sexual Stimuli in Graphics," *Journal of Advertising,* 16, 1, 1987, 26–31. [f] Kirk H. Smith and Martha Rogers, "Effectiveness of Subliminal Messages in Television Commercials: Two Experiments," *Journal of Applied Psychology,* 19, 6, 1994, 866–874. [g] Lisa Bannon, "How a Rumor Spread About Subliminal Sex in Disney's *Aladdin,*" *Wall Street Journal,* October 24, 1995, A-1; Bruce Orwall, "Disney Recalls *The Rescuers* Video Containing Images of Topless Woman," *Wall Street Journal Interactive Edition,* January 11, 1999.

Evaluating the Effectiveness of Subliminal Persuasion

Despite many studies by academics and researchers since the 1950s, there is no evidence that subliminal advertising persuades people to buy goods or services. A review of the literature reveals that subliminal perception research has been based on two theoretical approaches.

1. Constant repetition of very weak (i.e., sub-threshold) stimuli has an incremental effect, which over many responses, would lead to a response (or

behaviour). This would be the operative theory when weak stimuli are flashed repeatedly on a movie screen or played on a soundtrack or audiocassette.

2. Subliminal sexual stimuli may arouse unconscious sexual motivations. This is the theory behind the use of sexual embeds in print advertising.

But no studies have yet found that either of these theoretical approaches has been used successfully by advertisers to increase sales. However, there is some indication that subliminal advertising may provide new opportunities for modifying antisocial behaviour through public awareness campaigns that call for individuals to make generalized responses to suggestions that enhance their personal performance or improve their attitudes.[4] There is also some (though not definitive) evidence that subliminal methods can indirectly influence attitudes and feelings toward brands.[5]

In summary, although there is some evidence that subliminal stimuli may influence affective reactions, there is no evidence that they can influence consumption motives or actions. There continues to be a big gap between perception and persuasion. A recent review of the evidence on subliminal persuasion shows that the only way for subliminal techniques to have a significant persuasive effect would be through long-term repeated exposure under a limited set of circumstances, which would not be economically feasible or practical within an advertising context.[6]

As to sexual embeds, most researchers are of the opinion that "what you see is what you get"; that is, a vivid imagination can see whatever it wants to see in just about any situation. And that pretty much sums up the whole notion of perception: individuals see what they want to see (e.g., what they are motivated to see) and what they expect to see. Several studies concerned with public beliefs about subliminal advertising found that a large percentage of Americans know what subliminal advertising is, they believe it is used by advertisers, and they believe it does persuade people to buy.[7] To correct any misconceptions among the public that subliminal advertising does, in fact, exist, the advertising community occasionally sponsors ads, like the one shown in Exhibit 5-3, that ridicule the notion that subliminal techniques are effective or that they are used in advertising.

THE DYNAMICS OF PERCEPTION

The preceding section explained how the individual receives sensations from stimuli in the outside environment and how the human organism adapts to the level and intensity of sensory input. We now come to one of the major principles of perception: raw sensory input by itself does not produce or explain the coherent picture of the world that most adults possess. Indeed, the study of perception is largely the

EXHIBIT 5-3

SUBLIMINAL IMBEDS ARE IN THE EYE OF THE BEHOLDER

Courtesy of American Association of Advertising Agencies.

study of what we subconsciously add to or subtract from raw sensory inputs to produce our own private picture of the world. Thus, perception is the result of two different kinds of inputs—physical stimuli and the consumer's personal experience—which interact to form the personal pictures—the perceptions—that each individual experiences. The combination of these two very different kinds of inputs produces for each of us a very private, very personal picture of the world. Because each person is a unique individual, with unique experiences, needs, wants, desires, and expectations, it follows that each individual's perceptions are also unique. This explains why no two people see the world in precisely the same way.

Individuals are very selective as to which stimuli they "recognize"; they subconsciously organize the stimuli they do recognize according to widely held psychological principles, and they interpret such stimuli subjectively in accordance with their personal needs, expectations, and experiences. Let us examine in some detail each of these three aspects of perception: the *selection*, *organization*, and *interpretation of stimuli*.

Perceptual Selection

Consumers subconsciously exercise a great deal of selectivity as to which aspects of the environment (i.e., which stimuli) they perceive. An individual may look at some things, ignore others, and turn away from still others. In actuality, people receive (i.e., perceive) only a small fraction of the stimuli they are exposed to.

A shopper in a supermarket may be exposed to more than 20 000 products of different colours, sizes, and shapes; to perhaps 100 people (looking, walking, searching, talking); to smells (from fruit, meat, disinfectant, people); to sounds in the store (cash registers ringing, shopping carts rolling, air conditioners humming, and clerks sweeping, mopping aisles, and stocking shelves); and to sounds from outside the store (planes passing, cars honking, tires screeching, children shouting, car doors slamming). Yet the shopper regularly manages to visit her local supermarket, select the items she needs, pay for them, and leave, all in a relatively short time, without losing her sanity or her personal orientation to the world around her. This is because she exercises *selectivity* in perception or **selective perception**.

Selective perception: The conscious and subconscious screening of stimuli by consumers through selective exposure, selective attention, perceptive defence, and perceptual blocking.

How does she manage to do this? All of us make use of four types of selectivity to help us cope with our complex environment: selective exposure, selective attention, perceptual defence, and perceptual blocking.

Selective Exposure

Consumers actively seek out messages that they find pleasant or with which they are sympathetic, and they actively avoid painful or threatening ones. They also selectively expose themselves to advertisements that reassure them of the wisdom of their purchase decisions. For example, if the consumer in the supermarket were a vegetarian, she might refrain from walking by the meat or seafood to avoid exposing herself to "unpleasant' sights.

The fact that consumers choose the stimuli that they want to see has great implications for marketers. Marketers have to ensure that they choose the media that will ensure that consumers "tune in" to their messages; and even if marketers have chosen the right media, they need to pay close attention to the actual messages to make sure that consumers do not shut these messages out totally. Ensuring that marketing messages actually target the audiences is even more complex in the online environment, where consumers have greater control over what they expose themselves to. Internet Insight 5-1 discusses one way in which marketers can ensure that their online ads are seen without wasting too much money.

INTERNET INSIGHT 5-1
GETTING SELECTIVE EXPOSURE TO WORK FOR YOU

Advertising in any medium is expensive, and often it does not reach the target audience. Reaching the right consumers and making sure your ad dollars are working for you is even more difficult when you are advertising online, because consumers have greater control over what they see (and don't see!) online.

Google, the world's number-one search engine, has a pay-per-click advertising service called AdWords that can solve that problem for online marketers. Advertisers can buy the rights to words and terms relevant to their business. Whenever someone uses these terms while searching the internet, the advertiser's name, description, and URL appear next to the regular search results. What makes this service even more appealing to marketers is that they have to pay only when a searcher clicks on the ad. Although several companies can lay claims to the same words, AdWords lets only eight ads pop up for each search, with the higher positions going to the highest bidders. Companies can limit the exposure of their ads to users in their own country or let the ads to be seen by anyone searching the web with Google.

The cost per click was just five cents when the service began, but competition between advertisers has driven up the price in the United States for some key words to three dollars a click. In Canada, the service is yet to become popular, and consequently prices here are still low. Since the users clicking on the word have chosen the key terms for their search, companies can be sure that those users are interested in the firm's product or service.

The key to using AdWords effectively is to choose the words that you want to claim very carefully. If the words chosen are too general, too many consumers will see the ad and many of them may click on it, increasing your cost. As Mark Ive, president of Hallz.com, an online directory of reception venues based in Mississauga, Ontario, says, it is important to identify key search terms. "I don't go after the guy typing "'wedding'... it gets expensive." He holds the claim to more specific terms, such as "Ontario wedding" and "banquet hall." Ive prefers the latter term because it is a Canada expression and hence U.S. wedding magazines or suppliers have not bid for it (thus helping to keep the price low). Hallz.com ads generated 1400 clicks in a month (with displays of 40 000), and it cost the company only $71.80.[a]

[a] Kyle Marnoch, "Put Another Nickel In," *Profit Magazine*, March 2003, p. 53.

Source: The Strategic Council, Toronto. Quoted in Christopher Kelly, "What They Want, When They Want It," *Marketing Magazine*, May 5, 2003, p. 24.

Selective Attention

Consumers exercise a great deal of selectivity as to how much attention they give to commercial stimuli. They have a heightened awareness of stimuli that meet their needs or interests and minimal awareness of stimuli that are irrelevant to their needs. Thus, consumers are likely to notice ads for products that would satisfy their needs and disregard those in which they have no interest. Our hypothetical vegetarian supermarket consumer may not pay any attention to the pages that are devoted to meat or seafood ads in the weekly supermarket flyers.

http://adwords. google.com

There is nothing like a prolonged power interruption to create heightened awareness of our dependence on electricity and the disruptions to daily life caused by the loss of electricity. Two parts of Canada experienced power outages in the second half of 2003—the Toronto area had a blackout, and Nova Scotia was ravaged by Hurricane Juan. Hedonics, a company that markets unique products to Canadians through a catalogue, used the heightened awareness that Canadians had in the fall of 2003 to market battery-operated products. The cover of its fall-winter issue for the year (see Exhibit 5-4) asked, "Where were you when the lights went

EXHIBIT 5-4

AN AD MAKING USE OF SELECTIVE ATTENTION

Courtesy of Hedonics.

out?" and it featured a range of battery-powered products.

People also vary in the kinds of information they are interested in and the form of message and type of medium they prefer. Some people are more interested in price, some in appearance, and some in social acceptability. Some people like complex, sophisticated messages; others like simple graphics.

Perceptual Defence

Consumers subconsciously screen out stimuli that they find psychologically threatening, even though exposure has already taken place. Thus, threatening or otherwise damaging stimuli are less likely to be consciously perceived than are neutral stimuli at the same level of exposure. Furthermore, individuals sometimes unconsciously distort information that is not consistent with their needs, values, and beliefs. For example, teenagers and young adults who see the warning labels on cigarette packages are likely to block out these messages or distort the information to suit their beliefs, as indicated in the following statement from a teenager:

When asked about the impact of such anti-smoking warnings and ads on young people, Rhea, a 22-year-old who started smoking when she was 13, says she and her friends "make fun of those ads... they are not effective at all. Most people who smoke in their teens think they are never going to die and smoking isn't going to do anything because it hasn't done anything yet."[8]

Marketers often try to combat *perceptual defence* by varying and increasing the amount of sensory input.

Perceptual Blocking

Consumers protect themselves from being bombarded with stimuli by simply "tuning out"—blocking such stimuli from conscious awareness. They do so for self-protection because of the visually overwhelming nature of the world in which we live. The popularity of such devices as TiVo and ReplayTV, which enable viewers to skip over television commercials with great ease, is, in part, a result of **perceptual blocking**.

Personal video recorders (PVRs) have marketers scrambling to find new ways of getting consumers' attention. Unlike the traditional video recorders, PVRs have embedded hard drives that can store 30 to 80 hours of television programs. Even more worrisome to marketers is the fact that PVRs can be programmed to skip or "zap" commercials. The Bell ExpressVu model 5800, for example, can store up to 55 hours of programming on its 80-gigabyte hard drive. This has marketers worried about the usefulness of traditional commercials.[9]

Figure 5-5 provides information on other methods that consumers use to avoid advertising.

Factors Affecting Perceptual Selection

Since consumers are selective in what they perceive, marketers are interested in finding out how to make sure consumers see (or are exposed to) marketing stimuli

Perceptual blocking: The subconscious screening out stimuli that are threatening or inconsistent wih our needs, values, beliefs, or attributes.

| FIGURE 5-5 | How Consumers Block Messages from Marketers | | | | | |

WAY OF BLOCKING	TOTAL N = 1285	15–19 N = 120	20–29 N = 204	30–39 N = 246	40–49 N = 270	50+ N = 445
Change TV channels	61%	83%	79%	66%	64%	43%
Use mute button	18	7	7	14	14	29
Leave room or walk away	14	8	9	13	17	29
Shut down or delete pop-up ads	14	25	22	15	13	8
Switch radio stations	13	23	21	17	13	1
Do something else	12	7	7	11	13	15
Turn it off	7	10	8	6	6	7
Fast forward through ads	6	1	4	5	8	9
Get food or drink	6	3	2	5	7	10
Avoid the website	5	7	5	7	4	3
Do household task	4	2	3	3	4	5
Ignore it	4	2	4	2	3	6
Read something	3	1	1	1	2	7

N = the number of respondents; percentages do not add up to 100 as more than one response was accepted.
Source: Courtesy of *Marketing Magazine*

and pay attention to them. Which stimuli are selected by consumers depends on (1) the nature of the stimulus itself, (2) consumers' *previous experience* as it affects their *expectations* (what they are prepared, or "set," to see), and (3) their *motives* at the time (their needs, desires, interests, and so on). Each of these factors can increase or decrease the probability that a stimulus will be perceived.

Nature of the Stimulus Marketing stimuli include an enormous number of variables that affect the consumer's perception, such as the *nature* of the product, its *physical attributes,* the *package* design, the *brand* name, the *advertisements* and commercials (including claims made for the product, colour, level of contrast in the ad, choice and sex of model, positioning of model, size of ad, typography, use of white space, etc.), the *position* of a print ad or a commercial, and the *editorial* environment.

In general, *contrast* is one of the most attention-compelling attributes of a stimulus. Advertisers often use extreme attention-getting devices to achieve maximum contrast and, thus, penetrate the consumer's perceptual "screen." For example, a number of magazines and newspapers carry ads that readers can unfold to reveal oversized, poster-like advertisements for products ranging from cosmetics to cars, because of the "stopping power" of giant ads among more traditional-sized ones. However, advertising does not have to be unique to achieve a high degree of differentiation; it simply has to contrast with the environment in which it is run. The use of a dramatic image of the product against a white background with little copy in a print advertisement, the absence of sound in a commercial's opening scene, a 60-second commercial within a string of 20-second spots—all offer sufficient contrast from their environments to achieve differentiation and attract the consumer's attention. Exhibit 5-5 illustrates the attention-getting nature of a dramatic image of a product in an advertisement. In an effort to achieve contrast, advertisers are also using splashes of colour in black-and-white print ads to highlight the product they are advertising.

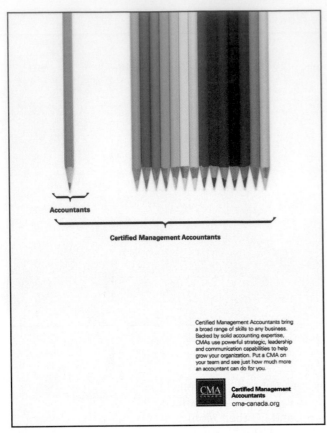

EXHIBIT 5-5

DRAMATIC IMAGES AND CONTRAST ATTRACT ATTENTION

Reprinted with the permission of Certified Management Accountants of Canada.

When they design packaging, astute marketers usually try to differentiate their packages to ensure that they are perceived rapidly by the consumer. Since the average package on the supermarket shelf has about one-tenth of a second to make an impression on the consumer, it is important that every aspect of the package—the name, shape, colour, label, and copy—provide sufficient sensory stimulation to be noted and remembered.

Sometimes advertisers capitalize on the lack of contrast (e.g., by making a television commercial so similar to the storyline of a program that viewers are unaware they are watching an advertisement until they are well into it). In print advertising, some advertisers run print ads (called *advertorials*) that closely resemble editorial matter, making it increasingly difficult for readers to tell them apart. Also, advertisers are producing 30-minute commercials (called *infomercials*) that appear to the average viewer as documentaries and, thus, command more attentive viewing than obvious commercials would receive.

Consumer Expectations People usually see what they expect to see, and what they expect to see is usually based on familiarity, previous experience, or preconditioned set (expectations). In a marketing context, people tend to perceive products and product attributes according to their own expectations. A student who has been told by his friends that a particular professor is interesting and dynamic will probably perceive the professor in that manner when the class begins; a teenager who attends a horror movie that has been billed as terrifying will probably find it so. However, stimuli that conflict sharply with expectations often receive more attention than those that conform to expectations (see Exhibit 5-6A and 5-6B).

For years, certain advertisers have used blatant sexuality in advertisements for products to which sex is not relevant, in the belief that such advertisements would attract a high degree of attention. However, ads containing irrelevant sexuality often defeat the marketer's objectives because readers tend to remember the sexual aspects of the ad (e.g., the innuendo or the model), not the product or brand advertised. Nevertheless, some advertisers continue to use erotic appeals in promoting a wide variety of products, from office furniture to jeans. (The use of sex in advertising is discussed in Chapter 8.)

Motives People tend to perceive the things they need or want: the stronger the need, the greater the tendency to ignore unrelated stimuli in the environment. A student who is looking for a new cell phone provider is more likely to notice and read carefully the ads for deals and special offers regarding such services than is his roommate, who may be satisfied with his present cellular service. In general, there is a heightened awareness of stimuli that are relevant to one's needs and interests and a decreased awareness of stimuli that are irrelevant to those needs. An indi-

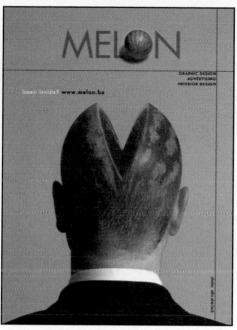

EXHIBIT 5-6

THE UNEXPECTED
ATTRACTS
ATTENTION

Courtesy of The Home Depot;
Courtesy of Melon. Photo by
John Sherlock.

vidual's perceptual process simply attunes itself more closely to those elements in the environment that are important to that person. Someone who is hungry is more likely to notice ads for food; a sexually repressed person may perceive sexual symbolism where none exists.

Marketing managers recognize the efficiency of targeting their products to the perceived needs of consumers. For example, a marketer can determine through marketing research what consumers consider to be the ideal attributes of the product category or what consumers perceive their needs to be in relation to the product category. The marketer can then segment the market on the basis of those needs and vary the product advertising so that consumers in each segment will perceive the product as meeting their own special needs, wants, and interests.

Perceptual Organization

People do not experience the numerous stimuli they select from the environment as separate and discrete sensations; rather, they tend to organize them into groups and perceive them as unified wholes. Thus, the perceived characteristics of even the simplest stimulus are viewed as a function of the whole to which the stimulus appears to belong. This method of perceptual organization simplifies life considerably for the individual.

The specific principles underlying perceptual organization are often referred to by the name given the school of psychology that first developed it: **Gestalt psychology.** (*Gestalt,* in German, means pattern or configuration.) Three of the most basic principles of perceptual organization are *figure and ground, grouping,* and *closure.*

Gestalt psychology: The study of principles of how people organize or configure stimuli.

Figure and Ground

As was noted earlier, stimuli that contrast with their environment are more likely to be noticed. A sound must be louder or softer to be noticed, a colour brighter or paler. The simplest visual illustration consists of a figure on a ground (i.e., background). The figure is perceived more clearly because, in contrast to its ground, it appears to be well defined, solid, and in the forefront. The ground is usually perceived as indefinite, hazy, and continuous. The common line that separates the figure and the ground is generally attributed to the figure rather than to the ground, which helps give the figure greater definition.

Consider the stimulus of music. People can either "bathe" in music or listen to music. In the first case, music is simply background to other activities; in the second, it is figure. Figure is more clearly perceived because it appears to be dominant; in contrast, ground appears to be subordinate and, therefore, less important.

People have a tendency to organize their perceptions into **figure-and-ground** relationships.

A short time after the terrorist attacks on the World Trade Center on September 11, 2001, a professor came across an ad for Lufthansa (Germany's national airline) that featured a photograph of a jet flying between two glass high-rise buildings. Rather than focusing on the brand and the jet (i.e., the "figure"), all the viewer could think about was the two tall glass towers in the background (i.e., the "ground"), and the possibility that the jet might crash into them. When the professor showed the ad to his students, many expressed the same thoughts. Clearly, this figure-ground reversal was the outcome of the painful events that occurred in September 2001.

Advertisers have to plan their advertisements carefully to make sure that the stimulus they want noted is seen as figure and not as ground. The musical background must not overwhelm the jingle; the background of an advertisement must not detract from the product. Print advertisers often silhouette their products against an indistinct background to make sure that the features they want noted are clearly perceived. We are all familiar with figure-ground patterns, such as the picture of the woman in Figure 5-6. How old would you say she is? Look again very carefully. Depending on how you perceived figure and how you perceived ground, she can be either in her early twenties or her late seventies.

Marketers sometimes run advertisements that confuse the consumer because there is no clear indication of which is figure and which is ground (see Exhibit 5-7). In this case, as in the well-known Absolut Vodka campaign, the blurring of figure and ground is deliberate. The Absolut campaign, which started more than 25 years ago, often runs print ads in which the figure (the shape of the Absolut bottle) is poorly delineated against its ground, challenging readers to search for the bottle; the resulting audience "participation" produces more intense scrutiny of the ad.

Figure and ground: The organization of perceptions into background and dominant (or figure) relationships.

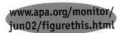
www.apa.org/monitor/jun02/figurethis.html

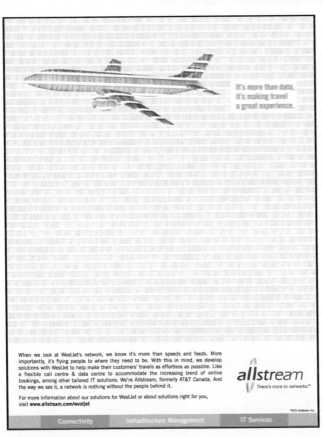

EXHIBIT 5-7

FIGURE-AND-GROUND REVERSAL

Courtesy of Allstream Corp.

Grouping

People tend to group stimuli so that they form a unified picture or impression. The perception of stimuli as groups or chunks of information, rather

FIGURE 5-6   Figure-and-Ground Reversal

than as discrete bits of information, makes them easier to remember. **Grouping** can be used advantageously by marketers to imply certain desired meanings in connection with their products. For example, an advertisement for tea may show a young man and woman sipping tea in a beautifully appointed room before a blazing hearth. The overall mood implied by the grouping of stimuli leads the consumer to associate the drinking of tea with romance, fine living, and winter warmth.

Most of us can remember and repeat our Social Insurance Number because we automatically group it into three "*chunks,*" rather than try to remember nine separate numbers. Similarly, we remember and say our phone number in three segments—the area code, first three digits, and last four digits.

Closure

Individuals have a need for **closure**. They express this need by organizing their perceptions so that they form a complete picture. If the pattern of stimuli to which individuals are exposed is incomplete, they tend to perceive it, nevertheless, as complete; that is, they consciously or subconsciously fill in the missing pieces. Thus, a circle with a section of its periphery missing is invariably perceived as a circle, not an arc.

Grouping:
The tendency to organize information into chunks or groups to facilitate memorization and recall.

Closure:
The need to complete incomplete patterns.

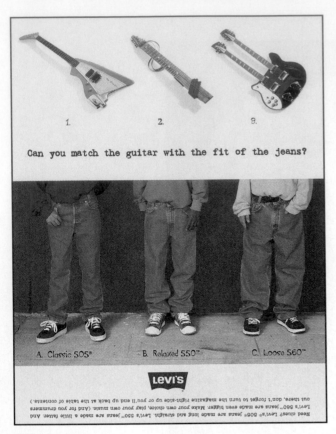

Can you match the guitar with the fit of the jeans?

A. Classic 505®   B. Relaxed 550™   C. Loose 560™

Levi's

Need closer? Levi's® 505® jeans are made long and straight. Levi's 550™ jeans are made a little fatter. And Levi's 560™ jeans are made even bigger. Make your own choice, play your own music. (And for you drummers out there, don't forget to turn the magazine right-side up or you'll end up back at the table of contents.)

EXHIBIT 5-8

USING THE NEED FOR CLOSURE TO INCREASE ATTENTION

© 1995 Levi Strauss & Company.

Incomplete messages or tasks are remembered better than completed ones. One explanation for this phenomenon is that a person who hears the beginning of a message or who begins a task develops a need to complete it. If he or she is prevented from doing so, a state of tension is created that manifests itself in improved memory for the incomplete task. For example, hearing the beginning of a message leads to the need to hear the rest of it—like waiting for the second shoe to drop.

The need for closure has interesting implications for marketers. Promotional messages in which viewers are required to "fill in" information beg for completion by consumers, and the very act of completion involves them more deeply in the message (see Exhibit 5-8). Similarly, advertisers have discovered that they can achieve excellent results by using the soundtrack of a well-known television commercial on radio. Consumers who are familiar with the television commercial perceive the audio track alone as incomplete; in their need for completion, they mentally play back the visual content from memory.

In summary, it is clear that perceptions are neither equivalent to the raw sensory input of discrete stimuli, nor equivalent to the sum total of discrete stimuli. Rather, people tend to add to or subtract from stimuli to which they are exposed on the basis of their expectations and motives, using generalized principles of organization that are explained by Gestalt theory.

Perceptual Interpretation

The preceding discussion has emphasized that perception is a personal phenomenon. People exercise selectivity as to which stimuli they perceive, and they organize these stimuli on the basis of certain psychological principles. The interpretation of stimuli is also uniquely individual, because it is based on

- what individuals expect to see in light of their previous experience;
- the number of plausible explanations they can envision; and
- their motives and interests at the time of perception.

Stimuli are often highly ambiguous. Some stimuli are weak because of such factors as poor visibility, brief exposure, high noise level, or constant fluctuation. Even stimuli that are strong tend to fluctuate dramatically because of different angles of viewing, varying distances, changing levels of illumination, and so on. Consumers usually attribute the sensory input they receive to sources they consider most likely to have caused the specific pattern of stimuli. Past experiences and social interactions help to form certain expectations that provide categories (or alternative explanations) that individuals use in interpreting stimuli. The narrower the individual's experience, the more limited the access to alternative categories.

When stimuli are highly ambiguous, an individual will usually interpret them in such a way that they serve to fulfill personal needs, wishes, interests, and so on. It is this principle that provides the rationale for the projective tests discussed in Chapter 3. Such tests provide ambiguous stimuli (such as incomplete sentences, unclear pictures, untitled cartoons, or ink blots) to respondents who are asked to interpret them. How a person describes a vague illustration, or what meaning the individual ascribes to an ink blot, is a reflection, not of the stimulus itself, but of the subject's own needs, wants, and desires. Through the interpretation of ambiguous stimuli, respondents reveal a great deal about themselves.

How close a person's interpretations are to reality, then, depends on the clarity of the stimulus, the past experiences of the perceiver, and his or her motives and interests at the time of perception.

Perceptual Distortion

Individuals are subject to a number of influences that tend to distort their perceptions; some of these are discussed next.

Physical Appearances People tend to attribute the qualities they associate with certain people to others who may resemble them, whether or not they consciously recognize the similarity. For this reason, the selection of models for print advertisements and television commercials can be a crucial element in their ultimate persuasiveness. Studies have found that attractive models are more persuasive and have a more positive influence on consumer attitudes and behaviour than average-looking models; attractive men are perceived as more successful businessmen than average-looking men. Some research suggests that models influence consumers' perceptions of physical attractiveness and, through comparisons, their own self-perceptions.[10] Recent research, however, has found that merely choosing a highly attractive model may not make a message more effective. One study revealed that highly attractive models are perceived as having more expertise regarding enhancing products (e.g., jewellery, lipstick, perfume) but not regarding problem-solving products (e.g., products that correct beauty flaws such as acne or dandruff).[11] Therefore, advertisers must ensure that there is a rational match between the product advertised and the physical attributes of the model used to promote it.

Stereotypes Individuals tend to carry pictures in their minds of the meanings of various kinds of stimuli. These stereotypes serve as expectations of what specific situations, people, or events will be like, and they are important determinants of how such stimuli are subsequently perceived.

An ad for Benetton featuring two men—one black and one white—handcuffed together, which was part of the "united colors of Benetton" campaign promoting racial harmony, produced a public outcry because people thought it depicted a white man arresting a black man.[12] Clearly, this perception was the result of stereotypes, since there was nothing in the ad to suggest that the white person was arresting the black person rather than the other way around.

www.benetton.com

First Impressions First impressions tend to be lasting; yet, in forming such impressions, the perceiver does not yet know which stimuli are relevant, important, or predictive of later behaviour. A shampoo commercial effectively used the line "You'll never have a second chance to make a first impression." Since first impressions are often lasting, it may prove fatal to the ultimate success of a new product to introduce it before it has been perfected; subsequent information about its advantages, even if true, will often be negated by the memory of its early performance.

Jumping to Conclusions Many people tend to jump to conclusions before examining all the relevant evidence. For example, the consumer may hear just the beginning of a commercial message and draw conclusions about the product or service being advertised. For this reason, some copywriters are careful to give their most persuasive arguments first.

In a recent study, a series of laboratory experiments tried to determine how the shape of food packaging affected consumers' perceptions of content volume. The study found that most consumers do not read the volume information on food labels; rather, they buy packages that they believe contain more of the product, whether or not this is actually so. For example, consumers perceived elongated packages to contain more than round packages. The studies also found a positive correlation between perceived product volume and consumption. Thus, the products inside packages that were perceived to hold more volume when purchased were also consumed faster after the purchase.[13]

Clearly, these findings have important implications for package design, advertising, and pricing.

Halo Effect Historically, the phenomenon of the halo effect has been used to describe situations in which the evaluation of a single object or person on a multitude of dimensions is based on the evaluation of just one or a few dimensions (e.g., a man is trustworthy, fine, and noble because he looks you in the eye when he speaks). Consumer behaviourists broaden the notion of the halo effect to include the evaluation of multiple objects (e.g., a product line) on the basis of the evaluation of just one dimension (a brand name or a spokesperson). Using this broader definition, marketers take advantage of the halo effect when they extend a brand name associated with one line of products to another. The lucrative field of *licensing* is based on the halo effect. Manufacturers and retailers hope to acquire instant recognition and status for their products by associating them with a well-known name. (Chapter 7 discusses licensing in greater detail.)

Despite the many subjective influences on perceptual interpretation, individuals usually resolve stimulus ambiguity somewhat realistically on the basis of their previous experiences. Only in situations of unusual or changing stimulus conditions do expectations lead to wrong interpretations.

CONSUMER IMAGERY

Consumer imagery: The enduring perceptions or images of products, prices, and product quality that consumers develop using various stimuli.

Consumers have a number of enduring perceptions, or images, that are particularly relevant to the study of consumer behaviour. Products and brands have symbolic value for individuals, who evaluate them on the basis of their consistency (congruence) with their personal pictures of themselves. Chapter 4 discussed consumer self-images and how consumers attempt to preserve or enhance their self-images by buying products and patronizing services that they believe are congruent with their self-images and by avoiding those that are not. The following section examines consumers' perceived images of products, brands, services, prices, and product quality.

Product Positioning

Positioning: Developing a distinct image for the product or service in the mind of the consumer in order to differentiate the offering from those of competitors.

The essence of successful marketing is the image that a product has in the mind of the consumer—that is, its **positioning**. Positioning is more important to the ultimate success of a product than are its actual characteristics, although products that are poorly made will not succeed in the long run on the basis of image alone. The core of effective positioning is a unique position that the product occupies in the mind of the consumer, usually relative to competition. Most new products fail because they are perceived as "me too" offerings that do not offer any advantages or unique benefits over competitive products.

Marketers of different brands in the same category can effectively differentiate their offerings only if they stress the *benefits* that their brands provide rather than their products' physical features. The benefits featured in a product's positioning must pertain to attributes that are important to and in keeping with the perceptions of the targeted consumer segment.

The two energy bars, NutriGrain and Balance, probably have quite similar nutritional composition and physical characteristics; however, each one of the two brands is clearly positioned to offer a distinct benefit. NutriGrain is positioned as an alternative to unhealthy snack foods in the morning, and Balance is positioned as an energy-providing product for the late afternoon.

Positioning strategy is the essence of the marketing mix; it complements the company's definition of the competition, its segmentation strategy, and its selection of target markets. For example, in its positioning as a breakfast food, NutriGrain competes with other breakfast foods. Through research, the manufacturer has determined the characteristics of persons who are concerned about their health and appearance (yet eat unhealthy breakfast foods such as doughnuts) and the media that they read, listen to, and watch. (The marketers of Balance must determine the characteristics of those who need a pick-me-up in the late afternoon and their media habits and develop a marketing plan that reflects all these elements.)

Positioning conveys the concept, or meaning, of the product or service in terms of how it fulfills a consumer need. A good positioning strategy should

- provide a meaning that is congruent with the consumer's needs; and
- feature the brand against its competition.

The classic 7-Up slogan "The Un-Cola" was designed to appeal to consumers' desire for an alternative to the most popular soft drink (by using the prefix *un*), while also elevating the product by placing it in the same league with its giant competitor (hence the word *cola*). A successful positioning strategy will

- create a distinctive brand image that consumers rely on when they choose a product;
- lead to consumer loyalty, positive beliefs about brand value, and a willingness to search for the brand;
- promote consumer interest in future brand promotions;
- *inoculate* consumers against competitors' marketing activities; and
- influence consumer beliefs about the brand's attributes and the prices consumers are willing to pay for it.[14]

In today's highly competitive environment, a distinctive product image is most important but also very difficult to create and maintain. As products become more complex and the marketplace more crowded, consumers rely more on the product's image and claimed benefits than on its actual attributes when they decide what to buy. The major positioning strategies are discussed in Figure 5-7. Which one of McDonald's positioning statements do you like? Why?

Product Repositioning

Regardless of how well positioned a product appears to be, the marketer may be forced to reposition it in response to market events, such as a competitor cutting into

Repositioning: Attempting to change the image that consumers have of a product.

FIGURE 5-7	Alternative Positioning Strategies
STRATEGY	**THEME AND EXAMPLE**
Umbrella positioning	Creating an overall image of the company around which a lot of products can be featured individually. Suitable for very large corporations with diversified product lines.
	McDonald's positioning approaches over the years: "You deserve a break today at McDonald's," "Nobody can do it like McDonald's can," "Good times, great taste," and the current "I'm lovin' it."
Positioning against the competition	Picking a competitor (usually the leader in the industry) and positioning a brand against it.
	Visa's former slogan "We make American Express green with envy."
Positioning based on a specific benefit	Depicting one crucial benefit of the brand.
	FedEx: "When it absolutely, positively has to be there overnight." Conveys the benefits of its reliable service.
Finding an "unowned" position	Finding a niche unfilled by other companies.
	Topol became a success because it was positioned as the smokers' toothpaste.
Filling several positions	Filling more than one unfilled gap or "unowned" perceptual position with more than one product offering in the same product category
	Tylenol's introduction of a number of products, such as Tylenol, Extra Strength Tylenol, Tylenol Arthritis Pain, Tylenol PM, and Aflexa.

the brand's market share or too many competitors stressing the same attribute. For example, rather than trying to meet the lower prices of high-quality private-label competition, some premium-brand marketers have repositioned their brands to justify their higher prices, playing up brand attributes that had previously been ignored.

Another reason to reposition a product or service is to satisfy changing consumer preferences.

When health-oriented consumers began to avoid high-fat foods, many fast food chains acted swiftly to reposition their images by offering salad bars and other supposedly healthy foods. Kentucky Fried Chicken changed its well-known corporate name to KFC so that it could omit the dreaded word "fried" from its advertising. Weight Watchers repositioned its line of frozen foods from "dietetic" to "healthy," maintaining its diet-thin imagery while responding to a shift in consumer values. As birthrates declined and consumers' preferences for gentler and purer products emerged, Johnson & Johnson repositioned its baby lotion, powder, and shampoo as products for grown-ups.

One of the most successful product repositionings is the promotion of Arm & Hammer washing soda as *the* standard for cleanliness and purity by showing it used to deodorize garbage cans, remove wax from fresh produce, remove the residue of hair styling products, and make a facial scrub.[15]

http://armandhammer.com/myhome/tour.asp

Perceptual mapping: A technique used to determine how consumers perceive a company's products—either in relation to other products or in regard to key attributes.

Perceptual Mapping

The technique of **perceptual mapping** helps marketers to determine just how their products or services appear to consumers in relation to competitive brands on one or more relevant characteristics. It enables marketers to see gaps in the positioning of all brands in the product or service class and to identify areas in which consumer needs are not being adequately met.

Research Insight 5-1 provides more details on how to develop perceptual maps.

RESEARCH INSIGHT 5-1
POSITIONING AND REPOSITIONING A PRODUCT WITH PERCEPTUAL MAPPING

Perceptual mapping is a way for companies to see how their products are perceived by consumers, and, if consumer perceptions are not positive, to find ways to reposition their products. There are two basic approaches to perceptual mapping:

- Attribute-based approaches, which assess products on key attributes.
- Non-attribute-based approaches, which use summary judgments of products based on the similarity of various brands.

Let us look each in more detail, using the toothpaste market as an example.

Attribute-Based Approach

The basic steps in an attribute-based approach to perceptual mapping are as follows:

- Identify the number of dimensions (or attributes) that consumers use to distinguish between brands.
- Rate the brands on these attributes.
- Ask consumers for their ideal level of these attributes.

For example, a survey of consumers might indicate that they use two attributes—ability to prevent cavities and freshen breath—to differentiate between brands. The next step would be to have consumers rate each brand on these two dimensions (on, for example, a five-point scale, with 1 being "poor" and 5 being "excellent"). For example, Crest and Colgate might get ratings of almost "5" on cavity prevention but only a "3" on the ability to freshen breath. Finally, you would ask each consumer to also state their ideal level of each attribute (on a five-point scale). This might result in a perceptual map similar to the one in Figure A.

Note that the size of the circle indicates the number of consumers who consider those to be the ideal levels of the attributes that a brand should possess. How would you interpret this perceptual map?

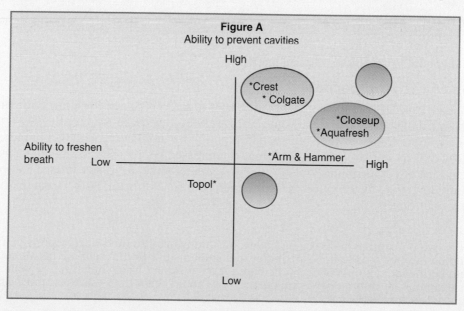

Figure A
Ability to prevent cavities

High

*Crest
* Colgate

*Closeup
*Aquafresh

Ability to freshen breath   Low ——————— *Arm & Hammer ——————— High

Topol*

Low

Non-Attribute-Based Approach

If you plan to use a non-attribute-based approach to perceptual mapping, you would do the following:

- List all brands and identify all possible pairs.
- Ask consumers to arrange the pairs in order of similarity (most similar, next most similar, etc). If there are too many brands, you can first ask them to arrange them in piles (extremely similar, similar, dissimilar, extremely dissimilar), and then rank the pairs in each pile.
- Identify the underlying dimensions by means of computer programs such as multi-dimensional scaling.

To illustrate, let us say that the following is a complete list of all toothpaste brands—Crest, Colgate, Aquafresh, Closeup, Topol, and Arm & Hammer. Then the total number of possible pairs would be 15 $[(n[n — 1])/2$ or $(6[5])/2]$. Consumers would be asked to rank the pairs in terms of similarity. Let us assume that Crest and Colgate were considered to be the most similar, while Crest and Topol were considered to be the most dissimilar. Aquafresh and Closeup may also be ranked as quite similar and somewhat similar to Topol and Arm & Hammer; the latter two may be ranked as similar to each other. With the help of a computer program, you might be able to develop a two-dimensional map of consumer perceptions similar to the one given in Figure B; however, you would have to name the dimensions yourself. Once you have named them, you can ask consumers for the ideal level of each attribute that a toothpaste should possess.

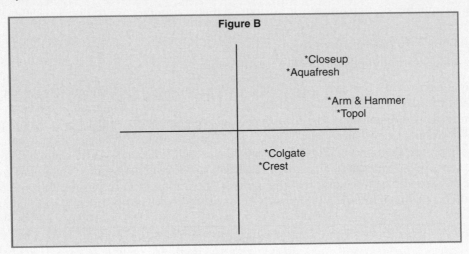

Figure B

How would you interpret this perceptual map?

Comparison of the Approaches

Attribute-based approaches lead to results that are easier to interpret since consumers rate the brands on pre-determined attributes. This approach would work well if (1) you can identify the key attributes that consumers use to differentiate between brands, and (2) if their overall perception of a brand is the sum of their perceptions of it on the key attributes. Non-attribute-based approaches assume that consumers may not have a clear idea of the attributes they use to differentiate between brands. It does not force them to use the attributes developed by the researcher. However, because of this, the results from this approach are often difficult to interpret.

QUESTIONS:

1. Interpret the two perceptual maps. Using Figure A, state which products need repositioning.
2. What would be the two most critical attributes that students use to differentiate between textbooks? What would be the ideal points of each attribute for a textbook? Using any three of your texts and this one as examples, develop a perceptual map of textbooks. How does this text score? Should it be repositioned? If so, how?

Perceived Price

How a consumer perceives a price—as high, low, or fair—has a strong influence on both purchase intentions and purchase satisfaction. Consider the perception of price fairness, for example. There is some evidence that customers do pay attention to the prices paid by other customers (such as senior citizens, frequent flyers, and affinity club members), and that the differential pricing strategies used by some marketers are considered unfair by customers not eligible for the special prices. No one is happy knowing he or she paid twice as much for an airplane ticket or a theatre ticket as the person in the next seat. Perceptions of price unfairness affect consumers' perceptions of product value and, ultimately, their willingness to patronize a store or a service. One study of the special challenges of service industries in pricing intangible products proposed three types of pricing strategies that are based on the customer's perception of the value provided by the purchase (see Figure 5-8).

Perceived price:
Consumers' perceptions of price as fair, high, or low.

Reference Prices

Products advertised as "on sale" tend to create enhanced customer perceptions of savings and value. Different formats used in sales advertisements have different impacts, depending on consumer **reference prices**. A reference price is any price that a consumer uses as a basis for comparison in judging another price. Reference prices can be external or internal. An advertiser generally uses a higher *external reference price* ("sold elsewhere at...") in an ad offering a lower sales price, to persuade the consumer that the product advertised is a really good buy. *Internal reference prices* are those prices (or price ranges) retrieved by the consumer from his or her memory. Internal reference points are thought to play a major role in consumers' evaluations of the value of an advertised (external) price deal, as well as the believability of any advertised reference price. Advertised prices (both reference and sales prices) are likely to affect consumers' internal reference prices (e.g., higher advertised prices lead to higher internal reference prices).[16]

Reference price:
The price that a consumer uses as a basis for comparison in judging another price.

Several studies have investigated the effects on consumer price perceptions of three types of advertised reference prices: plausible low, plausible high, and implausible high. *Plausible low* prices are well within the range of acceptable market prices; *plausible high* are near the outer limits of the range but not beyond the realm of believability, and *implausible high* are well above the consumer's perceived range of

---

FIGURE 5-8   Three Pricing Strategies Focused on Perceived Value

PRICING STRATEGY	PROVIDES VALUE BY . . .	IMPLEMENTED AS . . .
Satisfaction-based pricing	Recognizing and reducing customers' perceptions of uncertainty, which the intangible nature of services magnifies	Service guarantees Benefit-driven pricing Flat-rate pricing
Relationship pricing	Encouraging long-term relationships with the company that customers view as beneficial	Long-term contracts Price bundling
Efficiency pricing	Sharing with customers the cost savings that the company has achieved by understanding, managing, and reducing the costs of providing the service	Cost-leader pricing

Source: Leonard L. Berry and Yadav S. Manjit, "Capture and Communicate Value in the Pricing of Services," *Sloan Management Review*, Summer 1996, 41–51.

acceptable market prices. As long as an advertised reference price is within a given consumer's acceptable price range, it is considered plausible and is assimilated. (See assimilation-contrast theory in Chapter 7.) If the advertised reference point is outside the range of acceptable prices (i.e., implausible), it will be *contrasted* and thus will not be perceived as a valid reference point. This will adversely affect both consumer evaluations and the advertiser's image of credibility.[17]

Tensile and Objective Price Claims

The semantic cues (i.e., specific wording) of the phrase used to communicate the price-related information may affect consumers' price perceptions. **Tensile price claims** (e.g., "save 10 percent to 40 percent," "save up to 60 percent," "save 20 percent or more") are used to promote a range of price discounts for a product line, an entire department, or sometimes an entire store. In contrast to tensile cues, **objective price claims** provide a single discount level (e.g., "save 25 percent"). Because of the broader range of sale merchandise that is covered by both tensile and objective price claims, they are likely to generate more store traffic and sales than are reference price advertisements promoting individual products. Generally, ads that state a maximum discount level ("save up to 40 percent") are more effective than ads stating the minimum discount level ("save 10 percent or more") and ads stating a discount range ("save 10 percent to 40 percent").[18]

Consumer reactions to tensile price claims are affected by the *width* of the discount range. Several studies examined the effects of the three forms of tensile price claims (advertising a minimum, a maximum, or a range of savings) on consumers' price perceptions and on their search and shopping intentions. The studies found that, for *broader* discount ranges, tensile claims stating the maximum level of savings have more positive effects than those stating the minimum level or the entire savings range. For more *narrow* discount ranges, tensile claims stating the maximum level of savings appear to be no more effective than are claims stating the minimum level or the entire savings range.[19]

An experiment examining the effects of a "bundle price" (the marketing of two or more products or services in a single package for a special price) on consumer price perceptions found that additional savings offered directly on the bundle have a greater relative impact on buyers' perceptions of transaction value than do savings offered on the bundle's individual items.[20] Consumers are less sensitive to price when they use credit cards than when they use cash. Similarly, a recent study reported that consumers tend to be less sensitive to price when they shop online than when they shop in stores.[21]

Perceived Quality

Consumers often judge the quality of a product or service on the basis of a variety of informational cues that they associate with the product. Some of these cues are **intrinsic** to the product or service, whereas others are **extrinsic**. Either singly or in composite, such cues are the basis for perceptions of product and service quality.

Cues that are *intrinsic* concern the physical characteristics of the product itself, such as size, colour, flavour, or aroma. In some cases, consumers use physical characteristics (e.g., the flavour of ice cream or cake) to judge product quality. Consumers like to believe that they base their evaluations of product quality on intrinsic cues, because that enables them to justify their product decisions (either positive or negative) as being "rational" or "objective" product choices. More often than not, however, they use extrinsic characteristics to judge quality. For example, though many consumers claim they buy a brand because of its superior taste, they are often unable to identify that brand in blind taste tests.

Tensile price claims: Promoting a range of price discounts for an entire product line, department, or store.

Objective price claims: Promoting a single discount level.

Perceived quality: Consumers' perceptions of product quality.

Intrinsic cues: Physical characteristics of the product such as size, colour, or flavour.

Extrinsic cues: Cues such as price or country of origin that are external to the product.

One study discovered that the consumer's ability to identify the flavour of a powdered fruit drink was determined more by the colour than by the label or the actual taste. The study's subjects perceived the purple or grape-coloured versions of the powdered product "tart" in flavour and the orange-coloured version as "flavorful, sweet, and refreshing."[22]

Consumer Reports found that people often cannot differentiate among various cola beverages and that they base their preferences on such *extrinsic cues* as packaging, pricing, advertising, and even peer pressure.[23] In the absence of actual experience with a product, consumers often evaluate quality on the basis of cues that are external to the product itself, such as price, brand image, manufacturer's image, retail store image, or even the country of origin.

Many consumers use *country-of-origin* stereotypes to evaluate products (e.g., "German engineering is excellent" or "Japanese cars are reliable"). Many American consumers believe that a "Made in U.S.A." label means a product is "superior" or "very good." Yet for food products, a foreign image is often more enticing.

Haagen-Dazs, an American-made ice cream, has been incredibly successful with its made-up (and meaningless) Scandinavian-sounding name. And the success of Smirnoff vodka, made in Connecticut, can be attributed partly to its so-called Russian derivation.

There are many other examples that support the notion that North American consumers are much more impressed with foreign foods than they are with domestic foods.

Price-Quality Relationship

Perceived product value has been described as a trade-off between the product's perceived benefits (or quality) and the perceived sacrifice—both monetary and nonmonetary—necessary to acquire it. A number of research studies have found that consumers rely on price as an indicator of quality, that they attribute different qualities to identical products that carry different price tags, and that such consumer characteristics as age and income affect the perception of value.[24] One study suggested that consumers using a **price-quality relationship** are actually relying on a well-known (and, hence, more expensive) brand name as an indicator of quality without actually relying directly on price per se.[25] A later study found out that consumers use price and brand to evaluate the prestige of the product but do not generally use these cues when they evaluate the product's performance.[26] Because price is so often considered an indicator of quality, some product advertisements deliberately emphasize a high price to underscore the marketers' claims of quality. Marketers understand that products with lower prices may sometimes be assumed to be of poor quality. At the same time, when consumers evaluate more concrete attributes of a product, such as performance and durability, they rely less on the price and brand name as indicators of quality than when they evaluate the product's prestige and symbolic value.[27] For these reasons, marketers must understand all the attributes that customers use to evaluate a product and include all applicable information in order to counter any perceptions of negative quality associated with a lower price.

In most consumption situations, in addition to price, consumers also use such cues as the brand and the store in which the product is bought to evaluate its quality. Figure 5-9 presents a conceptual model of the effects of price, brand name, and store name on perceived product quality.

In summary, consumers use price as a surrogate indicator of quality if they have little information to go on, or if they have little confidence in their own ability to

Price-quality relationship: Perceived relationship between the price of a product and its quality.

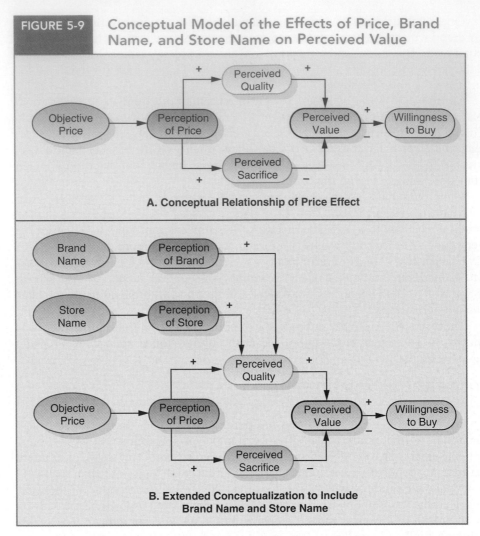

FIGURE 5-9   Conceptual Model of the Effects of Price, Brand Name, and Store Name on Perceived Value

A. Conceptual Relationship of Price Effect

B. Extended Conceptualization to Include Brand Name and Store Name

Source: W.B. Dodds, K.B. Monroe, and Dhruv Grewal, "Effects of Price, Brand and Store Information on Buyers' Product Evaluations," *Journal of Marketing Research,* 28, August 1991, 308. Reprinted by permission.

choose a product or service on other grounds. When the consumer is familiar with a brand name or has experience with a product (or service) or the store where it is sold, price declines as a determining factor in product evaluation and purchase.

Perceived Risk

Consumers must constantly decide what products or services to buy and where to buy them. Because the consequences of such decisions are often uncertain, the consumer perceives some "risk" in making a purchase decision. **Perceived risk** is defined as the uncertainty that consumers face when they cannot foresee the consequences of their purchase decisions. This definition highlights two relevant dimensions of perceived risk: uncertainty and consequences.

The degree of risk that consumers perceive and their own tolerance for taking risks are factors that influence their purchase strategies. It should be stressed that consumers are influenced by the risks they perceive, whether or not such risks actu-

Perceived risk:
The uncertainty that consumers face when they cannot foresee the consequences of their purchase decisions.

ally exist. A risk that is not perceived—no matter how real or how dangerous—will not influence consumer behaviour. The major types of risks that consumers perceive when making product decisions are *functional risk, physical risk, financial risk, social risk, psychological risk, and time risk* (see Figure 5-10).

Factors Affecting Risk Perception

Consumer perception of risk varies, depending on the person, the product, the situation, and the culture. The amount of risk perceived depends on the specific consumer. Some consumers tend to perceive high degrees of risk in various consumption situations; others tend to perceive little risk. For example, studies of risk perception among adolescents have found that adolescents who engage in high-risk consumption activities (such as smoking or using drugs) have a lower perception of risk than those who do not engage in high-risk activities.[28] *High-risk perceivers* are often described as **narrow categorizers** because they limit their choices (e.g., product choices) to a few safe alternatives. They would rather exclude some perfectly good alternatives than chance a poor selection. *Low-risk perceivers* have been described as **broad categorizers** because they tend to make their choices from a much wider range of alternatives. They would rather risk a poor selection than limit the number of alternatives from which they can choose. One study concluded that risk preference may be a stable personality trait, with experience a mediating factor in risk perception.[29]

Narrow categorizers: People who limit their choices to a few safe alternatives.

Broad categorizers: People who make their choices from a wide range of alternatives.

A person's perception of risk varies with product categories. For example, consumers are likely to perceive a higher degree of risk (e.g., functional risk, financial risk, or time risk) in the purchase of a plasma television set than in the purchase of a car. In addition to *product-category* perceived risk, researchers have identified *product-specific* perceived risk.[30] One study found that consumers perceive service decisions to be riskier than product decisions, particularly in terms of social risk, physical risk, and psychological risk.[31]

The degree of risk perceived by a consumer is also affected by the shopping situation (e.g., a traditional retail store, online, catalogue, direct-mail solicitations, or door-to-door sales). The sharp increase in mail order catalogue sales in recent years suggests that on the basis of positive experiences and word of mouth, consumers now tend to perceive less risk in mail order shopping than they once did, despite

---

FIGURE 5-10   Types of Perceived Risk

Functional risk is the risk that the product will not perform as expected. ("Can the new PDA operate a full week without needing to be recharged?")

Physical risk is the risk to self and others that the product may pose. ("Is a cellular phone really safe, or does it emit harmful radiation?")

Financial risk is the risk that the product will not be worth its cost. ("Will a new and cheaper model of a plasma TV monitor become available six months from now?")

Social risk is the risk that a poor product choice may result in social embarrassment. ("Will my classmates laugh at my purple mohawk haircut?")

Psychological risk is the risk that a poor product choice will bruise the consumer's ego. ("Will I be embarrassed when I invite friends to listen to music on my five-year-old stereo?")

Time risk is the risk that the time spent in product search may be wasted if the product does not perform as expected. ("Will I have to go through the shopping effort all over again?")

their inability to inspect the merchandise before ordering. High-risk perceivers are unlikely to buy online despite the geometric expansion of online retailing. However, as they gain experience in online purchasing, it is likely that their levels of perceived risk regarding electronic buying will decline.

How Consumers Handle Risk

Consumers characteristically develop their own strategies for reducing perceived risk. These risk-reduction strategies enable them to act with greater confidence when making product decisions, even though the consequences of such decisions remain somewhat uncertain. Some of the more common risk-reduction strategies are discussed in the following sections.

Consumers Seek Information Consumers seek information about the product and product category from friends and family and from other people whose opinions they value, from salespeople, and from the general media. They spend more time thinking about their choice and search for more information about the alternative products when they associate a high degree of risk with the purchase. This strategy is straightforward and logical because the more information the consumer has about the product and the product category, the more predictable the probable consequences and, thus, the lower the perceived risk.

Consumers Are Brand-Loyal Consumers avoid risk by remaining loyal to a brand they have been satisfied with instead of buying new or untried brands. High-risk perceivers, for example, are more likely to be loyal to their old brands and less likely to buy newly introduced products.

Consumers Select by Brand Image When consumers have had no experience with a product, they tend to "trust" a favoured or well-known brand name. They often think well-known brands are better and are worth buying for the implied assurance of quality, dependability, performance, and service. Marketers' promotional efforts supplement the perceived quality of their products by helping to build and sustain a favourable brand image.

Consumers Rely on Store Image If consumers have no other information about a product, they often trust the judgment of the merchandise buyers of a reputable store to have chosen good-quality products. Store image also imparts the implication of product testing and the assurance of service, return privileges, and adjustment in case of dissatisfaction.

Consumers Buy the Most Expensive Model When in doubt, consumers often feel that the most expensive model probably has the best quality; that is, they equate price with quality. (The price-quality relationship was discussed earlier in this chapter.)

www.csa.ca

Consumers Seek Reassurance Consumers who are uncertain about their ability to make a wise choice seek reassurance through money-back guarantees, test results from government and private laboratories, warranties, and pre-purchase trials. For example, it is unlikely that anyone would buy a new model car without a test drive. Products that do not easily lend themselves to free or limited trial (such as a refrigerator) present a challenge to marketers.

PERCEPTION AND MARKETING STRATEGY

Since the way consumers choose, organize, and interpret information has a great influence on the way they see products, marketers have to pay particular attention to the concept of perception. Marketers can use the concepts covered in the earlier sections of this chapter in many ways.

Make perceptual selection work in your favour: Selectivity in perception influences the stimuli that a consumer allows herself to be exposed to and the attention she pays to these stimuli. Marketers can increase the chance that consumers will see and pay attention to their products and promotion in several ways:

- *Increase accidental exposure to marketing stimuli by placing ads in places where consumers are a captive audience.* Where are you likely to be caught staring at a wall or a door without a choice? A washroom, of course! Two Canadian companies—Montreal's Zoom Media and Toronto's NewAD Media—specialize in washroom ads. Both companies specialize in reaching the 18–34 age group by advertising in bars, clubs, restaurants, university and college campuses, gyms, and fitness centres. NewAD is in 192 health clubs, 76 colleges or universities, and 1883 bars and restaurants across the country, while Zoom is in 200 fitness clubs, 71 colleges or universities, 1600 restaurants or bars, and several McDonald's restaurants in Quebec. Together, they are well positioned to reach the young adult market, which constitutes 27 percent of the Canadian population.[32]

  www.newad.com

  www.zoom-media.com

  To increase accidental exposure to their products and promotions, companies have also started placing ads in such strategic spots as dental offices, grocery checkout counters, and other spots where consumers are likely to be held captive.

- *Increase the chances of your product being noticed by using the principle of j.n.d.* As discussed earlier (refer to Figure 5-1), Weber's law or j.n.d can be used by marketers to draw attention to their products by making sure that the changes to their product are noticed. In certain instances, when a company does not want attention to be drawn to a particular feature of a product, it can achieve this by making sure that the changes to the product remain just under the j.n.d.

- *Make sure consumers pay attention to your promotion by using principles such as contrast and colour and through unusual promotional tactics.* Marketers have several ways of breaking through the clutter; they can create more interesting and eye-catching advertisements or use unusual ways of promoting their products. One novel way of getting through the clutter is to use unconventional—and often inexpensive—promotions, sometimes called "guerrilla marketing" to catch consumers' attention.

  Discovery Channel did a unique three-week promotion for its program *Frontiers of Construction*. In Toronto and Calgary, it had actors dress as construction workers in *Frontiers of Construction*–branded hard hats, tool belts, and vests, and put up posters and distribute Discovery Channel program guides and magnets to pedestrians. The actors also directed people to the channel's website. A dump truck towing a *Frontiers of Construction*–branded flatbed loaded with an excavator drove around downtown in both cities. What better way to catch people's attention?[33]

  Digital Ad Network gets the attention of mall shoppers while they are grabbing something to eat through its unique form of mall television advertising. Instead of using conventional television advertising in food courts, DAN runs full-motion billboards—a large, suspended billboard that runs full-motion video. "The effect is like seeing an outdoor ad with a woman in jeans, except that the palm trees sway and the waves actually crash on the beach," says DAN's executive vice-president and COO, Allan Safran.[34]

Other ways to increase the attention paid to your product include the effective use of principles of ad layout such as colour, contrast, and movement (Exhibit 5-9). Irving makes its ads stand out by the use of a bright colour—yellow; McDonald's used a bright yellow-and-red combination in its ad to get the attention of *Globe and Mail* readers when it started serving Heinz ketchup.

■ *Find creative ways to prevent consumers from blocking your messages.* As we saw earlier, consumers use perceptual blocking to avoid being exposed to too many stimuli. Although unconventional forms of promotion (such as the ones discussed above) may be able to break through the consumers' perceptual blocking, the increasing popularity of PVDs will necessitate creative ways of getting consumers to "see" the product without even being aware of it. One such method is the use of product placement in television shows and movies.

Examples of product placement include the appearance of Ruffles potato chips in *Degrassi: The Next Generation*; and the nine or ten placements of Windex due to the references to the product in the film *My Big Fat Greek Wedding*. However, the best examples of product placement are in Quebec, where a hybrid of product placement and sponsorships are part of the reality television phenomenon. For example, the TVA talk show *Le Grand Blond avec un show surnois* had contestants driving and sleeping in a Pontiac Vibe for a chance to win two of the cars; the show *Testosterone*, aimed at men, had segments where six men and six women battled to win a Sunfire, Grand Am, or Grand Prix by driving the cars in various challenging situations, including one where they had to pick up members of the opposite sex. The latter show's weekly audience of more than 500 000 male viewers was a perfect fit for GM's Pontiac cars.[35]

Ensure that consumers organize and interpret your messages correctly: Use the principles of closure, figure-ground, and grouping to help consumers organize the information that you provide. Similarly, make sure that messages are interpreted correctly by reducing perceptual distortions that are due to stereotypes or wrong first impressions.

What makes a doughnut fresh? Is it on-site baking? Can a doughnut that was baked (to "almost done") in Ontario and shipped across the country taste fresh? According to most Canadians,

EXHIBIT 5-9

USE OF BRIGHT COLOURS TO ATTRACT ATTENTION

Print advertisement used with permission of Whirlpool Corporation.

the answer is a definite no. Consumers have strong stereotypes that prevent them from believing that a pre-made, frozen doughnut that undergoes the final stages of preparation at the store is fresh or of good quality. That's the problem that Tim Hortons faced when the venerable Canadian doughnut maker was planning to ship doughnuts made and frozen at a central location in Ontario to the Atlantic provinces and British Columbia. When that became known, customers swore that the doughnut tasted different. For example, Doug Oneschuk of Kanata, Ontario, said, "I had a doughnut last week, and it's different from what I remember.... I wouldn't go there (anymore)."[36] Yet, the practice had been in effect in Ontario (and the rest of the country) for some time when the word got out about the new production process. Obviously, it was not the actual taste of the doughnut that was the problem, but consumers' stereotypes that "pre-baked" meant "not fresh."

Finally, use the halo effect to your advantage by leveraging brand equity in successful brands while introducing new products.

Develop suitable consumer imagery: Use price and quality perceptions to develop consumer imagery. As mentioned earlier, consumers develop images about products through their interpretations of various cues, including price; intrinsic cues about the product (e.g., its colour); extrinsic cues, such as product packaging; retail store environment; and other variables. Making sure that all such cues are in line with the desired image would help a company succeed in the marketplace.

TacoTime, the Canadian restaurant chain that aims to become "the dominant Mexican restaurant chain in Canada," has been successful in its attempts to re-brand its restaurants. As Ken Pattenden, the company's president, says "many of our stores were nondescript both in design and location.... It was a real leap of faith when you walked by one to assume it offered Mexican food."[37] The company conducted focus groups and asked consumers what came to mind when they thought of Mexico ("sunshine, beaches, and tequila") and what made a food look authentic and desirable (food served on a platter was considered more authentic than food wrapped in waxed paper). On the basis of the research findings, the company remodelled its restaurants to give them a more Mexican look and redesigned the way it presented its food. Even TacoTime's posters were redesigned—big, colourful pictures of its food platters went up in its outlets—and sales of its Casita platters jumped threefold.[38]

www.tacotimecanada.com

Evaluate the level of perceived risk and find ways of reducing it: Since the level of perceived risk is a key factor of consumer imagery, marketers need to understand the risk that a consumer feels when he or she is evaluating their product. If the risk is financial, then marketers can offer a liberal return policy ("satisfaction guaranteed or money refunded"); if the risk is functional or physical, it would be a good strategy to provide information about the product and get endorsements from neutral third parties (e.g., the Canadian Dental Association or the Heart and Stroke Foundation); for all other types of risks, an image as a trustworthy brand would provide reassurance to consumers.

SUMMARY

- Perception is the process by which individuals select, organize, and interpret stimuli into a meaningful and coherent picture of the world. Perception has implications for marketing strategy because consumers' decisions are based on what they perceive rather than on objective reality.

- The lowest level at which an individual can perceive a specific stimulus is that person's absolute threshold. The minimal difference that can be perceived between two stimuli is called the differential threshold or just noticeable difference (j.n.d.). Some researchers feel that even stimuli below the absolute threshold may be perceived subliminally.

- Consumers' selection of stimuli from the environment is based on the interaction of their expectations and motives with the stimulus itself.

- The principles of selective perception include the following concepts: selective exposure, selective attention, perceptual defence, and perceptual blocking.

- Consumers organize their perceptions into unified wholes according to the principles of Gestalt psychology: figure and ground, grouping, and closure.

- The interpretation of stimuli is highly subjective and is based on what the consumer expects to see in light of previous experience, his or her motives and interests at the time of perception, and the clarity of the stimulus itself. Influences that tend to distort objective interpretation include physical appearances, stereotypes, halo effects, irrelevant cues, first impressions, and the tendency to jump to conclusions.

- Just as individuals have images of themselves, they also have images of products and brands. Consumers often judge the quality of a product or service on the basis of a variety of informational cues; some are intrinsic to the product (such as colour, size, flavour, and aroma), while others are extrinsic (e.g., price, store image, brand image, and service environment).

- How a consumer perceives a price—as high, low, or fair—has a strong influence on his or her purchase intentions and satisfaction. Consumers rely on both internal and external reference prices when they assess the fairness of a price.

- Consumers often perceive risk (functional, physical, financial, social, psychological, or time) in making product selections because of uncertainty as to the consequences of their product decisions.

- Consumer strategies for reducing perceived risk include increased information search, brand loyalty, buying a well-known brand, buying from a reputable retailer, buying the most expensive brand, and seeking reassurance in the form of money-back guarantees, warranties, and prepurchase trials.

DISCUSSION QUESTIONS

1. How does sensory adaptation affect advertising effectiveness? How can marketers overcome sensory adaptation?

2. Define absolute and differential thresholds and j.n.d. How can a marketer use the concept of j.n.d. during periods of (a) rising ingredient and material costs and (b) increasing competition?

3. Define selective perception. Thinking back, relate one or two elements of this concept to your own attention patterns when you see print advertisements and television commercials.

4. How do advertisers use contrast to make sure that their ads are noticed? Would the lack of contrast between the ad and the medium in which it appears help or hinder the effectiveness of the ad? What are the ethical considerations in employing such strategies?

5. What are the implications of figure-ground relationships for print ads and for online ads? How can the figure-ground construct help or interfere with the communication of advertising messages?

6. What are the various types of perceived risk? Discuss four strategies that consumers use to handle perceived risk.

7. What is perceptual mapping? What are the approaches to developing a perceptual map?

CRITICAL THINKING QUESTIONS

1. What extrinsic cues and intrinsic cues would be used in assessing the perceived quality of the following products? How can a company use extrinsic cues to improve the perceived quality of these products?
   (a) wines
   (b) restaurants
   (c) plasma television monitors
   (d) post-graduate education

2. You have recently made the decision to attend a university. Was this a high-risk decision in your mind? Why? What strategies did you use to reduce the risk involved in this decision?

What could the university have done to reduce your perception of risk a little more?

3. As a university student, you must be faced with severe time constraints. What steps could a marketer of a new, "healthful" soft drink (i.e, containing real fruit juice and with added vitamins and minerals) take to make sure that students like you would be exposed to and pay attention to its advertising messages? What would help you organize and interpret the information provided by the firm in meaningful ways?

INTERNET EXERCISES

1. Visit the website of four companies in one of the following industries and identify the principles of perception used on these sites:

   (a) soft drinks   (b) beer or other alcohol
   (c) cars

2. Of the four companies that you chose in question (1), which one does the best job of getting your attention and conveying its message? Which one does the worst job, and why?

3. Visit the website of the *Globe and Mail* and click on some of the lead stories. Do you find any differences in the ads that accompany the different articles? Does this illustrate any concept covered in this chapter?

4. Visit the website of your university. Assume that you are a student just about to graduate from high school. What would your opinion of this website be? Does it use the principles of perception effectively? Why or why not?

KEY TERMS

Absolute threshold   (p. 145)
Broad categorizers   (p. 171)
Closure   (p. 159)
Consumer imagery   (p. 162)
Differential threshold (j.n.d.)
   (p. 146)
Extrinsic cues   (p. 168)
Figure and ground   (p. 158)
Gestalt psychology   (p. 157)
Grouping   (p. 159)
Intrinsic cues   (p. 168)
Just noticeable difference (j.n.d.)
   (p. 146)

Narrow categorizers   (p. 171)
Objective price claims   (p. 168)
Perceived price   (p. 167)
Perceived quality   (p. 168)
Perceived risk   (p. 170)
Perception   (p. 144)
Perceptual blocking   (p. 154)
Perceptual mapping   (p. 164)
Positioning   (p. 162)
Price-quality relationship   (p. 169)
Reference price   (p. 167)
Repositioning   (p. 163)
Selective perception   (p. 152)

Sensation   (p. 144)
Sensory adaptation   (p. 145)
Sensory receptors   (p. 144)
Subliminal perception   (p. 147)
Tensile price claims   (p. 168)
Weber's law   (p. 146)

CASE 5-1: BUYING MEDICINES ONLINE

Some U.S. consumers claim that they have been saving as much as 50 percent a month by buying their prescription drugs online from a Canadian mail order pharmacy. The prescriptions, written by physicians in the United States, are generally mailed to a Canadian pharmacy, where they are co-signed by a Canadian physician. This is done because it is illegal for a Canadian pharmacy to fill a prescription that is not written by a doctor licensed to practice medicine in Canada. After the prescription has been filled once, refills can be obtained routinely online.

Although appearing to be simple, buying prescription medicines from a Canadian pharmacy is not without controversy. Some studies have found that the savings are only 25 percent, whereas other studies have determined that some medicines actually cost more on the internet than they do at retail pharmacies in the United States. Furthermore, there is the issue of how long the consumer might have to wait for the Canadian pharmacy to fill the prescription and how long it will take the postal system to deliver it. A few individuals, for example, have reported receiving bills for their medications 30 to 90 days before the prescriptions were actually shipped.

QUESTIONS

1. Perceived risk is a powerful consumer behaviour concept. Explain how perceived risk and its various component risks are especially relevant in determining whether U.S. consumers would be willing to buy prescription medications from an online Canadian pharmacy.

2. As a Canadian company marketing prescription drugs online, what can you do to reduce the perceived risk that consumers may experience in this purchase situation?

NOTES

1   *Boomers, Beer, and a Healthy Lifestyle*, Ipsos-Reid, December 1, 2003.

2   Chris Daniels, "Carb-Charged Communications," *Marketing Magazine*, March 1, 2004.

3   Eric R. Spangenberg, Ayn E. Crowley, and Pamela W. Henderson, "Improving the Store Environment: Do Olfactory Cues Affect Evaluations and Behaviors?" *Journal of Marketing,* 60, April 1996, 67–80.

4   Kathryn T. Theus, "Subliminal Advertising and the Psychology of Processing Unconscious Stimuli: A Review of Research," *Psychology and Marketing,* 11, 3, May–June 1994, 271–290. See also Dennis L. Rosen and Surenra N. Singh, "An Investigation of Subliminal Embed Effect on Multiple Measures of Advertising Effectiveness," *Psychology and Marketing,* 9, 2, March–April 1992, 157–173.

5   For example, Andrew B. Aylesworth, Ronald C. Goodstein, and Ajay Kalra, "Effects of Archetypal Embeds of Feelings: An Indirect Route to Affecting Attitudes?" *Journal of Advertising,* Fall 1999, 73–81;

Nicholas Epley, Kenneth Savitsky, and Robert A. Kachelski, "What Every Skeptic Should Know about Subliminal Persuasion," *Skeptical Inquirer,* September–October 1999, 4–58.

6   Carl L. Witte, Madhavan Parthasarathy, and James W. Gentry, "Subliminal Perception versus Subliminal Persuasion: A Re-Examination of the Basic Issues," *American Marketing Association,* Summer 1995, 133–138. See also Jack Haberstroh, *Ice Cube Sex: The Truth about Subliminal Advertising* (Notre Dame, IN: Cross Cultural Publications, 1994).

7   Martha Rogers and Christine A. Seiler, "The Answer Is No: A National Survey of Advertising Practitioners and Their Clients about Whether They Use Subliminal Advertising," *Journal of Advertising Research,* March–April 1994, 36–45; Martha Rogers and Kirk H. Smith, "Public Perceptions of Subliminal Advertising: Why Practitioners Shouldn't Ignore This Issue," *Journal of Advertising Research,* March–April 1993, 10–18. See also Nicolas E. Synodinos, "Subliminal Stimulation: What Does the

Public Think about It?" in *Current Issues and Research in Advertising*, 11 (1 and 2), eds. James H. Leigh and Claude R. Martin Jr., 1988, 157–187.

8 Kevin Groves, "More Teen Girls Lighting Up," Halifax *Mail-Star*, September 9, 2003, p. B15.

9 Paul-Mark Rendon, "Zapping Power," *Marketing Magazine*, May 5, 2003, 20

10 Marsha L. Richins, "Social Comparison and the Idealized Images of Advertising," *Journal of Consumer Research*, 18, June 1991, 71–83. See also Mary C. Martin and James W. Gentry, "Stuck in the Model Trap: The Effects of Beautiful Models in Ads on Female Pre-Adolescents and Adolescents," *Journal of Advertising*, 26, 2, Summer 1997, 19–33.

11 Amanda B. Bower and Stacy Landreth, "Is Beauty Best? Highs versus Normally Attractive Models in Advertising," *Journal of Advertising*, 30, 1, Spring 2001, 1–12.

12 Kim Foltz, "Campaign on Harmony Backfires on Benetton," *New York Times*, November 20, 1989, D8.

13 Priya Raghubir and Aradhna Krishna, "Vital Dimensions in Volume Perception: Can the Eye Fool the Stomach?" *Journal of Marketing Research*, August 1999, 313–326.

14 Ajay Kalra and Ronald C. Goodstein, "The Impact of Advertising Positioning Strategies on Consumer Price Sensitivity," *Journal of Marketing Research*, 35, May 1998, 210–224.

15 **www.armandhammer.com/FrontPorch/fs.htm**.

16 Dhruv Grewal et al., "The Effects of Price Comparison Advertising on Buyers' Perceptions of Acquisition Value, Transaction Value, and Behavioral Intentions," *Journal of Marketing*, 62, April 1998, 46–59.

17 Katherine Fraccastoro, Scot Burton, and Abhijit Biswas, "Effective Use of Advertisements," *Journal of Consumer Marketing*, 10, 1, 1993, 61–79.

18 Ibid.

19 Abhijit Biswas and Scot Burton, "Consumer Perceptions of Tensile Price Claims in Advertisements: An Assessment of Claim Types across Different Discount Levels," *Journal of the Academy of Marketing Science*, 21, 3, 1993, 217–229.

20 Manjit S. Yadav and Kent B. Monroe, "How Buyers Perceive Savings in a Bundle Price: An Examination of a Bundle's Transaction Value," *Journal of Marketing Research*, 30, August 1993, 350–358.

21 Robert D. Hershey Jr., "Information Age? Maybe Not, When It Comes to Prices," *New York Times*, August 23, 1998, D10.

22 Lawrence L. Garber Jr., Eva M. Hyatt, and Richard G. Starr Jr., "The Effects of Food Color on Perceived Flavor," *Journal of Marketing Theory and Practice*, Fall 2000, 59–72.

23 Michael J. McCarthy, "Forget the Ads: Cola Is Cola, Magazine Finds," *Wall Street Journal*, February 24, 1991, B1.

24 For example, Kent Monroe, *Pricing: Making Profitable Decisions*, 2nd ed. (New York: McGraw Hill, 1990); William Dodds, Kent Monroe, and Dhruv Grewal, "Effects of Price, Brand, and Store Information on Buyers' Product Evaluations," *Journal of Marketing Research*, 28, August 1991, 307–319; Tung Zong Chang and Albert R. Wildt, "Price, Product Information, and Purchase Intention: An Empirical Study," *Journal of the Academy of Marketing Science*, 22, 1, 1994, 16–27; and Indrajit Sinha and Wayne S. DeSasrbo, "An Integrated Approach toward the Spatial Model of Perceived Customer Value," *Journal of Marketing Research*, 35, May 1998, 236–249.

25 Donald R. Liechtenstein, Nancy M. Ridgway, and Richard G. Nitemeyer, "Price Perception and Consumer Shopping Behavior: A Field Study," *Journal of Marketing Research*, 30, May 1993, 242.

26 Merrie Brucks and Valarie A. Zeithaml, "Price and Brand Name as Indicators of Quality Dimensions for Consumer Durables," *Journal of the Academy of Marketing Science*, Summer 2000, 359–374.

27 Ibid.

28 Herbert H. Severson, Paul Slovic, and Sarah Hampson, "Adolescents' Perception of Risk: Understanding and Preventing High Risk Behavior," *Advances in Consumer Research*, 20, 1993, 177–182.

29 Elke U. Weber and Richard A. Milliman, "Perceived Risk Attitudes: Relating Risk Perception to Risky Choice," *Management Science*, 43, 2, February 1997, 123–144.

30 Grahame R. Dowling and Richard Staelin, "A Model of Perceived Risk and Intended Risk Handling Activity," *Journal of Consumer Research*, 21, June 1994, 119–134.

31 Keith B. Murray and John L. Schlacter, "The Impact of Services versus Goods on Consumers' Assessment of Perceived Risk and Variability," *Journal of the Academy of Marketing Sciences*, 18, Winter 1990, 51–65

32 David Chilton, "Head to Head Competition," *Marketing Magazine*, March 10, 2003, pp. 11–12.

33 "Discovery Constructs Outdoor Promo," *Marketing Magazine*, March 10, 2003, 13.

34 James Careless, "A Reason to Look Up," *Marketing Magazine*, March 10, 2003, 21.

35 Danny Kucharksy, "A New Brand of Show," *Marketing Magazine*, May 5, 2003, 20.

36 Jennifer Stewart, "Tim's Says Pre-baked Doughnuts Always Fresh," Halifax *Mail-Star*, October 25, 2003, A2.

37 Norma Ramage, "TacoTime Dreams Grande," *Marketing Magazine*, March 3, 2003, 8.

38 Ibid.

Ocean Spray is a registered trademark. ©2004 Ocean Spray International, Inc.

NEW

Ocean Spray® Light Cocktails,
with ⅔ less calories and carbs.*

Try all 3:
Cranberry, White Cranberry and Ruby Red.

*compared to regular Ocean Spray® cocktails. Less than 8 carbs per 175 mL serving.

chapter 6
consumer learning

LEARNING OBJECTIVES

By the end of this chapter you should be able to:

1. Define learning.
2. Define behavioural learning and discuss classical and operant conditioning theories.
3. Define cognitive learning and discuss two cognitive learning theories.
4. Explain how consumers structure, retrieve, and retain information.
5. Discuss three different ways of measuring consumer learning.
6. Summarize the marketing implications of behavioural and cognitive learning theories.

6

listerine mouthwash has been on the market for many decades. Originally noted for its medicinal taste, Listerine mouthwash is now available in four flavours. The company has also introduced the hugely successful and highly publicized CoolMint Listerine PocketPaks—an extension of the product line in the form of thin, mint-like squares that melt in the mouth and eliminate bad breath. However, years ago, when the company first began making Listerine toothpaste, consumers did not buy it. Even when the manufacturer repackaged the product, reintroduced it, advertised it, and included free samples with its mouthwash products, Listerine toothpaste did not gain a significant market share, probably because consumers continued to associate it with the brand they knew so well—the medicinal-smelling, sharp-tasting Listerine mouthwash.

Most consumers associate the name Ben-Gay with a topical cream that relieves muscle and joint pain when rubbed on the skin. But Ben-Gay Aspirin flopped. Consumers were not prepared to take internally a product associated with a topical cream they had learned was for external use only.

Nabisco's Oreo Little Fudgies were smaller versions of its Oreo cookie, with an external chocolate coating. The original Oreo cookie inspired generations of consumers to pull the two halves of the cookie apart and lick out the creamy filling. But consumers found that pulling a chocolate-coated Oreo apart was very messy, and so the product did not sell.[1]

Listerine toothpaste, Ben-Gay Aspirin, and Nabisco's Oreo Little Fudgies were product extensions to successful products made by well-known and popular companies. They did not succeed because they required consumers to *learn* new consumption habits that *contradicted* previously learned and well-established patterns of product usage.

How individuals learn is a matter of great interest and importance to academics, psychologists, consumer researchers, and marketers. The reason that marketers are concerned with how individuals learn is that they are vitally interested in teaching them, as consumers, about products, product attributes, and their benefits: where to buy them, how to use them, how to maintain them, and even how to dispose of them. They are also vitally interested in how well they have taught consumers to prefer their brands and to differentiate their products from competitive offerings. Marketing strategies are based on communicating with the consumer, and marketers want their communications to be noticed, believed, and remembered. For those reasons, they are interested in every aspect of the learning process.

CHAPTER OVERVIEW

In this chapter, we will examine how consumers learn about products and ideas. We will begin with a look at two general categories of learning theory: behavioural learning theory and cognitive learning theory. Although these theories differ markedly in several ways, each theory offers insights to marketers on how to shape their messages to consumers so as to bring about desired purchase behaviour. We also discuss how consumers store, retain, and retrieve information, and how learning is measured. The chapter concludes with a discussion of how marketers use learning theories in their marketing strategies.

WHAT IS LEARNING?

Because not all learning theorists agree on how learning takes place, it is difficult to find a generally accepted definition of learning. From a marketing perspective, however, **consumer learning** can be thought of as the process by which individuals acquire the purchase and consumption knowledge and experience that they apply to future related behaviour. Several points in this definition are worth noting:

Consumer learning: The process by which individuals acquire the purchase and consumption knowledge and experience that they apply to future related behaviour.

■ Consumer learning is a *process;* that is, it continually evolves and changes as a result of newly acquired *knowledge*, which may be gained from reading, from discussions, from observation, from thinking, or from actual *experience.*

■ Newly acquired knowledge and personal experience serve as *feedback* to the individual and provide the basis for *future behaviour* in similar situations.

■ Not all learning is deliberately sought. Though much learning is *intentional* (i.e., it is acquired as the result of a careful search for information), a great deal of learning is also *incidental* (i.e., acquired by accident or without much effort). For example, some ads may induce learning (e.g., of brand names), even though the consumer's attention is elsewhere (on a magazine article rather than the advertisement on the facing page).

■ The term "learning" encompasses the total range of learning, from simple, almost reflexive responses to the learning of abstract concepts and complex problem solving.

Despite their different viewpoints, learning theorists in general agree that in order for learning to occur, certain basic elements must be present. The elements included in most learning theories are motivation, cues, response, and reinforcement. These concepts are discussed first because they tend to recur in the theories discussed later in this chapter.

Motivation

The concept of **motivation** is important to learning theory. Remember, motivation is based on needs and goals. Motivation acts as a spur to learning. For example, men and women who want to become good tennis players are motivated to learn all they can about tennis and to practise whenever they can. Conversely, people who are not interested in tennis are likely to ignore any information about the game. The goal object (proficiency in tennis) simply has no relevance for them. The degree of relevance, or *involvement,* determines how motivated a consumer is to search for knowledge or information about a product or service. (Involvement theory, as it has come to be known, was discussed in Chapter 3.) Uncovering consumer motives is thus essential to teaching consumers why and how a product will fulfill their needs.

Motivation: The driving force within individuals that impels them to action.

Cues

If learning is stimulated by motives, **cues** are the stimuli that give direction to these motives. An advertisement for a tennis camp may serve as a cue for tennis buffs, who may suddenly "recognize" that attending tennis camp is a concentrated way to improve their game while taking a vacation. The ad is the cue, or *stimulus,* that suggests a specific way to satisfy a salient motive. In the marketplace, price, styling, packaging, advertising, and store displays all serve as cues to help consumers fulfill their needs in product-specific ways.

Cues serve to direct consumer drives when they are consistent with consumer expectations. Marketers must be careful to provide cues that do not upset those expectations. For example, consumers expect designer clothes to be expensive and to be sold in upscale retail stores. Thus, a high-fashion designer should sell his or her clothes only through exclusive stores and advertise only in upscale fashion magazines. Each aspect of the marketing mix must reinforce the others if cues are to serve as the stimuli that guide consumer actions in the direction desired by the marketer.

Cues: The stimuli that give direction to motives.

Response

How individuals react to a drive or cue—how they behave—constitutes their **response**. Learning can occur even when responses are not overt. The car manufacturer that provides consistent cues to a consumer may not always succeed in stimulating a purchase. However, if the manufacturer succeeds in forming a favourable image of a particular model of car in the consumer's mind, when the consumer is ready to buy, it is likely that he or she will consider that make or model.

A response is not tied to a need in a one-to-one fashion. Indeed, as we saw in Chapter 3, a need or motive may evoke a whole variety of responses. For example, there are many ways to respond to the need for physical exercise besides playing tennis. Cues provide some direction, but there are many cues competing for the consumer's attention. Which response the consumer makes depends heavily on previous learning; that, in turn, depends on how related responses were reinforced previously.

Response: How individuals react to a drive or cue.

Reinforcement

Reinforcement increases the likelihood that a specific response will occur in the future as the result of particular cues or stimuli. For example, Exhibit 6-1 presents a three-step process for facial skin care based on three products (i.e., cues). This ad is instructional and designed to generate consumer learning. If a university student finds that the cleansing routine based on the three products featured in this ad

Reinforcement: A positive or negative outcome that influences the likelihood that a behaviour will be repeated in response to the same cue or stimulus.

EXHIBIT 6-1

PRODUCT USE LEADS TO REINFORCEMENT

Courtesy of Neutrogena Corporation.

Behavioural learning theory:
A theory that states that learning has happened when observable responses to external stimuli occur in a predictable way.

Classical conditioning:
Conditioned learning or learning that occurs through the pairing of stimuli.

Conditioned learning:
Learning that results when a stimulus is paired with another stimulus and draws the same response as that stimulus.

relieves his acne problem, he is likely to continue buying and using these products. Through positive reinforcement, learning has taken place, since the facial cleansing system lived up to expectations. However, if the products had not provided relief from the problem, the student would have no reason to associate the brand with acne relief in the future. Because of the absence of reinforcement, it is unlikely that he would buy that brand again.

Although learning is an individual process and may vary from person to person, psychologists have developed two major types of theories about consumer learning: behavioural and cognitive. Behavioural learning theories state that learning takes place through the connections established between stimuli based on past experience. Cognitive learning theories state that learning takes place through mental processes and without direct experience. The next two sections discuss these theories of learning.

BEHAVIOURAL LEARNING THEORIES

Behavioural learning theories are sometimes referred to as stimulus-response theories because they are based on the premise that observable responses to specific external stimuli signal that learning has taken place. When a person acts (responds) in a predictable way to a known stimulus, he or she is said to have "learned." Behavioural theories are not so much concerned with the *process* of learning as they are with the *inputs* and *outcomes* of learning, that is, with the stimuli that consumers select from the environment and the observable behaviour that results. Two behavioural theories with great relevance to marketing are classical conditioning and instrumental (or operant) conditioning.

Classical Conditioning

Classical conditioning is a behavioural learning theory that proposes that consumer learning takes place through the pairing of two stimuli. Early classical conditioning theorists regarded all organisms (both animal and human) as relatively passive entities that could be taught certain behaviour through repetition (or "conditioning"). In everyday speech, the word *conditioning* has come to mean a kind of "knee-jerk" (or automatic) response to a situation built up through repeated exposure. If you get a headache every time you think of visiting your Aunt Gertrude, your reaction may be conditioned from years of boring visits with her.

Ivan Pavlov, a Russian physiologist, was the first to describe conditioning and to propose it as a general model of how learning occurs. According to Pavlovian theory, **conditioned learning** results when a stimulus that is paired with another stimulus that elicits a known response produces the same response when used alone.

Pavlov demonstrated what he meant by conditioned learning in his studies with dogs. The dogs were hungry and eager to eat. In his experiments, Pavlov sounded a bell and then immediately applied a meat paste to the dogs' tongues, with the result that they began to salivate. Learning (conditioning) occurred when, after enough repetitions of the bell sound followed almost immediately by the food, the bell sound alone caused the dogs to salivate. The dogs associated the sound of the bell (the conditioned stimulus) with the meat paste (the unconditioned stimulus) and, after a number of pairings, gave the same unconditioned response (salivation) to the bell alone as they did to the meat paste. The unconditioned response to the meat paste became the conditioned response to the bell. Figure 6-1A models this relationship. If you usually listen to the 6 o'clock news while you wait for dinner to be served, you would tend to associate the 6 o'clock news with dinner, so that eventually the sounds of the 6 o'clock news alone might cause your mouth to water, even if dinner was not being prepared and even if you were not hungry. Figure 6-1B shows a diagram of this basic relationship.

In a consumer behaviour context, an unconditioned stimulus might consist of a known and well-liked object, such as a particular brand, Christmas decorations, or even an animal. For example, Royale brand bathroom tissue (now owned by the Irving group in Canada) uses fluffy white kittens in its ad; the kittens here would be the **unconditioned stimuli** toward which consumers are likely to have an unconditioned response (liking). The **conditioned stimuli** would be the bathroom tissue, and the conditioned response would be the positive feelings toward it. In the example given at the opening of the chapter, the brand name Listerine was the unconditioned stimulus associated with a medicinal taste, and avoiding Listerine brand toothpaste was the consumer's conditioned response.

Optimal conditioning—that is, the creation of a strong association between the conditioned stimulus (CS) and the unconditioned stimulus (US)—requires all of the following:

- forward conditioning (i.e., the CS should precede the US)
- repeated pairings of the CS and the US
- a CS and US that logically belong together
- a CS that is novel and unfamiliar
- a US that is biologically or symbolically salient

Contemporary behavioural scientists view classical conditioning as the learning of associations among events that allows the organism to anticipate and "represent" its environment. Classical conditioning, then, rather than being a reflexive action, is seen as the acquisition of new *knowledge* about the world.[2]

Key Concepts Derived from Classical Conditioning

Three basic concepts are derived from classical conditioning: *repetition, stimulus generalization,* and *stimulus discrimination.* Each of these concepts is important to the strategic applications of consumer behaviour.

Repetition Repetition increases the strength of the association between a conditioned stimulus and an unconditioned stimulus and slows the process of forgetting. However, research suggests that there is a limit to the amount of repetition that will aid retention. Although some over-learning (i.e., repetition beyond what is necessary for learning) aids retention, at some point an individual can become satiated with numerous exposures, and both attention and retention will decline. This effect,

Unconditioned stimuli: Stimuli that consumers already know and like.

Conditioned stimuli: Stimuli or objects that are linked to a previously known and liked stimulus (i.e., unconditioned stimuli) to elicit the same response.

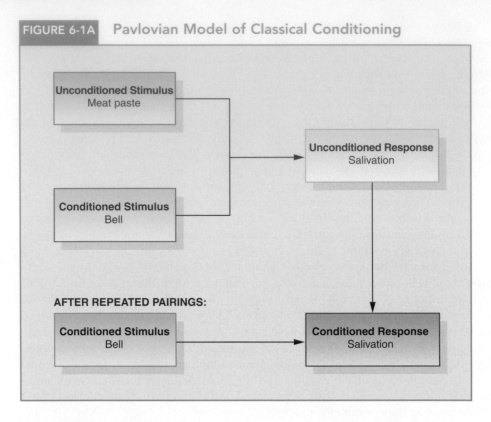

FIGURE 6-1A   Pavlovian Model of Classical Conditioning

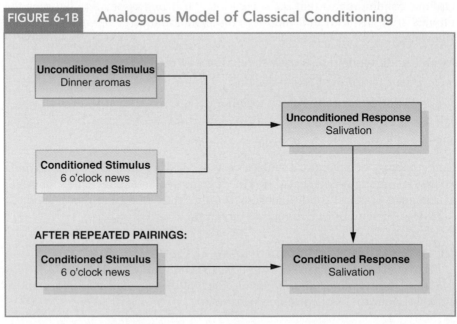

FIGURE 6-1B   Analogous Model of Classical Conditioning

Advertising wear-out: The reduction in attention and retention caused by overexposure to advertisements.

known as **advertising wear-out**, can be moderated by varying the advertising message. Marketers may prevent wear-out in two ways:

■ By using *cosmetic variations* in their ads (using different backgrounds, different styles of print, different advertising spokespersons) while repeating the same advertising theme. For example, the classic, decades-old Absolut Vodka campaign has used the same theme with highly creative and varied backgrounds, relating the product to holidays, trends, and cultural symbols in Canada and around the world (see Exhibit 6-2).

- By using *substantive variations* or changes in advertising content in different versions of an advertisement. For example, each of the two ads in Exhibit 6-3 stress a different attribute of the same product. Substantive variations in ads are likely to lead to greater information processing, more positive thoughts, and attitudes that are more resistant to change.[3]

Although the principle of repetition is well established among advertisers, not everyone agrees on how much repetition is enough, though there is general agreement that a minimum of three hits or exposures is needed.

Stimulus Generalization According to classical conditioning theorists, learning depends not only on repetition but also on the ability of individuals to generalize. Pavlov found, for example, that a dog could learn to salivate not only to the sound of a bell but also to the somewhat similar sound of jangling keys. If we were not capable of **stimulus generalization**—that is, of making the same response to slightly different stimuli—not much learning would take place.

Stimulus generalization: Making the same response to similar stimuli.

Stimulus generalization explains why some imitative products succeed in the marketplace (consumers confuse them with the original product they have seen advertised) and why manufacturers of private-label brands try to make their packaging resemble the national-brand leaders (consumers confuse them with national brands). Similarly packaged competitive products result in millions of lost sales for well-positioned and extensively advertised brands.

The principle of stimulus generalization is applied by marketers in several ways: *product line, form, and category extensions*. The marketer adds related products to an already established brand (product line extension—see Exhibit 6-4), adds new forms of a product (product form extension), and starts manufacturing related products (product category extension), knowing that the new product is more likely to be adopted when it is associated with a known and trusted brand name.

- Tylenol—a highly trusted brand—first introduced line extensions by making its products available in a number of different forms (tablets, capsules, and gelcaps), strengths (regular, extra strength, and children's), and package sizes.

- Crest has been successful at product form extensions—from Crest Toothpaste to Crest Whitestrips; Listerine has gone from mouthwash to ListerinePaks (see Exhibit 6-5), and Ivory from bath soap to liquid soap to shower gel.

- Olay has gone into product category extensions by introducing bar soaps; Neutrogena, the

EXHIBIT 6-2

ABSOLUT TARGETING A TECHNO-SAVVY CONSUMER

© 2000–2004 V&S Vin & Spirit AB. All Rights Reserved.

EXHIBIT 6-3

SUBSTANTIVE VARIATIONS IN TWO ADVERTISEMENTS FOR THE SAME PRODUCT

Courtesy of Grant Thornton LLP.

skin-care brand, has gone into product category extension by producing a line of men's care products (see Exhibit 6-6A); and Mr. Clean has started producing all-in-one mopping systems (see Exhibit 6-6B).

The success of product extensions depends on a number of factors, such as the image of the parent brand, the number of products associated with it, and the consistency of quality in various products in the category.

Family branding: the practice of marketing a whole line of company products under the same brand name—called **family branding**—is another strategy that capitalizes on the consumer's ability to generalize favourable brand associations from one product to others.

The Campbell's Soup Company, for example, continues to add new food products to its product line under the Campbell's brand name, achieving ready acceptance for the new products from satisfied consumers of other Campbell's food products. Kraft Foods sells salad dressings, cheeses, snacks, and toppings under the Kraft brand name. The Ralph Lauren designer label on men's and women's clothing helps to achieve ready acceptance for these products in the upscale sportswear market.

Retail private branding: The same effect as family branding can often be achieved by retail private branding. For example, Wal-Mart used to advertise that its stores carried only "brands you trust." Now the name Wal-Mart itself has become a "brand" that consumers have confidence in, and the name confers brand value on Wal-Mart's store brands.

Licensing: **Licensing**—allowing a well-known brand name to be affixed to products of another manufacturer—is a marketing strategy that operates on the principle of *stimulus generalization*. The names of designers, manufacturers, celebrities, corporations, and even cartoon characters are attached for a fee (i.e., "rented") to a variety of products, enabling the licencees to achieve instant recognition and implied quality for the licensed products. Exhibit 6-7 shows an ad for eyeglasses bearing the name of the well-known shoe manufacturer Kenneth Cole. Even Queen Elizabeth has agreed to extend the licensed name "House of Windsor" to

Family branding:
The marketing of an entire product line under the same brand name.

Licensing:
Affixing a well-known brand name to the products of other manufacturers.

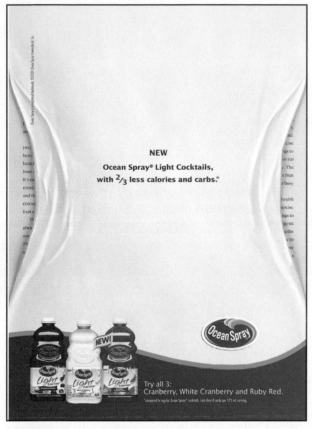

EXHIBIT 6-4

PRODUCT LINE EXTENSION—OCEANSPRAY
ADDS LIGHT COCKTAILS

Courtesy of Ocean Spray International.

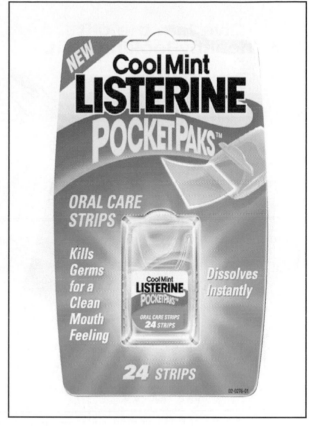

EXHIBIT 6-5

PRODUCT FORM EXTENSION

furniture and Scottish throw rugs. The increase in licensing has made counterfeiting a booming business, as counterfeiters add well-known licensor names to a variety of products without benefit of contract or quality control.[4]

Stimulus Discrimination *Stimulus discrimination* is the opposite of stimulus generalization; it results in the selection of a specific stimulus from among similar stimuli. The consumer's ability to discriminate among similar stimuli is the basis of positioning strategy (discussed in Chapter 5), which tries to establish a unique image for a brand in the consumer's mind.

> **Stimulus discrimination:**
> The ability to differentiate (or discriminate between) similar stimuli.

Unlike the imitator who hopes consumers will *generalize* their perceptions and attribute special characteristics of the market leader's products to its own products, market leaders want the consumer to *discriminate* among similar stimuli. Marketers can help consumers differentiate the marketers' products from competing brands through product differentiation strategies that emphasize an attribute that is relevant, meaningful, and valuable to consumers.

In 1998, half of Canadian grocery shoppers could not name a single brand of chicken; by 2001, 32 percent named Prime Naturally (by Maple Leaf Consumer Foods) in unaided recall surveys. How did Maple Leaf achieve this level of brand

EXHIBIT 6-6A

PRODUCT CATEGORY EXTENSION

Courtesy of Johnson & Johnson Inc.

EXHIBIT 6-6B

PRODUCT CATEGORY EXTENSION

Courtesy of Procter & Gamble.

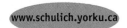

awareness? The answer is advertising that helped consumers discriminate between their brand and other branded or unbranded chickens. The ads for Prime emphasized that the chickens had been fed on vegetable grain. As Alan Middleton, of York University's Schulich School of Business notes, "The underlying strategy is so smart, which is, don't focus on the product and how delicious it is...but rather, take people back to what goes into it that makes it good and nutritious."[5] Prime ads consistently deviated from the norm—for example, one featured a robotic chicken being interviewed by a recruiter for Prime Naturally. Such "risky" advertising also helped consumers discriminate between Prime Naturally chicken and other brands.

Other marketers successfully differentiate their brands on an attribute that may actually be irrelevant to creating the implied benefit, such as a non-contributing ingredient or a colour.[6] Exhibit 6-8 shows an example of stimulus discrimination.

The principles of classical conditioning provide the theoretical underpinnings for many marketing applications. However, they do not explain all behavioural consumer learning. Our assessments of products are often based on how much satisfaction—the rewards—we experience as a result of making specific purchases, in other words, from instrumental conditioning.

Instrumental or Operant Conditioning

Instrumental conditioning (or operant conditioning) is a behavioural learning theory that requires a link between a stimulus and a response. However, in instrumental conditioning, the stimulus that results in the most satisfactory response is the one that is learned.

Instrumental learning theorists believe that learning takes place through trial and error and that habits are formed as a result of rewards received for certain responses or behaviour. For example, by shopping in a number of stores, consumers learn which ones carry the type of clothing they prefer and at prices they can afford. Once they find a store that carries clothing that meets their needs, they are likely to patronize that store to the exclusion of others. Every time they buy a shirt or a sweater there that they really like, their store loyalty is rewarded (*reinforced*), and their patronage of that store is more likely to be repeated. Although classical conditioning is useful in explaining how consumers learn very simple kinds of behaviour, instrumental conditioning is more helpful in explaining complex, goal-directed activities.

The name most closely associated with instrumental (or operant) conditioning is that of the American psychologist B.F. Skinner. According to Skinner, most individual learning occurs in a controlled environment in which individuals are

> **Instrumental or operant conditioning:** A theory that states that learning occurs through trial-and-error as a result of reinforcements received for specific behaviour.

EXHIBIT 6-7

SHOE MANUFACTURER LICENSES ITS NAME

Kenneth Cole Eyewear manufactured under trademark license by Clear Vision Optical.

EXHIBIT 6-8

STIMULUS DISCRIMINATION

Courtesy of Farmland Dairies.

"rewarded" for choosing the right kind of behaviour. Like Pavlov, Skinner developed his model of learning by working with animals. Small animals, such as rats and pigeons, were placed in his "Skinner box"; if they made the right movements (e.g., if they pressed levers or pecked keys), they received food (a positive reinforcement). Skinner and his many adherents have done amazing things with this simple learning model, including teaching pigeons to play ping-pong and even to dance. In consumer behaviour terms, instrumental conditioning suggests that consumers learn by means of a trial-and-error process in which some kinds of purchase behaviour result in more favourable outcomes (i.e., rewards) than do others. A favourable experience is "instrumental" in teaching the individual to repeat a specific behaviour. This model of instrumental conditioning is presented in Figure 6-2.

Types of Reinforcement

Skinner distinguished two types of reinforcement (or reward) that influence the likelihood that a response will be repeated. The first type, **positive reinforcement**, consists of events that strengthen the likelihood of a specific response. Using a shampoo that leaves your hair feeling silky and clean is likely to result in a repeat purchase of the shampoo. **Negative reinforcement** is an unpleasant or negative outcome that also serves to encourage a specific behaviour. An advertisement that shows a model with wrinkled skin is designed to encourage consumers to buy and use the advertised skin cream.

Either positive or negative reinforcement can be used to elicit a desired response. However, negative reinforcement should not be confused with punishment, which is designed to discourage behaviour. For example, parking tickets are not negative reinforcement; they are a form of "punishment" designed to discourage drivers from parking illegally.

Positive reinforcement: Outcomes that increase the likelihood of behaviour being repeated when the same stimuli are presented.

Negative reinforcement: Outcomes that decrease the likelihood of a behaviour being repeated when the same stimuli are presented.

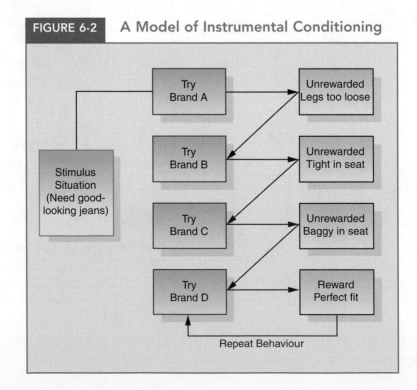

FIGURE 6-2   A Model of Instrumental Conditioning

Reinforcement Schedules

Marketers have identified three types of reinforcement schedules:

- *Continuous:* Continuous or total reinforcement gives a reward each time the consumer purchases a product (e.g., Zellers' Club Z points; Aeroplan points from Air Canada).

- *Fixed ratio:* A fixed ratio reinforcement schedule provides reinforcement every "*n*th" time the product or service is bought—say, every tenth time (e.g., a free meal after buying 10 meals at a restaurant). Exhibit 6-9 shows an example of fixed ratio reinforcement.

- *Variable ratio:* A reinforcement schedule that rewards consumers randomly (e.g., gambling machines, lotteries, sweepstakes, contests, door prizes). Gambling casinos operate on the basis of variable ratios. People pour money into slot machines, which are programmed to pay off on a variable ratio, hoping for the big win. Variable ratios tend to lead to high rates of desired behaviour and are somewhat resistant to extinction—perhaps because, for many consumers, hope springs eternal.

How do you know if a promotional campaign using operant conditioning is working? Research Insight 6-1 describes how a sweepstake promotion was tested.

EXHIBIT 6-9

ADVERTISEMENT SHOWING FIXED RATIO REINFORCEMENT

Courtesy of Delta Hotels.

Forgetting and Extinction

When a learned response is no longer reinforced, it diminishes to the point of *extinction,* that is, to the point at which there is no longer a link between the stimulus and the expected reward. When behaviour is no longer reinforced, it is "unlearned." There is a difference, however, between extinction and *forgetting.* A person who has not visited a once favourite restaurant for a very long time may have simply forgotten how much he used to enjoy eating there and not think to return. But a person who finds the food not to his satisfaction may no longer return because there is no reinforcement. Forgetting is often due to the passage of time; this is known as the process of *decay.* Marketers can overcome forgetting through repetition and can combat extinction through the deliberate enhancement of consumer satisfaction.

Massed versus Distributed Learning

As illustrated previously, *timing* has an important influence on consumer learning. Should a learning schedule be spread out over a period of time (**distributed learning**), or should it be "bunched up" all at once (**massed learning**)? The question is important for advertisers planning a media schedule, because massed advertising produces more initial learning, whereas a distributed schedule usually results in learning that lasts longer. When advertisers want an immediate impact (e.g., to introduce a new product or to counter a competitor's blitz campaign), they generally use a massed schedule to hasten consumer learning. However, a distributed

Distributed learning: A learning schedule that is spread out to facilitate retention of the material.

Massed learning: A learning schedule (or information presentation) that is compressed to facilitate fast learning.

RESEARCH INSIGHT 6-1
FINDING OUT THE EFFECTIVENESS
OF SWEEPSTAKES

Operant (or instrumental) conditioning, as you have just learned, involves the use of rewards—coupons, free trials, reward points, contests, and sweepstakes are all examples of the application of operant conditioning. Although reward points (e.g., Aeroplan, Club Z, Air miles) are examples of rewards offered for each purchase, sweepstakes are variable ratio reinforcements. How effective are such efforts? News Marketing Canada (NMC) of Mississauga, Ontario, recently conducted a study (using an independent research firm) on this topic.

The goal of the research was to examine how brand and category sales were influenced by a sweepstake offer advertised on ad pads placed on the shelf next to the product in mass merchandising stores, grocery chains, and drug stores. The store sample consisted of 20 stores; 10 were treated as control stores and 10 were test sites. The research design was as follows:

	PRETEST: 4 WEEKS	TEST: 4 WEEKS	POST-TEST: 4 WEEKS
Control stores	No consumer offers or ads on shelf	No consumer offers or ads on shelf	No consumer offers or ads on shelf
Test stores	No consumer offers or ads on shelf	Shelf: take one sweepstakes	No consumer offers or ads on shelf

The measures were

■ weighted percentage change in dollar and unit sales of the brand offering the sweepstake;
■ incremental changes in sales (additional units sold in terms of dollars and units) by the store; and
■ the change in sales in the category (to measure cannibalization effects).

After the 12 weeks, the following results were found:

■ Sales of the brand offering the sweepstake increased by 30 percent during the promotion.
■ Sales of competitive brands decreased by 2 percent.
■ Sales of the overall category increased by 28 percent.
■ The test period resulted in a 70.1% net percentage increase in unit sales in the test stores.
■ The post-test period saw the brand's sales increase by nearly 30 percent, compared with the pretest period.

What do the results indicate? Operant conditioning efforts like sweepstakes can result in increased sales even after the promotion ends. This is probably because of increased brand awareness and recall among consumers. Such promotions benefit not just the brand but also the category, thus benefiting the store as well as the sponsoring manufacturer.

Source: Wayne Mouland, "Sweeping Up Additional Sales," *Marketing Magazine*, October 6/13, 2003, 36. Courtesy of *Marketing Magazine*.

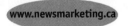
www.newsmarketing.ca

schedule, with ads repeated regularly, usually results in more long-term learning and is relatively immune to extinction.

COGNITIVE LEARNING THEORIES

Not all learning takes place as the result of repeated trials. A considerable amount of learning takes place as the result of thinking and problem solving by consumers. Sudden learning is also a reality. When confronted with a problem, we sometimes see the solution instantly. More often, however, we are likely to search for information on which to base a decision, and we carefully evaluate what we learn in order to make the best decision possible for our purposes.

Learning based on mental activity is called **cognitive learning**. Unlike behavioural learning theory, cognitive theory holds that learning involves complex *mental processing of information*. Instead of stressing the importance of repetition or the association of a reward with a specific response, cognitive theorists emphasize the role of motivation and mental processes in producing a desired response.

Three basic types of cognitive learning models exist. These are discussed in the following sections.

> **Cognitive learning:**
> Learning based on mental activity or processing of information.

Rote Learning

Rote learning (or iconic rote learning), is a form of cognitive learning in which consumers learn concepts or ideas by simple repetition without rewards or connection to other stimuli. Just as students learn concepts through rote memorization, consumers learn about products through repetition of advertising messages. This is how consumers learn about products and product attributes in several low-involvement conditions. For example, repeated ads by Heinz saying it is the best because it takes time to flow out of the bottle has led most of us to learn not only that Heinz is the best-tasting ketchup, but that thickness is the most important attribute for a ketchup. Similarly, Coca-Cola might be attempting to teach consumers that Coke is the leading soft drink and may be trying to make consumers learn that through its slogan "Coke is it"; do you think the company has been successful in achieving its goal?

> **Rote learning:**
> Learning of concepts or ideas through simple repetition.

Modelling or Observational Learning

Learning theorists have noticed that a considerable amount of learning takes place in the absence of direct reinforcement, either positive or negative, through a process psychologists call **modelling**, or observational learning (also called *vicarious learning*). Consumers often observe how others behave in response to certain situations (stimuli) and what the results are (reinforcement), and they imitate (model) the positively reinforced behaviour when they are in similar situations.

Advertisers recognize the importance of observational learning in their selection of models—whether celebrities or unknowns. If a teenager sees an ad that depicts social success as the outcome of using a certain brand of shampoo, she will want to buy it. If her brother sees a commercial that shows a muscular young athlete eating Wheaties—"the breakfast of champions"—he will want some, too. Indeed, vicarious (or observational) learning is the basis of much of today's advertising. Children learn much of their social behaviour and consumer behaviour by observing their older siblings or their parents. They imitate the behaviour of those they see rewarded, expecting to be rewarded similarly if they behave the same way (Exhibit 6-10).

Sometimes ads depict negative consequences for certain types of behaviour. This is particularly true of public policy ads, which may show the negative consequences of smoking, driving too fast, or taking drugs. By observing the actions of others and the consequences, consumers learn vicariously to recognize both desirable and undesirable behaviour.

> **Modelling:**
> The process through which individuals learn behaviour by observing the behaviour of others and the consequences of such behaviour.

www.antismokingads.org

Reasoning

At its highest level, cognitive learning involves the learning of concepts through creative thinking. Cognitive learning theory holds that the kind of learning most characteristic of human beings is the solving of problems by **reasoning**, which

> **Reasoning:**
> The highest form of cognitive learning, which involves creative thinking.

EXHIBIT 6-10

CONSUMERS LEARN BY MODELLING

Courtesy of Patek Philippe.

enables individuals to gain some control over their environment. This involves restructuring of existing knowledge and information to form new connections between concepts or objects. Cognitive learning helps us make sense of new situations and deal with complex stimuli.

Exhibit 6-11 presents an ad designed to appeal to cognitive processing.

Since learning, especially cognitive learning, depends on how consumers process information, store it, and retrieve it when the need arises, the next section will examine the nature of information processing in more detail.

INFORMATION PROCESSING

Just like a computer, the human mind processes the information it receives as input. Information processing is related to both the consumer's cognitive ability and the complexity of the information to be processed. Consumers process product information by attribute, brand, comparison between brands, or a combination of these factors. Consumers with higher cognitive ability apparently acquire more product information and are more capable of integrating information on several product attributes than are consumers with lesser ability. A consumer's cognitive ability can vary, depending upon the consumer's experience with the product (the more experience the greater the ability to process and use information) and his or her ability to use analogies, that is, the ability to transfer knowledge about familiar products to new or unfamiliar products.[7]

How Consumers Store, Retain, and Retrieve Information

Of central importance to the processing of information is the human memory. A basic research goal of most cognitive scientists is to discover how information is stored in memory, how it is retained, and how it is retrieved.

Structure of Memory

Because information processing is done in stages, it is generally believed that there are separate and sequential "storehouses" in memory where information is kept temporarily before further processing: a sensory store, a short-term store, and a long-term store.

Sensory store: All data come to us through our senses; however, the senses do not transmit whole images as a camera does. Instead, each sense receives a fragmented piece of information—such as the smell, colour, shape, and feel of a flower—and transmits it to the brain in parallel, where the perceptions of a single instant are synchronized and perceived as a single **image** and in a single moment. The image of a sensory input lasts for just a second or two in the mind's sensory

Imagery:
The ability of consumers to form mental pictures or images.

store. If it is not processed, it is lost immediately. For marketers, this means that although it is relatively easy to get information into the consumer's **sensory store**, it is difficult to make a lasting impression.

Short-term store: The **short-term store** (known as "working memory") is the stage of memory in which information is processed and held for just a short time. Anyone who has ever looked up a number in a telephone book, only to forget it just before dialling, knows how briefly information lasts in short-term storage. If information in the short-term store undergoes the process known as *rehearsal* (i.e., the silent, mental repetition of information), it is then transferred to the long-term store. The transfer process takes from two to ten seconds. If information is not rehearsed and transferred, it is lost in about 30 seconds or less. The amount of information that can be held in short-term storage is limited to about four or five items.

Long-term store: In contrast to the short-term store, where information lasts only a few seconds, the **long-term store** retains information for a relatively long time. Although it is possible to forget something within a few minutes after the information has reached long-term storage, it is more common for data in long-term storage to last for days, weeks, or even years. Almost all of us, for example, can remember the name of our grade one teacher. Figure 6-3 depicts the transfer of information received by the sensory store, through the short-term store, to long-term storage.

Rehearsal and Encoding

The amount of information available for delivery from short-term storage to long-term storage depends on the amount of rehearsal it is given. Failure to rehearse an input, either by repeating it or by relating it to other data, can result in fading and eventual loss of the information. Information can also be lost because of competition for attention. For example, if the short-term store receives a great number of inputs simultaneously from the sensory store, its capacity may be reduced to only two or three pieces of information.

The purpose of rehearsal is to hold information in short-term storage long enough for encoding to take place. **Encoding** is the process by which we choose a word or visual image to represent a perceived object. Marketers help consumers encode brands in several ways:

- **By using brand symbols**. Kellogg's uses Tony the Tiger on its Frosted Flakes; the Green Giant Company has its Jolly Green Giant. Dell Computer turns the *e* in its logo on its side for quick name recognition; Microsoft uses a stylized window, presumably on the world.

- **By using illustrations.** "Learning" a picture takes less time than learning verbal information, but both types of information are important in forming an overall

ADVERTISEMENT

GETTING TO THE

heart of the matter

What is cholesterol?

Cholesterol is a fat-like substance found in the blood, which is necessary for a variety of cellular functions within the body. There are several types of cholesterol in the bloodstream, including low-density lipoprotein cholesterol (LDL-C) and high-density lipoprotein cholesterol (HDL-C), as well as fatty particles called triglycerides.

Where does it come from?

About 20% of the cholesterol in your blood comes from your diet. The remaining 80% is made by your liver.

What do I need cholesterol for?

Your body uses cholesterol to make hormones, and it plays an important part in various cellular activities. Your body uses triglycerides to store energy.

What is meant by "good" and "bad" cholesterol?

Because cholesterol and triglyceride do not dissolve in blood, they cannot travel through the blood by themselves. Instead, they are carried by special proteins called lipoproteins:

- High-density lipoproteins (HDL) transport cholesterol from body tissues back to the liver, where it can be reused or eliminated from the body
- Low-density lipoproteins (LDL) transport cholesterol from the liver to the body tissues
- Very-low-density lipoproteins (VLDL) carry triglycerides from the liver to the tissues.

Cholesterol carried by HDL molecules (HDL cholesterol) is called "good" cholesterol, because it is moving from your body tissues back to your liver. You want high levels of HDL cholesterol.

Cholesterol carried by LDL molecules (LDL cholesterol) is called "bad" cholesterol because it can contribute to the clogging of your blood vessels, which can cause a heart attack or stroke. You want low levels of LDL cholesterol.

What is atherosclerosis? And how can it lead to a heart attack?

Atherosclerosis occurs when particles of cholesterol and other substances settle inside the walls of your blood vessels, forming blockages or "plaques". As the plaques build up, the

blood vessels become narrower and blood cannot move through them as easily.

If the atherosclerotic plaques in your arteries become large enough – or if a plaque breaks apart and a blood clot forms – a blood vessel may become completely blocked and prevent any blood from reaching the heart (causing a heart attack), the brain (causing a stroke) or other tissues.

Several factors can increase an individual's chance of developing atherosclerosis and these are known as "cardiovascular risk factors". They include elevated blood cholesterol, high blood pressure, diabetes, smoking, obesity, and a lack of physical exercise.

Can you inherit high cholesterol from your parents?

Yes. There are several inherited diseases that can cause abnormal blood levels of cholesterol or triglycerides. If you have close family members (parents, brothers or sisters) who have been diagnosed with heart disease or high levels of blood cholesterol, you should have your cholesterol and triglycerides checked in case you have an inherited form of high cholesterol.

How do I know that I have high cholesterol?

For many individuals, the first time they learn that they have high cholesterol is when they have their first heart attack. Having an abnormal cholesterol level does not cause any symptoms on its own – it is only once the individual develops a related health problem, such as heart disease, that symptoms will begin to occur. Because the liver produces cholesterol, it is possible to have abnormal cholesterol levels even if you eat a healthy diet, are physically active and maintain an ideal body weight.

The only way to find out whether you have a problem with your cholesterol is to have a blood test – and the results might surprise you. Not everyone needs to be tested for cholesterol levels, so ask your doctor whether this is a good idea for you.

Normal Blood Vessel

Blood Vessel with Atherosclerosis

Keri J. Kingsbury, MSN, RN, CCNIC Co-Chair, Canadian Lipid Nurse Network

Canadian Lipid Nurse Network

EXHIBIT 6-11

CANADIAN LIPID NURSE NETWORK AD: AD REQUIRING COGNITIVE PROCESSING

Courtesy of LaneLabs.

Sensory store:
The storing of sensory input for a few seconds in memory.

Short-term store or working memory:
The processing of information and its short-term storage.

Long-term store:
The retaining of processed information for extended periods of time.

Encoding:
The process of choosing a word or visual image to represent a perceived object.

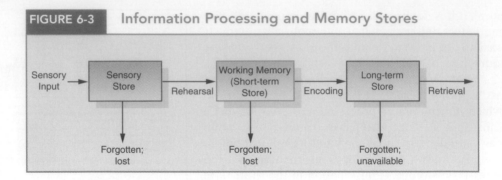

FIGURE 6-3   Information Processing and Memory Stores

mental image. A print ad with both an illustration and body copy is more likely to be encoded and stored than an illustration without verbal information.

What does a Japanese *sumo* wrestler have to do with hemlock? Hemlock—the American variety called "Bei Tsuga"—is extremely popular in Japan for building houses. But Canadian hemlock, though it is stronger, was not well known in Japan. To convey the qualities of Canadian hemlock (strength, greater bending stiffness, and greater nail-holding grip), the Coastal Forest and Lumber Association, which represents several west coast lumber companies, hired Mai-no-umi, a well-known *sumo* wrestler. Mai-no-umi, who, at five-feet five inches and 265 pounds, is a relatively "light-weight" sumo wrestler, is known for his ability to beat opponents more than three times his weight. By using Mai-no-umi in its ads, CFLA effectively conveyed the message that Canadian hemlock is stronger than its American counterpart.[8]

www.cfla.org

- ■ *By using high-imagery copy:* Another study found that high-imagery copy was remembered better than low-imagery copy, whether or not it was accompanied by an illustration. But for low-imagery copy, illustrations were an important factor in audience recall.[9]

- ■ *By placing messages in a suitable context:* Researchers have found that the encoding of a commercial is related to the context of the television program during (or before or after) which it is shown. Some parts of a program may require viewers to commit a larger portion of their cognitive resources to processing (e.g., when a dramatic event takes place as opposed to a casual conversation). When viewers commit more cognitive resources to the program itself, they encode and store less of the information conveyed by a commercial. This suggests that commercials that need a high level of cognitive processing may be less effective within or adjacent to a dramatic program than commercials that need less elaborate processing.[10] Other research indicates that viewers who are very involved with a television show respond more positively to commercials during or after that show and have more positive purchase intentions.[11]

- ■ *By using suitable message themes:* Men and women exhibit different encoding patterns. For example, women are more likely than men to remember television commercials depicting a social relationship. However, there is no difference in recall among men and women for commercials that focus on the product itself.[12]

When consumers are presented with too much information (a situation called *information overload*), they may have difficulty in encoding and storing it all. Findings suggest that it is difficult for consumers to remember product information from ads for new brands in heavily advertised categories.[13] Consumers can become cognitively overloaded when they are given a lot of information in a short time. The result of this overload is confusion, and they are unlikely to buy the product.

Retention

Information is stored in long-term memory in two ways: *episodically* (by the order in which it is acquired) and *semantically* (according to significant concepts). We may remember having gone to a movie last Saturday because of our ability to store data episodically, and we may remember the plot, the stars, and the director because of our ability to store data semantically. Learning theorists believe that memories stored semantically are organized into frameworks by which we integrate new data with previous experience. For information about a new brand or model of printer to enter our memory, for example, we would have to relate it to our previous experience with printers in terms of such qualities as speed, print quality, resolution, and memory.

Information does not just sit in long-term storage waiting to be retrieved. Instead, it is constantly organized and reorganized as new links between chunks of information are forged. In fact, many information-processing theorists view the long-term store as a network consisting of nodes (i.e., concepts), with links between and among them. The total package of associations brought to mind when a cue is **activated** is called a **schema**. Developing schemas with strong, easily activated links will aid the retention and retrieval of information. Consumer memory for the name of a product may also be activated by relating it to the spokesperson used in its advertising. For many people, Michael Jordan means Nike sneakers.

The ability of consumers to retain information also depends how similar the new information is to what is already stored in their memory. For example, people are more likely to remember the information they receive about new products if they bear a familiar brand name. People's knowledge and ability to code and recode information into larger pieces (called chunking) also influence how much information they can process and retain. Knowledgeable consumers can take in more complex chunks of information than those who are less knowledgeable in the product category. Thus, the amount and type of technological information contained in a computer ad can be much more detailed in a magazine such as *PC Magazine* or *Wired* than in a general-interest magazine such as *Time*.

Retrieval

Retrieval is the *process by which we recover information from long-term storage.* For example, when we are unable to remember something we are very familiar with, we are experiencing a failure of the retrieval system. Retrieval is made easy in the following situations:

- **When the benefits of the product (rather than its attributes) are stressed in advertising:** Consumers are likely to spend time interpreting and elaborating on information they find relevant to their needs (rather than product attributes) and to activate such relevant knowledge from long-term memory.[14]
- **When interference is lower:** The greater the number of competitive ads in a product category, the less the brand claims in a specific ad are remembered. Ads can also act as retrieval cues for a competitive brand.

An example of such consumer confusion occurred when consumers attributed the long-running and attention-getting television campaign featuring the Eveready Energizer Bunny to the leader in the field, Duracell. Advertising that creates a distinctive brand image can help in the retention and retrieval of the message.

Activation:
Relating new data to old ones to make the new material more meaningful.

Schema:
The whole package of associations brought to mind when a cue is activated.

Retrieval:
The process by which we recover information from long-term storage.

Elaboration likelihood model:
A theory that suggests that a person's level of involvement during message processing is a critical factor in determining which route to persuasion is likely to be effective.

Central route to persuasion:
The reaching of highly involved consumers through ads that focus on cognitive learning.

Peripheral route to persuasion:
The use of passive learning processes to reach consumers in a low-involvement situation.

Involvement and Information Processing

The level of consumer involvement in a purchase has considerable influence on the level and nature of information processing that occurs. The **elaboration likelihood model** provides insights into the connection between involvement and information processing. It suggests that the extent to which a person is involved (in the brand and in the decision) while processing a message is a critical factor in determining how information is processed, and that in turn affects learning and changes in attitude. For example, as the message becomes more personally relevant (i.e., as involvement increases), consumers are more likely to carefully evaluate the merits and weaknesses of a product, using many attributes, and to make the cognitive effort required to process the message arguments.[15] Thus, for high-involvement purchases, the **central route to persuasion**, which requires considered thought and cognitive processing, is likely to be the most effective marketing strategy. In such cases, the quality of the argument presented in the persuasive message is very influential in the decision.[16] When involvement is low, messages follow the **peripheral route to persuasion**; in such instances, consumers will engage in very little information search and evaluation and rely more heavily on other elements of the message (such as spokespersons or background music) to form attitudes or make product choices. In this instance, because the consumer is less motivated to make a cognitive effort, learning is more likely to occur through repetition, the passive processing of visual cues, and holistic perception.

The advertisement shown previously in Exhibit 6-11 to illustrate cognitive learning also illustrates the use of the central route to persuasion; Exhibit 6-12 shows an ad that takes the peripheral route. The central route to persuasion is more likely to happen with comparative ads since consumers are forced to process the arguments;[17] and when metaphors and other figures of speech that are unexpected are used ("It forced other car makers into the copier business" by Mercury Sable) as they place added processing demands on consumers.[18] Exhibit 6-13 uses a catchy metaphor headline to advertise a Dodge Durango.

The marketing implications of the elaboration likelihood model are clear: for high-involvement purchases, marketers should use arguments stressing the strong, solid, high-quality attributes of their products, thus using the central (or highly cognitive) route. For low-involvement purchases, marketers should use the peripheral route to persuasion, focusing on the method of presentation rather than on the content of the message (e.g., through the use of celebrity spokespersons or highly visual and symbolic advertisements).

The increasing use of the internet as a marketing vehicle poses interesting challenges and questions to marketers. In general, the internet is a high-involvement medium; can it be used to aid passive learning? For example, would mere expo-

THERE'S MORE THAN ONE WAY TO GET 100 GALLONS OF DRINKING WATER INTO YOUR HOME.

PŪR
WATER FILTRATION SYSTEM

YOUR WATER SHOULD BE PŪR.

The problem with bottled water is the bottles. Get as much clean, healthy water as you need right from your tap. PŪR faucet mount filters attach easily and turn off and on with a simple twist. Nothing to lug home, nothing to store. Find out more at www.purwater.com

EXHIBIT 6-12

AD USING PERIPHERAL ROUTE TO PERSUASION

Courtesy of The Procter & Gamble Company. Used by permission.

EXHIBIT 6-13

UNEXPECTED METAPHOR IN HEADLINE INCREASES IMPACT OF AN ADVERTISEMENT
Courtesy of DaimlerChrysler Corporation.

sure to banner advertising lead to some passive learning and brand awareness? Internet Insight 6-1 describes the results of a large study conducted by the Internet Advertising Bureau on the effectiveness of banner advertising.

www.iab.net

MEASURES OF CONSUMER LEARNING

For many marketers, their two goals for consumer learning are a larger market share and brand-loyal consumers. These goals are interdependent: brand-loyal customers provide the basis for a stable and growing market share, and brands with larger market shares have proportionately larger groups of loyal buyers.[19] Marketers devote their promotional budgets to trying to teach consumers that their brands are best and that their products will best solve the consumers' problems and satisfy their needs. Thus, it is important for the marketer to measure how effectively consumers have "learned" the message. The following sections examine various measures of consumer learning: *recognition and recall measures,* and *cognitive measures of learning.*

Measures of Recognition and Recall

Recognition and recall tests are conducted to determine whether consumers remember seeing an ad, to what extent they read it or saw it and can remember its content, what their resulting attitudes toward the product and the brand are, and whether they intend to buy it.

INTERNET INSIGHT 6-1
ARE BANNER ADVERTISEMENTS EFFECTIVE?

Canadians are a highly "connected" nation, with more than 16 million internet users.[a] This has led to the increasing popularity of online advertising. Companies are spending more and more money on all forms of online advertisements, including banner advertising, which is perhaps the most common form of online advertising. Banner advertising can be considered to be a form of low-involvement advertising since the ads are often highly visual and they aim to grab the consumer's attention with their layout and simple messages (as opposed to the complex, high-information ads). Are such ads effective?

One of the largest studies of banner ads and their effectiveness was conducted by the Internet Advertising Bureau (IAB). The IAB surveyed more than 16 000 respondents and studied 12 leading websites.[b] This is what was found:

- Awareness increased by 30 percent as a result of banner ads.
- Banner ads create a positive impression of the brand and change consumers' perceptions of the product.
- Banner ads are effective even when the viewers do not click on them.
- Banner ads are as effective as any other form of advertising in creating brand awareness.

Those findings show that even the mere exposure to online ads can lead to some passive learning. There is also some evidence that banner ads can produce impressive recall rates. One study found that ad recall with banner ads was an astounding 40 percent (compared with 41 percent for a 30-second TV spot).[c]

Of course, placing banner ads in a relevant context (i.e., in the right website and tied to relevant keywords in search engines), will result in greater learning since it will lead to proper encoding of the ads.

[a] "More Than Half of Canada and U.S. On-line," CyberAtlas, **http://cyberatlas.internet.com/big_picture/geographics/article/0,,5911_2200601,00.html**.

[b] IAB On-line Effectiveness Study," Internet Advertising Bureau (**www.iab.net**), 1997, quoted in Ramesh Venkat, *Canadian e-marketing: A Strategic Approach* (McGraw-Hill, 2003), 266.

[c] "Banner Ads Effective at Branding," Cyber Atlas, **www.cyberatlas.com**, accessed February 17, 1999.

Recognition tests:
Aided recall tests in which a consumer is shown an ad and asked whether he or she remembers seeing it and remembers its key points.

Recall tests:
Unaided recall tests in which consumers are asked if they have read a specific magazine (or watched a specific television show) and can remember any ads from it.

Comprehension:
The grasping of the intended message of an advertisement.

Recognition tests are based on *aided recall,* whereas **recall tests** use *unaided recall.* In recognition tests, the consumer is shown an ad and asked whether he or she remembers seeing it and can remember any of its salient points. In recall tests, the consumer is asked whether he or she has read a specific magazine or watched a specific television show, and if so, can remember any of the ads or commercials, the product advertised, the brand, and any salient points about the product. Generally, brand names that convey specific and relevant advantages are remembered more easily. For example, a recent study found that a brand name explicitly conveying a product benefit (such as Atlantic Mini-Storage) leads to higher recall of an advertised benefit claim than a non-suggestive brand name (Acme Storage).[20]

A number of syndicated research services conduct recognition and recall tests, such as those conducted by the Starch Readership Service, which evaluates the effectiveness of magazine advertisements. An advertiser can gauge the effectiveness of an ad by comparing its readership recognition scores with similar-sized ads, with competitive ads, and with the company's previous ads. Exhibit 6-14 shows an example of a "Starched" ad.

Cognitive Responses to Advertising

Another measure of consumer learning is the degree to which consumers accurately comprehend the advertising message. **Comprehension** depends on the characteristics of the message, the consumer's opportunity and ability to process the information, and the consumer's motivation (or level of involvement).[21] To ensure a high level of comprehension, many marketers conduct copy testing either *before* the advertising actually appears (called pretesting) or *after* it appears (post-testing). Pretests are used to determine which, if any, elements of an advertising message should be revised before large expenditures are made on advertising. Post-tests are used to evaluate the effectiveness of an ad that has already run and to determine which elements, if any, should be changed to give the ad more impact and to make future ads more memorable.

LEARNING AND MARKETING STRATEGY

Learning theories have been used by marketers in many ways. Both behavioural and cognitive learning theories have led to several marketing applications.

Classical Conditioning and Marketing Strategy

Identify and pair the product with a known, well-liked stimulus: Since classical conditioning is based on the assumption that consumers will transfer their feelings and behaviour toward the known stimulus to the unknown one, the implication of classical conditioning is that marketers need to identify the product with a well-known and well-liked stimulus. This could take the form of using celebrities to endorse a product,

EXHIBIT 6-14

STARCH READERSHIP SCORES MEASURE LEARNING THROUGH AD RECOGNITION TESTS
Courtesy of Buick.

using music that the target market knows and likes (e.g., popular songs, Christmas tunes in December), using pictures of living things that the target consumers like (e.g., puppies or other animals or babies in ads that target women); or using images of inanimate things (e.g., beautiful scenery) that might appeal to the target market. The key points to remember are (1) that the unconditioned stimulus has to suit the target market and the product, and (2) that the pairing has to be consistent (i.e., repeated over a long period). Such repeated pairing can have the following results:

- Consumers will pay more attention to the ad (as the unconditioned stimulus is something that is of interest to them) and to other promotions of the product.[22]
- Consumers develop favourable attitudes toward the product (because of the transfer of the positive feelings toward the unconditioned stimulus).
- Consumers develop greater intentions to purchase the product.
- Consumers learn the key attributes about the product. For example, they have learned that Royale bathroom tissues are soft because of the pairing of fluffy kittens with the product.

Use the concept of stimulus generalization effectively: As stated earlier, consumers learn to generalize from one stimulus to the other. This phenomenon can be used to the advantage of a new product (e.g., by using a well-known brand name while introducing the product) and for taking advantage of the brand equity that a company has developed by extending the product line, form, or category). Other examples of the application of this principle are the use of a family brand name, a retail brand name, and licensing.

Distinguish the company's products through effective use of stimulus discrimination: If consumers learn the similarity between products through stimulus *generalization*, they learn to distinguish between products through stimulus *discrimination*. Marketers can aid this by developing strong positioning strategies and through product differentiation (with colour, packaging, and other details). For example, Advil differentiates itself from other pain killers through the use of colour—a distinctive reddish brown. Similarly, Nexium (a medication for acid-reflux disease) is marketed as the purple pill.

Operant Conditioning and Marketing Strategy

Marketers effectively use the phenomenon of consumer instrumental learning when they provide positive reinforcement by assuring their prospective customers that they will be satisfied with the product, the service, and the total buying experience.

Make the product the ultimate reward: The objective of all marketing efforts should be to maximize customer satisfaction. Marketers must be certain to provide the best possible product for the money and to avoid raising consumer expectations for product (or service) performance beyond what the product can deliver. Aside from the experience of using the product itself, consumers can receive reinforcement from other elements in the purchase situation, such as the environment in which the transaction or service takes place, the attention and service provided by employees, and the amenities provided.

An upscale beauty salon, in addition to a beautiful environment, may offer coffee and soft drinks to the customers when they are waiting, and may provide free local telephone service at each hairdressing station. Even if the styling outcome is less than perfect, the customer may feel so pampered with the atmosphere and service that she looks forward to her next visit.

Some hotels provide reinforcement to guests in the form of small amenities, such as chocolates on the pillow or bottled water on the dresser; others send platters of fruit or even bottles of wine to returning guests to show their appreciation for their continued patronage.

Provide samples and free trials: If the product is the ultimate reward, then one way in which marketers can use operant conditioning is by providing free samples, which give the consumer a chance to try the product. If the product is good and provides positive reinforcement, this would lead to future purchases. Test driving, another form of sampling, is another example of the use of operant conditioning.

General Motors of Canada Ltd. has started offering 24-hour test drives in an effort to convince customers of the quality of GM cars. GM Canada president Michael Grimaldi says the company wants to "demonstrate to customers that this is a new GM."[23] Potential buyers can choose from eight to ten models to take home for 24 hours. GM spokesman Stew Low said the company wanted to "get bums in seats"[24] for enough time to let people get a good feel for the cars.

Practice relationship marketing: Another form of non-product reinforcement is to develop a close personal relationship with customers. This is known as relationship marketing. The knowledge that she will be notified of an upcoming sale or that selected merchandise will be set aside for her next visit cements the loyalty that a customer may have to a retail store. The ability to telephone his "personal" banker to transfer money between accounts or to do other banking transactions without going to the bank reinforces a customer's satisfaction with his bank.

Provide other non-product rewards (or reinforcements): Marketers have discovered that offering non-product rewards—even occasionally—serves as reinforcement and encourages consumer patronage. Offering samples of other related brands (e.g., free hair-frizz controller with a conditioner), free coupons for future purchases, "we pay the tax" sales, free upgrades for air travel, and other rewards that are tied to purchase are all examples of non-product rewards that marketers can offer. The promise of possibly receiving a reward provides positive reinforcement and encourages consumer patronage, especially when the reward is related to the product and enhances the consumer's experience with the product.

What do Canadians think of when they hear the word "ice"? If you are a young Canadian man in the 19–34 age group, you probably think of hockey and ice-cold beer—at least that is what Labatt's believed when it launched the "Crazy Coldie Program." During the NHL playoffs, the company included one of several NHL coldies, each shaped like the jersey of one hockey team. The results were extraordinary—a 300 percent growth in market share during the promotional period, and the ads that accompanied the promotion resulted in three times the usual consumer recall for the product category.[25]

www.labatt.ca

In an effort to connect with e-generation children, Kinder Surprise chocolate eggs, produced by Ferrero Canada, added a "magicode" inside every egg. The magicode directed children to the company's website, where they could play online games for 20 minutes free of charge. Not only did children visit the website, but so did their parents.[26]

www.magi-kinder.com

Shape behaviour through step-wise reinforcement: Reinforcement performed *before* the desired consumer behaviour (i.e, purchase) actually takes place is called **shaping**. Shaping makes it more likely that certain desired consumer behaviour will occur. For example, retailers recognize that they must first attract customers to their stores before they can expect them to do the bulk of their shopping there. Many retailers provide some form of preliminary reinforcement (shaping) to encourage consumers to visit their store. For example, car dealers recognize that in order to sell new model cars, they must first encourage people to visit their showrooms and then to test-drive their cars. So they encourage showroom visits by offering small gifts (such as key chains and DVDs), then larger gifts (e.g., a $10 cheque) for test-driving the car, and a rebate cheque upon placement of an order. They use a multi-step shaping process to achieve the desired consumer learning.

Shaping: The reinforcement of pre-purchase behaviour to lead the consumers slowly toward making a purchase.

Aeroplan and Land Rover Canada have formed a partnership to offer 250 Aeroplan miles to complete an online survey on vehicle purchase intentions, and another 5000 Aeroplan miles to test-drive a Land Rover within three months of completing the survey. Land Rover hopes that these initial pre-purchase reinforcements will shape consumer behaviour enough to lead to test-driving the vehicle and that the positive reinforcement from the test drive will lead to purchases.[27]

Cognitive Learning and Marketing Strategy

As we have seen, consumers do not learn only through connections or by learning the linkages between stimuli and behaviour. We also learn through mental processes such as reasoning or solving problems. We also learn through repetition (without pairing the new object with known stimuli) and by observing the behaviour of others (and outcomes that follow their behaviour). Marketers can make use of this knowledge in several ways.

Use rote learning to teach consumers about a brand: Most advertising is aimed at creating brand awareness and some learning about the brand through mere repetition. Rote learning is relevant to the advertising of low-involvement products; it is achieved through the repetition of simple messages (e.g., "Coke is it"), jingles, and slogans (e.g., Buckley's cough syrup—"It tastes awful. And it works.").

Use reasoning or problem solving to teach consumers about complex products and situations: In high-involvement situations, consumers are willing to process more information and use their ability to think, reorganize, and evaluate information to reach solutions to their problems. Under such circumstances, marketers can use complex messages to convey key points about a product or a service. As the elaboration-likelihood model suggests, in these situations marketers would do well to emphasize the strong, solid, high-quality attributes of their products, thus using the central (or highly cognitive) route to persuading consumers to use their product (see Exhibit 6-11 on page 197).

Use modelling to teach consumers about proper behaviour: Since consumers learn without direct experience—by observing how other people behave—marketers can teach consumers about new products and provide solutions to their problems through the use of modelling. For example, we have been taught, by modelling, not only that having dandruff is socially unacceptable, but also that Head and Shoulders is the solution to that problem. Several personal-hygiene products, such as deodorants, mouthwash, and more recently, teeth-whitening strips, are sold this way.

Use modelling to extinguish negative behaviour: Modelling is also widely used by marketers to teach consumers the consequences of potentially harmful behaviour such as smoking, using drugs, or drinking and driving. For example, recent ads against smoking showed a man who had been a smoker talking about how he lost his wife to cancer (as a result of second-hand smoke).

Help consumers store, retain, and retrieve messages through the effective use of information processing principles: As we saw earlier, marketers can use their understanding of information processing to aid consumer learning. Storage and encoding can be enhanced through high-imagery copy; retention can be enhanced through chunking and encouraging semantic coding of information, and retrieval can be enhanced through the reduction of interference.

SUMMARY

- Consumer learning is the process by which individuals acquire the purchase and consumption knowledge and experience they apply to future related behaviour. The basic elements that contribute to an understanding of learning are motivation, cues, response, and reinforcement.

- There are two schools of thought as to how people learn—behavioural theories and cognitive theories. Behavioural theorists view learning as observable responses to stimuli, whereas cognitive theorists believe that learning is a function of mental processing.

- Two major behavioural learning theories are classical conditioning and instrumental conditioning.

The principles of classical conditioning that provide the theoretical underpinnings for many marketing applications include repetition, stimulus generalization, and stimulus discrimination.

- Instrumental learning theorists believe that learning takes place through a trial-and-error process in which positive outcomes (i.e., rewards) result in the behaviour being repeated. Both positive and negative reinforcement can be used to encourage the desired behaviour. Reinforcement schedules can be total (consistent) or partial (fixed ratio or random).

- Cognitive learning theory holds that the kind of learning most characteristic of humans is problem solving. It can be at a rote learning level (when connections between two stimuli are learned through memorization) or at a higher, more complex level, when it is called reasoning.

- Vicarious learning or modelling is considered to be another form of cognitive learning because there is no direct experience involved. Modelling takes place when we learn by observing the behaviour of others and the outcomes that they experience.

- Learning requires the processing of information and storing of the information in memory. Memory has three storage units: the sensory store, the short-term store (or working memory), and the long-term store. The processes of memory are rehearsal, encoding, storage, and retrieval.

- Learning can be measured through recognition (aided recall) and recall measures or through cognitive measures (i.e., how well the message was understood), such as copy testing.

DISCUSSION QUESTIONS

1. What is learning? Explain behavioural and cognitive learning.

2. Explain classical conditioning theory. How can the principles of classical conditioning theory be applied to the development of marketing strategies?

3. Explain operant conditioning theory and discuss how it can be used by marketers.

4. What are the various forms of cognitive learning? When (or for what type of products) would you use each of these theories?

5. Describe in learning terms the conditions under which family branding is a good policy and those under which it is not.

6. (a) Define the following memory structures: sensory store, short-term store (working memory), and long-term store. Discuss how each of these concepts can be used in the development of an advertising strategy.

   (b) How does information overload affect the consumer's ability to comprehend an ad and store it in his or her memory?

7. What are some measures of learning?

CRITICAL THINKING QUESTIONS

1. Neutrogena, the cosmetics company, has introduced a new line of shaving products for men. How can the company use stimulus generalization and/or stimulus discrimination to market these products? Is instrumental conditioning applicable to this marketing situation? If so, how?

2. Which theory of learning (classical conditioning, instrumental conditioning, observational learning, or cognitive learning) best explains the following consumption behaviour: (a) buying a six-pack of Evian water, (b) preferring to buy clothes at Gap, (c) buying a digital camera for the first time, (d) buying a new car, and (e) switching from one cellular phone service to another? Explain your choices.

3. Assume that you are the marketing manager of a company that produces plasma television sets. How can you use the principles of encoding and retention to make sure that consumers learn and store information about this relatively new product category effectively?

4. Assume that you are in charge of introducing a new brand of pain reliever—one that targets migraine headaches—at a Canadian pharmaceutical company. Your company currently produces only one type of pain reliever: an acetominophen product (similar to Tylenol) in three forms (gelcaps, regular strength, and extra strength capsules).
   (a) Would you use the same brand name for the new product? Why or why not?

(b) What type of learning theory would you use to teach consumers about the new product? Why?

(c) How would you help consumers code, retain, and retrieve information about this product?

5. Imagine that you are the instructor in this course and you are trying to increase student participation in class discussions. How would you use reinforcement to achieve your objective?

INTERNET EXERCISES

1. Visit the websites of three cosmetic and beauty products manufacturers. Which one do you think makes the best use of learning principles? Which one makes very little use of learning principles? Justify your answers.

2. Visit some websites until you find one that attempts to shape consumer behaviour. How does the website do this? Is it effective? Why or why not?

3. Visit websites of some non-profit organizations (e.g., Canadian Wildlife Foundation, Canadian Cancer Society). Do these websites use any learning principles? If yes, which ones and how?

KEY TERMS

Activation   *(p. 199)*
Advertising wear-out   *(p. 186)*
Behavioural learning theory
   (p. 184)
Central route to persuasion
   (p. 200)
Classical conditioning   *(p. 184)*
Cognitive learning   *(p. 195)*
Comprehension   *(p. 202)*
Conditioned learning   *(p. 184)*
Conditioned stimuli   *(p. 185)*
Consumer learning   *(p. 182)*
Cues   *(p. 183)*
Distributed learning   *(p. 193)*
Elaboration likelihood model
   (ELM)   *(p. 200)*

Encoding   *(p. 197)*
Family branding   *(p. 188)*
Imagery   *(p. 196)*
Instrumental (or operant)
   conditioning   *(p. 191)*
Licensing   *(p. 188)*
Long-term store   *(p. 197)*
Massed learning   *(p. 193)*
Modelling   *(p. 195)*
Motivation   *(p. 183)*
Negative reinforcement   *(p. 192)*
Operant conditioning. *See*
   Instrumental conditioning
Peripheral route to persuasion
   (p. 200)
Positive reinforcement   *(p. 192)*

Reasoning   *(p. 195)*
Recall tests   *(p. 202)*
Recognition tests   *(p. 202)*
Reinforcement   *(p. 183)*
Response   *(p. 183)*
Retrieval   *(p. 199)*
Rote learning   *(p. 195)*
Schema   *(p. 199)*
Sensory store   *(p. 197)*
Shaping *(p. 205)*
Short-term store or working
   memory   *(p. 197)*
Stimulus discrimination   *(p. 189)*
Stimulus generalization   *(p. 187)*
Unconditioned stimuli   *(p. 185)*

CASE 6-1: THE PITFALLS OF REINFORCEMENT OF CUSTOMER BEHAVIOUR

Learning theory stresses that reinforcement is crucial in shaping future behaviour. Today, thanks to technology, service marketers can track the past behaviour of customers better than ever before and can easily reward desirable behaviour. Thus, the records of highly profitable customers are given special codes designed to provide them with faster and better service when they contact the company, move them ahead of other customers in service queues, and give them upgrades and special discounts that are unknown and unavailable to other customers. Furthermore, since many companies share data about customers' transactions, customers are often assigned to "reward tiers" before they even begin to do business with a company because their buying potential has already been measured.

However, rewarding the best customers also means that "lesser" customers receive inferior service. For example, the calls of selected customers calling a brokerage company are answered within 15 seconds, whereas other customers wait 10 minutes or more. At the websites of some banks, highly profitable customers have access to special links directing them to service agents and special phone lines, whereas other customers never even see these links. At many financial institutions, service agents are permitted to grant fee waivers to highly profitable customers while other patrons have no negotiating power. In addition, the special treatment of selected customers also means that other customers pay more service fees.

QUESTIONS

1. In the context of learning theory, what are the drawbacks of creating a reward system based entirely on measured past behaviour?

2. How can marketers create more effective reward systems to shape the future behaviour of less profitable customers?

Source: Diane Brady, "Why Service Stinks," Business Week, October 23, 2000, 118, 122, 124.

NOTES

1   The three product examples featured here are discussed in Robert M. McMath and Thom Forbes, *What Were They Thinking?* (New York: Time Business Random House, 1998).

2   N.J. Mackintosh, *Conditioning and Associative Learning* (New York: Oxford University Press, 1983), 10.

3   Curtis P. Haugtvedt, David W. Schumann, Wendy L. Schneier, and Wendy L. Warren, "Advertising Repetition and Variation Strategies: Implications for Understanding Attitude Strength," *Journal of Consumer Research,* 21, June 1994, 176–189.

4   Ken Bensinger, "Can You Spot the Fake?" *Wall Street Journal,* February 16, 2001, W1, W14.

5   Lesley Young, "Plucky Branding," *0*, October 6/13, 2003, 12.

6   Gregory S. Carpenter, Rashi Glazer, and Kent Nakamoto, "Meaningful Brands from Meaningless Differentiation: The Dependence on Irrelevant Attributes," *Journal of Marketing Research,* 31, August 1994, 339–350.

7   Jennifer Gregan Paxton and Deborah Roedder John, "Consumer Learning by Analogy: A Model of Internal Knowledge Transfer," *Journal of Consumer Research,* 24, December 1997, 266–284.

8   Eve Lazarus, "Branching Out," *Marketing Magazine,* October 20, 2003, 29.

9   H. Rao Unnava and Robert E. Burnkrant, "An Imagery-Processing View of the Role of Pictures in Print Advertisements," *Journal of Marketing Research,* 28, May 1991, 226–231.

10 Kenneth R. Lord and Robert E. Burnkrant, "Television Program Elaboration Effects on Commercial Processing," in *Advances in Consumer Research,* vol. 15, ed. Michael Houston (Provo, UT: Association for Consumer Research, 1988), 213–218.

11 Kevin J. Clancy, "CPMs Must Bow to 'Involvement' Measurement," *Advertising Age,* January 20, 1992, 26.

12 Joan Meyers-Levy and Durairaj Maheswaran, "Exploring Differences in Males' and Females'

Processing Strategies," *Journal of Consumer Research,* 18, June 1991, 63–70.

13 Robert J. Kent and Chris T. Allen, "Competitive Interference Effects in Consumer Memory for Advertising: The Role of Brand Familiarity," *Journal of Marketing,* 58, July 1994, 97–105.

14 Kevin Lane Keller, "Memory and Evaluation Effects in Competitive Advertising Environments," *Journal of Consumer Research,* 17, March 1991, 463–476.

15 John T. Cacioppo, Richard E. Petty, Chuan Feng Kao, and Regina Rodriguez, "Central and Peripheral Routes to Persuasion: An Individual Difference Perspective," *Journal of Personality and Social Psychology,* 51, 5, 1986, 1032–1043.

16 See, for example, Richard E. Petty and John T. Cacioppo, "Issues Involvement Can Increase or Decrease Persuasion by Enhancing Message-Relevant Cognitive Responses," *Journal of Personality and Social Psychology,* 37, 1979, 1915–1926; Cacioppo and Petty, "The Need for Cognition," *Journal of Personality and Social Psychology,* 42, 1982, 116–131; and John T. Cacioppo, Richard E. Petty, and Katherine J. Morris, "Effects of Need for Cognition on Message Evaluation, Recall and Persuasion," *Journal of Personality and Social Psychology,* 45, 1983, 805–818.

17 Sanjay Putrevu and Kenneth R. Lord, "Comparative and Noncomparative Advertising: Attitudinal Effects under Cognitive and Affective Involvement Conditions," *Journal of Advertising,* 23, 2, June 1994, 77–91.

18 Mark Toncar and James Munch, "Consumer Responses to Tropes in Print Advertising," *Journal of Advertising,* Spring 2001, 55–65.

19 For example, Alan Dick and Kunai Basu, "Customer Loyalty: Toward an Integrated Conceptual Framework," *Journal of the Academy of Marketing Science,* 22, Spring 1994, 99–113; and Grahame R. Dowling and Mark Uncles, "Do Customer Loyalty Programs Really Work?" *Sloan Management Review,* Summer 1997, 71–82.

20 Kevin Lane Keller, Susan E. Heckler, and Michael J. Houston, "The Effects of Brand Name Suggestiveness on Advertising Recall," *Journal of Marketing,* 62, January 1998, 48–57.

21 David Glen Mick, "Levels of Subjective Comprehension in Advertising Processing and Their Relations to Ad Perceptions, Attitudes, and Memory," *Journal of Consumer Research,* 18, March 1992, 411–424.

22 Chris Janiszewski and Luk Warlop, "The Influence of Classical Conditioning Procedures on Subsequent Attention to the Conditioned Brand," *Journal of Consumer Research,* 20, September 1993, 171–189.

23 Greg Keenan, "GM's 24-hour Test Drive Aims to Win Back Market Share," *I,* September 29, 2003.

24 Ibid.

25 Michelle Halpern, "Labatt's big PROMO! Score," *I,* October 6/13, 2003, 28.

26 Lesley Young, "A Kinder Surprise Found Online," *I,* October 20, 2003.

27 Lesley Young, "A New Flight Path," *Marketing Direct,* November 3, 2003, 9.

Now there's a Dove
of a different stripe.

©2001 Lever Brothers Company. *Deposits nutrients naturally found in skin.

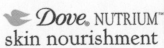 **Dove**. NUTRIUM™
skin nourishment

chapter 7
consumer attitude formation and change

LEARNING OBJECTIVES

By the end of this chapter, you should be able to:

1. Define attitudes and discuss five main characteristics of attitudes.
2. Explain the four functions of attitudes.
3. Explain how attitudes are formed.
4. Discuss at least four models of attitude formation and change.
5. Explain how marketers can create and change consumer attitudes.

7

two thousand and three was not a good year for the tourism industry in Canada. Several unforeseen events, the most important of which was probably the SARS scare, reduced the number of tourists coming to Canada. Although all Canadian cities were affected to some degree, the one most affected by SARS was Toronto. Initial reports indicated that most attractions in the city saw the number of visitors drop by 40 to 60 percent.[1] International tourists who had considered Toronto (and Canada) a safe place to visit were suddenly apprehensive about going there. Within a short span of two or three weeks, their attitude toward the city had changed.

Officials in the city's tourism department reacted by developing an integrated marketing campaign to change consumer attitudes toward the city. A new promotional campaign "Toronto—You Belong Here" was aimed at persuading Torontonians to start visiting local attractions;[2] a campaign aimed at tourists from the rest of Canada ("Canada Loves Toronto"), was cosponsored by Air Canada, which offered cheap air tickets to the city; the "It's time for a little T.O." promotion saw local businesses offering cheap packages including tickets to the Blue Jays' game for a dollar;[3] and the star-studded "Concert for Toronto" was aimed at attracting Americans.[4]

The purpose of all the ads was to change people's attitudes toward visiting the city—from a negative one due to health concerns to a positive one. The ads aimed at Torontonians and other Canadians probably tapped into the value-expressive functions of attitudes (by making them feel they could express their support for the city and, at the same time, convey to others that they were not easily frightened by the threat of SARS). Those aimed at international tourists tried to change brand beliefs, by perhaps showing that if it was safe enough for celebrities to visit Toronto, it must be safe for tourists too. And finally, the ads and the accompanying public relations campaign also attempted to influence consumer attributions by reassuring consumers, particularly inexperienced ones, that a visit to Toronto would not have any negative consequences but would make them heroes instead.

Mercedes-Benz, Canada, had a different, but perhaps even more interesting problem: consumers had very favourable attitudes toward their product, and yet many were not buying it. The company found during focus groups that most Canadians thought that Mercedes cars were well built, of high quality, and "top of the class." But when they were asked, they often said they would not buy one. What could account for this situation? As we will see later on in the chapter (in the section on the theory of reasoned action model of attitude formation), a positive attitude toward a behaviour and its outcomes—in this case, belief that buying a Mercedes would result in their owning a high-quality car— need not always result in an intention to buy. Although a positive attitude toward an object is a necessary condition for purchase or intention to purchase, consumers' purchase intentions can also be affected by other factors, such as their subjective norms about how others would view their actions.

In this chapter we will discuss the reasons that attitudes have such a pervasive influence on consumer behaviour. We also will discuss the properties that have made attitudes so attractive to consumer researchers. Particular attention will be paid to the central topics of attitude formation, attitude change, and related strategic marketing issues.

CHAPTER OVERVIEW

As consumers, each of us has a vast number of attitudes toward products, services, advertisements, direct mail, the internet, and retail stores. Whenever we are asked whether we like or dislike a product, a service, a particular store, or a specific direct marketer (e.g., Amazon), or an advertising theme (e.g., "Tommy girl—a declaration of independence"), we are being asked to express our attitudes.

This chapter examines the important role that attitudes play in shaping consumer behaviour. It also discusses the properties that have made attitudes so attractive to consumer researchers, as well as some of the common frustrations encountered in attitude research. Particular attention will be paid to the central topics of attitude formation, attitude change, and related strategic marketing issues.

WHAT ARE ATTITUDES?

Most marketing communications aim to create positive attitudes toward their products. Why are marketers so concerned about consumer attitudes? Can you think of the last time you bought a product (i.e., a brand) toward which you had a negative attitude? Let's leave out situations in which you had no choice—that eliminates textbooks, medicines, family decisions when you were not the person who made the decision, and products that you bought because those were the only ones that you could afford. What comes to mind now? If you are like most consumers, there will be very few cases when you bought a product toward which you had a negative attitude. Therein lies the importance of attitudes to marketers—usually a positive attitude is a necessary but not sufficient condition for purchase. Hence, marketers aim to create positive attitudes toward their products through their marketing efforts.

How can attitudes be defined? Although all of us have attitudes toward products, ideas, and people, in the context of consumer behaviour, an **attitude** has a specific meaning: *it is a learned predisposition to behave in a consistently favourable or unfavourable way with respect to a given object.* Each part of this definition describes an important property or characteristic of an attitude and is crucial to an understanding of the role of attitudes in consumer behaviour. These are discussed in the following sections.

> **Attitude:**
> A learned predisposition to behave in a consistently favourable or unfavourable way with respect to a given object.

Characteristics of Attitudes

Attitudes Have an "Object"

The word *object* in our consumer-oriented definition of attitude should be interpreted broadly to include specific consumption- or marketing-related concepts, such as product, product category, brand, service, possessions, product use, causes or issues, people, advertisement, internet site, price, medium, or retailer.

In conducting attitude research, we tend to be *object-specific.* For example, if we were interested in learning consumers' attitudes toward three major brands of DVD players, our "object" might include Sony, Toshiba, and Panasonic. If, however, we were interested in DVD players in general, we should examine consumer attitudes toward the product category of DVD players.

Attitudes Are Learned

There is general agreement that attitudes are *learned.* This means that attitudes relevant to purchase behaviour are formed as a result of direct experience with the product, word-of-mouth information acquired from others, or exposure to mass media advertising, the internet, and various forms of direct marketing (e.g., a retailer's catalogue).

Since attitudes are learned, they can be changed—not easily, of course, but with considerable effort.

Attitudes Have Behavioural, Evaluative, and Affective Components

The definition of attitudes provided earlier indicates that when we say that a person has a certain attitude toward an object, the person has made an evaluation of the object and has developed a feeling for it. It is also important to remember that although attitudes may result from behaviour, they are not synonymous with behaviour. Instead, they reflect either a favourable or an unfavourable evaluation of the attitude object. As *learned predispositions,* attitudes have a motivational quality; that is, they might propel a consumer *toward* a particular behaviour or repel the consumer *away* from a particular behaviour.

Attitudes Have Consistency

Another characteristic of attitudes is that they are relatively consistent with the behaviour they reflect. However, despite their *consistency,* attitudes are not necessarily permanent; they do change. (Attitude change is explored later in this chapter.)

It is important to illustrate what we mean by consistency. Normally, we expect consumers' behaviour to correspond with their attitudes. For example, if a French consumer reported preferring Japanese to Korean electronics, we would expect that he would be more likely to buy a Japanese brand when his current VCR needed to be replaced. In other words, when consumers are free to act as they wish, we expect that their actions will be consistent with their attitudes. However, circumstances often make that impossible. In the case of our French consumer, for example, the matter of affordability may intervene, and the consumer would find a particular

Korean VCR to be more cost-effective than a Japanese VCR. Therefore, we must consider possible *situational* influences on consumer attitudes and behaviour.

The consistency element of attitudes also make it possible for us to generalize from a person's attitude toward one object to his or her attitudes toward other related objects. For example, we would expect a person with a positive attitude toward environmentally friendly products to have a positive attitude toward other related behaviour and objects, such as recycling, composting, and products made with recycled materials.

Attitudes Have Direction, Degree, Strength, and Centrality

When a person says she has an attitude toward an object, she implies that she has a positive or negative feeling toward that object; thus, there is a *direction* to her feelings. However, two people with the same type of attitude (e.g., a positive attitude toward the singer Céline Dion and her songs) may have entirely different levels of the same attitude; Cathy might be extremely positive toward Céline Dion and her songs (and might give a rating of 10 on a 10-point scale with 10 being the most positive), while Brenda might be only slightly positive toward the artist and her songs (and might give a rating of 6 on the same scale). This is the *degree* of an attitude. Two people with the same degree of positiveness toward an object might still differ in the strength with which they hold an attitude. For example, although both Cathy and Denise might give Céline a rating of 10 as a musician, Cathy, who is a diehard Céline fan, might be unshakeable in her belief that Céline Dion is the greatest singer who ever lived, whereas Denise might consider Céline Dion to be at the same level as certain other singers. The *strength* of an attitude quite often depends on the *centrality* of the attitude to a person, or how close it is to the person's core cultural values. Attitudes that are strongly held reflect our core values and hence have high centrality to us; such values will be quite hard to change.

Attitudes Occur within a Situation

It is not immediately evident from our definition that attitudes occur within and are affected by the *situation*. By situation, we mean events or circumstances that, at a particular point in time, influence the relationship between an attitude and behaviour. A specific situation can cause consumers to behave in ways seemingly inconsistent with their attitudes.

For instance, let us assume that Reid buys a different brand of deodorant each time the brand he is using runs low. Although his brand switching may seem to reflect a negative attitude or dissatisfaction with the brands he tries, it actually may be influenced by a specific situation, for example, his wish to economize. Thus, he will buy whatever brand is the least expensive. Consider the recent slowdown in the North American economy. For the first time in more than 65 years, the market share of the popularly priced Suave brand hair care products topped 10 percent, while other manufacturers cut prices on their premium-priced offerings.[5]

The opposite can also be true. If Noah stays at a Hampton Inn each time he goes out of town on business, we may erroneously infer that he has a particularly favourable attitude toward Hampton Inn. On the contrary, Noah may find Hampton Inn to be "just okay." However, because he owns his own business and travels at his own expense, he may consider the Hampton Inn to be "good enough," given that he may be paying less than if he stayed at a Marriott, Sheraton, or Hilton hotel.

It is important to understand how consumer attitudes vary from situation to situation. For instance, it is useful to know whether consumer preferences for different burger chains (e.g., Burger King, McDonald's, or Wendy's) vary in terms of eating situations (e.g., lunch or snack, evening meal when rushed for time, or evening meal with family when not rushed for time). Consumer preferences for the various burger restaurants might depend on the eating situation. Wendy's, for example, might be favoured by a segment of consumers as a good place to have dinner with their families. Exhibit 7-1 is an example of Wendy's systematic effort to provide more main-course salads as a way of distancing itself from its more traditional competition. It also seems to be a logical way to win more dinnertime customers.

Radio Shack Canada launched new television spots to encourage consumers to think of Radio Shack as the store to go to for solving problems related to a variety of situations. The new ads, with the tag line "Radio Shack.... Just around the corner," emphasize the fact that most Canadians are within a 10 km drive of a Radio Shack, thus emphasizing the convenience aspect. The tag line is also adaptable to a wide variety of situations. One spot highlights how a bride rushing to a wedding could have bought an alarm clock from Radio Shack so that she would get to the church on time; it ends with "Radio Shack. Reliability is just around the corner." Another shows a man talking on a cell phone and driving into a bush; it ends with "Radio Shack. Safety is just around the corner."[6]

All consumers have attitudes toward a variety of products, product categories, and even ideas. Why do we have attitudes? Attitudes serve several functions. The next section deals with the functions of attitudes.

EXHIBIT 7-1

WENDY'S FEATURES MAIN COURSE SALADS TO DIFFERENTIATE ITSELF

© 2002 Oldemark LLC. All rights reserved.

FUNCTIONS OF ATTITUDES

Attitudes have four functions: the **utilitarian function**, the **ego-defensive function**, the **value-expressive function**, and the **knowledge function**.

The Utilitarian Function

Attitudes help us avoid punishments and seek rewards. For example, Martha may hold a positive attitude toward Sensodyne toothpaste because she has found that it helps prevent pain caused by her sensitive teeth. When a product has been useful or helped us in the past, our attitude toward it tends to be favourable. Ads that emphasize a product's benefits appeal to us because of their utilitarian benefits. The ad for Clorox Disinfecting Spray (Exhibit 7-2), for example, points out that this product will work for 24 hours, whereas its competitor, Lysol, will not.

The Ego-Defensive Function

Most people want to protect their self-images from inner feelings of doubt—they want to replace their uncertainty with a sense of security and self-confidence.[7] Our attitudes are a means by which we can defend ourselves against internal or external threats. Ads for cosmetics and personal care products, by acknowledging this

Utilitarian function: A component of the functional approach to attitude formation and change which suggests that consumers hold certain attitudes partly because of the brand.

Ego-defensive function: A component of the functional approach to attitude formation and change that suggests that consumers want to protect their self-concepts from inner feelings of doubt.

EXHIBIT 7-2

CLOROX USES A UTILITARIAN APPEAL WITH
ITS DISINFECTING SPRAY

Courtesy of The Procter & Gamble Company. Used by permission.

**Value-expressive
function:**
A component of the functional
approach to attitude for-
mation and change that
suggests that attitudes
express consumers' general
values, life style, and
outlook.

Knowledge function:
A component of the
functional approach to attitude formation and change
that suggests that consumers
have a strong need to know
and understand the people
and things with which they
come into contact.

need, increase both their relevance to the consumer and the likelihood of a favourable change by offering reassurance to the consumer's self-concept.

Suave Performance Series Anti-perspirant (Exhibit 7-3) emphasizes the security and increased self-confidence that comes of knowing that you are in control by stressing that consumers who use Suave "look smart."[8]

The Value-Expressive Function

Attitudes are an expression of the consumer's general values, life style, and outlook. By expressing their attitude, consumers can let others know what their values are; the opening vignette about Toronto's efforts to attract local consumers and other Canadians is an example of this function, for those efforts made Canadians feel that they could express their support for the city and, at the same time, convey to others that they were not easily frightened by such threats. By knowing target consumers' attitudes, marketers can better anticipate their values, life style, or outlook and can include these characteristics in their advertising and direct marketing.

ACDelco appeals to consumers who take pride in their health (and the associated strength) and reliability. The advertisement for ACDelco in Exhibit 7-4 addresses target consumers' attitudes and outlooks by stating, "You haven't missed a day of work in 12 years." It then appeals to the attitude by saying: "So it comes as no surprise that your auto parts are ACDelco."

The Knowledge Function

Individuals generally have a strong need to know and understand the people and things they encounter. Thus, attitudes serve as standards that help us understand the world around us. For example, if Karla bought an inexpensive wine and found it unsatisfactory, she may form a negative attitude toward low-priced wines and the next time she buys wine, she may avoid low-priced brands. Thus, her attitude has provided her with knowledge, which helps her simplify her decision making.

Most human beings have a cognitive need, a "need to know," and this is important to marketers concerned with product positioning. Indeed, many product and brand positionings are attempts to satisfy the *need to know* and to improve the consumer's attitudes toward the brand by providing knowledge that the consumer might find beneficial.

Celestial Seasonings states that green tea is loaded with antioxidants, which are good for you. It supports its claims with some evidence—the bar graph—and an incentive—a cents-off coupon (Exhibit 7-5). An important characteristic of the advertising is its appeal to consumers' *need to know.*

HOW ARE ATTITUDES FORMED?

How do people, especially young people, form their first *general* attitudes toward "things"? Consider their attitudes toward clothing they wear, such as underwear,

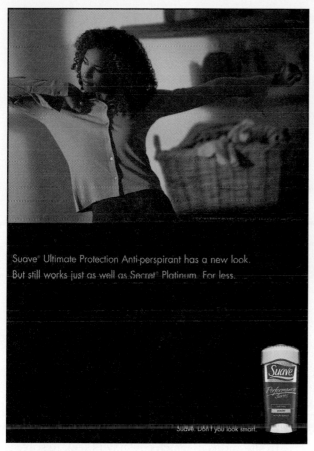

EXHIBIT 7-3

SUAVE USES AN EGO-DEFENSIVE APPEAL

Courtesy of Unilever.

EXHIBIT 7-4

ACDELCO USES A VALUE-EXPRESSIVE APPEAL

Courtesy of General Motors.

casual wear, and business attire. How do they form their attitudes toward Fruit of the Loom or Calvin Klein underwear, or Levi's or Gap casual wear, or Anne Klein or Emporium Armani business clothing? And what about where such clothing is bought? Would they buy their underwear, casual wear, and business clothing at Wal-Mart, Sears, the Bay, or Zellers? How do family members and friends, admired celebrities, mass media advertisements, even cultural membership, influence the formation of their attitudes about buying or not buying each of these types of apparel? The answers to such questions are of vital importance to marketers, for unless they know how attitudes are formed, they cannot understand or influence consumer attitudes or behaviour.

www.hbc.com

Our examination of attitude formation is divided into three areas: *how attitudes are learned,* the *sources of influence* on attitude formation, and the influence of *personality* on attitude formation.

How Attitudes Are Learned

When we speak of the formation of an attitude, we refer to the shift from having no attitude toward a given object, such as a digital camera, to having *some* attitude toward it—for example, having a digital camera is great when you want to

EXHIBIT 7-5

CELESTIAL SEASONINGS USES KNOWLEDGE
APPEAL

Courtesy of Celestial Seasonings.

email photos to friends. The shift from no attitude to an attitude (i.e., the *attitude formation*) is a result of learning (see Chapter 6 for a detailed examination of learning theories).

Consumers learn attitudes in different ways. Classical conditioning theory, discussed in Chapter 6, tells us that consumers learn about products and thus form attitudes by connecting them to a known (unconditioned) stimulus.

When Oil of Olay introduces a new moisturizing body wash, it is counting on an extension of the favourable attitude already associated with the brand name to the new product (see Exhibit 7-6). The company is counting on stimulus generalization from the brand name to the new product to lead to consumers' learning an attitude toward the body wash.

Conversely, operant conditioning theory suggests that sometimes attitudes *follow* the purchase and consumption of a product. For example, a shopper may try a food item being offered at a supermarket as a sample, and this may result in a positive attitude toward the product (provided it is satisfactory). Shoppers also make trial purchases of new brands from product categories in which they have little personal involvement (see Chapter 3). If they find the brand they bought to be satisfactory, then they are likely to develop a favourable attitude toward it.

In situations in which consumers seek to solve a problem or satisfy a need, they are likely to form attitudes (either positive or negative) about products on the basis of exposure to information and their own cognition (knowledge and beliefs). In general, the more information consumers have about a product or service, the more likely they are to form attitudes about it, either positive or negative. However, consumers often use only a small part of the information available to them. Research suggests that only two or three important beliefs about a product dominate in the formation of attitudes and that less important beliefs provide little additional input.[9] This important finding suggests that marketers should fight the impulse to include *all* the features of their products and services in their ads; rather, they should emphasize the few points that are at the heart of what distinguishes their product from the competition.

Sources of Influence on Attitude Formation

The formation of consumer attitudes is strongly influenced by *personal experience,* the *influence* of family and friends, *direct marketing,* and *mass media.*

The primary means by which attitudes toward goods and services are formed is the consumer's direct experience in trying and evaluating them.[10] Recognizing the importance of direct experience, marketers often try to persuade people to try their new products by offering cents-off coupons or even free samples. Exhibit 7-7 illustrates this strategy; the ad for Acuvue contact lenses includes a coupon for $50 off the consumer's first purchase of Acuvue Toric lenses.

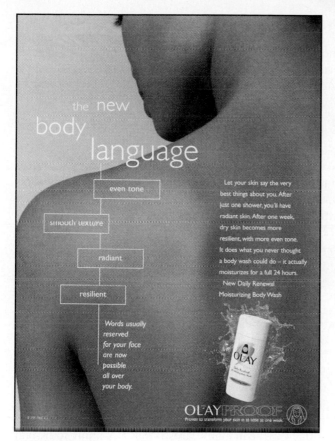

EXHIBIT 7-6

FORMING ATTITUDES THROUGH ASSOCIATION
WITH A WELL-REGARDED BRAND NAME

Courtesy of The Procter & Gamble Company. Used by permission.

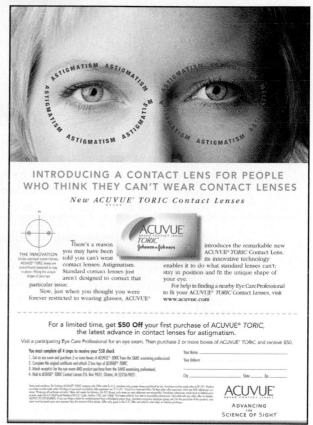

EXHIBIT 7-7

ACUVUE® TORIC USES A CENTS-OFF COUPON
TO ENCOURAGE TRIAL

Courtesy of Acuvue. Photograph © TORKIL GUDNASON.

As we come into contact with others, especially family, close friends, and people we admire, such as a respected teacher, we form attitudes that influence our lives.[11] The family is an extremely important influence on the formation of attitudes, for it is the family that gives us many of our basic values and a wide range of central beliefs. For instance, young children who are rewarded for good behaviour with sweet foods and candy often retain a taste for (and positive attitude toward) sweets as adults.

Mass media communications are an important source of information that influences the formation of consumer attitudes. Research shows that an emotionally appealing advertising message is more likely to create an attitude toward the product in consumers who lack direct experience with the product, than in consumers who have already had direct experience with the product category.[12] Research has also shown that attitudes that develop through *direct experience* (e.g., using a product) tend to be held more confidently and to be more enduring and more resistant to attack than those developed by *indirect experience* (e.g., reading a print ad).

Just as television provided the advertiser with more realism than is possible in a radio or print ad, the internet has an even greater ability to provide "telepresence,"

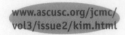

www.ascusc.org/jcmc/
vol3/issue2/kim.html

which is the simulated perception of direct experience. The internet can also provide the "flow experience," which is a cognitive state when an individual is so involved in an activity that nothing else matters. Research on telepresence suggests that "perceptions of telepresence grew stronger as levels of interactivity and levels of vividness (i.e., the way an environment presents information to the senses) of websites increased."[13]

Personality Factors

Personality also plays a critical role in attitude formation. Individuals with a high *need for cognition* (i.e., those who crave information and enjoy thinking) are likely to form positive attitudes in response to ads or direct mail that are rich in product-related information. Conversely, people who are relatively *low in need for cognition* are more likely to form positive attitudes in response to ads that feature an attractive model or well-known celebrity. Similarly, attitudes toward new products and new consumption situations are strongly influenced by specific personality characteristics of consumers.

ATTITUDE MODELS

Motivated by a desire to understand the relationship between attitudes and behaviour, psychologists have tried to construct models that capture all the underlying dimensions of an attitude.[14] To this end, the emphasis has been on specifying the composition of an attitude in order to explain or predict behaviour more accurately. The following section examines two important attitude models: the tri-component attitude model and the multi-attribute attitude models. These models assume a rational model of human behaviour—that is, attitude formation will precede behaviour. Although this may be true in many cases, it may not apply to certain situations. We will also cover two other theories of attitude formation—*cognitive dissonance theory* and *attribution theory*—that explain attitude formation under circumstances in which behaviour precedes attitude formation. Each of these models affords a somewhat different perspective on the component parts of an attitude and how those parts are arranged or related.

Tri-component Attitude Model

Tri-component attitude model:

An attitude model consisting of three parts: a cognitive (knowledge) part, an affective (feeling) part, and a conative (behavioural) part.

According to the **tri-component attitude model**, attitudes consist of three major components: a *cognitive* component, an *affective* component, and a *conative* component (see Figure 7-1).

The Cognitive Component

The first part of the tri-component attitude model consists of a person's *cognitions*, that is, the knowledge and perceptions that are acquired by a combination of direct experience with the *attitude object* and related information from various sources. This knowledge and resulting perceptions commonly take the form of *beliefs;* that is, the consumer believes that the attitude object possesses various attributes and that specific behaviour will lead to specific outcomes.

Although Figure 7-2 captures only part of the consumer Ralph's belief system about two types of broadband internet connections (i.e., cable and DSL), it illustrates the composition of his belief system about these two alternatives. Ralph's belief systems are based on four attributes: speed, availability, reliability, and "other" features. Ralph believes that the local cable company's broadband connection is much faster than DSL, but he does not like the fact that he will also have to subscribe to cable TV if he does not want to pay an extra $20 a month for the broadband internet connection. Ralph is thinking of asking a few of his friends about the differences between cable and DSL broadband internet service. He will also go online to a number of websites that discuss this topic.

www.cnet.com

The Affective Component

A consumer's *emotions* or *feelings* about a particular product or brand constitute the *affective component* of an attitude. These emotions and feelings are often treated by consumer researchers as primarily *evaluative*; that is, they capture an individual's

---

FIGURE 7-1   A Simple Representation of the Tri-component Attitude Model

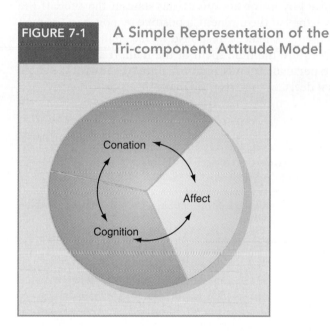

FIGURE 7-2   A Consumer's Belief System for Two Methods of Broadband Internet Access

Product	**BROADBAND INTERNET ACCESS**							
Brand	**Cable Internet Access**				**DSL Internet Access**			
Attributes	Speed	Availability	Reliability	Other Features	Speed	Availability	Reliability	Other Features
Beliefs	Faster than DSL	Offered now by my cable company	As reliable as my cable TV	No choice of provider and slows down when lots of subscribers are online	Slower than a cable modem but faster than dial-up service	Offered now by my local telephone company	Can be spotty	Bandwidth varies less than with a cable connection but can be more difficult to install and troubleshoot
Evaluations	(++++)	(+++)	(+++)	(−)	(++)	(+++)	(−)	(+)

Source: Adapted from Todd Spangler, "Crossing the Broadband Divide," *PC Magazine,* February 12, 2001, 92–103.

direct or global assessment of the attitude object (i.e., the extent to which the individual rates the attitude object as "favourable" or "unfavourable," "good" or "bad"). To illustrate, Figure 7-3 shows a series of evaluative (affective) scale items that might be used to assess consumers' attitudes toward Lubriderm Skin Therapy Moisturizing Lotion.

Affect-laden experiences also manifest themselves as *emotionally charged states* (e.g., happiness, sadness, shame, disgust, anger, distress, guilt, or surprise). Research shows that such emotional states may enhance or amplify positive or negative experiences and that later memories of such experiences may influence what comes to mind and how the individual acts.[15] For instance, a person visiting an outlet mall is likely to be influenced by his or her emotional state at the time. If the shopper is feeling particularly happy at the moment, a positive response to the mall may be amplified. The emotionally enhanced response to the mall may lead the shopper to recall with great pleasure the time spent at the mall. It also may influence the individual shopper to persuade friends and acquaintances to visit the same mall and to make the personal decision to revisit the mall.

FIGURE 7-3   Selected Evaluative Scale Used to Gauge Consumers' Attitudes toward Lubriderm Skin Therapy Moisturizing Lotion

Compared with other skin moisturizing lotions, Lubriderm Skin Therapy Moisturizing Lotion is:

Good	[1]	[2]	[3]	[4]	[5]	[6]	[7]	Bad
Positive	[1]	[2]	[3]	[4]	[5]	[6]	[7]	Negative
Pleasant	[1]	[2]	[3]	[4]	[5]	[6]	[7]	Unpleasant
Appealing	[1]	[2]	[3]	[4]	[5]	[6]	[7]	Unappealing

FIGURE 7-4   Measuring Consumers' Feelings and Emotions with Regard to Using Lubriderm Skin Therapy Moisturizing Lotion

For the past 30 days you have had a chance to try Lubriderm. We would appreciate it if you would identify how your skin felt after using the product during this 30-day trial period.

For each of the words below, we would appreciate it if you would mark an "X" in the box corresponding to how your skin felt after using Lubriderm during the past 30 days..

	VERY				NOT AT ALL
Relaxed	[ ]	[ ]	[ ]	[ ]	[ ]
Beautiful	[ ]	[ ]	[ ]	[ ]	[ ]
Tight	[ ]	[ ]	[ ]	[ ]	[ ]
Smooth	[ ]	[ ]	[ ]	[ ]	[ ]
Supple	[ ]	[ ]	[ ]	[ ]	[ ]
Clean	[ ]	[ ]	[ ]	[ ]	[ ]
Refreshed	[ ]	[ ]	[ ]	[ ]	[ ]
Younger	[ ]	[ ]	[ ]	[ ]	[ ]
Revived	[ ]	[ ]	[ ]	[ ]	[ ]
Renewed	[ ]	[ ]	[ ]	[ ]	[ ]

In addition to using direct or global evaluative measures of an attitude object, consumer researchers can also use a battery of affective response scales (scales that measure feelings and emotions) to construct a picture of consumers' overall feelings about a product, a service, or an ad. Figure 7-4 gives an example of a five-point scale that measures affective responses.

The Conative or Behavioural Component

Conation, the final component of the tri-component attitude model, is concerned with the *likelihood* or *tendency* that an individual will undertake a specific action or behave in a particular way with regard to the attitude object. According to some interpretations, the conative component may include the actual behaviour itself.

In marketing and consumer research, the conative component is often treated as an expression of the consumer's *intention to buy.* Buyer intention scales are used to assess the likelihood that a consumer will buy a product or behave in a certain way. Figure 7-5 provides two examples of common *intention-to-buy scales.* Interestingly enough, people who are asked an intention-to-buy question appear more likely to actually buy a brand that they have evaluated positively (e.g., by saying they would buy it) than are consumers who are not asked an intention question.[16] This suggests that a positive brand commitment in the form of a positive answer to an attitude intention question has a positive influence on the actual brand purchase.

Multi-attribute Attitude Models

Multi-attribute attitude models portray consumers' attitudes with regard to an attitude object (e.g., a product, a service, a direct-mail catalogue, or a cause or issue) as a function of consumers' perception and assessment of the key attributes of the attitude object or their beliefs about the object. Although there are many variations of this type of attitude model, we will briefly consider the following three: the *attitude-toward-object model,* the *attitude-toward-behaviour model,* and the *theory-of-reasoned-action model.*

The Attitude-toward-Object Model

The **attitude-toward-object model** is especially suitable for measuring attitudes toward a *product* (or *service*) category or specific *brands.*[17] According to this model, the consumer's attitude toward a product or specific brands of a product is

Multi-attribute attitude models:
Attitude models that examine the composition of consumer attitudes in terms of selected product attributes or beliefs.

Attitude-toward-object model:
A model that proposes that a consumer's attitude toward a product or brand is a function of the presence of certain attributes and the consumer's evaluation of these attributes.

FIGURE 7-5	Two Examples of Intention-to-Buy Scales

Which of the following statements best describes the chance that you will buy Lubriderm Lotion the next time you purchase a skin care product?

_____ I definitely will buy it.

_____ I probably will buy it.

_____ I am uncertain whether I will buy it.

_____ I probably will not buy it.

_____ I definitely will not buy it.

How likely are you to buy Lubriderm Lotion during the next three months?

_____ Very likely

_____ Likely

_____ Unlikely

_____ Very unlikely

a function of the presence (or absence) and evaluation of certain product-specific beliefs and/or attributes. This can be expressed in equation form:

Consumer attitude toward an object, or $A_o = \Sigma_{i=1}^{n} W_i X_{ib}$
where W_i = importance of attribute i
X_{ib} = belief that brand b has a certain level of attribute i

In other words, consumers generally have favourable attitudes toward those brands that they believe have an adequate level of attributes that they evaluate as positive, and they have unfavourable attitudes toward those brands they feel do not have an adequate level of desired attributes or have too many negative or undesired attributes.

Let us look at the broadband internet connection example (see Figure 7-2) again. If what Ralph is really looking for is speed and reliability, he will have a positive attitude toward cable internet access.

Some researchers consider the ad for a product itself to be an object. In other words, the consumer forms various feelings (affects) and judgments (cognitions) as the result of hearing or seeing an ad. These feelings and judgments in turn influence the consumer's *attitude toward the ad* and *beliefs about the brand* acquired from the ad. Finally, the consumer's attitude toward the ad and beliefs about the brand influence his or her *attitude toward the brand*.[18]

Research shows that attitude toward an ad can have a stronger impact on attitude toward the brand when the product is novel (e.g., contact lenses for pets) than when it is familiar (e.g., pet food).[19] Thus, it is important to consider the nature of the attitude object in assessing the potential impact of an advertisement.

The Attitude-toward-Behaviour Model

Attitude-toward-behaviour model:

A model that proposes that a consumer's attitude toward a specific behaviour is a function of how strongly he or she believes that the action will lead to a specific (favourable or unfavourable) outcome.

The **attitude-toward-behaviour** model attempts to explain the individual's *attitude toward behaving* or *acting* with respect to an object rather than the attitude toward the object itself.[20] The appeal of the attitude-toward-behaviour model is that it seems to correspond somewhat more closely to actual behaviour than does the attitude-toward-object model. For instance, knowing Howard's attitude about the act of buying a top-of-the-line BMW (i.e., his attitude toward the *behaviour*) reveals more about the act of buying than does simply knowing his attitude toward expensive German cars or specifically BMWs (i.e., the attitude toward the *object*). This seems logical, for a consumer might have a positive attitude toward an expensive BMW but a negative attitude about his prospects of buying such an expensive car.

Theory-of-Reasoned-Action Model

Theory of reasoned action:

A comprehensive theory of the interrelationship among attitudes, intentions, and behaviour.

The **theory of reasoned action** is a comprehensive integration of attitude components into a structure that is designed to lead both to better explanations and to better predictions of behaviour. Like the basic tri-component attitude model, the theory-of-reasoned-action model incorporates a *cognitive* component, an *affective* component, and a *conative* component; however, these are arranged in a pattern different from that of the tri-component model (see Figure 7-6).

In accordance with this expanded model, to understand *intention* we also need to measure the *subjective norms* that influence a person's intention to act. A subjective norm can be measured directly by assessing a consumer's feelings about what relevant others (family, friends, roommates, co-workers) would think of the action being contemplated; that is, would they look favourably or unfavourably on the action? For example, if a graduate student were considering buying a New (VW) Beetle and stopped to ask himself whether his parents or girlfriend would approve or disapprove, such a reflection would constitute his subjective norm.

FIGURE 7-6   A Simplified Version of the Theory of Reasoned Action

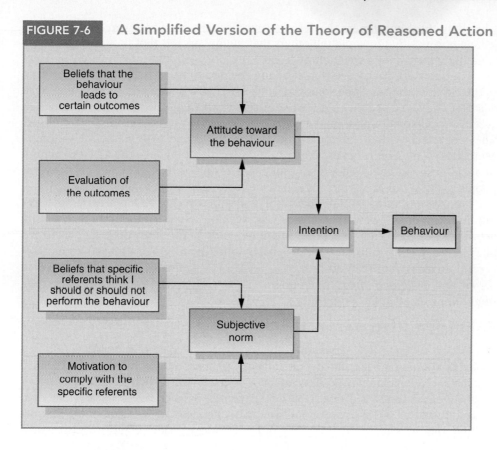

Consumer researchers can get behind the *subjective norm* to the underlying factors that are likely to produce it. They do this by assessing the *normative beliefs* that the individual attributes to relevant others, as well as the individual's *motivation to comply* with each of the relevant others. For instance, consider the graduate student contemplating the purchase of a New Beetle. To understand his subjective norm about the desired purchase, we would have to identify his relevant others (parents and girlfriend); his beliefs about how each would respond to his purchase of the Beetle (e.g., "Dad would consider the car an unnecessary luxury, but my girlfriend would love it"); and finally, his motivation to comply with the wishes of his parents or his girlfriend.[21]

Let us look at an example. Most Canadians would agree that Mercedes-Benz produces highly desirable cars that rate well in quality, construction, and status and that hold the top place in terms of luxury. Clearly, consumers' attitudes toward the object (a Mercedes) and the results of buying it (the behaviour) were positive. Yet, many young Canadians who could afford to buy the car were not doing so. What could account for this reluctance to buy a Mercedes?

www.mercedes-benz.ca

Extensive qualitative research discovered that many consumers felt that the cars represented "old money and prestige"; more important, they were delaying the purchase of a Mercedes because they felt that they had not yet "arrived" and hence had not "earned the privilege" and could not give themselves permission to "indulge" in a Mercedes. They were afraid that other people would think they were declaring that they had arrived, when in fact, they were unsure of their success.

Clearly, to these consumers, the desire to purchase the car was lowered by their subjective norms—that it would tell others that the buyers felt that they had "arrived," something they were not yet ready to do.

The solution? Mercedes-Benz Canada decided to try to make consumers think of the car as a journey rather than a destination. The company developed television ads that conveyed the message "you are ready" through the story of Raymond, a successful, 30-something Canadian who had postponed eating ice cream all his life. The spot ended with the announcer saying, "Don't spend your whole life waiting... Mercedes-Benz. You're ready." The results were phenomenal—the ads scored high on recall tests, on being emotionally stirring, and on conveying the message; several people even called to say the ads actually encouraged them to buy the car.[22]

Our discussion of attitude formation and attitude change has stressed the traditional "rational" view that consumers develop their attitudes before taking action; that is, they know what they are going to do before they do it. But there are alternatives to this "attitude precedes behaviour" perspective, alternatives that, on careful analysis, are likely to be just as logical and rational. *Cognitive dissonance theory* and *attribution theory* each offers a different explanation of why behaviour might precede attitude formation.

Cognitive Dissonance Theory

Cognitive dissonance theory:

The discomfort or dissonance that consumers experience as a result of conflicting information.

According to **cognitive dissonance theory**, when a consumer holds conflicting thoughts about a belief or an attitude object, the result is discomfort or dissonance. For instance, consumers who have made a commitment—such as making a down payment or ordering a product, particularly an expensive one such as a car or a computer—often begin to feel cognitive dissonance when they think of the unique, positive qualities of the brands they did not choose. When cognitive dissonance occurs after a purchase, it is called *post-purchase dissonance.* Because purchase decisions often require some amount of compromise, post-purchase dissonance is quite normal. Nevertheless, it is likely to leave consumers with an uneasy feeling about their prior beliefs or actions—a feeling that they would seek to resolve by changing their attitudes to conform with their behaviour.

Thus, in the case of post-purchase dissonance, attitude change is often an *outcome* of an action or behaviour. The conflicting thoughts and dissonant information following a purchase are prime factors that induce consumers to change their attitudes so that they will be consonant with their actual purchase behaviour.

What makes post-purchase dissonance relevant to marketing strategists is the premise that *dissonance* propels consumers to reduce the unpleasant feelings created by the rival thoughts. A variety of tactics are possible. The consumer can rationalize the decision as being wise, seek out advertisements that support the choice (while avoiding dissonance-creating competitive ads), try to persuade his or her friends of the positive features of the brand, or look to known satisfied owners for reassurance.

Consider how a man who just bought an engagement ring for his girlfriend would respond to the following headline: "How can you make two months' salary last forever?" (see Exhibit 7-8). This thought and the rest of the message are likely to catch his attention. It says to him that although an engagement ring costs a great deal of money, it lasts forever because the future bride will cherish it for the rest of her life. Such a message is bound to help him reduce any lingering dissonance that he might have about how much he just spent on the ring.

In addition to such consumer-initiated tactics to reduce post-purchase uncertainty, marketers can relieve consumer dissonance by including messages in their

advertising specifically aimed at reinforcing consumers' decisions by complimenting their wisdom,
offering stronger guarantees or warranties, increasing the number and effectiveness of their services, or
providing detailed brochures on how to use the
products correctly.

Attribution Theory

As a group of loosely interrelated social psychological principles, **attribution theory** tries to explain
how people assign causality (e.g., blame or credit) to
events on the basis of either their own behaviour or
the behaviour of others.[23] In other words, a person
might say, "I contributed to Care, Inc. because it
really helps people in need," or "She tried to persuade me to buy that unknown auto-focus camera
because she'd make a bigger commission." In attribution theory, the underlying question is why: "Why
did I do this?" "Why did she try to get me to switch
brands?" This process of making inferences about
one's own or someone else's behaviour is a large
part of attitude formation and change.

Self-Perception Theory

Of the various perspectives on attribution theory
that have been proposed, **self-perception theory**—
individuals' inferences or judgments as to the causes
of their own behaviour—is a good beginning point
for a discussion of attribution.

In terms of consumer behaviour, self-perception
theory suggests that attitudes develop as consumers
*look at and make judgments about their own behav-
iour.* Simply stated, if a physician observes that she routinely buys the *Globe and
Mail* on her way to the clinic, she is apt to conclude that she likes the *Globe and
Mail* (i.e., she has a positive attitude toward this newspaper).[24] Drawing inferences
from our own behaviour is not always as simple or as clear-cut as the newspaper
example might suggest. To appreciate the complexity of self-perception theory, it is
useful to distinguish between *internal and external attributions.*

Ralph has just finished using a popular computer presentation program (e.g.,
Microsoft's PowerPoint) for the first time, and his slide show was well received by his
audience. If, after the presentation, he says to himself, "I'm really a natural at making
great presentations," this statement would be an example of an *internal attribution.* It
is an internal attribution because he is giving himself credit for the outcome (because
of his ability, skill, or effort). That is, he is saying, "This slide presentation is good
because of me." Conversely, if Ralph concludes that the successful presentation was
due to factors beyond his control (e.g., a user-friendly program, the help of a friend,
or just luck), this would be an example of an *external attribution.* In this case, he might
be saying, "My great presentation is beginner's luck."

This distinction between internal and external attributions can be of strategic
marketing importance. For instance, it would generally be in the best interests of the
firm that produces the presentation program if the users, especially inexperienced

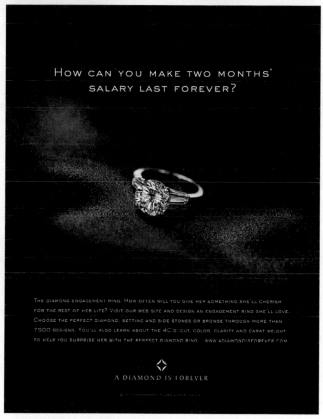

HOW CAN YOU MAKE TWO MONTHS'
SALARY LAST FOREVER?

THE DIAMOND ENGAGEMENT RING. HOW OFTEN WILL YOU GIVE HER SOMETHING SHE'LL CHERISH
FOR THE REST OF HER LIFE? VISIT OUR WEB SITE AND DESIGN AN ENGAGEMENT RING SHE'LL LOVE.
CHOOSE THE PERFECT DIAMOND, SETTING AND SIDE STONES OR BROWSE THROUGH MORE THAN
7500 DESIGNS. YOU'LL ALSO LEARN ABOUT THE 4C'S: CUT, COLOR, CLARITY AND CARAT WEIGHT,
TO HELP YOU SURPRISE HER WITH THE PERFECT DIAMOND RING.   WWW.ADIAMONDISFOREVER.COM

A DIAMOND IS FOREVER

EXHIBIT 7-8

HELPING RECENT CONSUMERS REDUCE THEIR
COGNITIVE DISSONANCE

Courtesy of the Diamond Trading Company and J. Walter Thompson.

Attribution theory:
A theory concerned with
how people assign causality
to events and form or alter
their attitudes as an outcome
of those attributions.

**Self-perception
theory:**
A theory that suggests that
consumers develop attitudes
by reflecting on their own
behaviour.

users, *internalized* their successful use of the graphics package. If they internalized such a positive experience, it is more likely that they will repeat the behaviour and become a satisfied regular user. However, if they were to *externalize* their success, it would be preferable that they attribute it to the particular program rather than to an incidental environmental factor such as "beginner's luck" or a friend's instructions.

According to the principle of *defensive attribution*, consumers are likely to take personal credit for a success (internal attribution) and to blame a failure on someone else or on outside events (external attribution). For this reason, it is crucial that marketers offer uniformly high-quality products that allow consumers to see themselves as the reason for the success, that is, to say to themselves, "I'm competent." Moreover, a company's advertising should reassure consumers, particularly inexperienced ones, that its products will not let them down but will make them heroes instead.

Foot-in-the-Door Technique   Self-perception theorists have studied situations in which a consumer's compliance with a minor request affects subsequent compliance with a more substantial request. This strategy, which is commonly referred to as the **foot-in-the-door technique**, is based on the premise that individuals look at their previous behaviour (e.g., compliance with a minor request) and conclude that they are the kind of person who says "yes" to such requests (i.e., an internal attribution). Such self-attribution makes it more likely that they will agree to a similar more substantial request. Someone who donates five dollars to cancer research might be persuaded to donate much more if she is approached properly. The initial donation is, in effect, the *foot in the door*.

Foot-in-the-door technique: A theory of attitude change that suggests individuals form attitudes that are consistent with their own prior behaviour.	

Research into the foot-in-the-door technique has concentrated on understanding how specific incentives, such as cents-off coupons of varying amounts, ultimately influence consumer attitudes and subsequent purchase behaviour. It appears that different-sized incentives create different degrees of internal attribution, which, in turn, lead to different amounts of attitude change. For instance, people who try a brand without any inducements or who buy a brand repeatedly are more likely to infer increasingly positive attitudes toward the brand from their own behaviour (e.g., "I buy this brand because I like it"). In contrast, people who try a free sample are less committed to changing their attitudes toward the brand ("I tried this brand because it was free").

Thus, contrary to what might be expected, it is not the biggest incentive that is most likely to lead to positive attitude change. If an incentive is too big, marketers run the risk that consumers may externalize the cause of their behaviour to the incentive and be *less* likely to change their attitudes and *less* likely to make future purchases of the brand. Instead, what seems most effective is a *moderate* incentive, one that is just big enough to stimulate an initial purchase of the brand but still small enough to encourage consumers to internalize their positive usage experience and allow a positive attitude change to occur.[25]

Attributions toward Others

In addition to understanding self-perception theory, it is important to understand **attributions toward others** because of the variety of applications to consumer behaviour and marketing. As already suggested, every time a person asks "why?" about a statement or action of another person—a family member, a friend, a salesperson, a direct marketer, a shipping company—attribution theory is relevant. To illustrate, in evaluating the words or deeds of, say, a salesperson, a consumer tries to

Attributions toward others: Consumers' perception that another person is responsible for either positive or negative product performance.	

determine whether the salesperson's motives are in the consumer's best interests. If the salesperson's motives are viewed as favourable to the consumer, the consumer is likely to respond favourably. Otherwise, the consumer is likely to reject the salesperson's words and go elsewhere to make a purchase. Consider the following example:

A consumer orders a new DVD player from a major direct marketer such as Amazon or Indigo. Because she wants it immediately, she agrees to pay an extra $5 to $10 for next-day delivery by FedEx. If the next day the package with the DVD player fails to show up as expected, the consumer has two possible "others" to which she may attribute the failure—that is, the direct marketer or the delivery service. In addition, she may blame them both (a dual failure); or if the weather is very bad, she may conclude that the reason is the bad weather (an attribution that neither of them was at fault).[26]

www.indigo.ca

The tendency of consumers to question the motives of a company can pose serious problems for marketers because this can make advertising less effective. Perhaps this explains why sponsorships (especially those where the company is not seen as directly benefiting) are effective, particularly on the internet, where ads are probably even more intrusive than in other situations. Internet Insight 7-1 provides additional details on the effectiveness of online sponsorships in increasing consumers' purchase intentions.

How We Test Our Attributions

After making initial attributions about a product's performance or a person's words or actions, we often try to determine whether our inference is correct. According to a leading attribution theorist, people acquire conviction about particular observations by acting like "naive scientists," that is, by collecting additional information in an attempt to confirm (or disconfirm) their prior inferences. In collecting such information, consumers often use the following criteria:[27]

www.coe.uga.edu/ echd/counpsy/ eminentpsychologists_ new.htm#kelley

- *Distinctiveness*—The consumer attributes an action to a particular product or person if the action occurs when the product (or person) is present and does not occur in its absence.

- *Consistency over time*—Whenever the person or product is present, the consumer's inference or reaction must be the same, or nearly so.

- *Consistency over modality*—The inference or reaction must be the same, even when the situation in which it occurs varies.

- *Consensus*—The action is perceived in the same way by other consumers.

The following example illustrates how each of these criteria might be used to make inferences about product performance and people's actions.

If Nancy, a retired elementary school teacher who loves to cook and bake, observes that her apple pies seem to bake more evenly in her new Whirlpool gas range/oven, she is likely to credit the new Whirlpool appliance with the improved appearance of her pies (i.e., distinctiveness). Furthermore, if she finds that her new Whirlpool gas range/oven produces the same high-quality results each time she uses it, she will tend to be more confident about her initial observation (i.e., the inference has consistency over time). Similarly, she will also be more confident if she finds that her satisfaction with the Whirlpool appliance extends across a wide range of other related tasks, from cooking turkeys in the oven to cooking pasta on the gas range (i.e., consistency over modality). Finally, Nancy will have still more confidence in her inferences to the extent that her friends who own Whirlpool gas ranges/ovens also have similar experiences (i.e., consensus).

www.whirlpool.com

INTERNET INSIGHT 7-1
DO ONLINE SPONSORSHIPS WORK?

Sponsorships, especially exclusive ones, have been a popular way for marketers to reach consumers, both in the online and in the traditional media. Research has found that sponsorships are an effective way of increasing ad recall—one study found that sponsorships led to 2.5 times higher recall over the traditional 30-second commercial.[a] Similar effects were found when CBS aired five sponsored programs in the 1990s (with sponsors like Reebok, Anheuser-Busch, and Pepsico); recall rates and intention to purchase measures were considerably higher than for traditional advertisements.[b] However, these studies were looking at television sponsorships; a recent IAB study of exclusive online sponsorships provides some interesting insights. The IAB study involved major internet companies (e.g., Yahoo!, Primedia, and StudioOne) and Volvo. These were the findings:

- Consumers were invited to participate in a survey that let them give some advice to the company conducting the survey; they were offered a key chain as a reward for participation.

- Fifty percent of respondents who agreed to take part in the survey were assigned to a control group (i.e., they were not exposed to the sponsorship), and 50 percent were assigned to the one of the test groups (i.e., they were exposed to either a shared sponsorship situation or an exclusive sponsorship situation).

- Each group had 1514 respondents, and each group answered the same questionnaire, which asked about car purchase habits and cars in the consideration set.

- The respondents were led to a site where they could watch the New York Auto Show for a specified time, after which they answered a questionnaire. Depending on the test situation, the site was co-sponsored, sponsored exclusively, or not sponsored at all.

The study found that exclusive sponsorships have a significant impact on purchase intentions. Specifically, it made the following findings:

- Shared sponsorships (i.e., when several companies were shown as sponsors of a site) did not lead to any statistically significant increases in the brand's ability to make it into the consideration set.

- Exclusive sponsorship (i.e., when the site was sponsored by one company) led to a 381 percent increase in the brand's inclusion in the consideration set (from 1.6 percent to 7.1 percent), a statistically significant increase.

Why do exclusive sponsorships work so well? One reason might be that consumers (who had chosen to participate in the study and were probably highly involved in the product category) saw the opportunity to see the show as a gift and, as the advertiser does not take advantage of this situation by advertising, they attribute positive qualities to the sponsor. Furthermore, the very fact of agreeing to participate in the study and the acceptance of the token (not large) gift might have acted as a "foot in the door" and made consumers more aware of (and positive toward) the sponsor.

Why did the shared sponsorship not have a similar effect? In the shared sponsorship situation, the identification of several sponsors may have had the same effect as traditional advertisements, which consumers often screen out. No one company is given total credit for bringing the content to the consumer, and the "gift" psychology may not have come into effect.

QUESTIONS:
1. Have you come across any examples of the foot-in-the-door technique on the internet?
2. Do you think that such sponsorships are ethical?

[a] IAB Volvo/Euro RSCG Sponsorship Effectiveness Study, Interactive Advertising Bureau, September 10, 2003. Courtesy of Interactive Advertising Bureau.

[b] Ibid.

Much like Nancy, we go about gathering additional information from our experiences with people and things, and we use this information to test our initial inferences.

ATTITUDES AND MARKETING STRATEGY

As we saw at the beginning of the chapter, a positive attitude is a necessary but not sufficient condition for purchase. In other words, just because a consumer has a positive attitude, we cannot be certain that she will buy a product. However, if her attitude toward a product is negative, it is extremely unlikely that she would buy it. Hence marketers try to do two things:

- maintain positive attitudes and make them even more positive
- alter negative (or neutral) attitudes and make consumers move toward a positive attitude

It is important to recognize that much of what has been said about *attitude formation* is also basically true of attitude change. That is, attitude changes are *learned;* they are influenced by *personal experience* and other *sources of information,* and *personality* affects both the receptivity and the speed with which attitudes are likely to be altered. Hence, most attitude change strategies are based on marketers' knowledge of attitude formation. These attitude change strategies can be grouped into seven categories: (1) appealing to the basic motivational functions of attitudes, (2) associating the product with an admired group or event, (3) resolving two conflicting attitudes, (4) influencing consumer attributions, (5) altering components of the multi-attribute models, (6) changing consumer beliefs about competitors' brands, and (7) attempting to change behaviour or affect first.

Appeal to the basic motivational functions of attitudes: An effective strategy for changing consumer attitudes toward a product or brand is to make particular needs or functions prominent. Marketers can change attitudes toward a brand by appealing to the value-expressive, knowledge, utilitarian, or ego-defensive functions. They can change consumers' attitude toward a product by showing how the product can fulfill one or more of the basic motivational functions of attitude. For example the tourism commission's ads, discussed at the beginning of this chapter, that tried to change the attitudes of Torontonians and other Canadians probably tapped into the value-expressive functions of attitudes—by making people feel that they could express their support for the city and, at the same time, convey to others that they were not easily scared by the threat of the SARS outbreak.

Associate the product with a special group, event, or cause: Attitudes are related, at least in part, to certain groups, social events, or causes. It is possible to alter attitudes toward products, services, and brands by pointing out their relationships to particular social groups, events, or causes.

The Canadian Imperial Bank of Commerce sponsors, along with other organizations, the annual Run for the Cure, which collects money for cancer research. Scotia Bank sponsors the Epilepsy Buskerfest in Toronto, and Junior Achievement sponsors the Economics of Staying in School program. Even smaller organizations such as Sobeys contribute to charitable causes—for example, Sobey's has a "School Is Cool" program through which participating stores donate money to local schools for computers and other equipment.

www.torontobusker
fest.com

Molson's sponsors anti-drinking-and-driving promotions across Canada. Called "Get the Picture: Remember Don't Drink and Drive," the program was launched in 2003 during frosh week and was aimed at demonstrating that Molson's was a good corporate citizen.[28]

Companies regularly make mention in their advertising of the civic and public acts that they sponsor to let the public know about the good they are trying to do. For instance, Folgers coffee sponsors a program, "Wakin' up the Music," which supports a music appreciation program for youngsters in grades one to three, created by the Grammy Foundation.

Resolving two conflicting attitudes: Attitude-change strategies can sometimes resolve actual or potential conflict between two attitudes. Specifically, if consumers can be made to see that changing their negative attitude toward a product, a specific brand, or its attributes is really not in conflict with another attitude, they may be induced to change their evaluation of the brand from negative to positive.

Stanley is a serious amateur photographer who has been thinking of moving from 35 mm photography into the realm of medium-format photography in order to take advantage of the larger negatives. However, with the growth of digital photography, he is unsure whether his move to the medium format will be worthwhile. He loves the idea of having a bigger negative to work with in his darkroom (attitude 1), but he may feel that a medium-format camera would be an unwise investment because these cameras may soon be supplanted by digital photography (attitude 2). However, if Stanley learns that Mamiya makes a medium-format camera that offers both a film capability and a digital capability, he might change his mind and thereby resolve his conflicting attitudes (see Exhibit 7-9).

Cognitive dissonance and post-purchase dissonance can affect consumers' attitudes toward products. If post-purchase dissonance is not reduced, consumers may end up with conflicting attitudes toward a purchase, and that may lead to problems later. Since consumers are likely to feel some post-purchase dissonance with all major purchases, that is, those involving a high amount of financial or non-financial risk, marketers should attempt to reduce this risk in the following ways:

- by assuring consumers through advertising that they have made the right choices
- by contacting buyers and providing reassurance and customer assistance
- by offering guarantees and warranties that reduce consumer anxiety

Influencing consumer attributions: As we saw earlier, consumer attributions can have a major influence on attitude formation and change. Companies can use a knowledge of consumer attributions by

- helping consumers develop internal attributions (i.e., attribute successes to themselves);
- making sure, when external attributions are inevitable, that consumers attribute positive outcomes to the product; and
- developing advertising that reassures consumers, particularly inexperienced ones, that the company's products will not let them down but will make them heroes instead.

EXHIBIT 7-9

RESOLVING TWO CONFLICTING ATTITUDES

Courtesy of Mamiya America Corporation.

Altering components of the multi-attribute models: Earlier in this chapter we discussed a number of multi-attribute attitude models. These models have implications for attitude-change strategies; specifically, they give us additional insights into how to change attitudes by (1) changing the relative evaluation of attributes, (2) changing brand beliefs, (3) adding an attribute, and (4) changing the overall brand rating.

Changing the relative evaluation of attributes: The overall market for many product categories is often naturally divided so that different consumer segments are offered different brands with different features or benefits. For instance, within a product category such as deodorants, there are brands like Mitchum that stress potency and brands like Secret that stress gentleness. Traditionally, these two brands of deodorants have appealed to different segments of the deodorant market. Similarly, when it comes to cola, the market can be divided into regular colas and diet colas, or when it comes to tea, there is the division between regular tea and herbal tea.

In general, when a product category is naturally divided according to distinct product features or benefits that appeal to different groups of consumers, marketers usually have an opportunity to persuade consumers to "cross over," that is, to persuade consumers who prefer one version of the product (e.g., a standard "soft" contact lens) to shift their favourable attitudes to another version of the product (e.g., a disposable contact lens) by changing their relative evaluation of attributes.

Changing brand beliefs: A second cognitive-oriented strategy for changing attitudes concentrates on changing beliefs or perceptions about the brand itself. This is by far the most common form of advertising appeal. Advertisers are constantly reminding us that their product has "more" or is "better" or "best" in relation to some important product attribute. As a variation on this theme of "more," ads for Palmolive dish detergent are designed to *extend* consumers' brand attitudes with regard to the product's gentleness by suggesting that it be used for hand washing of fine clothing.

The Hewlett Packard computer ad (see Exhibit 7-10) challenges the notion that computers have to be difficult to use and difficult for a firm's IT department to manage by saying the product is "Simple to the point of 'duh.'" It describes the computer as "fast and lean," and claims that this machine will prove that "if there is less to go wrong, less will."

Pantene hair care products challenge the notion that you have to be stuck with "flat hair." Pantene suggests that when consumers use its volume care products, they can increase the volume of their hair by as much as 80 percent.

Within the context of brand beliefs, there are forces working to stop or slow down attitude change. For instance, consumers often resist evidence that challenges a strongly held attitude or belief and tend to interpret any ambiguous infor-

EXHIBIT 7-10

CHANGING ATTITUDES BY ALTERING BELIEFS ABOUT A BRAND

Copyright 2000 Hewlett-Packard Company. Photos by John Offenbach/Stockalnd Martel. Reproduced with permission.

Now there's a Dove
of a different stripe.

Introducing Dove Nutrium,
the first dual formula nourishing bar.
The white stripes contain moisturizing cleansers.
This cleans and softens.
The pink stripes contain Vitamin E lotion.
This replenishes skin's nutrients.
This works with
this to give you a healthy glow.

©2001 Lever Brothers Company. *Deposits nutrients naturally found in skin.

Dove. NUTRIUM™
skin nourishment

EXHIBIT 7-11

CHANGING ATTITUDES BY ADDING AN ATTRIBUTE

Courtesy of Unilever.

mation in ways that reinforce their pre-existing attitudes.[29] Therefore, information suggesting a change in attitude needs to be compelling and repeated enough to overcome the natural resistance to letting go of established attitudes.

Adding an attribute: Another cognitive strategy consists of *adding an attribute*. This can be done either by adding an attribute that has previously been ignored or adding one that is an improvement or technological innovation.

The first method, adding a previously ignored attribute, is illustrated by the point that yogourt has more potassium than a banana does (a fruit known to have a high potassium content). For people interested in increasing their intake of potassium, the comparison of yogourt with bananas has the power of enhancing their attitudes toward yogourt.

The second method, adding an attribute that reflects an actual product change or technological innovation, is easier than stressing a previously ignored attribute.

Dove recently introduced Dove Nutrium. Not only does it clean and moisturize like regular Dove, but it also replenishes the skin's nutrients because it contains vitamin E lotion (see Exhibit 7-11).

Sometimes eliminating a characteristic or feature has the same enhancing outcome as adding one. A number of skin care or deodorant manufacturers, for instance, offer versions of their products that are unscented (i.e., *deleting an ingredient*). Indeed, Dove also markets an unscented version of its original Dove product.

Changing the overall brand rating: Still another cognitive-oriented strategy consists of trying to alter consumers' *overall assessment of the brand* directly, without trying to improve or change their evaluation of any single brand attribute. Such a strategy often relies on some form of global statement that "this is the largest-selling brand" or "the one all others try to imitate," or a similar claim that sets the brand apart from all its competitors.

Honda regularly advertises that its cars are used by other auto manufacturers as the "standard" to live up to. Excedrin Migraine says it is the number-one doctor-recommended brand for the relief of migraine pain.

Changing beliefs about competitors' brands: Another approach to attitude-change strategy is to change consumer beliefs about the *attributes of competitive* brands or product categories.

Advil often makes a dramatic assertion of product superiority over Aspirin and Tylenol: the ad claims that Advil lasts longer and is gentler than Aspirin and that two Advils work better than Extra Strength Tylenol. Similarly, Oracle uses advertising to create the attitude that the Oracle Small Business Suite is superior to QuickBooks, a principal competitor (Exhibit 7-12).

In general, this strategy must be used with caution. Comparative advertising can boomerang by giving visibility to competing brands and claims. (Chapter 8 discusses comparative advertising in greater depth.)

Changing affect or behaviour first: The strategies discussed so far generally focus on changing cognition or beliefs about the product first and, through a change in cognition, changing the attitude toward the product. However, the elaboration likelihood model (ELM) proposes the more global view that consumer attitudes are changed by one of two distinctly different "routes to persuasion": a central route or a peripheral route (see also Chapter 3).[30] In other words, the central route to attitude change is relevant only when a consumer's motivation or ability to assess the attitude object is *high* and he or she is ready to seek out information relevant to the attitude object (i.e., the product) itself. When this is not the case (i.e., in low-involvement situations), learning and attitude change tend to follow the *peripheral route* without the consumer focusing on information relevant to the attitude object itself. In such cases, attitudes often change when trial is encouraged (through cents-off coupons, free samples, etc.), or a positive feeling (i.e., affect) is created through classical conditioning, such as beautiful background scenery or a celebrity endorsement. Thus, in these circumstances, it might be more effective to change the affective and/or cognitive components of the attitude first.

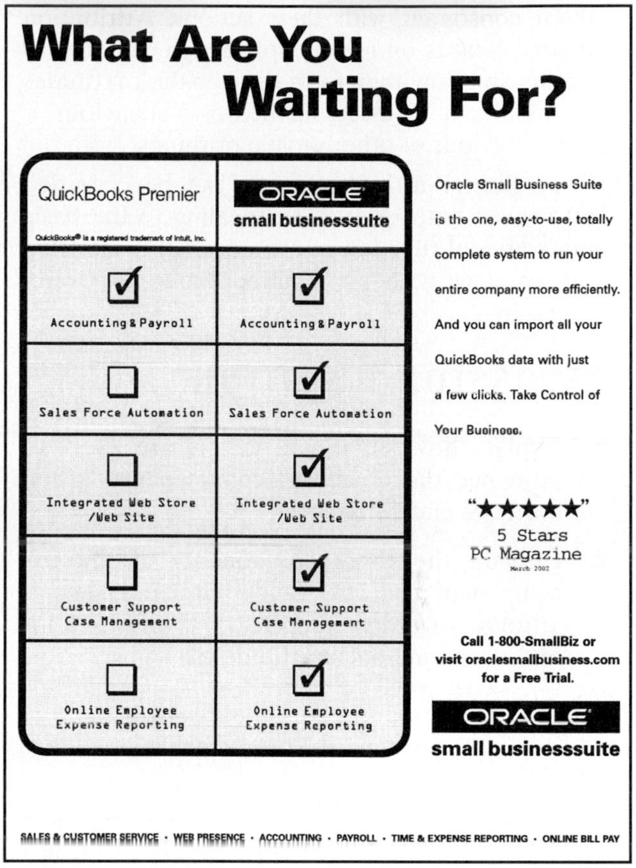

EXHIBIT 7-12

CHANGING ATTITUDES BY CHANGING BELIEFS ABOUT THE COMPETITOR'S BRAND

Courtesy of Oracle Netledger.

SUMMARY

- An attitude is a learned predisposition to behave in a consistently favourable or unfavourable way with respect to a given object (e.g., a product category, a brand, a service, an advertisement, a website, or a retail establishment).

- Two broad categories of attitude models have received attention: the tri-component attitude model and the multi-attribute attitude models.

- The tri-component model of attitudes consists of three parts: a cognitive (or knowledge and beliefs) component, an affective (or emotions or feelings) component, and a conative (or action tendency) component.

- As a group, multi-attribute attitude models (i.e., attitude-toward-object, attitude-toward-behaviour, and the theory-of-reasoned-action models) examine consumer beliefs about specific product attributes (e.g., product or brand features or benefits).

- Unlike the above models, both cognitive dissonance theory and attribution theory provide alternative explanations of attitude formation and change that suggest that behaviour might precede attitudes. Cognitive dissonance theory suggests that the conflicting thoughts, or dissonant information, following a purchase decision might propel consumers to change their attitudes to make them consonant with their actions. Attribution theory focuses on how people assign causality to events and how they form or alter their attitudes as an outcome of assessing their own behaviour or the behaviour of other people or things.

- Strategies of attitude change can be classified into seven categories: (1) appealing to the basic motivational function of attitudes, (2) associating the product with an admired group or event, (3) resolving two conflicting attitudes, (4) influencing consumer attributions, (5) altering components of the multi-attribute models, (6) changing beliefs about competitors' brands, and (7) changing the affective and/or behavioural components of an attitude first. Each of these strategies gives the marketer a different way of changing consumers' existing attitudes.

DISCUSSION QUESTIONS

1. Explain how situational factors are likely to influence the degree of consistency between attitudes and behaviour.

2. Explain the three components of the tri-component model of attitudes. Explain a person's attitude toward visiting Disney World in terms of the tri-component attitude model.

3. Explain the multi-attribute models of attitudes. How can a marketer use the models to change consumer attitudes?

4. What is cognitive dissonance? A university student has just bought a new computer. What might cause him to experience post-purchase dissonance? How might he try to overcome it? How can the retailer who sold the computer help reduce the student's dissonance? How can the computer's manufacturer help?

CRITICAL THINKING QUESTIONS

1. How can the marketer of a "nicotine patch" (a device that helps people to quit smoking) use the theory of reasoned action to segment its market? Using this theory, identify two segments that the marketer should target and suggest ways of positioning the product for each of the two segments.

2. Explain how the product manager of a breakfast cereal might change consumer attitudes toward the company's brand by (a) changing beliefs about the brand, (b) changing beliefs about competing brands, (c) changing the relative evaluation of attributes, and (d) adding an attribute.

3. The Department of Transportation of a large city is planning an advertising campaign that will encourage people to switch from private cars to mass transit. Give examples of how the department can use the following strategies to change commuters' attitudes: (a) changing the basic motivational function, (b) changing beliefs about public transportation, (c) using self-perception theory, and (d) using cognitive dissonance.

4. The Saturn Corporation is faced with the problem that many consumers consider compact and mid-sized North American cars to be of poorer quality than comparable Japanese cars. Assuming that Saturn produces cars that are as good as Japanese cars or better, how can the company persuade consumers of this fact?

5. Should the marketer of a popular computer graphics program prefer consumers to make internal or external attributions? Explain your answer.

6. Because attitudes are learned predispositions to respond a certain way, why don't marketers and consumer researchers just measure purchase behaviour and forget attitudes?

INTERNET EXERCISES

1. Find two online ads, one illustrating the use of the affective component and the other illustrating the cognitive component. Discuss each ad in the context of the tri-component model. In your view, why did each marketer take the approach it did in each of these ads?

2. Find an example of an exclusive online sponsorship. What was the brand and the event sponsored? Do you think it is effective? Why?

3. Visit some entertainment websites and some car manufacturers' websites. Do they use any attitude change strategies? If they do, do you see any difference in the types of strategies used?

4. Visit the websites of some non-profit organizations and examine the types of messages that they use. What types of attitude change strategies do they use?

KEY TERMS

Attitude   *(p. 215)*
Attitude-toward-behaviour model   *(p. 226)*
Attitude-toward-object model   *(p. 225)*
Attributions toward others   *(p. 230)*
Attribution theory   *(p. 229)*

Cognitive dissonance theory   *(p. 228)*
Ego-defensive function   *(p. 217)*
Foot-in-the-door technique   *(p. 230)*
Knowledge function   *(p. 218)*
Multi-attribute attitude models   *(p. 225)*

Self-perception theory   *(p. 229)*
Theory of reasoned action   *(p. 226)*
Tri-component attitude model   *(p. 222)*
Utilitarian function   *(p. 217)*
Value-expressive function   *(p. 218)*

CASE 7-1: IT'S RAINING, SO I'LL ORDER SOUP

Over the course of our lives, we all develop attitudes toward different foods—we like some and dislike others. While one person may love broccoli, another person might rather go hungry than eat broccoli. And there is one food category known as "comfort foods," that is, the foods that we "love" and that we eat in certain situations in order to obtain some measure of psychological comfort, to feel "safe" and "secure." So on a cold and rainy afternoon, a bowl of chicken soup or tomato soup might be "just what the doctor ordered." Interestingly enough, people are more likely to seek out comfort foods when they are happy (as a "reward" they give themselves) than when they are lonely, depressed, or bored.

According to a recent survey conducted by the Food and Brand Lab of the University of Illinois, the most popular comfort foods, in order of popularity, are (1) potato chips: 24 percent, (2) ice cream: 14 percent, (3) cookies: 12 percent, (4) candy and chocolate bars: 11 percent, (5) pizza and pasta: 11 percent, (6) beef or steak burgers: 9 percent, (7) fruits and vegetables: 7 percent, (8) soup: 4 percent, and (9) other: 9 percent. Moreover, people who are in a happy mood are more likely to seek out foods like pizza or steak, whereas people who are sad are more likely to reach for ice cream or cookies. Bored people often opt for a bag of potato chips.

QUESTION

1. What factors discussed in this chapter might help account for our need for comfort foods?

Source: Brian Wansink and Cynthia Sangerman, "The Taste of Comfort," *American Demographics*, July 2000, 66–67.

NOTES

1   David Bars, "Marketing after SARS," *Marketing Magazine*, July 28, 2003, 1.

2   Ibid. See also Paul-Mark Rendon, "BBDO Kicks Off Toronto SARS Effort," *Marketing Magazine*, May 19, 2003, 1.

3   Paul-Mark Rendon, "Toronto Steps Up Marketing Efforts," *Marketing Magazine*, May 5, 2003.

4   Paul-Mark Rendon, "Stars against SARS," *Marketing Magazine*, July 28, 2003.

5   Jack Neff, "Suave Strokes," *Advertising Age,* August 20, 2001, 12.

6   Lesley Young, "Radio Shack Corners New Ad Theme," *Marketing Magazine*, September 8, 2003, 3.

7   Maria Knight Lapinski and Franklin J. Boster, "Modeling the Ego-Defensive Function of Attitudes," *Communication Monographs,* 68, 3, September 2001, 314–324.

8   Cara Beardi, "Zippo's Eternal Flame," *Advertising Age,* August 13, 2001, 4.

9   Morris B. Holbrook, David A. Velez, and Gerard J. Tabouret, "Attitude Structure and Search: An Integrative Model of Importance-Directed Information Processing," in Kent B. Monroe, ed., *Advances in Consumer Research,* 8 (Ann Arbor, MI: Association for Consumer Research, 1981), 35–41.

10   Richard P. Bagozzi, Hans Baumgartner, and Youjae Yi, "Coupon Usage and the Theory of Reasoned Action," in Rebecca H. Holman and Michael R. Solomon, eds., *Advances in Consumer Research,* 18 (Provo, UT: Association for Consumer Research, 1991), 24–27.

11   For an interesting article on the impact of social interaction on attitude development, see Daniel J. Howard and Charles Gengler, "Emotional Contagion Effects on Product Attitudes," *Journal of Consumer Research,* 28, September 2001, 189–201.

12   Haksik Lee, Gilbert D. Harrell, and Cornelia L. Droge, "Product Experiences and Hierarchy of Advertising Effects," in *2000 AMA Winter Educators' Conference,* 11, eds. John P. Workman and William D. Perreault (Chicago: American Marketing Association, 2000), 41–42.

13   James R. Coyle and Esther Thorson, "The Effects of Progressive Levels of Interactivity and Vividness in Web Marketing Sites," *Journal of Advertising,* 30, 3, Fall 2001, 65–77; and Lynn C. Dailey and C. Edward Heath, "Creating the Flow Experience Online: The Role of Web Atmospherics," in *2000 AMA Winter Educators' Conference,* 11, eds. John P. Workman and William D. Perreault (Chicago: American Marketing Association, 2000), 58.

14   Richard J. Lutz, "The Role of Attitude Theory in Marketing," in Harold H. Kassarjian and Thomas S. Robertson, eds., *Perspectives in Consumer Behavior,* 4th ed. (Upper Saddle River, NJ: Prentice-Hall, 1991), 317–339.

15   Joel B. Cohen and Charles S. Areni, "Affect and Consumer Behavior," in Harold H. Kassarjian and Thomas S. Robertson, eds., *Perspectives in Consumer Behavior,* 188–240; and Madeline Johnson and George M. Zinkhan, "Emotional Responses to a Professional Service Encounter," *Journal of Service Marketing,* 5, Spring 1991, 5–16. See also John Kim, Jeen-Su Iim, and Mukesh Bhargava, "The Role of Affect in Attitude Formation: A Classical Condition Approach," *Journal of the Academy of Marketing Science,* 26 (1998), 143–152.

16   Jaideep Sengupta, "Perspectives on Attitude Strength" in Joseph W. Alba and J. Wesley Hutchinson, eds., *Advances in Consumer Research,* 25 (Provo, UT: Association for Consumer Research, 1998), 63–64.

17   Martin Fishbein, "An Investigation of the Relationships between Beliefs about an Object and the Attitude toward the Object," *Human Relations,* 16, (1963), 233–240; and Martin Fishbein, "A Behavioral Theory Approach to the Relations between Beliefs about an Object and the Attitude toward the Object," in Martin Fishbein, ed., *Readings in Attitude Theory and Measurement* (New York: Wiley, 1967), 389–400.

18   Rajeev Batra and Michael L. Ray, "Affective Responses Mediating Acceptance of Advertising," *Journal of Consumer Research,* 13, September 1986, 236–239; Julie A. Edell and Marian Chapman Burke, "The Power of Feelings in Understanding Advertising Effects," *Journal of Consumer Research,* 14, December 1987, 421–433; and Marian Chapman Burke and Julie A. Edell, "The Impact of Feelings on Ad-Based Affect and Cognition," *Journal of Marketing Research,* 26, February 1989, 69–83.

19   Dena Saliagas Cox and William B. Locander, "Product Novelty: Does It Moderate the Relationship between Ad Attitudes and Brand Attitudes?" *Journal of Advertising,* 16, 1987, 39–44. See also Cynthia B. Hanson and Gabriel J. Biehal, "Accessibility Effects on the Relationship between Attitude toward the Ad and Brand Choice," in Frank R. Kardes and Mita Sujan, eds., *Advances in Consumer Research,* 22 (Provo, UT: Association for Consumer Research, 1995), 152–158.

20   Icek Ajzen and Martin Fishbein, *Understanding Attitudes and Predicting Social Behavior* (Upper Saddle River, NJ: Prentice-Hall, 1980); and Martin Fishbein and Icek Ajzen, *Belief, Attitude, Intentions, and Behavior* (Reading, MA: Addison-Wesley, 1975), 62–63. See also Robert E. Burnkrant, H. Rao Unnava, and Thomas J. Page, Jr., "Effects of Experience on Attitude Structure," in Rebecca H. Holman and Michael R. Solomon, eds., *Advances in Consumer Research,* 18 (Provo, UT: Association for Consumer Research, 1991), 28–29.

21   Terence A. Shimp and Alican Kavas, "The Theory of Reasoned Action Applied to Coupon Usage," *Journal of Consumer Research,* 11, December 1984, 795–809; Blair H. Sheppard, Jon Hartwick, and Paul R. Warshaw, "The Theory of Reasoned Action: A Meta-Analysis of Past Research with Recommendations for Modifications and Future Research," *Journal of Consumer Research,* 15, September 1986, 325–343; Sharon E. Beatly and Lynn R. Kahle, "Alternative Hierarchies of the Attitude-Behavior Relationship: The Impact of Brand Commitment and Habit," *Journal of the Academy of Marketing Science,* 16, Summer 1988, 1–10; Richard P. Bagozzi, Hans Baumgartner, and Youjae Yi, "Coupon Usage and the Theory of Reasoned Action," in Rebecca H. Holman and Michael R. Solomon, eds., *Advances in Consumer Research,* 18 (Provo, UT: Association for Consumer Research, 1991), 24–27; and Hee Sun Park, "Relationships among Attitudes and Subjective Norms: Testing the Theory of Reasoned Action across Cultures," *Communication Studies,* 51, 2, Summer 2000, 162–175.

22   Joanne Caza, "From Destination to Journey" *Marketing Magazine,* September 8, 2003, p. 25.

23   Edward E. Jones et al., *Attribution: Perceiving the Causes of Behavior* (Morristown, NJ: General Learning Press, 1972); and Bernard Weiner, "Attributional Thoughts about Consumer Behavior," *Journal of Consumer Research,* 27, 3, December 2000, 382–387.

24   Chris T. Allen and William R. Dillon, "Self-Perception Development and Consumer Choice Criteria: Is There a Linkage?" in Richard P. Bagozzi and Alice M. Tybout, eds., *Advances in Consumer Research,* 10 (Ann Arbor, MI: Association for Consumer Research, 1983), 45–50.

25   See, for example, Leslie Lazar Kanuk, *Mail Questionnaire Response Behavior as a Function of Motivational Treatment* (New York: CUNY, 1974).

26   John R. O'Malley, Jr., "Consumer Attributions of Product Failures to Channel Members," in Kim P. Corfman and John F. Lynch, Jr., eds., *Advances in Consumer Research,* 23 (Provo, UT: Association for Consumer Research, 1996), 342–345. See also Charmine Hartel, Janet R. Mccoll-Kennedy, and Lyn McDonald, "Incorporating Attributional Theory and the Theory of Reasoned Action within an Affective Events Theory Framework to Produce a Contingency Predictive Model of Consumer Reactions to Organizational Mishaps," in Joseph W. Alba and J. Wesley Hutchinson, eds., *Advances in Consumer Research,* 25 (Provo, UT: Association for Consumer Research, 1998), 428–432.

27   Harold H. Kelley, "Attribution Theory in Social Psychology," in David Levine, ed., *Nebraska Symposium on Motivation,* 15 (Lincoln: University of Nebraska Press, 1967), 197.

28   Michelle Warren, "Taking Safe Drinking to School," *Marketing Magazine,* September 8, 2003, 1.

29   Geoffrey L. Cohen, Joshua Aronson, and Claude M. Steele, "When Beliefs Yield to Evidence: Reducing Biased Evaluation by Affirming the Self," *Personality and Social Psychology Bulletin,* 26, 9, September 2000, 1151–1164.

30   Richard E. Petty et al., "Theories of Attitude Change," in Harold Kassarjian and Thomas Robertson, eds., *Handbook of Consumer Theory and Research* (Upper Saddle River, NJ: Prentice Hall, 1991); and Richard E. Petty, John T. Cacioppo, and David Schumann, "Central and Peripheral Routes to Advertising Effectiveness: The Moderating Role of Involvement," *Journal of Consumer Research,* 10, September 1983, 135–146. See also Curtis P. Haugtvedt and Alan J. Strathman, "Situational Product Relevance and Attitude Persistence," in Marvin E. Goldberg, Gerald Gorn, and Richard W. Pollay, eds., *Advances in Consumer Research,* 17 (Provo, UT: Association for Consumer Research, 1990), 766–769; and Scott B. Mackenzie and Richard A. Spreng, "How Does Motivation Moderate the Impact of Central and Peripheral Processing on Brand Attitudes and Intentions?" *Journal of Consumer Research,* 18, March 1992, 519–529.

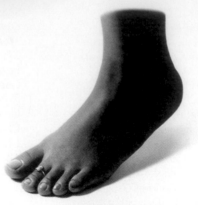

INDIA
Married

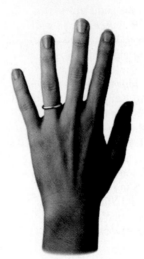

USA
Married

Never underestimate the importance of local knowledge.

Issued by HSBC Holdings plc

Photography By Richard Pullar

chapter 8
communication and consumer behaviour

LEARNING OBJECTIVES

By the end of this chapter, you should be able to:

1. List and explain the various elements of the communication process.
2. Discuss the characteristics of the sender, message, receiver, and feedback that can affect the effectiveness of marketing communications.
3. Discuss the major barriers to effective communication.
4. Discuss how marketers can use their knowledge of communication and barriers to communication to develop effective communication strategies.

8

for canada the year 2003 was an unusual one. First, there was the SARS outbreak; then came mad cow disease. Both decreased tourism to, and within, Canada and seriously harmed Canadian businesses. The impact of both these disasters was so severe partly because of rapid improvements in communication tools. The world has, in several ways, become a "global village"—a planet whose people increasingly adopt similar values and one in which events that occur half-way around the globe are quickly reported to the entire planet through highly visual media such as television and the internet. During the SARS outbreak, images of hospital staff with their noses and mouths covered were quickly flashed around the world, together with a warning from the World Health Organization, and this led to dramatic declines in travel to Canada. Similarly, news that one cow in Alberta was infected with the mad cow disease travelled around the world quickly; governments across the world banned Canadian beef.

www.who.int

If improvements in communications have resulted in the fast transmission of negative news and increased the impact of such events, they have also expanded the tools available to governments and industries to respond to such events. For example, the Government of Canada did several things to inform Canadians and non-Canadians of the steps that it had taken to protect the general public. In the case of the SARS outbreak, as mentioned in the previous chapter, Canada Tourism, the Government of Ontario, and private organizations tried to convince the public that Ontario, especially Toronto, was a safe place to visit. Communication strategies involved public relations campaigns such as the a new promotional campaign "Toronto—You Belong Here," which was intended to persuade Torontonians to get out and start visiting local attractions;[1] and the star-studded "Concert for Toronto," which was designed to

www.beefinfo.org

attract Americans.[2] These campaigns, too, got extensive news coverage. Similarly, as soon as the single case of mad cow disease was reported in Alberta, the Canadian Cattlemen's Association (CCA) and its marketing arm, the Canadian Beef Information Centre, issued press releases stating that the Canadian inspection system was one of the most advanced in the world. Health Canada updated its website to include a fact sheet about the disease, aimed at providing Canadians and visitors to the country with factual information that would reduce their fears about the safety of Canadian beef. The Government of Alberta even sent postcards to Albertans at the end of the year to thank them for continuing to buy Albertan beef.

Marketers have always relied on various forms of communication to persuade consumers to act in a desired way—to vote, to use certain products, and to stop using others. Communication can take many forms: it can be verbal, written, visual, or a combination of the three. It can even be symbolic, such as the image conveyed through packaging, premium price, or a logo. In short, communication is the bridge between marketers and consumers and between consumers and their socio-cultural environments.

CHAPTER OVERVIEW

Communicating effectively with consumers and other publics is essential for the success of any marketing manager. This chapter covers the communication process and discusses its various elements in more detail. It also discusses the different message structures, appeals, and presentations that a company can use to communicate effectively with its consumers. The final section deals with the marketing implications of the various concepts covered in the chapter.

WHAT IS COMMUNICATION?

Although there are many ways to define communication, most marketers agree that **communication** is *the transmission of a message from a sender to a receiver via a medium (or channel) of transmission.* In addition to these four basic components—sender, receiver, medium, and message—the fifth essential component of communication is *feedback,* which tells the sender whether the intended message was, in fact, received. Figure 8-1 depicts this basic communication model.

The Sender

The sender, as the initiator of the communication, can be a formal or an informal source. A **formal communications source** is likely to represent either a for-profit (commercial) organization or a not-for-profit organization; an **informal source** can be a parent or friend who gives information or advice about a product. Consumers often rely on informal communications sources in making purchase decisions because, unlike formal sources, the sender appears to have nothing to gain from the receiver's subsequent actions. For that reason, **word-of-mouth communications** tend to be highly persuasive. Many studies recommend that marketers should encourage detailed, positive word-of-mouth about their products and services among consumers.[3]

The Receiver

The receivers of formal marketing communications can be classified into three groups:

Communication:
The transmission of a message from a sender to a receiver via a medium (or channel) of transmission.

Formal communications source:
A for-profit or not-for-profit organization that sends a message to the consumer.

Informal communications source:
Parents, friends, or other personal sources of communication.

Word-of-mouth communications:
Informal conversations about a product or service.

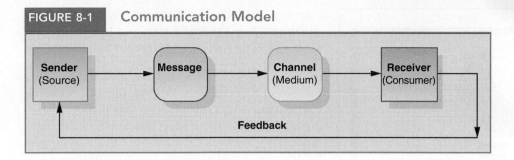

FIGURE 8-1   Communication Model

- the targeted prospects or customers (i.e., a member of the marketer's target audience)
- intermediary audiences (i.e., wholesalers, distributors, retailers, and relevant professionals)
- unintended audiences (i.e., publics that are important to the marketer, such as shareholders, creditors, suppliers, employees, bankers, and the local community)

It is important to remember that the audience—no matter how large or how diverse—is composed of individual receivers, each of whom interprets the message according to his or her own perceptions and experiences.

The Medium

The medium, or communications channel, can be classified into three categories:

- **impersonal communications** media, or mass media, such as *print* (newspapers, magazines, billboards), *broadcast* (radio, television), or *electronic* (primarily the internet). During the SARS outbreak, Canada Tourism used several television and newspaper ads to communicate the message that Toronto was a safe city to visit.
- **interpersonal communications**, a formal conversation between a salesperson and a customer or an informal conversation between two or more people that takes place face to face, by telephone, by mail, or online.
- **interactive communications** that permit the audiences of communication messages to provide direct feedback are beginning to blur the distinction between interpersonal and impersonal communications. Interactive communication can take place through websites, direct marketing (e.g., print, broadcast, or radio ads that seek individual responses from consumers), or direct mail. For example, during the mad cow incident, Health Canada used interactive communication through its website to provide factual information to consumers.

The Message

The *message* can be *verbal* (spoken or written), *non-verbal* (a photograph, an illustration, or a symbol), or a combination of the two. A verbal message, whether it is spoken or written, can usually contain more specific information about a product or service than can a non-verbal message. However, a combination of verbal and non-verbal messages often gives the receiver more information than either would alone.

Non-verbal communication takes place through both interpersonal and impersonal channels; it often takes the form of symbolic communication. Marketers often try to develop logos or symbols that are associated exclusively with their products and that achieve high recognition. The Coca-Cola Company, for example, has trademarked

Impersonal communications: Communications through mass media, such as television, newspapers, and magazines, that are directed toward large audiences.

Interpersonal communications: Communications that occur directly between people by telephone, email, or mail or in person.

Interactive communications: Impersonal or interpersonal communications that permit the audiences of communication messages to provide direct feedback.

www.hc-sc.gc.ca/english/diseases/bse

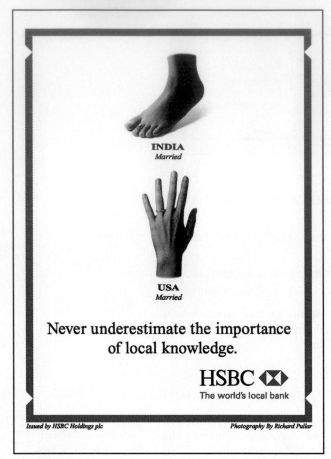

EXHIBIT 8-1

AD DEPICTING NON-VERBAL COMMUNICATION
Courtesy of HSBC Bank Canada. Photography by Richard Pullar.

Feedback:
Verbal or non-verbal communication from the receiver of a message back to the sender.

both the word *Coke* in a specific typographic style and the shape of the traditional Coke bottle, and both are instantly recognizable to consumers as symbols of the company's best-selling soft drink.[4] In some countries, the colour of a product can be registered as a trademark. For example, in 1994, the U.S. Supreme Court ruled that even a colour that distinguishes a product (and serves no other function) can be registered as a trademark.[5] Exhibit 8-1 depicts an ad portraying non-verbal, symbolic communication.

Feedback

Feedback is an essential component of both interpersonal and impersonal communications. Prompt feedback permits the sender to reinforce, change, or modify the message to ensure that it is understood in the intended way. Generally, it is easier to obtain feedback (both verbal and non-verbal) from interpersonal communications than from impersonal communications. For example, a good salesperson is usually alert to non-verbal feedback from customers. This may take the form of facial expressions, such as a smile, a frown, a look of total boredom, or an expression of disbelief; or body movements, such as finger tapping, head nodding, head shaking, or clenched hands. Because of the high cost of space and time in impersonal media, it is very important for sponsors of impersonal communications to devise methods to obtain feedback as promptly as possible, so that they may revise a message if its meaning is not being received as intended.

An excellent example of marketing based on shoppers' feedback, in the form of "body language," is the selling method employed at the rapidly growing Diesel jeans stores. Unlike other clothing stores, Diesel stores are not user-friendly because the company believes that a disoriented customer is the best prospect. Diesel stores feature loud techno music and large television screens playing videos unrelated to the merchandise. There are no signs directing customers to different departments, no obvious salespeople, and the clothing has strange names accompanied by confusing charts intended to explain the options. In the midst of this chaos, young and hip-looking salespeople who are trained to spot "wayward-looking," overwhelmed, and confused shoppers, "rescue" them by becoming their "shopping friends" and, of course, sell them as many pairs of jeans as possible.[6]

FACTORS THAT AFFECT THE COMMUNICATION PROCESS AND ITS EFFECTIVENESS

In general, a company's marketing communications are designed to make the consumer aware of the product, induce purchase or commitment, create a positive attitude toward the product, give the product a symbolic meaning, or show how it can solve the consumer's problem better than a competitive product or service. The communication process and its effectiveness are affected by the characteristics of the source (or message initiator), the characteristics of the message, the characteristics of the receiver, the nature of the medium selected to transmit the message, and the nature of the feedback provided by the audience. The following sections discuss these in more detail.

Characteristics of the Message Initiator (Source)

The sponsor (initiator) of the message must first decide to whom the message should be sent and what meaning it should convey. Then the sponsor must *encode* the message in such a way that its meaning is interpreted by the targeted audience in precisely the intended way. The sources of *impersonal communications* are usually organizations (either for-profit or not-for-profit) that develop and transmit messages through special departments (e.g., marketing or public relations) or spokespersons. The targets, or receivers, of such messages are usually a specific audience or several audiences that the organization is trying to inform, influence, or persuade. For example, AOL wants to attract both online users and advertisers; a museum may wish to target both donors and visitors; and a mail-order company may want to persuade consumers to call a toll-free number for a copy of its catalogue.

Marketers have a large arsenal from which to draw in encoding their messages: words, pictures, symbols, spokespersons, and special channels. They can buy advertising space or time in carefully selected media, or they can try to have their message appear in space or time usually reserved for editorial messages. (The latter, called **publicity**, is usually the result of public relations efforts and tends to be more believable because its commercial origins and intent are not readily apparent.)

Sources can be classified into four categories:

- personal, informal sources (e.g., friends and family members)
- impersonal, neutral sources (e.g., *Consumer Reports* and the Canadian Dental Association)
- commercial or marketer-related sources (the firm itself or its employees, CEO, etc.)
- celebrity sources

The communication process and its effectiveness depend to a great extent on the credibility of the sources since the decoding of the message is influenced by **source credibility**. The sponsor of the communication—and his or her apparent honesty and objectivity—has an enormous influence on how the communication is received by the receivers. When the source is well respected and highly regarded by the intended audience, the message is much more likely to be believed. Conversely, a message from a source considered unreliable or untrustworthy is likely to be received with skepticism and may be rejected.

Credibility is built on a number of factors, of which the most important are the perceived intentions of the source. Receivers ask themselves, "Just what does he (or she) stand to gain if I do what is suggested?" If the receiver believes there is any type of personal gain for the message sponsor as a result of the proposed action or advice, the message itself becomes suspect: "He wants me to buy that product just to earn a commission."

Credibility of Informal Sources

One of the main reasons that informal sources such as friends, neighbours, and relatives have a strong influence on a receiver's behaviour is simply that they seem to

Publicity:
Messages that appear in space or time usually reserved for editorial messages, usually through public relations efforts by the firm.

Source credibility:
The apparent honesty and objectivity of the source of communication.

Opinion leader:
The person in a word-of-mouth encounter who offers advice or information about a product or service.

have nothing to gain from a product transaction that they recommend. That is why word-of-mouth communication is so effective. Interestingly enough, some informal sources of communications, called **opinion leaders**, often do profit psychologically, if not tangibly, by giving product information to others. A person may obtain a great deal of ego satisfaction by offering both solicited and unsolicited information and advice to friends. This ego gratification may actually improve the quality of the information provided, because the opinion leader often deliberately seeks out the latest detailed information in order to enhance his or her position as an "expert" in a particular product category. The fact that the opinion leader does not receive material gain from the recommended action increases the likelihood that the advice will be considered seriously.

Even with informal sources, however, intentions are not always what they appear to be. People who experience post-purchase dissonance often try to alleviate their uncertainty by persuading others to make a similar purchase. Each time they persuade a friend or an acquaintance to choose the same brand as they did, they are somewhat reassured that their own choice was wise. The receiver, on the other hand, regards product advice from "the person who owns one" as totally objective, because the source is able to speak from actual experience. Thus, the increased credibility accorded the informal source may not really be warranted, despite the aura of objectivity.

Credibility of Impersonal, Neutral Sources

Not-for-profit sources generally have more credibility than for-profit (commercial) sources. Formal sources that are considered to be "neutral"—such as *Consumer Reports* or newspaper articles—have greater credibility than do commercial sources because of the perception that neutral sources are more objective in their product assessments. That is why publicity is so valuable to a manufacturer. Citations of a product in an editorial context, rather than in a paid advertisement, give the reader much more confidence in the message. One study discovered that the perceived trustworthiness of publicity was higher when the message stressed the company's altruistic motives (e.g., launching a recycling program because of "good corporate citizenship") than when the message stressed a commercial corporate motive (e.g., launching a recycling venture in the form of a subsidiary).[7]

Credibility of Commercial or Marketer-Related Sources

Because consumers recognize that the intentions of commercial sources, such as manufacturers, service companies, financial institutions, and retailers, are clearly profit-oriented, they judge the credibility of commercial sources by such factors as

- past performance,
- reputation,
- the kind and quality of service they are known to render,
- the quality and reputation of other products they manufacture,
- the image and attractiveness of the spokesperson used,
- the type of retail outlets through which they sell, and
- their position in the community (e.g., whether there is evidence that they are committed to such issues as social responsibility or equal employment).

Firms with well-established reputations generally have an easier time selling their products than do firms with lesser reputations. The ability of a quality image to invoke credibility is one of the reasons for the growth of family brands.

Manufacturers with favourable brand images prefer to give their new products the existing brand name in order to obtain ready acceptance from consumers. Furthermore, a quality image permits a company to experiment more freely in many more areas of marketing than would otherwise be considered prudent, such as free-standing retail outlets, new price levels, and innovative promotional techniques. Recognizing that a manufacturer with a good reputation generally has high credibility among consumers, many companies spend a sizeable part of their advertising budget on **institutional advertising**, which is designed to promote a favourable company image rather than specific products.

> **Institutional advertising:** Advertising that is intended to promote a favourable company image rather than specific products.

Many companies sponsor special entertainment and sports events to enhance their image and credibility with their target audiences. The nature and quality of these sponsorships constitute a subtle message to the consumer: "We're a great (kind, good-natured, socially responsible) company; we deserve your business." For example, such firms as American Express, Avon Products, and Estée Lauder sponsor free public concerts, athletic events, and walks to support cancer research. Other kinds of corporate-sponsored special events include marching bands, fireworks displays, parades, laser shows, and travelling art exhibits.

Let us look at some examples. L'Oreal Canada sponsored the *Canadian Idol* show and *Star Académie* in 2003. The company was also involved in marketing initiatives for International Women's Day, Toronto Fashion Week, the Cannes film festival, and Cirque du Soleil. The company feels that all these sponsorships are in line with the interests of their target audience and will gain them considerable exposure.[8]

> www.brandstorm.loreal.com

Kellogg Canada sponsors "Mission Nutrition" at elementary schools across the country. The program, a joint initiative between Kellogg and Dietitians of Canada, attempts to teach children about healthy living in an entertaining way. The program is linked to health curriculum in the schools.[9]

> www.missionnutrition.ca

Nike Canada won the hearts and minds of Canadians, especially those from Toronto, with its RunTO campaign. The biggest outdoor, out-of-home campaign that the company had ever run, the RunTO campaign was aimed at bringing some fun and energy into Toronto in the summer of 2003—a time when Torontonians were reeling under the negative publicity that their city received because of the SARS outbreak. Nike spent more than $1 million on the campaign. Was the expenditure effective? Thousands of runners joined the 10K race, but according to Caroline Whaley, Director of Marketing at Nike Canada, the benefits went far beyond that—"People really warmed to it, they liked the idea that we were doing something for Toronto, and it was more than just an advertising campaign."[10]

> www.runto.ca

Credibility of Spokespersons and Endorsers

Consumers sometimes regard the spokesperson who gives the product message as the source (or initiator) of the message. Thus, the "pitchman" (whether male or female) who appears in person or in a commercial or advertisement has a major influence on the credibility of the message. This accounts for the increasing use of celebrities to promote products. Many studies have investigated the relationship between the effectiveness of the message and the spokesperson or endorser. Here are some of the findings of this body of research:

The effectiveness of the spokesperson is related to the message itself: For example, when message comprehension is low, receivers rely on the spokesperson's credibility in forming attitudes toward the product, but when comprehension (and, thus, systematic information processing) is high, the expertise of the spokesperson has far less effect on a receiver's attitudes.[11]

The similarity between the endorser and the type of product or service adver-tised is an important factor: One study found that, for products that are related to attractiveness (such as cosmetics), a physically attractive celebrity spokesperson significantly enhanced the credibility of the message and attitudes toward the ad. But for other products, such as cameras, an attractive endorser had little or no effect. This suggests a "match-up" hypothesis for celebrity advertising.[12] Another study found that a celebrity endorser was more effective in terms of source credibility and consumer attitudes toward the ad for a hedonistic and "experiential" service, such as a restaurant, than for a utilitarian service like a bank.[13]

Similarity between endorsers and the target audience is crucial: Endorsers who have demographic characteristics (e.g., age, social class, and ethnicity) that are similar to those of the target audience are viewed as more credible and persuasive than those who do not. Moreover, consumers with a strong ethnic identification are more likely to be persuaded by endorsers with similar ethnicity than are people with a weaker ethnic identification.[14]

The endorser's credibility is not a substitute for corporate credibility: One study discovered that although the endorser's credibility strongly influences the audience's *attitudes toward the ad,* corporate credibility had a strong influence on *attitudes toward the advertised brand.*[15] This study supports the development of multiple measures to evaluate the credibility and persuasiveness of advertising messages, such as attitudes toward the ad, attitudes toward the brand, and consumer purchase intentions.

The product advertised should lie within the competence of the endorser: Marketers who use celebrities to give testimonials or endorse products must be sure that the specific wording of the endorsement lies within the recognized competence of the spokesperson. A tennis star can believably endorse a brand of analgesic with comments about how it relieves sore muscle pain; however, a recitation of medical evidence supporting the brand's superiority over other brands is beyond his expected knowledge and expertise and, thus, may reduce (rather than enhance) message credibility.

www.campbellsoup.ca/
en/kitchen/p2c_cook.
asp

Campbell's of Canada recently introduced the "Power2Cook" campaign aimed at encouraging men—especially young men—to cook with the company's products. The spokesperson for the campaign or the "Campbell's Cook" is Damon Runyan, a caterer, chef at a private club in Toronto, and star of a show on Canada's Food Network. Campbell's chose its new spokesperson carefully: he is demographically similar to the target audience, the product lies within his area of expertise (besides his practical expertise, he has undergone formal studies in food technology), he is physically attractive, and there is synergy between the product and Runyan. Can any company ask for more from a celebrity?[16]

Somewhat surprisingly, one study of advertising agencies found that none of the agencies surveyed had a written strategy for the selection of celebrity endorsers. The study's authors recommended a long list of factors to be considered in selecting celebrity endorsers, such as a careful match with the target audience, product, and brand, the celebrity's overall image, prior endorsements, trustworthiness, familiarity, expertise, profession, and physical attractiveness and whether the celebrity is a brand user.[17]

In interpersonal communications, consumers are more likely to be persuaded by salespersons who engender confidence and who give the impression of honesty and integrity. Consumer confidence in a salesperson is created in diverse ways, whether warranted or not. A salesperson who looks you in the eye is often considered to be more honest than one who does not. For many products, a sales representative who dresses well and drives an expensive, late-model car may have more credibility than one who has no such outward signs of success and doesn't appear to be the representation of a best-selling product. For some products, however, a salesperson may achieve more credibility by dressing the part of an expert. Thus a man selling home improvements may achieve more credibility by looking like someone who just climbed off a roof or out of a basement than by looking like a banker.

Effects of Time on Source Credibility: The Sleeper Effect

The persuasive effects of high-credibility sources do not last indefinitely. Although a high-credibility source is more influential than a low-credibility source, research suggests that both positive and negative credibility effects tend to disappear after six weeks or so. This phenomenon has been termed the **sleeper effect**.[18] Consumers simply forget the source of the message faster than they forget the message itself. Studies attribute the sleeper effect to dissociation (i.e., the consumer dissociates the message from its source) over time, which leaves just the content of the message. Interesting findings related to the sleeper effect include the following:

■ The memory of a negative cue (e.g., a low-credibility source) simply decays faster than the message itself, leaving behind the primary content of the message. (This observation is called the theory of *differential decay.)*[19]

■ A study applying the sleeper effect to political advertising showed that the effectiveness of the attack ad increases considerably over a period of weeks, whereas the audience's initial negative perception of the political assailant as having low credibility fades and has only a temporary negative impact on the ad.[20]

■ However, if the message is reintroduced, it jogs the audience's memory, and the original effect manifests itself again; that is, the high-credibility source remains more persuasive than the low-credibility source.[21]

The implication for marketers who use high-credibility spokespersons is that they must repeat the same series of ads or commercials regularly in order to maintain a high level of persuasiveness.

> **Sleeper effect:**
> The tendency of communications to lose the impact of source credibility over time.

Message Characteristics

Several characteristics of the message influence the effectiveness of the communication between customers and marketers. The most important are the credibility of the message, the structure and presentation of the message, and the type of appeal used by the marketer.

Credibility of the Message

Although the source of the message is a big factor in gaining the confidence of consumers (and making the message more credible), certain characteristics of the message itself have an impact on its credibility.

■ *The reputation of the retailer who sells the product has a major influence on the credibility of the message:* Products sold by well-known quality stores seem to carry the added endorsement (and implicit guarantee) of the store itself (e.g., "If Sears carries it, it must be good.").

■ *The consumer's previous experience with the product or the retailer:* Fulfilled product expectations tend to increase the credibility accorded future messages by the same advertiser; unfulfilled product claims or disappointing experiences with the product tend to reduce the credibility of future messages.

■ *The reputation of the medium that carries the advertisement also enhances the credibility of the advertiser:* For example, a medium's prestige, its reputation for honesty and objectivity, and its specialized knowledge and expertise all add to the credibility of a medium. Thus, advertisements in prestigious magazines such as *Fortune,* newspapers known for their honesty and objectivity (e.g., the *Globe and Mail*), and specialized media (e.g., *Canadian Geographic*) are more likely to be seen as credible by consumers.

However, there is no single answer as to which medium has the most credibility, especially at a time when new forms of media, such as the internet, and traditional media in new forms, such as online editions of well-established newspapers, are emerging and evolving. One study discovered that persons interested in politics are shifting from television to the web for political information.[22] Another study reported that the public generally considers opinion polls reported in traditional news media to be more credible than online polls,[23] and still another study reported that cable television newscasts are viewed as the most credible and that differences in the perceived credibility of various media were related to the age of the viewers.[24] As the number and types of media continue to evolve and grow, print, broadcast, and digital media executives should survey their audiences periodically about such factors as perceived fairness, balance, and accuracy in order to maximize their credibility with audiences and their attractiveness to advertisers.

Message Structure and Presentation

Some of the decisions that marketers must make in designing the message pertain to the use of *resonance, positive or negative message framing, one-sided or two-sided messages, comparative advertising, order of presentation*, and the use of *repetition*.

Advertising resonance:
Wordplay, often used to create a double meaning, used in combination with a relevant picture.

Resonance   **Advertising resonance** is defined as wordplay; it is often used to create a double meaning or is used in combination with a relevant picture (see Exhibit 8-2). Other examples of advertising resonance are the phrase "absolut masterpiece" appearing next to a bottle of Absolut Vodka, and Pepsi's slogan "hit the beach topless" next to a Pepsi bottle cap lying in the sand. Using insights provided by semiotics, researchers have found that by manipulating the resonance in an ad, they can improve consumer attitudes toward the ad and the brand and unaided recall of advertising headlines.[25] They also found that small changes in the ad format (resonance) can have a positive and measurable impact on consumer response.

Message Framing   Should a marketer stress the benefits to be gained by using a specific product (*positive message framing*) or the benefits to be lost by not using the product (*negative message framing*)? Research suggests that decisions about **message framing** depend on the consumer's attitudes and characteristics as well as the product itself. Positively framed messages have been found to be more effective in the following situations:

Message framing:
The designing of a message to stress either the benefits to be gained by using the products or the benefits that will be lost if the product is not used.

- in low-involvement situations in which there is little emphasis on detailed cognitive processing[26]
- when the target consumers have an independent self-image (i.e., they view themselves as defined by unique characteristics)[27]
- when the target market consists of older consumers; in such instances emotion-based, positively framed messages have been found to be more effective[28]

Negatively framed messages, conversely, have been found to be more effective in the following situations:

- when the product is a high-involvement one that encourages detailed information processing.[29]

■ when the target consumers have an interdependent self-view (i.e., view themselves as defined by others), perhaps because they find messages that stress avoidance goals more convincing (negative framing).[30]

■ when it is important to change subsequent usage behaviour. For example, a study of a credit card company's customers who had not used their cards in the preceding three months found that negative message framing (i.e., what the consumer might lose by not using the credit card) had a much stronger effect on subsequent usage behaviour than did positive message framing.[31]

■ when certain medical tests are being marketed. Negative ads were found to be more effective in persuading consumers to go for tests that aid the early detection of diseases especially when anecdotal messages are used.[32]

■ when the market is new: A study discovered that argument-based, negatively framed messages are particularly effective in new markets.[33]

Although most negatively framed ads stress a fear appeal, it is possible to have negatively framed ads that stress the benefits lost if a product is not used in an amusing and interesting way.

Why don't teenagers and young adults drink milk? There are several reasons, of course, not the least of which is their feeling that milk is just a boring commodity. To change their image of milk, the BC Dairy Foundation ran a series of ads that attempted to convey the message "Don't take your body for granted." To express the benefits lost by not drinking milk, it asked, "What would life be like without a body?" The ads, which showed bodiless heads in various situations, were extremely successful—80 percent of the target market remembered seeing at least one ad (as opposed to 56 percent achieved by similar spending by other companies), 92 percent agreed that it was unique and different, and 83 percent found the campaign enjoyable.[34]

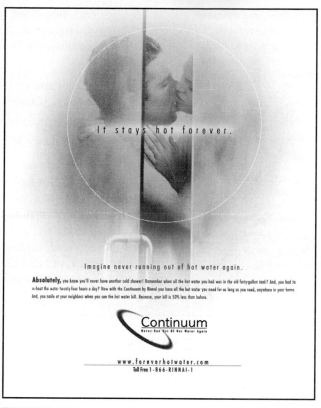

EXHIBIT 8-2

RESONANCE IN ADVERTISING
Courtesy of Rinnai Corporation.

www.bcdairyfoundation.ca

One-Sided versus Two-Sided Messages Should marketers tell their audiences only the good points about their products, or should they also tell them the bad (or the commonplace)? Should they pretend that their products are the only ones of their kind, or should they acknowledge competing products? These are very real strategic questions that marketers face every day, and the answers depend on the nature of the audience and the nature of the competition. **One-sided messages** (i.e., those that give only the arguments in favour or support of the product being advertised) have been found to be effective in the following situations:

■ when the audience is friendly (e.g., if it uses the advertiser's products)

■ if the audience initially favours the communicator's position

■ if the audience is not likely to hear an opposing argument

One-sided messages:
Messages that state only the positive features or benefits of the product.

Two-sided messages: Messages that state the positive and some negative features or benefits of the product.

Comparative advertising: Advertising that explicitly names or identifies a competitor for the purpose of claiming overall superiority or superiority on one or more attributes.

In general, **two-sided (refutational) message** tend to be more credible than one-sided advertising messages because they acknowledge that the advertised brand has shortcomings. Two-sided messages can be very effective in the following situations:

- when the target audience is likely to see competitors' negative counterclaims or when consumer attitudes toward the brand are already negative[35]
- if the target audience is critical or unfriendly (e.g., if it uses competitive products)
- if the target audience is well-educated

The credibility of an advertised claim can often be enhanced by actually stating that some features of the product are no better than those of a competing brand or by not claiming that the product will solve the buyer's every problem.

Rogaine ads often note that at the conclusion of a 12-month clinical test, almost half the men using the product experienced modest to dense hair regrowth, about a third experienced minimal hair regrowth, and about one-sixth had no regrowth whatever (see Exhibit 8-3). The admission that the product did not always work enhanced the credibility of the ad.

Comparative Advertising Comparative advertising is a widely used marketing strategy in which a marketer claims that its brand of a product is superior—either overall or in certain ways—to its competitors, which are named or identified implicitly (see Exhibits 8-4 and 8-5). Comparative advertising is useful for positioning products, choosing the target market, and positioning brands.

Both Telus Mobility and Bell Mobility recently targeted Fido consumers by means of comparative ads. Microcell (the company that markets Fido) introduced City Fido, a plan that aimed at replacing landlines with mobile phones through an offer of unlimited local calls. This led to comparative ad campaigns from both Telus Mobility and Bell Mobility. Bell began running ads inviting Microcell customers to move to Bell with a direct comparative ad that referred to "spotty coverage" from Fido. Why did Bell and Telus react so strongly? According to Ken Wong, a professor at Queen's University, "Fido is almost like a low-hanging fruit [because it is struggling financially]. It is much easier to go after a weaker competitor than one that is equal [to] or stronger than you."[36]

Some critics of the technique maintain that comparative ads often help consumers remember the competitor's brand at the expense of the advertised brand. However, the wide use of comparative advertising and the research into its strategic effects do not support this view. Studies have found that comparative ads are capable of exerting more positive effects on brand attitudes, purchase intentions, and purchase than are non-comparative advertise-

EXHIBIT 8-3

TWO-SIDED APPEAL

© 1994 The Upjohn Company.

ments.[37] Using an information-processing perspective, studies of comparative advertising found that comparative ads are effective because

- they elicit higher levels of cognitive processing,[38]
- they lead to better recall,[39]
- they are perceived as more relevant than non-comparative ads,[40] and
- they are more effective in positioning the product in consumers' minds.[41]

Is the use of negative comparative messages (i.e., messages that use negativity in the ads while referring to the product that is used as the basis for comparison) a good strategy? A study that tested the degree of negativity in comparative messages (by using positive, negative, and mildly negative comparative messages) for several products reported that negative elements in an ad contributed to its effectiveness as long as they were believable or were offset by some elements that made the ad appear neutral.[42]

There has been considerable concern expressed that comparative advertising may mislead consumers; in fact, several legal actions have been brought against companies by the Competition Bureau. A recent study advocates the development of concrete measures designed to gauge the ability of a comparative ad to mislead consumers.[43]

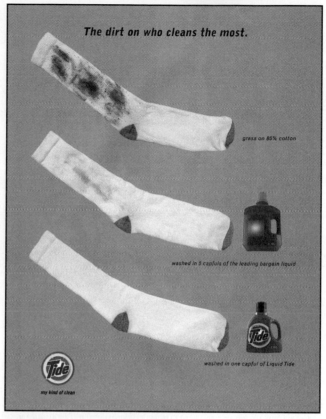

EXHIBIT 8-4

COMPARATIVE ADVERTISING
Courtesy of Procter & Gamble.

Order Effects Is it best to present your commercial first or last? Should you give the bad news first or last? Communications researchers have found that the order in which a message is presented (**order effect**) affects the audience's receptivity. For this reason, politicians and other professional communicators often jockey for position when several of them address an audience; they are aware that the first and last speeches are the most likely to remain in the audience's memory. On television, the position of a commercial in a commercial break can be critical. The commercials shown first are remembered the best, whereas those in the middle are remembered the least.

When just two competing messages are presented, one after the other, the evidence about which position is more effective is somewhat contradictory. Some researchers have found that the material presented first produces a greater effect (*primacy effect*); others have found that the material presented last is more effective (*recency effect*). One study found that in situations that foster high levels of cognitive processing, the first message tends to be more influential (primacy effect), whereas in situations of low message elaboration, the second message had a greater impact (recency effect).[44] Magazine publishers recognize the importance of order effects by charging more for ads on the front, back, and inside covers of magazines than for the inside pages. Order is also important in listing product benefits within an ad. If audience interest is low, the most important point should be made first to attract attention. However, if interest is high, that is not necessary, and so product benefits can be arranged in ascending order, with the most important mentioned

Order effect:
The effect of the order of presentation of the ad—that is, whether it is placed first, last, or in the middle of a set of ads.

www.cb_bc.gc.ca

Wake up with a whole new reason to smile.

Crest® Night Effects™
is clinically proven to give you

2x THE WHITENING*

of Colgate Simply White Night™ in 14 nights.
www.crestnighteffects.com SLEEP YOUR WAY TO A WHITER SMILE

EXHIBIT 8-5

COMPARATIVE ADVERTISING
Courtesy of Procter & Gamble.

last. When both favourable and unfavourable information are to be presented (as in an annual report to shareholders), placing the favourable material first often produces greater tolerance for the unfavourable news. It also produces greater acceptance and better understanding of the total message.

Repetition   *Repetition* is an important factor in learning. Thus, it is not surprising that repetition, or frequency of the ad, increases persuasion, ad recall, brand name recall, and brand preferences. It also increases the likelihood that the brand will be included in the consumer's *consideration set*. Repetition increases the effectiveness of advertising for the following reasons:

- Repeated exposure gives consumers more opportunity to internalize product attributes and to develop more or stronger cue associations, positive attitudes, and willingness to resist efforts at counter-persuasion by competitors.[45]

- In low-involvement situations, people are more likely to regard message claims that are repeated often as more truthful than those repeated less often.[46]

- Varied ad executions (as opposed to repetitions of the same ad) enhance memory for the brand name over repeated executions of the same ad.[47] This supports the *encoding variability hypothesis,* which attributes the superior memorability of varied executions to the multiple paths that are laid down in the memory between the brand

name and other concepts and that provide alternative retrieval routes to the brand name.[48]

Advertising Appeals

Sometimes objective, *factual appeals* are more effective; at other times *emotional appeals* are more effective. It depends on the kind of audience and their degree of involvement in the product category. In general, however, logical, reason-why appeals are more effective in persuading educated audiences, and emotional appeals are more effective in persuading less-educated consumers. The following section examines the effectiveness of several frequently used emotional appeals.

Fear   Fear is an effective appeal often used in marketing communications. Some researchers have found a negative relationship between the intensity of fear appeals and their ability to persuade; that is, strong fear appeals tend to be less effective than mild fear appeals. A number of explanations have been offered for this phenomenon. The theory of psychological reactance (discussed in Chapter 3) suggests that consumers may react negatively to attempts to control their behaviour by frightening them.

For example, a study of warning information labels affixed to full-fat, reduced-fat, and non-fat products concluded that, for products with credible and familiar risks, information labels were more effective than warning labels because they do not arouse *psychological reactance.*[49]

Strong fear appeals concerning a highly relevant topic (such as cigarette smoking) cause the individual to experience cognitive dissonance, which is resolved either by rejecting the practice or by rejecting the unwelcome information. Because giving up a comfortable habit is difficult, consumers more readily reject the threat. This they do by a variety of techniques, such as the following:

- denial of its validity ("There still is no real proof that smoking causes cancer.")
- the belief that they are immune to personal disaster ("It can't happen to me.")
- a diffusing process that robs the claim of its true significance ("I play it safe by smoking only filter cigarettes.")

Furthermore, fear appeals may not be effective with some target markets. A study of adolescent responses to fear communications found that adolescents are more persuaded to avoid drugs by messages that depict negative social consequences rather than physical threats to their bodies.[50] Finally, the effectiveness of fear appeals may also depend on the personality of the consumer. A high sensation seeker is more likely to use drugs and also to react negatively to fear-focused anti-drug messages, feeling that he or she is immortal.[51]

Humour Many marketers believe that humour will increase the acceptance and persuasiveness of their advertising communications. Although a big proportion of ads (up to 24 percent of television ads in the United States) use humour, there are some risks to using this appeal.[52] For example, the effects of humourous ads vary by the audience's demographics, level of involvement (humour is more effective for promoting low-involvement products), and attitudes (humour is more effective when the audience already has positive attitudes toward the brand).[53] Figure 8-2 summarizes some research findings on the impact of humour on advertising.

Marketers believe that younger, better-educated, upscale, and professional people tend to be receptive to humorous messages (see Exhibit 8-6). A study of how humour actually works in ads discovered that surprise is almost always needed to generate humour and that the effectiveness of humorous ads is also influenced by such message elements as warmth and playfulness.[54]

Abrasive Advertising How effective can **abrasive** (unpleasant or annoying) ads be? Studies of the sleeper effect, discussed earlier, suggest that the memory of an unpleasant commercial that antagonizes listeners or viewers may dissipate over time, leaving only the brand name in their minds.

EXHIBIT 8-6

HUMOUR TO BABY BOOMERS

For Irving Oil Canada by Target Marketing & Communications Inc.

Abrasive advertising: Advertising that is unpleasant or annoying.

FIGURE 8-2	Impact of Humour on Advertising

- Humour attracts attention.
- Humour does not harm comprehension. *(In some cases it may even aid comprehension.)*
- Humour is not more effective at increasing persuasion.
- Humour does not enhance source credibility.
- Humour enhances liking.
- Humour that is relevant to the product is superior to humour that is unrelated to the product.
- Audience demographic factors (e.g., gender, ethnicity, age) affect the response to humorous advertising appeals.
- The nature of the product affects the appropriateness of a humorous treatment.
- Humour is more effective with existing products than with new products.
- Humour is more appropriate for low-involvement products and feeling-oriented products than for high-involvement products.

Source: Marc G. Weinberger and Charles S. Gulas, "The Impact of Humor in Advertising: A Review," *Journal of Advertising* 21, no. 4, December 1992, 35–59. Reprinted by permission.

All of us have at one time or another been repelled by so-called agony commercials, which depict in diagrammatic detail the internal and intestinal effects of heartburn, indigestion, clogged sinus cavities, hammer-induced headaches, and the like. Nevertheless, pharmaceutical companies often run such commercials with great success because they appeal to a certain segment of the population that suffers from ailments that are not visible and thus elicit little sympathy from family and friends. Their complaints are legitimized by commercials with which they immediately identify. With the sponsor's credibility established ("They really understand the misery I'm going through"), the message itself tends to be highly successful in persuading consumers to buy the product.

Sex in Advertising In our highly permissive society, sensual advertising seems to permeate the print media and the airwaves. Advertisers are increasingly trying to provoke attention with suggestive illustrations, crude language, and nudity and trying to appear "hip" and contemporary. In today's advertising, there is a lot of explicit and daring sexual imagery, extending far beyond the traditional product categories of fashion and fragrance into such categories as shampoo, beer, cars, and home construction.

There is little doubt that sexual themes attract attention, but studies show that they rarely encourage actual consumption behaviour, for the following reasons:

- Sexual appeals interfere with comprehension of the message, particularly when there is substantial information to be processed.[55]

- More product-related thinking occurs in response to non-sexual appeals, and visual sexual elements in an ad are more likely to be processed than its verbal content, drawing cognitive processing away from product or message evaluation.[56]

- It has a negative impact on the product message.[57] This might also be partly because the visual sexual elements in an advertisement are more likely to be processed than are it verbal elements; thus the cognitive processing is drawn away from the product or message.[58]

These and other findings support the theory that sexual advertising appeals often detract from the processing of message content.

The type of interest that sexual advertising evokes often stops exactly where it starts—with sex. If a sexually suggestive or explicit illustration is not relevant to the product being advertised, it has little effect on consumers' buying intentions. This highlights the risk of sexually oriented advertising: The advertiser may be giving up persuasiveness to achieve "stopping power." When using sex to promote a product, the advertiser must be sure that the product, the ad, the target audience, and the use of sexual themes and elements all work together. When sex is relevant to the product, it can be an extremely potent copy theme. For example the advertisers of Perrier Jouët champagne show a beautiful nude tattooed with the company's logo and the single word "Unforgettable" to suggest a romantic, exciting, and unforgettable evening drinking their champagne (see Exhibit 8-7).

Characteristics of the Target Audience (Receivers)

Receivers decode the messages they receive on the basis of their personal experiences and personal characteristics. If Mrs. Brown receives shoddy merchandise from an online retailer, she may be reluctant to buy online again. At the same time, her neighbour, Mrs. Greene, may be so pleased with the merchandise she receives from a reliable online retailer in terms of quality, service, and fit that she vows to do even more of her shopping online in the future. The level of trust each neighbour displays toward online communications is based on her own experience.

EXHIBIT 8-7

SEXUAL APPEAL

© 2002 Champagne Perrier-Jouët Epornay.

The decoding and comprehension of persuasive messages is affected by a number of factors related to the receiver, including the receiver's personal characteristics, involvement with the product or product category, the congruence of the message with the medium, and the receiver's mood.

Personal Characteristics and Comprehension

The amount of meaning accurately derived from the message is a function of the message characteristics, the receiver's opportunity and ability to process the message, and the receiver's motivation. In fact, all of an individual's personal characteristics (described in earlier chapters) influence the accuracy with which the individual decodes a message. A person's demographics (such as age, sex, marital status), socio-cultural memberships (social class, race, religion), and life style are key determinants in how a message is interpreted. A bachelor may interpret a friendly comment from his unmarried neighbour as a "come-on"; a student may interpret a professor's comments as an indication of grading rigour. Personality, attitudes, and prior learning all affect how a message is decoded. Perception, based as it is on expectations, motivation, and past experience, certainly influences the interpretation of a message. Not everyone reads and understands the marketing communications they receive in the way that the sender intended.

One study, which examined the effect of illiteracy on comprehension, discovered that one-third of the recipients of a direct-mail advertising piece written at a grade 8 reading level could not understand the intended message.[59] Another study, of sex-based differences in responses to charity ads, reported that women found altruistic appeals that stressed helping others more persuasive, whereas men tended to choose self-oriented themes that stressed helping oneself.[60]

Involvement and Congruency

A person's level of involvement (see Chapter 6) has a crucial influence on how much attention is paid to the message and how carefully it is decoded. People who have little interest (i.e., a low level of involvement) in golf, for example, may not pay much attention to an ad for a specially designed putter; people who are very interested (highly involved) in golf may read every word of a highly technical advertisement describing the new golf club. Thus, a target audience's level of involvement is an important consideration in the design and content of persuasive communications. In the case of high-involvement products, marketers should do the following:

- present advertisements with strong, well-documented issue-related arguments that encourage cognitive processing (this follows from the elaboration likelihood model discussed earlier in Chapter 6)
- present messages that contrast the style of ad and its context (e.g., a humorous ad in a rational context such as a television documentary)[61] or present such products in cognitively involving programs and use cognitively involving messages[62]

In contrast, people with low involvement with the product preferred messages placed within a congruent context (e.g., a humorous ad within a humorous television series).[63]

Mood

Mood, or affect, has a significant influence on how a message is decoded. A consumer's mood (e.g., cheerfulness or unhappiness) affects the way in which an advertisement is perceived, recalled, and acted upon. Marketers of many image-centred products, such as perfume, clothing, and liquor, have found that appeals based on the emotions and feelings associated with these products are more effective than rational appeals depicting the product's benefits. Advertisers have found that emotional appeals work well even for technologically complex products. For example, Apple Computer encourages consumers to "Think Different."

Studies have reached the following conclusions:

- A positive mood enhanced the learning of brand names and the product categories to which they belong.[64]
- The consumer's mood is often influenced by the *content* of the ad and by the *context* in which the advertising message appears (such as the accompanying television program or adjacent newspaper story); these in turn affect the consumer's evaluation and memory of the message.[65]
- Consumers with low familiarity with a service category prefer ads based on story appeals rather than lists of attributes, and such appeals work better when the receivers are in a happy mood while decoding the message.[66]

Characteristics of the Medium

Besides the characteristics of the message, the nature of the medium selected for advertising can itself have a major impact on the effectiveness of marketing communications. For example, newspapers, although ads can be inserted quickly and at relatively low cost, are not able to appeal to several senses (as television can), and the production quality is lower. However, since it is easier to design ads for newspapers and as these ads can be inserted relatively quickly, newspapers are an effective medium for communicating information about sales and special promotions.

Even within a medium, different programs or sections may have very different impact on consumers. Thus, ads appearing in television news shows are likely to be seen as more credible by consumers than are those appearing in sitcoms. Similarly, ads appearing in the business section of a newspaper (e.g., the "Report on Business" section of the *Globe and Mail*) are likely to be viewed differently by its readers than are those appearing in some of its other sections.

Figure 8-3 takes a detailed look at the persuasiveness and limitations of the major advertising media.

FIGURE 8-3   Persuasive Capabilities and Limitations of Major Advertising Media

	TARGETING PRECISION	MESSAGE DEVELOPMENT AND EXECUTION	DEGREE OF PSYCHOLOGICAL NOISE	OBTAINING FEEDBACK	RELATIVE COST
Newspapers	Access to large audiences. Not very selective in reaching consumers with specific demographics. Effective for reaching local consumers.	Flexible. Messages can be designed and published quickly. Limited production quality and short message life.	High clutter. Many messages competing for attention.	Sales volume. Redemptions of special promotions and level of store traffic provide immediate feedback.	Determined by size of ad and the medium's circulation. Affordable for local businesses. Permits joint (cooperative) advertising by national manufacturers and local sellers.
Magazines	High geographic and demographic selectivity. *Selective binding*[a] allows more precise targeting of subscribers with the desired demographics.	High quality of production. High credibility of ads in special-interest magazines. Long message life and pass-along readership. Long lead time required.	High clutter. Some magazines may not guarantee ad placement in a particular position within the magazine.	Delayed and indirect feedback, such as the Starch scores that measure recall and attention.	Determined by cost of page and circulation. Top magazines charge very high rates.
Television	Reaches very large audiences. Many programs lack audience selectivity.	Appeals to several senses. Permits messages that draw attention and generate emotion. Short-duration messages must be repeated. Long lead time.	High clutter. Viewers can avoid message exposures by channel surfing or using advanced technologies such as TiVo.	Day-after recall tests measure how many consumers were exposed to the message and, to a lesser degree, their characteristics.	Costs very high; based on how many consumers watch a given program.

(continued)

FIGURE 8-3   Persuasive Capabilities and Limitations of Major Advertising Media (continued)

	TARGETING PRECISION	MESSAGE DEVELOPMENT AND EXECUTION	DEGREE OF PSYCHOLOGICAL NOISE	OBTAINING FEEDBACK	RELATIVE COST
Radio	High geographic and demographic audience selectivity.	Audio messages only. Short exposure. Relatively short lead time.	High clutter. Listeners can easily switch among stations during commercials.	Delayed feedback, such as day-after recall tests.	Based on size of the audience reached. Local radio may be relatively inexpensive.
Internet	Potential for great audience selectivity. Audience may be demographically skewed. Enables tracking of customers and building of databases. Privacy issues make targeting more difficult.	Increasingly more advanced messages can be designed and shown relatively quickly. Marketers recognize that their home pages are advertisements and must be designed as persuasive tools.	Very high degree of clutter. Visitors can easily escape promotional messages. Banner ads and home pages can reinforce and expand promotional messages featured in other media.	Interactive medium with potential for gathering immediate feedback. Click rates on ads do not measure their impact accurately (since exposure to the brands featured occurs even without a click).	Great variation in establishing advertising rates since there is no standard measure of the impact of online advertising.
Direct Mail[b]	High audience selectivity. Enables personalization. Perceived by many as "junk mail."	Enables novel, visually appealing, and dramatic messages (including the addition of sensory inputs).	No competing messages within the mailing.	Easy to measure feedback through limited pretests and cost per inquiry and cost per order. Delayed feedback.	Relatively high cost per person per mailing due to "junk mail" image.
Direct Marketing[c]	Marketers can build and constantly refine an electronic database of qualified buyers based on inquiries and direct orders. Permits the development of highly selective customer segments. Privacy concerns makes this practice difficult.	A function of the medium used to solicit the direct response from the customer.	Can be relatively free of clutter, even in media where there is generally a lot of noise. For example, infomercials provide advertisers with a "clutter-free" environment.	Generates measurable responses and enables marketers to measure the profitability of their efforts directly.	Determined through such variables as cost per inquiry, cost per sale, and revenue per advertisement.

[a] Selective binding is a technique that enables publishers to narrowly segment their subscription bases. When readers subscribe, they are asked to provide demographic information, which the publisher enters into a database. Through a sophisticated computerized system, the publisher is able to select specific subscribers, according to reader demographic profiles, to receive special sections that are bound into a limited number of magazines.

[b] Direct mail includes catalogues, letters, brochures, promotional offers, and any materials mailed directly to customers at their homes or offices.

[c] Direct marketing is not a medium but an interactive marketing technique that uses various media (such as mail, print, broadcast, telephone, and cyberspace) for the purpose of soliciting a direct response from a consumer. Electronic shopping (through home-shopping TV channels or interactive cable) is also considered direct marketing.

Feedback—The Receiver's Response

Since marketing communications are usually designed to persuade a target audience to act in a desired way (e.g., to buy a specific brand or product, to vote for a political candidate, to pay income taxes early), the ultimate test of marketing communications is the receiver's response. For this reason, it is essential for the sender to obtain *feedback* as promptly and as accurately as possible. Only feedback can tell the sender whether and how well the message has been received.

As noted earlier, an important advantage of interpersonal communications is the ability to obtain immediate feedback through verbal as well as non-verbal cues. Experienced speakers are very attentive to feedback and constantly modify their messages according to what they see and hear from the audience. Immediate feedback is what makes personal selling so effective. It enables the salesperson to tailor the sales pitch to the expressed needs and observed reactions of each prospect. Similarly, it enables a political candidate to stress specific aspects of his or her platform selectively in response to questions asked by voters in face-to-face meetings. Immediate feedback in the form of inattention alerts the university professor that she needs to jolt a dozing class awake, perhaps by making a provocative statement such as, "This material will probably appear on your final exam."

Obtaining feedback is as important in *impersonal* (mass) communications as it is in *interpersonal* communications. Indeed, because of the high costs of advertising space and time in mass media, many marketers consider impersonal communications feedback to be even more essential. The organization that initiates the message must develop in advance some method for determining whether its mass communications are received by the intended audience, are understood in the intended way, and are achieving the intended results.

Unlike interpersonal communications feedback, mass communications feedback is rarely direct; instead, it is usually inferred. Senders infer how persuasive their messages are from the resulting action (or inaction) of the targeted audience. Receivers buy (or do not buy) the advertised product; they renew (or do not renew) their magazine subscriptions; they vote (or do not vote) for the political candidate. Another type of feedback that companies seek from mass audiences is the degree of customer satisfaction (or dissatisfaction) with a product purchase. They try to discover, and correct as swiftly as possible, any problems with the product in order to retain their brand's image of reliability. Many companies have established 24-hour hot lines to encourage comments and questions from their consumers and also solicit consumer feedback through online contact. Figure 8-4 shows a comprehensive model of the options and relationships among the basic communications elements discussed above.

BARRIERS TO COMMUNICATION

Various barriers to communication may reduce the accuracy with which consumers interpret messages. These include selective perception and psychological noise.

Selective exposure to messages: Consumers perceive advertising messages selectively, and they tend to ignore advertisements that have no special interest or relevance for them. Furthermore, technology provides consumers with increasingly sophisticated means to control their exposure to media. Television remote controls offer viewers the ability to "wander" among programs with ease (often referred to as *grazing*), to *zap* commercials by muting the audio, and to *channel-surf*—switch channels during the commercials and take a look at other programs. Some marketers try to overcome channel surfing during commercials by *roadblocking* (i.e., playing the same commercial simultaneously on competing channels).

FIGURE 8-4   Comprehensive Communication Model

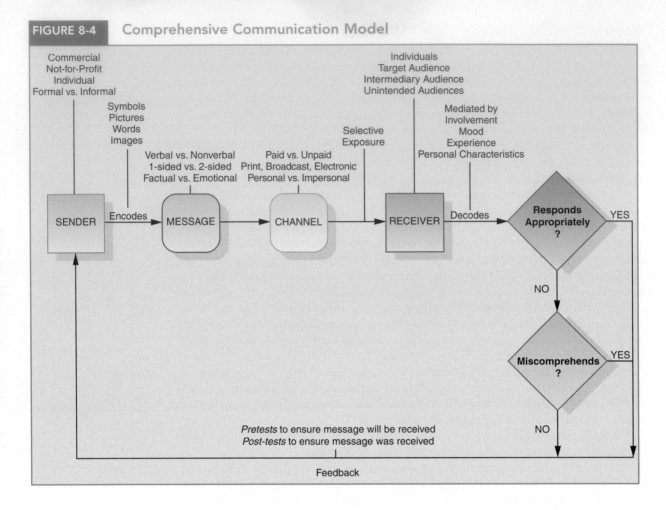

The VCR enables viewers to fast-forward (*zip*) through commercials of pre-recorded programs. Most people zip indiscriminately through videotapes to avoid all commercials, without first evaluating the commercials they zap. More recently, digital video recorders and services like TiVo and ReplayTV allow viewers to watch programs whenever they want. These devices are much easier to use than VCRs, and worried broadcasters are actively pursuing legislation that will limit their capacity to affect advertising exposure.[67] Caller ID, answering machines, and other devices allow consumers to screen out calls from telemarketers.

Psychological noise: Just as telephone static can impair reception of a message, so too can **psychological noise**, such as competing advertising messages or distracting thoughts. A viewer faced with the clutter of nine successive commercial messages during a program break may actually receive and retain almost nothing of what he has seen. Similarly, an executive planning a department meeting while driving to work may be too engrossed in her thoughts to "hear" a radio commercial. She is just as much a victim of noise—albeit psychological noise—as another who literally cannot hear the commercial because of construction noise from the building next door.

There are various strategies that marketers use to overcome psychological noise:

Psychological noise:
Barriers to message reception such as competing advertising messages or distracting thoughts.

- Exposing consumers repeatedly to an advertising message (through *repetition* or *redundancy* of the advertising appeal).

- Using *contrast* (e.g., featuring an unexpected outcome, increasing the amount of sensory input—such as colour, scent, or sound).

- Using *teasers* to overcome noise. For example, trivia quizzes shown at the beginning of a commercial break are designed to persuade viewers to stick with the channel in order to find out at the end of the break whether their answers were right.

- Placing ads in *specialized media* where there is less psychological noise. For example, studies show that ads placed in computer and video games and shown in movie theatres are remembered better than similar ads placed in more general media.[68]

Of course, the most effective way to ensure that a promotional message stands out and is received and decoded properly by the target audience is effective *positioning* and a *unique selling proposition*. Advertisements for products that appear to give better value than do competitive products are more likely to be received in their intended ways than other promotional messages in the advertising clutter.

COMMUNICATION AND MARKETING STRATEGY

In order to create persuasive communications, the sponsor (who may be an individual, a for-profit company, or a not-for-profit organization) must first establish the objectives of the communication, then select the right audiences for the message and the best media through which to reach them, and then design (encode) the message in a manner that is suitable for each medium and each audience. As noted earlier, the communications strategy should also include a feedback mechanism that alerts the sponsor to any need for modifications or adjustments to the media or the message.

Establish communications objectives: In developing its communications strategy, the sponsor must establish the primary communications objectives. These might consist of creating awareness of a service, promoting sales of a product, encouraging (or discouraging) certain practices, attracting retail patronage, reducing post-purchase dissonance, creating goodwill or a favourable image, or any combination of these and other communications objectives.

The ads for milk that BC Dairy Foundation (BCDF) ran, for example, started out with clear objectives for the communication strategy: to change the image of milk among the chosen target market (teens and young adults) from a nutritious but boring drink to one that was "hip and cool" and essential for their body. The last part of the message was left for the viewers to infer, since research showed that this target audience needed to draw their own message from ads rather than have one thrust upon them).[69]

Two thousand and three was a year of disasters for the Canadian tourism industry. SARS and mad cow disease decreased the number of visitors to Canada. What was even more worrisome to the industry was the decline in the number of American tourists. Since visitors from the U.S. account for more than 80 percent of the annual visitors to Canada, this was a serious concern for the Canadian tourism industry. What accounted for the decline? SARS and mad cow disease had an impact, of course, as did the higher Canadian dollar. But research found that Americans wanted to stay closer to home because of international events, including the war in Iraq. Research also found that Americans thought of Canada as "domestic." So the Canadian Tourism Commission (CTC) hired Palmer Jarvis DDB, a

www.travelcanada.ca

Vancouver company, with clear objectives in mind: to show Americans that Canada was a safe alternative to travelling in the States, yet, at the same time, an interesting alternative. The campaign, which consisted of one-page ads in popular newspapers had two halves. One half read, "Given the economy and worldwide uncertainty, maybe this is the summer to stay in the U.S. and visit those distant relations." The second half showed an unflattering family portrait. Having clear objectives led to a focused campaign that was highly successful.[70]

Select the target audience: An essential component of a communications strategy is selecting the audience. It is important to remember that an audience is made up of individuals—in many cases, great numbers of individuals. Because each individual has his or her own traits, characteristics, interests, needs, experience, and knowledge, it is essential for the sender to segment the audience into groups that are homogeneous in some relevant characteristic. Segmentation enables the sender to create specific messages for each target group and to run them in specific media that are seen, heard, or read by that group. It is unlikely that a marketer could develop a single message that would appeal simultaneously to its total audience. Efforts to use "universal" appeals phrased in simple language that everyone can understand invariably result in unsuccessful advertisements that few people relate to.

Robin Smith, executive director at the BCDF, notes, "Everybody drinks it [milk] so the big mistake people fall into is trying to become all things to all people." The BCDF got around this by designing different ads for different target markets—the "what would life be without a body?" ads aimed at a young audience, and other ads aimed at the older market.[71]

Companies that have many diverse audiences sometimes find it useful to develop a communications strategy that consists of an overall (or umbrella) communications message to all their audiences, from which they spin off a series of related messages targeted directly to the specific interests of individual segments. In addition, to maintain positive communications with all of their publics, most large organizations have public relations departments or employ public relations firms to provide favourable information about the company and to suppress unfavourable information.

Choose the best media: Media strategy is an essential part of a communications plan. It calls for the placement of ads in the specific media that are read, watched, or heard by each targeted audience. To do this, advertisers develop, through research, a **consumer profile** of their target customers that includes the specific media they read or watch. Media organizations regularly research their own audiences in order to develop descriptive **audience profiles**. A cost-effective media choice is one that closely matches the advertiser's consumer profile to the audience profile of a medium.

Consumer profile: Psycho-demographic profile of the target market of a product or service.

Audience profile: Psycho-demographic profile of the readers, viewers, or listeners of a medium.

Before choosing specific media vehicles, advertisers must choose general media categories that will enhance the message they want to convey. Which media categories the marketer selects depends on the product or service to be advertised, the market segments to be reached, and the marketer's advertising objectives. Rather than use one media category to the exclusion of others, many advertisers use a multimedia campaign strategy, with one primary media category carrying the major burden of the campaign and other categories providing supplemental support.

In the Nike Canada RunTO campaign, for example, billboards were the primary media category; however, the company also used radio and transit ads and even "guerilla marketing" in the form of a pack of Nike-clad joggers on the street.[72]

The BC Dairy Foundation used television as the main medium but supported their "What would life be like without a body?" campaign with print ads, two award-winning websites, and a sales promotion ("Trojan One") using the "Cold

Crew" street team to interact with teenagers.[73] Figure 8-3 on pages 261–262 compares the persuasiveness of various advertising media along the dimensions of *targeting precision* (i.e., the ability to reach exclusively the intended audience), constructing a *persuasive message*, degree of *psychological noise, feedback,* and relative *cost.*

   Develop suitable message strategies: The message is the thought, idea, attitude, image, or other information that the sender wishes to convey to the intended audience. In trying to encode the message in a form that will enable the audience to understand its precise meaning, the sender must do several things:

- ***Know exactly what he or she is trying to say and why.*** What are the objectives and what is the message intended to accomplish?

- ***Know the target audience's personal characteristics—education, interests, needs, and experience.*** The sender must then design a message strategy through words and/or pictures that will be noticed and accurately interpreted (decoded) by the targeted audience. Figure 8-5 presents a list of message elements designed to appeal to three personality types: the *righteous buyer* (who looks to recommendations from independent sources such as *Consumer Reports*), the *social buyer* (who relies on the recommendations of friends, celebrity endorsements,

FIGURE 8-5	The Righteous, Social, and Pragmatic Buyer: A Comparative Analysis		
	RIGHTEOUS	**SOCIAL**	**PRAGMATIC**
Copy Appeals	Describe quality. Note achievements, awards, community and environmental positions.	Offer quality-of-life enhancements, exclusivity.	Benefit-driven. Focus on bottom line.
Copy Length	Wants information. Detailed copy facilitates decisions.	Provide short, lively copy.	Repeat benefits and price. Keep it to the point. Bottom-line oriented.
Endorsements	Highly important when from an independent source.	Impressed with credible celebrity endorsements.	Not important.
Visuals	Show the product fully. Use detail in comparison charts.	Show people having fun. Whimsical!	Include charts for comparison. Show practical use of product.
Pricing	Emphasize fair price, value.	Full retail price easily accepted.	Offer a discount or a special deal.
Guarantees	Provide strongly worded guarantees.	Important, and a decision tie-breaker.	Provide strongly worded guarantees.
Free Trial	"I can test it myself!"	"I can show it off!"	"I can use it and return it if I don't like it!"
Shipping and Handling	Show fairness. Wants costs itemized.	Include in price.	Ship it free.
Premiums	Relate to purchase.	Appeal to the ego. Fun.	Emphasize giving something free.
Time Limits of Offer	Don't ever break your word.	Helps incite action now.	There's always another deal.
Sweepstakes/ Contests	No great appeal.	Dreams of winning and impressing others.	Wants something for nothing.
Charter Membership	Provides some appeal.	"I'm the first to have it!"	Appeals if there's a special deal.

Source: Adapted from Gary Hennerberg, "The Righteous, Social, and Pragmatic Buyer," *Direct Marketing*, May 1993, 31–32. Reprinted with permission from *Direct Marketing* magazine, 224 Seventh Street, Garden City, NY 11330, 516-746-6700.

and testimonials), and the *pragmatic buyer* (who looks for the best value for the money, though not necessarily the lowest price).[74]

■ *Use non-verbal stimuli effectively.* Non-verbal stimuli (such as photographs or illustrations) tend to reinforce verbal message arguments. A number of studies have tried to manipulate the proportions of visual and verbal information used in print ads to determine their relative influence on recall and persuasion, but the findings have been inconclusive. In some cases, body copy alone induces more favourable consumer evaluations than body copy and visuals used together; in other instances the reverse is true. One study found that when verbal information was low in imagery, the inclusion of visual examples in the ad increased consumer recall of the verbal information.[75]

■ *Choose a suitable structure and presentation style for the message*. As we saw earlier, the message sender has to decide whether to frame the message positively or negatively, whether to offer one-sided or two-sided messages, and what the order of the message presentation should be (i.e., first, middle, or last). The marketer should also decide whether the product should be compared with another brand or not.

■ *Choose a suitable appeal for its promotional messages.* Should the advertisement use a fear appeal or a humorous one? Should sexual appeals be used? How exactly, should fear, humour, or sex appeal be used in the ad? Earlier sections provided some guidelines for making these decisions. The choice of the appeal would depend, among other things, on the image of the company and the nature of the product.

Although there are no definitive answers to these issues, research (which has been discussed in earlier sections) can offer some guidelines to marketers.

Reduce barriers to effective communication: When developing marketing messages and distributing them, marketers have to take steps to reduce psychological noise and increase the level of exposure to their messages (by dealing with consumers' selectivity in exposure). Chapter 5 dealt with selective exposure (e.g., increasing accidental exposure) or finding creative ways (such as guerilla marketing).

Imperial Oil of Canada has started placing ads on tiny video screens near the gas pump. Consumers in the Greater Toronto area were the first to see the new ads, which only feature products that are sold in the on-site convenience store.[76]

Toyota Canada caught the attention of its target audience (young buyers) by putting cars on the street to be sampled by Canadians. The campaign, which ran in Quebec, invited listeners of Énergie radio station to flag down an Echo with the station's logo and take it for a test drive.[77] As we saw earlier in this chapter, psychological noise can be dealt with by repeating the message, using contrast effectively, using teaser campaigns, and placing ads in specialized media.

Measure the effectiveness of marketing communications: Once messages have been developed and communicated, marketers need to evaluate their effectiveness. In doing so, marketers must measure two things:

■ the *persuasion effects* (i.e., was the message received, understood, and interpreted correctly?)

■ the *sales effects* (i.e., did the ad increase sales?)

Advertisers gauge the *persuasion effects* of their messages by conducting audience research to find out which media are read, which television programs are watched, and which advertisements are remembered by their target audiences. If the feedback reveals that the audience does not notice an ad or misunderstands it, an alert sponsor modifies or revises the message so that the intended communication does, in fact, take place.

The campaign that the Canadian Tourism Commission ran to increase the number of Americans visiting Canada scored high on persuasion effects. Eighty-four percent of the Americans surveyed in the seven markets where the campaign ran found the ads appealing. The ads were clearly successful in persuading Americans to visit Canada—the likelihood of Americans in those seven markets increased by 13 percent.[78]

Generally, persuasion effects are measured through *exposure, attention, interpretation,* and *recall.* Selected measures of these factors are described in Research Insight 8-1.

www.pmb.ca

RESEARCH INSIGHT 8-1
MEASURES OF ADVERTISING EFFECTIVENESS

MEASURES OF MEDIA AND MESSAGE EXPOSURE

Exposure measures look at *how many* consumers received the message and/or *who* received it. The data collected by both types of measures are offered for sale by syndicated services, such as the following:

- The Print Measurement Bureau provides, for various magazines, data on *circulation* as well as descriptive *audience profiles* (a breakdown of readers by sex, median age, and household income).
- The weekly Nielsen Ratings rank television programs by the size of their audiences. A "top ranking" means that the program was watched by more people than any other program at that time during the week. This is done through the use of

  - *people meters* (small boxes that have buttons and lights assigned to each person in a household; the person presses a button when he or she starts watching and again when he or she has finished watching); and/or
  - *diaries* in which viewers record the programs they watched each day and who in the household watched each program.

- Nielsen//NetRatings uses a sample of consumers with internet access to determine which websites are visited most often and the average duration of visits to each site.[a]

ATTENTION MEASURES

Attention measures aim to track actual bodily responses—that is, physiological responses—to advertising.

- *Eye tracking* uses a camera to track the movement of the eye across a television commercial or a print ad. It records the sequence in which various parts of the ad are viewed, the parts that were studied or ignored, and how much time was spent on each part.
- *Brain wave analysis* tracks the degree of attention paid to the various parts of messages through headsets that viewers wear while watching commercials. These data are used to construct an "engagement index" showing the flow of attention across an ad.
- *Skin reaction analysis* measures subtle reactions by the skin to messages with tiny sensors placed on the upper palm of one hand. These data are used to generate a "viewer involvement profile" regarding the message tested.[b]

■ *Theatre tests* in which television programs or commercials are shown in a theatre and viewers use dials located in their armrests to indicate their levels of interest or lack of interest during the showing of the program or advertisement.

■ *Website usability tests* allow researchers to "peek over the shoulders" of visitors to record how quickly they find specific information, which parts of the site attract more attention, and which parts lead to more clicks.[c]

■ The *Starch Readership Survey* (discussed in Chapter 6) is a measure of attention as well as recall of advertisements in print media.

MESSAGE INTERPRETATION MEASURES

Attention measures, including sophisticated physiological techniques, do not assess the reasons for consumers' engagement with the messages tested. To do that, researchers have devised the following methods:

■ *Attitudinal measures* (see Figure 7-3 in Chapter 7), placed within *copy pretests* or *post-tests* to assess whether respondents like the message, understand it correctly, and regard it as effective and persuasive. Researchers are also interested in measuring the emotions and feelings provoked by ads.

■ *Facial electromyography* (Facial EMG)—a method that tracks the electrical activity and subtle movements of facial muscles—to gauge the emotions generated by different types of television commercials. EMG may measure emotional responses more accurately than self-reporting of cognitive responses, because it goes beyond the biases and limitations of the more common self-report technique (which, however, is much cheaper and easier to administer).[c]

MESSAGE RECALL MEASURES

In addition to the *recall and recognition* measures discussed in Chapter 6, researchers use *day-after recall tests* in which people who have watched television shows or listened to radio programs are interviewed a day later. The participants are asked to describe which commercials they remember. The recall of a commercial and its central theme is evidence of its attention-getting and persuasive power.

[a] www.mriplus.com, www.nielsenmedia.com.

[b] Patricia Winters Lauro, "Research Methods Are Being Developed to Help Advertisers Find Out What You Really Think," *New York Times*, April 13, 2000, p. C1.

[c] Richard H. Hazlett and Sasha Yassky, "Emotional Response to Television Commercials: Facial EMG vs. Self Reports," *Journal of Advertising Research*, March–April 1999, 7–23.

Unlike interpersonal communications between, say, a retail salesperson and a customer, in which the feedback (i.e., the customer's purchase or non-purchase) is immediate, impersonal communications feedback is much less timely. Therefore, the *sales effects* of mass communications are difficult to assess (although retailers can usually assess the effectiveness of their morning newspaper ads by midday on the basis of sales activity for the advertised product). Still, most companies use before-and-after sales figures to assess the effectiveness of specific promotional campaigns.

L'Oreal Canada believes that its sponsorships in 2003 were a major factor in the sales growth that it experienced that year. The company took a risk when it sponsored the *Canadian Idol* and *Star Académie* shows, but both sponsorships paid off very well for the company. Company sales increased 7.8 percent over the previous year's—much above the industry average of 5 percent and of its parent company the L'Oreal Group. Can all of the sales increase be attributed to the innovative marketing campaigns? Obviously, no; the company also introduced several new products and brand extensions during the period, and those would have also played a role in the company's increased sales.[79]

A widely used method of measuring the sales effects of food and other packaged goods advertising is based on the Universal Product Code (UPC), which is tied to computerized cash registers. Supermarket scanner data can be combined with data from other sources, such as media and promotional information, to measure the correlation between advertisements and special promotions and sales.

Measuring the Effectiveness of Web-based Communications Since the number of companies using the internet for communicating with their target audience is growing, there is greater interest in measuring the effectiveness of web campaigns. Unlike traditional mass media advertising, a big proportion of web-based advertising is oriented toward short-term promotions that have immediate sales effects. Of course, that is not the case with all web-based communication. In fact, many companies invest considerable time and energy into their web communications in order to build customer loyalty.

INTERNET INSIGHT 8-1
ASSESSING THE EFFECTIVENESS OF WEB-BASED COMMUNICATIONS

MEASURE	PROBLEMS
Hits or the number of files downloaded	Depends on number of image files on a site; if there are 10 image files, each one is counted as a hit. Hence this gives an unrealistically high impression of the traffic that the site attracts.
Page views or the number of pages downloaded	Gives an idea about the number of impressions an ad gets, but does not eliminate the multiple counting of an individual visiting the site several times.
Unique visitor count: uses the IP address of the visitor to count the number of visitors	Avoids counting of multiple visits by the one individual; however, if a computer is used by more than one person, this leads to a lower count and can result in the ad or site being viewed as less effective.
	The type of visitor cannot be evaluated—for example, a 12-year-old and a middle-aged professional visiting the website of an expensive automobile manufacturer would be counted as equal.
Number of registered users	Works well for sites with a lot of "content" or information; not relevant for other sites.
Repeat visitors: number of repeat visits by an individual	Provides a measure of loyalty and persuasiveness of the site and/or the value of the content that it hosts.
Attitude measures	Similar to attitude measures for other forms of communication; measures changes in attitudes, but not impact on sales.
Coupon redemption rates	Measures the sales effects of web-based coupons; works well for everyday, convenience items but not for others.
Return on investment: iterative analysis of web advertising purchases and sales that result	A bottom-line measure that serves the purpose of a direct marketer or an etailer, but not that of companies that use the web for other purposes.

Internet advertising usually takes the form of banner ads or promotional sites that feature company and product information along with sales promotion and other communications with the target audience. Internet Insight 8-1 provides details of how companies measure the effectiveness of their web-based communications.

SUMMARY

- There are five basic elements in communication: the sender, the receiver, the medium, the message, and feedback (the receiver's response). In the communications process, the sender, using words, pictures, symbols, or spokespersons, encodes the message and sends it through a selected channel (or medium). The receiver decodes (interprets) the message on the basis of his or her personal characteristics and experience and responds (or does not respond) on the basis of such factors as selective exposure, selective perception, comprehension, and psychological noise.

- There are four types of communications: interpersonal, neutral and impersonal, marketer-initiated (or mass), and interactive. Interpersonal communications take place in person, by telephone, by mail, or by email; mass communications take place through such impersonal media as television, radio, newspapers, and magazines. Interactive communications allow the receiver to communicate back to the sender.

- The persuasiveness of a message depends on the credibility of the source. Informal sources and neutral or editorial sources are considered to be highly objective and, thus, highly credible.

- The choice of media depends on the product, the audience, and the advertising objectives of the

campaign. Each medium has advantages and shortcomings that must be weighed in the selection of media for an advertising campaign.

- The manner in which a message is presented influences its impact. In some situations and with some audiences, one-sided messages are more effective; with others, two-sided messages are more effective.

- High-involvement products (those with great relevance to a consumer segment) are best advertised through the central route to persuasion, which encourages active cognitive effort. Low-involvement products are best promoted through peripheral cues, such as background scenery, music, or celebrity spokespersons.

- Emotional appeals frequently used in advertising include fear, humour, and sexual appeals. When sexual themes are relevant to the product, they can be very effective; when used solely to attract attention, they rarely achieve brand recall.

- Designing an effective communication strategy involves setting objectives, selecting the right target audience, choosing the best medium or media, developing the best message strategy and, once the campaign has been executed, measuring its effectiveness.

DISCUSSION QUESTIONS

1. Explain the differences between feedback from interpersonal communications and feedback from impersonal communications. How can the marketer obtain and use each kind of feedback?

2. List and discuss the effects of psychological noise on the communications process. What strategies can a marketer use to overcome psychological noise?

3. List and discuss factors that affect the credibility of formal communications sources of product information. What factors influence the credibility of an informal communications source?

4. What are the implications of the sleeper effect for the selection of spokespersons and the scheduling of advertising messages?

5. What are the advantages and disadvantages of using fear or humour in ads?

6. For what kinds of audiences would you consider using comparative advertising? Why?

CRITICAL THINKING QUESTIONS

1. Take any two ads, one illustrating a one-sided message and the other a two-sided message. Which of the measures discussed in the chapter would you use to evaluate the effectiveness of each ad? Explain your answers.

2. Assume that you are the manager of a company just entering the market with a new brand of laundry detergent. What type of message framing, presentation, and appeal would you use? Would you use a comparative message or not? Using concepts covered in this chapter, explain your answers.

3. Watch one hour of television on a single channel during prime time and also tape the broadcast. Immediately after watching the broadcast, list all the commercials you can remember seeing. Compare your list with the actual taped broadcast. Why were you able to remember some of the ads and not the others? Does the fact that you remember an ad make it more persuasive for you?

4. Assume that you are the marketing manager of a company producing chocolates and that you are looking for a celebrity to act as the spokesperson for your product. Would a celebrity be suitable for this product category? Who might the celebrity be? Explain your answers.

INTERNET EXERCISES

1. Visit the website of several companies in the automotive industry and see whether they are using celebrity sponsors. Which ones use celebrity sponsors? Are these sponsors effective? Why or why not?

2. Visit the website of Campbell's Canada (**www.campbellsoup.ca**). Examine the "Power2Cook" part of the website. What does this, and other parts of their website offer? Are the strategies used effective? Why?

3. Visit **www.dugg.com**, a website sponsored by McDonald's Canada. Do you find the website interesting? Do you feel that this is an effective way to communicate with a younger audience? Why?

4. Visit the website of several companies until you find one that uses two-sided appeals and one that uses one-sided appeals in their web advertising. Which one do you like? Why?

KEY TERMS

Abrasive advertising *(p. 257)*
Advertising resonance *(p. 252)*
Audience profile *(p. 266)*
Communication *(p. 244)*
Comparative advertising *(p. 254)*
Consumer profile *(p. 266)*
Feedback *(p. 246)*
Formal communications source *(p. 244)*
Impersonal communications *(p. 245)*

Informal communications source *(p. 244)*
Institutional advertising *(p. 249)*
Interactive communications *(p. 245)*
Interpersonal communications *(p. 245)*
Message framing *(p. 252)*
One-sided messages *(p. 253)*
Opinion leader *(p. 248)*
Order effect *(p. 255)*

Psychological noise *(p. 264)*
Publicity *(p. 247)*
Sleeper effect *(p. 251)*
Source credibility *(p. 247)*
Two-sided messages *(p. 254)*
Word-of-mouth communications *(p. 244)*

CASE 8-1: TARGET AUDIENCE

Effective media strategy is the placement of advertisements in specific media that are seen, heard, or read by selected target markets. And yet, in reality, this appears to be untrue regarding television programs. For example, in an effort to capture younger consumers, advertisers routinely pay significantly more to advertise on television programs with vastly lower ratings than other shows if those lower-rated programs nevertheless include marginally better or improving numbers in the 18- to 34-year-old demographic viewing group. Also, although people over 50 watch more television and generally have more disposable income than do younger people, the key factor in defining a network's success (and the ability to charge higher advertising rates) is its ability to deliver more programs that attract 18- to 49-year-olds than do other networks.

Whether the definition of "younger" adult viewer is 18 to 34 or 18 to 49, pursuing younger adults on television and paying much more to reach them than the older consumers who watch more television appears on the surface to be an unwise strategy. From their perspective, television executives are in the market of delivering a vehicle to reach the audiences that advertisers want to reach. Therefore, if advertisers are willing to pay $23.54 to reach 1000 viewers aged 18 to 34 but only $9.57 to reach 1000 consumers over 35, the television networks will continue to focus on this segment regardless of who actually watches more television.

Thus, television networks have pursued younger viewers because advertisers have done so. And advertisers have done so because they believe that, as consumers, these individuals buy more of the products advertised on television. They also believe that by "hooking" these consumers when they are young, they will make them brand-loyal for their offerings and keep them as consumers as they mature.

QUESTIONS

1. Do you think television producers should continue pursuing younger viewers even though market research findings suggest that older viewers watch more television? Explain your answer.

2. Watch a popular 30-minute television sitcom targeting 18- to 34-year-old viewers, and make a list of the products and brands advertised on the program. Go to the Statistics Canada website (**www.statscan.ca**) and find the link to population projections. Look at the projections for the age distribution in Canada, and discuss whether the marketers of the products and brands that you listed earlier should continue to advertise for the next five years on the type of sitcom that you watched earlier. How about the next 10 years?

Source: Jonathan Dee, "The Myth of '18 to 34,'" *New York Times Magazine*, October 13, 2002, section 6, 58–61.

NOTES

1   "BBDO Kicks Off Toronto SARS Effort,. *Marketing Magazine*, May 19, 2003, 1.

2   Ibid. See also Paul-Mark Rendon, "Stars against SARS, *Marketing Magazine*, July 28, 2003.

3   For example, L. Jean Harrison-Walker, "The Measurement of Word-of-Mouth Communication and an Investigation of Service Quality and Customer Commitment as Potential Antecedents," *Journal of Service Research,* August 2001, 60–75.

4   For an empirical analysis of some 200 logos designed to achieve corporate image and communication goals, see Pamela W. Henderson and Joseph A. Cote, "Guidelines for Selecting or Modifying Logos," *Journal of Marketing*, April 1998, 14–30.

5   See Paul N. Bloom and Torger Reve, "Transmitting Signals to Consumers for Competitive Advantage," *Business Horizons*, July–August 1990, 58–66; and Linda Greenhouse, "High Court Ruling Upholds

Trademarking of a Color," *New York Times*, March 29, 1994, D1.

6   Warren St. John, "A Store Lures Guys Who Are Graduating from Chinos," *New York Times on the Web*, July 14, 2002.

7   Lynne M. Sallot, "What the Public Thinks about Public Relations: An Impression Management Experiment," *Journalism and Mass Communication Quarterly*, Spring 2002, 150–171.

8   Danny Kucharsky, "Highlighting a Canadian Approach, *Marketing Magazine*, December 8–15, 2003, 25–26.

9   Eve Lazarus, "Cafeteria Blues, *Marketing Magazine*, January 19, 2004, 12.

10   Paul-Mark Rendon, "Nike's Top-scoring Campaign," *Marketing Magazine*, December 8–15, 2003, 23.

11   S. Ratneshwar and Shelly Chaiken, "Comprehension's Role in Persuasion: The Case of Its Moderating Effect on the Persuasive Impact of Source Cues," *Journal of Consumer Research* 18, June 1991, 52–62.

12   Michael A. Kamins, "An Investigation into the 'Match Up' Hypothesis in Celebrity Advertising: When Beauty May Be Only Skin Deep," *Journal of Advertising* 19, 1 (1990): 4–13. See also Marsha L. Richins, "Social Comparison and the Idealized Images of Advertising," *Journal of Consumer Research* 18, June 1991, 71–83.

13   Marla Royne Stafford, Thomas F. Stafford, and Ellen Day, "A Contingency Approach: The Effects of Spokesperson Type and Service Type on Service Advertising," *Journal of Advertising*, Summer 2000, 17–32.

14   Laura M. Arpan, "When in Rome? The Effects of Spokesperson Ethnicity on Audience Evaluation of Crisis," *Journal of Business Communication*, July 2002, 314–339; Osei Appiah, "Ethnic Identification and Adolescents' Evaluations of Advertisements," *Journal of Advertising Research*, September–October 2001, 7–22; Oscar W. DeShields Jr. and Ali Kara, "The Persuasive Effect of Spokesperson Similarity Moderated by Source Credibility," *2000 American Marketing Association Education Proceedings,* vol. 11, 132–143.

15   Ronald E. Goldsmith, Barbara A. Lafferty, and Stephen J. Newell, "The Impact of Corporate Credibility and Celebrity Credibility on Consumer Reaction to Advertisements and Brands," *Journal of Advertising*, Fall 2000, 43–54.

16   **http://www.campbellsoup.ca/en/kitchen/ p2c_cook.asp**. Accessed October 24, 2004.

17   B. Zafer Erdogan, Michael J. Baker, and Stephen Tagg, "Selecting Celebrity Endorsers: The Practitioner's Perspective," *Journal of Advertising Research*, May–June 2001, 39–48.

18   Carl I. Hovland, Arthur A. Lumsdaine, and Fred D. Sheffield, *Experiments on Mass Communication* (New York: Wiley, 1949): 182–200.

19   See Joseph W. Alba, Howard Marmorstein, and Amitava Chattopadhyay, "Transitions in Preference over Time: The Effects of Memory on Message Persuasiveness," *Journal of Marketing Research* 29, November 1992, 414.

20   Ruth Ann Weaver Lariscy and Spencer F. Tinkham, "The Sleeper Effect and Negative Political Advertising," *Journal of Advertising*, Winter 1999, 13–30.

21   Darlene B. Hannah and Brian Sternthal, "Detecting and Explaining the Sleeper Effect," *Journal of Consumer Research* 11, September 1984, 632–642.

22   Thomas J. Robinson and Barbara K. Kaye, "Using Is Believing: The Influence of Reliance on the Credibility of Online Political Information among Politically Interested Internet Users," *Journalism and Mass Communication Quarterly*, Winter 2000, 865–879.

23   Sung Tae Kim, David Weaver, and Lars Willnat, "Media Reporting and Perceived Credibility of Online Polls," *Journalism and Mass Communication Quarterly*, Winter 2000): 846–864.

24   Mineabere Ibelema and Lary Powell, "Cable Television News Viewed as Most Credible," *Newspaper Research Journal*, Winter 2001, 41–51.

25   Edward F. McQuarrie and David Glen Mick, "On Resonance: A Critical Pluralistic Inquiry into Advertising Rhetoric," *Journal of Consumer Research* 19, September 1992, 180–197.

26   Durairaj Maheswaran and Joan Meyers Levy, "The Influence of Message Framing and Issue Involvement," *Journal of Marketing Research* 27, August 1990, 361–367.

27   Jennifer L. Aaker and Angela Y. Lee, "'I' Seek Pleasure and 'We' Avoid Pains: The Role of Self-Regulatory Goals in Information Processing and Persuasion," *Journal of Consumer Research*, June 2001, 33–49.

28   Rajesh K. Chandy, Gerard J. Tellis, Deborah J. MaCinnis, and Pattana Thaivanich, "What to Say When: Advertising Appeals in Evolving Markets," *Journal of Marketing Research*, November 2001, 399–414.

29   Durairaj Maheswaran and Joan Meyers Levy, "The Influence of Message Framing and Issue Involvement," *Journal of Marketing Research* 27, August 1990, 361–367.

30   I. Jennifer L. Aaker and Angela Y. Lee, "'I' Seek Pleasure and 'We' Avoid Pains: The Role of Self-Regulatory Goals in Information Processing and Persuasion," *Journal of Consumer Research*, June 2001, 33–49.

31   Yoav Ganzach and Nili Karsahi, "Message Framing and Buying Behavior: A Field Experiment," *Journal of Business Research* 32, 1995, 11–17.

32   Dena Cox and Anthony D. Cox, "Communicating the Consequences of Early Detection: The Role of Evidence and Framing," *Journal of Marketing*, July 2001, 91–103.

33   Rajesh K. Chandy, Gerard J. Tellis, Deborah J. MaCinnis, and Pattana Thaivanich, "What to Say When: Advertising Appeals in Evolving Markets," *Journal of Marketing Research*, November 2001, 399–414.

34   Eve Lazarus, "The Cool Appeal of Milk," *Marketing Magazine*, December 8–15, 2003, 11.

35   Ayn E. Crowley and Wayne D. Hoyer, "An Integrative Framework for Understanding Two-Sided Persuasion," *Journal of Consumer Research* 20, March 1994, 561–574.

36   Lesley Young, "Wireless Marketers Unleash Hounds," *Marketing Magazine*, December 8–15, 2003, 4.

37   Randall L. Rose, Paul W. Miniard, Michael J. Barone, Kenneth C. Manning, and Brian D. Till, "When Persuasion Goes Undetected: The Case of Comparative Advertising," *Journal of Marketing Research* 30, August 1993, 315–330; see also Cornelia Pechmann and S. Ratneshwar, "The Use of Comparative Advertising for Brand Positioning: Association versus Differentiation," *Journal of Consumer Research* 18, September 1991, 145–160; and Cornelia Pechmann and David W. Stewart, "The Effects of Comparative Advertising on Attention, Memory, and Purchase Intentions," *Journal of Consumer Research* 17, September 1990, 180–191.

38   Darrel D. Muehling, Jeffrey J. Stoltman, and Sanford Grossbart, "The Impact of Comparative Advertising on Levels of Message Involvement," *Journal of Advertising* 19, 4, 1990, 41–50; see also Jerry B. Gotlieb and Dan Sarel, "Comparative Advertising Effectiveness: The Role of Involvement and Source Credibility," *Journal of Advertising* 20, 1, 1991, 38–45.

39   Ibid.

40   Ibid.

41   Kenneth C. Manning, Paul W. Miniard, Michael J. Barone, and Randall L. Rose, "Understanding the Mental Representations Created by Comparative Advertising," *Journal of Advertising*, Summer 2001, 27–39.

42   Alina B. Sorescu and Betsy D. Gelb, "Negative Comparative Advertising: Evidence Favoring Fine-Tuning," *Journal of Advertising*, Winter 2000, 25–40.

43   Michael J. Barone, Randall L. Rose, Paul W. Miniard, and Kenneth C. Manning, "Enhancing the Detection of Misleading Comparative Advertising," *Journal of Advertising Research*, September–October 1999, 43–50.

44   Curtis P. Haugtvedt and Duane T. Wegener, "Message Order Effect in Persuasion: An Attitude Strength Perspective," *Journal of Consumer Research* 21, June 1994, 205–218.

45   Curtis P. Haugtvedt et al., "Advertising Repetition and Variation Strategies: Implications for Understanding Attitude Strength," *Journal of Consumer Research* 21, June 1994, 176–189.

46   Scott A. Hawkins and Stephen J. Hoch, "Low Involvement Learning: Memory without Evaluation," *Journal of Consumer Research* 19, September 1992, 212–225.

47   H. Rao Unnava and Robert E. Burnkrant, "Effects of Repeating Varied Ad Executions on Brand Name Memory," *Journal of Marketing Research* 28, November 1991, 406–416.

48   Ibid.

49   Brad J. Bushman, "Effects of Warning and Information Labels on Consumption of Full Fat, Reduced Fat, and No Fat Products," *Journal of Applied Psychology* 83, 1, 1998, 97–101.

50   Denise D. Schoenbachler and Tommy E. Whittler, "Adolescent Processing of Social and Physical Threat Communications," *Journal of Advertising* 35, 4, Winter 1996, 37–54.

51   James B. Hunt, John F. Tanner Jr., and David R. Eppright, "Forty Years of Fear Appeal Research: Support for the Ordered Protection Motivation Model," *American Marketing Association* 6, Winter 1995, 147–153.

52   Dana L. Alden, Ashesh Mukherjee, and Wayne D. Hoyer, "The Effects of Incongruity, Surprise and Positive Moderators on Perceived Humor in Advertising," *Journal of Advertising*, Summer 2000, 1–15.

53   Ibid.

54   Ibid.

55   Jessica Severn, George E. Belch, and Michael A. Belch, "The Effects of Sexual and Non-Sexual Advertising Appeals and Information Level on Cognitive Processing and Communication Effectiveness," *Journal of Advertising* 19, 1, 1990, 14–22.

56   Ibid.

57   Michael S. LaTour, Robert E. Pitts, and David C. Snook Luther, "Female Nudity, Arousal, and Ad Response: An Experimental Investigation," *Journal of Advertising* 19, 4, 1990, 51–62.

58   Jessica Severn, George E. Belch, and Michael A. Belch, "The Effects of Sexual and Non-Sexual Advertising Appeals and Information Level on Cognitive Processing and Communication

Effectiveness," *Journal of Advertising,* 19, no. 1, 1990, 14–22.

59   Jean Harrison-Walker, "The Import of Illiteracy to Marketing Communication," *Journal of Consumer Marketing* 12, 1, 1995, 50–64.

60   Frédéric F. Brunel and Michelle R. Nelson, "Explaining Gender Responses to 'Help-Self' and 'Help-Others' Charity Ads Appeals: The Mediating Role of World-Views," *Journal of Advertising,* Fall 2000, 15–27.

61   Patrick De Pelsmacker, Maggie Geuens, and Pascal Anckaert, "Media Context and Advertising Effectiveness: The Role of Context Appreciation and Context/Ad Similarity," *Journal of Advertising,* Summer 2002, 49–61.

62   Andrew Sharma, "Recall of Television Commercials as a Function of Viewing Context: The Impact of Program-Commercial Congruity on Commercial Messages," *Journal of General Psychology,* October 2000, 383–396.

63   Patrick De Pelsmacker, Maggie Geuens, and Pascal Anckaert, "Media Context and Advertising Effectiveness: The Role of Context Appreciation and Context/Ad Similarity," *Journal of Advertising,* Summer 2002, 49–61.

64   Angela Y. Lee and Brian Sternthal, "The Effects of Positive Mood on Memory," *Journal of Consumer Research,* September 1999, 115–129.

65   See Mahima Mathur and Amitava Chattopadhyay, "The Impact of Moods Generated by Television Programs on Responses to Advertising," *Psychology and Marketing* 8, 1, Spring 1991, 59–77.

66   Anna S. Mattila, "The Role of Narratives in the Advertising of Experiential Services," *Journal of Service Research,* August 2000, 35–45.

67   Brad Stone, "The War over Your TV," *Newsweek,* July 29, 2002, 46–47.

68   For example, Michael T. Ewing, Erik Du Plessis, and Charles Foster, "Cinema Advertising Re-Considered," *Journal of Advertising Research,* January–February 2001, 78–85; and Michelle R. Nelson, "Recall of Brand Placements in Computer/Video Games," *Journal of Advertising Research,* March–April 2002, 80–92.

69   Eve Lazarus, "The Cool Appeal of Milk," *Marketing Magazine,* December 8–15, 2003, 11.

70   Chris Daniels, "Speedy Response to a Crisis," *Marketing Magazine,* December 8–15, 2003, 14–15.

71   Eve Lazarus, "The Cool Appeal of Milk," *Marketing Magazine,* December 8–15, 2003, 11.

72   Paul-Mark Rendon, "Nike's Top-scoring Campaign," *Marketing Magazine,* December 8–15, 2003, 23.

73   Eve Lazarus, "The Cool Appeal of Milk," *Marketing Magazine,* December 8–15, 2003, 11.

74   Gary Hennerberg, "The Righteous, Social, and Pragmatic Buyer," *Direct Marketing,* May 1993, 31–34.

75   H. Rao Unnava and Robert E. Burnkrant, "An Imagery Processing View of the Role of Pictures in Print Advertisements," *Journal of Marketing Research* 28, May 1991, 226–231.

76   Paul-Mark Rendon, "Fill 'er Up, and Check the Ads," *Marketing Magazine,* December 8–15, 2003, 4.

77   Paul Ferriss, "Attracting Young Drivers," *Marketing Magazine,* December 8–15, 2003, 27–28.

78   Chris Daniels, "Speedy Response to a Crisis," *Marketing Magazine,* December 8–15, 2003, 14–15.

79   Danny Kucharsky, "Highlighting a Canadian Approach," *Marketing Magazine,* December 8–15, 2003, 25–26.

part three
external influences on consumer behaviour

Part 3 examines external influences on consumer behaviour.

As members of society, all consumers are influenced by external (or socio-cultural) factors. This part will cover the influence of these societal factors on consumer behaviour. We will begin with the influence of the culture of the society at large (Chapter 9) and move on to the external factors that are closer to consumers. Thus, Chapter 10 will examine the role of subcultures, while Chapter 11 will deal with social class and its influence on consumer behaviour. Chapter 12 will deal with social influences that are closest to the consumer—reference groups and the family. The final chapter in this section (Chapter 13) will examine innovations and how innovations are diffused through a society.

3

COURSE RULES

1. IMPROPER GOLF ATTIRE ONLY.

2. NO MORE THAN 4 PLAYERS PER GROUP OR AS MANY AS YOU CAN FIT ON A CART.

3. ALL PLAYERS MUST START AT THE 1ST OR 19TH HOLE.

4. KEEP CARTS OFF GREENS. EVERYWHERE ELSE IS FAIR GAME.

5. THE 'FOOT WEDGE' IS DEFINITELY ALLOWED.

6. IF YOU GET A HOLE IN ONE, YOU'RE MY HERO.

Life's more fun when you make the rules.

starting from $24,700* base model.

PT TURBO

chrysler.ca

*Cash purchase price for 2003 PT Cruiser 28N; includes factory to retailer incentives. License, insurance, registration, $810 freight, retailer administration charges, and taxes not included. Retailer may sell for less. Chrysler is a registered trademark of DaimlerChrysler Corporation used under license by DaimlerChrysler Canada Inc.

chapter 9
the influence of culture on consumer behaviour

LEARNING OBJECTIVES

By the end of this chapter, you should be able to:

1. Define culture and its key characteristics.
2. Explain how culture is learned.
3. Explain how culture is communicated through language, symbols, and rituals.
4. Discuss core Canadian cultural values.
5. Discuss the qualitative and quantitative methods of measuring cultural values.
6. Explain how marketers can use their knowledge of cultural values to develop better marketing programs.

9

why do canadians buy more minivans than SUVs
while Americans buy far more SUVs than minivans? Are Canadians different from Americans? Do we have a national culture that is distinct from that of the United States? Canadians have long struggled with these questions, but at least according to one expert, we can rest assured not only that our values are different from those of Americans, but that they are also diverging from American values more and more. Environics Research Group, a major Canadian research firm, has been tracking Canadian and American social values since 1992. After three series of surveys (in 1992, 1996, and 2000) on 100 social values, the researchers state that not only are American and Canadian social values different, but they are diverging even more as time goes on. Americans value status and security more than Canadians do and are becoming more oriented toward exclusion and intensity, whereas Canadians are more idealistic and autonomy-seeking than their American counterparts. There are several specific value and attitude differences between the two populations. For example, while 49 percent of Americans agree that the father must be the head of the household, only 18 percent of Canadians do, and while 24 percent of Canadians consider men to be naturally superior to women, 38 percent of Americans think so. As regards religion, while 30 percent of Canadians consider themselves to be religious, only 20 percent go to church every week. However, nearly 59 percent of Americans consider themselves to be religious, and 42 percent attend church every week.[1]

How do these social values affect marketers? Besides the values to stress in advertising, Michael Adams, author of *Fire and Ice: The United States, Canada and the Myth of Conversing Values*, says that there are several specific issues that

http://erg.
environics.net

Canadian marketers have to recognize. For example, Canadians seem to place less value on owning things that other people admire (29 percent compared with 36 percent of Americans), and they seem to be moving in the direction of enjoying the experience of things rather than the possession of things.[2] Although Americans are much more outer-directed and take more risks, they are more concerned with maintaining social order and tradition. Canadians are more "inner directed, more security-seeking, and yet are more socially liberal and tolerant of individual diversity."[3]

The differences in social values also seem to be reflected in the types of products that Americans and Canadians buy and in their attitudes toward marketing.

Getting back to the issue of minivans, Adams says this might be a reflection of the differing social values of the two populations, for "minivan drivers are practical, pragmatic shoppers looking for a good deal over novelty and style, and are more concerned about the environment," whereas SUV owners are "confident, adaptable and not at all afraid of the future... feel financially secure and love to go shopping."[4]

CHAPTER OVERVIEW

The study of culture is a challenging undertaking because its subject is the broadest component of social behaviour—*an entire society*. In contrast to the psychologist, who is concerned principally with the study of individual behaviour, or the sociologist, who is concerned with the study of groups, the anthropologist is interested primarily in identifying the very fabric of society itself.

This chapter explores the basic concepts of culture, with particular emphasis on the influence of culture on consumer behaviour. We will first consider the specific dimensions of culture that make it a powerful force in regulating human behaviour. After reviewing several methods of measurement that researchers use to understand the influence of culture on consumption behaviour, we will show how a variety of core Canadian cultural values influence consumer behaviour.

This chapter is concerned with the general aspects of culture; the following chapter focuses on subcultures and shows how marketers can use a knowledge of subcultures to shape and modify their marketing strategies.

WHAT IS CULTURE?

Culture:
The sum total of learned beliefs, values, and customs that direct the consumer behaviour of members of a particular society.

Given the broad and pervasive nature of **culture**, its study generally requires a detailed examination of the character of the total society, including language, knowledge, laws, religions, food customs, music, art, technology, work patterns, products, and other artifacts that give a society its distinctive character. In a sense, culture is a society's personality. For this reason, it is not easy to define its boundaries.

Because our goal is to understand the influence of culture on consumer behaviour, we define culture as the *sum total of learned beliefs, values, and customs that direct the consumer behaviour of members of a particular society*.

The *belief* and *value* components of our definition refer to the accumulated feelings and priorities that individuals have about material things and possessions. More precisely, *beliefs* consist of the very large number of mental or verbal statements ("I believe...") that reflect a person's particular knowledge and assessment of something—another person, a store, a product, a brand. *Values* too are beliefs. Values differ from other beliefs, however, because they meet the following criteria: (1) they are relatively few in number; (2) they serve as a guide for culturally correct behaviour; (3) they are enduring or difficult to change; (4) they are not tied to specific objects or situations; and (5) they are widely accepted by the members of a society.

Therefore, in a broad sense, both values and beliefs are mental images that affect a wide range of specific attitudes that, in turn, influence the way a person is likely to respond in a specific situation.[5] For example, the criteria a person uses to evaluate various brands in a product category (such as Volvo versus Jaguar automobiles), or his or her eventual preference for one of these brands over the other, are influenced by both a person's general values (perceptions as to what constitutes quality and the meaning of country of origin) and specific beliefs (particular perceptions about the quality of Swedish compared with English cars).

In contrast to beliefs and values, customs are *overt modes of behaviour that constitute culturally approved or acceptable ways of behaving in specific situations.* Customs consist of everyday or routine behaviour. For example, a consumer's routine behaviour, such as adding sugar and milk to coffee, putting ketchup on hamburgers, putting mustard on frankfurters, and having a salad *after* rather than *before* the main course of a meal, are customs. Thus, whereas beliefs and values are guides for behaviour, customs are *usual and acceptable ways of behaving.*

By our definition, it is easy to see how an understanding of various cultures of a society helps marketers predict whether consumers will accept their products. Before we proceed further, let us examine some characteristics of culture.

Key Characteristics of Culture

The Impact of Culture Is Hard to Identify

The influence of culture is so natural and automatic that its influence on behaviour is usually taken for granted. When consumer researchers ask people why they do certain things, they frequently answer, "Because it's the right thing to do." This seemingly superficial response partially reflects the ingrained influence of culture on our behaviour. Often it is only when we are exposed to people with different cultural values or customs (as when visiting a different region or a different country) that we become aware of how culture has moulded our own behaviour. Thus, a true appreciation of the influence that culture has on our daily life requires some knowledge of at least one other society with different cultural characteristics. To understand, for example, that brushing our teeth twice a day with flavoured toothpaste is a cultural phenomenon requires some awareness that members of another society either do not brush their teeth at all or do so in a distinctly different manner from our own society.

Perhaps the following statement expresses it best:[6]

Consumers both view themselves in the context of their culture and react to their environment on the basis of the cultural framework that they bring to that experience. Each individual perceives the world through his own cultural lens.

Culture Offers Order, Direction, and Guidance to People

Culture exists to satisfy the needs of the people in a society. It offers order, direction, and guidance in all phases of human problem solving by providing "tried-and-true" methods of satisfying physiological, personal, and social needs. For example, culture provides standards and "rules" about when to eat ("not between meals"), what is normal to eat for breakfast (juice and cereal), lunch (a sandwich), dinner ("something hot and good and healthful"), and snacks ("something with quick energy"); and what to serve to guests at a dinner party ("a formal sit-down meal"), at a picnic (barbecued "franks and hamburgers"), or at a wedding (champagne).

Soft-drink companies would prefer that consumers received their morning "jolt" of caffeine from one of their products rather than from coffee. Because most Canadians do not consider soft drinks to be suitable as a breakfast beverage, the real challenge for soft-drink companies is to overcome culture, not competition. Indeed, coffee has been challenged on all fronts by juices, milk, tea (hot and iced), a host of different types of soft drinks, and now even caffeinated waters. Not resting on their "cultural advantage" as a breakfast drink and the namesake of the "coffee break," coffee marketers have been fighting back by targeting gourmet and specialty coffees (e.g., espresso, cappuccino, and café mocha) to young adults (those 18 to 24 years of age). These efforts have been paying off as young adults—an important segment of the soft-drink market—have been responding positively to gourmet coffees.[7]

Similarly, culture provides insights as to suitable dress for specific occasions, such as what to wear around the house, what to wear to school, to work, to church, at a fast food restaurant, or to a movie theatre.

Dress codes have changed dramatically; people are dressing more casually most of the time. Today, only a few big-city restaurants and clubs require business dress. With the relaxed dress code in the corporate work environment, fewer men are wearing dress shirts, ties, and business suits, and fewer women are wearing dresses, suits, and pantyhose. In their place casual slacks, sports shirts and blouses, jeans, and the emerging category of "casual dress" have been increasing in sales.

Thus, culture gradually but continually evolves to meet the needs of society.

Culture Is Dynamic

To fulfill its need-gratifying role, culture must continually evolve if it is to function in the best interests of a society. For this reason, the marketer must carefully monitor the socio-cultural environment in order to market an existing product more effectively or to develop promising new products.

This is not an easy task because many factors are likely to produce cultural changes in a society—new technology, population shifts, shortages of resources, wars, changing values, and customs borrowed from other cultures. For example, there are major and ongoing cultural changes in Canadian society that reflect the expanded role options open to women. Today, most women work outside the home, frequently in careers that once were considered exclusively male. More and more, these career women are not waiting for marriage and a man to buy them such luxuries as fur coats, expensive wristwatches, and diamond rings. More and more, such women are saying, "I earn a good living, why wait? I will buy it for myself."[8]

www.statcan.ca

In 1983, 26 percent of Canadians strongly agreed with the statement "The father of the family must be master in his own home"; in 2000, this percentage had come down to 18 percent. In the mid-1950s, 60 percent of Canadians went to church each Sunday; by 2000, only about 20 percent did.[9]

From time to time, a number of magazines publish lists of "what's hot" and "what's not." Figure 9-1 presents a recent example of such a comparative list of what is "in" and what is "out" when it comes to food. Such lists reveal the dynamic nature of a particular society or culture.

Culture Is Shared

To be considered a cultural characteristic, a particular belief, value, or practice must be shared by a significant portion of the society. Thus, culture is often viewed as group *customs* that link together the members of a society. Of course, common language is the crucial cultural component that makes it possible for people to share values, experiences, and customs.

FIGURE 9-1	Food: What's In and What's Out

WHAT'S IN WITH FOODS	WHAT'S OUT WITH FOODS
Multi-ethnic cuisine	Nouvelle cuisine
Artisanal cheeses	Flourless chocolate cake
Lemon butter sauces, salsa, au jus	Hollandaise, Béarnaise, heavy gravy
Comfort food, bistro cuisine	Fat-free foods
Soy beverages	Chai tea
Tapas	Sushi
Flavoured mashed potatoes	Rice pilaf
Prepared/partially prepared foods	Cooking from scratch
Authentic regional cuisine	Generic international cuisine
Hot and spicy dishes	Blackened fish and chicken

Source: *American Demographics*, November 2001, 24. Copyright © 2001 Media Central Inc., a Primedia Company. All rights reserved. Reprinted by permission.

Various social institutions in a society transmit the elements of culture and make the sharing of culture a reality:

- The *family*, which serves as the primary agent for enculturation—the passing along of basic cultural beliefs, values, and customs to society's newest members. A vital part of the enculturation role of the family is the consumer socialization of the young (see Chapter 12). This includes teaching such basic consumer-related values and skills as the meaning of money; the relationship between price and quality; the establishment of product tastes, preferences, and habits; and methods of responding to various promotional messages.

- *Educational institutions*, which impart basic learning skills, history, patriotism, citizenship, and the technical training needed to prepare people for significant roles in society.

- *Houses of worship*, which inculcate and perpetuate religious consciousness, spiritual guidance, and moral training.

- *The mass media*. The extensive exposure of the Canadian population to both print and broadcast media, as well as the easily digested, entertaining format in which the contents of such media usually are presented, make the mass media powerful vehicles for imparting a wide range of cultural values.

Consumers receive important cultural information from advertising. For example, it has been hypothesized that one of the roles of advertising in sophisticated magazines like *Vanity Fair*, *Wine Spectator*, and *Canadian Living* is to instruct readers about how to dress, how to decorate their homes, and what foods and wines to serve guests—in other words, what types of behaviour are most suitable for their particular social class.

www.vanityfair.com

www.winespectator.com

www.canadianliving.com

Culture Is Learned

Unlike innate biological characteristics (e.g., sex, skin, hair colour, or intelligence), culture is learned. At an early age, we begin to acquire from our social environment a set of beliefs, values, and customs that make up our culture. For children, the learning of these acceptable cultural values and customs is reinforced by playing with their toys. As children play, they act out and rehearse important cultural lessons and situations. This cultural learning prepares them for later real-life circumstances. The next section will examine the process by which human beings learn a society's cultural values, beliefs, and customs.

HOW CULTURE IS LEARNED

Anthropologists have identified three distinct forms of cultural learning:

- *formal learning,* in which adults and older siblings teach a young family member "how to behave"
- *informal learning,* in which a child learns primarily by imitating the behaviour of selected others, such as family, friends, or television heroes
- *technical learning,* in which teachers instruct the child in an educational environment about what should be done, how it should be done, and why it should be done

Although a firm's advertising can influence all three types of cultural learning, it is likely that many product advertisements enhance informal cultural learning by giving the audience a model of behaviour to imitate. This is especially true for visible or conspicuous products and products that are evaluated in public settings (such as designer clothing, cell phones, or status golf clubs), where peer influence is likely to be influential.[10]

The repetition of advertising messages creates and reinforces cultural beliefs and values. For example, many advertisers continually stress the same selected benefits of their products or services. Ads for wireless phone service often stress the clarity of their connection or the nationwide coverage of their service, as well as the flexibility of their pricing plans. It is difficult to say whether wireless phone subscribers *inherently* desire these benefits from their wireless service providers or whether, after several years of cumulative exposure to advertisements that stress these benefits, they have been taught by marketers to desire them. In a sense, although specific product advertising may reinforce the benefits that consumers want from the product (as determined by consumer behaviour research), such advertising also "teaches" future generations of consumers to expect the same benefits from the product category.

Figure 9-2 shows that cultural meaning moves from the culturally constituted world to consumer goods and from there to the individual consumer by means of various *consumption-related vehicles* (e.g., advertising or observing or imitating the behaviour of others).

Imagine the ever-popular T-shirt and how it can furnish cultural meaning and identity for wearers. A T-shirt can function as a *trophy* (as proof of participation in sports or travel) or as a self-proclaimed label of *belonging to a cultural category* (e.g., "Retired"). A T-shirt can also be used as a means of *self-expression,* which may give the wearer the additional benefit of serving as a "topic" initiating social dialogue with others. Still further, although we might expect that a Las Vegas T-shirt would be worn by a person who has been to Las Vegas (or has received it as a gift from someone else who has visited Las Vegas), this is not necessarily so. In such a world of "virtual identities," consumers can now just buy a Vancouver Island T-shirt at a local retailer and create the impression that they have been there.[11]

Enculturation and Acculturation

When discussing the acquisition of culture, anthropologists often distinguish between the learning of our own, or native, culture and the learning of some "new"

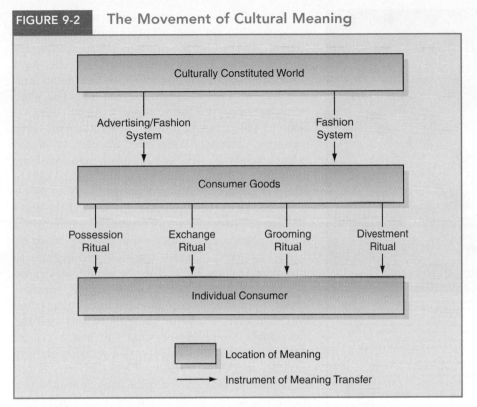

FIGURE 9-2   The Movement of Cultural Meaning

Source: Grant McCracken, "Culture and Consumption: A Theoretical Account of the Structure and Movement of the Cultural Meaning of Consumer Goods," *Journal of Consumer Research*, 13, June 1986, 72. Reprinted by permission of The University of Chicago Press as publishers.

(other) culture. The learning of one's own culture is known as **enculturation**. The learning of a new or foreign culture is known as **acculturation**. When entering foreign markets, marketers must study the specific culture of their potential target markets to determine whether their products will be acceptable to its members and, if so, how they can best persuade the target market to buy.

HOW CULTURE IS COMMUNICATED

Culture is communicated from one generation to another through a common language and through symbols, and rituals. In this section, we will examine each one in more detail.

Language and Symbols

To acquire a common culture, the members of a society must be able to communicate with each other in a common language. Without a common language, shared meaning could not exist and true communication would not take place (see Chapter 8).

To communicate with their audiences, marketers must use the right **symbols** to convey desired product images or characteristics (see Exhibit 9-1). These symbols can be verbal or non-verbal. Verbal symbols may include a television announcement or an advertisement in a magazine. Non-verbal communication includes the use of such symbols as figures, colours, shapes, and even textures to lend additional meaning to print or broadcast advertisements, trademarks, and packaging or product designs.

Enculturation:
The process of learning our own culture.

Acculturation:
The process of learning a new or foreign culture.

Symbol:
Anything that stands for something else.

EXHIBIT 9-1

AD USING VISUAL IMAGERY AS A SYMBOL

Ad reproduction courtesy of Singapore Airlines Limited.

Basically, the symbolic nature of human language sets it apart from all other animal communication. A symbol is anything that stands for something else. Any word is a symbol. The word *razor* calls forth a specific image related to an individual's own knowledge and experience. The word *hurricane* calls forth the notion of wind and rain and also has the power to stir us emotionally, arousing feelings of danger and the need for protection and safety. Similarly, the word *jaguar* has symbolic meaning: to some it suggests a fine luxury car; to others it implies wealth and status; to still others it suggests a sleek, wild animal to be seen at the zoo.

The capacity to learn symbolically is primarily a human phenomenon; most other animals learn by direct experience. Clearly, the ability of humans to understand symbolically how a product, service, or idea can satisfy their needs makes it easier for marketers to sell the features and benefits of their offerings. Through a shared language and culture, individuals already know what the image means; thus, an association can be made without actively thinking about it.

A symbol may have several, even contradictory, meanings; so the advertiser must ascertain exactly what the symbol is communicating to its intended audience. The advertiser who uses a trademark depicting an old craftsman to symbolize careful workmanship may instead be communicating an image of outmoded methods and lack of style. The marketer who uses slang in an advertisement to attract a teenage audience must do so with great care; slang that is misused or outdated will symbolically date the marketer's firm and product.

Price and channels of distribution also are significant symbols of the marketer and the marketer's product. Price often implies quality to potential buyers. For certain products, such as clothing, the type of store in which the product is sold also is an important symbol of quality. In fact, all the elements of the marketing mix—the product, its promotion, its price, and the stores that sell it—are symbols that communicate ranges of quality to potential buyers.

Ritual

In addition to language and symbols, culture includes various ritualized experiences and behaviours that until recently have been neglected by consumer researchers. A **ritual** is a type of symbolic activity consisting of a series of steps (multiple behaviours) that follow a fixed sequence and are repeated over time.[12]

In practice, rituals extend over the human life cycle from birth to death; they include a host of intermediate events, such as confirmation, graduation, and marriage. These rituals can be very public, elaborate, religious, or civil ceremonies, or they can be as mundane as an individual's grooming behaviour or flossing.[13] Ritualized behaviour is rather formal and is often scripted behaviour (such as a reli-

Ritual:
A type of symbolic activity consisting of a series of steps (multiple behaviours) that take place in a fixed sequence and are repeated over time.

gious service requiring a prayer book or the code of proper conduct in a court of law). It is also likely to occur repeatedly over time (such as the singing of the national anthem before a hockey game).

Most important from the standpoint of marketers is the fact that rituals tend to be replete with ritual artifacts (products) that are associated with or somehow enhance the performance of the ritual. For instance, tree ornaments, stockings, and various kinds of food are linked to the ritual of Christmas celebration. Other rituals, such as a bar mitzvah, a graduation, a wedding or wedding anniversary, a Thursday night card game (see Exhibit 9-2), or a Saturday afternoon visit to the hair salon, have their own specific artifacts associated with them. For special occasions, such as wedding anniversaries, some types of artifacts are considered more suitable as gifts than are others, for example, jewellery rather than everyday household articles (see Figure 9-3).

In addition to a ritual, which is the way that something is traditionally done, there is also **ritualistic behaviour**, which can be defined as any behaviour that is made into a ritual. For example, a baseball player may swing his bat a certain number of times and kick the dirt near home plate before a pitch to ensure a good swing. Figure 9-4 describes a young woman's ritualistic behaviour with respect to facial beauty care.

EXHIBIT 9-2

WEEK NIGHTS ARE RICH WITH RITUALS

© 2002 Hasbro, Inc. Used with permission.

CANADIAN CORE VALUES

What is the Canadian culture? In this section, we identify a number of **core values** that both affect and reflect the character of Canadian society. This is a difficult undertaking for several reasons. First, Canada is a diverse country, consisting of a variety of **subcultures** (religious, ethnic, regional, racial, and economic groups), each of which interprets and responds to society's basic beliefs and values in its own specific way. Second, Canada is a dynamic society that has undergone almost constant change in response to the development of new technology. This element of rapid change makes it especially difficult to monitor changes in cultural values. Finally, the existence of contradictory values in Canadian society is somewhat confusing. For instance, Canadians traditionally embrace freedom of choice and individualism, and yet simultaneously they show great tendencies to conform—in dress, in furnishings, and in fads—to the rest of society. In the context of consumer behaviour, Canadians like to have a wide choice of products, and they prefer those that express their unique personal life styles. Yet, there is often a considerable amount of implicit pressure to conform to the values of family members, friends, and other socially important groups. It is difficult to reconcile these seemingly inconsistent values; their existence, however, demonstrates that Canada is a complex society with numerous paradoxes.

Ritualistic behaviour:
Any behaviour that is made into a ritual.

Core values:
Criteria or values that both affect and reflect the character of a society.

Subculture:
A distinct cultural group that exists as an identifiable segment within a larger, more complex society.

When selecting the specific core values to be examined, we were guided by three criteria:

1. *The value must be pervasive.* A significant portion of the Canadian people must accept the value and use it as a guide for their attitudes and actions.

2. *The value must be enduring.* The specific value must have influenced the actions of the Canadian people over an extended period of time (as distinguished from a short-run trend).

3. *The value must be consumer-related.* The specific value must offer insights that help us to understand the consumption actions of the Canadian people.

FIGURE 9-3   Selected Rituals and Associated Artifacts

SELECTED RITUALS	TYPICAL ARTIFACTS
Wedding	White gown (something old, something new, something borrowed, something blue)
Birth of child	Canada Savings Bond, silver baby spoon
Birthday	Card, present, cake with candles
Fiftieth wedding anniversary	Catered party, card and gift, display of photos of the couple's life together
Graduation	Pen, Canada Savings Bond, card, wristwatch
Valentine's Day	Candy, card, flowers
New Year's Eve	Champagne, party, fancy dress
Thanksgiving	Turkey meal for family and friends
Going to the gym	Towel, exercise clothes, water, portable tape player
Saturday night hockey game	Beer, potato chips, pretzels
Grey Cup party	Same as Sunday football (just more)
Starting a new job	Get a haircut, buy some new clothing
Getting a job promotion	Taken out to lunch by co-workers, receive token gift
Retirement	Company party, watch, plaque
Death	Send a card, give to charity in the name of the deceased

FIGURE 9-4   Facial Beauty Ritual of a Young TV Advertising Sales Representative

1. I pull my hair back with a headband.
2. I take all my makeup off with L'Oréal eye makeup remover.
3. Next, I use a Q-tip with some moisturizer around my eyes to make sure all eye makeup is removed.
4. I wash my face with Noxzema facial wash.
5. I apply Clinique Dramatically Different Lotion to my face, neck, and throat.
6. If I have a blemish, I apply Clearasil Treatment to the area to dry it out.
7. Twice weekly (or as necessary) I use Aapri Facial Scrub to remove dry and dead skin.
8. Once a week I apply Clinique Clarifying Lotion 2 with a cotton ball to my face and throat to remove deep-down dirt and oils.
9. Once every three months I get a professional salon facial to deep-clean my pores.

Source: Adapted from "Culture and Consumption: A Theoretical Account of the Structure and Movement of the Cultural Meaning of Consumer Goods," by Grant McCracken in *Journal of Consumer Research,* Vol. 13, June 1986. Reprinted by permission of the publisher.

These criteria are met by a number of basic values that expert observers of the Canadian scene consider the "building blocks" of that rather elusive concept called the "Canadian character."

Achievement and Success

In a broad cultural context, achievement is a major Canadian value, with historical roots that can be traced to the traditional religious belief in the Protestant work ethic, which considers hard work to be wholesome, spiritually rewarding, and an end in itself. Indeed, substantial research evidence shows that the achievement orientation is closely associated with the technical development and general economic growth of North American society.[14]

People who consider a "sense of accomplishment" an important personal value tend to be achievers who strive hard for success. Although historically associated with men, especially male business executives, today *achievement* is very important for women, who are increasingly enrolled in undergraduate and graduate business programs and are more commonly seeking top-level business careers.

Success is a closely related Canadian cultural theme. However, achievement and success do differ. Specifically, achievement is its own direct reward (it is implicitly satisfying to the individual achiever), whereas success implies an extrinsic reward, such as luxury possessions, financial compensation, or status improvement. Both achievement and success influence consumption. They often serve as social and moral justification for the acquisition of goods and

EXHIBIT 9-3

AN ACHIEVEMENT-SUCCESS APPEAL
Courtesy of Land Rover.

services. For example, "You owe it to yourself," "You worked for it," and "You deserve it" are popular achievement themes used by advertisers to coax consumers into buying their products (see Exhibit 9-3). Regardless of their sex, achievement-oriented people often enjoy conspicuous consumption because it allows them to display symbols of their personal achievement. The values of achievement and success are also especially relevant when it comes to personal development and preparation for future careers.

It is of interest that the theories of colonialism and dependence were once used to explain the differences between the poor countries and the rich countries of the globe. However, these theories are given little credence today, and the current paradigm used to explain the differences between "have" and "have-not" nations is culture.

Activity

Canadians attach an extraordinary amount of importance to being *active* or *involved*. Keeping busy is widely accepted as a healthy and even necessary part of the Canadian life style. The hectic nature of Canadian life is attested to by foreign visitors, who frequently comment that they cannot understand why Canadians are always "on the run" and seemingly unable to relax.

The premium placed on activity has had both positive and negative effects on the popularity of various products. For example, a principal reason for the enormous growth of fast food chains, such as McDonald's and Kentucky Fried Chicken, is that so many people want quick meals when they are away from the house. Canadians rarely have a full breakfast because they usually are too rushed in the morning to prepare and eat a traditional morning meal. In fact, bagels have been stealing sales away from sit-down cereal breakfasts because they can be eaten on the run.[15]

Efficiency and Practicality

With a basic philosophy of down-to-earth pragmatism, Canadians pride themselves on being efficient and practical. When it comes to *efficiency,* they admire anything that saves time and effort. In terms of *practicality,* they are generally receptive to any new product that makes tasks easier and can help solve problems (see Exhibit 9-4). For example, today it is possible for manufacturers of many product categories to offer the public a wide range of interchangeable components. Thus, a consumer can design his or her own customized wall unit from such standard components as compatible metals and woods, legs, door facings, and style panels at a cost not much higher than a completely standardized unit. The capacity of manufacturers to create mass-produced components offers consumers the practical option of a customized product at a reasonable price. If you are unfamiliar with such furniture, just browse through an IKEA catalogue or the "virtual catalogue" on the IKEA website.

www.ikea.ca

Another illustration of Canadians' attentiveness to efficiency and practicality is the extreme importance attached to *time.* Canadians seem to be convinced that "time waits for no one," a belief that is seen in their habitual promptness.[16] Canadians, like their American neighbours, place a great deal of importance on the value of time itself, on the notion that time is money, on the importance of not wasting time, and on finding "more" time. One author has concluded that in our attempt to get more and more out of each day, we may become trapped in a vicious circle in which we feel as if we are getting less and less out of each day.[17]

The frequency with which Canadians look at their watches and the importance attached to having an accurate timepiece tend to support the Canadian value of *punctuality.* Similarly, the broad consumer acceptance of the microwave oven and microwaveable foods are also examples of Canadians' love affair with products that save time and effort by providing efficiency and practicality.

No time to marinade? No problem! Knorr 30 Minute Marinade won an award from Canadian consumers as the best new product in the category of sauces, dressings, and soups, because it helped consumers make efficient use of their time. One consumer said, "It works the same way as conventional marinades only faster and full of flavour."[18]

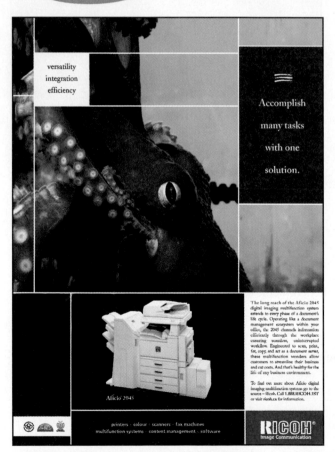

EXHIBIT 9-4

AD FOCUSING ON EFFICIENCY AND PRACTICALITY

Courtesy of Ricoh.

Similarly, Michelina's Salad Bowls became a big hit among consumers because "it is a quick lunch to grab and take to work when you don't have time."[19]

Progress

Progress is another watchword of Canadian society. Canadians respond favourably to the promise of progress. Receptivity to progress appears to be closely linked to the other core values already examined (*achievement, success, efficiency,* and *practicality*) and to the central belief that people can always improve themselves, that tomorrow should be better than today. In a consumption-oriented society, such as that of Canada or the United States, progress often means the acceptance of change, of new products or services designed to fulfill previously under-satisfied or unsatisfied needs. A new type of counsellor, the "life coach" or "personal coach," works with individuals in order to help them improve themselves and seek "fulfillment and balance in careers, family, health, and hobbies."[20] The coach tracks the client's progress and tries to keep the client heading in the direction of his or her fulfillment. Ideally, the coach makes the client excited about prospects for the future.

In the name of progress, Canadians appear to be receptive to product claims that stress "new," "improved," "longer-lasting," "speedier," "quicker," "smoother and closer," and "increased strength" (see Exhibit 9-5A).

EXHIBIT 9-5A

PROGRESS IS A WINNING APPEAL

Courtesy of Citizen Watch Company of America.

EXHIBIT 9-5B

AN AD APPEALING TO MATERIALISM

Courtesy of Infiniti and O'Regan's Infiniti, Halifax.

Material Comfort

For most Canadians (even young children), *material comfort* signifies the attainment of "the good life," a life that may include a new car (see Exhibit 9-5B), a dishwasher, an air conditioner, a hot tub, and an almost infinite variety of other convenience-oriented and pleasure-providing goods and services.[21] It appears that consumers' idea of material comfort is largely a *relative* view; that is, they tend to define their own satisfaction with the amount of material goods they have by comparing what they have with what others have. If a comparison suggests that they have more than others do, then they are more likely to be satisfied.[22]

Material comfort has often been associated with "bigger quantities of things" or "more of something." Recently, however, there has been a noticeable shift away from such a "more is better" viewpoint to a "better is better" vision—one that stresses better quality and better design. Canadians today increasingly want *better,* and *better-looking,* products. Such a state of affairs has been referred to as "the design economy"—that is, an economy that is based on the interaction of four elements: sustained prosperity, ongoing technology, a culture open to change, and marketing expertise.[23]

Individualism

Canadians place a strong value on "being themselves." Self-reliance, self-interest, self-confidence, self-esteem, and self-fulfillment are all exceedingly popular expressions of *individualism.* Striving for individualism seems to be linked to the rejection of dependency; that is, it is better to rely on yourself than on others (Exhibit 9-6).

In the context of consumer behaviour, an appeal to individualism often takes the form of reinforcing the consumer's sense of identity with products or services that both reflect and emphasize that identity. For example, advertisements for high-style clothing and cosmetics usually promise that their products will enhance the consumer's exclusive or distinctive character and set him or her apart from others.

Freedom

Freedom is another very strong Canadian value, with historical roots in such democratic ideals as freedom of speech, freedom of the press, and freedom of worship. As an outgrowth of these democratic beliefs in freedom, Canadians have a strong preference for *freedom of choice,* the opportunity to choose from a wide range of alternatives. This preference is seen in the large number of competitive brands and product variations that can be found on the shelves of the modern supermarket or department store. For many products, consumers can select from a wide variety of sizes, colours, flavours, features, styles, and even special ingredients (such as all-natural-ingredient toothpaste without sugar). It also explains why many companies offer consumers many choices (see Exhibits 9-7A and 9-7B).

EXHIBIT 9-6

AN APPEAL TO INDIVIDUALISM

© DaimlerChrysler Corporation.

EXHIBIT 9-7A

AD STRESSING FREEDOM OF CHOICE

Courtesy of Dean Foods.

EXHIBIT 9-7B

AD STRESSING FREEDOM OF CHOICE

Courtesy of RBC.

However, there are decision-making situations in which consumers are faced with too many choices. In such cases they may feel overwhelmed by the sheer number of choices and respond by running away from the stressful situation (see Chapter 14).

Recent research with 1000 English consumers found that many of them reported feeling bewildered and irritated by the fact that they were being offered "too much choice."[24]

External Conformity

Although Canadians deeply embrace freedom of choice and individualism, they nevertheless accept the reality of conformity. *External conformity* is a necessary process by which the individual adapts to society.

In the realm of consumer behaviour, conformity (or uniformity) takes the form of standardized goods and services. Standardized products have been made possible by mass production. The availability of a wide choice of standardized products places the consumer in the unique position of being *individualistic* (by selecting specific products that close friends do not have) or of *conforming* (by purchasing a similar or identical product). In this way, individualism and conformity exist side by side as choices for the consumer.

An interesting example of the "ping-pong" relationship between seeking individualism and accepting conformity is the widespread acceptance of more casual dressing in the workplace (already discussed in this chapter). For instance, male and female executives are conforming less to workplace dress codes (i.e., there are more "total" dress options open to business executives). Some male executives are wearing casual slacks and sport shirts to work; others are wearing blazers and slacks rather than business suits. Greater personal confidence and an emphasis on comfort appear to be the reasons that many executives are wearing less traditional business attire. Nevertheless, in some companies the appearance of male executives in blue blazers and grey slacks does seem like a business uniform (which is a kind of conformity). Consumer research examining the types of clothing that men and women wear to the office suggests that the majority of workers in Canada, as well as the U.S., are wearing some type of casual clothing to work.[25] For men, it is commonly "everyday casual" (jeans, shorts, T-shirts, etc.); for women it is "casual" (casual pants with or without a jacket, sweaters, separates, and pantsuits).

Humanitarianism

Canadians are often generous when it comes to giving to those in need. They support with a passion many humane and charitable causes, and they sympathize with the underdog who must overcome adversity to get ahead. They also tend to be charitable and willing to come to the aid of people who are less fortunate than they are. To make the study of charitable giving more fruitful, consumer researchers have recently validated two scales that deal with *attitudes toward helping others* (AHO) and *attitudes toward charitable organizations* (ACO).[26] Figure 9-5 presents the nine-item scale used to measure AHO and ACO.

Within the context of making charitable decisions, the website of the Planned Giving Design Center assists charities in their efforts to establish and cultivate rela-

www.pgdc.net

FIGURE 9-5	A Scale for Measuring Attitude toward Helping Others (AHO) and Attitude toward Charitable Organizations (ACO)

SCALE ITEM

ATTITUDE TOWARD HELPING OTHERS (AHO)

People should be willing to help others who are less fortunate.

Helping troubled people with their problems is very important to me.

People should be more charitable toward others in society.

People in need should receive support from others.

ATTITUDE TOWARD CHARITABLE ORGANIZATIONS (ACO)

The money given to charities goes for good causes.

Much of the money donated to charity is wasted. (R)

My image of charitable organizations is positive.

Charitable organizations have been quite successful in helping the needy.

Charity organizations perform a useful function for society.

Note: (R) = reverse scored.

Source: Deborah J. Webb, Corliss L. Green, and Thomas G. Brashear, "Development and Validation of Scales to Measure Attitudes Influencing Monetary Donations to Charitable Organizations," *Journal of the Academy of Marketing Science*, 28, no. 12, Spring 2000, 299–309. Reprinted by permission of the publisher.

tionships with professionals who advise clients in a position to make charitable contributions, such as lawyers, financial planners, and trust officers.[27] Other websites help individuals donate to specific charities.

Beyond charitable giving, other social issues have an impact on both what consumers buy and where they invest. Some investors prefer mutual funds that screen companies for such social issues as military contracts, pollution problems, and equal opportunity employment. Investments in socially conscious mutual funds are now quite commonplace. Many companies try to appeal to consumers by emphasizing their concern for environmental or social issues.

www.charityguide.org

www.guidestar.org

www.charitynavigator.org

Youthfulness

Canadians tend to place an almost sacred value on *youthfulness*. This emphasis is a reflection of the country's rapid technological development. In an atmosphere where "new" and "young" are constantly stressed, "old" is often equated with being outdated. This is in contrast to traditional European, African, and Asian societies, in which the elderly are revered for having the wisdom of experience that comes with age.

www.ethicalfunds.com

Youthfulness should not be confused with youth, which describes an age group. Canadians are preoccupied with *looking* and *acting* young, regardless of their chronological age. For Canadians, youthfulness is a state of mind and a state of being, sometimes expressed as being "young at heart," "young in spirit," or "young in appearance." Exhibit 9-8 presents an ad for Olay® Total Effects that depicts a woman who is "declaring war" on aging.

A great deal of advertising tries to create a sense of urgency about retaining one's youth and fearing aging.[28] Ads for hand cream talk about "young hands." Ads for skin treatment say, "I dreaded turning 30...." Ads for perfume and makeup promise that the consumer will look "sexy and young" or be able to "deny their age." Detergent ads ask the reader, "Can you match their hands with their ages?" These advertising themes, which promise the consumer the benefits of youthfulness, reveal the high premium Canadians place on appearing and acting young.

Fitness and Health

Canadians' preoccupation with *fitness* and *health* has emerged as a core value. This value has manifested itself in a number of ways, including the popularity of tennis, racquetball, and jogging, and the continued increases in sales of vitamins. Added to these trends is an enhanced consciousness on the part of Canadians that "you are what you eat" (see Exhibit 9-9).

Fitness and health are becoming life-style choices for many consumers. This trend has stimulated Reebok to open a series of exercise-retail complexes that try to build a cultural connection with consumers that goes beyond normal marketing. Traditional food

EXHIBIT 9-8

FIGHTING THE SIGNS OF AGING

Courtesy of The Procter & Gamble Company. Used by permission.

EXHIBIT 9-9

AD POINTING OUT THAT "YOU ARE WHAT YOU EAT"

© Nestlé USA. Reproduced with permission.

manufacturers have begun modifying their ingredients to cater to the health-conscious shopper. Frozen dinners have become more nutritious in recent years, and manufacturers of traditional "junk food" are trying to make it more healthful. "Light" or "fat-free" versions of snack chips or pretzels, along with "low-sodium," "no-cholesterol," "no-preservative" snack foods, are an attempt to provide consumers with tasty and healthful options. There are even websites for the fitness-minded consumer offering workout tips, nutritional information, and fitness-related products and services. Although there is no denying the "fitness and healthy living" trend in Canadian society, there is evidence that consumers find it difficult "to be good" when it comes to their own health. For instance, people miss their desserts. Research suggests that more than 75 percent of American consumers think about dessert between one and eight times a day. The main activities that seem to put people in the mood for desserts are exercise, working, entertainment, eating, and studying.[29] Also, many Canadians are unwilling to compromise on flavour for health benefits, with the result being a kind of reverse trend toward full-flavoured, rich foods. This counter-trend reveals the diversity of preferences that exist side by side in the marketplace.[30] It points out that low-fat and low-cholesterol food is not for everyone and that there is an important market segment whose members seek to indulge their taste buds and their waistlines. Indeed, AC Nielsen data for food, drug, and mass-merchandising outlet sales indicated recently that fat-free potato chip sales were down 33 percent, fat-free cookies and margarine sales were down 12 percent, and fat-free ice cream sales were down 22 percent.[31] And the World Health Organization reports that obesity is an increasing problem in both developed and developing countries.

Core Values Are Not a Canadian Phenomenon

The cultural values just examined are not all uniquely or originally Canadian. Some were borrowed, particularly from British and European society, as people emigrated to the country. Some values that originated in North America are now part of the fabric of other societies. In fact, there is evidence that the good life may be a universal notion and that global brands are used as an external sign of attaining the good life.[32]

In addition, not all Canadians necessarily accept each of these values. However, as a whole, these values do account for much of the Canadian character. Figure 9-6 summarizes a number of Canadian core values and their relevance to consumer behaviour.

Canadian versus American Core Values

Americans and Canadians do have a lot in common, though they also differ in significant ways (see Exhibit 9-10 on page 302). In fact, the values listed above are common to both Americans and Canadians.[33] What *is* different is the level or the

FIGURE 9-6　Summary of Canadian Core Values

VALUE	GENERAL FEATURES	RELEVANCE TO CONSUMER BEHAVIOUR
Achievement and Success, Activity	Hard work is good; success flows from hard work	Acts as a justification for acquisition of goods ("You deserve it").
	Keeping busy is healthy and natural	Stimulates interest in products that are time-savers and enhance leisure time.
Efficiency and Practicality	Admiration of things that solve problems (e.g., save time and effort)	Stimulates purchase of products that function well and save time.
	People can improve themselves; tomorrow should be better than today	Stimulates desire for new products that fulfill unsatisfied needs; ready acceptance of products that claim to be "new and improved."
Material Comfort	"The good life"	Fosters acceptance of convenience and luxury products that make life more comfortable and enjoyable.
Individualism	Being yourself (e.g., self-reliance, self-interest, self-esteem)	Stimulates acceptance of customized or unique products that enable a person to "express his or her own personality."
Freedom	Freedom of choice	Fosters interest in wide product lines and differentiated products.
External Conformity	Uniformity of observable behaviour; desire for acceptance	Stimulates interest in products that are used or owned by others in the same social group.
Humanitarianism	Caring for others, particularly the underdog	Stimulates patronage of firms that compete with market leaders.
Youthfulness	A state of mind that stresses being "young at heart" and having a youthful appearance	Stimulates acceptance of products that provide the illusion of maintaining or fostering youthfulness.
Fitness and Health	Caring about one's body, including the desire to be physically fit and healthy	Stimulates acceptance of food products, activities, and equipment perceived to maintain or increase physical fitness.

strength with which these values are held. Research indicates that there are some fundamental differences between the two nations. As Michael Adams points out in his recent book *Fire and Ice*, these differences "stem from differences in the founding values, experiences, and institutions in each country and how these initial differences express themselves"[34] in our everyday lives. The Environics surveys found the average Canadian to have the same social values at the same position as the most progressive American. Although Americans are indeed more risk-taking than Canadians, we are more willing to accept individual differences. Canadians are also (perhaps surprisingly) more emotionally informal and open than Americans.

Figures 9-7 A, B, and C provide more details of differences between Canadians and Americans by comparing their scores on 18 major cultural values. As can be seen from these tables, Canadians are more "liberal" than their American counterparts. For example, as shown in Figure 9-7A, in 2000 while nearly 50 percent of Americans thought the father should be the head of the household, only 8 percent of Canadians thought so. Canadians are also less likely to accept violence as a means of settling disputes and are more open to allowing immigrants from other racial groups to enter the country.

Furthermore, Adams states that Canada's cultural values are diverging from those of the United States. While Americans are becoming more exclusion- and intensity-oriented, Canadians are becoming more idealistic and autonomy-oriented.

FIGURE 9-7A   Canadian Values, 1992, 1996, 2000

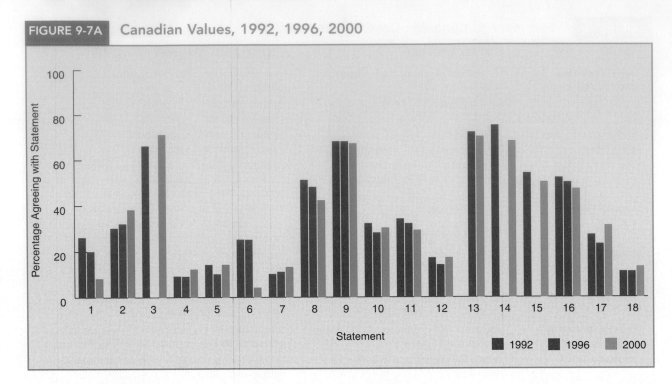

Note: Figures 9-7A, 9-7B, and 9-7C provide details of the average scores of Canadians or Americans on 18 major cultural values, listed below.

1. Father of the family must be the master in his own house.
2. Men are naturally superior to women.
3. Couples who share a home are a family.
4. Violence is a normal part of life.
5. When one is extremely tense/frustrated, a little violence can offer relief.
6. I am prepared to take great risks.
7. It is acceptable to use violence to get what you want.
8. I do not like changing my habits.
9. I relate to non-conformists.
10. I relate best to people who do not show their emotions.
11. It is important that other people admire what I own.
12. A widely advertised product is probably a good product.
13. I feel a personal responsibility to those worse off than myself.
14. I have trouble accomplishing things due to a hectic lifestyle.
15. It is important to get away from the responsibilities and burdens of one's life.
16. I discuss my problems and issues with other people.
17. I enjoy demonstrating my country's superiority.
18. Non-whites should not be able to immigrate to this country.

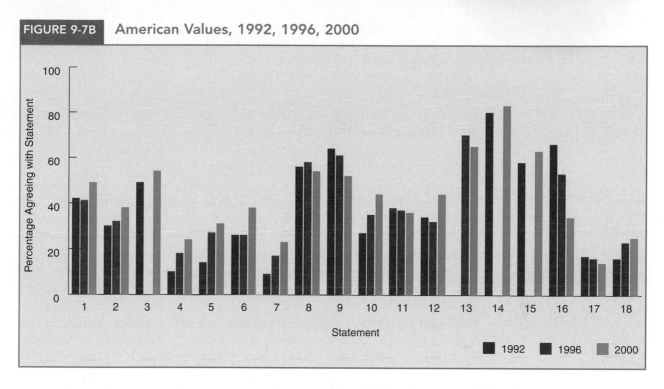

FIGURE 9-7B   American Values, 1992, 1996, 2000

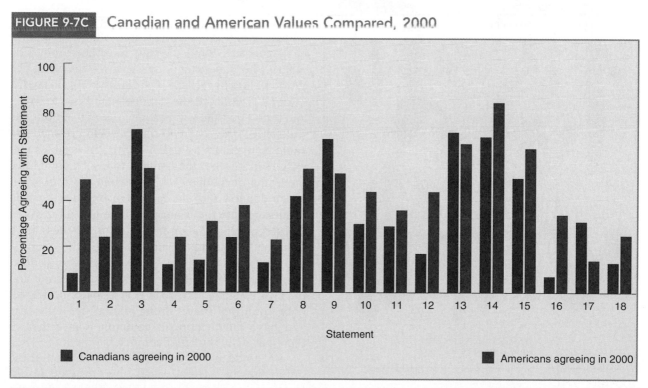

FIGURE 9-7C   Canadian and American Values Compared, 2000

Source: Figures 9-7A, 9-7B, and 9-7C adapted from *Fire and Ice* by Michael Adams. Copyright © Michael Adams, 2003. Reprinted by permission of Penguin Group (Canada).

For example, although the percentage of Canadians who think that men are naturally superior to women has been declining over the years, in the U.S., the percentage has actually risen a little over the years.

Adams also notes the following differences between Canadians and Americans:[35]

■ Canadians are less likely than Americans to say that religion is important to them (30 percent versus 59 percent in 2002).

■ There are more agnostics, atheists, and secular humanists among Canadians than among Americans (40 percent versus 25 percent in 2000).

■ Canadians are more likely than Americans to say that immigrants have a good influence on their country (77 percent versus 49 percent in 2000) and less likely to say that immigrants were bad for the country (18 percent versus 43 percent).

■ Canadians are more "liberal" in their values at every age than Americans. For example, while older Canadians and Americans tend to be more conformist than the younger generation in each country, older Canadians are more liberal than their American counterparts, and younger Canadians are more liberal than younger Americans.

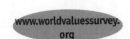
www.worldvaluessurvey.org

■ In Canada values vary by region far less than in the United States. In fact, the differences between Canadians from different regions are minimal. In the U.S. however, there is considerable variation in values among the different regions.

■ Even the most liberal Americans (New Englanders) are no more liberal than the *average* Canadian.

Adams argues that Canada and the United States are in fact diverging (rather than converging) in their values. Similar results have been found by others who have examined the three waves of the World Values Survey (WVS). Christian Boucher, for example, examined the data collected by the WVS and found that the gap between the two nations has widened in the past two decades. He grouped the value statements in the WVS into 28 variables and examined whether the United States or Canada was the leader of change in cultural values by looking at which country led the change in one decade. The results indicate that Canada led the U.S. in 12 of the 28 categories, including moral permissiveness, faith in non-governmental institutions, pride in country, and civil permissiveness.[36] It is important to note, however, that the differences between Canada and the U.S. are small and are largely a matter of degree; both countries share strong similarities in values and have much more in common than either of them has with any other country.

As noted at the beginning of this chapter, these differences in cultural values have resulted in differences in consumption patterns. Besides the higher ownership of minivans, Canadians also differ from American neighbours in television viewing

"You seem familiar, yet somehow strange—are you by any chance Canadian?"

EXHIBIT 9-10

© The New Yorker Collection 2001 Donald Reilly from cartoonbank.com. All rights reserved.

(Canadians watch much less television than Americans), church attendance (again, Canadians are less likely to go to church than Americans), obesity (fewer Canadians than Americans are obese), and other areas, including use of the internet (refer to Internet Insight 9-1).

THE MEASUREMENT OF CULTURAL VALUES

A wide range of measurement techniques are used in the study of culture. These include qualitative research methods, such as projective techniques, content analysis, consumer fieldwork, focus groups, and depth interviews. Besides these qualitative measures, there are quantitative value measurement instruments, such as the Rokeach Value Survey, the LOV (List of Vaues), and VALS (Values and Life Styles; discussed in the Appendix to Part 1). Research Insight 9-1 takes an in-depth look at some of the qualitative research methods used to measure consumer values; the more popular quantitative measurement instruments are discussed in the next section.

Value Measurement Survey Instruments

Anthropologists have traditionally observed the behaviour of members of a society and inferred from such behaviour the dominant or underlying values of the society. In recent years, however, there has been a gradual shift to measuring values directly by means of survey (questionnaire) research. Researchers use data collection instruments called *value instruments* to ask people how they feel about such basic personal and social concepts as freedom, comfort, national security, and peace.

INTERNET INSIGHT 9-1
AMERICANS AND CANADIANS ONLINE

Internet use in Canada surged during the 1990s but has levelled off in the past two years. This is probably because those who were interested in being connected have already established internet connections; those who have not done so already are less likely to do so in the near future. Thus, although internet use increased by 24 percent in 2000 and 19 percent in 2001, it increased by only 4 percent in 2002. However, the proportion of Canadians who use the internet regularly is fairly high (62 percent of all households or 7.5 million households).[a]

Among households with internet connections, a significant proportion reported that at least one member went online at least once every day; two-thirds of these households reported spending 20 hours a week or more online.

In 2002, Canadians spent $2.4 billion shopping on the internet and 37.3 percent of the households with internet connections had bought something on the web; an additional 1.7 million households had used the internet for gathering information, even though they had not actually made a purchase on the web. The most popular online purchases in 2002 were books, magazines, and newspapers; travel was the most popular category, followed by clothing and jewellery, according to the *Internet Advertising Handbook*[b] nearly 68 percent of Canadian internet users had bought at least one thing on the web at some time. This is lower than in the United States, where nearly 77 percent had reported buying something online. But whereas Americans are more likely than Canadians to shop online, they are less likely to bank online. Only 20 percent of Americans had done any online banking, while 61 percent of Canadian internet users had done so.

[a]All numbers in this Internet Insight are based on information provided by Statistics Canada.

[b]*Internet Advertising Handbook*, published by *Marketing Magazine*, p. 24.

RESEARCH INSIGHT 9-1
QUALITATIVE METHODS FOR MEASURING
CULTURAL VALUES

Chapter 2 covered some of the qualitative research methods used in consumer research, for example, focus groups, in-depth interviews, and projective techniques; these can also be used to measure cultural values. Besides these techniques, cultural values can also be measured with content analysis and fieldwork. These techniques are discussed in the following sections.

CONTENT ANALYSIS

We can sometimes draw conclusions about a society or specific aspects of a society, or compare two or more societies, by examining the content of particular messages. **Content analysis**, as the name implies, examines the content of verbal, written, and pictorial communications, such as the copy and art composition of an advertisement.

Content analysis can be a relatively objective means of determining what social and cultural changes have occurred in a specific society or of contrasting aspects of two different societies.

A content analysis of 263 ads appearing in eight issues of *Seventeen* magazine, four Japanese issues and four U.S. issues, found that teenage girls are portrayed differently in the two countries. The research concluded that these "differences correspond to each country's central concepts of self and society." Whereas American teen girls are often associated with images of "independence and determination," Japanese teen girls are most often portrayed with a "happy, playful, childlike girlish image."[37]

Content analysis is useful both to marketers and to public-policy makers interested in comparing the advertising claims of competitors in a specific industry, as well as for evaluating the nature of advertising targeted to specific audiences, such as women, the elderly, or children.

CONSUMER FIELDWORK

When examining a specific society, anthropologists often immerse themselves in the environment under study through **consumer fieldwork**. As trained researchers, they are likely to select a small sample of people from a particular society and carefully observe their behaviour. From their observations, researchers draw conclusions about the values, beliefs, and customs of the society under investigation.

If researchers were interested in how men choose neckties, they might put trained observers in department and clothing stores and note how neckties are selected (solid versus patterned, striped versus paisley, and so on). The researchers also may be interested in how much search accompanies the choice, that is, how often consumers tend to take a necktie off the display, examine it, compare it to other neckties in the store, and put it back again before choosing the necktie that they finally buy.

E-Lab LLC specializes in videotaping subjects at work, at home, in their cars, and in public places. Its research suggests: "Ask a teenager why he's buying a certain backpack, and you might not get a useful answer. Watch a teenager as he shops for that backpack, and you might learn a few things."

The distinct characteristics of **field observation** are that (1) it takes place in a natural environment; (2) it is sometimes done without the subject's knowledge; and (3) it focuses on observation of behaviour. Because the emphasis is on a natural environment and observable behaviour, field observation concerned with consumer behaviour often concentrates on in-store shopping behaviour and, less frequently, on in-home preparation and consumption.

In some cases, instead of just observing behaviour, researchers become **participant-observers**; that is, they become active members of the environment they are studying. For example, if researchers were interested in examining how consumers choose computer software, they might take a sales position in a computer superstore to observe directly and even to interact with customers in the transaction process.

Both field observation and participant-observer research require highly skilled researchers who can separate their own emotions from what they actually observe. Both techniques provide valuable insight that might not easily be obtained through survey research that simply asks consumers about their behaviour.

A variety of popular value instruments have been used in consumer behaviour studies. They include the *Rokeach Value Survey*, the *List of Values (LOV,)* and the *Values and Life Styles—VALS* (discussed in Chapter 1). The widely used **Rokeach Value Survey** is a self-administered value inventory that is divided into two parts, each part measuring different but complementary types of personal values (see Figure 9-8). The first part consists of 18 *terminal value* items, which are designed to measure the relative importance of end states of existence (or personal goals). The second part consists of 18 *instrumental value* items, which measure basic approaches an individual might take to reach end-state values. Thus, the first half of the measurement instrument deals with ends, and the second half considers means.

The LOV is a related measurement instrument that is also designed to be used in surveying consumers' personal values. The LOV scale asks consumers to choose their two most important values from a list of nine (such as "warm relationships with others," "a sense of belonging," or "a sense of accomplishment") that is based on the terminal values of the Rokeach Value Survey.[38] Perhaps the best-known survey of values in Canada is the Environics Survey of Social Values, which measures the social values of Canadians.

Although culture and cultural values have a significant influence on consumer behaviour, it is not a simple task to identify values that are relevant to the consumption of a product. And it takes considerable skill to use this knowledge while creating effective marketing programs. The next section examines the marketing implications of culture and cultural values.

Content analysis:
A method for systematically analyzing the content of verbal, written, and pictorial communication. Often used to study cultural values.

Consumer fieldwork:
Observational research by anthropologists of the behaviour of a small sample of people from a particular society.

Field observation:
A cultural observation technique that observes behaviour that takes place in a natural environment (sometimes without the subject's knowledge).

Participant-observer:
A researcher who participates in a study without informing those who are being observed.

FIGURE 9-8	The Rokeach Value Survey Instrument

TERMINAL VALUES	INSTRUMENTAL VALUES
A Comfortable Life (a prosperous life)	Ambitious (hardworking, aspiring)
An Exciting Life (a stimulating, active life)	Broad-Minded (open-minded)
A World at Peace (free of war and conflict)	Capable (competent, effective)
Equality (brotherhood, equal opportunity for all)	Cheerful (lighthearted, joyful)
Freedom (independence and free choice)	Clean (neat, tidy)
Happiness (contentedness)	Courageous (standing up for your beliefs)
National Security (protection from attack)	Forgiving (willing to pardon others)
Pleasure (an enjoyable life)	Helpful (working for the welfare of others)
Salvation (saved, eternal life)	Honest (sincere, truthful)
Social Recognition (respect and admiration)	Imaginative (daring, creative)
True Friendship (close companionship)	Independent (self-reliant, self-sufficient)
Wisdom (a mature understanding of life)	Intellectual (intelligent, reflective)
A World of Beauty (beauty of nature and the arts)	Logical (consistent, rational)
Family Security (taking care of loved ones)	Loving (affectionate, tender)
Mature Love (sexual and spiritual intimacy)	Obedient (dutiful, respectful)
Self-Respect (self-esteem)	Polite (courteous, well-mannered)
A Sense of Accomplishment (lasting contribution)	Responsible (dependable, reliable)
Inner Harmony (freedom from inner conflict)	Self-Controlled (restrained, self-disciplined)

Source: Modified and reproduced by special permission of the publisher, Consulting Psychologists Press, Inc., Palo Alto, CA 94303 from *Rokeach Value Survey* by Milton Research. Copyright 1983 by Milton Rokeach. All rights reserved. Further reproduction is prohibited without the publisher's written consent.

Rokeach Value Survey: A self-administered inventory consisting of 18 terminal values (or personal goals) and 18 instrumental values (or way of reading those personal goals).

CULTURE AND MARKETING STRATEGY

Identify cultural values that affect the consumption of your product: The first task for a marketer is to identify and understand the cultural values that are relevant in the consumption of the product category that it is dealing with. Both qualitative and quantitative methods can be used. Once these are identified, marketers have to find how they affect the purchase and consumption of their products.

Make sure that your marketing mix appeals to these values: Once a marketer identifies the core values of a society, it should use this knowledge to modify its marketing mix to suit the society's values. As we saw in the opening vignette, Canadians, compared with Americans, are more inward-looking, more security-consciousness, less concerned about other people admiring the products that they own, and more concerned about the environment. This not only converts to less interest in SUVs, but perhaps also requires a different approach to the marketing of SUVs. This explains why a marketer of luxury SUVs stresses prestige to the U.S. audience but "exploring the open road to Canadians."[39] This is perhaps one of the reasons that BMW chose to change its slogan from "The Ultimate Driving Machine" in the U.S. to "The Ultimate Driving Experience" in Canada.

Examine changes in cultural values that affect the consumption of your product, and make changes to the marketing mix as necessary: The changing nature of culture means that marketers have to reconsider continually why consumers are now doing what they do, who the purchasers and the users of their products are (males only, females only, or both), when they do their shopping, how and where they can be reached by the media, and what new product and service needs are emerging. Marketers who monitor cultural changes also often find new opportunities to increase corporate profitability. For example, marketers of such products and services as life insurance, financial and investment advice, casual clothing, toy electric trains, and cigars are among those who have attempted to take advantage of shifts in what is feminine and how to communicate with female consumers.

Examine whether a culture is homogeneous or heterogeneous: Some marketers make the assumption that all people living in a country share a common culture. As can be seen from the next chapter, though the residents of a country may have common core values, there are often differences between various subcultures within a country. For example, although Canadians may be more individualistic than people living in India or Japan, there are bound to be differences among Canadians belonging to different subcultures. And in fact, people living on the Prairies are less individualistic than those living in Quebec or British Columbia.

If a culture is highly heterogeneous, modifications to the marketing mix—especially promotion—may be necessary. For example, several firms marketing in Canada tend to develop separate advertising campaigns for Quebec, not just because of the language difference, but also because of value differences between English and French Canadians.

Be aware of symbols and consumption rituals and how they affect consumers' perception of products: As we saw earlier, each culture has its own symbols and consumption rituals. These have a major influence on the consumption patterns of its members. Savvy marketers use culturally acceptable symbols to appeal to their consumers.

When Kruger Inc., purchased Scott Paper from Kimberley Clark, it got a 10-year licence to use the Cottonelle brand name, after which Kimberley Clark was free to use the name on its own products. So Scott Paper had to find another name for its popular brand of bathroom tissue. After considerable consumer research, the company came up with "Cashmere," the expensive material traditionally made out of soft wool from goats found in Tibet, the Himalayas, and Kashmir. Scott Paper's research found that to most Canadian women (especially those from the eastern part of the country, where Cottonelle was popular) "Cashmere" symbolized the "ultimate in softness.... [The name] suggested that it was indulgent and luxurious and as soft as can be."[40]

SUMMARY

- In the context of consumer behaviour, culture is defined as the sum total of learned beliefs, values, and customs that serve to regulate the consumer behaviour of members of a particular society.

- Beliefs and values are guides for consumer behaviour; customs are usual and accepted ways of behaving.

- Culture offers order, direction, and guidance to members of society in all phases of human problem solving. Culture is dynamic; it evolves gradually and continually to meet the needs of society.

- Cultural values are learned or acquired through formal teaching, informal learning, and technical learning.

- The elements of culture are transmitted by three pervasive social institutions: family, church, and school. A fourth social institution that plays a major role in the transmission of culture is the mass media, both through editorial content and through advertising.

- Children acquire from their environment a set of beliefs, values, and customs that constitutes culture

(i.e., they are encultured). Immigrants and new entrants learn a culture through acculturation.

- Culture is transmitted to members of society through a common language and commonly shared symbols.

- All the elements in the marketing mix communicate symbolically with the audience. Products project an image of their own; promotion also projects a specific image. Price and retail outlets symbolically convey images concerning the quality of the product.

- A wide range of measurement techniques is used to study culture. They include projective techniques, attitude measurement, field observation, participant observation, content analysis, and value measurement surveys.

- A number of core values of the Canadian people are relevant to the study of consumer behaviour. These include achievement and success, activity, efficiency and practicality, progress, material comfort, individualism, freedom, conformity, humanitarianism, youthfulness, and fitness and health.

DISCUSSION QUESTIONS

1. Distinguish among beliefs, values, and customs. Illustrate how the clothing a person wears at different times or for different occasions is influenced by customs.

2. Think of various routines in your everyday life (such as grooming or preparing food). Identify one ritual and describe it. In your view, is this ritual shared by others? If so, to what extent? What are the implications of your ritualistic

behaviour to the marketers of the products you use during your routine?

3. Explain five core Canadian values and provide the relevance of each for marketers.

4. Discuss three qualitative techniques that can be used to measure cultural values. Which one

would you use if you were the marketer of clothing aimed at teenagers? Why?

5. What are terminal and instrumental values? Discuss any five terminal and any five instrumental values and their relevance for marketers.

CRITICAL THINKING QUESTIONS

1. A manufacturer of fat-free granola bars is considering targeting school-age children by positioning its product as a healthful, nutritious snack food. How can an understanding of the three forms of cultural learning be used in developing an effective strategy to target the intended market?

2. McCain Foods is planning a promotional campaign to encourage the drinking of orange and grapefruit juice in situations in which many people normally drink soft drinks. Using the Rokeach Value Survey (Figure 9-8), identify relevant cultural, consumption-specific, and product-specific values for citrus juices as an alternative to soft drinks. What are the implications of these values for an advertising campaign designed to increase the consumption of citrus juices?

3. For each of the products and activities, below
   (a) Name the core values most relevant to their purchase and use.
   (b) Determine whether these values encourage or discourage use or ownership.
   (c) Determine whether these core values are shifting and, if so, in what direction.
   The products and activities are:

(i) donating money to charities, (ii) donating blood, (iii) diet soft drinks, (iv) foreign travel, (v) suntan lotion, (vi) cellular phones, (vii) fat-free foods, (viii) products in recyclable packaging.

4. (a) Summarize an episode of a weekly television series that you watched recently. Describe how the program transmitted cultural beliefs, values, and customs.
   (b) Select and describe three commercials that were broadcast during the program mentioned in 4(a). Do these commercials create or reflect cultural values? Explain your answer.

5. (a) Find two different advertisements for deodorants in two magazines that are targeted to different audiences. Content-analyse the written and pictorial aspects of each ad, using any core values discussed in this chapter. How are these values portrayed to the target audiences?
   (b) Identify symbols used in these ads and discuss their effectiveness in conveying the desired product image or characteristics.

INTERNET EXERCISES

1. Visit the website of Environics Research Group (**http://erg.environics.net**). Go to their "Press Releases" section and then to the "Cars, Canada and Culture" report (hhtttp://erg.environics.net/news/default.asp?aID=541). Find the section on Canadian versus American vehicle owners. What differences in cultural values could account for these differences? Do the

differences between the two groups fit your expectations of Canadians and Americans?

2. Visit the website of Environics Research Group (**http://erg.environics.net**) and take the online survey. What do your answers say about your own values?

3. Go to the websites of two car manufacturers and examine the different models or lines (e.g.,

trucks, minivans, cars) that they offer. What values do these lines emphasize? Are there differences between the lines by the same manufacturer and/or between the same lines (or types of products) offered by the two manufacturers?

4. Go to the websites of several Canadian companies (e.g., McCain, Tim Hortons, WestJet). What Canadian values do these websites appeal to?

KEY TERMS

Acculturation   *(p. 287)*
Consumer fieldwork   *(p. 305)*
Content analysis   *(p. 305)*
Core values   *(p. 289)*
Culture   *(p. 282)*

Enculturation   *(p. 287)*
Field observation   *(p. 305)*
Participant-observer   *(p. 305)*
Ritual   *(p. 288)*
Ritualistic behaviour   *(p. 289)*

Rokeach Value Survey   *(p. 306)*
Subculture   *(p. 289)*
Symbol   *(p. 287)*

CASE 9-1: EAT AND RUN

Recently, a number of major food marketers have developed versions of their products for Canadians "on the go." General Mills introduced Nouriche, which turns its Yoplait yogourt into a non-fat yogourt smoothie bolstered with 20 vitamins and minerals. And Campbell Soup Company has launched four different flavours of its "Soup at Hand," microwaveable containers from which the single-serving size of soup can be sipped. Still further, Hershey's offers its portable puddings in tubes, and a number of food companies now market meals specifically designed to fit into the cup holder of a car.

We might imagine that the Canadian culture is changing and that it is no longer necessary or desirable to sit down at a table for a meal or, in many cases, even to have utensils in order to eat a meal. Just put your breakfast or lunch in your car's cup holder and drive off.

QUESTION

1. Do you think the introduction of these "meals on the go" constitutes a fundamental change in Canadian core values, or does it "fit in" with the core values examined in this chapter?

Source: Stephanie Thompson, "'To Go' Becoming the Way to Go," *Advertising Age,* May 13, 2002, 73.

NOTES

1   Michael Adams, *Fire and Ice: The United States, Canada and the Myth of Converging Values* (Penguin, 2004), x; and David MacDonald and Michael Adams, "We Are What We Drive," *Marketing Magazine,* March 15, 2004, 42.

2   Michael Adams, "Fire and Ice, 50–58.

3   Ibid., 56.

4   David MacDonald and Michael Adams, "We Are What We Drive," 42.

5   Thomas C. O'Guinn and L. J. Shrum, "The Role of Television in the Construction of Consumer Reality," *Journal of Consumer Research,* 23, March 1997, 278–295.

6   Linda C. Ueltschy and Robert F. Krampf, "Cultural Sensitivity to Satisfaction and Service Quality Measures," *Journal of Marketing Theory and Practice,* Summer 2001, 14–31.

7   "U.S. Coffee Consumption Highest in Decade—Survey," *Forbes.Com,* June 14, 2002, **www.forbes.com/business/newswire/2002/06/14rtr632507.html**.

8   Tara Parker-Pope, "All That Glitters Isn't Purchased by Men," *Wall Street Journal,* January 7, 1997, B1; and Dana Canedy, "As the Purchasing Power of Women Rises, Marketers Start to Pay Attention to Them," *New York Times,* July 2, 1998, D6.

9   Michael Adams, *Fire and Ice,* 51–59.

10   Gwen Rae Bachmann, Deborah Roedder John, and Akshay Rao, "Children's Susceptibility to Peer Group Purchase Influence: An Exploratory Investigation," in *Advances in Consumer Research,* vol. 20, eds. Leigh McAlister and Michael L. Rothschild (Provo, UT: Association for Consumer Research 1993), 463–468.

11   Shaila K. Dewan, "Can't Afford Hawaii? Get the Shirt," *New York Times,* July 21, 2001, B1, B6.

12   Dennis W. Rook, "The Ritual Dimension of Consumer Behavior," *Journal of Consumer Research,* 12, December 1985, 251–264.

13   Dennis W. Rook, "Ritual Behavior and Consumer Symbolism," in *Advances in Consumer Research,* vol. 11, ed. Thomas C. Kinnear (Ann Arbor, MI: Association for Consumer Research, 1984), 279–284.

14   David C. McClelland, *The Achieving Society* (New York: Free Press, 1961), 150–151.

15   James P. Miller, "Cereal Makers Fight Bagels with Price Cuts," *Wall Street Journal,* June 20, 1996, B1.

16   Corina Cristea, "Now Everybody's a Busy Body," *Brandweek,* July 6, 1998, 18–19.

17   Peter Rojas, "Time-Out Guide," *Red Herring,* December 1999, 114.

18   Lesley Young, "New and Approved," *Marketing Magazine*, April 5–12, 2004, 10.

19   Ibid.

20   Kate Gurnett, "Life Coaches Help People Move into Winner's Circle," *Times Union,* March 3, 2002, S21.

21   William J. Havlena and Susan L. Holak, "Children's Images and Symbols of Wealth: An Exploration Using Consumer Collages," *1997 AMA Winter Educators' Conference,* eds. Debbie Thorne LeClair and Michael Hartline (Chicago: American Marketing Association, 1997), 1–2.

22   Ramesh Venkat and Harold J. Ogden, "Material Satisfaction: The Effects of Social Comparison and Attribution," in *1995 AMA Educators' Proceedings,* eds. Barbara B. Stern and George M. Zinkan (Chicago: American Marketing Association, 1995), 314–349.

23   Frank Gibney, Jr., and Belinda Luscombe, "The Redesigning of America," *Time,* June 26, 2000, unpaginated insert section.

24   Virginia Matthews, "Simplicity Is the Consumer's Choice: Marketing Product Innovation: Shoppers Complain of Confusion as Companies Blitz Them with a Host of New Products, Writes Virginia Matthews," *Financial Times* (London), December 10, 1999, 16.

25   "Casual Clothes Are Workplace Trend," *Brandweek,* July 18, 1994, 17. See also Ellen Neuborne, "Fashion on Menu at T.G.I. Friday's," *USA Today,* February 27, 1996, B1.

26   Deborah J. Webb, Corliss L. Green, and Thomas G. Brashear, "Development and Validation of Scales to Measure Attitudes Influencing Monetary Donations to Charitable Organizations," *Journal of the Academy of Marketing Science,* 28, no. 2, Spring 2000, 299–309.

27   George R. Reis, "Building Bridges," *Fund Raising Management,* 30, no. 6, August 1999, 19–23.

28   Richard A. Lee "The Youth Bias in Advertising," *American Demographics,* January 1997, 47–50.

29   "The Big Scoop on Just Desserts," *Advertising Age,* October 2, 1995, 3.

30   Sean Mehegan, "As Indulgence Roars Back with a Vengeance, Low-Fat Candies Beat a Strategic Retreat," *Brandweek,* March 2, 1998, 12.

31   Jeffrey A. Tannenbaum, "Fat-Free Store Pushes to Gain Weight in U.S.—Small New York Firm Targets Shrinking Market," *Asian Wall Street Journal,* February 14, 2001, N5; and Normita Thongtham, "You Are What You Eat," *Bangkok Post,* March 2, 2002, 1.

32   George M. Zinkhan and Penelope J. Prenshaw, "Good Life Images and Brand Name Associations: Evidence from Asia, America, and Europe," in *Advances in Consumer Research,* vol. 21, eds. Chris T. Allen and Deborah Roedder John (Provo, UT: Association for Consumer Research, 1994), 496–500.

33   This section is based on the findings from the Environics Social Values Survey reported in Michael Adams, *Fire and Ice: The United States, Canada and the Myth of Converging Values*, Penguin Canada, 2004.

34   Michael Adams, *Fire and Ice,* 14.

35   Michael Adams, *Fire and Ice,* 47–76.

36   Christian Boucher, "Canada-US Values: Distinct, Inevitably Carbon Copy, or Narcissism of Small Differences?" *Horizons,* June 2004, 42–47.

37   Michael L. Maynard and Charles R. Taylor, "Girlish Images across Cultures: Analyzing Japanese versus

U.S. *Seventeen* Magazine Ads," *Journal of Advertising,* 28, no. 1, Spring 1999, 39–45.

38 Lynn R. Kahle, ed., *Social Values and Social Change: Adaption of Life in America* (New York: Praeger, 1983); Sharon E. Beatty et al., "Alternative Measurement Approaches to Consumer Values: The List of Values and the Rokeach Value Survey," *Psychology & Marketing,* 2, 1985, 181–200; and Lynn R. Kahle, Roger P. McIntyre, Reid P. Claxton, and David B. Jones, "Empirical Relationships between Cognitive Style and LOV: Implications for Values and Value Systems," in *Advances in Consumer Research,* vol. 22, eds. Frank R. Kardes and Mita Sujan (Provo, UT: Association for Consumer Research 1995), 141–146.

39 Stan Sutter, "Vive la différence," *Marketing Magazine,* January 26, 2004, 22.

40 Keith McCarthur, "Scott Flushes Cottonelle Name," *Globe and Mail,* August 17, 2004, B7.

Coming Soon!

www.newcanadian.com

Reporter

Indus

Indus Reporter
Let the journey begin.

**Responding to your needs - that's the *raison d'être* of
NewCanadian Publishing Inc.** And from this notion comes the
foundation for our latest magazine, the Indus Reporter. Following in
the footsteps of *The NewCanadian Magazine*, Indus Reporter will focus
on the ever-growing South Asian community in North America.

Join our team of writers and journalists as they explore the
politics, culture and ethos of this very successful community.
Visually appealing and incisive, Indus Reporter will deliver key
business news, impactful editorial and thought-provoking dialogue.

You've reached your destination, now enjoy the journey.

**Another insightful magazine from
NewCanadian Publishing Inc.**

Currently interviewing
writers/contributors/journalists.   Inquire at: jobs@newcanadian.com

Looking for new ways to reach
the South Asian community in
North America?   Contact us at: advertising@newcanadian.com

CAN $4.99   U.S. $3.99

0   56800 30264   0

www.newcanadian.com

chapter 10
subcultures and consumer behaviour

LEARNING OBJECTIVES

By the end of this chapter, you should be able to:

1. Define subcultures and list the major types of subcultures.
2. Discuss the unique features of the French-Canadian subculture and two other ethnic subcultures; explain how marketers can reach French Canadians effectively.
3. Discuss at least two of the following subcultures: subcultures based on age, sex, religion, or region.
4. Discuss how marketers can tailor their marketing strategies to reach specific subcultures.

canadian firms are trying hard to reach ethnic minorities in this country. Sears recently ran a "Postcard to India" event in Toronto, with the Eaton Centre in the heart of the city becoming India central for two weeks. Several exotic Indian specialties were showcased in the mall; the centre brought in Indian folk dancers and henna artists who decorated customers' hands with Indian designs.

Want to reach the youth market in Canada? Then Street Beat, a program developed and produced by Showbiz Productions of Markham, Ontario, which offers a mix of music and marketing, may be your best bet. Street Beat tours several hundred Canadian high schools each year and puts on video dance parties for teens. The sponsors (e.g., Pepsi-Cola, Mr. Sub, Blockbuster, and Nike) get the opportunity to interact with young consumers. Grassroots programs such as Street Beat are considered to be one of the best ways to reach young Canadians.

Both of the above are examples of how marketers are attempting to reach various subcultures in Canadian society.

CHAPTER OVERVIEW

Any society comprises subgroups or subcultures which share common values and beliefs. These subcultures provide important marketing opportunities for marketers. This chapter will examine the major subcultures in Canadian society. First, we will examine the French-Canadian culture—one of the founding groups of the country we have come to know as Canada. Then we will examine religious, regional, and ethnic groups within the Canadian mosaic. We will continue on to age- and gender-based subcultures and conclude the chapter with the implications of subcultures for marketers.

WHAT IS A SUBCULTURE?

Subculture:
A distinct cultural group that exists as an identifiable segment within a larger, more complex society.

The members of a specific **subculture** possess beliefs, values, and customs that set them apart from other members of the same society. In addition, they adhere to most of the dominant cultural beliefs, values, and behavioural patterns of the larger society. We define subculture, then, as *a distinct cultural group that exists as an identifiable segment within a larger, more complex society.*

Thus, the cultural profile of a society or nation is a composite of two distinct elements: (1) the unique beliefs, values, and customs subscribed to by members of specific subcultures; and (2) the central or core cultural themes that are shared by most of the population, regardless of what specific subcultures they belong to. Figure 10-1 presents a simple model of the relationship between two subcultural groups—French Canadians and English Canadians—and the larger culture. As the figure shows, each subculture has its own unique traits, and yet both groups share the dominant traits of the overall Canadian culture.

Let us look at it in another way: each Canadian is, in large part, a product of the "Canadian way of life." Each Canadian, however, is at the same time a member of various subcultures. An 11-year-old boy, for example, may simultaneously be a French Canadian, a Catholic, a preteen, and a Quebecker. We would expect that membership in each different subculture would provide its own set of specific beliefs, values, attitudes, and customs. Figure 10-2 lists typical subcultural categories and corresponding examples of specific subcultural groups. This list is by no means exhaustive: elementary school teachers, Liberals, Girl Guides, and millionaires—in fact, any group that shares common beliefs and customs—may be classified as a subculture.

Subcultural analysis enables the marketing manager to concentrate on sizeable and natural market segments. When carrying out such analyses, the marketer must determine whether the beliefs, values, and customs shared by members of a specific subgroup make them desirable candidates for special marketing attention. Subcultures, therefore, are relevant units of analysis for market research. And these subcultures are dynamic—the different ethnic groups that make up the Canadian population have been changing, and they will continue to change in size and economic power in the coming years. For instance, the total South-Asian population of Canada was 7000 in 1961, but by 2001 it had jumped to 917 075.[1]

FIGURE 10-1   Relationship between Culture and Subculture

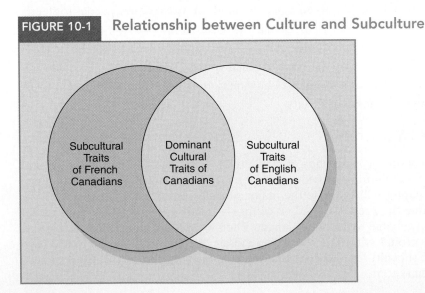

FIGURE 10-2	Major Subcultural Categories with Examples

Ethnic Origin: English, French, Aboriginal, Chinese, South-Asian, Greek, German, Irish
Religion: Protestant, Catholic, Muslim, Hindu
Geographic region: Atlantic Canadian, Western Canadian, Québécois
Race: Chinese, Caucasian, African
Age: Senior citizen, teenager, Xer
Gender: Female, male
Occupation: Bus driver, mechanic, engineer
Social class: Lower, middle, upper

The following sections examine a number of important subcultural categories: ethnicity, religion, geographic location, age, and sex. (Occupational and social-class subgroups are discussed in detail in Chapter 11.) Before we deal with the subcultures, it is important to remember that all consumers are simultaneously members of more than one subcultural segment (e.g., a consumer may be a young, Chinese-Canadian, Catholic homemaker living in Vancouver), and hence there would be considerable **subcultural interaction**. For this reason, marketers should strive to understand how multiple *subcultural* memberships *interact* to influence target consumers' consumption behaviour. Promotional strategy should not be limited to targeting a single subcultural membership.

Subcultural interaction: The interaction among the various subcultural memberships of consumers and its impact on their behaviour.

RACIO-ETHNIC SUBCULTURES

Whereas race refers to the genetically imparted physiognomical features of a person, especially colour of skin, ethnicity is a broader concept that includes race, origin or ancestry, identity, language, and religion.[2] Both race and ethnicity are dynamic concepts, as inter-racial marriage leads to racial blending and new identities being formed over a period. The subcultures that we are discussing are a combination of racial and ethnic groups, and hence they are called **racio-ethnic subcultures.**

For many people, ethnicity is an important subcultural reference that guides what they value and what they buy. This is especially true for the population of a country like Canada that has a history of attracting people from all over the globe—see Figure 10-3. (Interestingly enough, more than six million people—or 22.76 percent of the population—classified themselves as just "Canadian" rather than placing themselves in any ethnic category.) Supporting this pattern are the results of the 2001 census, which found that about one in five Canadians is foreign-born.[3] For these Canadians, as well as for Canadians born in Canada, there is frequently a strong sense of identification with and pride in the language and customs of their ancestors.

When it comes to consumer behaviour, this ancestral pride is manifested most strongly in the consumption of ethnic foods, in travel to the "old country," and in the purchase of numerous cultural artifacts (ethnic clothing, art, music, and foreign-language newspapers). Interest in these goods and services has expanded rapidly as younger Canadians attempt to understand their ethnic roots better and associate themselves more closely with those roots. We shall discuss four different ethnic subcultures in the following pages: French Canadians and the three largest visible-minority groups—Chinese Canadians, South Asians, and blacks.

Racio-ethnic subcultures: Subcultures based on race (genetically imparted physiognomical features such as colour of skin) and/or ethnicity (which includes race, origin or ancestry, language, and religion).

www12.statcan.ca/english/census01/home/index.cfm

French Canadians

According to Statistics Canada,[4] in 2001, there were 4 668 410 French Canadians, and they constituted 15.75 percent of the Canadian population. Although nearly

FIGURE 10-3	Ethnic Groups as a Percentage of the Canadian Population, 2001		
	TOTAL RESPONSES	**SINGLE RESPONSES**	**MULTIPLE RESPONSES**
Total population	29 639 035	18 307 545	11 331 490
Ethnic origin[a, b]			
Canadian	11 682 680	6 748 135	4 934 545
English	5 978 875	1 479 525	4 499 355
French	4 668 410	1 060 760	3 607 655
Scottish	4 157 210	607 235	3 549 975
Irish	3 822 660	496 865	3 325 795
German	2 742 765	705 600	2 037 170
Italian	1 270 370	726 275	544 090
Chinese	1 094 700	936 210	158 490
Ukrainian	1 071 060	326 195	744 860
North American Indian	1 000 890	455 805	545 085
Dutch (Netherlands)	923 310	316 220	607 090
Polish	817 085	260 415	556 665
East Indian	713 330	581 665	131 665
Norwegian	363 760	47 230	316 530
Portuguese	357 690	252 835	104 855
Welsh	350 365	28 445	321 920
Jewish	348 605	186 475	162 130
Russian	337 960	70 895	267 070
Filipino	327 550	266 140	61 405
Métis	307 845	72 210	235 635
Swedish	282 760	30 440	252 325
Hungarian (Magyar)	267 255	91 800	175 455
American (USA)	250 005	25 205	224 805
Greek	215 105	143 785	71 325
Spanish	213 105	66 545	146 555
Jamaican	211 720	138 180	73 545
Danish	170 780	33 795	136 985
Vietnamese	151 410	119 120	32 290

[a] Blacks are not included in this table because it is concerned with ethnicity (based on ancestry) rather than race. Statistics Canada figures indicate that there were more than 622 000 blacks in Canada in 2001, which makes them the third-largest visible-minority group in Canada. (Statistics Canada, "Blacks in Canada: A Long History," Spring 2004, p. 2–7., Catalogue No. 11-008.)
[b] Respondents were allowed to choose more than one category.

Source: Adapted from the Statistics Canada website: http://www.statcan.ca/english/Pgdb/demo53c.htm, http://www.statcan.ca/english/Pgdb/demo11a.htm. and http://www.statcan.ca/english/Pgdb/demo50a.htm.

half (2 111 570) of all Canadians of French origin live in Quebec, nearly a third live in Ontario; significant French populations also exist in New Brunswick (the Acadians) and Nova Scotia.

Although 2.9 million of Québécois (or 41 percent) are bilingual, nearly 54 percent speak only French. In spite of years of instruction in the other official language in school, only 17.7 percent of Canadians consider themselves to be fluent in both languages. Almost all (97 percent) of the Canadians who speak only French live in Quebec. Given that more than 6.7 million Quebeckers can speak French, communicating in French and in French-language media is extremely important for marketers.

Research shows that the values of French Canadians are different from those of English Canadians.[5] It has been suggested that French Canadians are more individualistic, liberal, and sensate than their English counterparts. Researchers studying Canadian values have found that Quebeckers are the most idealistic and autonomy-seeking of all Canadians. Perhaps because of their sensuousness, French Canadians are considered to have a higher appreciation of aesthetics and to be more fashion-conscious and hedonistic than are English Canadians. A recent Ipsos-Reid poll showed that French Canadians differ from other Canadians in the way they look at occupational success and related issues. Whereas 30 percent of Canadians rated "work-life balance" as a crucial measure of success, a significantly higher proportion (38 percent) of Quebeckers felt that way. And whereas 31 percent of Ontarians and 25 percent of Canadians in general thought a person's salary was a key measure of occupational success, only 20 percent of Quebeckers thought it was. Quebeckers are more willing than others to slow down their career plans to enjoy more free time, and they would accept a wage cut in exchange for a four-day work week.[6]

Some researchers, however, think that differences between English and French Canadians often disappear when other demographic factors, that is, income, social class, and education, are controlled for. For example, one study of differences between the values of French- and English-Canadian youth found that they differed on only two values—French Canadians valued being respected more than English Canadians did but placed less value on intellectual and cultural activities. However, research indicates that there are some differences between English and French Canadians in their consumption behaviour.

One area in which English and French Canadians differ significantly is their attitudes toward food. People living in Quebec (40 percent) and are more likely to mention a concern about the quality of food than are those from other provinces and territories, and this seems to be reflected in their daily food habits. French Canadians are more likely than others to cook all their main meals from scratch (32 percent compared with 27 percent for the rest of Canada). They are less likely to eat reheated refrigerated food (30 percent versus 41 percent) and are more likely to be actively trying to eat organic food than others in the country (42 percent versus 37 percent). French Canadians are less likely than others to be trying to maintain their weight (9 percent versus 14 percent), but nearly 33 percent admitted to having been on a diet in the past year, well above the national average of 28 percent.[7]

French Canadians are more likely than others to have breakfast every day (74 percent versus 60 percent). Interestingly enough, 79 percent of Quebeckers, as opposed to only 20 percent for all of Canada, would rather start the day with a good breakfast than with a romantic encounter! The differences in food habits also extend to the realm of beverages—French Canadians drink more coffee but less tea than others. Tea accounts for only 18 percent of hot beverages drunk in Quebec, and when Quebeckers do drink tea, the type most often preferred is not black tea (as in the rest of Canada). Quebeckers are also the most likely to agree with the statements "wine is good for your heart" (83 percent) and "liquor or distilled spirits is good for your heart" (37 percent). Quebeckers are also the most likely to have had at least one alcoholic beverage in the past month (68 percent compared with 55 percent for Atlantic Canadians).

There are also differences in attitudes toward healthy eating and exercising. Only 53 percent of Quebeckers had heard of "good carbs" and "bad carbs" (the national figure was 72 percent), and nearly 48 percent of Quebeckers admitted to taking 1000 or fewer steps each day (nearly 37 percent of Quebeckers could not estimate how many steps they took each day). Interestingly enough, in spite of their positive feelings for wine and distilled liquors, Quebeckers are the least likely group to have an accurate estimate of the calories in these drinks.

Similar differences have been found in several product categories. For example, Quebeckers are the most likely to read non-fiction books in the summer (52 percent versus 44 percent for the nation as a whole); they are also the most likely to start reading another book before finishing the first. Although several such differences exist, it is impossible to list all of them. Moreover, most studies only find differences between French Canadians and other groups but fail to discover why these differences exist. So although it is important for marketers to understand what the differences are (especially in their product category), it is less useful for us to look at such differences in detail. What is perhaps more interesting to a student of consumer behaviour is differences between French and English Canadians in media usage, attitudes toward advertising, and other related issues. We will examine these issues next.

Media Usage

The media habits of francophone Quebeckers are different from those of their anglophone neighbours.[8] They are more likely to turn to French magazines, newspapers, radio, and television for information and entertainment, and most of the programs they watch and listen to are produced locally. So, unlike their English-Canadian counterparts, they are less influenced by U.S. television. For example, whereas nine of the top ten shows watched by Ontarians are made in the United States, nine of the top ten shows watched by Quebeckers are written and produced in Quebec. The following are some other interesting facts about the media consumption patterns in Quebec:[9]

- Three French-language stations capture 75 percent of the market in Quebec.
- When French-language specialty channels are included, this percentage goes up to 85 percent.
- Top television shows in Quebec capture a significantly higher percentage of the market (more than 30 percent) than do top shows in other parts of Canada (20 percent).
- Twenty-seven of the top 30 television shows in Quebec are produced in the province.
- Quebeckers watch more television than do other Canadians—nearly 32 hours a week, compared with 29 hours for the rest of Canada.
- Quebeckers read more community newspapers than do other Canadians.
- The number of magazine readers is increasing in Quebec while it is dropping in the rest of the country.
- Sponsorship is a more important part of the promotional mix in Quebec than in other parts of Canada.
- Young Quebeckers listen to radio less than their English counterparts do (9.46 hours a week compared with 11.02 hours for the rest of Canada).

What does all of this mean to marketers interested in reaching Quebeckers? These are some implications:

- Use television advertising when possible since television is a popular medium in the province.
- Buy local advertising—most Quebeckers are watching television shows made in the province; this is also the case with other media (e.g., newspapers, magazines), so buying local media advertising is the best strategy for reaching Quebeckers.
- Appeal to Quebeckers' ethnic pride.
- Do not just translate ads; developing ads made for Quebec is a good strategy.

Chinese Canadians

Chinese Canadians are the largest visible minority group in Canada. According to Statistics Canada, there are more than one million people of Chinese descent in Canada and they make up 3.7 percent of the total Canadian population. Chinese is the third-most-spoken language in Canada, with more than 800 000 people giving it as their mother tongue in the 2001 census.

When discussing Chinese Canadians, it is important to remember that this is a diverse group made up of people from China, Taiwan, and Hong Kong. A variety of languages are spoken by this group: Mandarin and Cantonese Chinese are the most common. These are some features of the Chinese-Canadian population:[10]

- Chinese Canadians are concentrated in five cities: Toronto, Vancouver, Montreal, Calgary, and Edmonton.

- Toronto has the largest Chinese population (409 530). Vancouver is second with 342 665; however, Vancouver has a higher percentage of Chinese Canadians than Toronto (17.2 percent versus 8.7 percent). There were 51 850 Chinese Canadians in Calgary in 2001, where they made up 5.4 percent of the city's population. Montreal, with 52 110 Chinese Canadians (1.5 percent of the population), and Edmonton, with 41 285 (4.4 percent of the population), are the other cities with a large number of Chinese Canadians.

- Even in these cities, Chinese Canadians are concentrated in some areas. Figure 10-4 provides details of the geographic concentration of Chinese Canadians in Toronto and Vancouver.

- Sixty-eight percent of Chinese Canadians gave Cantonese as their mother tongue; 32 percent gave Mandarin as their mother tongue.

- Chinese Canadians are more likely than other minority groups to speak their mother tongue at home; 67 percent said their home language is Chinese.

- Like several other immigrant populations, Chinese Canadians are a young group; nearly 19 percent are under 15 years of age, 15.3 percent are in the 15–24 age category, and 14.7 percent are in the 25–34 age category compared with the total Canadian figures of 18.3 percent, 13.6 percent, and 13.7 percent, respectively.

FIGURE 10-4   Geographic Distribution of Chinese Canadians in Toronto and Vancouver

AREA	POPULATION	PERCENTAGE OF CITY'S POPULATION
Toronto Metropolitan Area (total)	**409 535**	**8.7%**
Markham	62 355	30
City of Toronto	259 710	10.6
Old City of Toronto	64 290	9.6
Mississauga	35 955	5.9
Vancouver Metropolitan Area (total)	**342 665**	**17.2**
Burnaby	50 135	26.2
Richmond	64 270	39.3
Vancouver	161 110	29.9

Source: Adapted from the Statistics Canada website: http://www.statcan.ca/english/Pgdb/demo53c.htm, http://www.statcan.ca/english/Pgdb/demo11a.htm, and http://www.statcan.ca/english/Pgdb/demo50a.htm.

Chinese Canadians are more likely than any other ethnic group to buy high-status, luxury brands in order to "show off, to astonish others, to stand out from others"[11] says one researcher (see Figure 10-5).They like displaying their wealth, and this may be one reason why they buy expensive brands. Ownership of expensive brands is also seen as a way of gaining respect from other members of the group. As can be seen from Figure 10-5, Chinese Canadians are above-average users of the internet, cell phones, and home computers. Their buying power is significant; in the Toronto market alone, Chinese Canadians spent more than $12.2 billion in 2003.[12]

South Asians

South Asians (people from India, Pakistan, Bangladesh, and Sri Lanka) are the second-largest visible-minority group in Canada. According to the 2001 census, there are nearly one million people of South Asian origin in Canada and they constitute nearly 3 percent of the Canadian population.

As in the case of Chinese Canadians, there are significant differences among South Asians, differences based on language, religion, and country of origin. Although most immigrants from India are Hindus, there are also other religious groups, in particular, Sikhs, Jains, and Muslims. Immigrants from Pakistan and Bangladesh are likely to be Muslims. Another element in the differences among subgroups is the different languages spoken by South Asians. Though most of the immigrants from India speak Punjabi or Gujarati, many speak other languages, such as Hindi, Tamil, and Bengali. Similarly, although some of the Sri Lankan immigrants speak Tamil, others speak Singhalese. Such differences in language, religion, and other factors make it difficult to generalize about this subculture. However, here are some interesting facts:

- There are more than 850 000 people of South Asian descent in Canada.

- Of these, 713 330 (2.47 percent of the Canadian population) are from India; nearly 50 000 are from Pakistan and Sri Lanka.

- Punjabi is the sixth-most-spoken language in Canada.

- South Asians are concentrated in Vancouver and Toronto. Toronto is home to nearly 50 percent (or 345 000) of Indo-Canadians and nearly 90 percent of Pakistanis and Sri Lankans. Vancouver has the next-highest Indo-Canadian pop-

FIGURE 10-5   Chinese Canadians and Product Ownership

PRODUCT	CHINESE CANADIANS IN TORONTO OWNING THE PRODUCT OR SERVICE (%)	OTHER CANADIANS OWNING THE PRODUCT OR SERVICE (%)
Car	91	64
House	77	65
Cell phone	86	48
Home computer	92	60
Internet access at home	79	50
High-speed/ADSL access	18	9
Cable access	55	12
Luxury brands (e.g., Gucci)	63	17

Source: Courtesy of Marketing Magazine.

ulation—about 142 000. Calgary, Edmonton, and Montreal also have sizeable Indo-Canadian populations.

- In Toronto, spending by South Asians—nearly $12.6 billion annually—exceeds spending by Chinese.

- South Asians, like the Chinese, are brand-conscious.

- South Asians spend a large amount of their income on food and recreation.

- Since bargaining is common in their native countries, South Asians like to shop around for the best price and to get a "deal."

Research in the U.S. has found that the use of Asian-American models in advertising is effective in reaching this market segment. Responses to an ad for stereo speakers featuring an Asian model were significantly more positive than responses to the same ad using a Caucasian model.[13] Additionally, the percentage of Asian Americans who prefer advertisements that are not in the English language varies among different Asian American groups. Exhibit 10-1 shows an ad targeting South-Asian Canadians.

EXHIBIT 10-1

TARGETING SOUTH-ASIAN CANADIANS

Courtesy of *The NewCanadian*.

Blacks or African Canadians

Unlike other visible minority groups, blacks have a long history in Canada. The first black person to arrive in Canada came in 1605—more than 400 years ago. In 1901, the black population of Canada was about 17 000; however, unlike the Chinese and Indo-Canadian populations, the black population did not grow until the late 1900s. In fact, even in 1971, the black population of Canada was only 34 000. Between 1980 and 2000, it grew exponentially, and it almost doubled between 1981 and 1991. By 2001, there were 662 000 blacks in Canada, making them the third-largest visible minority group in the country.[14]

Like the Chinese and South-Asian subcultures, blacks in Canada are a diverse group. In 1961, most of the blacks in Canada (72 percent) were from the Caribbean. In 2001, this percentage had dropped to 48 percent, and nearly the same proportion came from Africa. Here are some other interesting facts about blacks in Canada:

- Forty-seven percent of the blacks in Canada live in Toronto.

- Blacks account for 7 percent of Toronto's population—the highest concentration in any Census Metropolitan Area.

- Montreal has the next-highest concentration of blacks in Canada—nearly 140 000.

- Edmonton, Calgary, Hamilton, Halifax, and Ottawa have significant black populations (all 13 000 to 15 000). Halifax has been home to thousands of blacks for nearly three centuries. Ninety percent of blacks living in Halifax were born in Canada.

- Forty-six percent of black children under 14 live in single-parent families (that compares with 18 percent for all of Canada.

■ Although Canadian-born blacks are as likely to go to university as other Canadian-born groups, that is not true of recent immigrants.

■ The average salary of Canadian and foreign-born blacks is lower than that of other Canadian or foreign-born populations.

Blacks, as a group, have not been researched sufficiently. Part of the reason may be the relatively small number of blacks in Canada (where they make up only 2 percent of the population, compared with 13 percent in the United States) and their low level of economic power. Research shows that blacks are more likely to shop at stores that have black employees than at those that do not.

Besides race and ethnicity, there are several other variables that bind members of a subgroup together. These are religion, region, age, and sex. The next section discusses these subcultures.

OTHER MAJOR SUBCULTURES

There are several variables that can be used to group people into subcultures, but some are considered more important than others. In this section, we will look at subcultures that are based on religion, region, sex, and age. It is important to remember that other variables can also be used to define a subculture; in fact, social class is one such variable and we will devote an entire chapter to that (Chapter 11).

Religious Subcultures

Religious subcultures: People who are followers of a particular religion (e.g., Christianity, Judaism, Islam, Hinduism).

Canada is home to several **religious subcultures**.[15] Although Catholics are still the largest religious group in Canada (12.8 million, or 43 percent in 2001), there are a significant number of Protestants (8.7 million, or 35 percent). The number of Catholics has grown by 4 percent since 1991 primarily because of immigration, while the proportion of Protestants has declined by nearly 8 percent. Protestants are the dominant group in western Canada; Catholics are the largest religious group in Quebec and the Atlantic provinces. Ontario has almost equal numbers of Catholics and Protestants. New Brunswick and Quebec are the only provinces in which Catholics form the majority of the population. In British Columbia the largest group consists of people with no religion. Overall, 16 percent of Canadians did not identify with any religious group.

Although Canada is still a Christian nation, the 2001 census shows that the number of Canadians belonging to other religions is growing significantly. In fact, the religions showing the greatest increase in numbers since 1991 are Islam (129 percent), Hinduism (89 percent), Sikhism (89 percent), and small Christian denominations (121 percent). Although none of these groups accounts for more than 1.5 percent of the Canadian population, their influence is felt in cities like Toronto, Vancouver, and Montreal. The members of all these religious groups at times are likely to make purchase decisions that are influenced by their religious identity. Commonly, consumer behaviour is directly affected by religion in relation to products that are *symbolically* and *ritualistically* associated with the celebration of various religious holidays.

Religious requirements or practices sometimes take on an expanded meaning beyond their original purpose. For instance, dietary laws for an observant Jewish family represent an obligation, so there are toothpastes and artificial sweeteners that are kosher. A variety of symbols, such as COR, U, or MK, on food packaging signify that the food conforms to the Jewish dietary laws. For non-observant Jews and an increasing number of non-Jews, however, these marks often signify that the food is pure and wholesome—a kind of "Jewish *Good Housekeeping* Seal of Approval." In response to the broader meaning given to kosher-certified products,

RESEARCH INSIGHT 10-1
REACHING THE ETHNIC CONSUMER

As noted earlier, a significant proportion of the Canadian population is composed of visible minorities, and as a senior marketing executive notes, the sales growth in retailing is going to come from ethnic groups.[a] What makes marketing to ethnic groups even more important is the fact that in large urban markets like Toronto, Vancouver, and Montreal, ethnic groups are an even more significant presence. For example, of the approximately one million Canadians of Chinese origin in the country, 40 percent are in the greater Toronto area and another 34 percent are in the greater Vancouver area. Even within these cities, ethnic groups tend to be concentrated in certain neighbourhoods.[b] For example, whereas Chinese Canadians account for 20 percent of the total population of Vancouver, in Richmond, BC, 39 percent of the population is of Chinese origin. The retail potential of these ethnic subgroups is great. Nearly $42.3 billion of a total consumer retail spending of $316 billion (or 13.4 percent) is accounted for by visible minorities, and this proportion is even greater in large, metropolitan areas like Toronto and Vancouver.

How then can a marketer reach and research these groups? Here are some suggestions:

1. *Use ethnic media to reach and research visible minority consumers:* A significant proportion of immigrants from Asia and Africa speak their mother tongue at home and are loyal to ethnic media. For example, whereas only 15 percent of Italian Canadians speak their mother tongue at home, nearly 85 percent of Chinese Canadians do so. This is probably because the majority of Chinese Canadians are recent arrivals. There are several ethnic media in Canada today. Fairchild TV broadcasts Chinese-language television programs; *India Abroad*—a magazine aimed at Indo-Canadians—and several other publications serve the Indo-Canadian market. Vision TV, which markets itself as "Canada's multi-faith and multicultural broadcaster," broadcasts programs aimed at a variety of religious and ethnic minorities.

2. *Use ethnic associations and groups to reach visible minorities:* Cultural associations play a major role in helping visible minorities both to maintain their cultural identities and to become acculturated. As noted by a researcher, new Canadians tend to be loyal to their cultural roots because their ethnic identity is an important part of their self-concept.[c] For example, Kumkum Ramchandani says, "Cultural associations play a very big role in South Asian society.... These associations are a gathering place during religious festivals and ... keep traditions alive by offering religious classes and language training for children and adults."[d] An easy way for marketers to reach ethnic Canadians is to support the events run by these organizations, such as Chinese New Year celebrations or Indo-Canadian festivals like Diwali.

3. *Do not assume that all members of an ethnic group are the same:* A common misconception is that all members of an ethnic subgroup are basically the same, a misconception that leads to promotional campaigns that disregard subgroup variations. Take, for example, the South-Asian group in Canada, which consists mainly of people from India, Pakistan, and Sri Lanka. Although there are strong underlying similarities among these groups, there are also significant differences in language, religion, time of arrival in Canada, and cultural values.

    Indo-Canadians do not all speak the same language, for India is a country of many languages. Hence, to appeal to the Indo-Canadian community may require the use of more than one Indian language (e.g., Hindi, Punjabi or Gujarati) and/or English, since English is commonly spoken in India by the middle class. Thus, although Canadian Tire promotes its products in Mandarin and Cantonese to reach the Chinese-Canadian market, its ads to reach the Indo-Canadian market are in English.

4. *Go beyond the demographics:* As Sue MacGregor points out, although demographics are a good beginning, "demographics do not capture the social factors that affect people's buying patterns."[e] Although this is true of any group, it is particularly relevant in the case of ethnic minorities, and

most marketers are not familiar with the underlying values and motivations of these consumers. For example, although both Chinese Canadians and Indo-Canadians value ownership of luxury brands, their shopping patterns vary. Indo-Canadians are more likely to shop around to find the best price. And "Chinese-Canadians are more likely to display their wealth in the form of luxury brands to show their economic advancement."[f]

[a] Chris Daniels, "Shopping Mosaic," *Marketing Magazine*, May 17–24, 2004, 13–15.

[b] The figures on Chinese Canadians in this Research Insight are from Fairchild TV (**www.fairchildtv.com**).

[c] Sue MacGregor, "The New Canadian Consumer", p. 2, **http://www.cadillacfairview.com/CLIENT/CADILLAC/CF_UW_V500_MainEngine.nsf/resources/Retail+Newsletters/$file/CF+Space+Apr04Eng.pdf**.

[d] Kumkum Ramchandani, "Indian Origins," *The NewCanadian Magazine*, Summer 2004, 8–13.

[e] Sue MacGregor, "The New Canadian Consumer," 2, **http://www.cadillacfairview.com/CLIENT/CADILLAC/CF_UW_V500_MainEngine.nsf/resources/Retail+Newsletters/$file/CF+Space+Apr04Eng.pdf**.

[f] Quoted in Chris Daniels, "Shopping Mosaic," *Marketing Magazine*, May 17–24, 2004, 13–15.

a number of national brands have secured kosher certification for their products. Indeed, most kosher food in North America is eaten by non-Jews.[16] Exhibit 10-2 shows an ad for Hellmann's Real Mayonnaise. Note that the label displays a U inside a circle and the word *parve*. This tells the shopper that the product is kosher and that it can be eaten with either meat or dairy products (but not both).

Geographic and Regional Subcultures

Regional subcultures: Groups that identify with the regional or geographical areas in which they live.

Canada is a large country with a range of climatic and geographic conditions that give rise to **regional subcultures**. Given the country's size and physical diversity, it is only natural that many Canadians have a sense of regional identification and use this identification as a way of describing others (such as "he is a true Newfoundlander"). These labels often help us form a mental picture and supporting stereotype of the person in question.

Research shows that there are regional differences in values across Canada, though these differences are far less pronounced that those found in the United States. According to Michael Adams,[17] all of the 10 Canadian provinces (or seven regions) fall into the same values quandrant (Idealism and Autonomy), whereas the nine regions in the United States are divided among the four quadrants (Figure 10-6). However, there are some differences among the various Canadian provinces:

- Quebec is the most postmodern of all Canadian provinces. Of course, the differences between Quebec and the other regions are probably due more to differences in ethnicity than to regions.

- British Columbia's geographical position reflects the way of life and the relaxed attitude of its people. Residents of this province are known for being health-conscious and nature-loving; that probably explains why they score higher on statements that measure "effort toward health and spiritual quest," "importance of spontaneity," "discriminating consumerism," "ethical consumerism," and "skepticism of advertising."

- Ontario falls in the centre of the Canadian values map-space, with its residents scoring more or less the Canadian average on most statements.

- Atlantic Canadians and residents of the Prairie provinces are slightly more traditional than other Canadians. They are more respectful of authority and are more likely to go to church. The values in these regions resemble those of the small towns and small cities that are common in these areas—"social intimacy," "civic engagement," and "everyday ethics."

- Interestingly, there is a strong egalitarian bent among Atlantic Canadians; they score higher on "gender parity," "hierarchy," and "rejection of order."

- People from the Prairies and Alberta have above-average belief in the "traditional family," "traditional gender identity," and "duty."

Anyone who has travelled across Canada has probably noted many regional differences in consumption behaviour, especially when it comes to food and drink. For example, a *mug* of black coffee typifies the west, while a *cup* of coffee with milk and sugar is preferred in the east. There also are geographic differences in the consumption of a staple food such as bread.

Consumer research studies document regional differences in consumption patterns and attitudes toward consumption. Figure 10-7 illustrates some regional differences in food consumption and related factors. There are also regional differences in consumer spending patterns in other areas. In general, large metropolitan areas, with a substantial number of affluent middle-aged households, dominate many, but not all, consumer-spending categories. Two examples are the metropolitan Toronto and Montreal areas, which lead in apparel purchasing. Regional differences also exist with respect to entertainment and electronic products. For example, satellite dishes are more popular in Saskatchewan (35 percent of the homes have one) and lowest in British Columbia (15 percent). BC residents are below-average television viewers (20 hours a week), compared with other Canadians (nearly 24 hours a week).

EXHIBIT 10-2

AD FOR A PRODUCT CONTAINING A "U" ON THE LABEL SIGNIFYING THAT THE FOOD IS KOSHER

Reprinted with the permission of Unilever Bestfoods. All rights reserved.

Age Subcultures

It's not difficult to understand why each major age group of the population might be thought of as a separate subculture. After all, don't you listen to different music than your parents and grandparents do, dress differently, read different magazines, and enjoy different television shows? Clearly, important shifts occur in an individual's demand for specific types of products and services as he or she goes from being a dependent child to a retired senior citizen. In this chapter, we will limit our examination of **age subcultures** to four age groups: Generation Y, Generation X, baby boomers, and seniors. These four age segments have been singled out because their distinctive life styles qualify them for consideration as subcultural groups.

Age subculture:
Age subgroup of the population.

The Generation Y Market

The **Generation Y** age cohort (a cohort is a group of individuals born over a relatively short and continuous period of time) includes the approximately 6.9 million Canadians born between the years 1977 and 1994 (i.e., the children of baby

Generation Y:
People born between the years 1977 and 1994.

FIGURE 10-6   The Regions of North America on the Socio-cultural Map

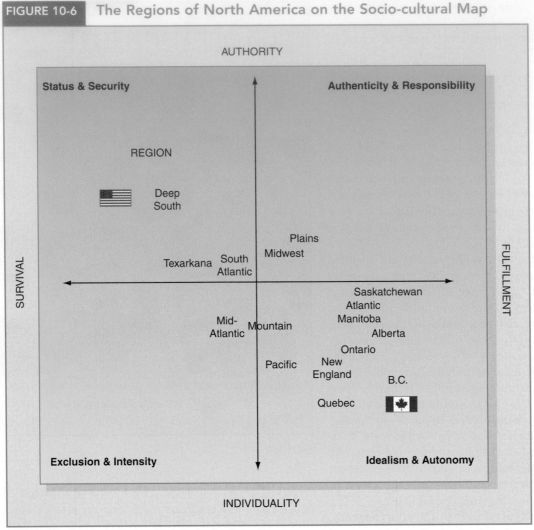

Source: From *Fire and Ice* by Michael Adams. Copyright © Michael Adams, 2003. Reprinted by permission of Penguin Group (Canada).

boomers). Members of Generation Y (also known as "echo boomers" and the "millennium generation") can be divided into three sub-segments: Gen Y adults (age 19–24), Gen Y teens (age 13–18), and Gen Y kids, or "tweens" (age 8–12).[18]

Members of Generation Y are often described as pragmatic, savvy, socially and environmentally aware, and open to new experiences.

Appealing to Generation Y   The teen segment of Generation Y has considerable buying power on their own and also influences purchases by their parents. They have grown up in a media-saturated environment and tend to be aware of "marketing hype." For example, they would tend to understand immediately that when a shopping centre locates popular teen stores at opposite ends of the mall, teens are being encouraged "to walk the mall."[19]

This age cohort has shifted some of its television viewing time to the internet, and, when compared with their parents, they are less likely to read newspapers and often do not trust the stores where their parents shop.[20] Smart retailers have found it profitable to develop websites specifically targeted to the interests of the Gen Y con-

FIGURE 10-7	Regional Variations Food Consumption and Related Issues

FOOD CONSUMPTION OR CONSUMPTION-RELATED ISSUE	PROVINCE OR REGION SCORING HIGHEST	PROVINCE SCORING LOWEST	CANADA
Made their main meal from scratch during the past seven days every day.[a]	Quebec and Atlantic Canada (32%)	Saskatchewan/Manitoba (16%)	27%
Used a frozen meal in the past 7 days at least once.[b]	Saskatchewan/Manitoba (22%)	Atlantic Canada (10%)	17%
Feel they eat a well-balanced and healthy diet.[c]	British Columbia (32%)	Alberta (18%)	26%
Agree they take vitamin supplements regularly.[d]	British Columbia (62%)	Atlantic Canada (37%)	52%
Have not eaten in a restaurant and had a fast food meal in the past seven days.[e]	British Columbia (72%)	Alberta and Quebec (52%)	56%
Agree that moderate drinking of alcohol is good for your health.[f]	Atlantic Canada (64%)	Alberta (51%)	58%
Agree that moderate consumption of wine is good for your health.[g]	British Columbia (84%)	Atlantic Canada (76%)	80%
Agree that moderate consumption of liquor/distilled spirits is good for you.[h]	Quebec (38%)	Alberta (22%)	31%
Have heard about "good carbs" and "bad carbs."[i]	Alberta (83%)	Quebec (52%)	72%
Consider themselves regular tea drinkers.[j]	Atlantic Canada (21%)	Quebec (9%)	15%
Eat breakfast every day.[k]	Quebec (74%)	Saskatchewan/Manitoba (52%)	60%
Prefer a complete hot breakfast to a romantic encounter to start off the day.[l]	Quebec (79%)	Alberta and Atlantic Canada (51%)	61%
Take more than 1000 steps on an average day.[m]	Saskatchewan/Manitoba and Atlantic Canada (57%)	Quebec (32%)	46%

Sources: Data compiled from the following polls conducted by Ipsos-Reid; please visit **www.ipsos.ca** for full tabular results. Courtesy of Ipsos-Reid.

[a-e] "So, What Foods Are Canadians Eating and How Healthy Do They Think They Are Eating? A Profile of Canada's Eating and Food Purchasing Habits," July 10, 2002.
[f-h] "Boomers, Beer, and a Healthy Lifestyle," December 1, 2003.
[i] "Canadians Aware of 'Good' and 'Bad' Carbohydrates but Do Not Really Understand Them," March 10, 2004.
[j] "Canadians and Tea: 'Good for Your Health' Is an Important Benefit for Drinking Tea for Just Under Half of Canadians (41%)," March 4, 2004.
[k-l] "Six in Ten Canadians (60%) Report Eating Breakfast Everyday," June 4, 2003.
[m] "Canadians Need to Get Moving," Januray 8, 2004.

www.limitedtoo.com

www.goravegirl.com

www.abercrombiekids.com

sumer. For example, Limited Too, Rave Girl, and Abercrombie & Fitch all have sites targeted to the tween market, despite the fact that a person is supposed to be at least 18 years old to place an order.[21] Exhibit 10-3 shows an ad aimed at Generation Y.

EXHIBIT 10-3

AD APPEALING TO THE YOUNG ADULT

Courtesy of Sprint.

Generation X:
People born between the years 1965 and 1977.

Research by the Environics Group shows that young Canadians are somewhat disengaged from their surroundings. They are only half as likely as older Canadians to read a newspaper or to go to church. They are also less likely to get married than their parents but are twice as likely to get divorced.[22] They are less likely than their parents to have children, and when they do, it is later in life. They have so few children that they are not replacing themselves. Most of them will live longer than their parents, well into their eighties and nineties.

The Generation X Market

This age group—often referred to as *Xers, busters,* or *slackers*—consists of the approximately 6.8 million individuals born between about 1965 and 1977 (different experts use different starting and ending years). As consumers, these 24- to 38-year-olds account for a significant proportion of consumer spending. They do not like labels, are cynical, and do not want to be singled out and marketed to. They matured during an era of soaring divorce rates and "latchkey children."[23]

Also, unlike their parents, who are are likely to be baby boomers, they are in no rush to marry, start a family, or work excessive hours to earn high salaries. For **Generation X** consumers, job satisfaction is more important than salary. It has been said, for example, that "Baby Boomers live to work, Gen Xers work to live!" Xers reject the values of older co-workers who may neglect their families while striving for higher salaries and career advancement, and many have observed their parents getting laid off after many years of loyalty to an employer. They therefore are not particularly interested in long-term employment with a single company but instead prefer to work for a company that can offer some work-life flexibility and can bring some fun into the environment. Gen Xers understand the necessity of money but do not view salary as a sufficient reason for staying with a company—the quality of the work itself and the relationships built on the job are much more important.[24] For Generation X, it is more important to enjoy life and to have a life style that provides freedom and flexibility.

Appealing to Generation X Members of Generation X often pride themselves on their sophistication. Although they are not necessarily materialistic, they do buy good brand names (such as Sony) but not necessarily designer labels. They want to be recognized by marketers as a group in their own right and not as mini–baby boomers. Therefore, advertisements targeted to this audience must focus on their style in music, fashions, and language. One key for marketers appears to be sincerity. Xers are not against advertising but only opposed to insincerity.

Baby boomer media do not work with members of Generation X. Younger Canadians are less likely to read newspapers and more likely to watch television than are older Canadians. Generation Xers are the MTV generation, and are more likely to be watching Fox television than the traditional major networks.

The Baby Boomer Market

Marketers have found **baby boomers** a particularly desirable target audience because (1) they are the largest distinctive age category alive today; (2) they frequently make important consumer purchase decisions; and (3) they contain small sub-segments of trend-setting consumers (sometimes known as yuppies, or young urban professionals) who have influence on the consumer tastes of other age segments of society.[25]

Baby boomers:
Persons born between 1946 and 1964.

Who Are the Baby Boomers?

The term *baby boomers* refers to the age segment of the population that was born between 1946 and 1964. Thus, baby boomers are in the broad age category that extends from about mid-30s to mid-50s. These 9.9 million or so baby boomers make up more than 30 percent of the adult population. Their numbers alone would make them a much sought-after market segment. However, they also are valued because they form a large part of all those in professional and managerial occupations and more than one-half of those with at least a university degree.

In addition, although each year more baby boomers turn 50 years of age (see Exhibit 10-4), they do not necessarily like the idea. Increases in health club memberships and a boom in the sales of vitamin and health supplements are evidence that these consumers are trying hard to look and feel young—they do not want to age gracefully but will fight and kick and pay whatever is necessary to look young. For example, 35- to 50-year-olds are the largest market for plastic surgery, and the majority of cosmetic-dentistry patients are 40 to 49 years of age.[26]

Consumer Characteristics of Baby Boomers

Baby boomers tend to be motivated consumers. They enjoy buying for themselves, for their houses or apartments, and for others—they are consumption-oriented. As baby boomers age, the nature of the products and services they most need or desire changes. For example, because of the aging of this market segment, sales of "relaxed fit" jeans, and "lineless" bifocal glasses are up substantially, as are the sales of walking shoes. Men's and women's pants with elastic waistbands are also enjoying strong sales. Recently, bank marketers and other financial institutions have also been paying more attention to boomers who are starting to think about retirement, St. Joseph's Aspirin has switched its target from babies to boomers, and Disney has ads to entice baby boomers to vacation at their theme parks without their children.[27]

Yuppies are by far the most sought-after subgroup of baby boomers. Although they make up only 5 percent of the population, they generally are well off financially, well educated, and in enviable professional or managerial careers. They are often associated with status brand names, such as BMWs

EXHIBIT 10-4

BABY BOOMERS' SENSE OF SELF

Courtesy of the American Cancer Society. All rights reserved.

EXHIBIT 10-5

APPEALING TO YUPPIES' SENSE OF SEEKING
ENRICHING EXPERIENCES

Courtesy of Williams Labadie.

or Volvo station wagons, Rolex watches, cable TV, and Cuisinart food processors. Today, as many yuppies are maturing, they are shifting their attention away from expensive status-type possessions to travel, physical fitness, planning for second careers, or some other form of new directions for their lives (see Exhibit 10-5).

Gen Yers, Gen Xers, and baby boomers differ in their purchasing behaviour, attitudes toward brands, and behaviour toward ads. Figure 10-8 captures some of the differences among these three age cohorts.

Older Consumer

Canada is aging. Some baby boomers are well into their 50s (or "mature adults"), and there are plenty of pre-boomers—those 57 to 65 years old. According to the 2001 Canadian census, there are about four million people in this country who are 65 or older (12.8 percent of the population).[28] More important, by the year 2026 one out of every five Canadians (about 7.75 million people) will be in this age bracket.[29] From the beginning to the end of the twentieth century, life expectancy in Canada rose to 79.7 years. And the 65-plus age segment of the Canadian population is projected to increase by 56 percent between 2001 and 2026 (as a large number of baby boomers turn 65).[30]

It should also be kept in mind that "later adulthood" (i.e., 50 years and over) is the longest adult life stage for most consumers—it often lasts 29 years or more).[31] This is in contrast to "early adulthood" (i.e., 18 to 34 years of age), a stage lasting 16 years, and "middle adulthood" (35 to 49, a stage lasting 14 years. Remember that people over 50 compose about 30 percent of the adult Canadian market.

Although some people think of older consumers as people without substantial financial resources, in generally poor health, and with plenty of time on their hands, the fact is that 11.5 percent of men and 4 percent of women aged 65 and over were employed in 2003. Additionally, thousands of seniors are involved in the daily care of a grandchild,[32] and many do volunteer work. The annual discretionary income of this group amounts to a significant proportion of the discretionary income of Canada, and these older consumers are major purchasers of luxury products such as cars, alcohol, vacations, and financial products.

Defining "Older" in Older Consumer Driving the growth of the elderly population in relation to other age groups are three factors: the declining birth rate, the aging of the huge baby boomer segment, and improved medical diagnoses and treatment. In Canada, "old age" is officially assumed to begin at age 65 (or when a person starts collecting Old Age Security). However, people over age 60 tend to view themselves as being 15 years younger than their chronological age.

FIGURE 10-8	Comparison of Selected Age Cohorts across Marketing-Related Issues		
THEMES	**GENERATION Y**	**GENERATION X**	**BOOMERS**
Purchasing behaviour	Savvy, pragmatic	Materialistic	Narcissistic
Coming-of-age technology	Computer in every home	Microwave in every home	TV in every home
Price-quality attitude	Value-oriented: weighing price-quality relationships	Price-oriented: concerned about the cost of individual items	Conspicuous consumption: buying for indulgence
Attitude toward brands	Brand embracing	Against branding	Brand-loyal
Behaviour toward ads	Rebel against hype	Rebel against hype	Respond to image-building type

Source: Stephanie M. Noble and Charles H. Noble, "Getting to Know Y: The Consumption Behaviors of a New Cohort," *AMA Winter Educators' Conference 11* (Chicago: American Marketing Association, 2000), *Marketing Theory,* Conference Proceedings, 294.

Research consistently suggests that people's perceptions of their ages are more important than their actual age in determining their behaviour.[33] In fact, people may at the same time have a number of different perceived or **cognitive ages**. Specifically, elderly consumers think of themselves as younger than their chronological ages on four perceived age dimensions: *feel age* (how old they feel); *look age* (how old they look); *do age* (how involved they are in activities favoured by members of a specific age group); and *interest age* (how similar their interests are to those of members of a specific age group).[34] The results support other research which has found that elderly consumers are likely to consider themselves younger (to have a younger cognitive age) than their chronological age.

For marketers, these findings underscore the importance of looking beyond chronological age to perceived or cognitive age when appealing to mature consumers and to the possibility that cognitive age might be used to segment the mature market. The "New-Age Elderly," when compared with the "Traditional Elderly," are more adventurous, more likely to be better off financially, and more receptive to marketing information.[35]

Cognitive age:
An individual's perceived age (usually 10 to 15 years younger than his or her chronological age.

Segmenting the Elderly Market The elderly are by no means a homogeneous subcultural group. There are those who, as a matter of choice, do not have colour TVs or touch-tone telephones, whereas others have the latest desktop computers and spend their time surfing the internet (cyberseniors will be discussed later in this section).

One consumer gerontologist has suggested that the elderly are more diverse in interests, opinions, and actions than other segments of the adult population.[36] Although this view runs counter to the popular myth that the elderly are uniform in attitudes and life styles, both gerontologists and market researchers have repeatedly demonstrated that age is not necessarily a major factor in determining how older consumers respond to marketing activities.

With an increased appreciation that the elderly constitute a diverse age segment, more attention is now being given to finding ways to segment the elderly into meaningful groups.[37] One relatively simple segmentation scheme partitions the elderly into three chronological age categories: the *young-old* (65 to 74 years of age), the *old* (those 75 to 84); and the *old-old* (those 85 years of age and older). This market segmentation approach provides useful consumer-relevant insights.

The elderly can also be segmented in terms of motivations and *quality-of-life orientation.* Figure 10-9 presents a side-by-side comparison of new-age elderly

| FIGURE 10-9 | Comparison of New-Age and Traditional Elderly |

NEW-AGE ELDERLY	TRADITIONAL OR STEREOTYPICAL ELDERLY
• Perceive themselves to be different in outlook from other people their age	• Perceive all older people to be about the same in outlook
• Age is seen as a state of mind	• See age as more of a physical state
• See themselves as younger than their chronological age	• See themselves at or near their chronological age
• Feel younger, think younger, and "do" younger	• Tend to feel, think, and do things that they feel match their chronological age
• Have a genuinely youthful outlook	• Feel that one should act one's age
• Feel there is a considerable adventure to living	
• Feel more in control of their own lives	• Normal sense of being in control of their own lives
• Have greater self-confidence when it comes to making consumer decisions	• Normal range of self-confidence when it comes to making consumer decisions
• Less concerned that they will make a mistake when buying something	• Some concern that they will make a mistake when buying something
• Especially knowledgeable and alert consumers	• Low-to-average consumer capabilities
• Selectively innovative	• Not innovative
• Seek new experiences and personal challenges	• Seek stability and a secure routine
• Less interested in accumulating possessions	• Normal range of interest in accumulating possessions
• Higher measured life satisfaction	• Lower measured life satisfaction
• Less likely to want to live their lives over differently	• Have some regrets as to how they lived their lives
• Perceive themselves to be healthier	• Perceive themselves to be of normal health for their age
• Feel financially more secure	• Somewhat concerned about financial security

Source: Reprinted by permission from "The Value Orientation of New-Age Elderly: The Coming of an Ageless Market" by Leon G. Schiffman and Elaine Sherman in *Journal of Business Research* 22, April 1991, 187–194. Copyright 1991 by Elsevier Science Publishing Co., Inc.

consumers and the more traditional older consumers. The increased presence of the new-age elderly suggests that marketers need to respond to the value orientations of older consumers whose life styles remain relatively ageless. Clearly, the new-age elderly are individuals who feel, think, and act according to a cognitive age that is younger than their chronological age. Several recent studies on aging suggests an "erosion of chronological age as a central indicator of the experience of aging."[38]

Although some people might think of older Americans as individuals who still use rotary phones and are generally resistant to change, this stereotype is far from the truth. Many of them, especially the new-age elderly, are comfortable with new technologies. However, research indicates that older Canadians are less likely than younger Canadians to go online. Internet Insight 10-1 provides further information on internet usage patterns of older Canadians.

Marketing to the Older Consumer Older consumers do want to be marketed to, but only for the "right" kinds of products and services and with the "right" advertising presentation. For example, older models tend to be under-represented in advertisements or are often shown as being infirm or feeble. Part of the problem, according to some writers on the subject, is that the advertising professionals who create the ads are often in their 20s and 30s and have little understanding of older consumers. Older people often want to be identified not for what they did in the past but by what they would like to accomplish in the future. Retiring or moving to

INTERNET INSIGHT 10-1
ARE OLDER CANADIANS BEING LEFT OUT OF THE INTERNET REVOLUTION?

Older Canadians are not totally afraid of new technologies. In fact, many of them are computer-savvy; yet, as a group, they are less likely to have internet connections or use the internet regularly. In fact, one survey found that only 13 percent of Canadians 60 years or older had used the internet in the past year, while 53 percent of those less than 60 years of age had done so. What is even more troublesome is the fact that, of those who are not online now, very few are interested in getting online. According to Statistics Canada, even in 2002, the percentage of older Canadians with online access from any location was less than one-third of the figure for Canadians under 35 years of age (refer to the table below). Of course, these numbers are likely to change as baby boomers age and enter the senior market.

Older consumers who do use the internet regularly are part of an elite group. These people are better educated and have higher incomes than other older consumers. They are also more likely to be male than female. But even when these consumers go online, they spend far less time online than younger people and their online activities do not affect their other daily activities in any way. They use the internet far less (only 5.7 hours per week), and more than half (57 percent) spend their online time on searching for information on goods and services. Not surprisingly, a significant proportion (38 percent) of older online consumers searched for medical information on the internet.

ONLINE ACCESS OF CANADIANS

Age of Householder	Online Access from Any Location				
	1998	1999	2000	2001	2002
	(percentage of households)				
All households	35.9	41.8	51.3	60.2	61.6
Less than age 35	45.3	53.0	66.3	76.2	75.4
Age 35 to 54	46.9	54.9	65.7	74.1	75.5
Age 55 to 64	27.5	32.7	42.4	52.5	56.3
Age 65 and over	7.2	10.1	13.9	19.3	21.6

Source: Adapted from the Statistics Connectedness Series "Internet Use Among Older Canadians," Catalogue 56F0004, No. 4, August 2001, and from Statistics Canada CANSIM database, Table 358-004.

What are the reasons for the lower online access and use among older Canadians? One reason may be the fact that older Canadians, who are likely to be retired, have not had the access to training and education in using the internet that younger people have had. They probably had to learn to use the computer on their own, unlike younger Canadians, who were taught to use computers at school or at work. Secondly, older Canadians are also likely to have lower household incomes, and income is a major factor affecting internet use. Finally, older consumers may not have the same time pressures that younger Canadians do and may thus be less interested in online activities like internet banking; this may further reduce their interest in getting online.

What's the attraction for seniors to go online? Certainly, the internet is a great way to keep in touch with friends and family members living far away, including grandchildren at university. But the web is also a place to find information (e.g., about the stock market or about health issues), entertainment, and a sense of community. There also appears to be a relationship between the amount of time an older adult spends on the internet and his or her ability to get out (using the internet may serve as a substitute for going out of the house). Having a computer and modem "empowers" older consumers—it allows them to regain some of the control that they may have lost owing to the physical deterioration or reduced social interaction. For example, with internet access, a person can pay bills, shop, and "talk" to their friends.

a milder part of the country is viewed as the opening of a new chapter in life and not a quiet withdrawal from life. In the same vein, the increase in the number of older adults taking vacation cruises and joining health clubs signifies a strong commitment to remaining "functionally young."[39]

Sex as a Subculture

Sex role:
The traits that are attributed to males and females.

Gender subcultures:
Subcultures based on gender or sex roles.

Because **sex roles** have an important cultural component, it is quite fitting to examine **gender** as a subcultural category.

Sex Roles and Consumer Behaviour

All societies tend to assign certain traits and roles to males and others to females. In Canadian society, for instance, aggressiveness and competitiveness were often considered traditional *masculine traits;* neatness, tactfulness, gentleness, and talkativeness were considered traditional *feminine traits.* In terms of role differences, women have historically been cast as homemakers with responsibility for child care, and men as the providers or breadwinners. Because such traits and roles are no longer relevant for many individuals, marketers are increasingly appealing to consumers' broader vision of gender-related role options.

Consumer Products and Sex Roles In every society, it is quite common to find products that are either exclusively or strongly associated with the members of one sex. In Canada, for example, shaving equipment, cigars, pants, ties, and work clothing were historically male products; bracelets, hair spray, hair dryers, and sweet-smelling colognes generally were considered feminine products. For most of these products, the *sex role* link has either diminished or disappeared; for others, the prohibition still lingers. An interesting product category with regard to the blurring of a gender appeal is men's fragrances. Although men are increasingly wearing fragrances, it is estimated that 30 percent of men's fragrances are worn by women.[40] Also, although women have historically been the major market for vitamins, men are increasingly being targeted for vitamins exclusively formulated for men.

As far as the internet is concerned, men and women seem to be attracted to it for different reasons. Women tend to go online to seek out reference materials, online books, medical information, cooking ideas, and government information and to chat. In contrast, men tend prefer exploring, making discoveries, finding free software, and making investments. This provides further support for the notion that men are "hunters," whereas women are "nurturers."[41] Still further, data from the U.S. shows that although men and women are equally likely to browse commercial sites, women are less likely to purchase online (32 percent for men versus 19 percent for women). Evidence suggests that the lower incidence of women purchasing online is due to their greater distrust of online security and privacy.[42] Figure 10-10 presents a gender-oriented segmentation scheme that accounts for the type of online materials favoured by specific sub-segments of males and specific sub-segments of females.

The Working Woman

Marketers are keenly interested in the *working woman*, especially the married working woman. They recognize that married women who work outside the home are a large and growing market segment, one whose needs differ from those of women who do not work outside the home (frequently self-labelled "stay-at-home

FIGURE 10-10	Male and Female Internet User Segments	
	KEY USAGE SITUATION	**FAVOURITE INTERNET MATERIALS**
FEMALE SEGMENTS		
Social Sally	Making friends	Chat and personal webpage
New Age Crusader	Fight for causes	Books and government information
Cautious Mom	Nurture children	Cooking and medical facts
Playful Pretender	Role play	Chat and games
Master Producer	Job productivity	White Pages and government information
MALE SEGMENTS		
Bits and Bytes	Computers and hobbies	Investments, discovery, software
Practical Pete	Personal productivity	Investments, company listings
Viking Gamer	Competing and winning	Games, chat, software
Sensitive Sam	Help family and friends	Investments, government information
World Citizen	Connecting with world	Discovery, software, investments

Source: Scott M. Smith and David B. Whitlark, "Men and Women Online: What Makes Them Click?" *Marketing Research*, 13, 2, Summer 2001, 23.

mothers"). It is the size of the working woman market that makes it so attractive. Approximately 62 percent of Canadian women 15 years of age and older are in the labour force; that is a market of more than 7.9 million individuals.

Because a significant proportion of all business travellers today are women, hotels have begun to realize that it pays to provide the services women want, such as healthy foods, gyms, and spas and wellness centres. Female business travellers are also concerned about hotel security and frequently use room service because they do not want to go to the hotel bar or restaurant. The Paris Hilton, for example, hands key cards to female patrons discreetly so that no one else sees or hears the room number, offers valet parking, and allows women to receive guests in an executive lounge located on the hotel's business floor. And bathrooms feature roses, shampoos, and bath gels.[43]

Segmenting the Working Woman Market To provide a richer framework for segmentation, marketers have developed categories that differentiate the motivations of working and non-working women. A number of studies have divided the female population into four segments: *stay-at-home* housewives; *plan-to-work* housewives; *just-a-job* working women; and *career-oriented* working women.[44] The distinction between "just-a-job" and "career-oriented" working women is particularly meaningful. "Just-a-job" working women seem to be motivated to work primarily by a sense that the family requires the additional income, whereas "career-oriented" working women, who tend to be in a managerial or professional positions, are driven more by a need to achieve and succeed in their careers. Today, though, with more and more female university graduates in the workforce, the percentage of career-oriented working women is on the rise.

Working women spend less time shopping than non-working women. They accomplish this "time economy" by shopping less often and by being loyal to certain brands and stores. Not surprisingly, working women also are likely to shop during the evening and on weekends, as well as to buy through direct-mail catalogues.

Businesses that advertise to women should also be aware that magazines are now delivering a larger women's audience than are television shows. Whereas early 1980s television shows had higher ratings than popular magazines, today the top 25 women's magazines have larger audiences than the top 25 television shows targeted to women.[45]

SUBCULTURES AND MARKETING STRATEGY

Subcultural analysis can play an important part in helping a firm develop successful marketing strategies. Although the cultural values of a nation shape the overall behaviour and attitudes of its population, the various subcultures within a nation often have slightly different values and attitudes. A knowledge of these subcultural differences can be of great help to a marketer who wants to reach specific groups of individuals in a country.

Segment the market using subcultures: Depending on the nature of the product, segmentation using subcultures may be an effective strategy. Subcultures have unique needs and expectations and different media usage patterns, and they value different things. For example, as mentioned earlier, a marketer appealing to the Chinese-Canadian community may need to emphasize the status that a brand name may provide, but when appealing to another subculture may need to stress the functionality of the product.

Some subcultures, especially ethnic subcultures, are concentrated in certain parts of the country and hence are easier to target and reach.

Use ethnic media to reach subcultural groups: Several of the ethnic subcultures in the country have their own media, and these are often the best vehicles for reaching people of that subculture. The Vancouver Chinese-Canadian community can be reached through ethnic media such as FTV, Ming Pao, Sing TAO, and radio stations such as AM 1470, AM 1320. Indo-Canadians can be reached by several local publications in Toronto and Vancouver and through more broad-based, widely circulated Indian papers such as *India Abroad*.

Be aware of segments within each subculture: One of the biggest mistakes that marketers can make is to treat everyone in a subculture—whether it is based on ethnicity, religion, gender, or age) as being similar. Quite often, the differences between members of a subgroup are great and what is appealing to one subgroup may be offensive to another. For example, Chinese Canadians from Hong Kong, Mainland China, and Taiwan differ from each other significantly. Hong Kong Chinese are more exposed to Western culture; they like pop culture, action thrillers, variety shows, teen idol shows, and game shows. Mainland and Taiwan Chinese, however, are more traditional and prefer romantic shows and traditional cultural programs. Hong Kong Chinese like *dim sum*; people from mainland China or Taiwan do not.

Similarly, treating all women or older Canadians alike would be a big mistake. The discussion earlier on segments within the female market or the older Canadian market pointed out how much variation exists within these groups.

Develop unique marketing mixes for subcultures: Some subcultures, but not all, require unique marketing mixes (especially promotional campaigns). For example, as stated earlier, French Canadians are a significant subculture—in population size, concentration, media usage, and values—and it is probably necessary to develop a separate promotional program for this subculture. Similarly, given the size of the Chinese-Canadian market and the popularity of Chinese as a home language among members of this group, separate programs may be feasible. Canadian

Tire runs Chinese language ads to cater to the Chinese-Canadian population and specially made ads (in English) to cater to the South-Asian community.

Even if totally new programs are not feasible, companies should consider adapting existing programs to the unique needs of subcultures. This might mean running ads in ethnic media or modifying current ads. Age and gender subcultures may also require special consideration; often, these subcultures need special promotional campaigns.

Incorporate members of different cultural groups in advertising: As a minimum, organizations can incorporate members of subcultures in their promotions. For example, Wal-Mart runs television ads that use models belonging to various ethnic minorities and also takes steps to ensure that employees from different groups are pictured in its ads.

SUMMARY

- Subcultural analysis enables marketers to segment their markets to meet the specific needs, motivations, perceptions, and attitudes shared by members of a specific subcultural group.

- A subculture is a distinct cultural group that exists as an identifiable segment within a larger, more complex society. Its members possess beliefs, values, and customs that set them apart from other members of the same society.

- The major subcultural categories in this country are ethnic origin, religion, geographic location, age, and sex.

- Each of these can be broken down into smaller segments that can be reached through special copy appeals and choice of media.

- In some cases (such as the elderly consumer), product characteristics can be tailored to the specialized needs of the market segment.

- Because all consumers are simultaneously members of several subcultural groups, the marketer must determine for the product category how specific subcultural memberships interact to influence the consumer's purchase decisions.

DISCUSSION QUESTIONS

1. Why is subcultural analysis especially important in a country such as Canada?

2. Chinese and South-Asian Canadians are a small proportion of the total Canadian population. Why are they an important market segment? How can a marketer of personal computers effectively target Chinese and South-Asian Canadians?

3. Marketers realize that people of the same age often have very different life styles. Using the evidence presented in this chapter, discuss how developers of retirement housing can use the life styles of older Canadians to segment their markets more effectively.

4. How should marketers promote products and services to working women? What appeals should they use? Explain.

5. As the owner of a Saturn car dealership, what kind of marketing strategies would you use to target working women?

CRITICAL THINKING QUESTIONS

1. How can marketers of the following products use the material presented in this chapter to develop promotional campaigns designed to increase market share among black, Chinese, and South-Asian Canadian consumers? The products are (a) compact disc players, (b) ready-to-eat cereals, and (c) designer jeans.

2. Sony is introducing a new 52-inch LCD television with a picture-in-picture feature. How should the company position and advertise the product to (a) Generation X consumers and (b) affluent baby boomers?

3. In view of the anticipated growth of the over-50 market, a leading cosmetics company is re-evaluating the marketing strategy for its best-selling moisturizing face cream for women. Should the company market the product to younger women (under 50) as well as older women? Would it be wiser to develop a new brand and formula for consumers over 50 rather than target both age groups with one product? Explain your answer.

4. Using one of the subculture categories listed in Figure 10-2, name a group that can be regarded as a subculture at your university or college.
   (a) Describe the norms, values, and behaviour of the members of that subculture.
   (b) Interview five members of that subculture about their attitudes toward the use of credit cards.
   (c) What are the implications of your findings for marketing credit cards to the group you selected?

INTERNET EXERCISES

1. Visit the website of Prime Advertising (**www.primead.com**) and look at the Canadian Tire ads the company developed for the Chinese-Canadian and South-Asian markets. Do these ads look different from those that Canadian Tire runs for the general population? If so, how?

2. Visit the website of Fairchild TV (**www.fairchildtv.com**) and examine the information provided on Chinese-Canadian markets. What insights have you gained into the Chinese-Canadian market from this site? How would you use this information if you were marketing technology products (e.g., Plasma televisions, laptop computers, digital video cameras)?

3. Visit the website of the milk marketing board of Quebec. Are the ads different from those run in other parts of Canada? What values do these ads seem to tap into?

4. Visit the website of an organization in an industry that caters to older Canadians (e.g., pharmaceuticals, travel). Would the site be appealing to older Canadians? Why or why not?

KEY TERMS

Age subculture   *(p. 325)*
Baby boomers   *(p. 329)*
Cognitive age   *(p. 331)*
Gender subcultures   *(p. 334)*

Generation X   *(p. 328)*
Generation Y   *(p. 325)*
Racio-ethnic subcultures   *(p. 315)*
Regional subcultures   *(p. 324)*

Religious subcultures   *(p. 322)*
Sex role   *(p. 334)*
Subcultural interaction   *(p. 315)*
Subculture   *(p. 314)*

CASE 10-1: AVON'S ANEW ULTIMATE

Avon (**www.avon.com**) is one of the largest direct sellers of beauty-related products (with worldwide sales of more than $6 billion), including skin-care and hair-care products and makeup. The company is known for selling its products through more than two million independent sales representatives living in more than 140 countries.

One of its emerging skin-care products is Anew Ultimate Skin Transforming Cream. This product is an outgrowth of some of the latest advances in skin-care technology. Anew Ultimate Skin Transforming Cream promises to fight aging of the skin.

Avon's Anew Ultimate Skin Transforming Cream promises to release powerful anti-aging ingredients—including an amalgam of pure gold, copper, and magnesium—to create a cream that contributes to the "growth, development, and maintenance of young skin."

In terms of consumer benefits, Anew Ultimate Skin Transforming Cream promises to (1) restore the skin's suppleness, (2) lift and firm the skin, (3) smooth out deep lines and wrinkles, and (4) enhance a natural skin brilliance.

Avon says its testing reveals that after one week of using Anew Ultimate Skin Transforming Cream, more than 90 percent of the women had improved skin texture and clarity, and 80 percent had improved skin tone. Still further, after one month, consumers experienced a positive change in the look and feel of their skin (e.g., a more sculpted or contoured look and a smoothing out of creases and folds).

The product price of $30 for a 1.7 fl. oz. jar moves Avon and Anew farther upscale in terms of a target market.

QUESTIONS

1. Cognitive age and the new-age elderly are two interrelated concepts explored in this chapter. How are these two concepts relevant to Avon in marketing this new product?

2. Do you feel that the $30 price of the product makes it an upscale product?

Source: **www.avon.com**; and Christine Bitter, "Avon's Anti-Aging Ultimate Gets a New Launch," *Brandweek*, vol. 43, 34, September 23, 2002, 4.

NOTES

1   Statistics Canada, as cited in Kumkum Ramchandani, "Indian Origins," *The New Canadian Magazine*, Summr 2004, 8–13.

2   Statistics Canada, "Definition of Concepts and Variables," Aug 5, 2003, **http://www.statcan.ca/ english/concepts/definitions/ethnicity.htm.**

3   Statistics Canada, Proportion of foreign-born population, census metropolitan areas, 2001 Census, **http://www.statcan.ca/english/Pgdb/demo46b.htm.**

4   Statistics Canada, "Population by Selected Ethnic Origins," April 28, 2003, **http://www.statcan.ca/english/Pgdb/demo28a.htm.**

5   For a detailed discussion of French-Canadian consumer behaviour, refer to Gurprit S. Kindra, Michel Laroches, and Thomas E. Muller, *Consumer Behaviour: The Canadian Perspective*, Nelson Canada: Toronto, 1995, 345–351.

6   Michael Adams, *Fire and Ice: The United States and Canada and the Myth of Converging Values* (Penguin Canada, 2004), 82–83; John Wright, "What Are Canadians' Top Indicators of Career Success?" (Toronto: Ipsos-Reid, May 7, 2003).

7   All information in this section is from the following Ipsos-Reid *Polls and Figures*: John Wright, "Canadians on Summer Reading," June 21, 2004; Geneviève Binet, "Canadians and Tea," March 4, 2004; Carla Flamer, "Canadians Need to Get Moving," January 8, 2004; and John Wright, "Boomers, Beer and a Healthy Lifestyle," December 1, 2003.

8   All information in this section is from Chris Powell, "Shopping Mosaic," *Marketing Magazine*, May 17–24, 2004, 12–15,

9   "C'est la Vie in Quebec 2004," *Marketing Magazine*, April 5–12, 2004. Unpaginated insert.

10   All figures are from Statistics Canada as reported in Census 2001, "Chinese Canadian Highlights," provided by Fairchild TV, **http://www.fairchildtv.com/english/**.

11   Joseph Chen, of Millward Brown Goldfarb, Toronto, quoted in "Shopping Mosaic," by Chris Powell, *Marketing Magazine*, May 17–24, 2004, 14.

12   Chris Powell, "Shopping Mosaic," *Marketing Magazine*, May 17–24, 2004, 12–15.

13   Judy Cohen, "White Consumer Response to Asian Models in Advertising," *Journal of Consumer Marketing*, Spring 1992, 17–27.

14   Statistics Canada, "Blacks in Canada: A Long History," Spring 2004, p. 27, Catalogue No. 11-008. (Blacks is the term used by Statistics Canada.)

15   This section is based on "Religion in Canada," Statistics Canada, Catalogue number 96F0030XIE2001015, May 2003.

16   Kevin Michael Grace, "Is This Kosher," *Report Newsmagazine*, 27, 1, May 8, 2000, 37; Laura Bird, "Major Brands Look for the Kosher Label," *Adweek's Marketing Week*, April 1, 1991, 18–19; and Judith Waldrop, "Everything's Kosher," *American Demographics*, March 1991, 4.

17   Michael Adams, *Fire and Ice: The United States and Canada and the Myth of Converging Values*, Penguin Canada, 2004, 79–85.

18   Stephanie M. Noble and Charles H. Noble, "Getting to Know Y: The Consumption Behaviors of a New Cohort," in *2000 AMA Winter Educators' Conference*, 11, eds. John P. Workman and William D. Perreault (Chicago: American Marketing Association, 2000), 293–303; and Pamela Paul, "Getting Inside Gen Y," *American Demographics*, 23, 9, September 2001, 42–49.

19   Lauren Keating, "The In Crowds," *Shopping Center World*, 29, 5, May 2000, 160–165.

20   Joyce M. Wolburg and James Pokrywczynski, "A Psychographic Analysis of Generation Y College Students," *Journal of Advertising Research*, 41, 5, September-October 2001, 33–52.

21   Chantal Todè, "Evolution of Tweens' Tastes Keeps Retailers on Their Toes," *Advertising Age*, February 12, 2001, S6.

22   Michael Adams and Christine de Panafieu, "God is Dead? 'Whatever,'" *Globe and Mail*, June 16, 2003.

23   Keating, "The In Crowds," 163.

24   Judi E. Loomis, "Generation X," *Rough Notes*, 143, 9, September 2000, 52–54.

25   "Boomer Facts," *American Demographics*, January 1996, 14. Also see Diane Crispell, "U.S. Population Forecasts Decline for 2000, but Rise Slightly for 2050," *Wall Street Journal*, March 25, 1996, B3.

26   Cindy Hearn and Doug Hammond, "Cosmetic Dentistry: The 'Boom' Is upon Us!" *Dental Economics*, 91, 9, September 2001, 118–122.

27   Abbey Klaassen, "St. Joseph: From Babies to Boomers," *Advertising Age*, July 9, 2001, 1, 38; and Bob Garfield, "Disney's Quest for Boomers Shows a Bit of Imagineering," *Advertising Age*, August 13, 2001, 29.

28   Statistics Canada, "Population by Age and Sex," **http://www.statcan.ca/english/Pgdb/demo10a.htm**.

29   Statistics Canada, "Population Projections for 2001 to 2026," **http://www.statcan.ca/english/Pgdb/demo23c.htm**.

30   Ibid.

31   John Nielson and Kathy Curry, "Creative Strategies for Connecting with Mature Individuals," *Journal of Consumer Marketing*, 14, 4, 1997, 320.

32   Anne Milan and Brian Hamm, "Across the Generations: Grandparents and Grandchildren," *Canadian Social Trends*, Winter 2003.

33   Kelly Tepper, "The Role of Labeling Processes in Elderly Consumers' Responses to Age Segmentation Cues," *Journal of Consumer Research*, March 1994, 503–519; and Candace Corlett, "Building a Successful 501 Marketing Program," *Marketing Review*, January 1996, 10–11, 19.

34   Benny Barak and Leon G. Schiffman, "Cognitive Age: A Nonchronological Age Variable," in *Advances in Consumer Research*, 8, ed. Kent B. Monroe (Ann Arbor, MI: Association for Consumer Research, 1981), 602–606; Elaine Sherman, Leon G. Schiffman, and William R. Dillon, "Age/Gender Segments and Quality of Life Differences," in *1988 Winter Educators' Conference*, ed. Stanley Shapiro and A.H. Walle (Chicago: American Marketing Association, 1988), 319–320; Stuart Van Auken and Thomas E. Barry, "An Assessment of the Trait Validity of Cognitive Age," *Journal of Consumer Psychology*, 1995, 107–132; Robert E. Wilkes, "A Structural Modeling Approach to the Measurement and Meaning of Cognitive Age," *Journal of Consumer Research*, September 1992, 292–301; and Chad Rubel, "Mature Market Often Misunderstood," *Marketing News*, August 28, 1995, 28–29.

35   Elaine Sherman, Leon G. Schiffman, and Anil Mathur, "The Influence of Gender on the New-Age Elderly's Consumption Orientation," *Psychology &Marketing*, 18, 10, October 2001, 1073–1089.

36   Elaine Sherman, quoted in David B. Wolfe, "The Ageless Market," *American Demographics*, July 1987, 26–28, 55–56.

37   Carol M. Morgan and Doran J. Levy, "Understanding Mature Consumers," *Marketing Review*, January 1996, 12–13, 25; and Elaine Sherman and Leon G. Schiffman, "Quality-of-Life (QOL) Assessment of Older Consumers: A Retrospective Review," *Journal of Business and Psychology*, Fall 1991, 107–119.

38   Don E. Bradley and Charles F. Longino, Jr., "How Older People Think about Images of Aging in Advertising and the Media," *Generations*, 25, 3, Fall 2001, 17–21.

39   Isabelle Szmigin and Marylyn Carrigan, "Learning to Love the Older Consumer," *Journal of Consumer Behaviour* (London), 1, 1, June 2001, 22–34; Bill Radford, "Age Old Trend/Health-Conscious Seniors Displacing Younger Fitness-Club Patrons," *The Gazette*, November 12, 2001, "Life" p.1; and Bradley and Longino, "How Older People Think...," 17–21

40   Maxine Wilkie, "Scent of a Market," *American Demographics*, August 1995, 40–49.

41   Scott M. Smith and David B. Whitlark, "Men and Women Online: What Makes Them Click?" *Marketing Research*, 13, 2, Summer 2001, 20–25.

42   Kara A. Arnold and Lyle R. Wetsch, "Sex Differences and Information Processing: Implications for Marketing on the Internet," in *2001 AMA Winter Educators' Conference*, 12, eds. Ram Krishnan and Madhu Viswanathan (Chicago: American Marketing Association 2001), 357–365.

43   Anjuman Ali, "Women Travelers: Marooned No More," *Wall Street Journal Europe*, July 6–7, 2001, 29.

44   Thomas Barry, Mary Gilly, and Lindley Doran, "Advertising to Women with Different Career Orientations," *Journal of Advertising Research*, 25, April–May 1985, 26–35.

45   Alison Stein Wellner, "The Female Persuasion," *American Demographics*, 24, 2, February 2002, 24–29.

MDX A MORE CIVILIZED LOOK AT NATURE. ⒶACUR

chapter 11
social class and consumer behaviour

LEARNING OBJECTIVES

By the end of this chapter you should be able to:

1. Define social class and explain the key features of a social-class system.
2. Explain how social class is measured in Canada, and describe the variables used to measure social class in this country.
3. Discuss the differences in life styles of the various social classes.
4. Explain the problems with using social class as a segmentation variable.
5. Discuss how social class affects marketing strategy.

11

have you read *Nuvo Magazine?* It is a glossy, oversized, expensive quarterly magazine published in Vancouver. The magazine rejects ads and products that do not match its image. Now in its sixth year of publication, *Nuvo* has generated two copycat magazines—*Luxury* and *Rich Guy*. What do these magazines have in common? All three of them target the super-affluent consumers in Canada, people with annual incomes of $100 000 and up. The annual household income of *Nuvo* readers is $173 000; 90 percent are university-educated, and a third of those have a graduate degree. *Nuvo* has a total circulation of 50 000, but only 2117 copies go to paid subscribers; the rest are delivered to carefully selected homes in upscale neighbourhoods and high-end hotels. Who advertises in *Nuvo*? Companies like Rolex, BMW, Escada, Aston Martin, Cartier, and Chanel. The owner of high-end jewellery stores Montecristo in Vancouver says he chose *Nuvo* because he wanted to reach the upscale, upper-class Canadian—or the top 2 percent of the population—who would appreciate his jewellery.[1]

www.nuvomagazine.com

CHAPTER OVERVIEW

Some form of class structure or social stratification has existed in all societies throughout human history. In contemporary societies, an indication that social classes exist is the common reality that people who are better educated or have more prestigious occupations, such as physician or lawyer, are often more highly valued than truck drivers and farmhands. In this chapter, we will examine the nature of social class, the variables and methods used to measure social class, and the various social class groups in Canadian society. We will also look at the consumers at either end of the social-class continuum (the affluent and the non-affluent consumer) and the influence of social class on marketing strategy.

WHAT IS SOCIAL CLASS?

Social class:
The division of members of a society into a hierarchy of distinct status classes, so that members of each class have the same relative status and members of all other classes have either more or less status.

Although **social class** can be thought of as a continuum—a range of social positions on which each member of society can be placed—researchers have preferred to divide the continuum into a small number of specific social classes, or *strata*. Social class is defined as *the division of members of a society into a hierarchy of distinct status classes, so that members of each class have the same relative status and members of all other classes have either more or less status.*

To appreciate more fully the complexity of social class, we will briefly consider several underlying concepts pertinent to this definition.

Social Class Is Hierarchical and a Natural Form of Market Segmentation

Social-class categories are usually ranked in a hierarchy, ranging from low- to high-status. Thus, members of a specific social class perceive members of other social classes as having either more or less status than they themselves do. To many people, therefore, social-class categories suggest that others are either equal to them (about the same social class), superior to them (higher social class), or inferior to them (lower social class).

The hierarchical aspect of social class is important to marketers. Consumers may buy a certain product, such as an imported luxury car, because it is favoured by members of either their own or a higher social class, and they may avoid other products, such as a digital readout wristwatch as a dress watch, because they consider the products to be "lower class." Thus, the various social-class strata provide a natural basis for market segmentation for many products and services. In many instances, consumer researchers have been able to relate aspects of product usage to membership in a particular social class.

Social Class Provides a Frame of Reference for Consumer Behaviour

Social-class membership serves consumers as a frame of reference (or a reference group) for the development of their attitudes and behaviour. Members of a specific social class may be expected to turn most often to other members of the same class for cues (or clues) as to proper behaviour. In other cases, members of a particular social class (e.g., upper-lower class) may aspire to advance their social-class standing by emulating the behaviour of members of the middle class. Thus, they might read middle-class magazines, do "middle-class things" (such as visit museums and advance their education), and eat at middle-class restaurants so that they can observe middle-class behaviour.[2]

The classification of society's members into a small number of social classes has also enabled researchers to note the existence of shared values, attitudes, and behavioural patterns among members within each social class and differences in values, attitudes, and behaviour *between* social classes. Consumer researchers have been able to relate social-class standing to consumer attitudes toward specific products and to examine social-class influences on the actual consumption of products.

Social Class Reflects a Person's Relative Social Status

Social status:
The amount of status the members of that class have in comparison with members of other social classes.

Researchers often measure social class in terms of **social status**; that is, they define each social class by the amount of status the members of that class have in comparison with members of other social classes. In social-class (sometimes called *social stratification*) research, *status is often thought of as the relative rankings of members of each social class in terms of specific status factors.* For example, relative *wealth* (amount of economic assets), *power* (the degree of personal choice or influence over others), and *prestige* (the degree of recognition received from others) are three status factors that are often used when estimating social class.

To understand how status operates in the minds of consumers, researchers have explored the idea of **social comparison theory**. According to this social-psychological concept, people quite normally compare their own material possessions with those owned by others in order to determine their own relative social standing. This is especially important in a marketing society, where status is often associated with consumers' purchasing power (or how much can be bought). Simply stated, individuals with more purchasing power or a greater ability to make purchases have more status. Those who have more restrictions on what they can or cannot buy have less status. Because visible or conspicuous possessions are easy to spot, they especially serve as markers or indicators of our status and the status of others. Not surprisingly, recent research has confirmed that a crucial ingredient of status is a consumer's possessions compared with similar things that are owned by other people (possibly a home compared with another person's home).[3]

A related concept is *status consumption*—the process by which consumers endeavour to increase their social standing through conspicuous consumption or possessions.[4] A number of research studies have validated the status consumption scale presented in Figure 11-1. As the market for luxury or status products continues to grow, there is an even greater need for marketers to identify and understand which consumers especially seek out such status-enhancing possessions, as well as the relationship between status consumption and social class.[5]

Although *social comparison theory* and its related activity of *status consumption* have the potential of being very enlightening about status and how it operates, consumer and marketing researchers most often approach the actual study of status by means of one or more of the following convenient demographic (more precisely, socio-economic) variables: *family income, occupational status,* and *educational attainment.* These socio-economic variables, as expressions of status, are used every day by marketing practitioners to measure social class.

> **Social comparison theory:**
>
> A social-psychological concept that states that individuals compare their own material possessions with those owned by others in order to determine their relative social standing.

Individuals Can Move Up or Down the Social Class Hierarchy

Social-class membership in Canada is not as hard and fixed as it is in some countries. Although people can move either up or down in social-class standing from the

---

FIGURE 11-1	A Five-Question Status Consumption Scale[a]

1. I would buy a product just because it has status.
2. I am interested in new products with status.
3. I would pay more for a product if it had status.
4. The status of a product is irrelevant to me. (reverse scored)
5. A product is more valuable to me if it has some snob appeal.

[a] Each of the five items is measured on a 7-point Likert (agree-disagree) scale.

Source: Jacqueline K. Eastman, Ronald E. Goldsmith, and Leisa Reinecke Flynn, "Status Consumption in Consumer Behavior: Scale Development and Validation," *Journal of Marketing Theory and Practice*, Summer 1999, 44.

MDX A MORE CIVILIZED LOOK AT NATURE.   ⊛ ACURA

EXHIBIT 11-1

AN AD APPEALING TO UPWARDLY MOBILE
CONSUMERS

Acura/Honda Canada Inc.

class position held by their parents, Canadians have primarily thought in terms of *upward mobility* because of the availability of free education and opportunities for self-development and self-advancement. Because upward mobility has commonly been attainable in North America, the higher social classes often become reference groups for ambitious men and women of lower social status. The advertisement in Exhibit 11-1 is targeted to successful upwardly mobile people striving to express their personal vision.

Recognizing that people often aspire to the life style and possessions enjoyed by members of a higher social class, marketers frequently incorporate the symbols of higher-class membership, both as products and props in advertisements targeted to the lower social classes. For example, ads often display the marketer's products in an upper-class setting: a board game on a table in front of a fireplace with a beautiful mantelpiece; a computer on the desk of an elegantly appointed executive office; a domestic wine being drunk by fashionably dressed European-looking models, a bottle of jam on an exquisitely set dining room table; a new-model car in front of a famous exclusive restaurant. Sometimes a more direct appeal to consumers' desire to have products that are normally restricted to members of other social classes is an effective message. For instance, if a direct marketer of consumer electronics were to promote a top-of-the-line flat-panel monitor (such as a high-end Sony 18-inch LCD display), which is usually bought by business executives, as "now it's your turn to have what business executives have enjoyed" (it's been marked down to 50 percent of the original price), this would be a marketing message that encourages household consumers to have a "dream monitor" on their desks.

Another characteristic of social-class mobility is that products and services traditionally within the realm of one social class may filter down to lower classes. For instance, plastic surgery was once affordable only for movie stars and other wealthy consumers. Today, however, people of all economic strata undergo cosmetic procedures.

Some Signs of Downward Mobility

Although Canada is often associated with *upward mobility,* because it was the "rule" for much of its history that each generation of a family tended to do better than the last generation, there now are signs of some *downward mobility.* Social commentators have suggested that some young adults (such as members of the X-Generation described in Chapter 10) are not only likely to find it difficult to do better than their successful parents (e.g., to get better jobs, own homes, have more disposable income, and have more savings) but also may not even do as well as their parents.

There is some evidence of such a slide in social-class mobility. Specifically, researchers have found that the odds that young men's income will reach middle-class levels by the time they reach their thirtieth birthday have been slowly declining.[6] This regressive pattern holds true regardless of race, parents' income, and a young person's educational level.

THE MEASUREMENT OF SOCIAL CLASS

There is no general agreement on how to measure social class. To a great extent, researchers are uncertain about the underlying elements of social-class structure. To attempt to resolve this dilemma, they have used a wide range of measurement techniques.

Systematic methods of measuring social class fall into the following broad categories: subjective measures, reputational measures, and objective measures.

Subjective Measures

Using **subjective measures** of social class, individuals are asked to estimate their own social-class positions. Typical of this approach is the following question:

Which one of the following four categories best describes your social class: the lower class, the lower-middle class, the upper-middle class, or the upper class?

Lower class	[ ]
Lower-middle class	[ ]
Upper-middle class	[ ]
Upper class	[ ]
Do not know/refuse to answer	[ ]

Subjective measures: Asking people to estimate their own social-class positions.

The resulting classification of social-class membership is based on the participants' self-perceptions or self-images. Social class is treated as a personal phenomenon, one that reflects an individual's sense of belonging or identification with others. This feeling of social-group membership is often referred to as **class consciousness.**

Class consciousness: An individual's sense of belonging to or identification with others of the same social class.

Subjective measures of social-class membership tend to produce an over-abundance of people who classify themselves as middle class (thus understating the number of people—the "fringe people"—who would, perhaps, be more correctly classified as either lower or upper class).[7] Moreover, it is likely that the subjective perception of social-class membership, as a reflection of a person's self-image, is related to product usage and consumption preferences (see Chapter 4). This is not only a North American phenomenon. Every year in Japan, a "Life of the Nation" survey asks citizens to place themselves into one of five social-class categories: upper, upper-middle, middle-middle, lower-middle, and lower. Whereas in the late 1950s more than 70 percent of respondents put themselves in one of the three middle-class categories, since the late 1960s, close to 90 percent categorize themselves as "middle class."[8] Again, this demonstrates the tendency for consumers to report seeing themselves as "middle class."

Reputational Measures

Using **reputational measures** of social class requires selected community informants to make initial judgments about which social class other members of the community belong to. The final task of assigning community members to social-class positions, however, belongs to the trained researcher.

Reputational measures: Using selected community informants to make judgments about which social class other members of the community belong to.

Sociologists have used the reputational approach to obtain a better understanding of the specific class structures of the communities under study. Consumer researchers, however, are interested in the measurement of social class in order to understand markets and consumption behaviour better, not social structure. For the purposes of that narrower goal, the reputational approach has proved to be impractical.

Objective Measures

Objective measures: Using selected demographic or socio-economic variables to measure a person's social class.

In contrast to the subjective and reputational methods, which require people to judge their own class standing or that of other community members, **objective measures** consist of selected demographic or socio-economic variables concerning the individuals under study. These variables are measured with questionnaires that ask respondents several factual questions about themselves, their families, or their places of residence. When selecting objective measures of social class, most researchers favour one or more of the following variables: occupation, amount of income, and education. To these socio-economic factors they sometimes add geo-demographic clustering data in the form of a postal code for and information about the neighbourhood where the person lives. These socio-economic indicators are especially important as a means of locating concentrations of consumers with specific social-class membership.

www.statcan.ca

Socio-economic measures of social class are of considerable value to marketers who are interested in segmenting markets. Marketing managers who have developed socio-economic profiles of their target markets can locate these markets (i.e., identify and measure them) by studying the socio-economic data periodically issued by Statistics Canada and numerous commercial geodemographic data services. To reach a desired target market, marketers match the *socio-economic profiles* of their target audiences to the *audience profiles* of selected advertising media. Socio-economic audience profiles are regularly developed and routinely made available to potential advertisers by most of the mass media (see Figure 11-2).

FIGURE 11-2	Socio-economic Profile of *Maclean's* Readers
Total number of readers	2 910 000
Percentage male	52%
Number of ESIs (Earners, Spenders, Investors)	1 000 000+
Median age	43
Post-graduates	273 000
Professionals	200 000
MOPEs (Managers, Owners, Professionals)	636 000
IT managers, specialists, professionals	267 000
Average household income	$72 310
Readers with household income of over $125 000 per year	366 000
Readers with personal incomes of over $60 000 per year	476 000
Readers who have invested in mutual funds in the last two years	385 000
Readers who invest $10 000 or more in RRSPs each year	198 000
Readers with savings/securities of over $100 000	209 000
Readers who bought an electronic organizer in the past 12 months	45 000
Readers who bought a home entertainment system in the past year	135 000
Readers with 21+ business trips in the past year	62 000

Source: Maclean's magazine, http://www.macleans.ca/advertising/print/sec3_2.htm. Courtesy of *Maclean's* magazine.

Objective measures of social class fall into two basic categories: *single-variable indexes* and *composite-variable indexes*.

Single-Variable Indexes

A **single-variable index** uses just one socio-economic variable to evaluate social-class membership. Some of the variables that are used for this purpose are discussed next.

Single-variable index: A measure of social class that uses just one socio-economic variable.

Occupation Occupation is a widely accepted and probably the best-documented measure of social class because it reveals occupational status.[9] The importance of occupation as a social-class indicator is dramatized by the frequency with which people ask someone they meet for the first time, "What do you do for a living?" The response to this question serves as a guide in sizing up (or evaluating and forming opinions of) others.

More important, marketers often think in terms of specific occupations or occupational categories when they define a target market for their products. They may say, "Teachers are our best customers for summer cruises" or "We target our vacation resort club to executives and professionals." Still further, the likelihood that particular occupations would be receptive to certain products or services is often the reason for screening prospective focus group participants for occupation. It is also the reason that marketers choose particular occupational databases to target with direct-marketing campaigns (e.g., a list of female lawyers practising in Calgary).

Within the domain of occupational status, there has also been an increasing trend toward self-employment among business and professional people. Specifically, it appears that business executives and professionals who are self-employed or entrepreneurs are substantially more likely to be *very wealthy* than their counterparts who work for someone else.[10] This link between self-employment and higher incomes is consistent with the trend of increasing numbers of business school graduates seeking to work for themselves rather than going to work for a "big business."

It is also noteworthy that although the status of a particular occupation may change significantly over time, the status of some 40 occupations in the United States (studied between 1976 and 2000) was found to be highly consistent.[11] Specifically, certain occupations (e.g., Supreme Court judges and physicians) were consistently ranked high over the many years of the research, whereas other occupations (e.g., farmhands and taxi drivers) were consistently ranked low during the same period of time.

Education A person's formal education is another commonly accepted approximation of social class. Generally speaking, the more education a person has, the more likely it is that he or she is well paid (or has a higher income) and has an admired or respected position (high occupational status).[12] Using Statistics Canada data, Figure 11-3 supports the close relationship between educational attainment and amount of household income.

Income Individual or family income is another socio-economic variable that is often used to approximate social-class standing. Researchers who favour income as a measure of social class use either *amount* or *source* of income. Available research suggests that income works best in accounting for leisure consumption when measured in terms of "engaging in" a particular leisure activity, such as skiing, bowling, or playing basketball or golf.[13]

Although income is a popular estimate of social-class standing, not all consumer researchers agree that it is an accurate index of social class. Some argue that

| FIGURE 11-3 | Relationship between Education and Income |

LEVEL OF EDUCATION	ANNUAL INCOME
Less than high school	$21 230
High school and/or some post-secondary education	$25 477
Trades diploma or certificate	$32 743
College certificate or diploma	$32 736
University certificate, diploma, or degree	$48 648

Source: Adapted from the Statistics Canada table "Number and Average Employment Income (2) in Constant (2000) Dollars, Sex (3), Work Activity (3), Age Groups (7) and Historical Highest Level of Schooling (6) for Population 15 Years and Over with Employment Income, for Canada, Provinces, Territories, Census Metropolitan Areas and Census Agglomerations, 1995 and 2000 - 20% Sample Data," Catalogue 97F0019, March 11, 2003.

a blue-collar car mechanic and a white-collar assistant bank manager may both earn $53 000 a year, and yet because of (or as a reflection of) social-class differences, each will spend that income in a different way. How they decide to spend their incomes expresses different values. From this point of view, it is the difference in values, not the amount of money they earn, that is an important discriminant of social class between people. Substantiating the importance of consumers' personal values, rather than amount of income, is the observation that affluence may be more a function of attitude or behaviour than of income level.[14] These "adaptational affluent" consumers constitute a broad segment who do not have the income needed to be considered affluent in today's society, and who nevertheless want to have the best. They buy less but buy better quality, assigning priorities and gradually working their way toward having everything they want.

Other Variables Quality of neighbourhood and dollar value of residence are rarely used as sole measures of social class. However, they are used informally to support or verify a social-class membership assigned on the basis of occupational status or income.

Finally, possessions have been used by sociologists as an index of social class.[15] The best-known and most elaborate rating scheme for evaluating possessions is *Chapin's Social Status Scale*, which uses the presence of certain items of furniture and accessories in the living room (types of floor or floor covering, curtains, fireplace, library table, telephone, or bookcases) and the condition of the room (cleanliness, organization, or general atmosphere).[16] Conclusions are drawn about a family's social class on the basis of such observations. To illustrate how home decorations reflect social-class standing, lower-class families are likely to put their television sets in the living room and bedrooms, whereas middle- and upper-class families usually put them in one or more of the following rooms: bedrooms, family room, or a media room (but *not* in the living room). The marketing implications of such insights suggest that advertisements for television sets targeted at lower-class consumers should show the set in a living room, whereas advertisements directed to middle- or upper-class consumers should show the set in a bedroom, a family room, or a media room. Exhibits 11-2A and 11-2B present ads that target upper-class consumers.

Composite-Variable Indexes

Composite-variable indexes systematically combine a number of socio-economic factors to form one overall measure of social-class standing. Such indexes are of interest to consumer researchers because they may reflect the complexity of social class better than single-variable indexes do. For instance, research reveals that the *higher* the socio-economic status (in terms of a composite of income, occupational status, and

Composite-variable indexes:
The systematic combining of a number of socio-economic factors to form one overall measure of social-class standing.

EXHIBIT 11-2A

AD TARGETING UPPER-CLASS
CONSUMERS

Courtesy of Land Rover & Silverhammer.

EXHIBIT 11-2B

AD TARGETING UPPER-CLASS CONSUMERS

Courtesy of General Motors of Canada.

education), the more positive are the consumers' ratings of mail order and phone buying, compared with in-store shopping.[17] The same research also found that downscale consumers (a composite of lower scores on the three variables) were less positive toward magazine and catalogue shopping and more positive toward in-store shopping than were more upscale socio-economic groupings. Armed with such information, retailers like Wal-Mart and Zellers that especially target *working-class* consumers would have real difficulty using catalogue and telephone selling. In contrast, retailers like Lands' End, which concentrates on upscale consumers, has been especially successful in developing catalogue programs targeted to specific segments of affluent or upscale consumers.

Two of the more important composite indexes are the **Index of Status Characteristics** and the **Socio-economic Status Score.**

Index of Status Characteristics. A classic composite measure of social class is Warner's Index of Status Characteristics (ISC).[18] The ISC is a weighted measure of the following socio-economic variables: occupation, source of income (not amount of income), house type, and dwelling area (quality of neighbourhood).

Socio-economic Status Score. The United States Bureau of the Census developed the Socioeconomic Status Score (SES), which combines three basic socio-economic variables: occupation, family income, and educational attainment.[19]

LIFE-STYLE PROFILES OF THE SOCIAL CLASSES

Consumer research has found that in each of the social classes, there is a constellation of specific life-style factors (shared beliefs, attitudes, activities, and behaviour) that tends to distinguish the members of each class from the members of all other social classes.

Index of Status Characteristics:

A weighted measure of occupation, source of income, house type, and dwelling area.

Socio-economic Status Score:

A measure using three basic socio-economic variables: occupation, family income, and educational attainment.

To capture the life-style composition of the various social-class groupings, Figure 11-4 presents a consolidated portrait, pieced together from numerous sources, of the members of the following six social classes: upper-upper class, lower-upper class, upper-middle class, lower-middle class, upper-lower class, and lower-lower class. Each of these profiles is only a generalized picture of the class. People in any class may possess values, attitudes, and behavioural patterns that are a hybrid of two or more classes.

Next, we will examine the life styles of three social class groups—the affluent (the upper classes), the middle class, and the lower class—in more detail. This will be followed by a discussion on the "techno class"—consumers who are computer-savvy.

The Affluent Consumer

Affluent households constitute an especially attractive target segment because its members have incomes that provide them with a disproportionately large share of all discretionary income—the extra money that allows the purchase of luxury cruises, foreign sports cars, time-sharing ski-resort condos, good jewellery, and ready access to home computers, laptops, and internet access. It has also been pointed out there is a strong positive relationship between health and economic status—that is, "the healthiest people are those who are economically advantaged" and "poverty is bad for you."[20]

The wealth of Canadians grew dramatically during the 1990s, partly because of the longest bull market in Canadian history. The affluent market is increasingly attracting marketers. Whirlpool Corporation, for example, realizes that as more and more consumers own household appliances, it can no longer rely on volume to increase its profits. So the firm now focuses on upscale products that are so profitable they can sell fewer appliances and still make money. Its Duet line, a $2800 washer-dryer set, sold so well in the first six months after its introduction that Whirlpool had to double its sales projections.[21]

Although affluent consumers (those with an annual family income of $100 000 or more) constitute only 20 percent of all Canadian households, this upscale market segment drinks more wine, takes more domestic airline flights, owns more vehicles, and holds more securities than the much larger segment of non-affluent households. This market can be divided into three groups: families with annual incomes of $100 000 to 124 999, $125 000 to $149 999, and $150 000 or more. The average household income for these consumers is $110 709, $135 708, and $242 929 respectively.[22] The most affluent segments of society are more likely than others to spend more on each product they buy. For instance, studies in the United States have found that when it comes to desktop, laptop, and handheld computers, the "least affluent" spent $1512 and the "medium affluent" spent $1816, whereas the "most affluent" spent $2911. Research in the United States has found that affluent customers have an affinity for technology, especially when it comes to the task of managing their finances.[23] As shown in Figure 11-5, affluent consumers in the U.S. (and probably in Canada) are more likely to take part in certain sports, especially snowboarding, sailing, golf, and hiking. The results reveal that the "most affluent" are more likely than members of the two other affluent consumer segments to participate in a sampling of sports.[24]

A growing subcategory of the affluent are *millionaires*. Contrary to common stereotypes, millionaires are quite similar to non-millionaires. They are usually the first generation to be rich, often working for themselves in "ordinary" unglamorous

FIGURE 11-4   Social-Class Profiles

The Upper-Upper Class—Country Club Establishment
- Small number of well-established families
- Belong to best country clubs and sponsor major charity events
- Serve as trustees for local universities and hospitals
- Prominent physicians and lawyers
- May be heads of major financial institutions, owners of major long-established firms
- Accustomed to wealth, so do not spend money conspicuously

The Lower-Upper Class—New Wealth
- Not quite accepted by the upper crust of society
- Represent "new money"
- Successful business executives
- Conspicuous users of their new wealth

The Upper-Middle Class—Achieving Professionals
- Have neither family status nor unusual wealth
- Career-oriented
- Young successful professionals, corporate managers, and business owners
- Most are university graduates, many with graduate degrees
- Active in professional, community, and social activities
- Have a keen interest in obtaining the "better things in life"
- Their homes serve as symbols of their achievements
- Consumption is often conspicuous
- Very child-oriented

The Lower-Middle Class—Faithful Followers
- Primarily non-managerial white-collar workers and highly paid blue-collar workers
- Want to achieve respectability and be accepted as good citizens
- Want their children to be well-behaved
- Tend to be churchgoers and are often involved in church-sponsored activities
- Prefer a neat and clean appearance and tend to avoid faddish or highly styled clothing
- Constitute a major market for do-it-yourself products

The Upper-Lower Class—Security-Minded Majority
- The largest social-class segment
- Solidly blue collar
- Strive for security (sometimes gained from union membership)
- View work as a means to "buy" enjoyment
- Want children to behave properly
- High wage earners in this group may spend impulsively
- Interested in items that enhance their leisure time (e.g., TV sets, hunting equipment)
- Husbands have a strong "macho" self-image
- Males are sports fans, heavy smokers, beer drinkers

The Lower-Lower Class—Strugglers
- Poorly educated, unskilled labourers
- Often out of work
- Children are often treated poorly
- Tend to live a day-to-day existence

FIGURE 11-5 Three Segments of Affluent Consumers' Average Household Expenditures (among purchasing households)

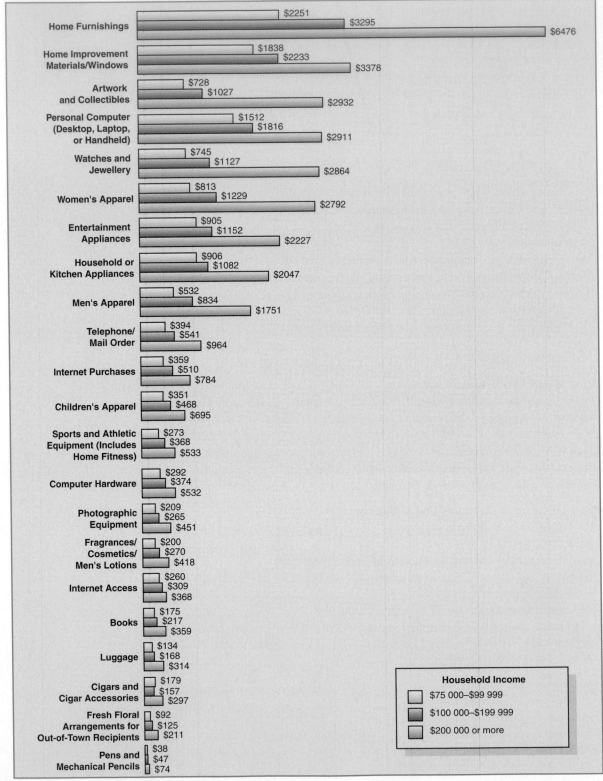

Source: 2002 Mendelsohn Affluent Survey (New York: Mendelsohn Media Research, Inc., 2002), 11.

businesses. They work hard and frequently live in unpretentious homes, often next door to non-millionaires.

In the United Kingdom, the affluent are often empty nesters with large disposable incomes and small or paid-off mortgages. They have an abundance of money, but are time-poor and are interested in improving the quality of their lives with overseas vacations and sports cars.[25] Moreover, researchers who have examined affluent consumers, in both the United Kingdom and the United States, have found that they are likely to concentrate on saving or reducing time and effort and, not surprisingly, are willing to pay for many things that provide that convenience.[26]

Research Insight 11-1 provides more information on how the affluent market can be segmented; Internet Insight 11-1 looks at how affluent consumers can be targeted using the internet.

Middle-Class Consumers

It is not easy to define the boundaries of the middle class. Although Statistics Canada does not have a definition of middle class, there have nevertheless been many attempts to define it. For instance, "middle market" has been defined as the "middle" 50 percent of household incomes.[27] Still another definition of "middle class" envisions households comprising university-educated adults, who in some way use computers to make a living, are involved in their children's education, and are confident that they can maintain the quality of their family's life.[28] For many marketers "middle class" can be thought of as including households that range from lower-middle to middle-middle class in terms of some acceptable variable or combination of variables (e.g., income, education, and occupation). This view of middle class does *not* include the upper-middle class, which over the years has increasingly been treated as a segment of affluent consumers.

Adding to the challenge of defining middle class is the fact that luxury and technological products have been becoming more affordable for more consumers (often because of the introduction of near-luxury models by luxury-brand firms and the downward price trend for many technology products) and, therefore, more middle-class consumers have access to products and brands that where once beyond their reach.[29]

Middle-class Canadians, who were not the traditional target market for high-end products, are forcing marketers to rethink their definition of the luxury consumer. Many middle-class Canadians are in two-income households and have fewer children than before. These factors, along with changing values, have increased their appetite for luxury goods. According to Peter Stanger, VP and director of Boston Consulting Group's Toronto office, "Most consumers feel this renewed sense of sophistication, meaning they believe they deserve something special on occasion. Luxury products just used to be marketed to the rich, but now there's a much broader market that can be targeted."[30] This is seen in the sales of high-end products like luxury cars. According to BCG, between 1997 and 2002, more Canadians than ever before traded up to European luxury cars, leading to growth rates of 151 percent for Mercedes-Benz and Jaguar and 133 percent for BMW.[31]

www.bcg.com/offices/
office_toronto.jsp

In Canada and the United States, the dynamic nature of social class has been working against the middle class. In particular, there is mounting evidence that the middle class in these countries is slowly disappearing. It appears that middle-class consumers are increasingly moving upstream to the ranks of the upper-middle class, and another smaller segment is losing ground and slipping backward to the ranks of the working class—creating a distribution that looks like an "hourglass."[32]

RESEARCH INSIGHT 11-1
SEGMENTING THE AFFLUENT MARKET

The affluent market is not one single market. Contrary to popular stereotypes, "the wealth in America is not found only in suburban clubs."[a]

Because not all affluent consumers share the same activities, interests, and opinions, various marketers have tried to isolate meaningful segments of the affluent market. One scheme has divided the affluent into two groups—the *upbeat enjoyers* who live for today and the *financial positives* who are conservative and look for value. It has been commented that "most people who have money are fairly conservative, and have accumulated wealth because they are very good savers."[b]

To assist the many marketers interested in reaching sub-segments of the affluent market, Mediamark Research, Inc. (MRI) has developed the following affluent market-segmentation schema for the "upper deck" consumers, who are defined as the top 10 percent of households in terms of income:[c]

- *Well-feathered nests:* Households that have at least one high-income earner and children present (38 percent of the upper deck).
- *No strings attached:* Households that have at least one high-income earner and no children (35 percent of the upper deck).
- *Nanny's in charge:* Households that have two or more earners, neither earning a high income, and children present (9 percent of the upper deck).
- *Two careers:* Households that have two or more earners, neither earning a high income, and no children present (11 percent of the upper deck).
- *The good life:* Households that have a high degree of affluence with no person employed or with the head of household not employed (7 percent of the upper deck).

Armed with information about such affluent life-style segments, MRI provides subscribing firms with profiles of users of a variety of goods and services often targeted to the affluent consumer, such as domestic and foreign travel, leisure clothing, lawn-care services, rental cars, and various types of recreational activities. For instance, the well-feathered nester can be found on the tennis court, the good lifer may be playing golf, while the two-career couple may be off sailing.[d]

With few local marketers vying for their business, the *rural affluent* are a sub-segment of the affluent market that is untapped and is somewhat difficult to pinpoint. The rural affluent fall into four categories:[e]

- *Suburban transplants:* Those who move to the country but still commute to high-paying urban jobs.
- *Equity-rich suburban expatriates:* Urbanites who sell their houses for a huge profit, buy a far less expensive house in a small town, and live on the difference.
- *City people with country homes:* Wealthy snowbirds and vacationers who spend the winter in a warm climate or the summer in a scenic cottage area.
- *Wealthy landowners:* Wealthy farmers and other local people who make a comfortable living off the land.

Note: The research referred to in this Research Insight is based on U.S. data. Although the affluent market in Canada may differ from the one in the United States in size and wealth, the general findings reported here are expected to hold true for Canada.

[a] "Marketing to Affluents: Hidden Pockets of Wealth," *Advertising Age*, July 9, 1990, S1.

[b] Jeanie Casison, "Wealthy and Wise," *Incentive*, January 1999, 78–81.

[c] *The Upper Deck* (Mediamark Research, Inc., 2001).

[d] For some further insights about the affluence of two-income households, see Diane Crispell, "The Very Rich Are Sort of Different," *American Demographics*, March 1994, 11–13.

[e] Sharon O'Malley, "Country Gold," *American Demographics*, July 1992, 26–34.

INTERNET INSIGHT 11-1
TARGETING THE ONLINE AFFLUENT CONSUMER

How would you use the internet to reach your target market if you were marketing a luxury car like Infiniti? Infiniti, like other luxury cars, is targeted at the affluent consumer, and indeed, the company needs to focus on this group to market its products successfully. The internet can be an effective medium for targeting the rich. A look at the internet campaign of Infiniti Canada can provide insights into how to target affluent Canadians.

The first rule in targeting any group on the internet is to find a suitable hub (or a site) that members of your target market are likely to visit or to partner with a company that has a strong web presence. Of course, this meant that Infiniti had to have a clear idea about the demographics of its target market. Since the firm was targeting the affluent consumer, it defined its target market as the upscale male professional between the ages of 25 and 55. The partner it chose was TD Waterhouse Canada, the internet banking and investment firm; Infiniti chose to cosponsor TD Waterhouse's fifth "Investor Rally" online stock market game. What better partner for a high-end car?

Secondly, to succeed in attracting the target consumer, a company has to engage his or her attention with a suitable incentive. In the case of Infiniti's target market, the incentive was a chance to win the grand prize—you guessed it—a brand new Infiniti—the 2000Q45 Platinum edition luxury sedan. The game was ideally suited to reach Infiniti's target market: it was a competitive environment that appealed to young, male professionals with high incomes. The top of the game page read "Presented by Infiniti. Powered by TD Waterhouse." The company also placed banner ads that linked it to the Infiniti site, which provided more information about the car offered as the grand prize.

There were additional incentives, like a $500 cash prize every week (to persuade consumers to play the game for the entire 12-week period) and a viral marketing email campaign that offered additional investment game money for anyone who invited a friend to join the game.

The results were very rewarding for Infiniti. Besides the people who had signed up for earlier Investor Rallies, 6000 new people signed on to the fifth one. Infiniti received 400 requests for a test drive; more important, perhaps, it received a databank of potential customers!

QUESTIONS:

1. Would this strategy have worked as well if the company's target market had been upscale women?
2. If you wanted to appeal to an upscale female market, whom would you partner with (or which hub would you choose)? Why?

The Working Class

Although many advertisers would prefer to show their products as part of an affluent life style, they cannot ignore working-class or blue-collar people, who account for a sizeable part of the market. Lower-income, or *downscale consumers* (frequently defined as having household incomes of $25 000 or less or in the lowest quartile) may actually be more brand-loyal than wealthier consumers, because they cannot afford to make mistakes by switching to unfamiliar brands.

Understanding the importance of talking to (not *at*) the downscale consumers, companies such as MasterCard and McDonald's target "average Joes" (and Janes) with ads portraying the modest life styles of some of their customers.[33] For instance, marketers need to be sensitive to the fact that downscale consumers often spend a higher percentage of their incomes on food than do their middle-class counterparts. Moreover, food is a particularly important purchase area for low-income consumers because it represents an area of self-indulgence. For this reason, they

www.nissan.ca/en

periodically trade up the foods they buy—especially favourite ethnic and natural foods—"where taste and authenticity matter."[34]

The "Techno Class"

Familiarity and competence with technology, especially computers and the internet, appears to be a new basis for a kind of "class standing" or status or prestige. Those who are unfamiliar with computers are being referred to as "technologically under-classed."[35] Educators, business leaders, and government officials have warned that the inability to use digital technology adequately is having a harmful effect on the lives of those who are not computer-literate.

Not wanting to see their children left out of the "sweep of computer technology," parents in all social-class groupings are seeking out early computer exposure for their children. Either because of their own positive experiences with computers (or possibly their own lack of personal computer experience), parents sense that an understanding of computers is a necessary tool of competitive achievement and success. At the other end of the life and age spectrum, even 55-year-old professionals, who were at first reluctant to "learn computers," are now seeking personal computer training—they no longer want to be left out, nor do they want to be further embarrassed by having to admit that they "don't know computers."

Consumers throughout the world have come to believe that it is essential to acquire a functional understanding of computers in order to ensure that they do not become obsolete or hinder themselves socially or professionally. In this sense, there is a technological class structure that is centred on the amount of computer skills that a person possesses. It appears that those without necessary computer skills will increasingly find themselves to be in an underclass and at a disadvantage. As *Wired* magazine wrote when it began publishing in 1993, "The Digital Revolution is whipping through our lives like a Bengali typhoon."[36] The importance of the computer and its prominence in our lives has resulted in somewhat of a reversal of fortune, in that the "geek" is now often viewed by his or her peers as "friendly and fun." The increasingly positive image of geeks has made them and their life styles the target of marketers' messages designed to appeal to their great appetite for novel technological products (see Exhibit 11-3).

Indeed, according to a recent British National Opinion Poll (NOP) of 7- to 16-year-olds, "Computer geeks are now the coolest kids in class."[37] The poll found that the archetypical geek is most commonly a 14- to 16-year-old boy who is the family computer expert, and he is willing to teach his parents, siblings, and teachers about computers. Interestingly enough, in an environment where children naturally take to computers, it is often the parents who find themselves technologi-

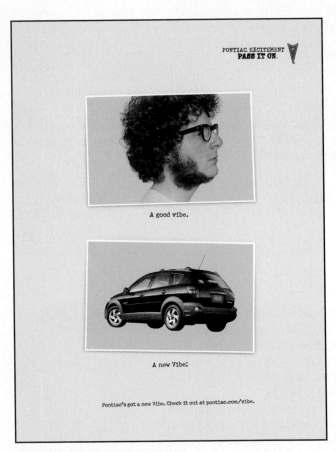

PONTIAC EXCITEMENT
PASS IT ON.

A good vibe.

A new Vibe.

Pontiac's got a new Vibe. Check it out at pontiac.com/vibe.

EXHIBIT 11-3

APPEALING TO THE GEEK-ORIENTED CONSUMER

Courtesy of General Motors.

cally disenfranchised. To remedy this situation, some schools are offering classes to bring parents up to speed in the use of computers.[38]

SOCIAL CLASS AND MARKETING STRATEGY

Social-class profiles provide a broad picture of the values, attitudes, and behaviour that distinguish the members of various social classes. This section examines specific consumer research that relates social class to the development of marketing strategy. Rather than looking at marketing strategy implications in the same manner as we have done in earlier chapters, in this one, we will examine how social-class status affects consumer behaviour in various product categories.

Clothing, Fashion, and Shopping

A Greek philosopher once said, "Know, first, who you are; and then adorn yourself accordingly."[39] This bit of wisdom is relevant to clothing marketers today, because most people dress to fit their self-image, which includes their perceptions of their own social-class membership. In fact, for many consumers, the notion of "keeping up with the Joneses" (i.e., trying to be like our neighbours) has been replaced by looking to more upscale reference groups that they would like to emulate (most often, people earning substantially more than they themselves do).

Members of specific social classes differ in what they consider fashionable or in good taste. For instance, lower-middle-class consumers have a strong preference for T-shirts, baseball caps, and other clothing that offers an *external point of identification,* such as the name of an admired person or group, such as the Toronto Blue Jays; a respected company or brand name like Budweiser; or a valued trademark like Tommy Hilfiger. These consumers are prime targets for licensed goods (bearing well-known logos). In contrast, upper-class consumers are likely to buy clothing that is free from such supporting associations. Upper-class consumers also seek clothing with a more subtle look, such as the kind of sportswear found in an L.L. Bean, Lands' End, or Talbots catalogue, rather than designer jeans.

Social class is also an important variable in determining where a consumer shops. People tend to avoid stores that have the image of appealing to a social class very different from their own. In the past, some mass merchandisers who tried to appeal to a higher class of consumer found themselves alienating their traditional customers. This implies that retailers should pay attention to the social class of their customer base and the social class of their store appeal to ensure that their advertisements send the right message.

Gap has been rapidly rolling out the Old Navy clothing stores in an effort to attract working-class families that usually buy their casual and active wear clothing from general merchandise retailers such as Zellers or Wal-Mart. For Gap, trading down to the lower-income consumer with Old Navy has resulted in bigger sales, more leverage with suppliers, and increased traffic volume. In effect, Gap created a "knock-off" of itself before anybody else got the chance.[40] However, in creating a lower-price alternative to itself, Gap has also tended to cannibalize itself—shifting loyal Gap customers to the Old Navy outlets.

Different department and clothing stores also target different social-class consumers. Harry Rosen targets upscale consumers, Sears and The Bay appeal to middle-class shoppers, and Zellers and Wal-Mart tend to target more of a working-class customer.

In exploring the social-class image or perception of retailers, researchers have discovered that consumers rate shirts purchased at Nordstrom, for example, to have higher status than shirts sold at Kmart.[41] Given that consumers' social-class perceptions of clothing brands and retail stores' prestige may affect their choices, researchers have developed a 19-item instrument (the PRECON scale) to gauge the following underlying factors of consumer preference: brand, quality, status, fashion involvement, and store atmosphere (see Figure 11-6).[42]

The Pursuit of Leisure

Social-class membership is also closely related to the choice of recreational and leisure-time activities. Upper-class consumers are likely to go to the opera, the theatre, and concerts, and to play bridge. Lower-class consumers tend to be avid television watchers and fishing enthusiasts, and they enjoy drive-in movies and hockey and baseball games. Furthermore, the lower-class consumer spends more time on commercial types of activities (like bowling, playing pool or billiards, or visiting taverns) and on crafts (such as model building and woodworking projects) than on intellectual activities like reading or going to museums. In any case, whether we are describing middle-class or working-class consumers, there appears to be a trend toward more spending on "experiences" that bring the family together, such as family vacations or other activities and less spending on "things."[43] Over the past decade or so, however, a number of changes are increasingly being observed that point to a further blurring of social-class lines with regard to leisure interests, especially preferences in the arts and media (see Figure 11-7). More specifically, only with the increased numbers of the suburban middle-class viewers could wrestling have become one of cable television's most popular programming areas. Similarly, the presumably sophisticated consumers who read magazines such as *The New Yorker* also like to attend theme parks and shoot billiards.[44]

FIGURE 11-6   The PRECON Scale for Measuring Clothing Preferences and Store Prestige

Brand	I consider the brand name when purchasing clothing for myself. I will pay a higher price for clothing that is made by a popular designer or manufacturer. I look my best when wearing brand-name clothing. Clothing made by a well-known designer or manufacturer is worth more money.
Quality	I prefer to shop at stores that carry high-quality merchandise. I usually buy high-quality clothing. When I buy clothes for others or as a gift, I buy clothes of superior quality.
Status	It is important to shop in the same clothing stores as my friends. Sometimes I would like to know where important people buy their clothes. I like to shop in the same clothing stores as people I admire. I often ask friends where they buy their clothes.
Fashion Involvement	Planning and selecting my wardrobe can be included among my favourite activities. I enjoy clothes as much as some people enjoy books, records, and movies. If I were to suddenly receive more money than I have now, I would spend it on clothes. I like to shop for clothes.
Store Atmosphere	It is important to me that a clothing store have a warm, inviting atmosphere. It is important to me that the clothing store I shop in have great service. Personal service is important to me when buying clothes. I shop at stores that have artistic-looking displays.

Source: Dawn R. Deeter-Schmelz, Jesse N. Moore, and Daniel J. Goebel, "Prestige Clothing Shopping by Consumers: A Confirmatory Assessment and Refinement of the PRECON Scale with Managerial Implications," *Journal of Marketing Theory and Practice*, Fall 2000, 51.

FIGURE 11-7   Preferences of Americans for 100 Arts, Media, and Leisure Pursuits

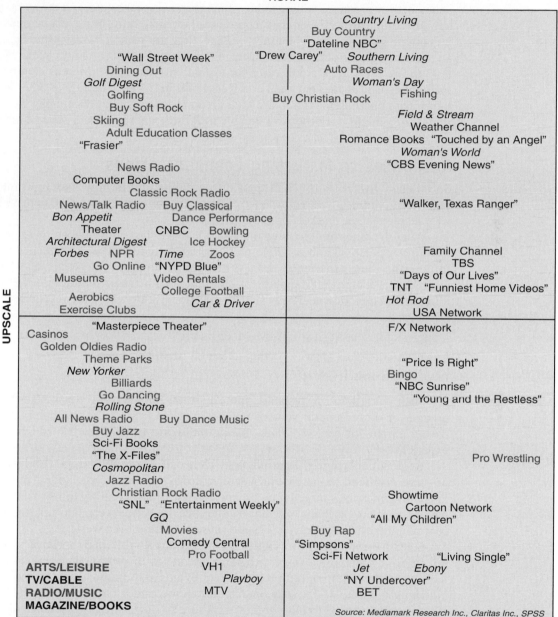

RURAL

Country Living
Buy Country
"Dateline NBC"
"Drew Carey"   *Southern Living*
"Wall Street Week"   Auto Races
Dining Out   *Woman's Day*
Golf Digest   Buy Christian Rock   Fishing
Golfing
Buy Soft Rock   *Field & Stream*
Skiing   Weather Channel
Adult Education Classes   Romance Books   "Touched by an Angel"
"Frasier"   *Woman's World*
"CBS Evening News"

News Radio
Computer Books
Classic Rock Radio
News/Talk Radio   Buy Classical   "Walker, Texas Ranger"
Bon Appetit   Dance Performance
Theater   CNBC   Bowling
Architectural Digest   Ice Hockey
Forbes   NPR   *Time*   Zoos   Family Channel
Go Online   "NYPD Blue"   TBS
Museums   Video Rentals   "Days of Our Lives"
College Football   TNT   "Funniest Home Videos"
Aerobics   *Car & Driver*   *Hot Rod*
Exercise Clubs   USA Network

UPSCALE / **DOWNSCALE**

"Masterpiece Theater"   F/X Network
Casinos
Golden Oldies Radio
Theme Parks   "Price Is Right"
New Yorker   Bingo
Billiards   "NBC Sunrise"
Go Dancing   "Young and the Restless"
Rolling Stone
All News Radio   Buy Dance Music
Buy Jazz
Sci-Fi Books
"The X-Files"   Pro Wrestling
Cosmopolitan
Jazz Radio
Christian Rock Radio   Showtime
"SNL"   "Entertainment Weekly"   Cartoon Network
GQ   "All My Children"
Movies   Buy Rap
Comedy Central   "Simpsons"
Pro Football   Sci-Fi Network   "Living Single"
ARTS/LEISURE   VH1   *Jet*   *Ebony*
TV/CABLE   *Playboy*   "NY Undercover"
RADIO/MUSIC   MTV   BET
MAGAZINE/BOOKS

Source: Mediamark Research Inc., Claritas Inc., SPSS

URBAN

The computer-generated preference space above, based on the preferences of Americans for 100 arts, media, and leisure pursuits, reveals omnivorous culture buffs among consumers who are upscale, downscale, urban, or rural.

Source: Michael J. Weiss, Morris B. Holbrook, and John Habich, "Death of the Arts Snob?" *American Demographics*, June 2001, 44. All rights reserved. Reprinted with permission.

Saving, Spending, and Credit

Saving, spending, and credit card use all seem to be related to social-class standing. Upper-class consumers are more future-oriented and confident of their financial acumen; they are more willing to invest in insurance, real estate, and the stock market. In comparison, lower-class consumers are generally more concerned with immediate gratification; when they do save, they are primarily interested in safety and security. Therefore, it is not surprising that members of the lower social classes tend to use their bank credit cards for instalment purchases, whereas members of the upper social classes pay their credit card bills in full each month. In other words, lower-class purchasers tend to use their credit cards to "buy now and pay later" for things they might not otherwise be able to afford, whereas upper-class purchasers use their credit cards as a convenient substitute for cash.

Responses to Marketing Communications

Social-class groupings differ in their media habits and in how they transmit and receive communications. Knowledge of these differences is invaluable to marketers who segment their markets on the basis of social class.

When it comes to describing their world, lower-class consumers tend to portray it in rather personal and concrete terms, whereas middle-class consumers are able to describe their experiences from a number of different perspectives. A simple example illustrates that members of different social classes tend to see the world differently. The following responses to a question asking where the respondent usually buys gasoline were received:

Upper-middle-class answer: At Mobil or Shell.

Lower-middle-class answer: At the station on Main and Fifth Street.

Lower-class answer: At Ed's.

Such variations in response indicate that middle-class consumers have a broader or more general view of the world, while lower-class consumers tend to have a narrow or personal view—seeing the world through their own immediate experiences.

Regional differences in terminology, choice of words and phrases, and patterns of usage also tend to increase as we move down the social-class ladder. Therefore, in creating messages targeted to the lower classes, marketers try to word advertisements to reflect particular regional preferences that exist (e.g., an "apartment" in central and eastern Canada is a "suite" in some parts of the west).

Selective exposure to various types of mass media differs by social class. In the selection of specific television programs and types of programs, members of the higher social classes tend to prefer current events and drama, whereas lower-class individuals tend to prefer soap operas, quiz shows, and situation comedies. Higher-class consumers tend to have greater exposure to magazines and newspapers than do their lower-class counterparts. Lower-class consumers are likely to have greater exposure to publications that dramatize romance and the lives of movie and television celebrities. For example, magazines such as *True Story* appeal heavily to blue-collar or working-class women, who enjoy reading about the problems, fame, and fortunes of others. Middle-class consumers are more likely to read a newspaper and to prefer movies and late-night programs than their lower-class counterparts.[45] Before we end the discussion of the implications of marketing strategy for social class, let us also look at the limitations of social class as a segmentation variable.

LIMITATIONS OF SOCIAL CLASS AS A SEGMENTATION VARIABLE

Although social class is a powerful influence on consumer behaviour, its relevance to marketing is being increasingly questioned by several practitioners. There are several reasons for this: (1) social class is more difficult to judge or measure than is income, (2) many kinds of purchase behaviour are related more to income than to social class, (3) consumers often consume according to their expected social class or their parents' social class rather than their present one, (4) dual incomes have made many activities and products that were accessible only to the upper classes open to middle-class consumers, and (5) individual dimensions of social class such as occupation, income, or education may be better predictors of certain behaviour than is social class itself.

SUMMARY

- Social stratification, the division of members of a society into a hierarchy of distinct social classes, exists in all societies and cultures.

- Social class reflects the amount of status that members of a specific class possess in relation to members of other classes; it also serves as a frame of reference (a reference group) for the development of consumer attitudes and behaviour.

- There are three basic methods for measuring social class: subjective measurement (an individual's perception), reputational measurement (perceptions of others), and objective measurement. Objective measures use specific socio-economic measures, either alone (as a single-variable index) or in combination with others (as a composite-variable index).

- The variables used to measure social class are income, occupation, education, and to a lesser extent, housing and possessions.

- A frequently used classification system consists of six classes: upper-upper, lower-upper, upper-middle, lower-middle, upper-lower, and lower-lower classes.

- Profiles of these classes indicate that the socio-economic differences among classes are reflected in differences in attitudes, in leisure activities, and in consumption habits. This is why segmentation by social class is of special interest to marketers.

- Particular attention is currently being directed to affluent consumers, who are the fastest-growing segment in our population; however, some marketers are finding it extremely profitable to cater to the needs of non-affluent consumers.

- Research has revealed social-class differences in clothing habits, home decoration, and leisure activities, as well as saving, spending, and credit habits. Thus, astute marketers tailor specific product and promotional strategies to each social-class target segment.

DISCUSSION QUESTIONS

1. What is social class? Why is social class a relevant segmentation variable for marketing products and services?

2. Marketing researchers generally use the objective method to measure social class rather than the subjective or reputational methods. Why is the objective method preferred by researchers?

3. Describe the correlation between social status (or prestige) and income. Which is a more useful segmentation variable? Discuss.

4. Discuss any three of the following social class groups and explain how a marketer can use this knowledge to develop marketing programs:

    upper-upper class   upper-middle class
    upper-lower class   lower-middle class
    lower-upper class   lower-lower class

5. What are some problems with using social class as a segmentation variable?

CRITICAL THINKING QUESTIONS

1. Which status-related variable—occupation, education, or income—is the most suitable segmentation base for (a) expensive vacations, (b) opera subscriptions, (c) subscriptions to *People* magazine, (d) fat-free foods, (e) personal computers, (f) pocket-size cellular telephones, and (g) health clubs?

2. How would you use the research evidence on affluent households presented in this chapter to segment the market for (a) home exercise equipment, (b) vacations, and (c) banking services?

3. You are the owner of two furniture stores, one catering to upper-middle-class consumers and the other to lower-class consumers. How do social-class differences influence each store's (a) product lines and styles, (b) advertising media selection, (c) copy and communications style used in the ads, and (d) payment policies?

4. Find three print ads in one of the following publications:
   Globe and Mail, Maclean's, Canadian Living, Report on Business, Reader's Digest, Canadian Geographic

   Using the social-class characteristics listed in this text, identify the social class targeted by each ad and evaluate the effectiveness of the advertising appeals used.

5. Select two households featured in two different television series or sitcoms. Classify each household into one of the social classes discussed in the text, and analyse its life style and consumption behaviour.

INTERNET EXERCISES

1. Visit the website of a high-end car manufacturer (e.g., Mercedes-Benz or Peugot) and that of a lower-priced car manufacturer (e.g., Kia or Hyundai). Do you see any differences between the two sites?

2. Visit the website of Statistics Canada (**www.statcan.ca**) and examine the differences in income between people with a university education and those with a high school education. Are these variables correlated?

3. Visit the websites of the *Financial Post* magazine and the *Globe and Mail*'s "Globe Investor." What kind of ads do you see on the websites? Which market do these ads seem to be catering to?

KEY TERMS

Class consciousness   *(p. 347)*
Composite-variable indexes   *(p. 350)*
Index of Status Characteristics   *(p. 351)*
Objective measures   *(p. 348)*
Reputational measures   *(p. 347)*
Single-variable index   *(p. 349)*
Social class   *(p. 344)*
Social comparison theory   *(p. 345)*
Social status   *(p. 344)*
Socio-economic Status Score   *(p. 351)*
Subjective measures   *(p. 347)*

CASE 11-1: MAKE MINE TOP LOADING

Canadians do a lot of laundry. Indeed, according to some experts, it is a uniquely North American phenomenon to consider clothing dirty after only one wearing. Because of this, Canadians tend to subject their clothing to frequent washing and drying, which, in turn, results in more wear and tear on their clothes.

To make matters worse, Canadians (and Americans) also prefer top-loading washing machines to front loaders. The reason for this seems to be an unwillingness to bend over in order to load or unload the machine. Top-loading washing machines also tend to have a larger capacity than front loaders, so it allows Canadians to wash larger loads.

However, top-loading washing machines tend to damage clothes more than front loaders because the garments are beaten by an agitator to get them clean. In contrast, front loaders are easier on clothing because they merely tumble the clothing inside their rotating tub. Procter and Gamble chemists experimented by washing one-half of the collar of a white dress shirt in a typical Canadian top-loading washing machine and the other half in a European front-loading machine. The half washed in the top loader ended up looking more worn and yellower.

So why haven't a substantial number of Canadians switched to front-loading washing machines if they are so much better? Perhaps the main reason is that a typical low-end top loader may be priced at $450 to $550, whereas a comparable front loader costs between $1000 and $1100—almost three times as much. Clearly, at such a price, it is probably safe to assume that only affluent households would consider such a purchase.

QUESTION

1. Assume that you work for an advertising agency whose client, an appliance manufacturer, has introduced a line of front-loading washing machines (to complement its line of top loaders). Considering the discussion of the affluent in this chapter, what types of magazines would you suggest be used to promote these front-loading washing machines to Canadian consumers?

Source: Emily Nelson, "In Doing Laundry, Americans Cling to Outmoded Ways," *The Wall Street Journal*, May 16, 2002, A1, A10.

NOTES

1   Eve Lazarus, "The Luxe Approach," *Marketing Magazine*, March 29, 2004, 6.

2   Douglas B. Holt, "Does Cultural Capital Structure American Consumption?" *Journal of Consumer Research,* 25, June 1998, 19.

3   Shaun Saunders, "Fromm's Marketing Character and Rokeach Values," *Social Behavior and Personality,* 29, no. 2, 2001, 191–196.

4   Jacqueline K. Eastman, Ronald E. Goldsmith, and Leisa Reinecke Flynn, "Status Consumption in Consumer Behavior: Scale Development and Validation," *Journal of Marketing Theory and Practice,* Summer 1999, 41–52.

5   Jacqueline K. Eastman, Ronald E. Goldsmith, and Leisa Reinecke Flynn, "Status Consumption in Consumer Behavior: Scale Development and Validation," *Journal of Marketing Theory and Practice,* Summer 1999, 43.

6   Randy Kennedy, "For Middle Class, New York Shrinks as Home Prices Soar," *New York Times,* April 1, 1998, A1, B6; "Two Tier Marketing," *Business Week,* March 17, 1997, 82–90; and Keith Bradsher, "America's Opportunity Gap," *New York Times,* June 4, 1995, 4.

7   Malcolm M. Knapp, "Believing 'Myth of the Middle Class' Can Be Costly Misreading of Consumer Spending," *Nation's Restaurant News,* January 1, 2001, 36.

8   Takashina Shuji, "The New Inequality," *Japan Echo,* August 2000, 38–39.

9   Rebecca Piirto Heath, "The New Working Class," *American Demographics,* January 1998, 52.

10   John P. Dickson and R. Bruce Lind, "The Stability of Occupational Prestige as a Key Variable in Determining Social Class Structure: A Longitudinal Study 1976–2000," in *2001 AMA Winter Educators' Conference,* 12, eds. Ram Krishnan and Madhu Viswanathan (Chicago: American Marketing Association, 2001), 38–44.

11   Rebecca Piirto Heath, "Life on Easy Street," *American Demographics,* April 1997, 33–38.

12   Diane Crispell, "The Real Middle Americans," *American Demographics,* October 1994, 28–35.

13   Eugene Sivadas, George Mathew, and David J. Curry, "A Preliminary Examination of the Continued Significance of Social Class to Marketing: A Geodemographic Replication," *Journal of Consumer Marketing,* 14, 6, 1997, 469.

14   Dennis Rodkin, "Wealthy Attitude Wins over Healthy Wallet: Consumers Prove Affluence Is a State of Mind," *Advertising Age,* July 9, 1990, S4, S6.

15   Janeen Arnold Costa and Russell W. Belk, "Nouveaux Riches as Quintessential Americans: Case Studies of Consumption in an Extended Family," *Advances in Nonprofit Marketing,* 3 (Greenwich, CT: JAI Press, 1990), 83–140.

16   F. Stuart Chapin, *Contemporary American Institutions* (New York: Harper, 1935), 373–397.

17   Robert B. Settle, Pamela L. Alreck, and Denny E. McCorkle, "Consumer Perceptions of Mail/Phone Order Shopping Media," *Journal of Direct Marketing,* 8, Summer 1994, 30–45.

18   W. Lloyd Warner, Marchia Meeker, and Kenneth Eells, *Social Class in America: Manual of Procedure for the Measurement of Social Status* (New York: Harper and Brothers, 1960).

19   *Methodology and Scores of Socioeconomic Status,* Working Paper No. 15 (Washington, DC: U.S. Bureau of the Census, 1963).

20   Paul Bruder, "Economic Health: The Key Ingredient in the Personal Health of Global Communities," *Hospital Topics,* 79, no. 1, Winter 2001, 32–35.

21   Lisa Singhania, "Whirlpool Looks to Innovation to Boost Appliance Sales," *The Grand Rapids Press,* February 6, 2000, F1; and Gregory L. White and Shirley Leung, "Stepping Up: Middle Market Shrinks as Americans Migrate toward the High End—Shifting Consumer Values Create 'Hourglass Effect'; Quality Gets Easier to Sell—Six Air Bags, 22 Bath Towels," *Wall Street Journal,* March 29, 2002, A1.

22   Statistics Canada, "Family Income Groups (21A) in Constant (2000) Dollars, Age Group of Lone Parent or Reference Person (5)...." Catalogue no. 97F0020XIE2001099. **www.statcan.ca**.

23   "New Forrester Report Advises How to Win Affluent Consumers in the Economic Slump," *Business Wire,* August 1, 2001, 1.

24   *The Mendelsohn Affluent Survey 2002* (New York: Mendelsohn Media Research, 2002).

25   Geoffrey Holliman, "Once a Teenager, Now Affluent and Best Not Ignored," *Marketing,* December 2, 1999, 22.

26   Martha R. McEnally and Charles Bodkin, "A Comparison of Convenience Orientation between U.S. and U.K. Households," in *2001 AMA Winter Educators' Conference,* 12, eds. Ram Krishnan and Madhu Viswanathan (Chicago: American Marketing Association, 2001), 332–338.

27   Gayle Gerhardt and Pete Jacques, "Is the Middle Market Still in the Middle?" *Life Insurance Marketing & Research Association's Market Facts Quarterly,* Fall 2001, 18–21.

28   Debra Goldman, "Paradox of Pleasure," *American Demographics,* May 1999, 50–53.

29   W. Michael Cox, "The Low Cost of Living," *The Voluntaryist,* October 1999, 3.

30   Chris Daniels, "Almost Rich," *Marketing Magazine,* April 26, 2004, 9.

31   Chris Daniels, "Almost Rich," *Marketing Magazine,* April 26, 2004, 9–12.

32   White and Leung, "Stepping Up," *Wall Street Journal,* March 29, 2002, A1.

33   Karen Benezra, "Hardworking RC Cola," *Brandweek,* May 25, 1998, 18–19.

34   "Small Budgets Yield Big Clout for Food Companies—10.1 Million Low Income Consumers Can't (or Shouldn't) Be Ignored," *PR Newswire,* August 22, 2002, 1.

35   Steve Rosenbush, "Techno Leaders Warn of a 'Great Divide,'" *USA Today,* June 17, 1998, B1.

36   Steve Lohr, "A Time Out for Technophilia," *New York Times,* November 18, 2001, 4.

37   "Computer Geeks Now the Cool Kids in Class," *The Press* (Christchurch, New Zealand), July 20, 2000, 31.

38   Sophia Lezin Jones, "Parent Technology Nights: Classes to Help Boost Computer Savvy Riverside Elementary Moms, Dads Invited," *The Atlanta Journal-Constitution,* October 19, 1999, JJ1.

39   Epictetus, "Discourses" (second century) in *The Enchiridon,* 2nd ed., trans. Thomas Higginson (Indianapolis: Bobbs-Merrill, 1955).

40   Mike Duff, "Old Navy: The Master of Downmarket Apparel Dollars," *DSN Retailing Today,* May 8, 2000, 89–90.

41   D.F. Baugh and L.L. Davis. "The Effect of Store Image on Consumers' Perceptions of Designer and Private Label Clothing," *Clothing and Textiles Research Journal,* 7, no. 3, 1989, 15–21.

42   Dawn R. Deeter-Schmelz, Jesse N. Moore, and Daniel J. Goebel, "Prestige Clothing Shopping by Consumers: A Confirmatory Assessment and Refinement of the PRECON Scale with Managerial Implications," *Journal of Marketing Theory and Practice,* Fall 2000, 43–58.

43   Christina Duff, "Indulging in Inconspicuous Consumption," *Wall Street Journal,* April 14, 1997,

B1, B2; and Christina Duff, "Two Family Budgets: Different Means, Similar Ends," *Wall Street Journal,* April 14, 1997, B1, B2.

44   Michael J. Weiss, Morris B. Holbrook, and John Habich, "Death of the Arts Snob?" *American Demographics,* June 2001, 40–42.

45   Kim and Han, "Perceived Images of Retail Store Brands," 59.

give them a future
we can all smile about

take david suzuki's nature challenge
www.davidsuzuki.org

David
Suzuki
Foundation

SOLUTIONS ARE IN OUR NATURE

chapter 12
reference groups and family

LEARNING OBJECTIVES

By the end of this chapter you should be able to:

1. Define reference groups and the various types of reference groups.
2. Discuss the three types of reference group influence.
3. Discuss the factors affecting the level of reference group influence.
4. Discuss at least three common reference groups and their influence on your behaviour.
5. Explain how marketers can use reference groups when designing the marketing strategy for their products.
6. Discuss traditional and non-traditional family life cycles.
7. Explain the principal consumption roles in a family and family decision making.
8. Discuss how marketers can use family influence to develop more effective marketing strategies.

12

www.griplimited.ca

what do you do when your target market views your brand of beer as "Dad's beer"? That was the problem facing the marketers of Labatt Blue—a brand with a half-century of tradition behind it. Labatt had carved out an image for itself as a young and exciting product and had become part of Canadian culture, but after several decades, the brand needed to reinvent itself in order to attract a younger audience and maintain its market share. Labatt hired Grip Limited, a fledgling Toronto advertising company, to alter consumer perceptions of its Blue brand.

The crucial issue was to attract young men—the beer's primary target market—by changing their impression of the brand as one for older people. The company and its advertising agency decided to focus the new campaign on what they considered to be important to their target market—friendships. The ad campaign, developed after extensive research, focused on what young men do *with* their friends, *to* their friends, and *for* their friends. Seventy scenarios were developed, and the company decided to give a realistic flavour to the ads by recruiting "real guys" from hockey and rugby clubs for a week-long shoot alongside professional actors.

The first ad, "Cheers. To Friends," aired during *Hockey Night in Canada*, showed what young men do when they are among friends (e.g., tying a naked pal to a telephone pole, filling an SUV with golf balls). The fact that the non-actors did not know what was planned made their reactions real and helped convey a brand image that was spontaneous, fun, and contemporary, for it showed images that, in the words of Andrew Howard, senior director of marketing at Labatt, were a "real part of what guys do together."[1]

Initial reactions to the ad campaign were extremely positive, and the company is hopeful that, with a consistent, long-running campaign, it will be able to attract younger men.

CHAPTER OVERVIEW

This chapter examines the groups that influence us.

With the exception of those very few people who are classified as hermits, most of us enjoy being part of a group and we interact with other people every day, especially with members of our own families.

In the first part of this chapter, we will consider how group involvements and memberships influence our actions as consumers—that is, influence consumers' decisions, shopping activities, and actual consumption. The second part of the chapter deals with how the family influences its members' consumer behaviour. The chapter will also examine the marketing implications of the family and reference groups on consumer decision making.

WHAT ARE REFERENCE GROUPS?

Reference group:
A person or group that serves as a point of comparison (or reference) for an individual in forming either general or specific values or attitudes, or as a specific guide for behaviour.

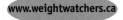
www.weightwatchers.ca

Symbolic group:
A group that a person identifies with by adopting its values, attitudes, and behaviour in spite of knowing that he or she cannot belong to that group.

Although a *group* may be defined as two or more people who interact to accomplish either individual or mutual goals, a **reference group** is any person or group that serves as a point of comparison (or reference) when an individual is forming either general or specific values or attitudes, or serves as a specific guide for behaviour. The broad scope of this definition includes an intimate group of two co-workers who each week attend a Weight Watchers class together and a larger, more formal group, such as a local scuba diving club, whose members are all interested in scuba equipment, scuba training, and scuba diving trips and vacations. Included in this definition, too, is a kind of "one-sided grouping" in which an individual consumer observes the appearance or actions of others, who unknowingly serve as consumption-related role models.

Reference groups can be classified in many ways:

- ■ *By membership status:* Reference groups can be classified on the basis of membership status into membership groups and symbolic groups. A group that a person either belongs to or would qualify for membership in is called a *membership group*. For example, the group of women that a young executive plays tennis with every week would be considered, for her, a membership group.

   There are also groups in which an individual is not likely to receive membership, despite acting like a member by adopting the group's values, attitudes, and behaviour. This is considered a **symbolic group.**

   For instance, professional golfers may constitute a symbolic group for an amateur golfer who identifies with certain players by imitating their behaviour whenever possible (e.g., by buying a specific brand of golf balls or golf clubs). However, the amateur golfer does not (and probably never will) qualify for membership as a professional golfer because he has neither the skill nor the opportunity to compete professionally.

■ *By extent of interaction:* Originally, reference groups were defined narrowly to include only those groups with which a person interacted directly, such as family and close friends. Although these **direct reference groups** play an important role in our lives, the concept has gradually broadened to include both direct and indirect individual or group influences. **Indirect reference groups** consist of those individuals or groups with whom a person does not have direct face-to-face contact, such as movie stars, sports heroes, political leaders, television personalities, or even well-dressed and interesting-looking people on the street. Symbolic groups (mentioned earlier) are indirect reference groups. It is the power of the indirect reference group that helps sell the Nike clothing, golf balls, and golf equipment used by Tiger Woods.

■ *By nature of attraction:* There are some groups that we want to belong to (positive or aspirational groups); we try to do everything possible to belong to these groups and to avoid being rejected by them. But there are also groups that we do not want to belong to; these negative (or dissociative) groups may also affect our behaviour because we want to be seen as distinct from them and may go out of our way to show that we don't belong to them.

■ *By degree of formality:* **Informal reference groups** include friendship groups, relationships with neighbours, and so on. There are no formal membership rules or mechanisms, and yet we know we are part of these groups. **Formal reference groups** are groups in which there is an official membership and that follow a more formal structure. For example, if you are an accountant, you would belong to several accounting groups or organizations such as the Certified General Accountants of Canada. Similarly, while you might belong to an informal friendship group at university, you are also likely to be part of other formal membership groups, such as the Business Society or other student organizations.

Regardless of the type of reference group, from a marketing perspective, it is important to remember that all these groups serve as *frames of reference* for individuals in their purchase or consumption decisions. The usefulness of this concept is enhanced by the fact that it places no restrictions on the size of the group or its membership. Nor does it require that consumers identify with a tangible group (i.e., the group can be symbolic, such as owners of successful small businesses, leading corporate chief executive officers, rock stars, or golf celebrities).

TYPES OF REFERENCE GROUP INFLUENCE

Reference groups influence us in three ways. They provide information about brands or product categories (informational influence). They let us know what patterns of behaviour we are expected to follow to meet the group's expectations (normative influence). And they also influence us because we identify with them and their behaviour, not because they expect us to, but because we want to (identification influence). Each type of influence is described in more detail in the following sections.

Informational Influence

This type of reference group influence occurs when a member of the reference group member provides information that is used to make purchase decisions. Reference groups give us a lot of information about the products we consume. For example, other students may tell you that a particular course is very difficult or that a particular professor is a difficult grader. Often, **informational influence** takes place informally (e.g., a friend tells you that she bought a new computer at a really good

Direct reference groups: Groups within which a person interacts on a direct basis, such as family and close friends.

Indirect reference groups: Groups with which a person does not come into face-to-face contact.

www.nike.com

Informal reference groups: Groups in which there are no official memberships or formal structures.

Formal reference groups: Groups with formal membership structures and rules.

Informational influence: A type of reference group influence that occurs when a member of a reference group provides information that is used to make purchase decisions.

EXHIBIT 12-1

INFORMATIONAL REFERENCE GROUP INFLUENCE

NESQUIK advertorial from *Today's Parent* magazine, 2004.

Normative influence:
A type of influence that occurs when we conform to a group's norms or expectations in order to belong to that group.

Identification influence:
A type of reference group influence that occurs because we identify with, and have internalized, the group's values and behaviour.

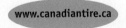

www.canadiantire.ca

price from Future Shop, and hence you decide to visit the store since you are in the market for a computer). But it can also take place in a more formal way because consumers often ask reference group members for advice on their purchase decisions. For example, when you are in the market for a computer, you might go to a friend who is considered to be a "computer nerd" and ask her for some advice. Exhibit 12-1 provides an example of informational reference group influence.

Normative Influence

Normative influence occurs when we conform to a group's norms or expectations because we want to belong to that group; in other words, the reference group influences us through the use of rewards (membership in the group) or punishment (banishment from the group). To exert such influence, membership in a group must be very important to the consumer. Several consumer products are sold by means of normative influence (e.g., personal hygiene products such as deodorants and mouthwash). Exhibit 12-2 gives an example of normative reference group influence.

Identification Influence

Often, we base our behaviour on that of people who belong to a reference group, not because we are afraid of being punished or losing the benefit of group membership, but because we truly identify with (and agree with) the group's values and behaviour. In other words, we want to be like them because we like them, not because we are afraid of being rejected by them. Under **identification influence**, we have accepted and internalized the group's values and, because we value the same things now, we behave in the same way. Often, typical consumers are used in ads because they provide identification influence to others. Universities, for example, use current students or recent graduates in their ads in the hope that potential students will identify with these people (Exhibit 12-3).

Canadian Tire, the venerable Canadian retailer, used an imaginary couple—Ted and Gloria—when it launched its new advertising campaign to reposition the store. The company decided to reposition its store as one that carries exclusive products that help consumers solve their problems. The ads actually show viewers what a product does, why it is different, and how it helps a typical suburban family solve its problem. The suburban couple have taken centre stage in the ads; the company is hoping that millions of Canadians will identify with them.[2]

The ad campaign by Labatt that showed "real guys recruited from hockey and rugby clubs" having fun celebrated the friendships among young men. The target market could identify with the people in the ad, and hence consumer reaction has been strong, with initial research indicating that the target market could relate well to the ad.[3]

Which type of reference group influence would come into play in a particular situation? That depends to a great extent on the nature of the product. For example, complex, technological products are often sold by means of informational influence, whereas products that we use to express ourselves, such as clothes or makeup, are sold through identification influence. Normative influence works best in situations where we are concerned about public acceptance (e.g., personal hygiene products or home maintenance). Figure 12-1 provides details of the types of reference group influence and examples of each.

Regardless of the nature of reference group influence, to achieve consumer conformity, a reference group must do the following:

- inform or make the individual aware of a specific product or brand
- give the individual the opportunity to compare his or her own thinking with the attitudes and behaviour of the group
- influence the individual to adopt attitudes and behaviour that are consistent with the norms of the group
- legitimize the decision to use the same products as the group

In contrast, marketers, especially those responsible for a new brand or a brand that is not the market leader, may wish to choose a strategy that asks consumers to strike out and be different and not just follow the crowd when making a purchase decision.

EXHIBIT 12-2

NORMATIVE REFERENCE GROUP INFLUENCE
Courtesy of *Maclean's* magazine.

FACTORS THAT AFFECT REFERENCE GROUP INFLUENCE

The amount of influence that a reference group exerts on an individual's behaviour usually depends on the nature of the individual and the product and on factors related to the reference group itself. This section discusses how and why some of these factors influence consumer behaviour. Figure 12-2 presents a broad view of the factors that influence conformity.

Information and experience: An individual who has first-hand experience with a product or service, or can easily obtain full information about it, is less likely to be influenced by the advice or example of others. For instance, when a young corporate sales rep wants to impress his client, he may take her to a restaurant that he knows from experience to be good or to one that has been highly recommended by the local newspaper's Dining Out Guide. If he has neither personal experience nor information he regards as valid, he may ask the advice of a friend or a parent or imitate the behaviour of others by taking her to a restaurant he knows is frequented by young business executives whom he admires.

Level of purchase confidence: A consumer who is less confident about making purchase decisions is more likely to be influenced by a reference group. This lower

"Success is what you make of it. When I graduate from MSVU, I'll have at least three successful businesses on my resume. I'll be ready for the job market. I'll be ready to make a living as an entrepreneur."

Halifax, Nova Scotia
www.msvu.ca

- Dave Reynolds is studying Business Administration and participating in MSVU's Entrepreneurial Skills Program. He is also President and CEO of Quicksnap Inc., which manufactures a patented sneaker clip he invented.

MOUNT SAINT VINCENT UNIVERSITY

Excellence · Innovation · Discovery

Discover the difference.   GO

EXHIBIT 12-3

IDENTIFICATION REFERENCE GROUP INFLUENCE

Mount Saint Vincent University, 2003.

purchase confidence may be the result of lack of experience or information; it might also be a personality variable. Some consumers are more likely than others to have lower levels of self-confidence.

Commitment to the group: People who are strongly committed to a group are more likely to be influenced by group norms, to be concerned about group rewards or sanctions, or to approach the group for information.

Research has found that among those attending a sporting event, such as a hockey or baseball game, the more an individual identifies with a particular team, the greater the likelihood that he or she will buy the products of the companies that sponsor that team—such as a particular brand of beer or hot dog, or particular newspapers.[4]

Credibility, attractiveness, and power of the group: A reference group that is seen as credible, attractive, or powerful can induce changes in consumer attitude and behaviour. When consumers want to obtain accurate information about the performance or quality of a product or service, they are likely to be persuaded by those whom they consider trustworthy and knowledgeable. That is, they are more likely to be persuaded by sources with *high credibility.*

When consumers are primarily concerned with the acceptance or approval of others they like, with whom they identify, or who offer them status or other benefits, they are likely to adopt their product, brand, or other behavioural characteristics. They are concerned primarily with the power that a person or group can exert over them, so they might choose products or services that conform to the norms of that person or group in order to avoid ridicule or punishment. However, unlike other reference groups that consumers follow because they are credible or attractive, *power groups* are not as likely to cause attitude change. Individuals may conform to the behaviour of a powerful person or group, but they are not as likely to change their own attitudes.

Conspicuousness of the product: The potential influence of a reference group on a purchase decision varies according to how visually or verbally conspicuous the product is to others. A *visually conspicuous* product is one that will stand out and be noticed—such as a luxury item or novelty product. A *verbally conspicuous* product may be highly interesting, or it may be easily described to others. Products that are especially conspicuous and revealing of status, such as a new car, fashion clothing, a sleek laptop computer, or home furniture, are most likely to be bought with an eye to the reactions of relevant others. Privately consumed products that are less conspicuous, such as yogourt or laundry soap are less likely to be bought with a reference group in mind.

Walk down any street in Canada (and almost anywhere else) and you are likely to see someone wearing a hat, T-shirt, or jacket emblazoned with the logo of a favourite sports team. Similarly, while in a car, just look at the licence plates of other

FIGURE 12-1	Types of Reference Group Influences	
TYPE OF REFERENCE GROUP INFLUENCE	**TYPICAL STATEMENTS MADE BY CONSUMERS**	**EXAMPLES OF PRODUCTS**
Informational influence	*"I asked Tom what would be a good place to buy a computer and went to the store he suggested."* *"I heard my friends talking about what to look for when you buy a computer, and I looked for those features when I was in the market for a computer."* *"I noticed that all the computer experts in our department had Dell laptops, so I bought one too."*	Big ticket items such as cars Complex items such as computers or other technology-oriented products Services because their quality is difficult to judge before purchase Socially risky items such as a dress for a wedding; health-related items
Normative influence	*"I noticed that the popular students in my class wore a particular brand, and I thought I would fit in better if I wore that brand name too."* *"My friends told me that my outfit looks really old-fashioned, so I went out and got something different."* *"My friends were talking about someone and laughing at his bad breath, so I decided to buy mouthwash and Listerine strips."*	Personal-hygiene products like mouthwash or deodorant Clothing and other visible items of attire such as hats Clothing for special occasions
Identification influence	*"My friends wear jeans to school every day; I think it is cool, so I wear jeans every day too."* *"All the successful business people I know wear dark-coloured suits, so I decided to get one myself."* *"My friends are big believers in physical activity and are members of a gym. I've seen the improvement in their fitness and thought I'd join a gym too."*	Products that are visible in use such as clothing and jewellery, soft drinks, beer, etc.

cars on the road. It will not be long before you start seeing licence plates bearing the name and logo of universities, favourite sports teams, environmental groups, and many other institutions and causes.

Whether or not the product is a necessity: In general, the less of a necessity a product is, the more likely it is to be affected by reference group influences. For example, reference group influences are stronger for products such as snowboards, designer clothes, and yachts, than for utilitarian products like a can of soup or even big-ticket necessities like stoves and microwave ovens.

Interestingly enough, when a product is a necessity, the reference group influence on purchase of the product category is weak, although reference groups may still exert some influence on the brand bought *if it is a public necessity.* For

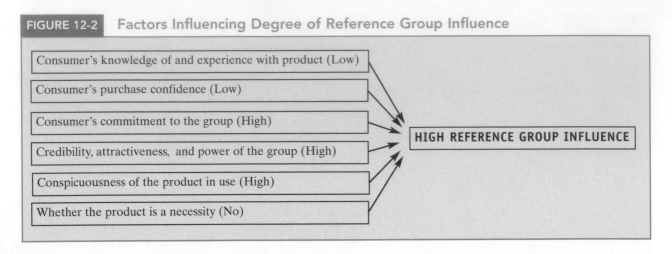

FIGURE 12-2   Factors Influencing Degree of Reference Group Influence

example, although you might buy a house brand of cola to drink at home, when you are with friends, you might choose Pepsi or Coke, depending on the group's preference. Luxury (or non-necessity) items, conversely, are more prone to product category influence; for example, people might buy a hot tub (a non-necessary item) because they want to impress their friends, but the brand of hot tub may not matter very much. Of course, when a luxury product is also highly visible when it is used, it becomes important to own the right brand.

SELECTED CONSUMER-RELATED REFERENCE GROUPS

As already mentioned, consumers may be influenced by a diverse range of people whom they come in contact with or observe. We will consider the following seven specific reference groups because they are a kind of cross-section of the types of groups that influence consumers' attitudes and behaviour: (1) friendship groups, (2) shopping groups, (3) work groups, (4) virtual groups or communities, (5) brand communities (6) consumer-action groups, and (7) celebrities. The family, possibly the most compelling reference group for consumer behaviour, will be covered fully in the second part of this chapter.

Friendship Groups

Friendship groups are classified as informal groups because they are usually unstructured and lack specific authority levels. In relative influence on a person's purchase decisions, friends come right after an individual's family.

Seeking and maintaining friendships is a basic drive of most people. Friends fulfill a wide range of needs: they provide companionship, security, and opportunities to discuss problems that an individual may be reluctant to discuss with family members. Friendships are also a sign of maturity and independence, for they represent a breaking away from the family and the forming of social ties with the outside world.

The opinions and preferences of friends are an important influence in determining the products or brands a consumer ultimately selects. Marketers of products such as brand-name clothing, fine jewellery, snack foods, and alcoholic beverages, recognize the power of peer group influence, and they often depict friendship situations in their ads.

Shopping Groups

Two or more people who shop together, whether for food, for clothing, or simply to pass the time, can be called a **shopping group.** Such groups are often offshoots of family or friendship groups, and therefore they function as what has been referred to as *purchase pals.*[5] The reasons for shopping with a purchase pal range from a primarily social motive (to share time together and enjoy lunch after shopping) to helping reduce the risk when making an important decision, since having someone along with expertise will reduce the chance of making an unwise purchase. In cases where none of the members of the shopping group knows much about the product under consideration, a shopping group may form for defensive reasons; members may feel more confident with a collective decision.

A special type of shopping group is the *in-home shopping party*, which consists of a group that gathers in the home of a friend to attend a "party" devoted to demonstrating and evaluating a specific line of products. The in-home party approach allows marketers to demonstrate the features of their products to a number of potential customers simultaneously. Early purchasers tend to create a bandwagon effect: undecided guests often overcome a reluctance to buy when they see their friends deciding to make purchases. Furthermore, some of the guests may feel obliged to buy because they are in the home of the sponsoring host or hostess. Given the spirit and excitement of "consumer gatherings" or "parties," Tupperware, for example, generates 90 percent of its billion dollars in annual sales from such consumer parties.[6]

> **Shopping group:**
> Two or more people who shop together, whether for food, for clothing, or simply to pass the time.

Work Groups

The sheer amount of time that people spend at their jobs, often more than 35 hours a week, provides ample opportunity for work groups to serve as a major influence on the consumption behaviour of their members.

Both the formal work group and the informal friendship-work group can influence consumer behaviour. The *formal work group* consists of people who work together as part of a team and, thus, have a sustained opportunity to influence each other's consumption-related attitudes and actions. *Informal friendship-work groups* consist of people who have become friends as a result of working for the same firm, whether or not they actually work together. Members of informal work groups may influence the consumption behaviour of other members during coffee or lunch breaks or at after-work meetings.

Recognizing that work groups influence consumers' brand choices and that many women now work outside of their homes, firms that in the past sold their products exclusively through direct calls on women in their homes now are redirecting their sales efforts to offices and plants during lunch-hour visits. For instance, Avon and Tupperware, two leading direct-to-home marketers, encourage their sales representatives to reach working women at their places of employment.

www.avon.ca

www.tupperware.ca

Virtual Groups or Communities

Thanks to computers and the internet, we are witnessing the emergence of a new type of group—**virtual groups** or communities. Both adults and children are turning on their computers, logging on to the web, and visiting special-interest websites, often with chat rooms. If you're a skier, you can chat online with other skiers; if you're an amateur photographer, you can chat online with others who share your interest. Local newspapers everywhere run stories from time to time about singles

> **Virtual groups:**
> Groups that exist by virtue of using the internet as the medium of communication.

who met online and are now married. An internet provider such as America Online even lets its members create "Buddy Lists," so that when they sign on to AOL they immediately know which of their friends are currently online and can send and receive instant messages. An elderly person in Winnipeg, for example, might not make it to the local senior citizens' centre when it's freezing outside and snowing, but he or she can always log on to the centre's website.[7] Internet Insight 12-1 provides more information on web-based reference groups.

INTERNET INSIGHT 12-1
VIRTUAL REFERENCE GROUPS

Whereas 50 years ago the definition of a community stressed the notion of geographic proximity and face-to-face relationships, today's communities are defined much more broadly as "sets of social relations among people."[8] In this spirit, there is also today rather wide-scale access to what is known as "internet communities" or "virtual communities." These terms refer to web-based consumer groups. These communities give their members access to extensive amounts of information, fellowship, and social interaction covering an extremely wide range of topics and issues—vegetarianism, cooking, collecting, trading, finance, filmmaking, romance, politics, technology, art, hobbies, spiritualism, age grouping, online game playing, voice-video chats, free email, tech assistance, travel and vacations, educational opportunities, living with illnesses, and a host of life-style options, to name but a few. Virtual communities enable marketers to address consumers with a particular common interest, can be one of the primary pleasures a consumer has online, and can also enhance the consumption experience (through discussions with others).[9]

The exchange of knowledge that can take place in a virtual community can help a good product sell faster and a poor product fail faster. Indeed, there are a number of "knowledge exchanges" that permit registered members and others to ask questions of experts on subjects germane to that exchange. For example, **EXP.com** offers expertise in 300 subjects and does so without a subscription fee—the customer or expert can determine the prices for answers.[10] And some virtual communities, hosted by a commercial source, are aimed at particular ethnic groups and contain online content targeted to a distinct ethnic community. Startec Global Communications Corporation already operates virtual communities for Arab, Iranian, Turkish, Indian, and Chinese consumers. Its **DragonSurf.com** site, for instance, concentrates on the needs and interests of young, educated Chinese web surfers in China and elsewhere around the world.[11]

Why are people attracted to virtual groups? When visiting such communities, it does not matter if you are tall or short, thin or fat, handsome or plain. On the internet, people are free to express their thoughts, to be emotional and intimate with those they do not know and have never met, and even to escape from those they normally interact with by spending time on the internet. The anonymity of the web gives its users the freedom to express whatever views they wish and also to benefit from savouring the views of others. Because of this anonymity, internet users can say things that they would not say in face-to-face interactions.[12] Communicating over the internet permits people to explore the boundaries of their personalities (see the related discussion in Chapter 4) and to shift from one persona to another. For example, investigators have found that a surprisingly large number of men adopt female personas online ("gender swapping").[13] Some community websites have attempted to control the limits of what is deemed acceptable and unacceptable by instituting codes of behaviour. For example, when fans of the cancelled television program *Dr. Quinn, Medicine Woman* subscribe to an email discussion list devoted to that program, they receive a "conduct code."[14]

Brand Communities

The next step in the evolution of relationship marketing (discussed in more detail in Chapter 15) is the establishment of **brand communities**. One recent newspaper article noted, "There is a definite feeling among marketers that if you want to build up loyalty to your brand, your product has to have an active social life."[15] Among such brand communities are the group of runners who get together at the Niketown store in Boston on Wednesday evenings for a run, Saturn automobile reunions and barbecues, and Harley-Davidson owner groups. A *brand community* has been defined as "a specialized, non-geographically bound community, based on a structured set of social relationships among admirers of a brand.... It is marked by a shared consciousness, rituals and traditions, and a sense of moral responsibility."[16] It is this sense of community, for example, that causes Saab owners to beep or flash their lights at another Saab on the road (i.e., in a greeting ritual).

Consider how Jeep has developed its brand community. The company offers multiple opportunities for Jeep owners to get to know each other, their vehicles, and the company. Jeep conducts Jeep Jamborees (regional rallies that concentrate on off-road driving), Camp Jeep (national rallies offering off-road driving and product-related activities), and Jeep 101 (an off-road driving course with product-related activities and displays). At both Camp Jeep and Jeep 101, there are "camp counsellors" who provide participants with free beverages, free product information, and free off-road trail recommendations.[17] The result is that Jeep has fostered an involvement in its brand community, so that a bond exists between the Jeep owner and (1) the product, (2) the brand, (3) the company, and (4) other Jeep owners. The brand community is, therefore, "customer-centric"; it is the customer experience rather than the brand itself that gives meaning to the brand community. Consider the following comment from a Jeep owner attending Jeep 101:[18]

> I've been very happy. I get a lot of communications from Jeep, which I've been so impressed with. Usually you buy a car and then you're a forgotten soul. Its kinda like they want you to be part of the family. As soon as I got the invitation for Jeep 101, I registered. I was very excited. But I was nervous. I didn't think I would end up driving. I was very relieved to see someone in the car with you, 'cause it gave you the confidence to do what you're supposed to. Otherwise, I had visions of abandoning the truck on the hill and saying, 'I can't do it!' I thought I might wimp out, but I didn't.

Consumer-Action Groups

A particular kind of consumer group—a **consumer-action group**—has emerged in response to the consumerist movement. Today there are a very large number of such groups that are dedicated to helping consumers make the right purchase decisions, consume products and services in a healthy and responsible manner, and generally add to the overall quality of their lives. The following are just a few examples of the diverse range of consumer issues being addressed by private and public consumer-action groups: neighbourhood crime watch, youth development, forests and wildlife conservation, children and advertising, race and ethnicity, community volunteerism, legal assistance, public health, disaster relief, energy conservation, education, smoking, the environment, access to telecommunications, science in the public interest, credit counselling, privacy issues, and children and the internet.

Brand community:
A group of consumers whose social bonds are based on their interest in and usage of a brand.

www.nike.com

www.saturncanada.com

www.harleydavidson.com

www.jeep.ca

Consumer-action group:
A group that is dedicated to helping consumers make the right purchase decisions, use products and services, and improve the quality of their lives.

Consumer-action groups can be divided into two broad categories:

- *Groups that organize to correct a specific consumer abuse:* A group of irate parents who band together to protest the opening of an X-rated movie theatre in their neighbourhood or a group of neighbours who attend a meeting of the local municipal council to protest how poorly the streets in their area are being plowed in winter are examples of temporary, cause-specific consumer-action groups. These groups are short-lived, and they usually disband once their goals have been achieved.

- *Groups that organize to address broader, more pervasive problem areas:* Unlike the previous groups, these groups have more enduring concerns or common interests, and they operate over an extended or indefinite period.

www.madd.ca

An example of an enduring consumer-action group is Mothers Against Drunk Driving (MADD), a group founded in 1980 and still operating today throughout the United States and Canada through local community groups. MADD representatives serve on numerous public advisory boards and help establish local task forces to combat drunk driving. Additionally, the organization supports actions to restrict advertising of alcoholic beverages and is opposed in general to any advertising of products that may have a negative impact on youth.

The overriding objective of many consumer-action groups is to bring sufficient pressure to bear on selected members of the business community and government agencies to make them correct alleged abuses of consumers.

Celebrities

Do you or one of your friends own a Microsoft Xbox? When the Xbox was introduced into the Japanese market in February 2002, 50 000 limited-edition versions were available. In addition to a black translucent case, the limited-edition versions included a silver-plated key chain with the engraved signature of Bill Gates, CEO of Microsoft. It was hoped that this key chain would separate the Xbox from its Sony and Nintendo rivals.[19]

Celebrities, particularly movie stars, television personalities, popular entertainers, and sports icons, provide a very common type of reference group appeal. Indeed, it has been estimated that 25 percent of U.S. commercials use celebrity endorsers;[20] although Canadian figures are not available, it is likely that they are similar to those in the United States. To their loyal followers and to much of the general public, celebrities represent an idealization of life that most people imagine they would love to live.

Do you remember when Michael Jordan first retired from basketball for about two years? His return to the NBA resulted in an increase of $1 billion in the value of the shares of the firms whose products he endorses, and he is under contract with Nike until 2023.[21] But many experts believe that today it is Tiger Woods, and not Michael Jordan, who is the number-one celebrity endorser. His five-year deal with Buick is estimated at $30 million, and his $40 million deal with Nike is expected to double because he has now switched to Nike-brand golf balls.[22]

Advertisers spend enormous sums of money to have celebrities promote their products, with the expectation that the reading or viewing audience will react positively to the celebrity's association with the products. One discussion about celebrity endorsers noted that "famous people hold the viewer's attention," and this is why the World Chiropractic Alliance recently began a search to find doctors with famous patients and to use such associations in their marketing efforts.[23]

FIGURE 12-3	Types of Celebrity Appeals

TYPES	DEFINITION
Testimonial	Referring to personal use, a celebrity attests to the quality of the product or service.
Endorsement	Celebrity lends his or her name and appears on behalf of a product or service in which he or she may or may not be an expert.
Actor	Celebrity presents a product or service as part of character endorsement.
Spokesperson	Celebrity represents the brand or company over an extended period of time.

And are you aware that the number of Americans who practised yoga in 1998 increased by 300 percent over 1990? This was due in part to celebrities such as actress Gwyneth Paltrow and model Christy Turlington, who helped to popularize yoga, and to Madonna, who played a yoga instructor in her film *The Next Best Thing*.[24]

A firm that decides to employ a celebrity to promote its product or service has the choice of using the celebrity to give either a *testimonial* or an *endorsement* as an actor in a commercial or as a company spokesperson. Figure 12-3 describes the various types of celebrity appeals; Exhibits 12-4A and 12-4B show examples of celebrities being used in advertising.

Why are consumers influenced by celebrities? Consumers often see celebrities as having credibility. By **celebrity credibility** we mean the audience's perception of both the celebrity's *expertise* (how much the celebrity knows about the product area) and *trustworthiness* (how honest the celebrity is about what he or she says about the product).[25] To illustrate, when a celebrity endorses only one product, consumers are likely to see the product in a highly favourable light and express a greater intention to purchase it. In contrast, when a celebrity endorses a variety of products, his or her credibility is reduced because of the apparent financial motive for the celebrity's efforts.[26] A recent study also found that the endorser's credibility had its strongest influence on a consumer's attitude toward the ad. However, corporate credibility (the credibility of the company paying for the advertisement) had a stronger influence on attitude toward the brand.[27]

Celebrity credibility: The audience's perception of both the celebrity's expertise and trustworthiness.

The nature of the product influences the importance of celebrity credibility. Figure 12-4 presents the findings of a recent study of what marketing practitioners in the United Kingdom look for in choosing a celebrity endorser. What is apparent is that the importance of certain celebrity characteristics depends on whether the product being promoted is technical (e.g., PCs) or non-technical (e.g., jeans). Specifically, for a product like a PC the "trustworthiness" of a celebrity is considered to be most important, whereas for clothing the "physical attractiveness" of the celebrity is most important.

Not all companies think that using celebrity endorsers is the best way to advertise. Some companies avoid celebrities because they fear that if the celebrity gets involved in some undesirable act or event—an ugly divorce, a scandal, or a criminal case—the publicity will harm sales of the brand. For example, researchers recently compiled a list of 48 undesirable events occurring between 1980 and 1994 that involved celebrity endorsers hired by publicly traded companies. The list included such notables as Mike Tyson, Michael Jackson, and Jennifer Capriati.[28]

EXHIBIT 12-4A

CELEBRITY ENDORSEMENT

Courtesy of Trans Canada Trail.

EXHIBIT 12-4B

CELEBRITY SPOKESPERSON

Courtesy of Subaru Canada.

REFERENCE GROUPS AND MARKETING STRATEGY

Reference groups are widely used by marketers to promote their products. A significant proportion of the ads that we see use some form of reference group influence. In order to make full use of reference group influence, marketers need to take the following steps:

Recognize the extent of reference group influence in a situation: The first step in using reference group influence is to think about whether or not the product is prone to reference group influence at all, and if it is, what the influence of the reference groups is on decision making. As we saw earlier, reference group influence is greater when the product is visible, is a non-necessity, and is important to a group that has considerable credibility and power. Reference groups also have influence when the person buying the product does not know much about it.

By examining the product and the purchase situation in light of the above factors, marketers can decide whether reference group influence may be applicable to a product. If the product is prone to reference group influence, the marketer can move on to the next stage.

Identify the type of reference group influence that would be most effective in a particular situation. As shown in Figure 12-1, the types of reference group influences may depend on the nature of the product. While some products are more

FIGURE 12-4 Importance of Celebrity Characteristics for Two Types of Products

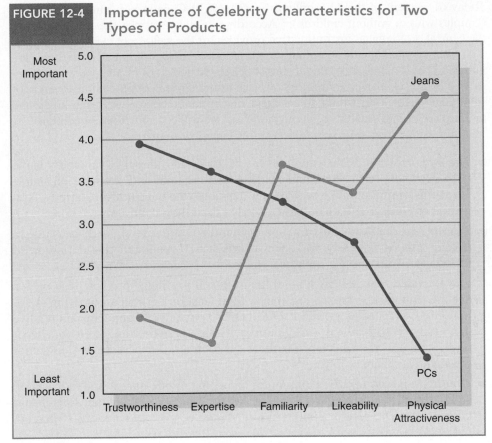

Source: B. Zafer Erdogan, Michael J. Baker, and Stephen Tagg, "Selecting Celebrity Endorsers: The Practitioner's Perspective," *Journal of Advertising Research*, May/June 2001, 46.

prone to normative influence, others may be subject to informational influence. Of course, if all advertisers use normative influence to market a product, it might make sense for you to choose a different approach. For example, most deodorant ads use normative reference group influence; can you develop a deodorant ad that uses informational or identification influence?

Identify possible reference group members to use in your promotions: Once a marketer has identified the extent and type of reference group influence, she has to choose suitable reference group members to portray in advertisements. When you have identified that the best way to introduce your product—say, a soft drink—is through identification influence, you have to pick the reference group members that your target market identifies with. Depending on your target market, the best reference group to use might be friends, work groups, or even a celebrity.

THE FAMILY

Although the term *family* is a basic concept, it is not easy to define because family composition and structure, as well as the roles played by family members, are almost always in transition. Traditionally, however, **family** is defined as *two or more persons related by blood, marriage, or adoption who live together.* In a more dynamic sense, the individuals who constitute a family might be described as members of the most basic social group who live together and interact to satisfy their personal and mutual needs.

Family:
Two or more persons related by blood, marriage, or adoption who live together.

Today 61 percent of the 11.6 million households in Canada are family households (couples with or without children).[29] According to many sources, the *family* remains the central or dominant institution that provides for the welfare of individuals.

Although *families* are sometimes referred to as *households*, not all households are families. That is, a household might consist of a single person or of persons who are not related by blood, marriage, or adoption, such as unmarried couples, family friends, or roommates. However, within the context of consumer behaviour, households and families are usually treated as synonymous, and we will continue this convention.

In most Western societies, four types of families dominate:

- *The married couple:* The simplest type of family, in number of members, is the *married couple*—a husband and a wife. As a household unit, the married couple is generally representative both of new marrieds who have not yet started a family and of older couples who have already raised their children.

- *The nuclear family:* A husband and wife and one or more children constitute a *nuclear family*. Recently, Canadian courts have broadened this definition to include same-sex couples and their children.

- *The extended family:* This type of family is still prevalent but has been on the decline. The nuclear family, together with at least one grandparent living in the household, is called an *extended family*. Only 3 percent of Canadian children live in households with at least one grandparent. However, because of divorce, separation, and out-of-wedlock births, there has been a rapid increase in the number of *single-parent households*.

- *The single-parent family:* Households consisting of one parent and at least one child. Although most single-parent families are headed by a woman, a significant number of single-parent families in Canada are headed by men—18.75 percent (245 825) in 2001.[30]

In the past 30 years the incidence of the extended family has also declined because of the geographic mobility that splits up families. Moreover, not surprisingly, the type of family that is most typical can vary considerably from culture to culture. In an individualistic society like Canada, the nuclear family is most common. In a country such a Thailand with a kinship culture (with extended families), a family would commonly include a head of household, married adult children, and grandchildren.[31]

Canadian families are changing rapidly. Changes in social values, the influx of women into the workforce, changing economic conditions, and other factors have altered the face of the Canadian family. More details of this are provided later in the chapter under the section on non-traditional families.

THE FAMILY LIFE CYCLE

Family life cycle: Classification of families into distinct and significant stages.

Sociologists and consumer researchers have long been attracted to the concept of the **family life cycle (FLC)** as a means of depicting what was once a rather steady and predictable series of stages through which most families progressed. However, with the advent of many diverse family and life-style arrangements, what was the rule has been on the decline. This decline in the percentage of families that progress through a traditional FLC (to be discussed below) seems to be caused by a host of societal factors, including a rising divorce rate, the explosive number of out-of-wedlock births, and the 35-year decline in the number of extended families as many young families moved to advance their job and career opportunities.

The notion of the FLC remains a useful marketing tool when we keep in mind that there are family and life-style arrangements that are not fully accounted for by the traditional definition. FLC analysis enables marketers to segment families into a series of stages spanning the life course of a family unit. The FLC is a composite variable created by systematically combining such commonly used demographic variables as *marital status, size of family, age of family members* (focusing on the age of the oldest or youngest child), and *employment status* of the head of household. The ages of the parents and the relative amount of disposable income usually are inferred from the stage in the family life cycle.

To recognize the current realities of a wide range of family and life-style arrangements, our treatment of the FLC concept is divided into two sections. The first section considers the traditional FLC schema. This model is increasingly being challenged because it fails to account for various important family living arrangements. To rectify these limitations, the second section focuses on alternative FLC stages, including increasingly important non-traditional family structures.

Traditional Family Life Cycle

The **traditional family life cycle** is a progression of stages through which many families pass, starting with bachelorhood, moving on to marriage (and the creation of the basic family unit), then to family growth (with the birth of children), to family contraction (as grown children leave home), and ending with the dissolution of the basic unit (upon the death of one spouse). Although different researchers prefer different numbers of FLC stages, the traditional FLC models proposed over the years can be synthesized into just five basic stages, as follows:

Traditional family life cycle:

A progression of stages through which many families pass, starting with bachelorhood, moving on to marriage, then to family growth (with the birth of children), to family contraction, and ending with the dissolution of the basic unit.

Stage I: Bachelorhood—young single adult living apart from parents

Stage II: Honeymooners—young married couple

Stage III: Parenthood—married couple with at least one child living at home

Stage IV: Post-parenthood—an older married couple with no children living at home

Stage V: Dissolution—one surviving spouse

The following discussion examines the five stages in detail and shows how they lend themselves to market segmentation strategies.

Stage I: Bachelorhood

The first FLC stage consists of young single men and women who have established households apart from their parents. Although most members of this FLC stage are fully employed, many are university or college students. Young single adults are apt to spend their incomes on rent, basic home furnishings, the purchase and maintenance of cars, travel and entertainment, and clothing and accessories. Members of the bachelorhood stage often have enough disposable income for considerable self-indulgence. Marketers target singles for a wide variety of products and services.

In most large cities, there are travel agents, housing developments, health clubs, sports clubs, and other service and product marketers that find this FLC stage a lucrative target niche. *Meeting, dating,* and *mating* are prominent concerns of many young adults who are beginning their working lives after recently completing university or some other form of career or job training. It is relatively easy to reach this segment because they are targeted by many special-interest publications. For example, *GQ, Details,* and *Playboy* are directed to a young, sophisticated, single male audience, whereas *Cosmopolitan, Allure,* and *Glamour* are directed to young single women.

How do you know it's the right dress?
The same way you know he's the right guy.

The perfect dress is out there, that with the finest retailers for
and we can help you find it. gift registry, a comprehensive
WeddingChannel.com has a local directory of preferred
comprehensive selection of over wedding vendors searchable by
20,000 photos of beautiful bridal city or zip code, and expert
gowns and accessories categorized advice and information and
and organized to make your you've got the perfect wedding
search simple and fun. Combine resource: WeddingChannel.com.

Featuring the registries of all these fine stores:

Tiffany & Co.	Bloomingdale's
Crate & Barrel	Macy's
Williams-Sonoma	The Bon Marché
Neiman Marcus	Burdines
Pottery Barn	Goldsmith's
Restoration Hardware	Lazarus
REI	Rich's
Gump's	

WeddingChannel.com™
Everything you need to plan the perfect wedding. Yours.

EXHIBIT 12-5

TARGETING THE "TO BE MARRIED" MARKET

Courtesy of WeddingChannel.com, Inc.

It is interesting to note how the attitude of 20- to 34-year-olds toward marriage have been changing. Whereas most Canadians a couple of decades ago would have thought that happiness in life depends on being married or being part of a couple, by 2001, a large proportion of them (26 percent) felt that being part of a couple was not necessary to be happy.[32]

Marriage marks the transition from the bachelorhood stage to the honeymooner stage. Engaged and soon-to-be-married couples are likely to have larger combined incomes than singles; therefore, they are the target for many products and services. The bridal industry is a $32-billion-a-year market in North America, and many companies compete to serve this market. Exhibit 12-5 provides an example of this.[33]

Stage II: Honeymooners

The *honeymoon* stage starts immediately after the marriage vows are taken and generally continues until the arrival of the couple's first child. This FLC stage serves as a period of adjustment to married life. Because many young husbands and wives both work, these couples have a combined income that often allows them to make self-indulgent purchases, to accumulate considerable savings, or to invest their extra income.

Honeymooners have considerable start-up expenses when establishing a new home (major and minor appliances, bedroom and living room furniture, carpeting, curtains, dishes, and a host of utensils and accessory items). During this stage, the advice and experience of other married couples are likely to be important to newlyweds. Also important as sources of new product information are the so-called shelter magazines, such as *Better Homes and Gardens* and *Metropolitan Home.*

Stage III: Parenthood

When a couple has its first child, the honeymoon is considered over. The *parenthood* stage (sometimes called the full-nest stage) usually extends over more than 20 years. Because of its long duration, this stage can be divided into shorter phases: the preschool phase, the elementary school phase, the high school phase, and the college or university phase. Throughout these parenthood phases, the relationships between family members and the structure of the family gradually change. Furthermore, the financial resources of the family change significantly, as one (or both) parents progress in a career and as child-rearing and educational responsibilities gradually increase and finally decrease as children become self-supporting.

An increase in the number of births among baby boomers (born between 1946 and 1964) has resulted in a what has been called the "baby boom echo." These parents are older, better educated, more affluent, and more socially aware than previous generations of parents. Many feel that they are better parents to their children than their parents were to them. Their children often become the focus of their lives, and they spend money accordingly. "Boomer" parents have become an important target for companies that serve the baby market. They also are an important market for many investment and insurance services. There are even companies that distributed product samples, coupons, and other promotions to boomer parents and their preschool children at daycare centres.[34] Their purpose was to secure product and service exposure among this important group of consumers.

Many magazines cater to the information and entertainment needs of parents and children. There are many other special-interest magazines, such as *Humpty Dumpty's,* for the young child just learning to read; *Owl Magazine,* for the elementary school pupil; *Boy's Life,* for young boys; and *American Girl, Seventeen, Glamour,* and *Mademoiselle,* for teenage girls and young women interested in fashion.

www.owlkids.com

Stage IV: Post-parenthood

Because parenthood extends over many years, it is only natural to find that *post-parenthood,* when all the children have left home, is traumatic for some parents and liberating for others. This so-called *empty-nest stage* signifies for many parents almost a "rebirth," a time for doing all the things they could not do while the children were at home and they had to worry about soaring child-related expenses. For the mother, it may be a time to further her education, to enter or re-enter the job market, or to seek new interests. For the father, it is a time to indulge in new hobbies. For both, it is the time to travel, to entertain, perhaps to refurnish their home, or to sell it in favour of a smaller house or condominium.

It is during this stage that married couples tend to be most comfortable financially. Today's empty nesters have more leisure time than previous generations. They travel more often, take long vacations, and are likely to buy a second home in a warmer climate. They have higher disposable incomes because of savings and investments, and they have fewer expenses (no mortgage or university tuition bills). They look forward to being involved grandparents. For this reason, families in the post-parenthood stage are an important market for luxury goods, new cars, expensive furniture, and vacations in faraway places.

Many empty nesters retire while they are still in good health. Retirement provides the opportunity to pursue new interests, to travel, and to fulfill unsatisfied needs. Hotels, airlines, and car-leasing companies have responded to this market with discounts to consumers over 60; some airlines have established special travel clubs with unlimited mileage for a flat fee. Adult communities have sprung up in many parts of the country. Of course, for older retired couples who do not have adequate savings or income, retirement is far different and very restrictive.

Older consumers tend to use television as an important source of information and entertainment. They like programs that provide the opportunity to "keep up with what's happening," especially news and public affairs programs. In addition, a number of special-interest magazines cater exclusively to this market, such as *Modern Maturity*. (Chapter 10 contains a more detailed discussion of the older consumer as a subcultural market segment.)

Stage V: Dissolution

Dissolution of the basic family unit occurs with the death of one spouse. When the surviving spouse is in good health, is working or has adequate savings, and has supportive family and friends, the adjustment is easier. The surviving spouse (usually the wife) often tends to lead a more economical life. Many surviving spouses seek each other out for companionship; others enter into second (or third and even fourth) marriages.

Modifications—The Non-traditional FLC

As we already noted, the traditional FLC model can no longer fully represent the progression of stages through which current family and life-style arrangements move. To compensate for these limitations, consumer researchers have been attempting to search out expanded FLC models that reflect better the diversity of family and life-style arrangements.[35] Figure 12-5 presents an FLC model that depicts along the main horizontal row the stages of the traditional FLC and, above and below the main horizontal row, selected alternative FLC stages that account for some important non-traditional family households that marketers are increasingly targeting. The underlying socio-demographic forces that drive this expanded FLC model include divorce and later marriages, with and without the presence of children. Although this modified FLC model is somewhat more realistic, it only recognizes families that started in marriage, ignoring such single-parent households as unmarried mothers and families formed because a single person or single persons adopt a child.

Non-traditional FLC Stages

Figure 12-5 presents an extensive categorization of non-traditional FLC stages that are derived from the dynamic socio-demographic forces (e.g., women entering the workforce, later marriages) operating during the past 25 years or so. These have resulted in changes in values and demographic changes in the Canadian population. The following are some of those changes:

- In 2001, 35 percent of Canadians felt that having a child is not necessary for happiness in life. Perhaps this explains why the fertility rate for Canadian women has dropped from 3.5 children in 1921 to 1.5 in 1999. Not only are women having fewer children, but many are choosing not to have children at all.[36]

    Coaticook, a small town in rural Quebec, has decided to do something about the low fertility rate among its population. Every year, the town hosts an unusual holiday raffle with cash prizes of up to $1000. To be eligible for the big prize, you have to have at least three children. The town gives $100 for the first child, $200 for the second, and $1000 for the third and subsequent children. It also offers $500 per child when a couple buys a home, gives a 50 percent discount for families with three children or more on recreation and cultural activities, and

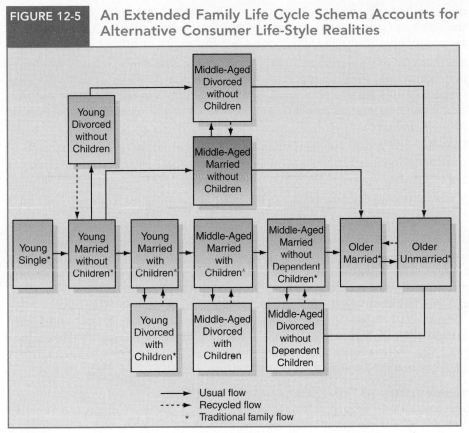

FIGURE 12-5   An Extended Family Life Cycle Schema Accounts for Alternative Consumer Life-Style Realities

Source: Patrick E. Murphy and William A. Staples, "A Modern-Sized Family Life Cycle," *Journal of Consumer Research,* 6 June 1979, 17. Reprinted by permission of The University of Chicago Press as publisher.

pays for 50 percent of cloth diaper cleaning. Have these measures worked? Fourteen percent of Coaticook families have three or more children, compared with only 9 percent for Quebec as a whole.[37]

■ Sixty-two percent of unmarried Canadian men are agreeable to common-law unions and 36 percent of women feel the same way.

■ One in 12 Canadians in a relationship lives in a separate residence while maintaining an intimate relationship with a non-resident partner. In fact, Statistics Canada uses the term "living apart together," or LAT, to refer to these arrangements. Such arrangements are prevalent not just among the young; more than 19 percent of such couples were in their thirties, 14 percent were in their forties, and more than 11 percent were 50 years or older.[38]

■ The percentage of children living in common-law and single-parent families has been rising. In 1981, 84 percent of children lived in married households; by 2001, that number had fallen to 68 percent. In contrast, the proportion of children living in common-law households had risen from 3 percent in 1981 to 13 percent in 2001, and those living in lone-parent households had risen from 13 percent in 1981 to 19 percent in 2001.[39]

■ More young adults are living with their parents. In 1981, only 34 percent of men and 21 percent of women 20–29 years old lived with their parents; by 2001, these numbers had increased to 47 percent and 35 percent, respectively. This might be the result of an increased need for higher education (and the higher cost of post-secondary education), failed marriages, job instability, or other factors.[40]

■ The number of stay-at-home fathers is increasing. The average father who stays at home to look after the children is 42 years old. He is less likely to have a post-secondary education than is a father who is earning outside the home (40 percent compared with 55 percent), and less likely to have been in a managerial or professional job.[41]

■ Families in Canada are becoming smaller. Whereas in 1961, 16 percent of Canadians lived in families with six or more members, by 1999, only 3.8 percent did.

■ Three percent of Canadian children live in families with at least one grandparent.[42]

These changes have led to non-traditional family life cycle stages and non-family households: those consisting of a single individual and those consisting of two or more unrelated individuals. At one time, non-family households were so uncommon that it was not really important whether they were considered or not. Figure 12-6 shows a modified family life cycle, which takes into account these non-traditional family structures that are becoming more common in Canada.

Figure 12-7 shows the percentages of Canadians in family and non-family households. As the figure reveals, more than 30 percent of all households are currently non-family households (i.e., men or women living alone or with another person as an unmarried couple).

Consumption in Non-traditional Families

When households undergo changes in status—as a result of divorce, temporary retirement, a new person moving into the household, or the death of a spouse—they often undergo spontaneous changes in consumption-related preferences, and thus they become attractive targets for many marketers. For example, divorce often requires that one (or both) former spouses find a new home, get new telephones (with new telephone numbers), buy new furniture, and perhaps find a job. These requirements mean that a divorced person might need to contact real estate agents, call the local and long-distance telephone companies, visit furniture stores, and possibly contact a personnel agency or career consultant. There are also the special needs of the children who are experiencing the divorce.

In another sphere, the substantial increase in two-income households (in which both the husband and the wife work) has also tended to muddy the life-style assumptions implicit in the traditional FLC. Most two-income families have children (the majority of whom are between 11 and 20 years of age). The most affluent two-income segment is, not surprisingly, the "crowded nesters." This two-income couple with an adult child living at home has the advantage of an additional potential source of income to contribute to the general well-being of the household.

The side-by-side existence of traditional and non-traditional FLC stages is another example of our recurring observation that the contemporary marketplace is complex in its diversity and is a challenge to segment and serve.

FAMILY DECISION MAKING AND CONSUMPTION-RELATED ROLES

Although many marketers recognize the family as the basic consumer decision-making unit, they most often examine the attitudes and behaviour of the one family

FIGURE 12-6   Noteworthy Non-traditional FLC Stages

ALTERNATIVE FLC STAGES	DEFINITION/COMMENTARY
Family Households	
Childless couples	It is increasingly acceptable for married couples to elect not to have children. Contributing forces are more career-oriented married women and delayed marriages.
Couples who marry later in life (in their late 30s or later)	More career-oriented men and women and greater occurrence of couples living together. Likely to have fewer or even no children.
Couples who have first child later in life (in their late 30s or later)	Likely to have fewer children. Stress quality life style: "Only the best is good enough."
Single parents I	High divorce rates (about 50 percent) contribute to a portion of single-parent households.
Single parents II	Young man or woman who has one or more children out of wedlock.
Single parents III	A single person who adopts one or more children.
Extended family	Young single-adult children who return home to avoid the expenses of living alone while establishing their careers. Divorced daughter or son with grandchild(ren) returns home to parents. Frail elderly parents who move in with children. Newlyweds living with in-laws.
Non-family Households	
Unmarried couples	Increased acceptance of heterosexual and homosexual couples.
Divorced persons (no children)	High divorce rate contributes to dissolution of households before children are born.
Single persons (most are young)	Primarily a result of delaying first marriage; also, men and women who never marry.
Widowed persons (most are elderly)	Longer life expectancy, especially for women, means more over-75 single-person households.

FIGURE 12-7   Family and Non-family Households

NUMBER OF HOUSEHOLDS BY TYPE IN 2001

Family Households	**8 371 020**
Married couples:	5 901 430
with children	3 469 700
without children	2 431 725
Common-law couples:	1 158 410
with children	530 905
without children	627 505
Lone-parent households:	1 311 190
Female householder	1 065 365
Male householder	245 825
Average family size = 3.0	
Total number of Canadians living in households:	29 522 300
Canadians living in family households:	25 586 660
Canadians living in non-family households:	3 935 640
Canadians living alone	2 976 880
Other arrangements	948 760

Source: Adapted from the Statistics Canada website: http//www.statcan.ca/english/Pgdb/famil40a.htm.

member whom they believe to be the major *decision maker*. In some cases, they also examine the attitudes and behaviour of the person most likely to be the primary *user* of the product or service. For instance, in the case of men's underwear, which is often bought by women for their husbands and unmarried sons, it is common to seek the views of both the men who wear the underwear and the women who buy it. By considering both the likely user and the likely purchaser, the marketer obtains a richer picture of the consumption process.

Primary Family Consumption Roles

For a family to function as a cohesive unit, tasks such as doing the laundry, preparing meals, setting the dinner table, taking out the garbage, and walking the dog must be done by one or more family members. In a dynamic society, family-related duties are constantly changing—for example, men are doing more housework than they used to do. However, we can identify eight distinct roles in the *family decision-making process,* as presented in Figure 12-8. A look at these roles provides further insight into how family members interact in their various consumption-related roles.

Although there are distinct roles in a family's consumption process, it is important to remember the following facts:

- The number and identity of the family members who fill these roles vary from family to family and from product to product.
- One member of a family may independently assume a number of roles.
- A single role may be performed jointly by two or more family members.
- In some cases, one or more of these basic roles may not be required. For example, a man may be walking down the snack food aisle at a local supermarket when he picks out an interesting new kind of chocolate candy. His selection does not directly involve the influence of other family members. He is the *decider,* the

FIGURE 12-8	The Eight Roles in the Family Decision-Making Process

ROLE	DESCRIPTION
Influencers	Family member(s) who provide information to other members about a product or service
Gatekeepers	Family member(s) who control the flow of information about a product or service into the family
Deciders	Family member(s) with the power to determine unilaterally or jointly whether to shop for, purchase, use, consume, or dispose of a specific product or service
Buyers	Family member(s) who make the actual purchase of a particular product or service
Preparers	Family member(s) who transform the product into a form suitable for consumption by other family members
Users	Family member(s) who use or consume a particular product or service
Maintainers	Family member(s) who service or repair the product so that it will provide continued satisfaction
Disposers	Family member(s) who initiate or carry out the disposal or discontinuation of a particular product or service

buyer and, in a sense, the *gatekeeper;* however, he may or may not be the sole consumer (or user).

■ Products may be consumed by a single family member (deodorant or razors), consumed or used directly by two or more family members (orange juice or shampoo), or consumed indirectly by the entire family (central air conditioning, a DVD player, or a collection of art glass).

Take the example of a common family consumption behaviour—eating out. Who makes the decision in your family? A study of children's influence on family decisions about eating out found that about 17 percent of the 9- to 12-year-old children studied considered themselves to be the main decision maker with respect to the decision to go to a restaurant, and 40 percent thought of themselves as the main decision maker with respect to the choice of restaurants. In contrast, 30 percent of the parents of these children felt that their offspring were the main decision makers in deciding to eat out, and almost an equal number, 29 percent, felt that the child (or children) also was the main decision maker with regard to which restaurant was patronized. Interestingly, in traditional families, children most often thought it was the father who made the decision to go to a restaurant, whereas in non-traditional families it was most often the mother (see Figure 12-9). The results also reveal that in non-traditional households a child was twice as likely to make the decision to go to a restaurant than in a traditional household.[43]

Research Insight 12-1 takes a look at how Catelli, a company that makes pasta products, used its knowledge of family decision making to market a new line of pasta products for children.

Husband-and-Wife Decision Making

Marketers are interested in the relative amount of influence that a husband and a wife have when it comes to family consumption choices. Most husband-wife influence studies classify family consumption decisions as **husband-dominated**, **wife-dominated**, **joint** (either equal or syncratic), and **autonomic** (either solitary or unilateral).[44]

The relative influence of a husband or wife on a particular consumer decision depends in part on the product and service category. For instance, during the 1950s, the purchase of a new car was strongly husband-dominated, whereas food and financial banking decisions were more often wife-dominated. Forty years later, the purchase of the family's principal car is still often husband-dominated in many households. Sometimes, however, such as in the case of a second car or a car for a

Husband-dominated decisions:
Family purchase decisions in which the husband is the key decision maker.

Wife-dominated decisions:
Family purchase decisions in which the wife is the key decision maker.

Joint decisions:
Family purchase decisions in which the final decision is made with equal involvement from both spouses.

Autonomic decisions:
Family purchase decisions in which the final decision is made by either spouse individually.

FIGURE 12-9	Who Decides to Go to a Restaurant? Children's Perceptions by Family Type			
	CHILD	**FATHER**	**MOTHER**	**TOTAL**
Traditional	12.0%	52.0%	36.0%	100% 75.8
Non-traditional	25.0%	12.5%	62.5%	100% 24.2
Total	15.2%	42.4%	42.4%	100% 100

Source: JoAnne Labrecque and Line Ricard, "Children's Influence on Family Decision Making: A Restaurant Study," *Journal of Business Research*, 54, November 2001, 175. With permission of Elsevier Service.

RESEARCH INSIGHT 12-1
CAN YOU MAKE PASTA THAT IS FUN AND "APPROVED BY MOM"?

One thing that most mothers know is that all children love pasta. So Catelli, the leader in the pasta industry, knew it had a winning idea when it decided to introduce a new line of pasta products aimed at children. The only question was how to develop a product that catered not just to the children's need for fun and adventure in a food item but also to parents' desire to give their children wholesome food.

The product development team at Catelli had several interesting ideas—all from adults trying to identify what children would like. The company decided to do some primary qualitative research into what their target market—the children themselves—had to say. They started out by testing the product ideas they had with small groups of children. Though some of the ideas were found to test well with children, the company decided that the best thing to do was to ask children to create their ideal pasta meal. The children they interviewed wanted to have "fun shapes" and "cool colours"; they wanted it to be simple.

Although children are the consumers or users of this product, the company realized that mothers are the gatekeepers, buyers, preparers, and in many instances, the deciders for this product category. So they decided to conduct focus groups with mothers to find out what they were looking for in a food product for their children. Two major criteria kept coming up: convenience and nutrition. One mother said, "Getting my kids to eat is a challenge. Entertaining them helps them eat properly. At the same time, I want a fast meal that needs to be nutritious. After all, pasta is a main meal, not a snack. I want to feel good about serving this as a meal for kids." The company went back to the drawing board and developed two popular shapes that all the children loved: aliens and sea creatures. The products were named "Aliens" and "Sea Creatures" with the additional tag line "Adventure pasta." The colours chosen had to be fun and bright enough to attract children, but, at the same time, be ones that can be made with natural ingredients that parents would feel comfortable with. The company chose purple, orange, and green for the pasta and made sure that these colours were made with all natural ingredients. The next step was to design a package that was appealing to children and reassuring to parents. The package had pictures on the cover that would catch the children's eye, but to satisfy the parents, it also conveyed the message that the product was "enriched with vitamins and iron."

The company decided to concentrate on gaining awareness and trial through its promotional campaign. To get the attention of young children and their parents (especially the mothers), the company advertised the product on Teletoon Network during the back-to-school period in September so that young children and their parents would catch the ads. To further increase awareness among mothers, the company used in-store promotions such as point-of-purchase displays. To encourage trial, samples and coupons were used.

An additional feature of the promotional campaign was a tie-in with Boston Pizza (a British Columbia company) and Pacini Restaurant (of Montreal). These partners gave Catelli the opportunity to gain attention and credibility among parents because they are well-established businesses. In return for being put on the children's menu of these restaurants, Catelli provided colouring placemats and other "at-table" promotional items. Thus, the arrangement was mutually beneficial.

The results were extremely satisfying. Awareness and trial among children and parents was high, and sales picked up fairly quickly.

Source: Will Stenason, "Pasta That's an Adventure for Kids," *Marketing Magazine*, March 17, 2003, 21.

www.catelli.com

single or working woman, this is not true. Female car buyers are a rapidly expanding segment of the automobile market, a segment to which many car manufacturers are currently paying separate marketing attention. And in the case of financial decision making, there has been a general trend over the past decade for the female head of the household to make financial decisions.[45]

Husband-wife decision making also appears to be related to cultural influence. Research comparing husband-wife decision-making patterns in the People's Republic of China and in the United States reveals that among Chinese there were substantially fewer "joint" decisions and more "husband-dominated" decisions for many household purchases.[46] When the comparison was limited to households in China, the research showed that in married couples in big cities like Beijing were more likely than rural couples to share equally in purchase decisions. Still further, because of China's one-child policy and the ensuing custom of treating a single child as a "little emperor," many of the parents' purchase decisions are influenced by the their child.[47]

In another recent cross-cultural study, husband-wife decision making was studied among three groups: Asian Indians living in India, Asian Indians living in the United States, and American nationals. Results show a decrease in husband-dominated decisions and an increase in wife-dominated decisions, going from Asian Indians in India, to Asian Indians in the United States, to American nationals. This pattern seems to indicate the impact of assimilation on decision making.[48]

It is important to recognize that the type of roles that family members play in a household is often related to early childhood socialization. In fact, while families perform several functions, such as providing for the economic well-being of their members, giving them emotional support, and encouraging suitable life styles, the key function of a family—from the marketer's point of view—is the role it plays in the socialization of family members. The next section takes a more detailed look at consumer socialization by the family.

SOCIALIZATION OF FAMILY MEMBERS

The **socialization of family members**, ranging from young children to adults, is a central family function. In the case of young children, this process includes imparting to children the basic values and modes of behaviour consistent with the culture. These generally include moral and religious principles, interpersonal skills, standards of dressing and grooming, manners and speech, and the selection of educational and occupational or career goals. Figure 12-10 represents the results of a study by "SmartGirl Internette" that looks at the household chores performed by American girls 11 to 17 years of age. The findings indicate that more than one-half of the girls in this age category say that they "dust and sweep."

A recent Dutch study found that younger juveniles spend most of their leisure time with their families, whereas older juveniles spend most of their leisure time with their peers.[49] The transition period among these two age groups was 13, with 13-year-olds dividing their leisure time between parents, peers, and being alone. The results further indicate that 12- and 15-year-old boys, especially from the higher social classes, were strongly focused on peer groups, whereas girls the same age tended to have close friendships with one best friend. This emphasis on peers (to the exclusion of family) has led not only to some troubled times for teenagers, but also to distinct consumption patterns, especially in products like clothing, which are prone to reference group influence.[50]

Parental socialization responsibility seems to be constantly expanding. For instance, parents are often anxious to see their young children possess adequate computer skills, almost before they are able to talk or walk—as early as 12 months after their birth. Because of parents' intense desire that their young children learn to use computers, hardware and software developers are regularly developing products targeted at parents seeking to buy such items for their children.

Socialization of family members:
A process of imparting to children the basic values and modes of behaviour consistent with the culture.

FIGURE 12-10	Household Chores Done by Girls Aged 11 to 17

CHORE	% WHO SAY THEY PERFORM IT
Picking things up in my room	95
Picking things up around the house	84
Vacuuming	72
Washing or drying the dishes	66
Loading or unloading the dishwasher	65
Doing laundry	61
Sweeping	55
Dusting	55
Cleaning the bathtub, shower, or sink	54
Washing the windows or mirrors	48
Cleaning the kitchen	46
Cleaning the toilet	41
Mopping the bathroom or kitchen floor	39
Ironing	37

Source: Marketing to Women, January 2000, 3. Courtesy of SmartGirl.org. Copyright 2002 SmartGirl Internette Inc.

Another sign of parents' constant pressure to help their young children secure an "advantage" or "keep ahead" are the demanding daily schedules that rule the lives of many children—daily preschool classes, after-school classes, play dates, weekend enrichment, and sports programs. Such hectic schedules foster a concentration on competition and results and not on having fun or on being creative. In contrast, when they were children, their parents may have built forts out of blankets or pillows. However, with the structured activities of today and with the child constantly surrounded by media, there is little opportunity for the child to explore his or her world in such an imaginative fashion.[51]

Marketers often target parents looking for help in the task of socializing their children. To this end, marketers are sensitive to the fact that the socialization of young children provides an opportunity to establish a foundation on which later experiences continue to build throughout life. These experiences are reinforced and modified as the child grows into adolescence and eventually into adulthood.

Consumer Socialization of Children

Consumer socialization:
The process by which children acquire the skills, knowledge, attitudes, and experiences necessary to function as consumers.

The aspect of childhood socialization that is particularly relevant to the study of consumer behaviour is **consumer socialization**, which is defined as the *process by which children acquire the skills, knowledge, attitudes, and experiences necessary to function as consumers* (see Exhibit 12-6). A variety of studies have looked at how children develop consumption skills. Many pre-adolescent children acquire their *consumer behaviour norms* by observing their parents and older siblings, who function as role models and sources of cues for basic consumption learning. In contrast, adolescents and teenagers are likely to look to their friends for models of acceptable consumption behaviour.[52] Other research has shown that younger children generally react positively to advertisements employing a spokesperson who seems to fulfill a parental role, whereas teens often like products for the simple reason that their parents disapprove of them.[53]

Shared shopping experiences (i.e., "co-shopping" when mother and child shop together) also give children the opportunity to acquire in-store shopping skills. Possibly because of their more harried lives, working mothers are more likely than non-working mothers to go shopping with their children. Co-shopping is a way of spending time with the children while at the same time accomplishing a necessary task. Research has also shown that children influence family purchases for many different types of products and that this influence can be significant.[54]

Consumer socialization also serves as a tool by which parents influence other aspects of the socialization process. For instance, parents often use the promise or reward of material goods to modify or control a child's behaviour. A mother may reward her child with a present when the child does something to please her, or she may withhold or remove it when the child disobeys. Research conducted by one of the authors supports this behaviour-controlling function. Specifically, adolescents reported that their parents often used the promise of chocolate candy as a means of controlling the adolescents' behaviour (such as getting them to finish their homework or clean their rooms).

It is important to mention that consumer socialization of children does not function identically in all cultures. A recent study found that American mothers emphasize autonomy more than Japanese mothers do and want their children to develop independent consumption skills at an early age. In contrast, Japanese mothers maintain greater control over their children's consumption and, therefore, their offspring's understanding of how advertising works and other consumer-related skills develop at a somewhat later age.[55]

The training wheels of good nutrition.

Get them started on the road to healthy snacking. Great fruity taste. And no artificial flavors.

www.dannon.com

EXHIBIT 12-6

CONSUMER- AND CONSUMPTION-RELATED SOCIALIZATION

Courtesy of Dannon.

Adult Consumer Socialization

The socialization process is not confined to childhood; rather, it is an ongoing process. It is now accepted that although socialization begins in early childhood, it lasts throughout a person's life. For example, when a newly married couple establishes their own household, their adjustment to living and consuming together is part of this continuing process. Similarly, the adjustment of a retired couple who decide to move to Vancouver Island or to another city to be closer to their children is also part of the ongoing socialization process. Even a family that welcomes a pet into their home as a new family member has the task of socializing the pet so that it fits into the family. Recent survey research reveals that pet owners commonly treat their pets as full-fledged family members. For instance, 58 percent of those surveyed said that they have sent or received a holiday card from their dog or cat; and 78 percent regularly talk to their pets the way would talk to a child.[56]

Intergenerational Socialization

It appears to be quite common for certain product loyalties or brand preferences to be transferred from one generation to another, maybe for even three or four generations within the same family. (This is known as *intergenerational brand transfer.*) For instance, peanut butter, mayonnaise, ketchup, coffee, and canned soup are all product categories for which brand preferences are often passed on from one generation to another. The following are selected comments from research with college-aged consumers as to how they feel about product usage extending over several generations:[57]

"My mother stills buys almost every brand that her mother did. She is scared to try anything else, for fear it will not meet the standards, and (she) would feel bad not buying something that has been with her so long." (Respondent is an Italian-American male in his early twenties.)

"I find it hard to break away from the things I've been using since I was little, like Vaseline products, Ivory soap, Lipton tea, and corn flakes. I live on campus so I have to do my own shopping, and when I do I see a lot of my mother in myself. I buy things I'm accustomed to using...products my mother buys for the house." (Respondent is a West Indian American female.)

Figure 12-11 presents a simple model of the socialization process for young children; it can be extended to family members of all ages. Note that the arrows run both ways between the young person and other family members and between the young person and his or her friends. This two-directional arrow signifies that socialization is really a two-way street, in which the young person is both socialized and influences those who are doing the socializing. Supporting this view is the fact that children of all ages often influence the opinions and behaviour of their parents. As an example, recent research with elementary-school-aged children has found that parental warmth relates positively to (1) the extent to which a child's interest in the internet serves as a catalyst for increased parental internet interest, (2) how much the child teaches a parent about the internet, and (3) whether the child acts as the parent's internet broker (e.g., the child shops for the parent on the internet).[58] Because children are often more comfortable than their parents with digital and electronic media, they are often the ones in the family who do the teaching.

Other Functions of the Family

Three other basic functions provided by the family are particularly relevant to a discussion of consumer behaviour. These are economic well-being (see Exhibit 12-7), emotional support, and suitable family life styles. It is important to note that the ways a family fulfills each one of these functions has evolved over time. For example, until recently, the economic well-being of a family was seen as the responsibility of the husband; as more and more women entered the workforce, this responsibility came to be shared by both partners in a family.

FAMILY INFLUENCE AND MARKETING STRATEGY

Marketers understand the importance of the family in influencing consumption behaviour. Of all the groups that influence a person's behaviour, the family is perhaps the most important, though most consumers are not aware of the influence that their family members have on their behaviour. This is because a lot of our behaviour is shaped by early childhood socialization and the values inculcated in us by our family.

FIGURE 12-11 A Simple Model of the Socialization Process

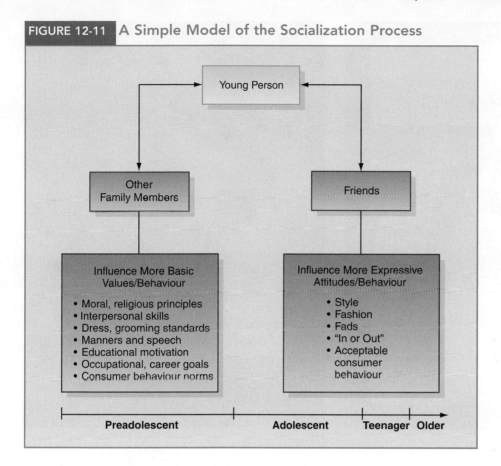

Marketers can use their knowledge of family influence in many ways. Specifically, they need to do the following:

Use the FLC for segmentation and positioning: Our consumption patterns are shaped by the stage of our family life cycle. Not only are we more likely to be in the market for certain products at certain stages of our FLC (e.g., homes in the young married with children), but even the attributes we value in a particular product is likely to depend on our FLC (see Exhibits 12-8 and 12-9). In other words, it is also possible to trace how the FLC concept influences a single product or service over time. Both these factors make the FLC an ideal segmentation variable for many products.

A recent study employed an eight-stage FLC scheme to investigate how consumers choose a bank.[59] As part of the research, the 3100 respondents were asked to rate the relative importance of 18 product and service characteristics that might affect their choice of a bank. Figure 12-12 presents the findings of the study. The research reveals that location is very important to all respondents (i.e., it was always ranked either first or second), but other bank attributes tended to be much more important to some FLC segments than to others. For instance, "fast service" was ranked fifth by bachelor-stage individuals and twelfth or thirteenth by full-nest II, empty-nest I, and empty-nest II respondents.

Recognize the diverse consumption roles within the family: As mentioned earlier, in each family there are eight distinct roles in the family decision-making

EXHIBIT 12-7

APPEALING TO THE RESPONSIBILITY OF
PROVIDING FOR THE FAMILY'S FUTURE
FINANCIAL NEEDS

Courtesy of State Farm Life Insurance Company (Canada).

EXHIBIT 12-8

AN ADVERTISEMENT APPEALING TO FULL-NEST I

Used with the permission of the David Suzuki Foundation.
Design by Alaris Design.

process. Recognizing who plays each role will enable marketers to target their communications more effectively.

Marketers need to recognize that they may have to target their communications at more than one person in the family. Since the needs and decision criteria of the members playing a role are likely to be different from those of other family members, advertisers have to create ads that cater to each one of the critical decision makers within the family.

Understand and use the dynamics of husband-wife decision making: It is essential for marketers to recognize the different roles played by the spouses in family decision making. For example, if the product in question is a husband-dominant one, the marketer has to develop ads that cater to the male in the family without alienating the female.

Recognize the influence that children have on household consumption: research shows that children influence nearly $20 million worth of purchases made by Canadian households every year. Even more interesting is the finding that by age 10, the average Canadian child has memorized more than 300 brand names. Ninety-one percent of tweens had asked their parents to buy snack food in the past six months, and 90 percent had asked to go to a specific fast food restaurant.[60]

Nest empty? Time to fly.

TOYOTA
the feeling never ends

All-New 2004 Camry Solara

You've spent years taking care of the kids. Now how about the one screaming inside you? Introducing the all-new Camry Solara SE V6. Its 225 hp VVT-i engine posts a 0-60 in a mere 7.1 seconds. For even more liberation, the 5-speed automatic transmission can be moved from the normal Drive position into the sequential shifting of the well-named Sport mode. Keeping all this under parental guidance is a 4-wheel independent suspension. And to listen to some good music for a change, a premium audio system comes standard with a 6-Disc CD changer. For details, see your Toyota dealer or call 1-888-TOYOTA-8 or visit www.toyota.ca.

EXHIBIT 12-9

AN AD APPEALING TO EMPTY NESTERS

Reproduced with the permission of Toyota Canada Inc., all rights reserved.

Radio Shack, which targets 25- to 54-year-old men, started advertising on youth channels such as YTV and Teletoon. The ads, which were for ZipZaps micro remote-control cars, ran first exclusively on YTV before being aired on other channels. According to Lindsay Walter, VP of advertising at the company, the company wanted to get to the influencers. "We understand that children are a big influence on where the shopping is going to be done and what items are going to be the hot items. We thought that by getting out into the market and getting visibility early... we could start to encourage that 'bug factor' early." The results were very positive; the company had its best year as far as sell-through of toys was concerned, and achieved a 100 percent sell through of the ZipZap cars.[61]

Understand and use the consumer socialization role played by the family: By recognizing the crucial role played by the family in socializing the individual, marketers will be better able to reach and influence consumers. For example, since consumer values such as attitudes toward money or savings are influenced by early childhood socialization, it would make sense for marketers to evoke such memories and use relevant family members in ads for such products.

www.radioshack.ca

FIGURE 12-12   Choosing a Bank—Importance of Service Attributes by FLC Stage

Attitude	Bachelor Stage: Young, single S1 Rank	Newly married couples: Young, no children S2 Rank	Full-nest I: Youngest child under 6 S3 Rank	Full-nest II: Youngest child 6 or over S4 Rank	Full-nest III: Older married couples with children S5 Rank	Empty-nest I: Older married couples, no children with them, head in labour force S6 Rank	Empty-nest II: Older married couples, no children living at home, head retired S7 Rank	Single heads of households S8 Rank
Located near home	1	2	1	1	1	1	2	1
Overall quality of service	2	9	7	7	6	7	10	4
Good reputation	3	1	2	2	8	6	9	2
Ease of qualifying for free chequing account by maintaining a minimum balance	4	10	9	13	11	11	5	3
Fast service	5	8	10	12	10	12	13	10
Being able to obtain all financial services at one location	6	11	11	10	13	9	8	12
Paying highest rates on savings	7	5	8	8	5	5	4	5
Availability of auto/personal loans	8	7	6	4	12	10	14	7

Source: Rajshekhar G. Javalgi and Paul Dion, "A Life Cycle Segmentation Approach to Marketing Financial Products and Services," *The Services Industries Journal,* 19, no. 3, July 1999, 78–79. Reprinted by permission.

Recognize that Canadian families are changing in nature, and modify their marketing mixes as needed: As mentioned earlier, the Canadian family is changing dramatically. Several new types of family structures are coming into existence as the social values of our country change. Changing family lifestyle commitments, including the allocation of time, are greatly influencing consumption patterns. For example, a series of diverse pressures on mothers has reduced the time that they have available for household chores and has created a market for convenience products and fast food restaurants. Also, with both parents working, an increased emphasis is being placed on the notion of "quality time" rather than on the "quantity of time" spent with children and other family members. Realizing the importance of quality family time, the Cayman Islands is telling its audience that you can "come back from your family vacation without needing one" (see Exhibit 12-10).

Even the notion of "quality family time" has been evolving. Researchers have identified a shift in the nature of family "togetherness." Whereas a family being together once meant doing things together, today it means being in the same household and each person doing his or her own thing.[62]

EXHIBIT 12-10

AD TELLING READERS THAT A GREAT VACATION IS FAMILY TIME

Reprinted by permission of the Cayman Islands Department of Tourism.

SUMMARY

- Consumer reference groups are groups that serve as frames of reference for individuals in their purchase decisions. Reference groups include (1) friendship groups, (2) shopping groups, (3) work groups, (4) virtual groups or communities, (5) brand communities, (6) consumer-action groups, and (7) celebrities.

- Reference groups can exert three types of influence: information influence (providing information about products), identification influence (when consumers identify with and internalize the values of the reference group), and normative influence (when consumers conform to get rewards or avoid punishments from reference groups).

- Reference group are influential for six reasons: (1) consumers lack information about the product, (2) consumers lack the confidence to make a purchase, (3) the product is a non-necessity, (4) the product is highly visible in use, (5) there is a reference group with high credibility and power, and/or (6) the consumer has a high level of commitment to the group.

- The concept of consumer reference groups has been broadened to include groups with which consumers have no direct face-to-face contact, such as celebrities, political figures, and social classes.

- The credibility, attractiveness, and power of the reference group affect the degree of influence it has.

- Celebrities are used to give testimonials or endorsements as actors or as company spokespersons. Increasingly, firms are using their top executives as spokespersons because their appearance in company advertisements seems to imply that someone at the top is watching over the consumer's interests.

- For many consumers their family is their primary reference group for many attitudes and behaviours. The family is the prime target market for most products and product categories.

- There are three types of families: married couples, nuclear families, and extended families.

- The members of a family assume specific roles in their everyday functioning; such roles or tasks extend to the realm of consumer purchase decisions. The main consumer-related roles of family members are influencers, gatekeepers, deciders, buyers, preparers, users, maintainers, and disposers. A family's decision-making style often is influenced by its life style, its roles, and cultural factors.

- Family consumption decisions can be classified as husband-dominated, wife-dominated, joint, or autonomic. The extent and nature of husband-wife influence in family decisions depend, in part, on the specific product or service and selected cultural influences.

- Classification of families by stage in the family life cycle (FLC) provides valuable insights into family consumption-related behaviour. The traditional FLC begins with bachelorhood and moves on to marriage, then to an expanding family, to a contracting family, and to an end with the death of a spouse.

- Dynamic socio-demographic changes in society have resulted in many non-traditional stages that a family or non-family household might pass through (such as childless couples, couples marrying later in life, single parents, unmarried couples, or single-person households). These non-traditional stages are becoming increasingly important to marketers as opportunities for specific market niches.

- Socialization is a core function of the family. Other functions of the family are the provision of economic and emotional support and the pursuit of a suitable life style for its members.

DISCUSSION QUESTIONS

1. How does the family influence the consumer socialization of children? What role does television advertising play in consumer socialization?

2. Make a list of formal and informal groups to which you belong, and give examples of purchases for which each served as a reference group. In which of the groups you listed is the pressure to conform the greatest? Why?

3. Think of a recent major purchase your family has made. Analyse the roles performed by the various family members in terms of the following consumption roles: influencers, gatekeepers, deciders, buyers, preparers, users, maintainers, and disposers.

4. Select three product categories and compare the brands you prefer with those your parents prefer. To what extent are the preferences similar? Discuss the similarities in the context of consumer socialization.

CRITICAL THINKING QUESTIONS

1. As a marketing consultant, you have been asked to evaluate a new promotional campaign for a large retail chain. The campaign strategy is aimed at increasing group shopping. What recommendations would you make?

2. You are the marketing vice-president of a large soft-drink company. Your company's advertising agency is in the process of negotiating a contract to employ a superstar female singer to promote your product. Discuss the reference group factors that you would mention before the celebrity is hired.

3. As a marketing consultant, you were retained by the Walt Disney Company to design a study investigating how families make vacation decisions. Whom, within the family, would you interview? What kind of questions would you ask? How would you assess the relative power

of each family member in making vacation-related decisions?

4. Which of the five stages of the traditional family life cycle constitute the most lucrative segments for the following products and services: (a) telephone party lines, (b) a Club Med vacation, (c) Domino's pizza, (d) CD players, (e) mutual funds, and (f) motor homes? Explain your answers.

5. As the marketing manager of a high-quality, fairly expensive line of frozen dinners, how would you use the non-family household information listed in the text (Figure 12-6) to segment the market and position your product?

INTERNET EXERCISES

1. Visit any chat group or bulletin board that is of interest to you for a week. Do you feel that the participants are reference group members for you? What would they influence you on? Why?

2. Visit the website for Jeep that the text referred to. What is the firm doing to foster a brand community? Do you feel these efforts are effective? Why or why not?

3. Go to the website of a product that is consumed by the entire family (e.g., food items) and one that is primarily of interest to one or two members in the family (e.g., household cleaners, children's products). Are there differ-

ences in the type of information and activities on the websites? What are the differences, and do you think they are suitable given the target market?

4. Go to the website of Kraft Canada (**www.kraft.ca**) or a company marketing similar products. Does the company use reference group influence? How? Who in the family is the company marketing to? What roles does the person(s) targeted play in household consumption decisions? Is the company targeting the right family member and using the best reference group influence? Why?

KEY TERMS

Autonomic decisions   *(p. 393)*
Brand community   *(p. 379)*
Celebrity credibility   *(p. 381)*
Consumer-action group   *(p. 379)*
Consumer socialization   *(p. 396)*
Direct reference groups   *(p. 371)*
Family   *(p. 383)*
Family life cycle   *(p. 384)*
Formal reference groups   *(p. 371)*

Husband-dominated decisions   *(p. 393)*
Identification influence   *(p. 372)*
Indirect reference groups   *(p. 371)*
Informal reference groups   *(p. 371)*
Informational influence   *(p. 371)*
Joint decisions   *(p. 393)*

Normative influence   *(p. 372)*
Reference group   *(p. 370)*
Shopping group   *(p. 377)*
Socialization of family members   *(p. 395)*
Symbolic group   *(p. 370)*
Traditional family life cycle   *(p. 385)*
Virtual groups   *(p. 377)*
Wife-dominated decisions   *(p. 393)*

CASE 12-1: CHILD-FREE, NOT CHILDLESS

In a recent *Canadian Social Trends,* Statistics Canada reported that about 7 percent of Canadian women in the 20- to 34-year age group intend to stay child-free. Although this is similar to the figures in the United States (where 6.6 percent of women in child-bearing years felt that way), all available data suggest that this figure is going to climb. The trend toward a desire to be child-free appears to cover all the age ranges in the 20- to 44-year-old group for women. For example, of those in the 20- to 24-year-old bracket 8 percent of women intend to remain child-free; this number comes down only slightly among 25- to 29-year-olds (7 percent). What is even more interesting is that a whopping 35 percent of Canadians in a lasting couple relationship felt that their happiness in life was not dependent on having a child.

Statistics Canada reports that the intention to remain child-free is highest among Canadians without any religious affiliation (12 percent), those born in Canada (8 percent), and those who are single (9 percent). The desire to be child-free does not seem to be related to the person's educational level, for across all educational levels, the percentage is 7 percent.

The increasing interest in being child-free by choice has led to several books on the subject and even a website (**www.childfree.net**).

QUESTIONS

1. What opportunities does this increasing market segment provide to marketers? In other words, what kind of products would be in demand as this proportion of the population continues to grow?

2. How would you imagine that the consumption of products and services of this group might differ from that by couples with children?

3. Visit the website **www.childfree.net** and look at the information posted. Does this qualify as a reference group?

NOTES

1   Michelle Warren, "Labatt Smiling over New Blue Work," *Marketing Magazine,* March 3, 2003, 3.

2   Marina Strauss, "Canadian Tire Ads Demonstrate Smarts," *Globe and Mail,* October 18, 2003, p. B10.

3   Michelle Warren, "Labatt Smiling over New Blue Work," *Marketing Magazine,* March 3, 2003, p.3.

4   Robert Madrigal, "The Influence of Social Alliances with Sports Teams on Intentions to Purchase Corporate Sponsors' Products," *Journal of Advertising,* 29, Winter 2000, 13–24.

5   Pamela Kicker and Cathy L. Hartman, "Purchase Pal Use: Why Buyers Choose to Shop with Others," in *1993 AMA Winter Educators' Proceedings,* 4, eds. Rajan Varadarajan and Bernard Jaworski (Chicago: American Marketing Association, 1993), 378–384.

6   Eve M. Kahn and Julie Lasky, "Out of the Pantry and Partying On," *New York Times,* November 8, 2001, F9.

7   Amitai Etzioni, "E-Communities Build New Ties, but Ties That Bind," *New York Times,* February 10, 2000, G7.

8   Cara Okleshen and Sanford Grossbart, "Usenet Groups, Virtual Community and Consumer Behavior," in *Advances in Consumer Research,* 25, eds. Joseph W. Alba and J. Wesley Hutchinson (Provo, UT: Association for Consumer Research, 1998), 276–282.

9   Birud Sindhav, "A Sociological Perspective on Web-Related Consumer Marketing," in *1999 AMA Educators Proceedings,* 10, eds., Stephen P. Brown and D. Sudharshan (Chicago: American Marketing Association, 1999), 226–227.

10   John Harney, "Cyber Bazaars," *IntelligentKM,* March 8, 2001, 58–62.

11   "Startec Acquires Chinese Web Community," *PR Newswire,* March 7, 2000, 1.

12   Eileen Fischer, Julia Bristor, and Brenda Gainer, "Creating or Escaping Community? An Exploratory Study of Internet Consumers' Behaviors," *Advances in Consumer Research,* 23 (Provo, UT: Association for Consumer Research, 1996), 178–182; and Siok Kuan Tambyah, "Life on the

Net: The Reconstruction of Self and Community," *Advances in Consumer Research,* 23 (Provo, UT: Association for Consumer Research, 1996), 172–177.

13   "Is the Net Redefining Our Identity?" *Business Week,* May 12, 1997, 100–101.

14   S. Elizabeth Bird, "Chatting on Cynthia's Porch: Creating Community in an E-Mail Fan Group," *Southern Communication Journal,* 65, no. 1, Fall 1999, 49–65.

15   Kendra Nordin, *Christian Science Monitor,* February 26, 2001, 16.

16   Albert M. Muniz, Jr. and Thomas C. O'Guinn, "Brand Community," *Journal of Consumer Research,* 27, March 2001, 412–432.

17   James H. McAlexander, John W. Schouten, and Harold F. Koenig, "Building Brand Community," *Journal of Marketing,* 66, January 2002, 38–54.

18   Ibid., 46.

19   Jay Greene, "Next, Bill Gates Air Fresheners?" *Business Week,* February 11, 2002, 16.

20   B. Zafer Erdogan, Michael J. Baker, and Stephen Tagg, "Selecting Celebrity Endorsers: The Practitioner's Perspective," *Journal of Advertising Research,* May/June 2001, 39–48.

21   Lynette Knowles Mathur, Ike Mathur, and Nanda Rangan, "The Wealth Effects Associated with a Celebrity Endorser: The Michael Jordan Phenomenon," *Journal of Advertising Research,* 37, 3, May–June 1997, 25; and Jeff Manning, "Jordan, Nike Linked Until 2023," *The Oregonian,* January 14, 1999, D1.

22   David Nielsen, "Tiger on Verge of Becoming No. 1 Pitchman in Sports," *Cincinnati Post,* June 21, 2000, 8B.

23   "D.C.s with Celebrity Patients Sought for PR Campaign," *Chiropractic Journal,* March 2002, 26.

24   Bonnie Tsui, "Yoga Magazine Gets Boost from Spirituality Surge," *Advertising Age,* September 4, 2000, 20.

25   Roobina Ohanian, "The Impact of Celebrity Spokespersons: Perceived Image on Consumers' Intention to Purchase," *Journal of Advertising Research,* February–March, 1991, 46–54.

26   Carolyn Tripp, Thomas D. Jensen, and Les Carlson, "The Effects of Multiple Product Endorsements by Celebrities on Consumers' Attitudes and Intentions," *Journal of Consumer Research,* 20, March 1994, 535–547; and David C. Bojanic, Patricia K. Voli, and James B. Hunt, "Can Consumers Match Celebrity Endorsers with Products?" in *Developments in Marketing Science,* ed. Robert L. King (Richmond, VA: Academy of Marketing Science, 1991), 303–307.

27   Ronald E. Goldsmith, Barbara A. Lafferty, and Stephen J. Newell, "The Impact of Corporate Credibility and Celebrity Credibility on Consumer Reaction to Advertisements and Brands," *Journal of Advertising,* 29, no. 3, Fall 2000, 43–54.

28   Richard Morin, "When Celebrity Endorsers Go Bad," *Washington Post,* February 3, 2002, B5.

29   Calculated from data provided in the following Statistics Canada tables: "Census families by number of children at home, Provinces and Territories," 2001 Census, **http://www.statcan.ca/english/Pgdb/famil50a.htm**; and "Household size, by provinces and territories,"2001 Census, **http://www.statcan.ca/english/Pgdb/famil53a.htm**.

30   **http://www.statcan.ca/english/Pgdb/famil54a.htm**, Statistics Canada, 2001 census.

31   Terry L. Childers and Akshay R. Rao, "The Influence of Familial and Peer-Based Reference Groups on Consumer Decisions," *Journal of Consumer Research,* 19, September 1992, 198–211.

32   Susan Stobert and Anna Kemeny, "Childfree by Choice," *Canadian Social Trends*, Summer 2003, 7–10.

33   Dee Miller, "'Till Death Do They Part," *Marketing News,* March 27, 1995, 1–2; and Nellie S. Huang, "No More Toasters, Please," *Smart Money,* April 1993, 133–135.

34   Paulette Thomas, "Show and Tell: Advertisers Take Pitches to Preschools," *Wall Street Journal,* October 28, 1996, B1, B5.

35   Charles M. Schaninger and William D. Danko, "A Conceptual and Empirical Comparison of Alternative Household Life Cycle Models," *Journal of Consumer Research,* 19, March 1993, 580–594.

36   Susan Stobert and Anna Kemeny, "Childfree by Choice," *Canadian Social Trends*, Summer 2003, 7–10.

37   Ingrid Peritz, "Bundle of Joy Worth a Bundle," *Globe and Mail*, February 7, 2004, pp. A1, A5.

38   Anne Milan and Alice Peters, "Couples Living Apart," *Canadian Social Trends*, Summer, 2003, 2–5.

39   "Update on Families," *Canadian Social Trends*, Summer, 2003, 11–13.

40   Ibid.

41   Canadian e-book, Statistics Canada.

42   Statistics Canada, "Grandparents and Grandchildren," *The Daily*, December 9, 2003.

43   J. Labrecque and L. Ricard, "Children's Influence on Family Decision-Making: A Restaurant Study," *Journal of Business Research,* 54, November 2001, 173–176.

44   Kim P. Corfman, "Perceptions of Relative Influence: Formation and Measurement," *Journal of Marketing Research,* 28, May 1991, 125–136. For additional articles on family decision-making roles and structures, see Christina Kwai-Choi and Roger Marshall, "Who Do We Ask and When: A Pilot Study about Research in Family Decision

Making," in *Developments in Marketing Science,* 16, eds. Michael Levy and Dhruv Grewal (Coral Gables, FL: Academy of Marketing Science, 1993), 30–35.

45   Joan Raymond, "For Richer and for Poorer," *American Demographics,* July 2000, 58–64.

46   John B. Ford, Michael S. LaTour, and Tony L. Henthorne, "Perception of Marital Roles in Purchase Decision Processes: A Cross-Cultural Study," *Journal of the Academy of Marketing Science,* 23, no. 2, 1995, 120–131; and Tony L. Henthorne, Michael S. LaTour, and Robert Matthews, "Perception of Marital Roles in Purchase Decision Making: A Study of Japanese Couples," *Proceedings* (Chicago: American Marketing Association, 1995), 321–322.

47   James U. McNeal and Chyon-Hwa Yeh, "Development of Consumer Behavior Patterns among Chinese Children," *Journal of Consumer Marketing,* 14, 1997, 45–59.

48   Gopala Ganesh, "Spousal Influence in Consumer Decisions: A Study of Cultural Assimilation," *Journal of Consumer Marketing,* 14 (1997), 132–145.

49   Elke Zeijl, Yolanda te Poel, Manuela du Bois-Reymond, Janita Ravesloot, and Jacqueline J. Meulman, "The Role of Parents and Peers in the Leisure Activities of Young Adolescents," *Journal of Leisure Research,* 32, no. 3, 2000, 281–302.

50   Alanna Mitchell, "Unglued," *Globe and Mail,* January 31, 2004, F1.

51   Pamela Kruger, "Why Johnny Can't Play," *Fast Company,* August 2000, 271–272.

52   Deborah Roedder John, "Consumer Socialization of Children: A Retrospective Look at Twenty-Five Years of Research," *Journal of Consumer Research,* 26, December 1999, 183–213.

53   Amy Rummel, John Howard, Jennifer M. Swinton, and D. Bradley Seymour, "You Can't Have That! A Study of Reactance Effects and Children's Consumer Behavior," *Journal of Marketing Theory and Practice,* Winter 2000, 38–45.

54   Kay M. Palan and Russell N. Laczniak, "The Relationship between Advertising Exposure and Children's Influence Strategies," in *2001 AMA Winter Educators' Conference,* 12, eds. Ram Krishnan and Madhu Viswanathan (Chicago: American Marketing Association, 2001), 28–36.

55   Gregory M. Rose, "Consumer Socialization, Parental Style, and Developmental Timetables in the United States and Japan," *Journal of Marketing,* 63, July 1999, 105–119.

56   John Fetto, "Woof Woof" Means, "I Love You," *American Demographics,* February 2002, 11.

57   Barbara Olsen, "Brand Loyalty and Lineage: Exploring New Dimensions for Research," in *Advances in Consumer Research,* 20, eds. Leigh McAlister and Michael L. Rothschild (Provo, UT: Association for Consumer Research, 1993), 575–579; Marilyn Lavin, "Husband-Dominant, Wife-Dominant, Joint," *Journal of Consumer Marketing,* 10 (1993), 33–42; and Vern L. Bengtson, "Beyond the Nuclear Family: The Increasing Importance of Multigenerational Bond," *Journal of Marriage and Family* (February 2001), 1–16.

58   Sanford Grossbart, Stephanie McConnell Hughes, Cara Okleshen, Stephanie Nelson, Les Carlson, Russell N. Laczniak, and Darrel Muehling, "Parents, Children, and the Internet: Socialization Perspectives," in *2001 AMA Winter Educators' Conference,* 12, eds. Ram Krishnan and Madhu Viswanathan (Chicago: American Marketing Association, 2001), 379–385.

59   Rajshekhar G. Javalgi and Paul Dion, "A Life Cycle Segmentation Approach to Marketing Financial Products and Services," *The Services Industries Journal,* 19, no. 3, July 1999, 74–96.

60   Chris Powell, "Under the Influence," *Marketing Magazine,* February 16, 2004, 9.

61   Ibid.

62   Leah Haran, "Families Together Differently Today," *Advertising Age,* October 23, 1995, 1, 12.

Easy, effective nighttime whitening.

It has everyone smiling.

So effective, you just apply it once at bedtime. There's no need to let it dry. Simply White™ Night is fast-drying and whitens effortlessly as you drift off to sleep. In two weeks, wake up to whiter teeth.

Dramatically whiter teeth made even simpler.™

Colgate®
Simply White™ NIGHT
Clear Whitening GEL

Guaranteed.†

† See product package for guarantee details.

chapter 13
consumer influence and the diffusion of innovations

LEARNING OBJECTIVES

By the end of this chapter, you should be able to:

1. Define opinion leadership and differentiate opinion leaders from surrogate buyers and market mavens.
2. Explain why opinion leadership occurs.
3. Discuss three different ways of measuring opinion leadership.
4. Explain why opinion leadership is effective.
5. Describe the profile of an opinion leader.
6. Explain how opinion leadership can be used by marketers to create effective marketing strategies.
7. Define an innovation and discuss the various types of innovations.
8. Describe the five adopter categories and the differences in the rate of adoption of consumer products.
9. Provide a profile of an innovative consumer.
10. Discuss the marketing strategy implications of the adoption process.

13

how do you make a Canadian television series set in small-town Saskatchewan popular? That was the problem facing the makers of *Corner Gas*, a CTV series, in 2003. The lead character is the owner of a corner gas station in a fictitious Saskatchewan small town called Dog River—definitely not the typical setting for a sitcom! Yet, the show was reaching more than 1.5 million viewers by the eleventh episode, which placed it in the top 15 of all programs watched on Canadian television.

www.cornergas.ca

How did the series manage to be so successful? To kick-start word-of-mouth publicity for the program, CTV sent out preview screeners to members of the media, as well as people who were identified as buzz-generators or "connectors." The cast appeared on CTV programs such as *Canada AM* and *Off the Record*. The company also distributed branded ice-scrapers, air fresheners, and a car safety kit as part of its promotional campaign. Finally, they gave away free gas at a Canadian Tire gas station in Toronto and, in return, asked for pledges to watch the show. Krispy Kreme provided 6000 doughnuts and free coffee at the gas station. The show was also promoted heavily on the internet.

Often, the success or failure of a new product depends on the manufacturer's ability to promote it by using opinion leaders and word-of-mouth communication. The success of *Corner Gas* can be attributed to a great extent to its ability in generating a considerable amount of word-of-mouth publicity or "buzz" through its unusual kinds of promotion. In this chapter, we will discuss both opinion leadership and the related topic of innovation diffusion.

CHAPTER OVERVIEW

This chapter deals with two interrelated issues of considerable importance to consumers and marketers alike—the informal influence that others have on consumers' behaviour and the dynamic processes that influence consumers' acceptance of new products and services.

In the first part of this chapter we examine the nature and dynamics of the influence that friends, neighbours, and acquaintances have on our consumer-related decisions. This influence is often called *word-of-mouth communications* or the *opinion leadership process* (the two terms will be used interchangeably here). We also consider the personality and motivations of those who influence (opinion leaders) and those who are influenced (opinion receivers). The second part of the chapter examines factors that encourage and discourage acceptance (or rejection) of new products and services.

OPINION LEADERSHIP

What Is Opinion Leadership?

The power and importance of personal influence are captured in the following comment by an ad agency executive: "Perhaps the most important thing for marketers to understand about word of mouth is its huge potential economic impact."[1]

Opinion leadership is the process by which one person (the opinion leader) informally influences the actions or attitudes of others, who may be opinion seekers or merely opinion recipients. The influence has several essential characteristics:

- It is interpersonal.
- It is informal.
- It takes place between two or more people.
- None of the people concerned represents a commercial selling source that would gain directly from the sale of something.
- It implies personal, or face-to-face, communication, although it may also take place in a telephone conversation or in emails or an internet chat group.
- It is likely to be reinforced by non-verbal actions.

One of the parties in a word-of-mouth encounter usually offers advice or information about a product or service, such as which of several brands is best or how a particular product may be used. This person, the **opinion leader**, may become an *opinion receiver* when another product or service is brought up as part of the conversation.

People who actively seek information and advice about products are sometimes called **opinion seekers**. For the sake of simplicity, the terms *opinion receiver* and *opinion recipient* are used interchangeably in the following discussion to refer both to those who actively seek product information from others and to those who

Opinion leadership: The process by which one person (the opinion leader) informally influences the actions or attitudes of others, who may be opinion seekers or merely opinion recipients.

Opinion leader: The person in a word-of-mouth encounter who offers advice or information about a product or service.

Opinion seeker: Individual who actively seeks information and advice about products from others.

receive unsolicited information. The following situations are some simple examples of opinion leadership at work:

- During a coffee break, a co-worker talks about the movie he saw last night and recommends seeing it.

- A person shows a friend photographs of his recent vacation in the Australian Outback, and the friend suggests that using a polarizing filter might produce better pictures of outdoor scenery.

- A family decides they would like a swimming pool for their backyard, and they ask neighbours who have pools which contractor they should use.

Most studies of opinion leadership are concerned with the measurement of the behavioural influence that opinion leaders have on the consumption habits of others. Available research, for example, suggests that "influentials," or opinion leaders, are almost four times as likely as others to be asked about political and government issues, as well as how to handle teenagers; three times as likely to be asked about computers or investments; and twice likely to be asked about health issues and restaurants.[2] There is also research to suggest that when an information seeker feels that he or she knows little about a particular product or service, a "strong-tie source" will be sought (such as a friend or family member), but when the consumer has some prior knowledge of the subject area, then a "weak-tie source" is acceptable (acquaintances or strangers).[3] Opinion leadership is not a rare phenomenon. Often more than one-third of the people studied in a consumer research project are classified as opinion leaders with respect to some self-selected product category.

Opinion Leaders Are Different from Purchase Pals and Surrogate Buyers

Before we discuss opinion leadership in more detail, let us examine two terms that are closely related to opinion leadership—purchase pals and surrogate buyers.

Purchase pals **Purchase pals** are information sources who actually accompany friends or acquaintances on shopping trips. Though they may be opinion leaders, they need not be. Research shows that the nature of the product influences the use of purchase pals. Although purchase pals were used only 9 percent of the time for groceries, they were used 25 percent of the time for electronic equipment (e.g., computers, VCRs, television sets).[4] Interestingly enough, male purchase pals are more likely to be used as sources of product category expertise, product information, and retail store and price information. Female purchase pals are more often used for moral support and to increase the buyer's confidence in his or her decisions. Similarly, when the tie between the purchase pal and the shopper is weak (e.g., when they are neighbours, classmates, or co-workers), the purchase pal's main contribution tends to be functional—the source's specific product experiences and general marketplace knowledge are being relied on. In contrast, when the ties are strong (as in the case of a mother, son, husband, or wife), what is relied on is the purchase pal's familiarity with and understanding of the buyer's individual characteristics and needs (or tastes and preferences).[5]

Surrogate Buyers Although the traditional model of new product adoption shows opinion leaders influencing the purchase of many new products and services, sometimes opinion leaders are replaced by **surrogate buyers**. For example, working women are increasingly turning to wardrobe consultants for help in buying business clothes, most new drugs start out requiring a doctor's prescription, and many service providers make decisions for their clients (e.g., your service station decides which brand of disk brake pads to install on your car). Consequently, in an increasing

Purchase pal:
An information source who accompanies a consumer on shopping trips; may or may not be an opinion leader.

Surrogate buyers:
Professional buyers who help buyers purchase products; often, they act as opinion leaders.

number of decision situations, it is a surrogate buyer who primarily influences the purchase.[6] Figure 13-1 presents the main differences between opinion leaders and surrogate buyers.

Market Mavens: A Special Category of Opinion Leaders

Market maven:
A person whose influence stems from general knowledge and market expertise, which lead to an early awareness of a wide range of new products and services.

Research suggests the existence of a special category of opinion leader, the **market maven**.[7] These consumers possess a wide range of information about many different types of products, retail outlets, and other dimensions of markets. They both initiate discussions with other consumers and respond to requests for market information. Market mavens like to shop, and they also like to share their shopping expertise with others. However, although they appear to fit the profile of opinion leaders in that they have high levels of brand awareness and tend to try more brands, unlike opinion leaders their influence extends beyond the realm of high-involvement products. For example, market mavens may help to spread information about such low-involvement products as razor blades and laundry detergent.[8] A recent study also found that market mavens are value-conscious, a characteristic that explains why they are very likely to redeem coupons.[9]

Market mavens are also distinguishable from other opinion leaders because their influence stems not so much from product experience but from a more general knowledge or *market expertise* that leads them to an early awareness of a wide array of new products and services. Part of this early awareness may come from the fact that market mavens have a more favourable attitude than non-mavens toward direct mail as a source of information.

The Situational Environment of Opinion Leadership

Discussions of products between two people do not take place in a vacuum. Two people are not likely to meet and spontaneously break into a discussion in which

FIGURE 13-1   Differences between Opinion Leaders and Surrogate Buyers

OPINION LEADER	SURROGATE BUYER
1. Informal relationship with end users	1. Formal relationship; occupation-related status
2. Information exchange occurs in the context of a casual interaction	2. Information exchange in the form of formal instructions/advice
3. Homophilous (to a certain extent) to end users	3. Heterophilous to end users (that in fact is the source of power)
4. Does not get paid for advice	4. Usually hired, therefore gets paid
5. Usually socially more active than end users	5. Not necessarily socially more active than end users
6. Accountability limited regarding the outcome of advice	6. High level of accountability
7. As accountability limited, rigour in search and screening of alternatives low	7. Search and screening of alternatives more rigorous
8. Likely to have (although not always) used the product personally	8. May not have used the product for personal consumption
9. More than one can be consulted before making a final decision	9. Second opinion taken on rare occasions
10. Same person can be an opinion leader for a variety of related product categories	10. Usually specializes for a specific product/service category

Source: Praveen Aggarwal and Taihoon Cha, "Surrogate Buyers and the New Product Adoption Process: A Conceptualization and Managerial Framework," *Journal of Consumer Marketing,* 14, 5, 1997; 394. Reprinted by permission.

information about products is asked for or offered. Rather, such discussions generally occur in a relevant situation (for example, when a specific product or a similar product is used or served) or as an outgrowth of a more general conversation that touches on the product category. For example, while drinking tea, one person might tell the other person about her favourite brand of tea.

Moreover, it is not surprising that opinion leaders and opinion receivers are often friends, neighbours, or work associates, for existing friendships provide numerous opportunities for conversation about products. Close physical proximity is likely to increase the occurrences of product-related conversations. A local health club or community centre, for example, or even the local supermarket, provides opportunities for neighbours to meet and have informal conversations about products or services.

Similarly, the rapid growth in the use of the internet is also creating a type of close "electronic proximity" or "community"—one in which people of like minds, attitudes, concerns, backgrounds, and experiences are coming together in "chat sessions" to talk about their common interests. As Figure 13-2 shows, Canada has the highest proportion of internet users in the world—15.2 million Canadians have access to the internet,[10] and more than 51 percent have access from home.[11] Furthermore, the popularity of instant messaging (see Figure 13-3) has increased the "electronic proximity" of people.

The increasing popularity of the internet has made it an important part of the opinion leadership process. The internet is proving to be a fertile environment for word-of-mouth communications of the kind that consumer marketers are interested in influencing. A recent study found personal involvement and a continuing relationship to be two important factors when it examined reactions to a website; it commented, "Information becomes a relationship on the WWW" (World Wide Web).[12] Internet Insight 13-1 provides more details on how the digital revolution has changed the nature and use of opinion leadership.

FIGURE 13-2 Top 15 Countries in Number of Internet Users by End of 2000

COUNTRY	NUMBER OF INTERNET USERS (IN MILLIONS)	INTERNET USERS AS PERCENTAGE OF POPULATION	INTERNET USERS IN THE COUNTRY AS PERCENTAGE OF ALL INTERNET USERS
United States	135.7	46.2	36.2
Japan	26.9	21.0	7.2
Germany	19.1	23.3	5.1
United Kingdom	17.9	30.1	4.8
China	15.8	12.2	4.2
Canada	15.2	49.0	4.1
South Korea	14.8	30.2	3.9
Italy	11.6	20.0	3.1
Brazil	10.1	5.6	2.8
France	9.0	15.0	2.8
Australia	8.1	40.1	2.2
Russia	6.6	4.5	1.8
Taiwan	6.5	28.8	1.7
Netherlands	5.4	33.0	1.5
Spain	5.2	12.4	1.4

Source: Based on U.S. Census Data.

FIGURE 13-3	A Profile of Adult Instant Messenger (IM) Users	
		PERCENT
GENDER		
Men		50
Women		50
AGE		
18–29 years of age[a]		30
30–49 years of age		50
50 plus years of age		19
EDUCATION		
No college		36
Some college		34
College graduate		30
ANNUAL HOUSEHOLD INCOME[a]		
Less than $50 000		45
$50 000 to $75 000		19
More than $75 000		24

[a] Some respondents did not know or declined to answer.

Source: Marc Weingarten, "The Medium Is the Instant Message" (based on Pew Internet & American Life Project, March 2001), *Business 2.0,* February 2002, 99.

www.strategis.ic.gc.ca/
epic/internet/
inoca-bc.nsf/en/
h_ca00864e.html

The opinion leadership process is a very dynamic and powerful consumer force. As informal communication sources, opinion leaders are remarkably effective at influencing consumers in their product-related decisions. In the next section, we look at some of the reasons for the effectiveness of opinion.

Why Does Opinion Leadership Happen?

To understand the phenomenon of opinion leadership, it is useful to examine the motivation of those who provide and those who receive product-related information. In other words, we need to look at why people seek opinion leadership and why people become opinion leaders.

Why Do People Seek Opinion Leaders?

Opinion receivers satisfy a variety of needs by engaging in product-related conversations. In general, consumers seek opinion leaders for the following reasons:

- to obtain new-product or new-usage information
- to reduce their risk by receiving first-hand knowledge from a user about a specific product or brand
- to reduce the search time entailed in the finding the right product or service
- to receive the approval of the opinion leader if they follow that person's advice and buy the product

For all of these reasons, people often look to friends, neighbours, and other acquaintances for product information. Indeed, research examining the importance

INTERNET INSIGHT 13-1
OPINION LEADERSHIP IN TODAY'S ALWAYS-IN-CONTACT WORLD

Over the past decade, with the proliferation of cell phones and email (and the invention of combination devices like the BlackBerry and web-capable cell phones), many people find themselves, by choice, to be always available to friends, family, and business associates. Because of this, a number of firms, such as Snap Portal, Xoom.com, Participate.com, TalkCity, and Prospero, now offer chat room management services to businesses. For example, Participate.com was hired by the health site Accenthealth.com to manage its chat rooms, so that Accenthealth editors could concentrate on writing and health issues.[13] This has also led to the popularity of what is often called **viral marketing**.

Viral Marketing

Also known as "buzz marketing," "wildfire marketing," "avalanche marketing," or any one of a dozen other names, *viral marketing* "describes any strategy that encourages individuals to pass on a marketing message to others, creating the potential for exponential growth in the message's exposure and influence."[14] Viral marketing is the marriage of email and word of mouth. It is named "viral" because it allows a message to spread like a virus. Consider HotMail, the first free eweb email service. By giving away free email addresses and services, and by attaching a tag to the bottom of every message that read, "Get your private, free e-mail at **http://www.hotmail.com**," Microsoft ensured that every time a HotMail user sent an email, there was a good chance the receiver of the email would consider signing up for a free HotMail account. And with the expectation of 150 million Instant Messenger (IM) users by the year 2004, companies like ActiveBuddy created custom software applications to connect IM users to information that they want, while "mimicking, in a crude way, the banter of a fellow IM user at the other end of the data link."[15] Figure 13-3 presents the demographic characteristics of adult Instant Messenger users.

---

of four specific sources of information about a hypothetical $100 purchase of consumer services revealed that *advice from others* was more important than the combined effect of sales representatives, advertising and promotion, and other sources.[16] Figure 13-4 compares the motivations of opinion receivers with those of opinion leaders.

Viral marketing:
Encouraging consumers to spread a marketing message to others; can lead to exponential growth in message exposure.

Why Do People Act as Opinion Leaders?

What motivates a person to talk about a product or service? Motivation theory suggests that people may give information or advice to others to satisfy some basic need of their own (see Chapter 3). However, opinion leaders may be unaware of their own motives. Some of the common reasons for people acting as opinion leaders are:

- *to reduce their own post-purchase dissonance:* Giving information and advice to others and influencing them to buy the same product may reduce consumers' post-purchase dissonance by confirming that their own buying decisions were right.

  For instance, if Noah subscribes to DSL broadband service and then is uncertain whether he made the right choice, he may try to reassure himself by "talking up" the service's advantages to others. In this way, he relieves his own psychological discomfort. Furthermore, when he can influence a friend or neighbour to also get DSL, he confirms his own good judgment in selecting the service first. Thus, the opinion leader's motivation may really be self-confirmation or self-involvement.

■ *for tangential personal benefits:* It may bring attention, imply some type of status, grant superiority, demonstrate awareness and expertise, and give the feeling of possessing inside information and the satisfaction of "converting" less adventurous souls.

■ *because of high levels of product involvement:* In addition to *self*-involvement, the opinion leader may also be motivated by *product involvement*. Opinion leaders who are motivated by product involvement may find themselves so pleased or so disappointed with a product that they simply must tell others about it.

■ *because of social involvement:* Those who are motivated by social involvement need to share product-related experiences. In this type of situation, opinion leaders use their product-related conversations as expressions of friendship, neighbourliness, and love.[17]

■ *because of message involvement:* The pervasiveness of advertising in our society encourages message involvement. People who are bombarded with advertising messages and slogans tend to discuss them and the products they are designed to sell. Such word-of-mouth conversation is typified by the popular use in everyday conversation of slogans such as Microsoft's "Where do you want to go today?"; Nike's "Just do it!"; or Chevrolet's "Like a rock."

Figure 13-4 compares the motivations of opinion leaders and opinion receivers.

Why Is Opinion Leadership Effective?

Marketers have long been aware of the influence that opinion leaders have on consumers, and they have been using opinion leadership effectively in the marketing of their products. In this section, we look at why opinion leadership is so effective in changing consumer behaviour.

FIGURE 13-4   A Comparison of the Motivations of Opinion Leaders and Opinion Receivers

OPINION LEADERS	OPINION RECEIVERS
SELF-IMPROVEMENT MOTIVATIONS	
• Reduce post-purchase uncertainty or dissonance	• Reduce the risk of making a purchase commitment
• Gain attention or status	• Reduce search time (e.g., avoid the necessity of shopping around)
• Assert superiority and expertise	
• Feel like an adventurer	
• Experience the power of "converting" others	
PRODUCT-INVOLVEMENT MOTIVATIONS	
• Express satisfaction or dissatisfaction with a product or service	• Learn how to use or consume a product
	• Learn what products are new in the marketplace
SOCIAL-INVOLVEMENT MOTIVATIONS	
• Express neighbourliness and friendship by discussing products or services that may be useful to others	• Buy products that have the approval of others, thereby ensuring acceptance
MESSAGE-INVOLVEMENT MOTIVATIONS	
• Express one's reaction to a stimulating advertisement by telling others about it	

Opinion Leaders Have Credibility

Opinion leaders are highly credible sources of information because they are usually considered to be objective when they dispense information or advice about products. They are considered to be acting in the best interests of the opinion recipients because they aren't paid for the advice and apparently have no axe to grind. Because opinion leaders often base their product comments on first-hand experience, their advice reduces for opinion receivers the perceived risk or anxiety inherent in buying new products. The average person is exposed to anywhere from 200 to 1000 sales communications a day, but he or she is thousands of times more likely to act on the basis of a friend's or colleague's recommendation. Whereas the advertiser has a vested interest in the message being advertised, the opinion leader has no commercial motive.[18] However, the opinion leader may be offering a subjective or biased opinion.

Opinion Leaders Provide both Positive and Negative Product Information

Information provided by marketers is invariably favourable to the product and/or brand. Thus, the very fact that opinion leaders offer both favourable and unfavourable information adds to their credibility. An example of an unfavourable or negative product comment is "The problem with those inexpensive digital cameras is that the images they produce aren't nearly as sharp as those from a small point-and-shoot 35 mm camera." Compared with positive or even neutral comments, negative comments are relatively uncommon. For this reason, consumers are especially likely to note such information and to avoid products or brands that receive negative evaluations. Over the years, a number of motion pictures have failed because of negative "buzz" about the film, and one study found that negative word of mouth about a food product retarded sales more than twice as much as positive word of mouth promoted sales.[19] Consumers, it turns out, are generally three to ten times more likely to share a negative experience than a positive one.[20] Figure 13-5 highlights the factors that lead to positive word-of-mouth behaviour.

Opinion Leaders Provide Information and Advice

Opinion leaders are the source of both information and advice. They may simply talk about their *experience* with a product, relate what they know about a product, or, more aggressively, *advise* others to buy or to avoid a specific product. The kinds of product or service information that opinion leaders are likely to convey during a conversation include the following:

- Which of several brands is best: *"In my opinion, when you consider cost, RCA offers the best value in TV."*
- How best to use a specific product: *"I find that my photos look best when I use genuine Kodak processing."*
- Where to shop: *"When The Bay has a sale, the values are terrific."*
- Who provides the best service: *"Over the last 10 years, I've had my car serviced and repaired at Canadian Tire, and I think its service can't be beaten."*

Many of the messages being sent and received these days deal with movies, restaurants, shopping, computer games, and other matters of interest to young adults—word-of-mouth communication in the form of telephone or email.

Figure 13-6 presents the results of a survey estimating the percentage of consumers who acted on a referral from an opinion leader for selected important product and service categories during the past year.

FIGURE 13-5   Factors Leading to Positive Word-of-Mouth Behaviour

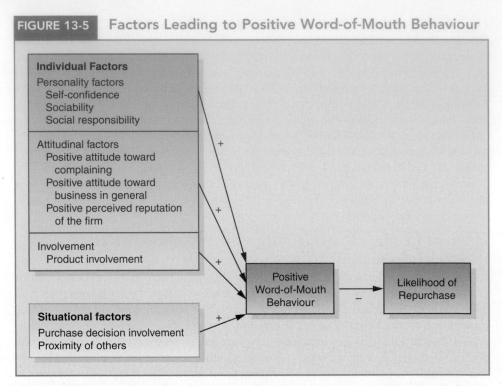

Source: Geok Theng Lau and Sophia Ng, "Individual and Situational Factors Influencing Negative Word-of-Mouth Behaviour," *Revue Canadienne des Sciences de l'Administration (Montreal),* 18, September 2001, 169.

FIGURE 13-6   Word of Mouth in Action

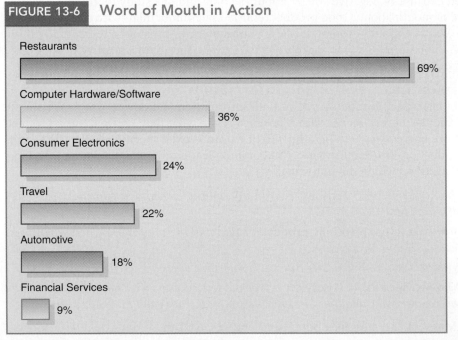

Source: Business Week (based on an online survey of 1000 adults, February 2002, Goodmind LLC), May 6, 2002, 10.

Opinion Leaders Are Specialists

Opinion leadership tends to be *category-specific;* that is, opinion leaders often "specialize" in certain product categories about which they offer information and advice. When other product categories are discussed, however, they are just as likely to become opinion receivers. A person who is considered particularly knowledgeable about boats may be an opinion leader in that subject; but when it comes to VCRs, the same person may seek advice from someone else—perhaps even from someone who has asked his advice about boats.

This leads to an interesting question: Do opinion leaders in one product category tend to be opinion leaders in other product categories? The answer to this question comes from an area of research aptly referred to as *opinion leadership overlap*. It has been found that opinion leadership tends to overlap across certain combinations of interest areas. Overlap is likely to be highest among product categories that involve similar interests (such as televisions and VCRs, high-fashion clothing and cosmetics, household cleansers and detergents, expensive wristwatches and writing instruments, hunting gear and fishing tackle). Thus, opinion leaders in one product area are often opinion leaders in related areas that they are also interested in or have specialized knowledge about.

Opinion Leadership Is a Two-Way Street

As the preceding example suggests, consumers who are opinion leaders in one product-related situation may become opinion receivers in another situation, even for the same product. Consider the following example:

Bradley, a new homeowner contemplating the purchase of a lawn mower, may ask for information and advice from other people to reduce his indecision about which brand to choose. Once the lawn mower has been bought, however, he may experience post-purchase dissonance (see Chapter 7) and have a compelling need to talk favourably about the purchase to other people to confirm the correctness of his own choice. In the first case, he is an opinion receiver (seeker); in the second, he is an opinion leader.

An opinion leader may also be influenced by an opinion receiver as the result of a product-related conversation. For example, a person may tell a friend about a favourite hotel getaway in Maui, Hawaii, and, in response to comments from the opinion receiver, come to realize that the hotel is too small and too isolated, and offers fewer amenities than other hotels.

A Profile of the Opinion Leader

Just who are opinion leaders? Can they be recognized by any distinctive characteristics? Can they be reached through specific media? Marketers have long tried to find answers to these questions, for if they are able to identify the relevant opinion leaders for their products, they can design marketing messages that encourage them to talk to other people and influence their consumption behaviour. For this reason, consumer researchers have attempted to develop a realistic profile of the opinion leader. This has not been easy to do. As was pointed out earlier, opinion leadership tends to be category-specific; that is, a person who is an opinion *leader* in one product category may be an opinion *receiver* in another product category. Thus, the generalized profile of opinion leaders is likely to be influenced by the context of specific product categories.

Although it is difficult to construct a generalized profile of the opinion leader without considering a particular category of interest (or a specific product or service category), Figure 13-7 does present a summary of the generalized characteristics that appear to hold true regardless of product category. The evidence shows that opinion leaders across all product categories generally share certain defining characteristics. First, they reveal a keen sense of knowledge and interest in the particular product or service area, and they are likely to be consumer innovators. They are

FIGURE 13-7   Profile of Opinion Leaders

GENERALIZED ATTRIBUTES ACROSS PRODUCT CATEGORIES	CATEGORY-SPECIFIC ATTRIBUTES
Innovativeness	Interest
Willingness to talk	Knowledge or expertise
Self-confidence	Special-interest media exposure
Gregariousness	Same age
	Same social status
	Social exposure outside group

also more willing to talk about the product, service, or topic; they are more self-confident; and they are more outgoing and gregarious, or sociable. Furthermore, within a specific subject area, opinion leaders receive more information from non-personal sources and are considered by members of their groups to have expertise in their area of influence. Indeed, a recent study found the expertise of the opinion leader to be strongly associated with likely influence on the information seeker's decision-making process.[21] They also usually belong to the same socio-economic and age groups as their opinion receivers.

When it comes to their mass media exposure or habits, opinion leaders are likely to read publications devoted to the specific topic or product category in which they "specialize." For example, photography opinion leaders read publications such as *Popular Photography, Balian's Outdoor and Nature PhotoWorld,* and *Petersen's Photographic.* These special-interest magazines serve not only to inform photography-oriented consumers about new cameras, films, and accessories that may be of personal interest but also provide them with the specialized knowledge that enables them to make recommendations to relatives, friends, and neighbours. Thus, the opinion leader tends to have greater exposure to media specifically relevant to his or her area of interest than does the non-leader.

The Interpersonal Flow of Communication, or How Opinion Leadership Happens

Two-step flow of communication theory:
A theory that portrays opinion leaders as direct receivers of information from impersonal mass media sources who in turn transmit (and interpret) this information to the masses.

A classic study of voting behaviour concluded that ideas often flow from radio and print media to opinion leaders, and from them to the general public.[22] This so-called **two-step flow of communication theory** portrays opinion leaders as direct receivers of information from impersonal mass-media sources, who in turn transmit (and interpret) this information to the masses. This theory views the opinion leader as an intermediary between the impersonal mass media and the majority of society. Figure 13-8 presents a model of the two-step flow of communication theory. Information is depicted as flowing in a single direction (or one way) from the mass media to opinion leaders (Step 1) and then from the opinion leaders (who interpret, legitimize, and transmit the information) to friends, neighbours, and acquaintances, who constitute the "masses" (Step 2).

Multi-step Flow of Communication Theory

A more comprehensive model of the interpersonal flow of communication depicts the transmission of information from the media as a multi-step flow. This revised model takes into account the fact that information and influence are often two-way

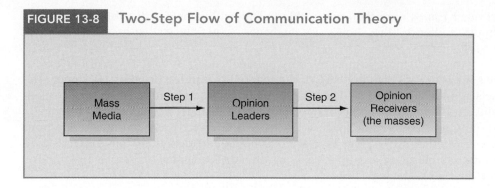

FIGURE 13-8   Two-Step Flow of Communication Theory

processes in which opinion leaders both influence and are influenced by opinion receivers. Figure 13-9 presents a model of the **multi-step flow of communication theory.** Steps 1a and 1b depict the flow of information from the mass media simultaneously to opinion leaders, opinion receivers and seekers, and information receivers (who neither influence nor are influenced by others). Step 2 shows the transmission of information and influence from opinion leaders to opinion receivers and seekers. Step 3 represents the transfer of information and influence from opinion receivers to opinion leaders.

Multi-step flow of communication theory: A modification of the two-step theory, the multi-step theory views the interpersonal flow of communication as a multi-step process in which information flows both ways between opinion leaders and opinion receivers, and between opinion receivers and information receivers.

Opinion Leadership and Marketing Strategy

Marketers have long been aware of the power that opinion leadership exerts on consumers' preferences and actual purchase behaviour. And many marketers look for an opportunity to encourage word-of-mouth communications and other favourable informal conversations about their products, because they recognize that consumers give more credence to informal sources of information than to paid advertisements or a company's salespeople.

Identify and provide samples to opinion leaders: As mentioned earlier, opinion leaders have a significant influence on the speed with which a product is accepted by the general population. Thus, it is important for marketers to identify opinion leaders for their products. By giving free samples to these opinion leaders, marketers can generate interest in their products and gain consumer acceptance for them. Marketers can easily find celebrities or experts who could act as opinion leaders. Look at the following example:

Tickle Me Elmo's huge success was helped when Tyco Toys rushed the doll to the popular talk show host Rosie O'Donnell, to give to her year-old son. Hundreds

FIGURE 13-9   Multi-step Flow of Communication

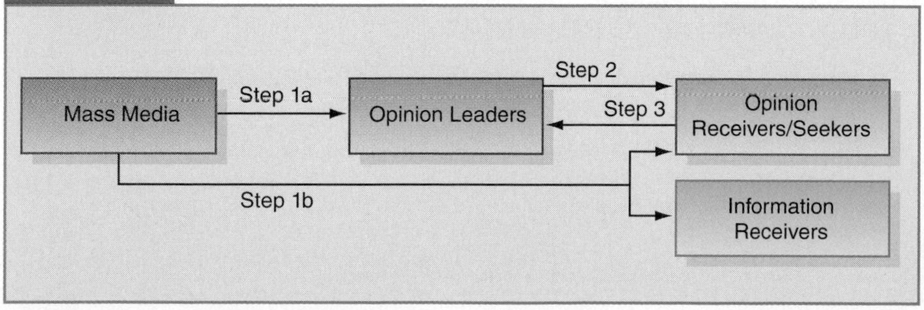

of other Elmos were then sent to Ms. O'Donnell's show for distribution to the in-studio audience (the show's TV audience is mainly stay-at-home mothers of preschoolers).[23]

However, since the most effective opinion leaders are often typical consumers, this is easier said than done. How can marketers find the ordinary consumer who acts as an opinion leader? The best approach seems to be to recognize the personality traits and media habits of the typical opinion leader and use this knowledge to identify possible opinion leaders. One way is to directly ask consumers questions about whether or not they have acted as opinion leaders in the past. Figure 13-10 shows sample questions for measuring opinion leadership. Research Insight 13-1 provides more details.

When informal word-of-mouth publicity does not spontaneously emerge from the uniqueness of the product or its marketing strategy, some marketers have deliberately attempted to stimulate or to simulate opinion leadership.

Design programs to stimulate opinion leadership: Advertising and promotional programs designed to persuade consumers to "tell your friends how much you like our product" are one way in which marketers encourage consumer discussions of their products or services. For instance, Daffy's, an off-price retailer operating in the New York metropolitan area, used an outdoor poster (at bus shelters and subway stations) to say boldly that "friends don't let friends pay retail." Here the implication is that you should share your knowledge and experience with others.

In a promotional campaign for Hennessy Cognac, actors were paid to visit Manhattan bars and nightclubs and order Cognac martinis made with Hennessy. Although they were instructed to act as if they were ordering a new fad drink, in reality they were attempting to create a new fad drink.[24]

Big Fat Inc., a Manhattan firm, places undercover employees in stores and other public places to talk up new books, beverages, records, and so on.[25]

The purpose of a promotional strategy of stimulation is to run advertisements or a direct-marketing program that is interesting and informative enough to provoke consumers into discussing the benefits of the product with others.

Develop advertisements simulating opinion leadership: A firm's advertisements can also be designed to simulate product discussions by portraying people in

---

FIGURE 13-10   Self-Designating Questions for Measuring Opinion Leadership

SINGLE-QUESTION APPROACH:
1.   In the last six months have you been asked your advice or opinion about *golf equipment*?*
     Yes _____ No _____

MULTIPLE-QUESTION APPROACH:
(Measured on a 5-point bipolar "Agree/Disagree" scale)

1.   Friends and neighbours frequently ask my advice about *golf equipment*.
2.   I sometimes influence the types of *golf equipment* friends buy.
3.   My friends come to me more often than I go to them about *golf equipment*.
4.   I feel that I am generally regarded by my friends as a good source of advice about *golf equipment*.
5.   I can think of at least three people whom I have spoken to about *golf equipment* in the past six months.

*Researchers can insert their own relevant product-service or product-service category.

RESEARCH INSIGHT 13-1
HOW DO YOU IDENTIFY OPINION LEADERS?

Consumer researchers are interested in identifying and measuring the effect of the opinion leadership process on consumption behaviour. In measuring opinion leadership, the researcher has a choice of four basic measurement techniques: (1) the *self-designating method,* (2) the *sociometric method,* (3) the *key informant method,* and (4) the *objective method.*

SELF-DESIGNATING METHOD

In the self-designating method, respondents are asked to evaluate the extent to which they have provided others with information about a product category or specific brand or have otherwise influenced the purchase decisions of others. Respondents can be asked either a single question or a series of questions to determine whether, in their opinion, they have acted as opinion leaders (refer to Figure 13-10).

The use of multiple questions enables the researcher to determine a respondent's opinion leadership more reliably because the statements are interrelated.[26] The self-designating technique is used more often than other methods because consumer researchers find it easy to include in market research questionnaires. But since this method relies on the respondent's self-evaluation, it may be open to bias should respondents consider "opinion leadership" (even though the term is not used) to be a desirable characteristic and, thus, overestimate their own roles as opinion leaders.

SOCIOMETRIC METHOD

The sociometric method measures the person-to-person informal communication of consumers concerning products or product categories. In this method, respondents are asked to name (1) the specific individuals (if any) to whom they gave advice or information about the product or brand under study and (2) the specific individuals (if any) who gave them advice or information about the product or brand under study.

In the first instance, if respondents name one or more individuals to whom they have given some form of product information, they are tentatively classified as opinion leaders. In the second instance, respondents are asked to name the individuals (if any) who gave them information about a product under investigation. Individuals designated by the primary respondent are tentatively classified as opinion leaders. In both cases, the researcher tries to validate the determination by asking the individuals named whether they did, in fact, either provide or receive the relevant product information.

KEY INFORMANT METHOD

Opinion leadership can also be measured through the use of a key informant, a person who is keenly aware of, or knowledgeable about, social communications among members of a specific group. The key informant is asked to identify those individuals in the group who are most likely to be opinion leaders. The key informant does not have to be a member of the group under study. For example, a professor may serve as the key informant for a university class, identifying those students who are most likely to be opinion leaders with regard to a particular issue. In the study of consumers, possible key informants include knowledgeable community members, such as the president of a women's club, the head of the local school board, or a prominent local businessperson.

This research method has several advantages and disadvantages. On the positive side, it is (1) relatively inexpensive because only one person or at most several people need to be intensively interviewed, whereas with the self-designating and sociometric methods, a consumer sample or entire community must be interviewed, and (2) it is very useful in the study of industrial or institutional opinion leadership. For example, a firm's salespeople might serve as key informants in the identification of specific customers who are most likely to influence the purchase decisions of other potential customers. Similarly, the purchasing agent of a firm might serve as a key informant by giving a supplier's salesperson the names of those persons in the firm who are most likely to influence the purchase decision.

On the negative side, it is difficult to find a person who can objectively identify opinion leaders in a relevant consumer group and, for that reason, it is rarely used by marketers.

OBJECTIVE METHOD

Finally, the objective method of determining opinion leadership is much like a "controlled experiment"—it involves placing new products or new-product information with selected individuals and then tracing the resulting "web" of interpersonal communication concerning the relevant products.

A new restaurant in a downtown business district might apply this approach to speed up the creation of a core customer base by sending out invitations to young, influential business executives to dine with their friends at a reduced introductory price any time during the first month of the restaurant's operations. If the restaurant's food and drink are judged to be superior, the restaurant is likely to enjoy the benefits of enhanced positive word-of-mouth publicity generated by the systematic encouragement of the young clientele to "try it out" and "talk it up" to their friends after experiencing the new restaurant.

the act of informal communication. This promotional tactic suggests that it is acceptable to discuss a particular subject or product. For example, simulated informal communications encounters between two or more women are often portrayed in televison advertising for personal-care products to persuade women to discuss their use or contemplated use of a product. Because these simulations often function as convenient substitutes for real opinion leadership, they reduce the need for consumers to actually seek product advice from others.

Create opinion leaders: Marketing strategists agree that promotional efforts would be significantly improved if they could segment their markets into opinion leaders and opinion receivers.[27] Then they could direct their promotional messages directly to the people most likely to "carry the word" to the masses. Because of the difficulty of determining who are the opinion leaders, however, some researchers have suggested that it might be more fruitful to "create" product-specific opinion leaders.

In one classic study, a group of socially influential high school students (class presidents and sports captains) were asked to become members of a panel that would rate newly released musical recordings. As part of their responsibilities, the panel participants were encouraged to discuss their record choices with friends. Preliminary examination suggested that these influentials would not qualify as opinion leaders for musical recordings because of their relatively meagre ownership of the product category.[28] However, some of the records the group evaluated made the top 10 charts in the cities in which the members of the group lived; these same recordings did not make the top 10 charts in any other city. This study suggests that product-specific opinion leaders can be created by taking socially involved or influential people and deliberately increasing their enthusiasm for a product category.

A recent research effort explored the notion of increasing enthusiasm for a product category. Over a 12-week period, half the participants were assigned to look at corporate websites (i.e., marketer-generated information sources), and half were asked to look at online discussions (e.g., in chat rooms and forums). Those who got their information from online discussions reported greater interest in the product category. It is felt that chat rooms and other forums provide consumers with personal experiences and may offer greater credibility, trustworthiness, relevance, and empathy than marketer-generated websites.[29]

Develop new products with "buzz potential": New-product designers take advantage of the effectiveness of word-of-mouth communication by deliberately designing products to have word-of-mouth potential. A new product should give customers something to talk about ("buzz potential"). Some examples of products and services that have had such word-of-mouth appeal are the Polaroid camera, the Sony Walkman, the Motorola StarTAC cellular phone, Swatch watch, America Online, and Microsoft Windows programs. These revolutionary products have attained market share because consumers "sell" them to each other by means of word of mouth. Motion pictures also appear to be one form of entertainment in which word of mouth operates with some regularity and a large impact. It is very common to be part of such a conversation or to overhear people discussing which movies they liked and which movies they advise others to skip. Proof of the power of word of mouth is those cases in which critics hate a movie and the viewing public like it and tell their friends.

Consider Penny Nirider, who lives in Thorntown, Indiana. Several years ago she took a day job at Enduron handling the firm's accounts payables. Shortly thereafter, the company purchased Wilmarc, a small firm that manufactures a number of plastic products, including the Snow-Ease, a shovel that does not require the user to bend over. When Penny received a call from an elderly woman who wanted to buy another Snow-Ease (and couldn't find one locally), she put one in a box and shipped it to the woman for $10 below retail (these shovels had never before been distributed by mail order). After a particularly large snowstorm, the elderly purchaser called a radio talk show and praised her shovel. As a result of word of mouth, Wilmarc sold 2100 snow shovels by mail order within the next four months—even after raising the price to its normal $29.95 level.[30]

Control negative word-of-mouth communication: Although most marketing managers believe that word-of-mouth communication is extremely effective, one problem they sometimes overlook is the fact that informal communication is difficult to control. Negative comments, often in the form of untrue rumours, can sweep through the marketplace to the detriment of a product.

Indeed, a recent study in the U.S. found that 90 percent or more of unhappy customers will not do business again with the company that is the source of their dissatisfaction. To make matters even worse, each dissatisfied customer will share his or her grievance with at least nine other people, and 13 percent of unhappy customers will tell more than 20 people about their bad experience.[31]

Common rumour themes that have plagued marketers in recent years and unfavourably influenced sales include the following: (1) The product was produced under unsanitary conditions, (2) the product contained an unwholesome or culturally unacceptable ingredient, (3) the product functioned as an undesirable depressant or stimulant, (4) the product contained a cancer-causing element or agent, and (5) the firm was owned or influenced by an unfriendly or misguided foreign country, governmental agency, or religious cult.

Some marketers have used toll-free telephone numbers in an attempt to head off negative word of mouth, displaying an 800 number prominently on the labels of their products labels. Customer relations managers want dissatisfied customers to call their companies' 800 numbers and receive "satisfaction" instead of telling their friends and relatives how dissatisfied they are. A particularly challenging form of "negative" word of mouth can be generated today over the internet, when a dissatisfied consumer decides to post his or her story on a bulletin board for all to see.

A recent newspaper article described a number of false internet postings, including ones by a former Sears employee who implied that the company ran sweatshops; a former Gateway 2000 employee who established a website to disparage the company's computer products; and a bulletin board posting that accused

www.adstandards.com

Tommy Hilfiger (the fashion designer) of making racist comments on the *Oprah Winfrey Show.*[32]

One consumer noted after she had complained about Blockbuster Video over the internet, "Five minutes of my time to complain to thousands of people is a good turnaround.... I vented and I felt better."[33]

And just as every large firm today has its own internet website, for many of these companies there is a corresponding "negative" website created by a disgruntled consumer. Such sites, which often take the form of chat rooms, enable customers who have had bad experiences with a product, service, or government agency to tell their "horror" stories to others.

www.sucks500.com

Diffusion of innovations:
The framework for examining consumer acceptance of new products throughout the social system.

Diffusion process:
A macro process concerned with the spread of a new product (an innovation) from its source to the consuming public.

Adoption process:
A micro process that focuses on the stages through which an individual consumer passes when deciding to accept or reject a new product.

Consumer innovators:
People who are likely to be the first to try new products, services, or practices.

www.gillette.com

www.hp.ca

Innovation:
A totally new product, service, idea, or practice.

DIFFUSION OF INNOVATIONS

The second part of this chapter examines a major issue in marketing and consumer behaviour—the acceptance of new products and services. The framework for examining consumer acceptance of new products is drawn from the area of research known as the **diffusion of innovations.** Consumer researchers who specialize in the diffusion of innovations are interested primarily in understanding two closely related processes: the **diffusion process** and the **adoption process.** In the broadest sense, diffusion is a macro process by which a new product (an innovation) spreads from its source to the consuming public. In contrast, adoption is a micro process by which an individual consumer passes through several stages when deciding to accept or reject a new product. In addition to an examination of these two related processes, we present a profile of **consumer innovators,** those who are the first to buy a new product. The ability of marketers to identify and reach this important group of consumers plays a large part in the success or failure of new-product introductions.

And why are new-product introductions so important? New products are essential for a company's growth and long-term well-being. For example, Gillette expects 40 percent of its sales to come from products introduced within the past five years; in fact, this is an organizational goal. Similarly, fully half of Hewlett Packard's revenues are derived from products introduced to the market within the past 24 months.[34]

It is also of interest to note that diffusion models for particular types of goods and services may change over time. For example, until the 1960s, it was assumed that new fashions diffused in a top-down or trickle-down manner—new styles are first adopted by the upper-class elites and gradually spread to the middle and lower classes. However, since the 1960s, the bottom-up model has served as the better explanation of fashion diffusion—new styles develop in lower-status groups and are later adopted by higher-status groups. These innovative fashions usually emanate from urban communities that also serve as the seedbeds for other innovations, such as art and popular music.[35]

Before we proceed further, let us look at what constitutes an innovation.

What Is an Innovation?

According to the Canadian government, an "innovation occurs when a business introduces new products or services to the marketplace, or adopts new ways of making products or services."[36] Although this is a useful definition of an innovation, there is no universally accepted definition of the terms product **innovation** or *new product*. Instead, new products or services can be defined in various ways. They can be classified as *firm-, product-, market-,* and *consumer-oriented definitions of innovations*. Thus, a product can be termed an innovation under the following circumstances:

■ *When the product is "new" to the company (firm-oriented approach):* From this point of view, copies or modifications of a competitor's product would qualify as new.

■ *When consumers have not had very much exposure to the new product—a market-oriented approach:* This can be assessed in two ways: when the product has been bought by only a small percentage of the potential market, or when the product has been in the market for only a short time. Both of these criteria (percentage penetration and time on the market) are subjectively decided on by the researcher.

■ *When a potential consumer judges the product to be new:* In other words, newness is based on the consumer's perception of the product rather than on physical features or market realities. Although some researchers have favoured such a *consumer-oriented* approach in defining an innovation,[37] it has received very little systematic attention from researchers.

■ *When a product is likely to change consumers' established patterns of usage—a product- and usage-based definition:* In contrast to the above definitions, a *product- and usage-based* definition looks at the features inherent in the product itself and at the effects these features are likely to have on consumers' established patterns of use. Using the product- and usage-based definition, we can define the following three types of product innovations:[38]

Continuous innovation: A new product that is an improved or modified version of an existing product; this has the least disruptive influence on consumer consumption patterns.

Dynamically continuous innovation: A new product entry that is innovative enough to have some disruptive effects on established consumption practices.

Discontinuous innovation: A dramatically new product entry that requires the establishment of new consumption practices.

1. A **continuous innovation** has the least disruptive influence on established patterns. It involves the introduction of a modified product rather than a totally new product. Examples include the redesigned Toyota Camry, the latest version of Microsoft PowerPoint, reduced-fat Oreo cookies, the BOSE Wave radio, and Teflon (see Exhibit 13-1).

2. A **dynamically continuous innovation** is somewhat more disruptive than a continuous innovation but still does not alter established behaviour patterns. It may involve the creation of a new product or the modification of an existing product. Examples include 8 mm camcorders, compact disc players, antilock automobile brakes, erasable-ink pens, and disposable diapers.

3. A **discontinuous innovation** requires consumers to adopt new habits. It usually involves the creation of a new product. Examples include airplanes, radios, television, cars, fax machines, home computers, videocassette recorders, medical self-test kits, and the internet.

Figure 13-11 shows how the telephone, a discontinuous innovation of major magnitude, has produced a variety of both dynamically continuous and continuous innovations and has even stimulated the development of other discontinuous innovations.

It should also be pointed out that although this part of the chapter deals primarily with what might

EXHIBIT 13-1

A CONTINUOUS INNOVATION

Reprinted by permission of DuPont and David Monaco.

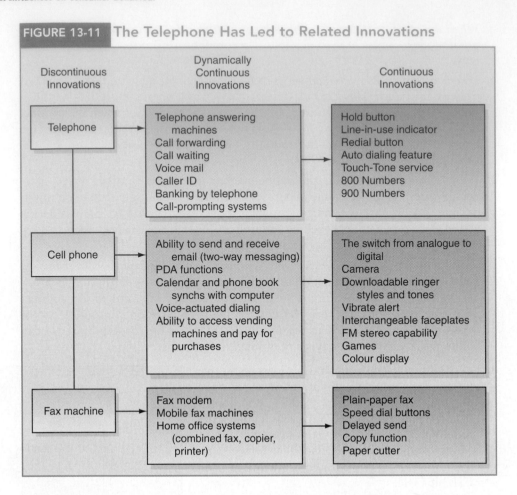

FIGURE 13-11 The Telephone Has Led to Related Innovations

	Dynamically Continuous Innovations	
Discontinuous Innovations		Continuous Innovations
Telephone	Telephone answering machines Call forwarding Call waiting Voice mail Caller ID Banking by telephone Call-prompting systems	Hold button Line-in-use indicator Redial button Auto dialing feature Touch-Tone service 800 Numbers 900 Numbers
Cell phone	Ability to send and receive email (two-way messaging) PDA functions Calendar and phone book synchs with computer Voice-actuated dialing Ability to access vending machines and pay for purchases	The switch from analogue to digital Camera Downloadable ringer styles and tones Vibrate alert Interchangeable faceplates FM stereo capability Games Colour display
Fax machine	Fax modem Mobile fax machines Home office systems (combined fax, copier, printer)	Plain-paper fax Speed dial buttons Delayed send Copy function Paper cutter

be described as "purchase" innovativeness (or time of adoption), a second type of innovativeness, "use innovativeness," has been the subject of some thought and research. A consumer is being *use-innovative* when he or she uses a product adopted previously in a novel or unusual way. In one study of the adoption of VCRs and PCs, early adopters showed significantly higher use-innovativeness than those who adopted somewhat later along the cycle of acceptance of the innovation.[39]

Factors That Affect the Diffusion of Innovations

www.canadianeconomy. gc.ca

The diffusion process is the way in which innovations spread, that is, how they are assimilated within a market. More precisely, it is the process by which the acceptance of an innovation (a new product, service, idea, or practice) is spread by communication (mass media, salespeople, or informal conversations) to members of a social system (a target market) over a period of time. This definition includes the four basic elements of the diffusion process: (1) product characteristics, (2) the channels of communication, (3) the social system, and (4) time.

Product Characteristics That Influence Diffusion

Not all products that are new have equal potential for consumer acceptance. Some products, like cordless telephones, seem to catch on almost overnight, whereas others, such as garbage compactors, take a very long time to gain acceptance or never seem to achieve widespread consumer acceptance.

The uncertainties of product marketing would be reduced if marketers could foresee how consumers will react to their products. For example, if a marketer knew that a product contained inherent features that were likely to inhibit its acceptance, the marketer could develop a promotional strategy that would compensate for these features or decide not to market the product at all. Pickup trucks are now being designed for the female driver, and manufacturers are careful to design door handles that do not break nails. Ford even offers adjustable gas and brake pedals.[40]

Although there are no precise formulas by which marketers can evaluate a new product's likely acceptance, diffusion researchers have identified five product characteristics that seem to influence consumer acceptance of new products: relative advantage, compatibility, complexity, trialability, and observability.[41] From the available research, it has been estimated that these five product characteristics account for much of the rate or speed of adoption.[42] Besides these, the felt need for the product, the amount of risk that it poses, and consumers' resistance to innovation also affect the speed with which a product will be adopted.

Relative Advantage The degree to which potential customers see a new product as superior to existing substitutes is its *relative advantage*. For example, although many people carry beepers so that their offices or families can reach them, a cellular telephone enables users to be in nearly instant communication with the world and to both receive and make calls. The fax machine is another example of an innovation that offers users a significant advantage in terms of its ability to communicate. A document can be transmitted in as little as 15 to 18 seconds at perhaps one-tenth the cost of an overnight express service, which will not deliver the document until the following day.

Compatibility The degree to which potential consumers feel a new product is consistent with their present needs, values, and practices is a measure of its *compatibility*. For example, Canadian men have made the transition from traditional razors to inexpensive disposable razors and products like the MACH3 by Gillette. However, it is difficult to imagine male shavers shifting to a new depilatory cream designed to remove facial hair. Although simpler to use, a cream would be basically *incompatible* with most men's current values regarding daily shaving practices. General Mills recently introduced Berry Burst Cheerios. Although hardly a major innovation, this new product is likely to succeed because it fits in well with Canadians' notions of what constitutes a good breakfast. General Mills' research had found that 90 percent of Canadians have, at some point, added fresh fruit to their cereal.[43]

www.generalmills.com

A study of purchasers of CD players and other technology-based products (such as computers, VCRs, and telephone answering machines) found that the main factors inhibiting product adoption were incompatibility with existing values and poor product quality.[44] And although it is possible, in theory, to make a cellular telephone the size of a button (personal phones the size of a hairclip are popular in Japan), North American consumers, according to phone manufacturer Ericsson, do not like the feeling of talking into empty space.[45]

It is also important to recognize that a particular innovation may diffuse differently throughout different cultures. For example, although shelf-stable milk (milk that does not require refrigeration) has been successfully sold for years in Europe, North Americans thus far have resisted the aseptic milk package.[46]

Complexity *Complexity,* the degree to which a new product is difficult to understand or use, affects product acceptance. Clearly, the easier a product is to understand and use, the more likely it is to be accepted. For example, the acceptance of convenience foods like frozen French fries, instant puddings, and microwave din-

Easy, effective nighttime whitening.

It has everyone smiling.

So effective, you just apply it once at bedtime. There's no need to let it dry. Simply White™ Night is fast-drying and whitens effortlessly as you drift off to sleep. In two weeks, wake up to whiter teeth.

Dramatically whiter teeth made even simpler.   Guaranteed.'

Colgate
Simply White
NIGHT
Clear Whitening Gel

EXHIBIT 13-2

AN AD STRESSING EASE AND CONVENIENCE

Courtesy of Colgate Palmolive.

ners is generally due to their ease of preparation and use. Interestingly enough, although VCRs can be found in most Canadian homes, millions of adults still need help from their children in programming the machine to record a program. The recognition of this need has made the VCR Plus1 device a success.

The issue of complexity is especially important when a company is trying to gain market acceptance for high-tech consumer products. Four predominant types of "technological fear" act as barriers to new product acceptance: (1) fear of technical complexity, (2) fear of rapid obsolescence, (3) fear of social rejection, and (4) fear of physical harm. Of the four, *technological complexity* was the most widespread concern of consumer innovators.[47] Exhibit 13-2 presents an advertisement for Colgate Simply White Night, a product that aids the whitening of teeth, that makes the point that it is easy to use and convenient.

Trialability *Trialability* refers to the extent to which a new product is capable of being tried on a limited basis. The greater the opportunity to try a new product, the easier it is for consumers to evaluate it and ultimately adopt it. In general, frequently purchased household products tend to have qualities that make trial relatively easy, since a small or "trial" size is usually available. Because a computer program cannot be packaged in a smaller size, many computer software companies offer free working models of their latest software online to encourage computer users to try the program and subsequently buy it.

Aware of the importance of trial, marketers of new supermarket products commonly use substantial cents-off coupons or free samples to give consumers a direct experience with the product (Exhibit 13-3).

However, durable articles, such as refrigerators or ovens, are difficult to try without making a major commitment. This may explain why publications such as *Consumer Reports* are so widely consulted for their ratings of infrequently purchased durable goods.

Observability *Observability* (or communicability) is the ease with which a product's benefits or attributes can be observed, imagined, or described to potential consumers. Products that have a high degree of social visibility, such as fashion items, are more easily diffused than products that are used in private, such as a new type of deodorant. Similarly, a tangible product is promoted more easily than an intangible product (such as a service).

Felt Need If a product satisfies consumers' unmet needs—that is, if current products are not satisfactory and consumers have been waiting for a better way to satisfy their needs—then there is a high degree of felt need for a product and the product will diffuse at a faster rate. For example, many consumers who had fireplaces in their homes were probably dissatisfied with the current options available for starting a fire (in most cases, crumpled newspapers!); so when firms started offering small pieces of "starter wood," consumers were quick to adopt the new offering.

Have you felt the need for a bandage that could be used on spots that are hard to cover, such as finger tips, knuckles, or elbows? If so, Montreal-based Beiersdorf Canada has just the solution for you—a spray bandage named Elastoplast. The product can be sprayed on to wounds and disappears in a short time without leaving a residue.[48]

Risk Some products, such as new high-tech products, pose a high level of financial risk; others, such as clothing in a new and very unusual style, involve social risk; and still others, such as laser surgery to correct vision problems, involve a physical risk. In such circumstances, consumers are likely to weigh the relative advantages of these products very carefully and may be reluctant to adopt the new innovation until it has been proved to be safe, for example, until many of their friends have tried laser surgery, or the financial risk has been reduced to an acceptable level, as in the case of video cameras, which came down in price from nearly $3000 to $1000 in a few years. Figure 13-12 summarizes the characteristics of products that influence diffusion.

Resistance to Innovation In a world in which consumers often find themselves with too little time and too much stress, the increased complexity of products wastes time and may delay the acceptance

EXHIBIT 13-3

SAMPLE EMPHASIZED

Courtesy of Avon.

FIGURE 13-12	Product Characteristics That Influence Diffusion	
CHARACTERISTICS	**DEFINITION**	**EXAMPLE**
Relative advantage	The degree to which potential customers perceive a new product as superior to existing substitutes	Air travel over train travel, cordless phones over corded telephones
Compatibility	The degree to which potential consumers feel a new product is consistent with their present needs, values, and practices	Gillette MACH3 over disposable razors, digital telephone answering machines over machines using tape to make recordings
Complexity	The degree to which a new product is difficult to understand or use	Products low in complexity, including frozen TV dinners, electric shavers, instant puddings
Trialability	The degree to which a new product is capable of being tried on a limited basis	Trial-size jars and bottles of new products, free trials of software, free samples, cents-off coupons
Observability	The degree to which a product's benefits or attributes can be observed, imagined, or described to potential customers	Clothing, such as a new Tommy Hilfiger jacket, a car, wristwatches, eyeglasses
Felt need for the product	The degree to which a product satisfies consumers' unmet needs	Starter wood for fireplaces
Risk associated with purchase	The degree of risk associated with using the product (e.g., financial/social/physical risk)	Unusual styles of clothing, expensive items like plasma TV sets

of the product.[49] Consider the fate of Sony's MiniDisc. Although a huge success in Japan, the product flopped in the United States a few years ago and is just now being reintroduced. The MiniDisc (MD) is small and thin and can hold 74 minutes of music. But most people in the United States are satisfied with their CDs and cassettes, and MDs cannot be played in a car without an adapter. Added to the MD's problems is the existence of recordable CD units for personal computers (CD "burners").[50]

The Channels of Communication

How quickly an innovation spreads through a market depends to a great extent on communications between the marketer and consumers, as well as communication among consumers (word-of-mouth communication). Of central concern is the uncovering of the relative influence of impersonal sources (advertising and editorial matter) and interpersonal sources (salespeople and informal opinion leaders).

In recent years, a variety of new channels of communication have been developed to inform consumers of innovative products and services. Consider the growth of interactive marketing messages, in which the consumer becomes an important part of the communication rather than just a passive recipient of the message. For example, for the past several years, an increasing number of companies, such as Ford, General Motors, and other major automobile manufactures, have used floppy disks or CD-ROMs to promote their products. Many websites currently ask the internet user if he or she would like to be informed about new products, discount offers, and so on, relevant to the focus of the site. If the answer is "yes," the consumer provides an email address and will then receive periodic information from this source.

Consider Nike's Presto line of sneakers. Although the company spends about $1 billion annually to promote its products, it was word of mouth that caused sales of the Presto to soar. Instead of ads in major publications and prime-time television, Nike used MTV and Comedy Central, offered a page of stickers in *YM* magazine, and rented a studio in Manhattan to display a wall containing 200 Presto sneakers. The firm also encouraged teenagers to log on to the Nike website to select Presto graphics, pair the graphics with music, and then email the mini–music videos to their friends (i.e., an example of viral marketing).[51]

The Social System

The diffusion of a new product usually takes place in a social setting, which is often referred to as a *social system.* In connection with consumer behaviour, the terms *market segment* and target market may be more relevant than the term *social system* used in diffusion research. A social system is a physical, social, or cultural environment to which people belong and within which they function. For example, for a new hybrid variety of corn, the social system might consist of all farmers in a number of local communities. For a new drug, the social system might consist of all physicians within a specific medical specialty (e.g., all neurologists). For a new special diet product, the social system might be all residents of a geriatric community. As these examples indicate, the social system serves as the *boundary* within which the diffusion of a new product is examined.

The orientation of a social system, with its own special values or norms, is likely to influence the acceptance or rejection of new products. When a social system is modern in orientation, the acceptance of innovations is likely to be high. In contrast, when a social system is traditional in orientation, innovations that are considered to be radical or to be infringements on established customs are likely to be avoided. According to one authority, the following characteristics typify a *modern social system*:[52]

- a positive attitude toward change
- an advanced technology and skilled labour force
- a general respect for education and science
- an emphasis on rational and ordered social relationships rather than on emotional ones
- an outreach perspective, in which members of the system frequently interact with outsiders, thus facilitating the entrance of new ideas into the social system
- the ability of members of the social system to readily see themselves in quite different roles

The orientations of a social system (either modern or traditional) may be national in scope and may influence members of an entire society, or it may exist at the local level and influence only those who live in a specific community. The point to remember is that a social system's orientation is the climate in which marketers must operate to gain acceptance for their new products. For example, in recent years, Canada and the United States have seen a decline in the demand for beef. The growing interest in health and fitness in both these countries has created a climate in which beef is considered too high in fat and in calories. At the same time, the consumption of chicken and fish has increased because these foods satisfy the prevailing nutritional values of a great number of consumers.

Time

Time is the backbone of the diffusion process. Purchase time refers to the amount of time that elapses between consumers' initial awareness of a new product or service and the point at which they buy it or reject it. Figure 13-13 illustrates the scope of purchase time by tracking a hypothetical family's purchase of a new car.

Figure 13-13 illustrates not only the length and complexity of consumer decision making but also how different information sources become important at successive steps in the process. Purchase time is an important concept because the average time a consumer takes to adopt a new product is a predictor of the overall length of time it will take for the new product to achieve widespread adoption. When the individual purchase time is short, a marketer can expect that the overall rate of diffusion will be faster than when the individual purchase time is long. Compare the purchase of a car with the purchase of an inexpensive innovation such as the Swiffer multi-purpose duster and mop; consumers probably saw an ad for the product, got a coupon in the mail, saw a product display in the supermarket, and bought the product—all in a matter of a couple of weeks.

ADOPTER CATEGORIES AND THE RATE OF ADOPTION

Adopter Categories

The concept of **adopter categories** involves a classification scheme that shows where a consumer stands in relation to other consumers in terms of time (or when the consumer adopts a new product). Five adopter categories are often cited in the diffusion literature: *innovators, early adopters, early majority, late majority,* and *laggards.* Figure 13-14 describes each of these adopter categories and estimates their relative proportions within the total population that eventually adopts the new product. It should also be mentioned that the first person to buy an innovation is often someone who serves as a bridge to other networks, an opinion broker between groups, rather than within groups.[53]

Adopter categories:
A classification scheme that shows where a consumer stands in relation to other consumers in terms of time (or when the consumer adopts a new product).

FIGURE 13-13   Timeline for Choosing a New Car

WEEK	PRECIPITATING SITUATIONS OR FACTORS
0	The family (Mom and Dad are both school teachers and have two elementary-school-aged children) currently owns one car, a mid-sized sedan, which is six years old and has 120 000 km on its odometer. The wife's parents, who retired recently, moved to Florida for the winter. They hope that their daughter and her family will visit them for Christmas week. But there is some concern that the family's current vehicle is too old to drive from Montreal to Tampa.

DECISION PROCESS BEGINS

1–4	For a few Saturday mornings, the family drives to a number of car dealerships to see, gather information about, test-drive, and price a number of mid-price, mid-sized family sedans.
5–9	The family's home gas furnace breaks and has to be replaced. Because of the expense involved, the family puts the notion of buying a new car on the back burner for a while.

INTEREST IS RETRIGGERED

10	As Christmas is now only two months away, the couple keeps being prodded by the wife's parents about driving down and spending the Christmas vacation with them in Florida. So they decide to once again think about buying a new car in time for such a vacation trip.

CONSUMER ACQUIRES A MENTOR (OPINION LEADER)

The husband asks one of his co-workers, a fellow teacher who knows a great deal about cars, to serve as his mentor (opinion leader) with respect to cars, and the co-worker agrees.

FEATURES AND BRAND OPTIONS ARE REVIEWED

11	With the advice of the mentor, the couple narrows down their search to vehicles that have four-cylinder engines (for good gas mileage), offer cruise control (for the long trip to Florida), and are equipped with air bags and antilock braking systems. Consequently, the choice has narrowed to the Toyota Camry, Honda Accord, and VW Passat.
12–13	The couple spends time on the internet at the manufacturers' websites and the websites of independent auto services, such as www.autoweb.com. They also return to their local Toyota, Honda, and VW dealers to test-drive these three vehicles again.
14–15	After spending evenings poring over brochures and information downloaded from the internet, the couple decides that the VW Passat is the car they want to buy.

ORDERING THE CAR

The couple visits four VW dealers located in the greater Montreal area, and three of them have the desired car (colour, options, etc.) in stock. Volkswagen, through its dealers, is currently offering a low-interest, four-year financing plan, which the couple decides is the best way for them to pay for the car. After negotiating with the three dealerships that have the car they want, they decide to pay $100 more for the car (considering what the dealer wants for the new vehicle and what the dealer is willing to give them for their trade-in) than the lowest price they received, in order to buy it from the dealership closest to their home. After signing the purchase agreement, the couple leave the dealership singing, "Florida, here we come!"

As Figure 13-15 shows, the adopter categories are generally depicted as taking on the characteristics of a normal distribution (a bell-shaped curve), which describes the total population that ultimately adopts a product. Some argue that the bell curve is an erroneous depiction because it may lead to the inaccurate conclusion that 100 percent of the members of the social system under study (the target market) will eventually accept the product innovation. This assumption is not in keeping with marketers' experiences, because very few, if any, products fit the precise needs of all potential consumers.

Instead of the classic five-category adopter scheme, many consumer researchers have used other classification schemes, most of which consist of two or three categories that compare *innovators* or *early triers* with *later triers* or *non-*

FIGURE 13-14   Adopter Categories

ADOPTER CATEGORY	DESCRIPTION	RELATIVE PERCENTAGE WITHIN THE POPULATION THAT EVENTUALLY ADOPTS
Innovators	*Venturesome*—very eager to try new ideas; acceptable if risk is daring; more cosmopolitan social relationships; communicate with other innovators	2.5%
Early Adopters	*Respect*—more integrated into the local social system; the persons to check with before adopting a new idea; category contains greatest number of opinion leaders; are role models	13.5
Early Majority	*Deliberate*—adopt new ideas just prior to the average time; seldom hold leadership positions; deliberate for some time before adopting	34.0
Late Majority	*Skeptical*—adopt new ideas just after the average time; adopting may be both an economic necessity and a reaction to peer pressures; innovations approached cautiously	34.0
Laggards	*Traditional*—the last people to adopt an innovation; most "localite" in outlook; oriented to the past; suspicious of the new	16.0
		100.0%

Source: Adapted/Reprinted with the permission of The Free Press, a division of Simon & Schuster, from *Diffusion of Innovations*, 3rd edition, by Everett M. Rogers. Copyright © 1995 by Everett M. Rogers. Copyright © 1962, 1971, 1983 by The Free Press.

triers. As we will see, this emphasis on the innovator or early trier has produced several important generalizations that have practical significance for marketers planning the introduction of new products.

Whereas the adopter categories describe the speed with which consumers adopt an innovation, there is another related concept—the rate of adoption—which describes the speed at which the entire adoption process happens. The next section gives more details about the rate of adoption.

Rate of Adoption

The rate of adoption refers to the length of time it takes for a new product or service to be adopted by members of a social system, that is, how quickly a new product is accepted by those who will ultimately adopt it. The general view is that the rate of adoption for new products is getting faster or shorter. Fashion adoption is a form of diffusion, one in which the rate of adoption is important. Cyclical fashion trends or "fads" are extremely "fast," whereas "fashion classics" may have extremely slow or "long" cycles.

In general, the diffusion of products around the world is becoming a more rapid phenomenon. For example, it took black-and-white television about 12 years longer to reach the same level of penetration in Europe and Japan as in the United States

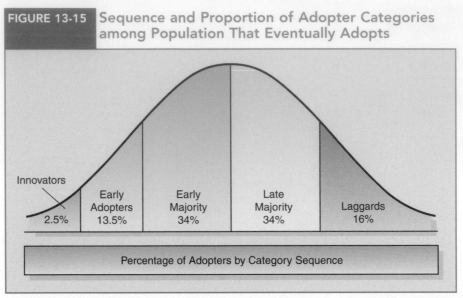

FIGURE 13-15   Sequence and Proportion of Adopter Categories among Population That Eventually Adopts

Innovators
2.5%

Early Adopters
13.5%

Early Majority
34%

Late Majority
34%

Laggards
16%

Percentage of Adopters by Category Sequence

Source: Adapted/reprinted with the permission of The Free Press, a division of Simon & Schuster, from *Diffusion of Innovations,* 3rd edition, by Everett M. Rogers. Copyright © 1995 by Everett M. Rogers. Copyright © 1962, 1971, 1983 by The Free Press.

or Canada. For colour television, the lag time dropped to about five years for Japan and several more years for Europe. In contrast, for VCRs there was only a three- or four-year spread, with the United States (with its emphasis on cable television) lagging behind Europe and Japan. Finally, for compact disc players, penetration levels in most developed countries were about even after only three years.[54]

The objective in marketing new products is usually to gain wide acceptance of the product as quickly as possible. Marketers desire a rapid rate of product adoption so that they can quickly establish market leadership (obtain the largest share of the market) before competition takes hold. A *penetration policy* is usually accompanied by a relatively low introductory price designed to discourage competition from entering the market. Rapid product adoption also demonstrates to marketing intermediaries (wholesalers and retailers) that the product is worthy of their full and continued support.

Under certain circumstances, however, marketers might prefer to avoid a rapid rate of adoption for a new product. For example, marketers who wish to use a pricing strategy that will enable them to recoup their development costs quickly might follow a *skimming policy:* they first make the product available at a very high price to consumers who are willing to pay top dollar, and then they gradually lower the price to attract additional market segments at each price reduction plateau. For example, a four-head, cable-ready, remote-control VCR could be had for $300 or less after a few years, but when VCRs were first marketed, two-head models, with no remote control, sold for $1000 or more.

Although sales graphs depicting the adoption categories (again, see Figure 13-15) are usually thought of as having a normal distribution in which sales continue to increase before reaching a peak (at the top of the curve), some research evidence indicates that a third to a half of such sales curves, at least in the consumer electronics industry, involve an initial peak, a trough, and then another sales increase. Such a "saddle" in the sales curve has been attributed to the early market adopters and the main market adopters being two separate markets.[55] Figure 13-16 presents three examples of sales curves with saddles—PCs, VCR decks with stereo, and cordless telephones.

FIGURE 13-16 "Sales Saddle" Differentiates Early Market Adopters from the Main Market Adopters

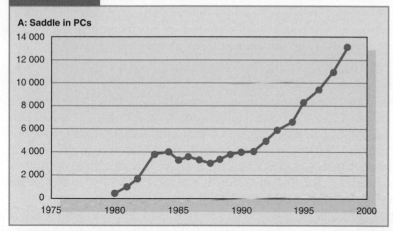

A: Saddle in PCs

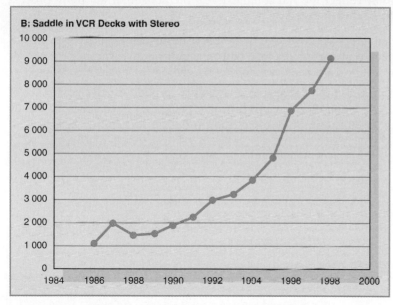

B: Saddle in VCR Decks with Stereo

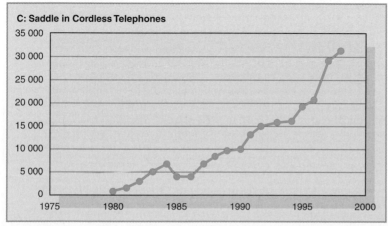

C: Saddle in Cordless Telephones

Source: Jacob Goldenberg, Barak Libai, and Eitan Muller, "Riding the Saddle: How Cross-Market Communications Can Create a Major Slump in Sales," *Journal of Marketing,* 66, April 2002, 5.

The Adoption Process

The second major process in the diffusion of innovations is *adoption*. The emphasis in the study of this process is on the stages that an individual consumer passes through while arriving at a decision to try or not to try or to continue using or to stop using a new product. (The *adoption process* should not be confused with *adopter categories*.)

Stages in the Adoption Process

Stages in the adoption process:
The process by which an individual moves from product awareness to interest, evaluation, trial, and finally, adoption.

It is often assumed that the consumer moves through five stages in arriving at a decision to buy or reject a new product: (1) awareness, (2) interest, (3) evaluation, (4) trial, and (5) adoption (or rejection). The assumption underlying the adoption process is that consumers engage in extensive information search, whereas consumer involvement theory suggests that for some products, a limited information search is more likely (for low-involvement products). The five **stages in the adoption process** are described in Figure 13-17.

Although the traditional adoption process model is insightful in its simplicity, it does not adequately reflect the full complexity of the consumer adoption process for the following reasons:

- It does not adequately acknowledge that there is quite often a need or problem-recognition stage that consumers face before acquiring an awareness of potential options or solutions (a need recognition preceding the awareness stage).

- The adoption process model does not adequately provide for the possibility of evaluation and rejection of a new product or service after each stage, especially after trial (e.g., a consumer may reject the product after trial or never use it continuously).

FIGURE 13-17   Stages in the Adoption Process

NAME OF STAGE	WHAT HAPPENS DURING THIS STAGE	EXAMPLE
Awareness	Consumer is first exposed to the product innovation.	Janet sees an ad for a new MP3 player in a magazine she is reading.
Interest	Consumer is interested in the product and searches for additional information.	Janet reads about the MP3 player on the manufacturer's website and then goes to an electronics store near her apartment and has a salesperson show her the unit.
Evaluation	Consumer decides whether or not to believe that this product or service will satisfy the need—a kind of "mental trial."	After talking to a knowledgeable friend, Janet decides that this MP3 player will allow her to easily download the MP3 files that she has on her computer. She also feels that the unit's size is small enough to easily fit into her beltpack.
Trial	Consumer uses the product on a limited basis.	Since an MP3 player cannot be "tried" like a small tube of toothpaste, Janet buys the MP3 player online from Amazon.com, which offers a 30-day (from the date of shipment) full-refund policy.
Adoption (Rejection)	If trial is favourable, consumer decides to use the product on a full rather than a limited basis—if unfavourable, the consumer decides to reject it.	Janet finds that the MP3 player is easy to use and that the sound quality is excellent. She keeps the MP3 player.

■ It does not explicitly include post-adoption or post-purchase evaluation, which can lead to a strengthened commitment or to a decision to discontinue use.

Figure 13-18 presents an enhanced representation of the adoption process model, one that includes the additional dimensions or actions described here.

The adoption of some products and services may have minimal consequences, whereas the adoption of other innovations may lead to major behavioural and life-style changes. Examples of innovations with major impacts on society include the car, the telephone, the electric refrigerator, the television, the airplane, and the personal computer.

The Adoption Process and Information Sources

The adoption process provides a framework for determining which types of information sources consumers find most important at specific decision stages. For example, early subscribers to a computer-linked data service, such as CompuServe, might first become aware of the service from mass media sources (magazines and radio publicity). Then these early subscribers' final pretrial information might be an outcome of informal discussions with personal sources. The important point is that impersonal mass media sources tend to be most valuable for creating an initial awareness of a product; as the purchase decision progresses, however, the relative importance of these sources declines, while the relative importance of interpersonal sources (friends, salespeople, and others) increases. Figure 13-19 depicts this relationship.

A Profile of the Consumer Innovator

Who is the consumer innovator? What characteristics set the innovator apart from later adopters and from those who never purchase? How can the marketer reach and influence the innovator? These are crucial questions for the marketing practitioner about to introduce a new product or service.

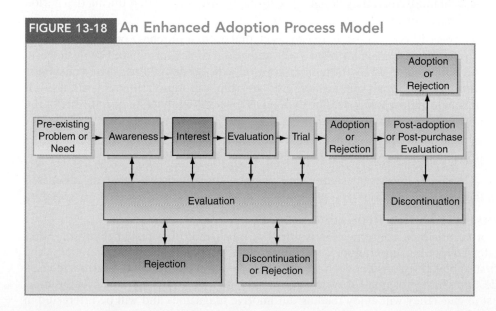

FIGURE 13-18   An Enhanced Adoption Process Model

FIGURE 13-19   Relative Importance of Different Types of Information Sources in the Adoption Process

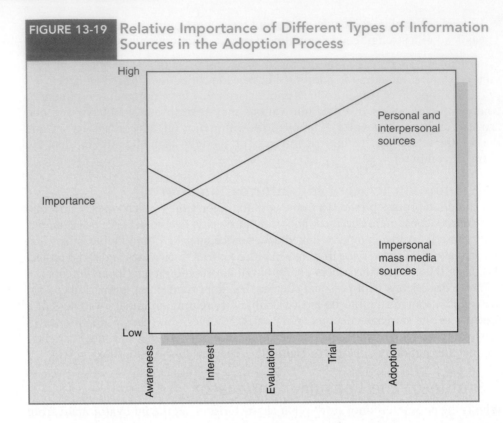

Consumer innovators can be defined as the relatively small group of consumers who are the earliest purchasers of a new product. The concept of *earliest* has been defined in many ways:

■ as the first 2.5 percent of the social system to adopt an innovation.

■ from the status of the new product under investigation. For example, if researchers define a new product as an innovation for the first three months of its availability, then they define the consumers who purchase it during this period as "innovators."

■ in terms of a consumers' *innovativeness,* that is, their purchase of some minimum number of new products from a selected group of new products. For instance, in the adoption of a new fashion, innovators can be defined as those consumers who buy more than one fashion product from a group of 10 new fashion products. Non-innovators would be defined as those who buy none or only one of the new fashion products.

■ as an arbitrary proportion of the total market, such as the first 10 percent of the population in a specified geographic area to buy the new product.

Consumer innovators share some common characteristics, which are discussed in the following sections.

Interest in the Product Category

Not surprisingly, consumer innovators are much more interested than are either later adopters or non-adopters in the product categories that they are among the first to buy. If what is known from diffusion theory holds true in the future, the earliest purchasers of small electric cars are likely to have a substantially greater interest in cars (they will enjoy reading automotive magazines and will be interested in the performance and functioning of cars) than will those who bought conventional small cars during the same period or those who bought small electric cars during a later period. Recent research into early adopters of products containing a non-fat synthetic cooking oil in the United States found them to have a high interest in such a product because of health and diet concerns.[56]

This higher level of interest leads to two actions on the part of consumer innovators: greater search for information (from a variety of informal and mass media sources), and greater deliberation (or extended decision making) about the purchase of new products or services in their areas of interest than non-innovators.

Although innovators have generally been portrayed as heavy users of the product category, this may be true only for relatively continuous innovations. A recent study found that for discontinuous innovations, it is often novices who buy the product, whereas experts in the field are often laggards with respect to product adoption. For example, serious amateur photographers with a great deal of camera knowledge and little computer literacy were found to be least likely to buy a digital camera. The people most likely to buy these cameras were those with high computer literacy and low photographic knowledge.[57] Therefore, it might be more important for the digital camera manufacturer to advertise in *PC Magazine* than in *Popular Photography*.

The Innovator Is an Opinion Leader

When discussing the characteristics of the opinion leader earlier in this chapter, we referred to a strong tendency for consumer opinion leaders to be innovators. An impressive amount of research on the diffusion of innovations has found that consumer innovators provide other consumers with information and advice about new products and that those who receive such advice often follow it. Thus, in the role of opinion leader, the consumer innovator often influences the acceptance or rejection of new products.

When innovators are enthusiastic about a new product and encourage others to try it, the product is likely to receive broader and quicker acceptance. When consumer innovators are dissatisfied with a new product and discourage others from trying it, its acceptance will be severely limited, and it may die a quick death. For products that do not generate much excitement (either positive or negative), consumer innovators may not be sufficiently motivated to provide advice. In such cases, the marketer must rely almost entirely on mass media and personal selling to influence future purchasers; the absence of informal influence is also likely to result in a somewhat slower rate of acceptance (or rejection) of the new product. Because motivated consumer innovators can influence the rate of acceptance or rejection of a new product, they influence its eventual success or failure.

Personality Traits

In Chapter 5, we examined the personality traits that distinguish the consumer innovator from the non-innovator. In this section, we will briefly highlight what researchers have learned about the personality of the consumer innovator.

- Consumer innovators are generally *less dogmatic* than non-innovators. They tend to approach new or unfamiliar products with considerable openness and little anxiety.

- They are people with a high *need for uniqueness*.[58] Those new products, both branded and unbranded, that represent a greater change in a person's consumption habits, were viewed as superior when it came to satisfying the need for uniqueness. Therefore, to gain more rapid acceptance of a new product, marketers might consider appealing to a consumer's need for uniqueness.

- They are *inner-directed;* that is, they rely on their own values or standards when making a decision about a new product. Thus, the first buyers of a new line of cars might be inner-directed, whereas the later purchasers might be other-directed. This suggests that as acceptance of a product progresses from early to later adopters, a gradual shift occurs in the personality type of adopters from inner-directedness to other-directedness.

- They are likely to have a higher *optimum stimulation level*. Specifically, people who seek a life rich with novel, complex, and unusual experiences (high optimum stimulation levels) are more willing to risk trying new products, to be innovative, to look for purchase-related information, and to accept new retail facilities.

- They are higher in *variety seeking*. Variety-seeking consumers tend to be brand switchers and purchasers of innovative products and services. They also possess the following innovator-related personality traits: they are open-minded (or low in dogmatism), extroverts, liberal, low in authoritarianism, able to deal with complex or ambiguous stimuli, and creative.[59]

- They have a lower *perceived risk*. Perceived risk, which is discussed in detail in Chapter 5, is another measure of a consumer's likelihood to try new brands or products. Perceived risk is the amount of uncertainty or fear about the consequences of a purchase that a consumer feels when considering buying a new product. For example, consumers experience uncertainty when they are afraid that a new product will not work properly or as well as other alternatives. Research on perceived risk and the trial of new products overwhelmingly indicates that consumer innovators are low-risk perceivers; that is, they experience little fear of trying new products or services. Consumers who see little or no risk in the purchase of a new product are much more likely to make innovative purchases than are consumers who perceive a great deal of risk. In other words, high-risk perception limits innovativeness.

- They are more *venturesome*. Venturesomeness is a broad-based measure of a consumer's willingness to accept the risk of purchasing new products. Measures of venturesomeness have been used to evaluate a person's general values or attitudes toward trying new products. A typical measurement scale might include statements such as these:

  - I prefer to (try a toothpaste when it first comes out) (wait and learn how good it is before trying it).

  - When I am shopping and see a brand of paper towels I know about but have never used, I am (very anxious or willing to try it), (hesitant about trying it), (very unwilling to try it).

  - I like to be among the first people to buy and use new products that are on the market (measured on a five-point "agreement" scale).

  Research into venturesomeness has generally found that consumers who indicate a willingness to try new products tend to be consumer innovators (as measured by their actual purchase of new products). Conversely, consumers who express a reluctance to try new products are, in fact, less likely to buy new products. Therefore, venturesomeness seems to be an effective barometer of actual innovative behaviour.

  To sum up, consumer innovators seem to be more receptive to the unfamiliar and the unique; they are more willing to rely on their own values or standards than on the judgment of others. They also are willing to run the risk of a poor product choice to increase their exposure to new products that will be satisfying. For the marketer, the personality traits that distinguish innovators from non-innovators suggest the need for separate promotional campaigns for innovators and for later adopters.

Purchase and Consumption Characteristics

Consumer innovators possess purchase and use traits that set them apart from non-innovators. For example, consumer innovators are *less* brand-loyal; that is, they are more apt to switch brands. This is not surprising, for brand loyalty would seriously impede a consumer's willingness to try new products.

Consumer innovators are more likely to be *deal-prone* (to take advantage of special promotional offers such as free samples and cents-off coupons). They are also likely to be *heavy users* of the product category in which they innovate. Specifically, they buy larger quantities and consume more of the product than non-innovators. Finally, for products like VCRs, PCs, microwave ovens, 35 mm cameras, and food processors, usage variety is likely to be a relevant dimension of new-product diffusion. An understanding of how consumers might be "usage innovators"—that is, finding or "inventing" new uses for an innovation—might create entirely new market opportunities for marketers' products.

To sum up, a positive relationship exists between innovative behaviour and heavy usage. Consumer innovators are not only an important market segment from the standpoint of being the first to use a new product, but they also represent a substantial market in terms of product volume. However, their propensity to switch brands or to use products in different or unique ways and their positive response to promotional deals also suggest that innovators will continue to use a specific brand only as long as they do not perceive that a new and potentially better alternative is available.

Media Habits

Comparisons of the media habits of innovators and non-innovators across such widely diverse areas of consumption as fashion clothing and new automotive services suggest that innovators have somewhat greater total exposure to magazines than do non-innovators, particularly to special-interest magazines devoted to the product category in which they innovate. For example, fashion innovators are more likely to read magazines such as *Gentlemen's Quarterly* and *Vogue* than are non-innovators; financial services innovators have greater exposure to such special-interest magazines as *Money* and *Financial World.* Exhibit 13-4 shows an ad that targets fashion innovators

Consumer innovators are also less likely to watch television than are non-innovators. This observation is consistently supported by research that over the past decade or so has compared the magazine and television exposure levels of consumer innovators. The evidence indicates that consumer innovators have higher-than-average magazine exposure (see Figure 13-20) and lower-than-average television exposure. It will be interesting, though, to

EXHIBIT 13-4

ADIDAS AD CALLS OUT TO THOSE WHO WOULD BE FASHION INNOVATORS

Reprinted by permission of Adidas America, Inc.

observe over the next few years what the impact of the convergence of computers and television will be. Studies of the relationship between innovative behaviour and exposure to other mass media, such as radio and newspapers, have been too few, and the results have been too varied to draw any useful conclusions.

Social Characteristics

Consumer innovators are more socially integrated into the community, better accepted by others, and more socially involved; that is, they belong to more social groups and organizations than do non-innovators. This greater social acceptance and involvement of consumer innovators may help explain why they function as effective opinion leaders.

Demographic Characteristics

www.gdsourcing.ca/
works/demographics
statscan.htm

It is reasonable to assume that the age of the consumer innovator is related to the specific product category in which he or she innovates; however, research suggests that consumer innovators tend to be younger than either late adopters or non-innovators. This is no doubt because many of the products selected for research attention (such as fashion, convenience grocery products, or new cars) are particularly attractive to younger consumers.

Consumer innovators have more formal education, have higher personal or family incomes, and are more likely to have higher occupational status (to be professionals or hold managerial positions) than are late adopters or non-innovators. In other words, innovators tend to be more upscale than other consumer segments are and can, therefore, better afford to make a mistake should the innovative new product or service being purchased prove to be unacceptable.

Figure 13-20 summarizes the major differences between consumer innovators and late adopters or non-innovators. The table includes the major distinctions examined in our current presentation of the *consumer innovator profile*.

Are There Generalized Consumer Innovators?

Do consumer innovators in one product category tend to be consumer innovators in other product categories? The answer to this strategically important question is a guarded "no." The overlap of innovativeness across product categories, like opinion leadership, seems to be limited to product categories that are closely related to the same basic interest area. Consumers who are innovators in relation to one new food product or one new appliance are more likely to be innovators in relation to other new products in the same general product category. In other words, although no single or generalized consumer-innovativeness trait seems to operate *across* broadly different product categories, evidence suggests that consumers who innovate *within* a specific product category will innovate again within the same product category. For example, up to the point of "innovator burnout" (i.e., "what I have is good enough"), a person who was an innovator in buying an original IBM PC for his or her home office in the early 1980s was most likely again an innovator in buying a PC with an Intel 80286 microprocessor, an Intel 80386 microprocessor, an Intel 80486 microprocessor, and an Intel Pentium microprocessor and is likely to be an innovator again when it comes to the next generation of microprocessors for personal computers. For the marketer, such a pattern suggests that it is generally a good marketing strategy to target a new product to consumers who were the first to try other products in the same basic product category.

In the realm of high-tech innovations, the evidence suggests there is a generalized "high-tech" innovator—known as a "change leader."[60] Such people tend to embrace and popularize many of the innovations that are ultimately accepted by

FIGURE 13-20	Comparative Profiles of the Consumer Innovator and the Non-innovator or Late Adopter

CHARACTERISTIC	INNOVATOR	NON-INNOVATOR (OR LATE ADOPTER)
Product Interest	More	Less
Opinion Leadership	More	Less
Personality		
Dogmatism	Open-minded	Closed-minded
Need for uniqueness	Higher	Lower
Social character	Inner-directed	Other-directed
Optimum stimulation level	Higher	Lower
Variety seeking	Higher	Lower
Perceived risk	Less	More
Venturesomeness	More	Less
Purchase and Consumption Traits		
Brand loyalty	Less	More
Deal proneness	More	Less
Usage	More	Less
Media Habits		
Total magazine exposure	More	Less
Special-interest magazines	More	Less
Television	Less	More
Social Characteristics		
Social integration	More	Less
Social striving (e.g., social, physical, and occupational mobility)	More	Less
Group memberships	More	Less
Demographic Characteristics		
Age	Younger	Older
Income	Higher	Lower
Education	More	Less
Occupational status	Higher	Lower

the mainstream population, such as computers, cellular telephones, and fax machines. They tend to have a wide range of personal and professional contacts representing different occupational and social groups; most often these contacts tend to be "weak ties" or acquaintances. Change leaders also appear to fall into one of two distinct groups: a *younger group* that can be characterized as being stimulation seeking, sociable, and having high levels of fashion awareness, or a *middle-aged group* that is highly self-confident and has very high information-seeking needs.

Like change leaders, "technophiles" are people who buy technologically advanced products soon after their market debut. Such individuals tend to be technically curious people. Also, another group responding to technology are adults who are categorized as "techthusiasts"—people who are most likely to buy or subscribe to emerging products and services that are technologically oriented. These consumers tend to be younger, better-educated, and more affluent.[61]

Diffusion Process and Marketing Strategy

Understanding the diffusion process is critical for successful marketing, for it will enable the marketer to successfully penetrate the market. The following are some of the marketing strategies that are implied by the diffusion process:

Identify the product characteristics that would inhibit its diffusion and find ways to compensate for these weaknesses: As we saw earlier, there are seven product characteristics that affect the diffusion of a product. By first evaluating how their product scores on these characteristics and then trying to compensate for product weaknesses (in terms of diffusion), marketers can hasten the diffusion of their new product. For example, if the product is complex, training personal salespeople well (to communicate product qualities) and having product demonstrations in retail outlets would help the diffusion process. However, if the product is low in relative advantage, then lowering the price or redesigning the product to increase its relative advantage may be necessary.

Identify the possible innovators and early adopters of the product and cater to them: As we saw earlier, innovators and early adopters are critical to the success of a product because they act as opinion leaders to other consumers. By using their knowledge of innovators, marketers can reach out to them and first persuade them to try the product. Marketers can use the knowledge that innovators are highly interested in the product and are heavy users of relevant media to identify these consumers. Knowledge of other innovator characteristics (e.g., venturesomeness) can be incorporated into advertising and other marketing communications to attract innovators.

www.sabian.com

Sabian, based in Meductic, NB, is known around the world for its cymbals. How did a small New Brunswick company achieve this status in an industry with well-established competitors like Paiste (a Swiss company) and Zildjian? One of the reasons for its success is its innovative promotional campaign. Sabian invited well-known drummers to its Meductic plant and asked them to invent new cymbals. These signature cymbals and their creators were featured in ads. The ads showed the drummers in unusual ways, having fun doing something they enjoyed. They also ran a series of ads which showed drummers who had switched to Sabian with the tag line "Join the Sabian Switchers."

Use forms of communication effectively to move the consumer through the adoption process: Consumers move from awareness to adoption incrementally; this is particularly true in the case of extended decision-making situations. When digital cameras first came on the market, marketers had to make consumers aware of the new product and create interest in it. This is effectively done through mass media; once consumers are aware of the product, evaluation and trial are most likely to be aided by the use of personal salespeople. So marketers have to advertise the product heavily and effectively to create awareness.

Make effective use of word-of-mouth communications: Since the spread of an innovation depends not only on marketing communications but also on word-of-mouth or interpersonal communications, marketers should attempt to create effective word-of-mouth communications for their product. This can be done through the use of viral marketing techniques, rewarding consumers for passing on the word to their friends (e.g., benefits to consumers who introduce a possible new customer) and offering free trials to opinion leaders and innovators.

SUMMARY

- Opinion leadership is the process by which one person (the opinion leader) informally influences the actions or attitudes of others, who may be opinion seekers or merely opinion recipients.

- Opinion receivers consider the opinion leader to be a highly credible, objective source of product information who can help reduce their search time and perceived risk.

- Opinion leaders give information or advice to others partly because doing so enhances their own status and self-image and because such advice tends to reduce any post-purchase dissonance they may have. Other motives include product involvement, "other" involvement, and message involvement.

- Market researchers identify opinion leaders by such methods as self-designation, key informants, the sociometric method, and the objective method.

- Studies of opinion leadership show that this phenomenon tends to be product-specific; that is, individuals "specialize" in a product or product category that they are very interested in.

- Generally, opinion leaders are gregarious, self-confident, innovative people who like to talk; they feel different from others and acquire information by reading special-interest magazines.

- The market mavens are opinion leaders across a wide range of products; they initiate discussions with other consumers and respond to requests for market information over a wide range of products and services.

- The opinion leadership process usually takes place among friends, neighbours, and work associates who are in frequent physical proximity and, thus, have ample opportunity to hold informal conversations about products.

- Marketers try to both simulate and stimulate opinion leadership. They have also found that they can create opinion leaders for their products by taking socially involved or influential people and deliberately increasing their enthusiasm for a product category.

- The diffusion process and the adoption process are two closely related concepts concerned with the acceptance of new products by consumers. The diffusion process is a macro process by which an innovation—a new product, service, or idea—spreads from its source to the consuming public. The adoption process is a micro process by which an individual consumer passes through several stages when making a decision to accept or reject a new product.

- Seven product characteristics influence the consumer's acceptance of a new product: relative advantage, compatibility, complexity, trialability, observability (or communicability), the felt need for the product, and the risk involved in buying it; the consumers' resistance to innovation also plays a role.

- Diffusion is also affected by the channels through which word of a new product is spread to the consuming public, the nature of the market in which the firm operates, and the time taken to buy the product.

- The five adopter categories are innovators, early adopters, early majority, late majority, and laggards.

- The traditional adoption process model describes five stages through which an individual consumer passes to arrive at the decision to adopt or reject a new product: awareness, interest, evaluation, trial, and adoption or rejection.

- The enhanced adoption process model considers the possibility of a pre-existing need or problem, the likelihood that some form of evaluation might occur through the entire process, and that even after adoption there will be post-adoption or post-purchase evaluation that might either strengthen the commitment or lead the consumer to stop using it.

- Consumer research has identified a number of consumer-related characteristics, including interest in the product, opinion leadership, personality factors, purchase and consumption traits, media habits, social characteristics, and demographic variables that distinguish consumer innovators from later adopters.

DISCUSSION QUESTIONS

1. (a) Why is an opinion leader a more credible source of product information than is an advertisement for the same product?
    (b) Are there any circumstances in which information from advertisements is likely to be more influential than word of mouth?

2. Why would a consumer who has just bought an expensive fax machine for home use attempt to influence the purchase behaviour of others?

3. Do you have any "market mavens" among your friends? Describe their personality traits and behaviour. Describe a situation in which a market maven has given you advice about a product or service, and discuss what you believe was his or her motivation for doing so.

4. Describe how a manufacturer might use knowledge of the following product characteristics to speed up the acceptance of pocket-sized cellular telephones:
    (a) relative advantage
    (b) compatibility
    (c) complexity
    (d) trialability
    (e) observability
    (f) felt need for the product
    (g) risk associated with buying the product

CRITICAL THINKING QUESTIONS

1. Toshiba has introduced an ultra-slim laptop computer that weighs about two pounds, has a colour screen, and has a powerful processor into which a full-size desktop screen and keyboard can be easily plugged. How can the company use the diffusion-of-innovations framework to develop promotional, pricing, and distribution strategies targeted to the following adopter categories?
    (a) innovators
    (b) early adopters
    (c) early majority
    (d) late majority
    (e) laggards

2. A company that owns and operates health clubs across the country is opening a health club in your town. The company has retained you as its marketing research consultant and has asked you to identify opinion leaders for its service. Which of the following identification methods would you recommend: the self-designating method, the sociometric method, the key informant method, or the objective method? Explain your selection. In your answer, be sure to discuss the advantages and disadvantages of the four techniques as they pertain to the marketing situation just described.

3. Sony is introducing a 27-inch television with a built-in VCR, a picture-in-picture feature, and a feature that allows the viewer to simultaneously view frozen frames of the last signals received from 12 channels.
    (a) What recommendations would you make to Sony about the initial target market for the new television model?
    (b) How would you identify the innovators for this product?
    (c) Select three characteristics of consumer innovators (as summarized in Figure 13-20). Explain how Sony might use each of these characteristics to influence the adoption process and speed up the diffusion of the new product.
    (d) Should Sony follow a penetration or a skimming policy in introducing the product? Why?

4. Describe two situations in which you served as an opinion leader and two situations in which you sought consumption-related advice or information from an opinion leader. State your relationship to the persons you interacted with. Are the circumstances during which you engaged in word-of-mouth communications consistent with those in the text's material? Explain.

5. With the advance of digital technology, some companies plan to introduce interactive television systems that will allow viewers to select films from video libraries and watch them on

demand. Among people you know, identify two who are likely to be the innovators for such a new service, and construct consumer profiles using the characteristics of consumer innovators discussed in the text.

INTERNET EXERCISES

1. Name a consumption-based internet group, find out about its activities, and submit a report.

2. Choose an innovation (a dynamically continuous or discontinuous one) and go to the company's website. How does the company use its website to diffuse this innovation through the market? How is it attempting to reach innovators or early adopters?

3. Go to the website of *Corner Gas*, the CTV series (**www.cornergas.ca**). Is the website doing anything to create "buzz"? What else could be done to create further word-of-mouth publicity for the series?

4. Look on the web for two examples of companies seeking opinion leaders and submit a report.

KEY TERMS

Adopter categories   *(p. 435)*
Adoption process   *(p. 428)*
Consumer innovators   *(p. 428)*
Continuous innovation   *(p. 429)*
Diffusion of innovations   *(p. 428)*
Diffusion process   *(p. 428)*
Discontinuous innovation   *(p. 429)*
Dynamically continuous
   innovation   *(p. 429)*

Innovation   *(p. 428)*
Market maven   *(p. 414)*
Multi-step flow of
   communication theory   *(p. 423)*
Opinion leader   *(p. 412)*
Opinion leadership   *(p. 412)*
Opinion seeker   *(p. 412)*
Purchase pal   *(p. 413)*

Stages in the adoption process
   (p. 440)
Surrogate buyers   *(p. 413)*
Two-step flow of communication
   theory   *(p. 422)*
Viral marketing   *(p. 417)*

CASE 13-1: LET THE ROBOT PICK IT UP

Although currently available in Europe and Japan, robot vacuums are just starting to be sold in North America. Dyson's DC06 vacuum, sold in the United Kingdom, has been called "the first fully autonomous household appliance." In Sweden, AB Electrolux (which owns Eureka, a U.S. brand) sells its Trilobite vacuum robot, a red, disk-shaped appliance, for approximately $1300. The price of the Trilobite is well below that of the $3800 robot vacuum that Matsushita sells in Japan. In the United States, The Sharper Image offers the Roomba Floor Vac Robot for $199.95.

A robot vacuum is cordless (it uses rechargeable batteries to avoid problems with tangled or snared power cords) and has some type of sensor (often infrared) that allows it to avoid bumping into furniture and walls. Alternatively, several manufacturers have developed robots that offer a vacuum feature or that are capable of operating a standard household vacuum cleaner (although the power cord can still present a problem). These more robot-like devices are often programmed by their owners via a standard personal computer; the consumer uses the computer's mouse and special software to "teach" the robot the location of doorways, furniture, and walls.

QUESTION

1. Seven product characteristics appear to influence consumer acceptance of new products—relative advantage, compatibility, complexity, trialability, observability, felt need for the product, and perceived risk. How would you relate each of these characteristics to the acceptance of a robot vacuum cleaner by consumers?

Source: Jack Neff, "Race for the Robot Intensifies in U.S.," *Advertising Age,* April; www.sharperimage.com/us/en/catalog/productview.jhtml?pid= 40660800; and www. personalrobots.com/inthenews/online/zdnet.html.

NOTES

1   Chip Walker, "Word of Mouth," *American Demographics,* July 1995, 40.
2   Ibid., 42.
3   Dale F. Duhan, Scott D. Johnson, James B. Wilcox, and Gilbert D. Harrell, "Influences on Consumer Use of Word-of-Mouth Recommendation Sources," *Journal of the Academy of Marketing Science,* 25, 4, 1997, 283–295.
4   Cathy L. Hartman and Pamela L. Kiecker, "Marketplace Influencers at the Point of Purchase: The Role of Purchase Pals in Consumer Decision Making," in *1991 AMA Educators' Proceedings,* eds. Mary C. Gilly and F. Robert Dwyer, et al. (Chicago: American Marketing Association, 1991), 461–467.
5   Pamela Kiecker and Cathy L. Hartman, "Predicting Buyers' Selection of Interpersonal Sources: The Role of Strong Ties and Weak Ties," in *Advances in Consumer Research,* 21, eds. Chris T. Allen and Deborah Roedder John (Provo, UT: Association for Consumer Research, 1994), 464–469.
6   Praveen Aggarwal and Taihoon Cha, "Surrogate Buyers and the New Product Adoption Process: A Conceptualization and Managerial Framework," *Journal of Consumer Marketing,* 14, no. 5, 1997, 391–400; and Stanley C. Hollander and Kathleen M. Rassuli, "Shopping with Other People's Money: The Marketing Management Implications of Surrogate-Mediated Consumer Decision Making," *Journal of Marketing,* 63, 2, April 1999, 102–118.
7   Lawrence F. Feick and Linda L. Price, "The Market Maven: A Diffuser of Marketplace Information," *Journal of Marketing,* 51, January 1987, 85.
8   Michael T. Elliott and Anne E. Warfield, "Do Market Mavens Categorize Brands Differently?" in *Advances in Consumer Research,* 20, eds. Leigh McAlister and Michael L. Rothschild (Provo, UT: Association for Consumer Research 1993), 202–208; and Frank Alpert, "Consumer Market

Beliefs and Their Managerial Implications: An Empirical Examination," *Journal of Consumer Marketing,* 10, 2, (1993), 56–70.
9   Brian T. Engelland, Christopher D. Hopkins, and Dee Anne Larson, "Market Mavenship as an Influencer of Service Quality Evaluation," *Journal of Marketing Theory and Practice,* 9, 4, Fall 2001, 15–26.
10   Eric Chi-Chung Shiu and John A. Dawson, "Cross-National Consumer Segmentation of Internet Shopping for Britain and Taiwan," *Service Industries Journal* (London), 22, 1, January 2002, 147–166.
11   Statistics Canada, "Internet Use Rates, by Location of Access and Household Income" CANSIM, table 358-0017 and Catalogue no. 56F0004MIE.
12   John Eighmey and Lola McCord, "Adding Value in the Information Age: Uses and Gratifications of Sites on the World Wide Web," *Journal of Business Research,* 41, 1998, 187–194.
13   Patricia Riedman, "Marketers Harvest Web Communities' Concealed Treasure," *Advertising Age,* February 14, 2000, 58.
14   Ralph F. Wilson, "The Six Simple Principles of Viral Marketing," *Web Marketing Today,* 70, February 1, 2000, accessed at **www.wilsonweb.com/wmt5/viral-principles.htm**; and **searchcrm.techtarget.com/sDefinition/0,sid11_gci213514,00.html**.
15   Marc Weingarten, "The Medium Is the Instant Message," *Business 2.0,* February 2002, 98–99.
16   Pamala L. Alreck and Robert B. Settle, "The Importance of Word-of-Mouth Communications to Service Buyers," in *1995 AMA Winter Educators' Proceedings,* eds. David W. Stewart and Naufel J. Vilcassim (Chicago: American Marketing Association, 1995), 188–193.
17   S. Ramesh Kumar, "The Might of the Word," *Businessline,* September 2, 1999, 1–2.

18   George Silverman, "The Power of Word of Mouth," *Direct Marketing,* 64, no. 5, September 2001, 47–52.

19   Geok Theng Lau and Sophia Ng, "Individual and Situational Factors Influencing Negative Word-of-Mouth Behaviour," *Revue canadienne des sciences de l'administration* (Montreal), 18, 3, September 2001, 163–178.

20   Silverman, "The Power of Word of Mouth."

21   Mary C. Gilly, John L. Graham, Mary Finley Wolfinbarger, and Laura J. Yale, "A Dyadic Study of Interpersonal Information Search," *Journal of the Academy of Marketing Science,* 26, no. 2, 1998, 83–100.

22   Paul F. Lazarsfeld, Bernard Berelson, and Hazel Gaudet, *The People's Choice,* 2nd ed. (New York: Columbia University Press, 1948), 151.

23   Joseph Pereira, "Toy Story: How Shrewd Marketing Made Elmo a Hit," *Wall Street Journal,* December 16, 1997, B1, B7.

24   "In the News: Ploys," *New York Times Magazine,* February 13, 1994, 19.

25   Gaffney, "The Cool Kids Are Doing It," 141.

26   Leisa Reinecke Flynn, Ronald E. Goldsmith, and Jacqueline K. Eastman, "The King and Summers Opinion Leadership Scale: Revision and Refinement," *Journal of Business Research,* 31, 1994, 55–64.

27   See, for example, Thomas W. Valente and Rebecca L. Davis, "Accelerating the Diffusion of Innovations Using Opinion Leaders," *Annals of the American Academy of Political and Social Science,* 566, November 1999, 55–67.

28   Joseph R. Mancuso, "Why Not Create Opinion Leaders for New Product Introduction?" *Journal of Marketing,* 33, July 1969, 20–25.

29   Barbara Bickart and Robert M. Schindler, "internet Forums as Influential Sources of Consumer Information," *Journal of Interactive Marketing,* 15, 3, Summer 2001, 31–39.

30   Thomas Petzinger, Jr., "The Front Lines," *Wall Street Journal,* November 11, 1997, B9.

31   Walker, "Starbucks' Word-of-Mouth Wonder," 40.

32   Roy Furchgott, "Surfing for Satisfaction: Consumer Complaints Go On-Line," *New York Times,* June 8, 1997, 8.

33   Ibid.

34   Jan-Benedict E.M. Steenkamp, Frankel ter Hofstede, and Michael Wedel, "A Cross-National Investigation into the Individual and National Cultural Antecedents of Consumer Innovativeness," *Journal of Marketing,* 63, 2, April 1999, 55–69.

35   Diane Crane, "Diffusion Models and Fashion: A Reassessment," *Annals of the American Academy of Political and Social Sciences,* 566, November 1999, 13–24.

36   Economic Concepts—Innovation, Government of Canada website, **http://www.canadianeconomy.gc.ca/english/economy/innovation.html**.

37   Everett M. Rogers, *Diffusion of Innovations,* 4th ed. (New York: Free Press, 1995); and Hubert Gatignon and Thomas S. Robertson, "Innovative Decision Processes," in *Handbook of Consumer Behavior,* eds. Thomas S. Robertson and Harold H. Kassarjian (Upper Saddle River, NJ: Prentice Hall, 1991), 316–348.

38   Thomas S. Robertson, "The Process of Innovation and the Diffusion of Innovation," *Journal of Marketing,* 31, January 1967, 14–19.

39   S. Ram and Hyung-Shik Jung, "Innovativeness in Product Usage: A Comparison of Early Adopters and Early Majority," *Psychology and Marketing,* 11, January–February 1994, 57–67; A. R. Petrosky, "Gender and Use Innovation: An Inquiry into the Socialization of Innovative Behavior," in *1995 AMA Educators' Proceedings,* eds. Barbara B. Stern and George M. Zinkan (Chicago: American Marketing Association, 1995), 299–307; and Kyungae Park and Carl L. Dyer, "Consumer Use Innovative Behavior: An Approach Toward Its Causes," in *Advances in Consumer Research,* 22, eds. Frank R. Kardes and Mita Sujan (Provo, UT: Association for Consumer Research 1995), 566–572.

40   Earle Eldridge, "Pickups Get Women's Touch," *USA Today,* June 13, 2001, 1B, 2B.

41   Rogers, *Diffusion of Innovations,* 15–16.

42   Hsiang Chen and Kevin Crowston, "Comparative Diffusion of the Telephone and the World Wide Web: An Analysis of Rates of Adoption," in Suave Lobodzinski and Ivan Tomek (eds.), *Proceedings of WebNet '97—World Conference of the WWW, Internet and Intranet,* Toronto, Canada, 110–115.

43   Paul-Mark Rendon, "Berry New Cheerios," *Marketing Magazine,* April 19, 2004, p. 10.

44   Tina M. Lowrey, "The Use of Diffusion Theory in Marketing: A Qualitative Approach to Innovative Consumer Behavior," in *Advances in Consumer Research,* 18, eds. Rebecca H. Holman and Michael R. Solomon (Provo, UT: Association for Consumer Research, 1991), 644–650.

45   Quentin Hardy, "Will Miniature Phones Ring Up Bigger Sales?" *Wall Street Journal,* December 4, 1996, B1, B4.

46   Richard Gibson, "Shelf Stable Foods Seek to Freshen Sales," *Wall Street Journal,* November 2, 1990, B1.

47   Susan H. Higgins and William L. Shanklin, "Seeding Mass Market Acceptance for High Technology Consumer Products," *Journal of Consumer Marketing,* 9, Winter 1992, 5–14.

48   Chris Powell, "Cut Care in a Can," *Marketing Magazine*, March 22, 2004, 6.

49   Paul A. Herbig and Hugh Kramer, "The Effect of Information Overload on the Innovation Choice Process," *Journal of Consumer Marketing*, 11, 2, 1994, 45–54.

50   Walter S. Mossberg, "Sony Again Attempts to Sell Its Mini-CD, Focusing on Recording," *Wall Street Journal*, May 28, 1998, B1.

51   Erin White, "Word of Mouth Makes Nike Slip-On Sneakers Take Off," *Wall Street Journal*, June 7, 2001, B1.

52   Everett M. Rogers and F. Floyd Shoemaker, *Communication of Innovations*, 2nd ed. (New York: Free Press, 1971), 32–33; see also Elizabeth C. Hirschman, "Consumer Modernity, Cognitive Complexity, Creativity and Innovativeness," in *Marketing in the 80's: Changes and Challenges*, ed. Richard P. Bagozzi et al. (Chicago: American Marketing Association, 1980), 135–139.

53   Thomas W. Valente and Rebecca L. Davis, "Accelerating the Diffusion of Innovations Using Opinion Leaders," *Annals of the American Academy of Political and Social Sciences*, 566, November 1999, 55–67; and Ronald S. Burt, "The Social Capital of Opinion Leaders," *Annals of the American Academy of Political and Social Sciences*, 566, November 1999, 37–54.

54   Kenichi Ohmae, "Managing in a Borderless World," *Harvard Business Review*, May–June 1989, 152–161.

55   Jacob Goldenberg, Barak Libai, and Eitan Muller, "Riding the Saddle: How Cross-Market Communications Can Create a Major Slump in Sales," *Journal of Marketing*, 66, 2, April 2002, 1–16.

56   Dianne Neumark-Sztainer, et al., "Early Adopters of Olestra-Containing Foods: Who Are They?" *Journal of the American Dietetic Association*, 100, 2, February 2000, 198–204.

57   C. Page Moreau, Donald R. Lehmann, and Arthur B. Markman, "Entrenched Knowledge Structures and Consumer Response to New Products," *Journal of Marketing Research*, 38, 1, February 2001, 14–29.

58   David J. Burns and Robert F. Krampf, "A Semiotic Perspective on Innovative Behavior," in *Developments in Marketing Science*, ed. Robert L. King (Richmond, VA: Academy of Marketing Science, 1991), 32–35.

59   Wayne D. Hoyer and Nancy M. Ridgway, "Variety Seeking as an Explanation for Exploratory Purchase Behavior: A Theoretical Model," in *Advances in Consumer Research*, 11, ed. Thomas C. Kinnear (Provo, UT: Association for Consumer Research, 1984), 114–119.

60   Bruce MacEvoy, "Change Leaders and the New Media," *American Demographics*, January 1994, 42–48.

61   Susan Mitchell, "Technophiles and Technophobes," *American Demographics*, February 1994, 36–42.

part four
consumer decision making

Part 4 discusses the various aspects of consumer decision making.

The final part of this book will deal with consumer decision making. As shown in the simplified model of consumer behaviour presented in Chapter 1, consumers' decision making is affected by both internal and external factors. Chapter 14 will look at the first three stages in consumer decision making—problem recognition, information search, and evaluation of alternatives. The last chapter (Chapter 15) will examine the outcomes of this decision making—purchase and post-purchase evaluation.

Nothing lasts forever.

Not even your tube of Polysporin*.
So check the expiry date to make sure you're getting
effective infection protection for your family.

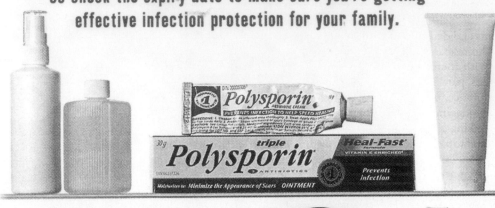

Polysporin Triple Antibiotic is specially designed to help prevent infection.
The Heal-Fast formula helps heal minor cuts and is enriched with Vitamin E.*
Polysporin moisturizes to minimize the appearance of scars.

ENTER THE GREAT POLYSPORIN* HUNT CONTEST!

If you have an old tube of Polysporin (and even if you don't!), you could win a fabulous 3.2 Megapixel Digital Camera and photo printer bundle, valued at approximately $565. or one of nine (9) secondary prizes of gift certificates†, each valued at $150.

Contest closing date is November 30, 2003. Odds of winning are based on number of entries received. Rules available online at www.polysporin.ca. To enter online – just visit www.polysporin.ca.

And here's a special bonus... we have TWO GRAND PRIZES! To enter for a chance to win a second camera package, add the expiry date of your tube of Polysporin to the entry form! It's that simple.

Grand prizes courtesy of

The Shopping Channel
TELEVISION · CATALOGUE · INTERNET

No purchase necessary. Contest open to all Canadian residents excluding residents of Quebec.
†Gift certificate redeemable at a major Canadian department store.
*TM Pfizer Canada Inc., Toronto, ON M1L 2N3

Save $1.00
On Polysporin* Plus Pain 30 g
or Polysporin* Triple 30 g

TO THE RETAILER: Pfizer Canada Inc., Pfizer Consumer Healthcare Division will reimburse you the face value of this coupon plus our specified handling fee, provided it is redeemed by a consumer at the time of the purchase of the product specified. Other applications may constitute fraud. Failure to send in, on request, evidence that sufficient stock was purchased in previous 90 days to cover coupons presented, will void coupons. Reproduction of this coupon is expressly prohibited. Coupons submitted become our property. For redemption, mail to: Pfizer Canada Inc., Pfizer Consumer Healthcare Division, Box 3000, Saint John, N.B. E2L 4L3.
TO THE CUSTOMER: Provincial law may require the retailer to collect tax on the full price of the item before deduction of the coupon value. A reduction on GST/HST payable, where applicable, is included in the coupon face value.
LIMIT ONE COUPON PER PURCHASE. ONLY VALID IN CANADA.
OFFER NOT VALID IN QUEBEC
EXPIRY DATE: FEBRUARY 15, 2004
*TM Pfizer Canada Inc., Toronto, ON M1L 2N3

8623 8029

chapter 14
consumer decision making I: the process—problem recognition, information search, and alternative evaluation

LEARNING OBJECTIVES

By the end of this chapter, you should be able to:

1. Explain what consumer decisions are and the various levels of consumer decision making.

2. Define problem or need recognition; discuss the various types of problems and explain how marketers can use their knowledge of problem recognition to develop marketing strategies.

3. Discuss consumers' pre-purchase search process, including the types of information sources, types of information sought, and the factors affecting the extent of pre-purchase search that consumers go through.

4. Explain attribute-based and attitude-based choices and discuss four types of consumer decision rules.

5. Discuss the marketing strategy implications of pre-purchase information search and alternative evaluation processes used by consumers.

14

have you ever been frustrated with all the remotes that are lying around in your house? If your household is like the typical Canadian one, it probably has three or four remotes—one for the television, one for the satellite dish, one for the VCR, one for the DVD player, and perhaps one for the music system. Although there are several universal remotes, most of them are not quite universal; they might do some of the functions of the individual remote, but not all of them. Worse still, many of them are difficult to use; it probably would take a technical wizard to learn to use these remotes (or, for that matter, to use many of today's electronic gadgets!). The difficulties in learning to use universal remotes arise because most universal remotes function by addressing each component individually—that is, you need to work your way to the component first and learn to program it.

What can be done to solve this problem? Intrigue Technologies, a Mississauga, Ontario, company has created the ideal solution—Harmony, a remote control that works the way you think. It asks you what you want to do and coordinates the functions of the units, depending on your request (rather than making you choose a unit first and work through its operations). For example, it displays activities ("watch a videotape," "watch a DVD," etc.) from which you can choose. If you choose "watch a DVD," Harmony will turn on your television and your DVD player. It can even be programmed to set the volume to suit your preferences, and it lets you choose the speaker that you want the sound to come through (television speakers or your stereo speakers). Even the setup has been simplified. As soon as you open the package and put in the batteries, Harmony's LCD screen says, "Hello, I am your Harmony. My scroll wheel is on my right side. Scroll down now." It asks you to go to a website for a clear tutorial and lets you create an online list of all your equipment so that the remote can be totally customized to your needs. This lets Harmony's help desk technicians know all your products when they check your account and enables them to answer your questions effectively.

As one user noted, Harmony passes the ultimate test: the in-law test! His 77-year-old mother-in-law—a woman raised on an island mountain with no electricity—got it working within seconds.[1]

CHAPTER OVERVIEW

This chapter, and the next one, draw together many of the psychological, social, and cultural concepts covered throughout the book into an overview framework for understanding how consumers make decisions. Together, these chapters examine **consumer decision making** in the context of all types of *consumption choices,* ranging from the consumption of new products to the use of old and established ones. Consumers' decisions are not considered as end points but rather as the beginning point of a consumption process.

This chapter examines the nature of consumer decision making and the first three steps of the consumer decision making (or the consumer decision-making process): problem recognition, information search, and alternative evaluation. We will begin with an analysis of consumer decision making, including models of consumer decision making and various levels of decision making. Next, we will look at how a consumer first recognizes that there is a problem, the type of consumer problems (from a decision-making point of view), and ways of activating problem recognition.

The second half of the chapter deals with information search and alternative evaluation. First, we will examine the types of information search processes, the types of information sought by consumers, and the factors that affect information search. Then we will move on to the way consumers evaluate the various products (or services) available to them. We will examine the decision rules that consumers use to make choices. The chapter ends with a look at the marketing strategy implications of consumers' information search and alternative evaluation processes.

WHAT IS A DECISION?

Every day, each of us makes numerous decisions concerning every aspect of our daily lives. However, we generally make these decisions without stopping to think about how we make them and what is involved in the particular decision-making process itself. In the most general terms, a decision is the selection of an option from two or more alternative choices. In other words, for a person to make a decision, a choice of alternatives must be available. When a person has a choice between mak-

http://harmonyremote.com

Consumer decision making:
Two distinct but interlocking stages: the process (recognition of problem, pre-purchase search, and evaluation of alternatives) and its outcomes (purchase and post-purchase processes). Both stages are influenced by factors internal and external to the consumer.

ing a purchase and not making a purchase, a choice between brand X and brand Y, or a choice of spending time doing A or B, that person is in a position to make a decision. For example, in the case of remote controls, we have the option of living with separate remote controls for each piece of electronic equipment, buying the typical low-end universal remote for about $70, or buying one of the three models of Harmony at prices ranging from $299 to $449. Conversely, if the consumer has no alternatives from which to choose and is literally *forced* to make a particular purchase or take a particular action (e.g., use a prescribed medication), then this single "no-choice" instance does not constitute a decision; such a no-choice decision is commonly referred to as a "Hobson's choice."

In actuality, no-choice purchase or consumption situations are fairly rare. For example, one core Canadian cultural value is *freedom*; as we saw in Chapter 9, *freedom* can be expressed in terms of a wide range of product choices. Thus, if there is almost always a choice, there is almost always an opportunity for consumers to make decisions. Moreover, experimental research reveals that giving consumers a choice when there was originally none can be a very good business strategy, one that can substantially increase sales.[2] For instance, when a direct-mail electrical appliance catalogue displayed two coffee makers instead of just one (the original coffee maker at $149 and a "new" only slightly larger one at $229), the addition of the second *comparison* coffee maker seemed to stimulate consumer evaluation, which significantly increased the sales of the original coffee maker.

Figure 14-1 summarizes various types of consumption and purchase-related decisions. Although not exhaustive, this list does demonstrate that the scope of consumer decision making is far broader than the mere selection of one brand from a number of brands.

Levels of Consumer Decision Making

Not all consumer decision-making situations receive (or require) the same degree of information search. If all purchase decisions required extensive effort, consumer decision making would be an exhausting process that left little time for anything else. Conversely, if all purchases were routine, they would tend to be monotonous and would provide little pleasure or novelty. On a continuum of effort ranging from very high to very low, we can distinguish three specific levels of consumer decision making: extensive problem solving, limited problem solving, and routinized-response behaviour.[3]

Extensive Problem Solving

When consumers have no established criteria for evaluating a product category or specific brands in that category or have not narrowed the number of brands they will consider to a small, manageable subset, their decision-making efforts can be classified as **extensive problem solving**. At this level, the consumer needs a great deal of information to establish a set of criteria on which to judge specific brands and a correspondingly large amount of information concerning each of the brands to be considered.

Extensive decision making is likely to occur when consumers are faced with high-value decisions—that is, decisions that involve high financial, social, or physical risk. It is also likely to occur when the consumer is faced with a totally new problem. Under such circumstances, consumers would be willing to spend considerable time and effort to seek a great deal of information (to establish criteria on which to judge brands and about the brands themselves) and to go through a detailed evaluation of alternatives before they make a final choice.

Extensive problem solving:
Consumer decision-making situations in which there are no established criteria for evaluating a product category or brand or those in which the number of brands have not been narrowed to a small subset.

FIGURE 14-1	Types of Purchase or Consumption Decisions	
DECISION CATEGORY	**ALTERNATIVE A**	**ALTERNATIVE B**
Basic Purchase or Consumption Decision	To purchase or consume a product (or service)	Not to purchase or consume a product (or service)
	To purchase or consume a specific brand	To purchase or consume another brand
	To purchase or consume one's usual brand	To purchase or consume another established brand (possibly with special features)
	To purchase or consume a basic model	To purchase or consume a luxury or status model
	To purchase or consume a new brand	To purchase or consume one's usual brand or some other established brand
	To purchase or consume a standard quantity	To purchase or consume more or less than a standard quantity
	To purchase or consume an on-sale brand	To purchase or consume a non-sale brand
Channel Purchase Decisions	To purchase or consume a national brand	To purchase or consume a store brand
	To purchase from a specific type of store (e.g., a department store)	To purchase from some other type of store (e.g., a discount store)
	To purchase from one's usual store	To purchase from some other store
	To purchase in-home (by phone or catalogue or internet)	To purchase in-store merchandise
	To purchase from a local store	To purchase from a store requiring some travel (outshopping)
Payment Purchase Decisions	To pay for the purchase with cash	To pay for the purchase with a credit card
	To pay the bill in full when it arrives	To pay for the purchase in instalments

Limited Problem Solving

Limited problem solving:

Consumer decision-making situations in which basic criteria for product evaluation have been established, but fully established preferences about a select group of brands have not been set.

At the level of **limited problem solving**, consumers already have established the basic criteria for evaluating the product category (perhaps because they have made such decisions before) and the various brands in the category. However, they have not fully established their preferences concerning a select group of brands. Their search for additional information is more like "fine-tuning"; they must gather additional brand information to discriminate among the various brands.

Routinized-Response Behaviour

Routinized-response behaviour:

Decision-making situations in which consumers have experience with the product category and a well-established set of criteria with which to evaluate brands they are considering.

At this level, consumers have experience with the product category and a well-established set of criteria with which to evaluate the brands they are considering. In some **routinized-response behaviour** situations, consumers may search for a small amount of additional information; in others, they simply review what they already know. Such decisions are the common, everyday buying decisions that all of us make; examples include most grocery and drug-store purchases.

Factors that Affect Choice of Decision-Making Process

Just how extensive a consumer's problem-solving task is depends on several factors:

- the importance of the decision
- the extent of previous experience (which influences the next two items)

- how well-established his or her criteria for selection are
- how much information he or she has about each brand being considered
- how narrow the set of brands is from which the choice will be made
- whether or not the consumer is following an emotional model of consumption

Clearly, extensive problem solving implies that the consumer must seek more information to make a choice (either because of previous experience or because of the importance of the decision), whereas routinized-response behaviour implies little need for additional information. Let us go back to the problem of too many remotes. What kind of decision-making process do you think a typical consumer would go through while buying a remote control?

When a consumer makes what is basically an emotional purchase decision, less emphasis is placed on the search for pre-purchase information. Instead, more emphasis is placed on current mood and feelings ("Go for it!"). This is not to say that emotional decisions are not rational. As Chapter 3 pointed out, buying products that afford emotional satisfaction is a perfectly rational consumer decision. Some emotional decisions are expressions that "you deserve it" or "treat yourself." For instance, many consumers buy designer-label clothing not because they look any better in it, but because status labels make them feel better. This is a rational decision. Of course, if a man with a wife and three children buys a two-seater BMW Z3 for himself, the neighbours might wonder about his rationality (although some might think it was deviously high). No such question would arise if the same man selected a box of Godiva chocolate instead of a Whitman Sampler, although in both instances each might be an impulsive, emotional purchase decision.

www.bmw.ca

www.godiva.com

www.whitmans.com

Not all decisions in our lives can be complex and require extensive search and consideration—we just cannot exert the effort required. Some decisions have to be easy ones.

A SIMPLIFIED MODEL OF DECISION MAKING

As mentioned in Chapter 1, consumer decision making can be thought of as consisting of two parts: the process of decision making (need recognition, pre-purchase information search, and alternative evaluation) and its outcomes (purchase and post-purchase processes). The process of decision making starts with the recognition of a need (or a problem); this is followed by search for information (about the criteria to be used to evaluate the alternatives and about the alternatives—or brands—themselves). The information gathered is used to evaluate the alternatives; consumers use various decision rules to go through this alternative evaluation process.

The second part of consumer decision making looks at the outcomes of this process: the actual purchase; in some situations, this may be preceded by a trial of the product or service. As a result of the trial, consumers may decide to try out the product; and their satisfaction or dissatisfaction with the product will lead to repeat purchase or a negative attitude toward the product. These outcomes will, in turn, have an impact on the way consumers would view the inputs (especially the marketing inputs) into their decision making.

Figure 14-2 provides details of the consumer decision-making process. The rest of this chapter will focus on the first part of consumer decision making—need recognition, pre-purchase search, and alternative evaluation. The next chapter will cover the outcomes of the consumer decision-making process.

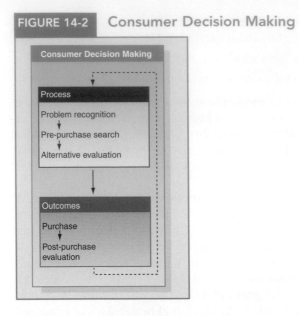

FIGURE 14-2 Consumer Decision Making

Consumer Decision Making

Process

Problem recognition
↓
Pre-purchase search
↓
Alternative evaluation

Outcomes

Purchase
↓
Post-purchase
evaluation

NEED OR PROBLEM RECOGNITION

Need recognition:
The realization by a consumer that there is a difference between his or her actual and desired states.

As pictured in the *process* component of the overview decision model (Figure 14-2), the act of making a consumer decision consists of three stages, and **need recognition** is the very first stage in this process.

The *recognition of a need* is likely to happen when a consumer is faced with a "problem." Unless the consumer recognizes a need or feels that there is a problem, there will be no decision making. Such problem or need recognition happens when there is a discrepancy between the actual and desired states of a consumer. In other words, when what we have and what we want are different, we face a problem or recognize a need.

Consider the case of Richard, a 35-year-old businessman working for a mid-sized marketing research firm in Edmonton. Richard is often out of town two or three days a week in order to moderate focus groups for his firm's clients, and he travels with his three-year-old laptop computer. Richard is a bit of a techno-geek; he frequently visits website chat rooms to discuss high-tech, computer-related topics, such as new programs and new computers. He enjoys unconventional, unique "wow" technology. For example, he drives a Volkswagen Beetle and takes notes at meetings with his 40-year-old Parker fountain pen, which he bought from a pen shop in Toronto that sells vintage fountain pens. He schedules his life, both professional and personal, with his Palm Pilot.

For Richard, the problem is that his current laptop (supplied by his employer), with its 15-inch screen, heavy battery, and built-in floppy disk and CD-ROM drives, weighs almost four kilograms (more than eight pounds). When encased in its genuine leather carrying case there is another kilogram (two pounds) of weight, and when combined with his briefcase and his 21-inch carry-on piece of luggage, he has found that it is all just too much for him to carry comfortably in airplane aisles, airports, and taxis. Also he has found his laptop very heavy when he has to walk more than several blocks. Therefore, he normally leaves it on his desk when attending local business meetings outside his office. Maybe more than anything else, Richard does not feel that a large and bulky laptop fits his persona—which is to be thought of and known for using high-tech and eye-catching technology. Indeed, Richard feels that he is known by his family and friends to "love tech-toys." Moreover, reflecting on his current laptop, he realizes he needs to leave it in the office and buy an ultra-light smaller laptop (one to one and a half kilograms, or about two to three and a half pounds) to carry with him when he is fulfilling his role as a "road warrior." It is fair to say that he has *recognized the need* for a smaller, lighter computer. And when he introduces the idea of a smaller computer to his boss, Richard is told he can go out and buy whatever he feels will do the job, and the firm will pay for it.

Among consumers, there seem to be two different need or problem-recognition styles. Some consumers are *actual state* types, who perceive that they have a problem when a product fails to work satisfactorily (as a cordless telephone that develops constant static). In contrast, other consumers are *desired state* types, for whom the desire for something new may trigger the decision process.[4] Since Richard's current laptop can do the job, albeit painfully, he appears to be a desired-state consumer.

Another factor that triggers problem recognition is the size of the gap between the actual and the desired states of a consumer. When the gap is small, even though the consumer may have a problem, she may not be motivated to take any action. When the gap is great, she recognizes a need that requires some action to fulfill it.

Going back to Richard's case, if his laptop weighed two kilograms (four pounds) instead of one and a half kilograms (three pounds), though he might experience some dissatisfaction, he would be unlikely to take any action. However, since the difference between his ideal laptop and his present one is significant, he is likely to look for a new one.

Note that the desired state is influenced by several variables that we have discussed in earlier chapters. For example, Richard's personality and life style (e.g., his need for unique products), his self-concept (as a "road warrior"), and his occupation and social class have all had an influences on his desire for a light-weight laptop.

Type of Problems

Not all consumer problems are the same. The nature of the problem has a great impact on the type of pre-purchase search and decision-making process that a consumer would follow; hence, understanding the nature of consumer problems is critical for the success of a marketing program.

Consumer problems can be classified into four categories based on two dimensions: the first deals with consumer awareness of the problem, and the second deals with the time span for a solution for the problem. Active problems are those the consumer is aware of or would become aware of in the normal course of events. Inactive problems are those that a consumer is unaware of and may never become aware of in the normal course of events. Problems can also be classified into those that require an immediate solution and those that do not. So we have four types of problems:

- *Active problems that require an immediate solution* (e.g., while pouring herself a glass of milk, Amanda notices that there is no more milk in the refrigerator; since she has two young children, she decides to go out and get some milk from the corner grocery store)

- *Active problems that do not require an immediate solution* (e.g., while driving out of her garage, Mary notices that the lawn needs to be mowed; she decides that it can wait a few days—until the weekend)

- *Inactive problems that require an immediate solution* (e.g., one of the tires on John's Subaru has a small hole in it and is going to be totally flat in a few minutes; however, John did not check the tires out before he got into the car and is unaware of the problem)

- *Inactive problems that do not require an immediate solution* (e.g., Jim does not know that there is a small dent in the back of his car; even if he knew it, since it is not a big dent, he need not fix it immediately)

Going back to the issue of universal remote controls, what type of a problem or need recognition happens here? Is it an active problem or an inactive problem? One that requires an immediate solution or one that can wait for a solution?

Problem Recognition and Marketing Strategy

Problem or need recognition is the beginning of the consumer decision-making process, and as such, it is important for marketers to trigger problem recognition. Since problem recognition occurs when the actual state differs from the desired state (and especially when the actual state is lower than the desired state), marketers can trigger problem recognition by the following methods:

Identify existing consumer problems and find solutions for them: Simple as it sounds, there are several consumer problems that marketers have not taken the trouble to find out about. There are several product categories that we are not totally satisfied with or ones in which there could be significant improvements made in the current offerings. By asking consumers what type of issues or problems they face with their current products, marketers may be able to identify product improvements or totally new offerings to solve consumers' problems.

What irritates you most about storing soft drinks in a fridge? If your fridge is like the average Canadian's, it is probably too full, and finding the soft drink after searching through all the other things in the fridge can be a frustrating experience. Although it is true that manufacturers of refrigerators have provided us with convenient spots in the doors to solve this problem, most of us store milk, yogourt, sauces, and other things in these spots and have no room for several cans of soft drinks.

The Canadian division of Coca-Cola has not only identified this problem, but has found a solution to it! Recently, Coke Canada introduced Fridge Mate, its long and lean 12-can box for storing Coca-Cola. Consumer research found that the old box, with its three rows of four cans each, was too big to fit into a fridge. This meant that consumers broke up the package and started storing individual cans (some rather than all) in various parts of the fridge. Fridge Mate solves this problem with its longer, leaner concept, which makes it easier to store in the fridge; it will also dispense the can by moving unused cans to the front as cans are taken out.[5]

Lower the actual state: The gap between actual and desired states can be influenced by changing consumers' perceptions of the actual state, or by making them realize that their actual state is not as good as they think it is. Consider the following situation: Total cereal runs ads comparing the percentage of daily requirements of several vitamins and minerals in a bowl of Total with what can be found in other popular cereals such as Kellogg's Cornflakes. By showing consumers how many bowls of the other brands would be required to match the vitamin and mineral content in one bowl of Total, the company made consumers realize that the actual state (the nutritional quality) of the other brands was not as good as they perceived it to be.

Marketers who follow this strategy tend to focus on making consumers aware of the inadequacies of their current products or ways of solving their problems. The emphasis here is on telling consumers that their current solutions (or products) are not as good as they think they are. Often, marketers who use this strategy tend to use comparative ads that emphasize the weaknesses of their competitors' products. Exhibit 14-1 provides another example of this strategy. As can be seen from the exhibit, the makers of Polysporin are attempting to make consumers realize that their tube of antibacterial cream (and other medicines) may not be effective anymore as it might have expired.

Increase the desired state: Marketers can also make consumers recognize a problem by telling them there are better solutions to their problems—that is, that their desired state can be much better than it actually is. This strategy is usually followed by marketers who have developed new and better ways of solving consumer problems. For example, when digital cameras first came onto the market, camera manufacturers had to convince consumers that digital cameras produced better-quality pictures and had other advantages over the current options (the desired state could be much better in terms of picture quality, ease of sharing the pictures with family and friends, etc.). Note that in this instance, the emphasis is on showing consumers how much better things can be.

Samsung recently introduced a wide-screen digital-light processing (DLP) technology television with picture quality that is visibly better than any conventional television set. As one technology critic puts it, the Samsung DLP television has "jaw-dropping visuals and audio,"[6] which would raise any consumer's expectations about the picture quality offered by television sets. In fact, Samsung's ads for the model highlight this by saying, "Your perception of television, and reality, may never be the same."[7]

Often, this is the strategy that manufacturers of innovative products use. When the product is brand new, consumers are often not aware that a better alternative exists and hence are not looking for a replacement for their current alternative. By showing consumers how much better life can be if they purchased the new product, marketers hope to trigger problem recognition.

Increase the importance of the gap: Sometimes, what consumers need to recognize is that although the difference between their actual and desired states

EXHIBIT 14-1

AD TRIGGERING PROBLEM RECOGNITION

Courtesy of Pfizer Canada Inc., Pfizer Consumer Healthcare Division. All rights reserved.

may be slight, this difference can be critical and can have serious consequences. For example, although the tires of your car may still be in working condition, it is important for you to have tires in very good condition, especially if you are going on a long trip. Michelin used to run ads with a baby in the middle of a tire with a tag line that emphasized that the safety of your family depended on the quality of your tires.

Convert inactive problems into active ones: Though the above three strategies focus on the difference between actual and desired states and the gap between them, marketers can also use their knowledge of problem recognition in different ways. Since many consumer problems are inactive (i.e., the consumer does not recognize their existence), marketers can trigger problem recognition by converting these problems into active ones.

Most women believe that breast cancer is the disease that they have to be most concerned about. As the Heart and Stroke Foundation of New Brunswick found through its research, most women think of heart disease as a "man's disease" and consider breast cancer (and other forms of cancer) to be the top threat to women's health. However, heart disease has become increasingly common among women and surpasses cancer as a threat to their health. So the Foundation ran a series of ads that showed a good-looking man who starts out saying, "Ladies, this one is for you." As the ad progresses, the man's statements become more menacing, and the tag line says, "If heart disease were this obvious, you'd do something about it." The Foundation is effectively trying to convert what is an inactive problem to many women to an active one that requires some immediate action—a checkup.[8]

Convert problems into ones requiring an immediate solution: Consumers often postpone making purchases or deciding on brands. Marketers can make them realize the cost of postponing a purchase decision and persuade them to look for a solution immediately. For example, consumers often postpone checking the "winter-readiness" of their cars; Canadian Tire ran ads in late fall and early winter highlighting the consequences of not having the car checked before the onset of winter.

PRE-PURCHASE SEARCH

Pre-purchase search:
The stage in consumer decision making in which the consumer perceives a need and actively seeks out information about products that will help satisfy that need.

The **pre-purchase search** begins when a consumer perceives a need that might be satisfied by the purchase and consumption of a product. The recollection of past experiences (drawn from storage in long-term memory) might provide the consumer with adequate information to make the present choice. However, when the consumer has had no prior experience, he or she may have to engage in an extensive search of the outside environment for useful information on which to base a choice. In this section, we look at the sources of information, the type of information that consumers search for, and the factors that lead to increased pre-purchase search.

Types of Information Sources

Consumers gather information about products and services from various sources; these can be broadly classified into *internal* and *external* sources. As mentioned earlier, past experiences (stored in long-term memory) provide valuable information that consumers use to make product choices. Past experiences (or internal information) can include experiences with the product category (e.g., the way your old computer performed, what it lacked), information gathered during past searches (e.g., the computer you have was bought from Future Shop, and you learned while you were buying it that Future Shop has a wider range of computers than other stores), and passive or low-involvement learning (e.g., you have learned over the years that Dell is a good source for laptops). If internal information gathered by the consumer through past experiences is found to be inadequate, then the consumer will go to external sources to gather more information. For example, if you are not very involved with computers and have not looked at what is available for five years (when you bought your old computer), you might feel that you need to gather new information before you make the purchase rather than rely on your past experience. However, if you need to buy tomato ketchup, you are unlikely to gather information from any external source, since your store of past information on the product category would be more than adequate for the decision.

Let's consider several of the external pre-purchase information sources open to a computer buyer. At the most fundamental level, search alternatives can be classified as either personal or impersonal. *Personal* search alternatives include more than a consumer's past experience with the product or service. They also include asking for information and advice from friends, relatives, co-workers, and sales representatives. Besides these personal sources, there are *impersonal* sources of information such as independent groups that provide valuable, impartial information to consumers (e.g., *Consumer Reports*). Companies provide a considerable amount of information to consumers in many ways (e.g., ads, company websites). Finally, consumers may also gather external information through experiential means (e.g., test-driving a car). Any or all of these sources might be used as part of a consumer's search process.

For instance, Richard spoke to a few friends and co-workers and asked them what they know about ultra-lightweight laptops. He also investigated whether PC-related publications, such as *PC Magazine* or *Laptops*, might have rated the various brands or types of laptops. Figure 14-3 presents some of the sources of information that Richard might use as part of his pre-purchase search.

Types of Information Sought

When you buy a computer, what kind of information would you collect? Would you collect the same kinds of information as if you were interested in buying a new brand of laundry detergent? Probably not, for the type of information that you collect depends on several factors, such as familiarity with the product category (i.e., your past experience and involvement), the importance of the purchase to you (which might depend on its price, the risks involved, whether it is a durable or a non-durable product, etc.), and your personality. With the purchase of a computer, most consumers would seek more information on a variety of factors than with a laundry detergent because a computer is a high-value, durable item that the average consumer would have had experience with. In this section, we will look at the types of information that consumers normally look for before making a decision.

Consumers tend to look for three basic types of information: (1) brands or alternatives that are available, (2) evaluative criteria (generally product features) that they should employ while making a choice, and (3) how products fare on these evaluative criteria.

For example, before deciding which computer to buy, Richard is likely to seek information on various brands of laptops that are on the market now, the features that he should be looking for in laptops, and how the different brands rank on these features. Note that in the case of a laundry detergent, consumers are likely to be aware of the various brands on the market and what to look for in a laundry detergent; the reason for seeking information (internal or external) might be their dissatisfaction with their present brand of laundry detergent. Hence, they might only seek information on how the brands fare on their evaluative criteria.

Let us examine each one of these types of information in more detail.

FIGURE 14-3 Various Sources of Pre-purchase Information for an Ultra-light Computer

PERSONAL	IMPERSONAL
Friends	Newspaper articles
Neighbours	Magazine articles
Relatives	*Consumer Reports*
Co-workers	Direct-mail brochures
Computer salespeople	Information from product advertisements
	External websites

www.consumerreports.org

Brands or Alternatives Available

Consumer awareness of brands in a product category varies with the product category, their past experience, and other factors. As shown in the above example, most consumers have a list of brands of laundry detergents that they are familiar with and would choose from without searching for other brands. This list of alternative brands is called the **evoked set** or the consideration set. When there are not enough brands in the evoked set or if the consumers are not happy with those in the evoked set, they are likely to get involved in an external search to find out if other brands are available.

A consumer's evoked set is distinguished from his or her **inept set**, which consists of brands (or models) the consumer excludes from consideration because they are felt to be unacceptable (or they are seen as "inferior"), and from the **inert set**, which consists of brands (or models) the consumer is indifferent toward because they are perceived as not having any particular advantages. Regardless of the total number of brands (or models) in a product category, a consumer's evoked set tends to be quite small on average, often consisting of only three to five brands (or models). However, research indicates that a consumer's consideration set increases in size as experience with a product category grows.[9]

The evoked set consists of the small number of brands the consumer is familiar with, remembers, and finds acceptable. Figure 14-4 depicts the evoked set as a subset of all available brands in a product category. As the figure shows, it is essential that a product be part of a consumer's evoked set if it is to be considered at all. The five terminal positions in the model that do not end in purchase would appear to have perceptual problems:

- *Unknown brands* (or models): brands that have not broken through a consumer's selective perception (because of selective exposure to advertising media and selective perception of advertising stimuli)

- *Unacceptable brands* (or models): brands that are perceived as being of poor quality or are deemed unsuitable because of poor positioning in either advertising or product characteristics

- *Indifferent brands* (or models): those that are perceived as not having any special benefits and are regarded *indifferently* by the consumer

- *Overlooked brands* (or models): those that have not been clearly positioned or sharply targeted at the consumer market segment under study

- *Inept brands* (or models): brands that may not be chosen because they are perceived by consumers as *unable to satisfy* perceived needs as fully as the brand that is chosen

In each of these instances, the implication for marketers is that promotional techniques should be designed to impart a more favourable, perhaps more relevant, product image to the target consumer. This may also require a change in product features or attributes (i.e., more or better features). An alternative strategy is to invite consumers in a particular target segment to consider a specific offering and possibly put it in their evoked set.

It should also be pointed out that at times a consumer may feel as if he or she is being offered too many choices. For example, the brand proliferation on supermarket shelves is such that a shopper may try a new brand, like it, and then never be able to find it again.[10]

Evaluative Criteria to Be Used

As in the case of brands or alternatives available, consumers may also have knowledge of the evaluative criteria to be used to make a decision. In such cases, they may

Evoked set:
The set of brands that the consumer considers while making a choice.

Inept set:
Brands that the consumer is aware of but excludes from purchase consideration.

Inert set:
Brands that the consumer is aware of but is indifferent toward and hence does not consider while making a choice.

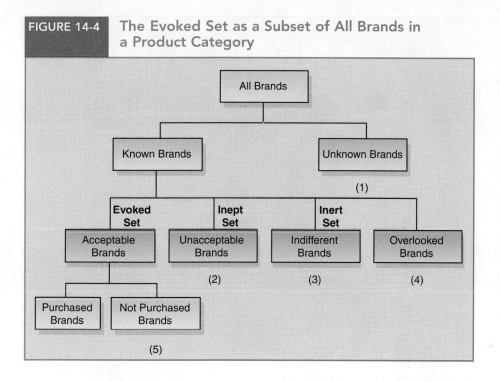

FIGURE 14-4 The Evoked Set as a Subset of All Brands in a Product Category

not conduct any external search to find out what evaluative criteria they should use to make a decision. However, if they are unfamiliar with the product category or are dissatisfied with the current brand, or if other situational or personality characteristics intervene, consumers are likely to search for additional information to determine what evaluative criteria to use in a particular situation.

Evaluative criteria are usually the features or attributes that consumers want in a product. Marketers can influence the evaluative criteria used by consumers through advertising. When a company knows that consumers will be evaluating alternatives, it sometimes advertises in a way that recommends the criteria that consumers should use in assessing product or service options. For example, Exhibit 14-2 presents an ad for Hartz Advanced Care Brand that compares its product, in terms of selected benefits, with two competitive products. The comparison points to Hartz's advantages. Such information is designed to educate and assist potential consumers in their decision making. Of course, marketers are likely to present evaluative criteria that favour their brand over others. Consumers can also refer to external sources such as *Consumer Reports* or other magazines for a more impartial list of evaluative criteria.

Research reveals that if evaluations are made online, information acquired later (the recency effect) is given more weight than information that had been acquired earlier (although this effect decreases with the amount of knowledge that consumers already possess).[11] In another study, the mere possession of a rebate coupon (whether it is used or not) for a product purchase enhances consumers' preference for that object.[12] There is also evidence that when making a "remote" purchase (i.e., the consumer is shopping from home or work rather than in the actual store), the leniency of the retailer's return policy can influence the decision process because it reduces consumer risk.[13]

EXHIBIT 14-2

AD PROVIDING EVALUATIVE CRITERIA
Courtesy of The Hartz Mountain Corporation.

Research Insight 14-1 provides details on how marketers can identify the evaluative criteria used by consumers.

Rating of Alternatives

The final factor about which consumers search for information is the way that different alternatives perform on evaluative criteria. Since evaluative criteria are often product characteristics (e.g., price, memory, weight, speed, repair service for a laptop), consumers may refer to external sources—company websites, retail salespeople, brochures, third parties like *Consumer Reports*, or family and friends for information on how a particular brand would perform on these evaluative criteria. Sometimes consumers might actually try a brand (e.g., test-drive a car or try how a camera "feels" in a store) to gather information and make judgments on various brands. In the case of inexpensive consumer items that they have bought several times before, consumers may depend on their past experience and limit their information search to retrieving this information from their memory.

Not all consumers will resort to a detailed external search process even if they are in the market for the same product category. For those who do get involved in a detailed information search, there are several third-party sources of information.

RESEARCH INSIGHT 14-1
IDENTIFYING EVALUATIVE CRITERIA—
HOW DO YOU FIND OUT WHAT CONSUMERS
ARE LOOKING FOR?

Evaluative criteria are the factors that consumers take into consideration when they choose between alternatives. Generally, these are product attributes or features, though other factors, such as after-sales service provided by the retailer or the status a brand offers, are also used by consumers to weigh different product options and make a decision. Knowing the evaluative criteria used by consumers is critical to marketers because they have to convince consumers that the product performs well by these criteria.

How then do marketers go about finding the evaluative criteria used by consumers? The most common techniques are surveys, focus groups, perceptual mapping, and conjoint analysis. Surveys and focus groups are direct methods of obtaining information about evaluative criteria; marketers ask people directly (in surveys or focus groups) what they are looking for when they buy a particular product. Conjoint analysis and perceptual mapping are indirect means of obtaining that information; researchers using these methods do not ask consumers directly about their evaluative criteria but try to determine these by indirect means.

Surveys: By far the most commonly used technique to identify evaluative criteria used by consumers is a survey, which is easy to do. These surveys can be administered by mail, by telephone, or in person. Consumers are usually asked direct questions about what they look for when they buy a particular product. For example, Maritz Canada conducted a survey of 1000 Canadian adults and asked them what they looked for when they chose a bank. They found out that the criteria that the Canadians were looking for were timely service (23 percent), courteous and knowledgeable staff at the local branch (22 percent), better interest rates (7 percent), better fee structures (6 percent), and a wide variety of financial services and products (1 percent).[14]

Focus groups: Focus groups are often used to find what consumers are looking for while buying products. Unlike surveys, focus groups tend to provide more qualitative information; this can be both a positive and a negative feature. On the one hand, focus groups can provide information on the intangible aspects of what consumers are looking for while buying a brand; on the other hand, the data collected can be harder to analyse and interpret.

Perceptual mapping: Researchers using perceptual mapping to identify the evaluative criteria used by consumers ask consumers to rate pairs of alternatives. Alternatives (or brands) are offered in pairs to consumers, and they are asked to pick the most similar pair, the next most similar one, and so on until all pairs have been evaluated. This results in a perceptual map (similar to the one shown in Chapter 6). This information is fed into a statistical program, which groups the various brands on a map. The technique does not say what the dimensions or product attributes are; the marketers have to make informed judgments about what the axes represent.

Conjoint analysis: Another indirect technique is conjoint analysis, which is used to evaluate the importance or ranking of evaluative criteria. Consumers are given written descriptions of various product alternatives in pairs; once all possible combinations of product attributes are evaluated, the information is entered into a computer program, which identifies the importance that consumers attach to each evaluative criterion.

Marketers can also judge the importance of evaluative criteria with what is called a Constant Sum Scale. Consumers are given a total number of points (say 100) to be allocated among various attributes. Since the total number of points is limited, the way consumers allocate the points between various attributes is an indication of the importance that they place on these.

In fact, the Canadian magazine industry has recently introduced a range of magazines aimed at women who want information about products, evaluative criteria, and how individual products do by these criteria. These so-called shopping magazines are gaining considerable market share.

www.louloumagazine.
com/english/index.jsp

Unlike the typical fashion magazine, shopping magazines like *Loulou* and *Lucky* focus on the nitty-gritty of shopping. Targeting 18- to 35-year-old women, these magazines do not publish stories. As Lise Ravary, publisher of *Loulou*, says, "No stories.... The copy is blurbs and cutlines explaining the products."[15] These magazines are not just about the products but about where to get them. *Lucky* even sends out stickers marked "Yes!" and "Maybe?" so that consumers can flag their choices in the magazine.

Other firms, like Cadillac Fairview, have started regular enewsletters for their registered shoppers. These newsletters, like their magazine counterparts, publish product information and editorial content that help consumers make decisions and give them the third-party endorsement they want.[16]

Would all consumers look to shopping magazines or other external sources for gathering information? The next section will look at the factors, that affect the degree of pre-purchase search that consumers get involved in.

Factors Affecting the Extent of Pre-purchase Search

The extent of an external search depends on several factors. These can be broadly classified into three categories—product factors, situational factors, and consumer factors—which are discussed below.

Product Factors

Several characteristics of the product such as its price, the availability of a variety of brands, the variation in features between them, the number of units being bought, the frequency between purchases, the degree of risk involved in buying it, and so on, can have a great impact on the extent of a consumer's pre-purchase search. For example, research reveals that price considerations can also help determine the extent of the search process. When significant price differences exist, consumers may engage in *smart shopping*; that is, they will invest considerable time and effort in looking for and using promotion-related information in order to obtain a price savings. For such consumers, this search constitutes doing their "homework" before making a purchase.[17]

The degree of risk involved in buying a product can also influence the extent of the pre-purchase search. In high-risk situations, that is, when the product is expensive, durable, or highly visible, consumers are likely to engage in complex and extensive information search and evaluation. In low-risk situations, they are likely to use very simple or limited search and evaluation tactics.

Situational Factors

The extent of the pre-purchase search is also affected by a variety of situational factors, such as the past experience that a consumer has in buying the product, whether or not it is a gift purchase, the influence of family and friends, and several other situational factors. The experience that a consumer has in buying a product has a major influence on the amount of pre-purchase search that he or she is willing to do. The consumer usually searches his or her memory (part of the internal influences depicted in the model) before seeking external sources of information regarding a given consumption-related need. Past experience is considered an internal source of information. The greater the relevant past experience, the less external information the consumer is likely to need to reach a decision. Many consumer decisions are based on a combination of past experience (internal sources) and marketing and non-commercial information (external sources).

An examination of the external search effort preceding the purchase of different product categories (televisions, VCRs, or personal computers) found that the external search effort was greatest for consumers who knew the least about the product category.[18] Conversely, research studies have found that consumers high in subjective knowledge (as judged by self-assessment) rely more on their own evaluations than on dealer recommendations.[19]

How much information a consumer will gather also depends on other situational factors. For example, someone who normally does not do much of an external search may spend hours on such a search because he or she is bored. Sometimes the search is a way avoiding routine things or less pleasurable activities, such as studying, and these factors may increase the amount of search conducted. Similarly, the influence of family and friends may tend to increase the amount of external search. For example, a consumer in need of a digital camera who would have normally gone out and bought one without much search from Future Shop may search for several hours because a sister who is an avid photographer is in town and influences the search process.

Consumer Factors

Besides product and situational factors, several consumer characteristics (both demographic and those related to personality) are also likely to affect the extent of a consumer's pre-purchase search. For example, younger, better-educated consumers are likely to indulge in greater pre-purchase search. Besides such demographic characteristics, personality traits such as a consumer's risk perception and dogmatism also influence the degree of pre-purchase search. As we saw in Chapter 5, consumers who are high-risk perceivers (or narrow categorizers) are likely to limit their choices to a few safe alternatives and may not indulge in an extensive pre-purchase search process. Conversely, consumers who are low-risk perceivers may conduct an extensive pre-purchase search in order to broaden the number of alternatives they have to choose from.

Other consumer characteristics such as attitude toward shopping can also influence a consumer's pre-purchase search process. The act of shopping is an important way of collecting external information. According to a recent consumer study, there is a big difference between the way men and women respond to shopping. Whereas most men do not like to shop, most women say they like the experience of shopping. Although the majority of women found shopping to be relaxing and enjoyable, the majority of men did not.[20]

Figure 14-5 provides additional information on the factors that lead to increased pre-purchase search.

Influence of the Internet

It is also important to point out that the internet has had a great impact on pre-purchase search. Rather than visiting a store to find out about a product or calling the manufacturer and asking for a brochure, consumers can obtain much of the information they need about the products and services they are considering from the manufacturers' websites. Many automobile websites, for example, give information about product specifications, sticker prices, and dealer cost, as well as reviews and even comparisons with competing vehicles. Jaguar's website lets you "build" your own Jaguar and see how it would look, for example, in different colours. Some websites even list a particular car dealer's new- and used-car inventory. And then there are websites such as Reflect.com that allow women to customize any number of cosmetic and beauty-care products.[21]

www.jaguar.ca

www.reflect.com

More and more Canadians are using the internet to gather information on a wide variety of products. However, as Internet Insight 14-1 points out, searching for information on the web also has disadvantages.

| FIGURE 14-5 | Factors Likely to Increase Pre-purchase Search |

PRODUCT FACTORS

Long inter-purchase time (a long-lasting or infrequently used product)
Frequent changes in product styling
Frequent price changes
Volume purchasing (large number of units)
High price
Many alternative brands
Much variation in features

SITUATIONAL FACTORS

Experience

First-time purchase
No past experience because the product is new
Unsatisfactory past experience within the product category

Social Acceptability

The purchase is for a gift
The product is socially visible

Value-Related Considerations

Purchase is discretionary rather than necessary
All alternatives have both desirable and undesirable consequences
Family members disagree on product requirements or evaluation of alternatives
Product usage deviates from important reference groups
The purchase involves ecological considerations
Many sources of conflicting information

CONSUMER FACTORS

Demographic Characteristics of Consumer

Well-educated
High income
White-collar occupation
Under 35 years of age

Personality

Low dogmatic
Low-risk perceiver (broad categorizer)
Other personal factors such as high product involvement and enjoyment of shopping
and search

As Figure 14-5 shows, a number of factors are likely to increase consumers' pre-purchase search. For some products and services, the consumer may have ongoing experience on which to draw, such as when a skier buys a "better" pair of skis. Or the purchase may essentially be discretionary rather than necessary, and so there is

INTERNET INSIGHT 14-1
INFORMATION SEARCH ON THE INTERNET

What do you do when you want to gather information about a rare disease? Or when you are in the market for a car? If you are like a lot of Canadians, you probably go online to search for information. In fact, according to Ipsos-Reid's *Canadian Inter@ctive Reid Report*, in 2001, looking for medical information was the most frequent online activity (67 percent of all online Canadians have visited a health website).[a] And, according to Ipsos-Reid, more Canadians used the internet to search for information about buying a car (63 percent) than about real estate (51 percent), online banking (53 percent), or comparison shopping (49 percent). Among those who have recently bought a vehicle, this number rises to 80 percent.[b]

Why is the web increasingly becoming the medium of choice for information search? Perhaps one consumer's comments drawn from a recent research study summarize the reasons: "I like to use the Web because it's so easy to find information, and it's really easy to use. The information is at my finger-tips and I don't have to search books in libraries."[c] Let us look at the specific advantages and disadvantages of the internet as a search medium for consumer purchases.

The Ipsos-Reid survey quoted earlier asked Canadians what they thought were the advantages that the internet had as a search medium over more traditional information sources. According to the study, the main advantage of the internet as a buying resource is the ability to shop and compare vehicles and vehicle prices—42 percent of respondents gave this as an advantage. The internet was also seen as a good source of information (31 percent), and let consumers avoid dealing with salespeople (28 percent). Saving time and being easier was mentioned by 13 percent of the respondents; the accessibility of the internet was also mentioned by many (10 percent). The other reasons given (e.g., convenience, flexibility in terms of timing, access to a lot of choices) were mentioned by 4 percent to 6 percent of respondents.[d]

Of course, Canadians also recognize the limitations of the internet as a search medium. The physical absence of the product (in this case, the car), the inability to test-drive, and concern about whether the information has been updated regularly were mentioned as the disadvantages of the internet as a buying resource. Interestingly enough, some Canadians value personal contact with the salesperson; 7 percent mentioned the lack of contact with a salesperson as a disadvantage of internet searches.[e]

Similar results were found when Ipsos-Reid examined the use of the internet as a tool in the purchase of a new home. Eighty-three percent say that the internet allowed them to look at more houses, 65 percent said it saved them time in the search process, and 57 percent said it made it easier for them to find their ideal property.[f]

What type of information are Canadians searching for online? In the case of cars, people used the internet to gather information on prices, features of the various brands, comparisons of prices and features, and other information.

QUESTION:

1. What kind of products have you searched for information about online?
2. Which information search was the most productive? Why?

[a] Ipsos-Reid, "Two-Thirds of All Online Canadians Have Visited a Health Website, Up from 55% In 2000," *Canadian Inter@ctive Reid Report*, December 17, 2002.

[b] Ipsos-Reid, "Driving a Better Deal: The Internet is Changing the Face of Buying Cars in Canada," July 18, 2003.

[c] Niranjan V. Raman, "A Qualitative Investigation of Web-Browsing Behavior," in *Advances in Consumer Research*, eds. Merrie Brucks and Deborah J. MacInnis, Provo, UT: Association for Consumer Research, 511–516.

[d] Ipsos-Reid, "Driving a Better Deal."

[e] Ibid.

[f] Ipsos-Reid, "The Internet is a Key Tool in Looking for a New House," October 7, 2003.

no rush to make a decision. In the case of Richard, our market researcher, while he is home in Edmonton this week and looking ahead to a busy month of business travel he is, therefore, excited about the prospects of buying a new ultra-light laptop before leaving on his trip.

The next section will look at how consumers evaluate alternatives.

EVALUATION OF ALTERNATIVES

When evaluating potential alternatives, consumers tend to use two kinds of information: (1) a "list" of brands (or models) from which they plan to make their selection (the evoked set) and (2) the criteria they will use to evaluate each brand or model. Making a selection from a *sample* of all possible brands or models is a human characteristic that helps simplify the decision. The type of decision-making process they are involved in (nominal, limited, or extensive) will also influence the way a consumer evaluates alternatives. For example, if they are in a nominal decision-making mode (e.g., while buying everyday items such as canned soup from a supermarket), consumers are likely to have strong brand preferences and a set list of evaluative criteria. In such cases, evaluation of alternatives might be limited to looking at two or three acceptable brands and choosing among them on the basis of price. However, if the consumer is interested in buying a large-screen television set, she may go through a detailed search process as well as a detailed evaluation of alternatives.

Before we consider the nature of evaluative criteria and the types of decision rules that consumers use to make choices, let us look at two broad categories of consumer choices: affective and attribute-based choices.

Types of Consumer Choice Processes

Economists consider human beings to be rational decision makers who collect information, evaluate alternatives, and make a decision that will maximize their satisfaction. No doubt, all of us do make decisions by such elaborate processes; these would be called attribute-based decisions. However, there are several times when we make decisions that are based not on a detailed evaluation of alternatives, but on emotions or feelings; these are considered affective choices. Let us look at affective and attribute-based choices in more detail.

Affective Choices

Affective choices are more holistic—that is, they do not involve detailed evaluation of alternatives but are based on an overall evaluation of the product. Even this evaluation is based on an emotional response to the product more than anything else. Affective choices tend to be based on how the consumer feels about the choice. They are often used for products that are intrinsically rewarding, such as perfume, clothing, or food, rather than those that are bought as a means to an end, such as computers.

We have probably all had the experience of comparing or evaluating different brands or models of a product and finding the one that just feels and looks "right" or performs the right way. Interestingly, research shows that when consumers discuss such "right products," there is little or no mention of price; brand names are not often uppermost in people's minds; the thing bought often reflects personality characteristics or childhood experiences; and it is often "love at first sight." In one study, the products claimed by research participants to "just feel right" included Big Bertha golf clubs, old leather briefcases, Post-it notes, and the Honda Accord.[22]

Attribute-Based Choices

Attribute-based choices are those in which consumers have pre-determined evaluative criteria and evaluate each alternative against these criteria before they arrive at a decision. Such a decision-making process need not involve external search processes or necessarily take a long time, though they often tend to require both external search and more time. For example, when we go grocery shopping, we choose between different desserts—for example, cakes, pies, ice cream, or the ingredients for a more elaborate homemade dessert—very quickly and using no outside information. We might follow simple rules—if it is for an everyday dessert, we might just go with our knowledge of what everyone in the family likes (chocolate ice cream and apple pie) and buy one of them depending on a few simple evaluative criteria (e.g., price and variety). However, if we are buying a laptop computer, we might collect information on what evaluative criteria are suitable, evaluate the performance or ratings of various brands on each evaluative criteria, and make a final decision based on a more complicated decision rule.

Nature of Evaluative Criteria

Regardless of the nature of the decision making, the criteria consumers use to evaluate the alternative products that constitute their evoked sets are usually expressed in terms of important product attributes. Examples of product attributes that consumers have used as criteria in evaluating nine product categories are listed in Figure 14-6.

What do you look for when you choose a telephone service provider? Sprint Canada did some qualitative and quantitative research to find out what consumers are looking for while they make choices in this category. They discovered that people want simple flexible bundles, with a single invoice and one company to call for sales and support. In other words, consumers were trying to simplify their lives by having long distance, local service, internet, and wireless all in one bundle at a reasonable price.[23]

As can be seen from the table, some of the evaluative criteria that consumers use are tangible ones, like size and memory, while others are intangible, like appearance, feel, quality, and taste. In most cases, consumers use a combination of tangible and intangible criteria. Intangible criteria are often judged by using surrogate measures. **Surrogate indicators** are attributes that are used as indicators of another attribute. For example, if you are presented with a food that you are not familiar with, how would evaluate its taste before eating it? Most people would do a visual inspection of the product and smell it to judge its taste. Here, both smell and visual characteristics (e.g., its colour and the way it is presented) are surrogate indicators of its taste.

Some of the tangible criteria used by consumers are also surrogate indicators of another attribute that is difficult to measure. Perhaps the surrogate measure of quality (an intangible and often difficult attribute to measure) used most often is price. Most people assume that a brand that is extremely low in price cannot be of good quality, and a brand that is high in price has to be high in quality too. Other surrogate indicators of quality are brand image, country of origin, and even the packaging. For example, cars made in Japan and Germany are considered to be of good quality, as are Swiss watches and French wines. And how do you judge the quality of an unknown brand? Besides country of origin, consumers often use the kind of packaging and wrapping to judge the quality of chocolates. Individually wrapped chocolates are considered to be of better quality than those that are not; similarly, chocolates that come in black or gold packaging often have the image of being better.

Surrogate indicators: Attributes that are used as indicators of another attribute.

Finally, consumers often rank evaluative criteria in order of importance. Consumers might differ in the ranking given to the same evaluative criteria; the same consumer might rank a decision criterion more important one day and less important another day depending on situational factors. For example, when you are buying a dessert for everyday use, price might be an important criterion, but if it is for a party, quality and appearance might rank much higher than price.

Let's return for a moment to Richard and his search for an ultra-lightweight laptop. As part of his search process, he has acquired information about a number of relevant issues (or attributes) that could influence his final choice. He has learned that the overall size of a notebook or laptop computer is very much a function of the size of its screen and that the weight of the machine is determined to a great extent by size and capacity of the battery (e.g., two hours or four hours of battery life), as well as what comes built into the machine itself—internal or external floppy disk drive; internal or external CD-ROM or CD-ROM/DVD; internal parallel, serial, and/or video ports; or just USB ports and anything else requiring a docking station.

As part of his search process, Richard has also acquired information about other relevant issues (or attributes) that could influence his final choice (see Figure 14-7). He has learned that some ultra-light Japanese laptops have keyboards that do not have the "feel" of most laptops sold in the U.S. market and are, therefore, harder to type on.

FIGURE 14-6   Possible Product Attributes Used as Purchase Criteria for Nine Product Categories

PERSONAL COMPUTERS	CD PLAYERS	WRISTWATCHES
Processing speed	Mega bass	Watchband
Price	Electronic shock protection	Alarm feature
Type of display	Length of play on batteries	Price
Hard-disk size	Random play feature	Water-resistance
Amount of memory	Water-resistance	Quartz movement
Laptop or desktop	Size of dial	
VCRs	**COLOUR TVS**	**FROZEN DINNERS**
Ease of programming	Picture quality	Taste
Number of heads	Length of warranty	Type of main course
Number of tape speeds	Cable-readiness	Types of side dishes
Slow-motion feature	Price	Price
Automatic tracking	Size of screen	Preparation requirements
35 MM CAMERAS	**FOUNTAIN PENS**	**COLOUR INKJET PRINTERS**
Autofocus	Balance	Output speed
Built-in flash	Price	Number of ink colours
Automatic film loading	Gold nib	Resolution (DPI)
Lens type	Smoothness	Length of warranty
Size and weight	Ink reserve	USB capability

On the basis of his information search, Richard realizes that he is going to have to make a decision about what he really wants from this new computer. Does he want just a lighter-weight version of his current laptop, or is he willing to sacrifice some features for a computer that is substantially smaller and lighter than the typical notebook machine? He comes to realize that on the road he uses the computer mainly for sending and receiving emails and making relatively minor changes in discussion guides for focus groups. These uses involve no serious typing and no great length of time spent looking at the computer screen. Occasionally he is also asked to review a proposal that has to be sent to a client, but Richard learned years ago that to do this properly he has to print out the proposal, read it, make changes, and then email the revised proposal back to his office. Thus, he realizes that he is willing to give up some functionality (such as a built-in floppy drive) in exchange for reduced size and weight.

But having a list of evaluative criteria and knowing how products perform on these does not enable consumers to make a decision. All of us require decision rules or strategies to help us sort through the information that we have collected on brands or alternatives. The next part of this section will examine the decision rules that consumers employ.

Consumer Decision Rules

Consumer decision rules, often referred to as **heuristics**, *decision strategies,* and *information-processing strategies,* are procedures used by consumers to facilitate brand (or other consumption-related) choices. These rules reduce the burden of making complex decisions by providing guidelines or routines that make the process less taxing.

Consumer decision rules have been broadly classified into two categories: **compensatory** and **non-compensatory decision rules**. In following a compensatory decision rule, a consumer evaluates brand or model options in terms of each relevant attribute and computes a weighted or summated score for each brand. The computed score reflects the brand's relative merit as a potential purchase choice. The assumption is that the consumer will choose the brand that scores highest among the alternatives evaluated. Referring to Figure 14-8, it is clear that when using a compensatory decision rule, the Toshiba Libretto L scores highest.

Consumer decision rules or heuristics:
Procedures used by consumers to facilitate brand (or other consumption-related) choices.

Compensatory decision rules:
Decision rules in which consumers evaluate each brand in terms of each relevant attribute and then select the brand with the highest weighted score.

Non-compensatory decision rules:
Rules in which a positive evaluation of an attribute does not compensate for a negative evaluation of the same brand on another attribute.

FIGURE 14-7 Comparison of Selected Characteristics of Ultra-light Laptop Computers

FEATURE	DELL LATITUDE C400	COMPAQ EVO N200	TOSHIBA LIBRETTO L
Weight	1.7 kg / 3.7 lb.	1.2 kg / 2.7 lb.	1 kg / 2.4 lb.
Dimensions (HWD, inches)	1 × 11.4 × 9.5	0.8 × 9.9 × 7.8	0.81 × 10.5 × 6.6
Processor	866MHz Pentium III	700 MHz Pentium III	800 MHz Crusoe
Display	12.1-inch TFT	10.4-inch TFT	10-inch TFT
RAM	256 MB	192 MB	256 MB
Hard Drive	20 GB	20 GB	20 GB
Battery Life	2.5 hours	2.5 hours	4 hours
Other Features	Built-in wireless and built-in Ethernet port	Needs PC card for wireless Has built-in Ethernet port	Built-in wireless and built-in Ethernet port
Price	$2256	$2238	$1999

Source: Adapted from Jonathan Blackwood, "The Jet Set," *Computer Shopper,* 22, 3, March 2002, 144–147; Dan Costa, "The Lighter Side," *PC Magazine,* 21, 6, March 26, 2002, 94–106; and accessed from www.dynamism.com.

A unique feature of a compensatory decision rule is that it allows a positive evaluation of a brand on one attribute to balance out a negative evaluation on some other attribute. For example, a positive assessment of the energy savings made possible by a particular brand or type of light bulb may offset an unacceptable assessment in terms of the bulb's diminished light output.

In contrast, non-compensatory decision rules do not allow consumers to balance positive evaluations of a brand on one attribute against a negative evaluation on some other attribute. For instance, in the case of an energy-saving light bulb, the product's negative (unacceptable) rating on its light output would not be offset by a positive evaluation of its energy savings. Instead, this particular light bulb would be disqualified from further consideration. If Richard's choice of a laptop computer had been based on the desire to have a built-in wireless capability (Wi-Fi) (refer again to Figure 14-7), a non-compensatory decision rule would have eliminated the Compaq Evo N200.

Three non-compensatory rules are considered briefly here: the *conjunctive* rule, the *disjunctive* rule, and the *lexicographic* rule.

Conjunctive Decision Rule

Consumers using this rule follow these steps:

Conjunctive decision rule:

A non-compensatory decision rule in which minimum criteria are established and brands that do not meet these minimum cutoffs are eliminated from further consideration.

- identify product attributes
- establish a separate, minimally acceptable level as a cutoff point for each attribute
- eliminate brands that fall below the cutoff on *any one* attribute.

Because the **conjunctive decision rule** can result in several acceptable alternatives, it becomes necessary in such cases for the consumer to apply an additional decision rule to arrive at a final selection, for example, to accept the first satisfactory brand. The conjunctive rule is particularly useful in quickly reducing the number of alternatives to be considered. The consumer can then apply another more refined decision rule to arrive at a final choice.

Disjunctive Decision Rule

Disjunctive decision rule:

A non-compensatory decision rule in which minimally acceptable cutoffs are set and any brand that meets or surpasses any cutoff is chosen.

The **disjunctive decision rule** is the "mirror image" of the conjunctive rule. In applying this decision rule, the consumers:

FIGURE 14-8	Hypothetical Ratings for Ultra-light Laptops		
FEATURE	**DELL LATITUDE C400**	**COMPAQ EVO N200**	**TOSHIBA LIBRETTO L**
Weight	4	8	10
Dimensions	3	7	10
Processor	7	5	6
Display	10	7	6
RAM	10	8	10
Hard Drive	8	8	8
Battery Life	6	6	8
Other Features	8	5	8
Price	7	7	8
Total	63	61	74

- identify product attributes
- establish a separate, acceptable cutoff level for each attribute (normally higher than the one established for a conjunctive rule)
- accept brands that meet or exceed the cutoff established for *any one* attribute

Here again, a number of brands or models might exceed the cutoff point, producing a situation in which another decision rule is required. When this happens, the consumer may accept the first satisfactory alternative as the final choice or apply another decision rule that is perhaps more suitable.

Lexicographic Decision Rule

Consumers who use the **lexicographic decision rule** go through the following steps:

- identify product attributes
- rank the attributes in terms of perceived relevance or importance
- compare the various alternatives in terms of the single attribute that is considered most important
- if one option scores high enough on this top-ranked attribute (regardless of the score on any of the other attributes), it is chosen and the process ends
- if there are two or more surviving alternatives, the process is repeated with the second highest-ranked attribute (and so on), until reaching the point that one of the options is chosen because it exceeds the others on a particular attribute

Lexicographic decision rule:
A non-compensatory rule in which attributes are first ranked in terms of importance, brands are compared on the most important attribute first, and the brand that scores the highest is chosen. The process is repeated if necessary.

With the lexicographic rule, the highest-ranked attribute (the one applied first) may reveal something about the individual's basic consumer (or shopping) orientation. For instance, a "buy the best" rule might indicate that the consumer is *quality-oriented;* a "buy the most prestigious brand" rule might indicate that the consumer is *status-oriented;* a "buy the least expensive" rule might reveal that the consumer is *economy-minded.*

A variety of decision rules appear quite commonplace. According to a consumer survey, nine out of ten shoppers who go to the store for things they buy often have a specific shopping strategy for saving money. The following are the consumer segments and the specific shopping rules that these segments employ:[24]

1. *Practical loyalists*—those who look for ways to save on the brands and products they would buy anyway.
2. *Bottom-line price shoppers*—those who buy the lowest-priced item with little or no regard for brand.
3. *Opportunistic switchers*—those who use coupons or sales to decide among brands and products that fall within their evoked set.
4. *Deal hunters*—those who look for the best bargain and are not brand-loyal.

We have considered only the most basic of an almost infinite number of consumer decision rules. Most of the decision rules described here can be combined to form new variations, such as conjunctive-compensatory, conjunctive-disjunctive, and disjunctive-conjunctive rules. It is likely that for many purchase decisions, consumers maintain in long-term memory overall evaluations of the brands in their evoked sets.

Figure 14-9 summarizes the essence of many of the decision rules considered in this chapter in terms of the kind of mental statements that Richard might make in selecting a notebook computer.

FIGURE 14-9	Hypothetical Use of Popular Decision Rules in Deciding to Buy an Ultra-light Laptop Computer

DECISION RULE	MENTAL STATEMENT
Compensatory rule	"I selected the computer that came out best when I balanced the good ratings against the bad ratings."
Conjunctive rule	"I selected the computer that had no bad features."
Disjunctive rule	"I picked the computer that excelled in at least one attribute."
Lexicographic rule	"I looked at the feature that was most important to me and chose the computer that ranked highest on that attribute."

Going Online to Find Help in Decision Making

For the past several years researchers have been examining how the use of the internet has affected the way consumers make decisions. It is often hypothesized that because consumers have limited information-processing capacity, they must develop a choice strategy based on both individual factors (e.g., knowledge, personality traits, and demographics) and contextual factors (characteristics of the decision tasks). The three major contextual factors that have been researched are *task complexity* (number of alternatives and amount of information available for each alternative), *information organization* (presentation, format, and content), and *time constraint* (more or less time to decide).[25] Figure 14-10 compares these contextual factors for both the electronic and traditional environments.

Life Styles as a Consumer Decision Strategy

An individual's or family's decisions to be committed to a particular life style (e.g., devoted followers of a particular religion) affects a wide range of specific everyday consumer behaviour. For instance, the Trends Research Institute has identified "voluntary simplicity" as one of the top 10 life-style trends.[26] Researchers there estimate that 15 percent of all "boomers" seek a simpler life style with reduced emphasis on ownership and possessions. Voluntary simplifiers are making do with less clothing and fewer credit cards (with no outstanding balances) and moving to smaller, yet still adequate, houses or apartments in smaller communities. Most important, it is not that these consumers can no longer afford their affluence or "life style of abundance"; rather, they are seeking new, "reduced," less extravagant lives. As part of this new life-style commitment, some people are looking for less stressful and lower-paying jobs. In a telephone survey, for example, 33 percent of those contacted claimed that they would be willing to take a 20 percent pay cut in return for working fewer hours.[27] Time pressure may also play a role in the consumer's decision process, for research has positively associated this factor with both sale proneness (i.e., respond positively to cents-off coupons or special offers) and display proneness (e.g., respond positively to in-store displays offering a special price).[28]

www.loblaws.ca

Loblaws is one Canadian company that recognizes consumers' need to simplify their lives and reduce some of the complications of modern life. Geoffrey Wilson, VP of industry and investor relations, says that Loblaws is "very cognizant of the time-value constraints in today's lifestyle...(and is) trying to meet that by having a

FIGURE 14-10	Comparison of Electronic and Traditional Information Environments

		ELECTRONIC ENVIRONMENT	TRADITIONAL ENVIRONMENT
Assumption		Consumers Use Both "Heads" and Computers to Make Decisions. The Total Capacity Is Extended.	Consumers Use "Heads" to Make Decisions. Their Cognitive Capacity Is Fixed.
Contextual Factors	Task Complexity	More alternatives and more information for each alternative are available. Information is more accessible.	Information is scattered and information search is costly.
	Information Organization	Information presentation format is flexible. It can be reorganized and controlled by consumers. Product utilities can be calculated by computers without consumers' direct examination of the attributes.	Information presentation format and organization are fixed. They can only be "edited" by consumers manually (e.g., using pencil and paper).
	Time Constraint	Time is saved by using computers to execute the decision rules; extra time is needed to learn how to use the application.	Complex choice strategies require more time to formulate and execute.

Source: Lan Xia, "Consumer Choice Strategies and Choice Confidence in the Electronic Environment," *American Marketing Association Conference Proceedings*, American Marketing Association, 10, 1999, 272.

meaningful, all encompassing store environment."[29] Loblaws tries to do this with its Live Life Well series of ads, which showcases President's Choice Organics and Natural Values products; recipes and health tips are included. Loblaws is moving its President's Choice brand from a grocery brand to a life-style focus.

Indigo is another company attempting to help its customers reduce the stress of modern-day living. The bookseller now carries products such as body lotion, health-oriented DVDs, tea, and incense and advertises them with pictures of women in yoga poses with "Simplify" and in-store signs that promote "tranquillity" and "Renewed Balance to Your Life."[30]

Incomplete Information and Non-comparable Alternatives

In many choice situations, consumers do not have enough information on which to base a decision and must use other strategies to cope with the missing elements. Information may be missing as a result of advertisements or packaging that mention only certain attributes, the consumer's own imperfect memory of attributes for alternatives that aren't present, or because some attributes are experiential and can be evaluated only after the product has been used.[31] There are at least four different strategies that consumers can use for coping with missing information:[32]

1. Consumers may delay the decision until they can obtain the missing information. This strategy is likely to be used for high-risk decisions.

2. Consumers may ignore missing information and decide to continue with the current decision rule (e.g., compensatory or non-compensatory), using the attribute information they have.

3. Consumers may change the decision strategy they are accustomed to using to one that better accommodates missing information.

4. Consumers may infer ("construct") the missing information.

Recent research has demonstrated that consumers tend to deal with missing information by buying the option that is deemed to be superior on the common attributes (i.e., basing the decision on the information that is available for all of the options or brands being considered). For marketers, therefore, the decision as to what information to provide or not to provide can help determine the product's success or failure in the marketplace.[33]

In discussing consumer decision rules, we have assumed that a choice is made from among the brands or models evaluated. Of course, a consumer also may conclude that none of the alternatives offers enough benefits and decide not to buy any of them. If this happened with a necessity, such as a refrigerator, the consumer would probably either lower his or her expectations and settle for the best of the available alternatives or look for information about additional brands, hoping to find one that more closely met his or her pre-determined criteria. However, if the purchase is more discretionary, the consumer probably would postpone the purchase. In this case, information gained from the search up to that point would be transferred to long-term storage (in the psychological field) and retrieved and re-introduced as input if the consumer regains interest in making such a purchase.

It should be noted that, in applying decision rules, consumers may at times attempt to compare dissimilar (non-comparable) alternatives. For example, a consumer may be undecided about whether to buy a large-screen, high-definition television set or a new set of scuba gear, because he can afford one or the other but not both. Or a consumer may try to decide between buying a new sweater or a new raincoat. When there is great dissimilarity in the alternative ways of allocating available funds, consumers abstract the products to a level in which comparisons are possible. In the foregoing examples, a consumer might weigh the alternatives (television versus scuba gear or sweater versus raincoat) in terms of which alternative would offer more pleasure or which, if either, is more of a "necessity."

A Series of Decisions

Although we have discussed the purchase decision as if it were a single decision, in reality, a purchase can involve a number of decisions. For example, when buying a car, people are involved in multiple decisions, such as choosing the make or country of origin of the car (foreign versus domestic), the dealer, the financing, and the particular options. In the case of a replacement car, these decisions must be preceded by a decision as to whether or not to trade in the current car. A study found that the attitudes and search behaviour of consumers who replace their cars after only a few years (early replacement buyers) differ greatly from those who replace them after many years (late replacement buyers). In particular, early car replacement buyers were more concerned with the car's style and image or status and were less concerned with cost. In contrast, late car replacement buyers undertook a greater amount of information and dealer search and were greatly influenced by friends.[34]

Since deciding how to pay for a purchase is one of the decisions facing consumers, it is of interest to point out that the use of debit cards has been gaining popularity in the United States as a payment option. Whereas in 1999, according to one study, 22 percent of purchases were made with credit cards and 21 percent with debit cards, by 2001 credit cards accounted for only 21 percent of purchases and debit card usage had risen to 26 percent.[35] Canadians seem even more attracted to debit cards than their American neighbours. In 2002, Canadians made 76.4 debit card transactions per person; in fact, Canadians are the highest users of debit cards in the world.[36]

INFORMATION SEARCH, ALTERNATIVE EVALUATION, AND MARKETING STRATEGY

An understanding of how and why consumers search for information, and the way they evaluate alternatives can help a marketer design effective marketing strategies. Since these processes are closely related to each other, we will examine the strategy implications of information search and alternative evaluation together in this section.

Get products into consumers' evoked set: As mentioned earlier, unless a brand is in a consumer's evoked set, it will not be considered at all. So the first thing a company has to do is try to get its brand in the consumer's evoked set. This is particularly important in the case of nominal and limited decision-making situations, in which people are less likely to search for alternative brands and may resort to their evoked set of alternatives quickly. In such circumstances, marketers should attempt to get their brands into the evoked set through ads that stand out, getting consumers to think about their brands *before* they get to the retail store (through the use of coupons, rebates, and free samples), and the use of comparative advertising that forces consumers to take a second look at their preferred brands. Marketers should also try to understand how, when, and where consumers get their information and should use the relevant media for their promotions.

If you were the president of an online dating service, how would you get your target market to consider your service? How would you get into their evoked set? To Mark Pavan, the president and CEO of Lemontonic, a Toronto online dating service, the answer was obvious. Instead of spending hundreds of thousands of dollars on the typical television commercial, he decided to hook up with *Hooked Up* (pun intended!), a reality show produced by Toronto Lone Eagle Entertainment. The show features 10 men and 10 women trying to find love during an adventurous stay in the Rocky Mountains. Pavan says the show's audience was a natural fit for the company's service since it targets young, single men and women; Christopher Geddes of Lone Eagle agrees; he says the "show speaks directly to their product offering."[37]

www.lemontonic.com

Limit the information search if your brand is the preferred brand: If a company is in the fortunate position of being the favourite brand of the consumer, then it should attempt to limit any information search as it could lead to other brands being placed in the evoked set or another brand in the evoked set being preferred. Companies often try to do this by making consumers buy in bulk (by offering them cash rebates or discounts for bulk buying), or encouraging them to do their decision making in advance. For example, lawn care companies try to get consumers to sign up for the next year in late fall when no one is looking for lawn-care options.

Use point-of-purchase advertising effectively: Since a lot of decisions are made at the retail level (especially in nominal and limited decision-making situations), marketers who have established brand loyalty and those who are attempting to get their brands into the evoked set would benefit by using point-of-purchase (POP) displays, coupons, and other retail advertising effectively. For example, POP

Diets Rich In
Tomato Products
May Help Reduce
The Risk Of
Certain Types Of
Cancer

© 2001 Campbell Soup Company

Did you know
Campbell's® Tomato soup is full of tomato goodness, all eight velvety smooth varieties from classic condensed to ready-to-serve.

www.campbellsoup.com/eatsmart

M'm!
M'm!
Good!®

EXHIBIT 14-3

CAMPBELL'S SEEKS TO CREATE AWARENESS AND INTEREST

Courtesy of Campbell Soup Company.

www.swisswater.com

displays that advertise a sale can attract price-conscious consumers and make them switch brands.

Understand consumer decision rules and use suitable promotional messages: An understanding of which decision rules consumers apply in choosing a particular product or service is useful to marketers concerned with formulating a promotional program. A marketer familiar with the prevailing decision rule can prepare a promotional message in a format that would facilitate consumer information processing. The promotional message might even suggest how potential consumers should make a decision. For instance, a direct-mail piece for a desktop computer might tell potential consumers "what to look for in a new PC." This mail piece might specifically ask consumers to consider the attributes of hard disk size, amount of memory, processor speed, monitor size and maximum resolution, video card memory, and CD burner speed.

Influence the choice of evaluative criteria: Since the number and type of evaluative criteria have a major role in the way consumers evaluate brands, marketers need to make sure the criteria on which their brand is strongest gets on to the consumers' list of evaluative criteria. If your brand's strongest attribute is the speed with which it delivers results, then unless speed is one of the evaluative criteria (and preferably the most important one) that consumers use, your brand is unlikely to be purchased. Companies can get their strongest attribute on the consumers' list of criteria through effective advertising. Take the example of Tums, the antacid. Since many women in the baby boomer age group are getting to the stage where osteoporosis is a matter of concern for them, Tums advertises the fact that it contains calcium. The brand is hoping that by making the presence of calcium an important evaluative criterion, women would choose Tums over other antacids. Similarly, Campbell's has been emphasizing the beneficial effects of a diet rich in tomato to influence the evaluative criteria used by consumers when selecting soups (Exhibit 14-3). Here's another example:

Swiss Water Decaffeinated Coffee Company, a small specialty brand with headquarters in Burnaby, BC, has been able to get consumers to buy its brand by incorporating an evaluative criterion into the consumers' minds when they look for coffee. What is even more interesting is that the company has been successful in making consumers value an attribute that is normally "hidden" from consumers. The company's product had very little brand-awareness; very few consumers had even heard of the Swiss water process, which enables the company, unlike most of its competitors, to decaffeinate coffee with water instead of chemicals. The company and its advertising agency, Saatchi Drum (based in Vancouver, BC), developed, a series of ads with the tag line "Decaf without the chemistry." The ads encouraged consumers to think of how the caffeine is taken out of their coffee; the ads were so successful that consumers asked for copies of the advertising! The company effectively influenced consumers' choice of evaluative criteria for coffee purchases by adding a new one on which their product scored high.[38]

Influence the rating of your product on evaluative criteria: One of the most important aims of advertising is to influence consumers' perceptions of how a product performs on key evaluative criteria. Marketers attempt to do this through comparative advertising as well as by emphasizing the key attributes of their brand over long periods of time. The assumption being made is that consistent advertising of a product's features and attributes will lead to low-involvement learning and positive attitude formation. These, in turn, can lead to positive evaluations of the brand.

Use surrogate indicators effectively: Marketers need to understand and use surrogate indicators effectively. For example, a brand that is being positioned as high in quality has to use the proper pricing (higher than average or the highest) and packaging. It also has to spend money on developing a strong brand image through consistent high-quality advertising in the right media. Similarly, a restaurant that aims to be seen as a high-quality restaurant has to ensure that its decor, its table settings, the attire of its employees, the menu card, and other features are in line with the image of a high-class restaurant.

Make effective use of consumption vision: Researchers have recently proposed "consumption vision" as an unorthodox, but potentially accurate, portrayal of decision making for those situations in which the consumer has little experience and the problems are not well structured, as well as for decisions in which there is a considerable amount of emotion. Under such circumstances, the consumer may turn to a consumption vision, a mental picture of the consequences of using a particular product.[39] Such visions allow consumers to imagine or vicariously participate in the consumption of the product or service before making an actual decision. A new university graduate may imagine himself working for a large corporation rather than for his Dad's small manufacturing firm. Or a consumer may visualize herself lying on a beach in Cuba. After "trying out" a number of different alternatives in his or her mind, so to speak, the consumer then makes his or her decision.[40] In a recent study, consumers were more likely to construct consumption visions when they saw an advertisement presenting the product's attributes in concrete and detailed language or in pictures.[41] There is also research evidence that a consumer's preferences may depend on the degree to which anticipated satisfaction is evoked. When anticipating satisfaction, the consumer forms mental images—consumption visions—of one or more of the options, and the final decision is very likely going to be based on this imagery. A real estate agent selling an expensive house might encourage her clients to ask themselves (i.e., "envision") how satisfied they would be to live in such a home.[42]

SUMMARY

- Marketers are particularly interested in the consumer's decision-making process. For a consumer to make a decision, more than one alternative must be available. (The decision not to buy is also an alternative.)

- Consumer decision making has two major parts: the process (recognition of a need or problem, pre-purchase information search, and alternative evaluation) and the outputs (purchase, consumption, and post-purchase processes).

- Consumer decision making can be classified into three groups—nominal, limited, and extensive—depending on how a consumer goes through the decision-making process (the steps covered, the time and effort spent on information search, and the nature of the alternative evaluation process).

- Consumer decision making starts with problem recognition. Problem recognition is the recognition of a gap between the expected and actual states of a consumer. Consumer problems can be active or inactive; they may need immediate solutions or can be deferred.

- Marketers can trigger problem recognition in many ways, including lowering the consumer's actual state, raising her expected or ideal state, and increasing the importance of the gap between these and other means.

- Pre-purchase information search can be internal or external. Consumers can get information from marketers, neutral sources (e.g., *Consumer Reports*), family and friends, or their past experiences.

- Consumers seek information about the alternatives or brands available, the evaluative criteria that they need to use to make a decision, and how the various alternatives rank on these criteria.

- When product attributes, especially product quality, is difficult to judge, consumers use surrogate indicators (attributes that stand in for another attribute) to evaluate the alternatives. Price and country of origin are examples of surrogate indicators often used by consumers to judge product quality.

- Once the alternatives have been evaluated, consumers still need to use decision rules to choose from among them. The most common decision rules used are compensatory, lexicographic, conjunctive, and disjunctive rules.

DISCUSSION QUESTIONS

1. Define extensive problem solving, limited problem solving, and routinized-response behaviour. What are the differences among the three decision-making approaches?

2. (a) Choose three different products that you believe require a reasonably intensive pre-purchase search by a consumer. Then, using Figure 14-5 as a guide, identify the specific characteristics of these products that make an intensive pre-purchase search likely.
   (b) For each of the products that you listed, identify the perceived risks that a consumer is likely to experience before a purchase. Discuss how the marketers of these products can reduce these perceived risks.

3. How can a marketer of very light, very powerful laptop computers use its knowledge of customers' expectations in designing a marketing strategy?

4. Describe the need-recognition process that took place before you bought your last soft drink. How did it differ from the process that preceded the purchase of a new pair of sneakers? What role, if any, did advertising play in your need recognition?

5. What are the various types of information sources that a consumer has? Which one would you use if you were in the market for these products? Why? (a) Home insurance (b) A new car (c) An MBA program (d) A high-definition television

6. Explain compensatory and non-compensatory decision rules and discuss two non-compensatory decision rules.

CRITICAL THINKING QUESTIONS

1. What kind of decision process would you expect most consumers to follow in their first purchase of a new product or brand in each of the following areas: (a) chewing gum, (b) sugar, (c) men's aftershave lotion, (d) carpeting, (e) paper towels, (f) a cellular telephone, and (g) a luxury car? Explain your answers.

2. Let's assume that this coming summer you are planning to spend a month touring Europe and are, therefore, in need of a good 35 mm camera.

(a) Develop a list of product attributes that you will use as the purchase criteria in evaluating various 35 mm cameras. (b) Distinguish the differences that would occur in your decision process if you were to use compensatory versus non-compensatory decision rules.

3. List the universities that you considered attending and the criteria that you used to evaluate them. Describe how you acquired information about the different attributes of

universities and how you made your decision. Be sure to specify whether you used compensatory or non-compensatory decision rules.

4. Select one of the following product categories: compact disc players, fast food restaurants, or shampoo. (a) Write down the brands that constitute your evoked set. (b) Identify brands that are not part of your evoked set. (c) Discuss how the brands included in your evoked set differ from those that are not included in terms of important attributes.

5. Choose a newspaper or magazine advertisement that attempts (a) to give the consumer a decision strategy to follow in making a purchase decision or (b) to reduce the perceived risk(s) associated with a purchase. Evaluate the effectiveness of the ad you have chosen.

INTERNET EXERCISES

1. Conduct an information search on the internet for laptop computers by going to the sites of two manufacturers (such as Dell, IBM, Apple, Gateway, or Hewlett-Packard). Which site do you like more and why? Once you have completed this, go to the website of *Consumer Reports* (**www.consumerreports.org**), and then to their web e-ratings section and click on the company that you chose as having the better website. How does *Consumer Reports* rate this company's website?

2. Go to the site of one manufacturer of packaged consumer goods (e.g., Kellogg's Canada or General Foods) and one automobile manufacturer (e.g., Ford Canada or Honda Canada). Does the information provided by these manufacturer regarding their products differ? How?

What other differences can you find between the sites?

3. What would your evaluative criteria be if you were choosing an MBA program? Go to the websites of two Canadian universities that offer MBA programs and submit a report on whether they provide enough information for you to evaluate them using your evaluative criteria.

4. Go to the website of *Consumer Reports* (**www.consumerreports.org**) and their web e-ratings section. Click on any product category and look at the "how we evaluate" section which provides details on how the organization evaluates sites. Is it similar to the way you would evaluate websites? Why or why not?

KEY TERMS

Compensatory decision rules
  (p. 479)
Conjunctive decision rule   *(p. 480)*
Consumer decision making
  (p. 458)
Consumer decision rules or
  heuristics   *(p. 479)*
Disjunctive decision rule   *(p. 480)*

Evoked set   *(p. 468)*
Extensive problem solving
  (p. 459)
Inept set   *(p. 468)*
Inert set   *(p. 468)*
Lexicographic decision rule
  (p. 481)
Limited problem solving   *(p. 460)*

Need recognition   *(p. 462)*
Non-compensatory decision rules
  (p. 479)
Pre-purchase search   *(p. 466)*
Routinized-response behaviour
  (p. 460)
Surrogate indicators   *(p. 477)*

CASE 14-1: MAKING PAPER OBSOLETE

One of the latest devices vying for our consumer dollars is the tablet PC (hint: search "tablet PC" in **www.google.ca** or some other search engine for the most up-to-date information). Although these computers allow the user to write directly onto the screen (with a stylist or "pen"), most versions of the product do include a keyboard. Compared with previous efforts to digitize handwriting, this new breed of writing tablet does not try to convert handwritten documents into text; instead, it stores and retrieves these files as handwritten notes, using a new Microsoft note-taking utility called Journal. With this software, for example, any handwritten word that you cross out on the screen is automatically erased.

Several versions of the tablet PC are on sale for about $2000 to $2500. The Compaq Evo Tablet PC is the size of a piece of paper and allows both pen and keyboard input, the Fujitsu Stylistic Tablet PC turns into a desktop PC when placed on its docking station, and the Viewsonic Tablet PC has a built-in Wi-Fi card and a wireless keyboard. For about $2500, the Acer Travelmate, which resembles a standard notebook computer, has a rotating screen that a user can write on with a stylist.

Consider the typical "road warriors" (i.e., frequent business travellers). In addition to taking their laptops on business trips, they carry in their briefcases a lot of handwritten notes on legal pads and printouts that have been marked up with a highlighter. It is believed that the tablet PC can reduce and perhaps even eliminate the need to carry these papers.

QUESTIONS

1. What would trigger a need in someone like you for a tablet PC?

2. What sources of information would you use if you were in the market for this product?

3. If you were considering the purchase of a tablet PC, which possible product attributes (discussed in this chapter) might you use as purchase criteria for this product category?

Source: Chris Taylor, "The Pen as Mighty as the Keyboard," *Business 2.0*, August 2002, 104.

NOTES

1   George Emerson, "One Size Fits All," *Report on Business*, December, 2003, 97–98.

2   Itamar Simonson, "Shoppers' Easily Influenced Choices," *New York Times*, November 6, 1994, 11.

3   John A. Howard and Jagdish N. Sheth, *The Theory of Buyer Behavior* (New York: Wiley, 1969), 46–47; see also John Howard, *Consumer Behavior in Marketing Strategy* (Upper Saddle River, NJ: Prentice Hall, 1989).

4   Gordon C. Bruner, II, "The Effect of Problem-Recognition Style on Information Seeking," *Journal of the Academy of Marketing Science,* 15, Winter 1987, 33–41.

5   "To the Fridge, Mate!" *Marketing Magazine*, April 26, 2004, 6.

6   George Emerson, "One Size Fits All," *Canadian Business,* December, 2003, 97.

7   Samsung ad, *Canadian Business*, December, 2003, 23.

8   Michelle Warren, "Menacing Character Speaks to Women about Heart Disease," *Marketing Daily*, April 19, 2004, 1

9   Michael D. Johnson and Donald R. Lehmann, "Consumer Experience and Consideration Sets for Brands and Product Categories," in *Advances in Consumer Research,* eds. Merrie Brucks and Deborah J. MacInnis (Provo, UT: Association for Consumer Research), 295–300.

10   Thomas T. Semon, "Too Much Choice Not Ideal, but Not Enough Choice Likely Worse," *Marketing News,* November 5, 2001, 9.

11   Gita Venkataramani Johar, Kamel Jedidi, and Jacob Jacoby, "A Varying-Parameter Averaging Model on

On-Line Brand Evaluations," *Journal of Consumer Research*, 24, September 1997, 232–247.

12   Sankar Sen and Eric J. Johnson, "Mere-Possession Effects without Possession in Consumer Choice," *Journal of Consumer Research*, 24, June 1997, 105–117.

13   Stacy L. Wood, "Remote Purchase Environments: The Influence of Return Policy Leniency on Two-Stage Decision Processes," *Journal of Marketing Research*, 38, 2, May 2001, 157–169.

14   Paul-Mark Rendon, "Canadians Happy with Their Banks," *Marketing Magazine*, February 13, 2004.

15   Andrea Zoe Aster, "Shopping Basics," *Marketing Magazine*, 21–22.

16   Ibid.

17   Haim Mano and Michael T. Elliott, "Smart Shopping: The Origins and Consequences of Price Savings," in *Advances in Consumer Research*, eds. Merrie Brucks and Deborah J. MacInnis (Provo, UT: Association for Consumer Research), 504–510.

18   Sharon E. Beatty and Scott M. Smith, "External Search Effort: An Investigation across Several Product Categories," *Journal of Consumer Research*, 14, June 1987, 83–95.

19   Richard A. Spreng, Richard L. Divine, and Thomas J. Page, Jr., "An Empirical Examination of the Differential Effects of Objective and Subjective Knowledge on Information Processing," in *2001 AMA Educators' Proceedings*, 12, eds. Greg W. Marshall and Stephen J. Grove (Chicago: American Marketing Association, 2001), 329.

20   Matthew Klein, "He Shops, She Shops," *American Demographics*, March 1998, 34–35.

21   Ken Krizner, "Individuality Extends into Manufacturing," *Frontline Solutions*, 2, 3, March 2001, 1, 18.

22   Jeffrey F. Durgee, "Why Some Products 'Just Feel Right,' or, the Phenomenology of Product Rightness," in *Advances in Consumer Research*, 22, eds. Frank R. Kardes and Mita Sujan (Provo, UT: Association for Consumer Research, 1995), 650–652.

23   Michelle Warren, "Sprint Grows Up," *Marketing Magazine*, April 19, 2004, 19.

24   Laurie Peterson, "The Strategic Shopper," *Adweek's Marketing Week*, March 30, 1992, 18–20.

25   Lan Xia, "Consumer Choice Strategies and Choice Confidence in the Electronic Environment," in *1999 AMA Educators Proceedings*, 10, eds. Stephen P. Brown and D. Sudharshan (Chicago: American Marketing Association, 1999), 270–277.

26   Carey Goldberg, "Choosing the Joys of a Simplified Life," *New York Times*, September 21, 1995, C1, C9.

27   Ibid.

28   Nancy Spears, "The Time Pressured Consumer and Deal Proneness: Theoretical Framework and Empirical Evidence," in *2000 AMA Winter Educators' Conference*, 11, eds., John P. Workman and William D. Perreault (Chicago: American Marketing Association, 2000), 35–40.

29   Sarah Dobson, "Pitching Calm: Balance as the New Mantra," *Marketing Magazine*, May 17/24, 2004, 6.

30   Ibid.

31   Sandra J. Burke, "The Effects of Missing Information on Decision Strategy Selection," in *Advances in Consumer Research*, 17, eds. Marvin E. Goldberg, Gerald Gorn, and Richard W. Pollay (Provo, UT: Association for Consumer Research, 1990), 250–256.

32   Sarah Fisher Gardial and David W. Schumann, "In Search of the Elusive Consumer Inference," in *Advances in Consumer Research*, 17, eds. Marvin E. Goldberg, Gerald Gorn, and Richard W. Pollay, 283–287. See also Sandra Burke, "The Effects of Missing Information," 250–256.

33   Ran Kivetz and Itamar Simonson, "The Effects of Incomplete Information on Consumer Choice," *Journal of Marketing Research*, 37, 4, November 2000, 427–448.

34   Barry L. Bayus, "The Consumer Durable Replacement Buyer," *Journal of Marketing*, 55, January 1991, 42–51.

35   Calmetta Coleman, "Debit Cards Look to Give Credit Cards a Run for Consumers' Money," *Wall Street Journal*, December 3, 2001, B1, B4; "Understanding Debit Cards," **www.aarp.org/confacts/ money/debitcards/html**; and "Debit Cards," **www. mcvisa.com/debi.html**.

36   Canadian Bankers Association website, "Quick Facts" section, **http://www.cba.ca/en/viewdocu-ment.asp?fl=3&sl=174&docid=413&pg=1**.

37   Chris Powell, "Lemontonic Connects to Hooked Up," *Marketing Magazine*, February 16, 2004, 4.

38   Frank Dennis, "Selling Hidden Brands," *Marketing Magazine*, May 10, 2004, 23.

39   Diane M. Phillips, Jerry C. Olson, and Hans Baumgartner, "Consumption Visions in Consumer Decision Making," in *Advances in Consumer Research*, 22, eds. Frank R. Kardes and Mita Sujan (Provo, UT: Association for Consumer Research, 1995), 280.

40   Ibid., 280–284.

41   Diane M. Phillips, "Anticipating the Future: The Role of Consumption Visions in Consumer Behavior," in *Advances in Consumer Research*, vol. 23, eds. Kim P. Corfman and John G. Lynch, Jr. (Provo, UT: Association for Consumer Research, 1996), 70–75.

42   Baba Shiv and Joel Huber, "The Impact of Anticipating Satisfaction on Consumer Choice," *Journal of Consumer Research*, 27, 2, September 2000, 202–216.

Santa's favourite helper

sears.ca

chapter 15
consumer decision making II: the outcomes—purchase, post-purchase

LEARNING OBJECTIVES

By the end of this chapter, you should be able to:

1. Explain the different types of purchase decisions that consumers have to make.
2. Discuss at least three outlet-related factors and how they affect consumers' purchase behaviour.
3. Discuss the four types of in-store decisions.
4. Discuss the five types of consumer gift-giving situations.
5. Explain the importance of consumption and the meanings that consumers attach to the acts of consumption and possession.
6. Define brand loyalty and identify four ways of creating brand loyalty.
7. Define post-purchase dissonance and ways of reducing it.
8. Define customer satisfaction and dissatisfaction, and explain how marketers can decrease customer dissatisfaction.
9. Define relationship marketing and ways in which marketers can establish a relationship with their customers.
10. Discuss the marketing strategy implications of consumer purchase and post-purchase processes.

15

the marketing team at Cavendish Farms knew they had a good product. The company's French fries were made from high-quality PEI potatoes. Consumer research had shown that the brand was a strong one, with consumers seeing Cavendish as a potato specialist. Yet, the company trailed market leader McCain in sales. Given the mergers and consolidations occurring in the industry, and the growth of private label brands, the company knew it had to do something to strengthen its brand.

Focus groups revealed that consumers saw French fries as not just fast food but as a product that "contributes to feelings of nostalgia, joy, fun, contentment, comfort, being together as a family and showing your family you care about them."[1] The company also found that consumers rated their brand highest on taste, and then on its appetizing golden yellow colour and consistent quality. However, the company was also seen as a little too laid back and not very innovative. But the main problem was to get consumers to try the brand.

www.cavendishfarms.
com

So Cossette Communication-Marketing, Cavendish's advertising agency, was asked to devise a set of new commercials that would position the brand as innovative and the product as tasty. Their solution? The "Sample Lady" commercials: entertaining, delivering the key product message (that it is tasty), and encouraging trial. The ads showed a father and son in a grocery store, where the father lets the son try one French fry from the sample lady. They both like the taste so much that they go back for more, but the sample lady doesn't let them try another sample. The father goes to elaborate lengths (e.g., switching off the store lights) and both dad and son are caught with their mouths full of fries. The commercial also led in nicely to in-store sampling, which triggered trial. The result? Post-advertising research found that brand awareness, trial, and use had all increased; the company exceeded its sales targets, and its market share showed significant gains.

CHAPTER OVERVIEW

This chapter deals with the outputs of the consumer decision-making process—purchase and post-purchase processes. We will begin the chapter with a look at how consumers go about the actual act of purchasing and the outlet factors that influence this process. In this part, we will also cover gift giving since it is a large part of consumer buying. We will also examine the meanings consumers assign to consuming and possessing products. Then, we will look at what happens after purchase—post-purchase dissonance, consumer satisfaction and dissatisfaction, and brand loyalty. Relationship marketing, which marketers use to foster customer satisfaction, will also be discussed. The chapter will end with the implications for marketing strategy of the outcomes of consumer decision making.

PURCHASE BEHAVIOUR

Purchase behaviour:
The outcome of a consumer's decision-making process, including brand, store, and payment option choices.

Purchase behaviour is the outcome of a consumer's decision-making process.

There are several types of purchase decisions that consumers have to make; at one level, consumers have to make brand choices, store choices, and payment option choices. They can also make the decision to make a trial purchase, go for a repeat purchase, or make long-term commitment purchases. We will look at these in more detail in this section.

Trial, Repeat, and Long-Term Commitment Purchases

When a consumer buys a product or brand for the first time and buys a smaller quantity than usual, this purchase would be considered a trial. Thus, a trial is the exploratory phase of purchase behaviour in which consumers attempt to evaluate a product through direct use. For instance, when people buy a new brand of laundry detergent about which they may be uncertain, they are likely to buy smaller trial quantities than if it were a familiar brand. Consumers can also be encouraged to try a new product through such promotional tactics as free samples (as in the case of Cavendish Farms French fries), coupons, and sale prices.

When a new brand in an established product category, such as toothpaste, chewing gum, or cola, is found by trial to be more satisfactory or better than other brands, consumers are likely to repeat the purchase. Repeat purchase behaviour is closely related to the concept of *brand loyalty,* which most firms try to encourage because it contributes to greater stability in the marketplace. Unlike trial (in which the consumer uses the product on a small scale and without any commitment), or even an initial purchase, a repeat purchase usually signifies that the product meets with the consumer's approval and that he or she is willing to use it again and in larger quantities.

Trial, of course, is not always feasible. For example, with most durable goods—refrigerators, washing machines, or electric ranges—a consumer usually moves directly from evaluation to a long-term commitment (through purchase) without the opportunity for an actual trial. While purchasers of the new Volkswagen Beetle were awaiting delivery of their just purchased cars, they were kept "warm" by being sent a mailing that included a psychographic tool called "Total Visual Imagery" that was personalized to the point that it showed them the precise model and colour they had ordered.[2]

It should be noted that some observers believe that eventually there will be almost universal internet access, at least in Canada and the United States. As a result, some authorities are forecasting that very soon, consumers will be buying food and other household staples through in-home television computer systems. Choices will be made by the shopper after viewing brands and prices on the screen. So the purchasing process itself may change dramatically in the coming decades.[3]

Consider Richard and his decision concerning the selection of an ultra-light laptop. There is really no way that he can try all three computers that he has been considering because the Toshiba Libretto L is not sold in traditional retail stores. So what does Richard do? First of all, a number of his co-workers use Dell laptops, and he knows that they are very good computers and come with a terrific warranty. He goes to one of his co-workers and tries out her Dell laptop. However, he decides that at 1.7 kilograms (3.7 pounds), the Dell Latitude C400 is just too heavy for his needs. Next, he calls several local computer retailers in the Edmonton area and finds a store that carries the Compaq Evo N200 and has one on display. On his lunch break, Richard visits this retailer and "plays" with the Compaq. He finds that, although the display is acceptable to him, the keyboard is too small for his hands. He also dislikes the fact that he would have to carry an external card for wireless internet access (Wi-Fi).

Now Richard starts to seriously consider the Toshiba Libretto L, a computer that he found listed on the Dynamism website. Let's start with the fact that this Libretto laptop, at 1 kilogram (2.4 pounds), admirably addresses the issue of weight and also offers a fairly speedy processor, a lot of memory, a good-sized hard drive, and more battery life than many other laptops (see Figure 14-7 in Chapter 14). And Richard likes the idea that not very many people have ever heard of or seen the Libretto (it's unique and he is, therefore, unique). However, he also has to be practical because his firm is going to be paying for it. Dynamism is not a traditional retailer selling traditional products—it offers a range of sub-notebooks that are available on the Japanese market and converts them for use by English-speaking consumers. These sub-notebook computers are often available in Japan up to one or two years before they may be offered by their manufacturers for sale in North America. And Dynamism is not the only place to buy such computers. Richard visits the eBay website and finds a few listings for the latest Toshiba Libretto L, some offering the machine for several hundred dollars less than Dynamism is asking. So what should Richard do?

www.ebay.ca

Richard next visits a Yahoo! chat room devoted to the Toshiba Libretto L computer. The computer series started with the Libretto L1 and progressed through a series of Ls. There are hundreds of postings on the websites with some owners asking questions and other owners providing answers. Richard reads dozens of these "chats" and decides that the Libretto L will meet his need for an ultra-light laptop. It also

http://groups.yahoo.com/group/libretto-L1

satisfies his desire to be unique. Users of the Libretto chat room are generally thrilled with the performance of the computer, and the keyboard was considered by a number of chat room participants to be outstanding. But now Richard must decide if he should save his firm a few hundred dollars by buying the computer on eBay or buy it through Dynamism. He posts this question to the chat room participants, and the overwhelming response is that the advantages of buying from Dynamism far outweigh the cost differential. Chat room participants praise Dynamism for the conversion job the firm does to make the computer usable to an English-speaking owner, provide stories of how the technical support staff at Dynamism helped them solve problems with this and other Japanese computers that they have owned, and how Dynamism's warranty is worth its weight in gold. Consequently, Richard decides to buy the current Toshiba Libretto L from Dynamism, along with a spare battery and an external CD-RW drive. Three days after placing the order, the FedEx second-day air package from Dynamism is sitting on his office desk.

Brand Choice, Store Choice, and Payment Option Choices

Not only do consumers have to decide on a brand (using decision rules discussed in the previous chapter), but they also have to decide where to buy the chosen

EXHIBIT 15-1

SEARS POSITIONS ITSELF AS A CHRISTMAS GIFT STORE

Courtesy of Sears Canada.

brand and how to pay for it. Although for the purposes of discussion, we have divided them into three separate categories, these choices are often interrelated and may occur in varying sequences. For example, consumers may decide on a store first and then decide on a brand once they are in the store; or they may decide on a brand first and try to find a store that carries that brand at a reasonable price or provides other benefits, such as good after-sales service. Both the choice of the store and the brand may be influenced by the type of payment options available.

Store-first decisions are made when the consumer's evoked set consists of stores rather than brands. For example, if a consumer is in need of a toaster, then he or she is likely to think about stores that are good places to buy such products (e.g., Wal-Mart, Zellers, The Bay, and Sears), will decide on a store first, and will then choose from among the brands available in that store. (Exhibit 15-1 shows an ad by Sears which attempts to position it as the store for buying Christmas presents for everyone on your list.) For other purchases, the same consumer might first decide on a brand (e.g., a Sony big-screen television) and then look at stores that carry the brand, note the prices in each store, and choose the store that has the lowest price and/or the best after-sales service.

When firms are devising their marketing strategy, they should consider whether consumers choose a store first or a brand. If consumers are deciding on the store first, then a manufacturer has to

- make sure that the product is distributed in all the outlets for that product category;
- develop good point-of-purchase materials and in-store promotional materials;
- make efforts to secure good shelf space in the main outlets; and
- work with retailers to strengthen co-operative advertising programs.

If, however, consumers choose the brand first, then marketers can focus on

- exclusive distribution in a few prominent outlets; and
- developing brand image through promotion.

Finally, some consumer purchases are driven by the availability of flexible payment options. This is particularly true of big ticket items such as cars, furniture, and major appliances. For such items, marketers have to ensure that their payment options are similar to (or better than) those offered by their competitors. "Buy now, pay later," or "No payments until next January," or "No money down" are payment options aimed at making purchase easier and a company's brand more attractive to consumers.

www.retailcouncil.org

As mentioned earlier, it is important to remember that consumers may make brand and store choices sequentially (in any order) or at the same time. In other words, consumers may go to a particular store without having decided on a brand or having decided to buy from that store. Both brand and store choices could be made simultaneously. For example, while in the market for a computer, a consumer might decide to go to Future Shop first (because it is the closest store) with the intention of then going to Business Depot-Staples, and with no brand in mind. But at the store, a Compaq laptop on sale might catch the consumer's eye, and he might buy it on the spot. Here, both store choice and brand choice are being made at the same time.

www.staples.ca

Since store choice is a large part of a consumer's purchase decision, the next section will examine how retail store image, retail environment, and other factors influence consumer decision making.

OUTLET FACTORS AND PURCHASE

Several factors related to the retail store influence consumer decision making, especially purchase. Retailers have a major role to play in the actual shopping experience; the retail store image and retail environment are key factors that shape consumers' purchase decisions. We will discuss each of these in this section.

Retail Store Image

Retail stores have images of their own that serve to influence the perceived quality of products they carry and the decisions of consumers as to where to shop. These images stem from the stores' design and physical environment, pricing strategies, promotional strategies, and product assortments. A study that examined the effects of specific store environmental factors on quality inferences found that consumer perceptions were more heavily influenced by ambient factors (such as the number, type, and behaviour of other customers in the store and the sales personnel) than by store design features.[4]

www.sears.ca

Retailers are finding it increasingly difficult to be all things to all people and still be successful. Large retailers such as The Bay and Sears, which offer a wide range of products and are known as "middle-of-the-road" department stores, are being squeezed by discounters like Wal-Mart on one side and specialty chains such as Winners and Home Depot on the other side. These stores have retaliated by opening their own specialty stores: Hudson's Bay has opened Home Outfitters, and Sears has opened several furniture and appliance specialty stores.[5]

Pricing Strategies and Retail Image

A study of retail store image based on comparative *pricing strategies* found that consumers tend to perceive stores that offer a small discount on a large number of items (i.e., *frequency of price advantage*) as having lower prices overall than competing stores that offer larger discounts on a smaller number of products (i.e., *magnitude of price advantage*). Thus, frequent advertising that presents large numbers of price specials reinforces consumer beliefs about the competitiveness of a store's prices.[6] This finding has important implications for retailers' *positioning strategies*. In times of heavy competition, when it is tempting to hold frequent, large sales covering many items, such strategies may result in an unwanted change in store image. Lord and Taylor's in New York, formerly positioned as an upscale, high-class department store, advertises sales so often and has so many aisles filled with sales racks proclaiming bargain prices, that its upscale image has been tarnished, and its customer mix has changed.

Product Assortment and Retail Image

The width of product assortment also affects retail store image. Grocery retailers, for example, are often reluctant to reduce the number of products they carry for fear that the smaller assortment will make consumers less likely to shop in their stores.[7] Conversely, Whole Foods Markets—a relatively small supermarket chain—has carved out a profitable niche for itself by carrying a much smaller but more highly selective range of products than conventional supermarkets. Whole Foods stores carry organic products (perceived as more healthful), many of which are bought from mom-and-pop producers; all food products carried are screened for artificial ingredients; and the chain is phasing out all food containing hydrogenated fats. The chain has been much more profitable than conventional supermarkets in spite of its limited product assortment.[8] Clearly, the unique benefit that a store provides is more important than the number of items it carries in forming a favourable store image in consumers' minds.

The type of product the consumer wishes to buy influences his or her selection of a retail outlet. And conversely, the consumer's evaluation of a product is often influenced by the knowledge of where it was bought. A woman wishing to buy an elegant dress for a special occasion may go to a store with an elegant, high-fashion image. Regardless of what she actually pays for the dress she chooses, she will probably consider its quality to be high. However, she may consider the quality of the identical dress to be much lower if she buys it in an off-price store with a low-price image.

Most studies of the effects of extrinsic cues on perceived product quality have focused on just one variable—either price *or* store image. However, when a second extrinsic cue is available (such as price *and* store image), perceived quality is sometimes a function of the interaction of both cues. For example, when brand and retailer images become associated, the less favourable image becomes enhanced at the expense of the more favourable image. Thus, when a low-priced store carries a brand with a high-priced image, the image of the store will improve, whereas the image of the brand will be adversely affected. For that reason, marketers of prestigious designer goods often attempt to control the outlets where these products are sold. Also, when upscale stores sell leftover expensive items to discount stores, they remove the designer labels from these goods as part of the agreements they have with the manufacturers of these products.

Although the retail environment affects the retail store's image, it is discussed separately in the next section because it is a variable that shapes where and how many purchases are made by a consumer.

Retail Environment

Several factors affect the consumer's shopping experience but the most important is perhaps the retail environment. The environment in a retail store is affected by the layout of the store, in-store stimuli, and, to some extent, its location. We will discuss these in more detail in the following sections.

Store Layout

A retail store's layout can have significant impact on the route a consumer takes in the store; this, in turn, affects the number of items that the consumer gets to see and the length of time that a consumer spends in the store. There are several store layouts, but the most common ones are the grid layout and the free-form layout. In the grid layout, there are well-defined parallel aisles at regular intervals; at the back of the store are rows at right angles to the aisles. Grid layouts are used in supermarkets to make the shoppers go through the aisles and force them to go to the sides and the back of the store where meat, dairy, and produce are kept. This layout is also used in department stores (especially low-end ones).

www.ikea.ca

In the free-form layout, items are grouped together by type in a way that encourages unstructured flow of traffic. Signs and fixtures help consumers see where items are placed. In a free-form layout, the entire store is visible to the consumer. This feature makes it more suitable for smaller stores such as specialty stores and boutiques. This layout also makes it possible for store personnel to see the customers while they are shopping and to guide them to the various parts of the store.

In-Store Stimuli

In-store stimuli such as the signs used, lighting, music, colours, shelf space, width of aisles, displays, and scent affect consumers' impressions of the store and their purchase behaviour. For example, research shows that when an item is on sale, having a sale price sign and a benefits sign (what the product can do for you) increases sales more than either sign alone.[9] Similarly, the colours used in a store can have a strong influence on consumers' shopping behaviour. One study found that although consumers preferred warm colours (e.g., red and yellow), these colours made consumers make quick decisions and not linger in the store. The researchers suggest that cool colours may be better suited to retail stores, or sections of retail stores (e.g., clothing), where consumers have to deliberate and think through the various options presented.[10]

Wal-Mart Canada recently conducted a large study, the Customer Understanding Project, to understand how consumers react to in-store signs. The company employed a qualitative research method for the project; it followed 20 consumers for one hour as they shopped in a Wal-Mart, interviewing them as they worked their way through the store. Results indicated that consumers wanted better placement of signs (at eye level), less clutter, and more "goosenecks" or signs that stick out every eight feet or so, which would let them see what is in an aisle without having to walk through it.[11]

Music and scent also affect consumers' impressions of the store and their in-store behaviour. Research has found that slow music makes consumers move more slowly through the store than fast music. Interestingly enough, this slower movement also led to increased sales (38.2 percent percent).[12] Finally, the type of scent used in a store can influence consumer behaviour. Ambient scent or scent that is present in the store environment (as opposed to scent from products in the store) can influence a consumer's perception of the store. One study found that scents such as lavender, ginger, spearmint, and orange had an influence on how consumers evaluated the store and its products.[13]

In-Store Decisions

As the above discussion indicates, in-store stimuli seem to have a major impact on consumer decision making. In fact, research has found that a huge proportion of consumer purchase decisions are actually made in the store.[14] Consumer decisions made in the store can be classified into three categories:

- *Generally planned*—product category decided on before entering the store, but specific brand or item not decided on. For example, a consumer might have decided to buy a dessert but not the exact type or brand.

- *Substitute purchases*—one brand or product is substituted for another because of lack of availability, better options, or other reasons. For example, even if the customer had decided to buy ice cream for dessert and normally buys Farmer's ice cream (a Maritime brand), she might find that Breyer's is on sale and might decide to try it instead.

- *Totally unplanned*—this includes impulse purchases (e.g., candy or magazines at the checkout counter), ones that were not on the list but are items the consumer might have bought anyway, and purchases that were not planned but carried out as a result of in-store promotions. For example, many of us have, at one time or another, bought things that were on sale because the price was attractive and after thinking about it, we felt that it was something we would need soon (e.g., a winter coat that is on sale and our old one is in bad shape).

www.popai.com

In fact, research by Point of Purchase Advertising International (POPAI) shows that 60 percent of supermarket purchases and 53 percent of department store purchases are unplanned ones and are the result of in-store decisions. If substitute purchases and generally planned purchases are added to this list, then nearly 70 percent of supermarket purchase decisions and 74 percent of department store decisions are made in the store.[15] Of course, some products are more likely to be in-store decisions than others. For example, purchases of magazines, first aid products, hair care products, and motor oil were found to be more likely than the average product to be in-store decisions.[16] This indicates that marketers need to focus on retail-level promotions and have to take product category and type of retail outlet into consideration when making these decisions.

CONSUMER GIFT BEHAVIOUR

In terms of both dollars spent each year and how they make givers and receivers feel, gifts are a particularly interesting part of consumer behaviour. Products and services chosen as gifts represent more than ordinary everyday purchases. Because of their symbolic meaning, they are associated with such important events as Mother's Day, births and birthdays, engagements, weddings, graduations, and many other accomplishments and milestones.

Gifting behaviour has been defined as "the process of *gift exchange* that takes place between a giver and a recipient."[17]. The definition is broad and embraces gifts given voluntarily ("just to let you know I'm thinking of you"), as well as gifts that are an obligation ("I had to get him a gift").[18] It includes gifts given to (and received from) others and gifts to ourselves, or **self-gifts.** Indeed, although almost all Canadians bought at least one "gift" last year, the majority of products that we refer to as "gifts" are bought by the purchaser for herself or himself.[19] Furthermore, gift purchases represent 10 percent of all retail purchases in Canada and the United States.[20]

The giving of presents is an act of symbolic communication, with explicit and implicit meanings ranging from congratulations, love, and regret to obligation and dominance. The nature of the relationship between giver and gift receiver is an important consideration in choosing a gift. Indeed, gift giving often affects the relationship between the giver and the recipient.[21] Figure 15-1 enumerates of the relationships between various combinations of gift givers and gift receivers in the consumer gifting process. The model reveals the following five gifting subdivisions: (1) inter-group gifting, (2) inter-category gifting, (3) intra-group gifting, (4) inter-personal gifting, and (5) intra-personal gifting.

Inter-group gifting behaviour occurs whenever one group exchanges gifts with another group (such as one family with another). You will recall from Chapter 12 that the process and outcome of family decision making is different from individual decision making. Similarly, gifts given to families will be different from those given to individual family members. For example, a "common" wedding gift for a bride *and* a groom may include products for setting up a household rather than a present

Gifting behaviour:
The process of exchanging gifts between two or more individuals.

Self-gifts:
Gifts to ourselves.

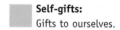

FIGURE 15-1	Five Giver-Receiver Subdivisions

		RECEIVERS "OTHER"	
GIVERS	INDIVIDUAL	GROUP	SELF[a]
Individual	Interpersonal gifting	Inter-category gifting	Intra-personal gifting
Group	Inter-category gifting	Inter-group gifting	Intra-group gifting

[a] This "self" can be either singular self ("me") or plural ("us").

Source: Based on Deborah Y. Cohn and Leon G. Schiffman, "Gifting: A Taxonomy of Private Realm Giver and Recipient Relationships," Working Paper, City University of New York, Baruch College, 1996, 2–7.

Inter-category gifting: Gifts from an individual to a group or from a group to an individual.

that would personally be used by either the bride *or* the groom. When it comes to **inter-category gifting**, either an individual is giving a gift to a group (a single friend is giving a couple an anniversary gift) or a group is giving an individual a present (friends chip in and give another friend a joint birthday present). The gift selection strategies "buy for joint recipients" or "buy with someone" (creating inter-category gifting) are especially useful when the recipient is difficult to buy for.[22] These strategies can also reduce some of the time pressure associated with shopping for the great number of presents exchanged during the Canadian ritual of giving Christmas presents. For example, a consumer may choose to buy five inter-category presents for five aunt and uncle pairs (inter-category gifting) instead of buying 10 personal gifts for five aunts and five uncles (interpersonal gifting). In this way, less time, money, and effort may be expended.

Intra-group gifting: Gifts by a group to itself or its members.

An **intra-group gift** can be characterized by the sentiment "we gave this to ourselves"; that is, a group gives a present to itself or its members. For example, a two-income couple may find that their demanding work schedules limit the time they can spend together as husband and wife. Therefore, they might give themselves an anniversary present of a Caribbean vacation; that would be an intra-group gift. It would also remedy the couple's problem of not spending enough time together. In contrast, **interpersonal gifting** occurs between just two individuals, a giver and a receiver. By their very nature, interpersonal gifts are "intimate" because they are an opportunity for the giver to reveal what he or she thinks of the recipient. Successful gifts are those that communicate that the giver knows and understands the receiver and their relationship. For example, a pair of earrings given to a friend in just the right shape and size can mean that "he really knows me." In contrast, a toaster oven given as a Valentine's Day present, when the recipient is expecting a more "intimate" gift, can mean the deterioration of a relationship.[23]

Interpersonal gifting: Gifts exchanged between individuals.

Researchers have found that both male and female gift givers feel more comfortable in giving gifts to the same sex. However, givers of both sexes reported that they felt more intensely about presents they gave to members of the opposite sex.[24] Additionally, although women get more pleasure than men from giving presents and generally play the dominant role in gift exchanges, both sexes are strongly motivated by feelings of obligation.[25] Moreover, research has also found that interpersonal giving can be the cause of "gifting anxiety" (which is related to social anxiety) on the part of the givers, the recipients, and the gift situations themselves.[26] A knowledge of such gender differences is useful for marketers because it implies that additional help might be appreciated at the point of purchase when a shopper is considering a gift for someone of the opposite sex.

Gift giving behaviour is influenced by a society's values and traditions. One study examined the giving of presents to their children by mothers (*interpersonal gifting*) in three different cultures: (1) Anglo-Celtic (mothers born in Australia), (2) Sino-Vietnamese (mothers born in Vietnam), and (3) Israeli (mothers born in Israel).[27] Whereas in all three of these cultures the mother plays a central role in family gift giving, there were important differences (see Figure 15-2). Anglo-Celtic mothers were found to choose status or prestige gifts, whereas Sino-Vietnamese mothers were likely to pick practical gifts, and Israeli mothers tended to select gifts that they felt would be important to the recipient.

Self-gifting Behaviour

Intra-personal gifting: Gifts given to ourselves.

Intra-personal gifting, or a self-gift (also called "monadic giving"), occurs when the giver and the receiver are the same individual.[28] To some extent a present to oneself is a "state of mind." If a consumer sees a purchase as the buying of something he or

FIGURE 15-2	Major Differences in Gift Giving across Three Cultures

GIFT-GIVING ELEMENTS	ANGLO-CELTIC MOTHERS	SINO-VIETNAMESE MOTHERS	ISRAELI MOTHERS
1. Motivation			
Justification	Short-term goals	Long-term goals	Long-term/short-term goals
Significance	Prestige gifts	Practical gifts	Importance to recipient
	Birthday gifts	Lucky money	
Timing	Special occasions (e.g., birthdays, Christmas)	Chinese New Year and academic reward	Birthdays and general needs
2. Selection			
Involvement	High priority	Low priority	Low priority
	Social and psychological risks	Financial risks	
Family Influences	Children	Mother	Mother dominant with younger children and influenced by older children
Promotional Influences	Status symbols	Sale items	Sale items
Gift Attributes	Quality	Price	Price
	Money unsuitable	Money suitable	Money suitable
3. Presentation			
Presentation Messages	Immediate self-gratification	Delayed self-gratification	Immediate self-gratification
Allocation Messages	Multiple gifts	Single gifts	Single gifts
	Mothers favoured	Eldest child favoured	
Understanding of Messages	Always	Not always	Never
4. Reaction			
Achievement	Often	Most of the time	Never
Feedback	More expressive	Less expressive	Least expressive
Usage	Often private	Often shared	Never shared

Source: Constance Hill and Celia T. Romm, "The Role of Mothers as Gift Givers: A Comparison Across Three Cultures," in *Advances in Consumer Research,* 23, ed. Kim P. Corfman and John G. Lynch, Jr. (Provo, UT: Association for Consumer Research, 1996), 26. Reprinted by permission.

she needs, then it is simply a purchase. However, if the same person sees the same purchase as a present to him- or herself, it is something special, with special meaning. People may treat themselves to presents that are products (such as clothing, compact discs, or jewellery), services (such as hair styling, restaurant meals, or spa membership), or experiences (such as socializing with friends).[29] For example, while buying Christmas presents for other people, some consumers find themselves in stores that they might not otherwise visit or find themselves looking at merchandise that they want but would not ordinarily buy, and they take the opportunity to buy a present for themselves.[30] Such intra-personal gifts have their own special range of meaning and context. Figure 15-3 illustrates specific circumstances and motivations that might lead a consumer to buy a gift for himself or herself. Research has found that when college students had the money to spend and when

FIGURE 15-3   Circumstances and Motivation for Self-Gift Behaviour

CIRCUMSTANCE	MOTIVATION
Personal accomplishment	To reward oneself
Feeling down	To be nice to oneself
Holiday	To cheer oneself up
Feeling stressed	To fulfill a need
Have some extra money	To celebrate
Need	To relieve stress
Had not bought for self in a while	To maintain a good feeling
Attainment of a desired goal	To provide an incentive toward a goal
Others	Others

Source: David Glen Mick and Mitchelle DeMoss, "To Me from Me: A Descriptive Phenomenology of Self-Gifts," in *Advances in Consumer Research*, 23. Marvin E. Goldberg, Gerald Gorn, and Richard W. Pollay, ed. (Provo, UT: Association for Consumer Research, 1990), 677–682. Reprinted by permission.

they either felt good or wanted to cheer themselves up, they were particularly likely to buy presents for themselves.[31]

Figure 15-4 summarizes the five gifting behaviour subdivisions discussed earlier.

The internet has had considerable impact on gift giving in Canada. By 2002, Canadians were spending nearly a billion dollars buying presents on the internet. (See Internet Insight 15-1.)

BEYOND THE DECISION: CONSUMING AND POSSESSING

Historically, the emphasis in consumer behaviour studies has been on product, service, and brand choice decisions. As shown throughout this book, however, there are many more facets to consumer behaviour. The experience of using products and services, as well as the pleasure of *possessing, collecting,* or *consuming* "things" and

FIGURE 15-4   Gifting Relationship Categories

GIFTING RELATIONSHIP	DEFINITION	EXAMPLE
Inter-group	A group giving a gift to another group	A Christmas gift from one family to another family
Inter-category	An individual giving a gift to a group or a group giving a gift to an individual	A group of friends chips in to buy a new mother a baby gift
Intra-group	A group giving a gift to itself or its members	A family buys a VCR for itself as a Christmas gift
Interpersonal	An individual giving a gift to another individual	Boyfriend gives Valentine's Day chocolates to a girlfriend
Intra-personal	Self-gift	A woman buys herself jewellery to cheer herself up

Source: Adapted from Deborah Y. Cohn and Leon G. Schiffman, "Gifting: A Taxonomy of Private Realm Giver and Recipient Relationships," Working Paper, City University of New York, Baruch College, 1996, 2.

INTERNET INSIGHT 15-1
INTERNET AND CONSUMER GIFT GIVING

What do you do to make your Christmas shopping easier? Do you go online and buy some presents from web-based retailers? Or are you one who prefers brick-and-mortar stores?

The internet was expected to change Canadians' gift buying habits significantly. And though many of us have turned to online stores to help reduce the stress we face at Christmastime, most Canadians seem to still prefer buying from a traditional retailer. Compared with our American counterparts, Canadians have been reluctant to buy gifts online. During the 2003 holiday season, Canadians spent $972 million online buying presents, but the amount was practically the same as they spent in 2002—in fact, it was marginally lower (the 2002 figure was $990 million). Americans, however, increased their online gift purchases by about 30 percent between 2002 and 2003.

The figures are surprising, because Canadians are world leaders in internet access and online banking. What makes the lower gift purchases even more interesting is the fact that online shopping increased from 39 percent of internet subscribers in 2002 to 47 percent in 2003. Of course, this is much lower than the American figure of 75 percent. Why don't Canadians shop online for gifts? Perhaps the Canadian conservatism and risk-averseness has something to do with this phenomenon. As a nation, we seem to be more concerned with security issues related to online shopping, which might explain our reluctance to do our gift shopping online. It is also quite likely that we like the personal touch that retail shopping provides. (Although some Canadians liked the fact that online shopping let them avoid contact with retail salespeople, an almost equal number missed this contact.) Finally, perhaps we just like going to the shopping mall more than our American counterparts do!

When they do buy gifts online, what do Canadians buy? Books are the most often purchased online gift item; nearly a third of online gift purchases were books. CDs or music (25 percent), DVDs or videos (18 percent), and toys or games (16 percent) are the next most popular online gift items. All of these are items that need not be touched, seen, or experienced before purchase; furthermore, these items, especially CDs, DVDs, and toys, are sold in sealed packages in stores and hence can only be experienced to the same extent in a retail environment. Perhaps these factors account for the popularity of these products as online gifts.

Source: This Internet Insight is based on an Ipsos-Reid article entitled "Canadian Online Gift Purchasing Flat During 2003 Holiday Season," January 19, 2004.

"experiences" (mechanical watches, old fountain pens, or a baseball card collection) contributes to consumer satisfaction and overall quality of life. These consumption outcomes or experiences, in turn, affect consumers' future decision processes.

Thus, given the importance of possessions and experiences, a broader perspective of consumer behaviour might view consumer choices as the beginning of a **consumption process**, not merely the end of a consumer decision-making effort. In this context, the choice or purchase decision is an *input* into a process of consumption. The input stage includes the establishment of a *consumption set* (an assortment or portfolio of products and their attributes) and a *consuming style* (the "rules" by which the individual or household fulfills consumption requirements). The *process* stage of a simple model of consumption might include, from the consumer's perspective, the *using, possessing* (or having), *collecting,* and *disposing of* things and experiences. The output stage of this process would include changes in a wide range of feelings, moods, attitudes, and behaviour, as well as reinforcement (positive or negative) of a particular life style (e.g., a devotion to physical fitness), enhancement of a sense of self, and the level of consumer satisfaction and quality of life.[32] Figure 15-5 presents a simple *model of consumption* that reflects the ideas discussed here and throughout the book.

Consumption process: The input (consumption set and consuming style), process (using, possessing, collecting, and disposing of), and output stages (feelings moods, attitudes, and behaviour) that follow the purchase decision.

FIGURE 15-5   A Simple Model of Consumption

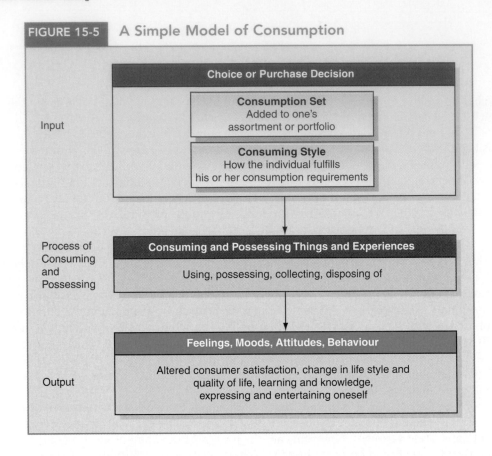

Products Have Special Meaning and Memories

Consuming is a diverse and complex concept.[33] It includes the simple utility derived from the continued use of a superior toothpaste, the relaxation of an island holiday, the stored memories of a video from childhood, the "sacred" meaning or "magic" of a grandparent's wristwatch, the symbol of membership gained from wearing a school tie, the pleasure and sense of accomplishment that comes from building a model airplane, and the fun and even financial rewards that come from collecting almost anything (even jokers from decks of cards). In fact, one man's hobby of collecting old earthenware drain tiles has become the Mike Weaver Drain Tile Museum.[34] There are special possessions that consumers resist replacing, even with an exact replica, because the replica cannot possibly hold the same meaning as the original. Such possessions are often tied, in the consumer's mind, to a specific physical time or person.[35]

www.swatch.com

Consider how some consumers have a fascination with Swatch watches. For example, there is the story of how one woman hid in a department store for the lunch shift so that the person filling in at the Swatch counter would sell her a second Swatch watch, or the man who paid someone $100 to stand in line overnight in front of a New York City food store where 999 special edition Swatch watches were to go on sale the next morning. Such collecting can be "both rational and irrational, deliberate and uncontrollable, cooperative and competitive, passive and aggressive, and tension producing and tension reducing."[36] In fact, with respect to Swatch watches, the company has changed its "limited-edition" strategy from offering 30 000 pieces worldwide to now offering certain designs in only a single outlet.[37]

Some possessions (such as photographs, souvenirs, trophies, and everyday objects) help people to create "personal meaning" and to maintain a sense of the past, which is essential for a sense of self.[38] For instance, objects from the past are often acquired and saved intentionally (some become antiques or even heirlooms) to memorialize pleasant or momentous times and people in one's past.

Why are some consumers so interested in the past? It has been suggested that nostalgia permits people to maintain their identity after some major change in their life. This nostalgia can be based on family and friends; on objects such as toys, books, jewellery, and cars; or on special events, such as graduations, weddings, and holidays.[39] Providing the triple benefits of a sense of nostalgia, the fun of collecting and the attraction of a potential return on investment, there is a strong interest in collecting Barbie dolls. It is estimated that there are more than 100 000 Barbie doll collectors, who are dedicated to hunting down rare and valuable Barbie dolls to add to their collections.

And it appears that you're never too young to start collecting, as evidenced by the following story about a child who started collecting at the age of two:[40]

> Cars have always interested Kevin LaLuzerne, a fifth-grader at Oakhurst Elementary in Largo. He has boxes and boxes of Hot Wheels, Micro Machines, and other cars—more than 600! He started collecting them when he was just two, and he still enjoys seeing all of the different cars and trucks he has collected over the years. He even has a "Weinermobile," the Oscar Meyer hot dog car. Kevin's newest addition to his collection is a limited-edition Chevron car that has a cartoon mouth, eyes, and ears.

Even the Smithsonian gives tips on collecting. They have developed a website designed to teach children how to start and care for a collection.[41]

http://kids.si.edu/collecting

At the other end of the age continuum, older consumers are often faced with the problem of how they should dispose of such special possessions. Indeed, in the past several years, a number of researchers have examined this subject. Sometimes it is some precipitating event, such as the death of a spouse, illness, or moving to a nursing home or retirement community, that gets a person thinking about how to dispose of his or her possessions. Often the older person wants to pass a family legacy on to a child, ensure a good home for a cherished collection, or influence the lives of others.[42]

Brand Loyalty

Brand loyalty is the ultimate outcome of consumer learning and decision making that is desired by marketers. However, there is no single definition of this concept. The varied definitions of brand loyalty reflect the varied models of consumer learning and information processing that were covered in Chapter 6. They are summarized in Figure 15-6, together with their shortcomings and weaknesses in the context of potential competitive responses.

Behavioural scientists, who favour the theory of instrumental conditioning, believe that brand loyalty results from an initial product trial that is reinforced through satisfaction, leading to repeat purchase. *Cognitive* researchers, however, emphasize the role of mental processes in building brand loyalty. They believe that consumers engage in extensive problem-solving behaviour involving brand and attribute comparisons, leading to a strong brand preference and repeat purchase behaviour. A recent study maintains that linking consumer satisfaction only to brand loyalty, as many marketers do, is shortsighted. The researchers argue that brand loyalty is a combination of interrelated attitudinal components, such as

Brand loyalty:
Consistent preference and/or purchase of the same brand in a specific product/service category.

FIGURE 15-6	Definitions of Brand Loyalty and Their Shortcomings	
STAGE	**IDENTIFYING MARKER**	**VULNERABILITIES**
Cognitive	Loyalty to information such as price, features, and so forth.	Actual or imagined better competitive features or price through communication (e.g., advertising) and vicarious or personal experience. Deterioration in brand features or price. Variety seeking and voluntary trial.
Affective	Loyalty to a liking: "I buy it because I like it."	Cognitively induced dissatisfaction. Enhanced liking for competitive brands, perhaps conveyed through imagery and association. Variety seeking and voluntary trial. Deteriorating performance.
Conative	Loyalty to an intention: "I'm committed to buying it."	Persuasive counter-argumentative competitive messages. Induced trial (e.g., coupons, sampling, point-of-purchase promotions). Deteriorating performance.
Action	Loyalty to action, coupled with the overcoming of obstacles.	Induced unavailability (e.g., stocklifts—purchasing the entire inventory of a competitor's product from a merchant). Increased obstacles generally. Deteriorating performance.

Source: Richard L. Oliver, "Whence Brand Loyalty?" *Journal of Marketing,* 63, 1999, 33–44.

perceived product superiority, personal fortitude, and bonding with the product or company.[43] However, we must not discount the value of satisfaction alone. A syndicated research company reported that 74 percent of its respondents resist promotional efforts by rival brands once they find a brand they are satisfied with.[44]

Behavioural definitions, such as frequency of purchase or proportion of total purchases, lack precision, because they do not distinguish between the "real" brand-loyal buyer who is intentionally faithful and the spurious brand-loyal buyer who repeats a brand purchase because it is the only one available at the store. Often consumers buy a variety of brands within their acceptable range (i.e., their *evoked set*, see Chapter 14). The greater the number of acceptable brands in a specific product category, the less likely the consumer is to be loyal to one specific brand. Conversely, products having few competitors, as well as those purchased with great frequency, are likely to have greater brand loyalty. Thus, a more favourable attitude toward a brand, service, or store, compared with potential alternatives, together with repeat patronage, are seen as the requisite components of customer loyalty. A recent study related the attitudinal and purchase aspects of brand loyalty to market share and the relative prices of brands. The study showed that brand trust and brand affect, combined, determine purchase loyalty and attitudinal loyalty. Purchase loyalty leads to a higher market share, and attitudinal loyalty often enables the marketer to charge a higher price for the brand relative to the competition.[45]

An integrated conceptual framework views consumer loyalty as the relationship between an individual's relative attitude toward an entity (brand, service, and store or vendor) and patronage behaviour.[46] The consumer's relative attitude consists of two dimensions: the strength of the attitude and the degree of attitudinal differentiation among competing brands. As Figure 15-7 shows, a consumer with a high relative attitude and high degree of repeat purchase behaviour would be defined as *brand-loyal;* a consumer with a low relative attitude and high repeat patronage would be considered *spuriously loyal.* This framework also shows a correlation between brand loyalty and consumer involvement. High involvement leads to extensive information search and, ultimately, to brand loyalty, whereas low involvement leads to exposure and brand awareness and then possibly to brand habit (or spurious loyalty). Spuriously loyal consumers see little difference among brands and buy the same brand repeatedly because of situational cues, such as package familiarity, shelf positioning, or special prices. Conversely, truly brand-loyal consumers have a strong commitment to the brand and are less likely to switch to other brands in spite of the persuasive, promotional efforts of competitors.

Are Canadians loyal to their brand of beer? That depends on how you define brand loyalty and whether you are talking about Canadians in general or those in particular regions of the country. Although 74 percent were really loyal to their favourite brand of beer, further investigation into brand-switching behaviour indicates that only some of these consumers are truly brand-loyal. There are quite a few Canadians who are repeat buyers of a brand but who would switch for a promotional offer from another brand; that indicates that there is some spurious brand loyalty. Brand switching varies from one region to another. Atlantic Canadians are the most likely ones to switch brands for a promotional offer (42 percent), and Ontarians are not far behind (41 percent). Quebeckers are the most committed beer drinkers; 70 percent of them said "no way" when asked if they would switch brands for a promotional offer.[47]

Unlike tangible products where switching to another brand is relatively easy, it is often difficult to switch to another "brand" of service. For example, it is costly and time consuming to transfer one's business to a new lawyer or accountant or even to get used to a new hair dresser. One study showed that the reasons that customers switch service providers play a role in their loyalty toward subsequent providers. Thus, service marketers should research past customer behaviour and use these data to increase the loyalty of new customers.[48]

Loyalty programs are generally designed with the intention of forming and maintaining brand loyalty. One researcher argues that the objective of a sound loyalty program should be to build loyalty to the brand and product and not just the program itself. The study classifies loyalty programs into the four groups shown in Figure 15-8. The researcher argues that customers prefer immediate-gratification programs (see sections 1 and 3 of the figure) to programs with delayed gratification (sections 2 and 4). However, marketers prefer programs that explicitly link the product and the program (sections 1 and 2) because they have a greater influence on purchase behaviour.[49] It is essential to consider both perspectives in designing a

FIGURE 15-7   Brand Loyalty as a Function of Relative Attitude and Patronage Behaviour

Source: Alan S. Dick and Kunal Basu, "Customer Loyalty: Toward an Integrated Conceptual Framework," *Journal of the Academy of Marketing Science,* 22, 2 (1994), 101. Copyright © 1994 by *Journal of the Academy of Marketing Science.* Reprinted by permission of Sage Publications.

| FIGURE 15-8 | Four Kinds of Loyalty Programs |

Timing of Reward

		Immediate	Delayed
Directly Supports the Product's Value Position		**1** Retailer/Brand Manufacturer Promotions (Price Promotions)	**2** Airline Frequent Flyer Clubs, Coupons, and Tokens (GM card)
Type of Reward Other Indirect Types of Reward		**3** Competitions and Lotteries (Instant Scratches)	**4** Multiproduct Frequent Buyer Clubs (Fly Buys)

Source: Grahame R. Dowling and Mark Uncles, "Do Customer Loyalty Programs Really Work?" *Sloan Management Review,* Summer 1997, 71–82.

loyalty program. Another study points out that loyalty programs for packaged goods are more effective when they offer more knowledge about the brand and increase the association between the loyalty program and the brand.[50]

Measuring Brand Loyalty

Given the variations in definitions of brand loyalty, how can marketers measure the level of brand loyalty of their customers? Marketers agree that brand loyalty consists of both attitudes and actual behaviour toward a brand and that both must be measured. *Attitudinal measures* are concerned with consumers' overall feelings (i.e., evaluation) about the product and the brand and their purchase intentions. *Behavioural measures* are based on observable responses to promotional stimuli—repeat purchase behaviour rather than attitude toward the product or brand. So marketers who use behavioural measures ask for (1) number of repeat purchases of a brand within a certain purchase period and (2) number of brands that were considered as potential buys.

A recent study pointed out that marketers must distinguish between two attitudinal measures of brand loyalty; the study demonstrated that the degree of commitment toward buying the brand and the propensity to be brand-loyal are two *separate* dimensions but did not conclusively determine which construct is more useful for explaining buying behaviour.[51]

Research Insight 15-1 provides more details on measuring brand loyalty.

POST-PURCHASE EVALUATION

As consumers use a product, particularly during a trial purchase, they evaluate its performance in light of their own expectations. There are three possible outcomes of these evaluations: (1) actual performance matches expectations, leading to a neutral feeling; (2) performance exceeds expectations, causing what is known as *positive disconfirmation of expectations* (which leads to satisfaction); and (3) performance is below expectations, causing *negative disconfirmation of expectations* and dissatisfaction.[52] For each of these three outcomes, consumers' expectations and satisfaction are closely linked; that is, consumers tend to judge their experience against their expectations when performing a post-purchase evaluation. We will examine consumer satisfaction and dissatisfaction in more detail later in this chapter.

RESEARCH INSIGHT 15-1
TWO ATTITUDINAL MEASURES OF BRAND LOYALTY

Although marketers agree that attitudinal measures of brand loyalty are important, there is no agreement on the attitudes that need to be measured. Should we be measuring attitude toward the act of purchasing or attitude toward being loyal to the brand? Each of these tools measures slightly different aspects of brand loyalty. Attitude toward the act of purchasing the brand is probably a measure of the tendency to buy the brand repeatedly; the propensity to be brand-loyal measures the consumer's willingness to switch brands. Given below are sample scales of both types of attitudinal measures of brand loyalty.

ATTITUDE TOWARD THE ACT OF BUYING THE BRAND

Using a scale from 1 to 5, please tell me how committed you are to purchasing your preferred brand of directory advertising.

Uncommitted	1	2	3	4	5	Committed

Purchasing advertising with my preferred brand of directory in the next issue would be:

Bad	1	2	3	4	5	Good
Unpleasant	1	2	3	4	5	Pleasant
Unfavourable	1	2	3	4	5	Favourable
Negative	1	2	3	4	5	Positive
Undesirable	1	2	3	4	5	Desirable
Unwise	1	2	3	4	5	Wise
Unlikely	1	2	3	4	5	Likely

I would recommend my main brand to other people.

Unlikely	1	2	3	4	5	Likely

PROPENSITY TO BE LOYAL

I would rather stick with a brand I usually buy than try something I am not very sure of.

If I like a brand, I rarely switch from it just to try something different.

I rarely introduce new brands and products to my colleagues.

I rarely take chances by buying unfamiliar brands even if it means sacrificing variety.

I buy the same brands even if they are only average.

I would rather wait for others to try a new brand than try it myself.

I would rather stick to well-known brands when purchasing directory advertising.

Source: Rebekah Bennett and Sharyn Rundle-Thiele, "A Comparison of Attitudinal Loyalty Measurement Approaches," *Journal of Brand Management,* January 2002, 193–209.

Post-purchase Dissonance

An important component of post-purchase evaluation is the reduction of any uncertainty or doubt that the consumer might have had about the selection. As part of their post-purchase analysis, consumers try to reassure themselves that their choice was a wise one; that is, they attempt to reduce **post-purchase cognitive dissonance**. As Chapter 7 indicated, they do this by adopting one of the following strategies: They may rationalize the decision as being wise; they may seek advertisements that support their choice and avoid those of competitive brands; they may

Post-purchase cognitive dissonance: The discomfort or dissonance that consumers experience after purchase about whether or not they made the right decision.

attempt to persuade friends or neighbours to buy the same brand (and, thus, confirm their own choice); or they may turn to other satisfied owners for reassurance.

The degree of post-purchase analysis that consumers undertake depends on the importance of the product decision and the experience acquired in using the product. When the product lives up to expectations, they probably will buy it again. When the product's performance is disappointing or does not meet expectations, however, they will search for alternatives. Thus, the consumer's post-purchase evaluation "feeds back" as *experience* to his or her psychological field and serves to influence future related decisions. Although it would be logical to assume that customer satisfaction is related to customer retention (i.e., if a consumer is satisfied with his Brooks Brothers suit he will buy other Brooks Brothers products), a recent study found no direct relationship between satisfaction and retention. The findings show that customer retention may be more a matter of the brand's reputation—especially for products consumers find difficult to evaluate.[53]

Consumer Satisfaction and Dissatisfaction

As mentioned earlier, when the actual performance of a product exceeds what was expected, consumers experience satisfaction. Overall satisfaction with the product includes satisfaction with its performance and satisfaction with the shopping experience. At times, deficiencies in one area (e.g., poor service) can affect or even counteract positive performance in the other (e.g., excellent product performance). Since satisfied consumers are more likely to become repeat buyers and brand-loyal customers, it is imperative that marketers attempt to make the actual performance exceed the expected one. This can be done by developing realistic expectations, or not overstating the product's benefits or attributes in promotional campaigns. Consumer satisfaction can lead to positive word-of-mouth communication and repeat purchases.

When consumers talk about performance expectations, they are thinking of three different types of performance expectations:[54]

- *Instrumental performance:* the way a product actually functions (e.g., the way a computer works in terms of speed, memory available, the ease with which you can type on a keyboard)
- *Symbolic performance:* the style, appearance, and overall aesthetics of a product (e.g., the physical appearance of the monitor, keyboard, and "tower," and how the appearance fits in with your furniture)
- *Affective performance:* the way owning the product makes you feel (e.g., owning a brand-new Apple computer may make you feel that you are in tune with technological innovations)

Research has found that consumers move away from services (and perhaps products), not because they have found better alternatives, but because they were dissatisfied with their present service. In the case of services, although core service failure (e.g., a bad haircut) account for nearly half of the service switching, other factors (e.g., bad service in general, poor pricing strategies, poor responses to service problems) cause many consumers to change to other service providers. In other words, maintaining the quality of the peripheral aspects of a product or service is also important to keeping customers.

As the above discussion indicated, preventing consumer dissatisfaction is probably just as important as ensuring consumer satisfaction. This is because dissatisfied consumers are more likely than satisfied ones to talk about the product, and negative word-of-mouth is hard to deal with. Although dissatisfied customers have several other options open to them (e.g., not take any action but hold a less favourable attitude toward the product, complain to the manufacturer or retailer, complain to third-party agencies like the Better Business Bureau, or stop buying the brand), studies find that nearly half of the dissatisfied consumers are likely to warn their friends against buying the product.[55]

What is Richard's post-purchase evaluation of his new laptop? He absolutely loves it! First of all, because of his personality, the fact that nobody he knows has this same computer has done wonders for his ego (affective performance). But from a practical standpoint, the computer has also been a huge success. It is so small and light that he can carry it in his normal business briefcase rather than needing a separate piece of computer luggage (instrumental performance). The screen, even though it is only 10 inches in size, is bright and clear and large enough for his needs when he is travelling, and the pointer, which is integrated into the keyboard, works so well that he sees no need to purchase a small mouse (symbolic performance). Furthermore, when he first got the Libretto and had a number of questions about it, he was able to get through to the technical support staff at Dynamism by telephone with no long waits, and all of his questions were answered and his concerns were resolved.

RELATIONSHIP MARKETING

Many firms have established **relationship marketing** programs (sometimes called *loyalty programs*) to foster usage loyalty and a commitment to their company's products and services. Relationship marketing is exceedingly logical when we realize credit card research has shown that "75 percent of college students keep their first card for 15 years, and 60 percent keep that card for life."[56] This kind of loyalty is enhanced by relationship marketing, which at its heart is all about building *trust* (between the firm and its customers) and keeping *promises* ("making promises," "enabling promises," and "keeping promises" on the part of the firm and, possibly, on the part of the customer).[57]

Indeed, it is the aim of relationship marketing to create strong, lasting relationships with a core group of customers. The emphasis is on developing long-term bonds with customers by making them feel good about how the company interacts (or does business) with them and by giving them some kind of personal connection to the business. A review of the composition of 66 consumer relationship marketing programs revealed three elements shared by more than 50 percent of the programs. They are (1) fostering ongoing communication with customers (73 percent of the programs); (2) furnishing loyalty by building in extras like upgrades and other perks (68 percent of the programs); and (3) stimulating a sense of belonging by providing a "club membership" format (50 percent of the programs).[58] A real relationship marketing program is more than the use of database marketing tactics to target customers better. Rather, the consumer must feel that he or she has received something for being a participant in the relationship.[59] In a positive vein, businesses have been finding that the internet is an inexpensive, efficient, and productive way to extend customer services.[60] This has resulted in the new phrase "permission marketing." It is the "art of asking consumers if they would like to receive a targeted email ad, promotion, or message *before* it appears in their inbox." The opposite tack, sending a consumer spam and offering the option to "Click here to opt out," annoys consumers and is not permission marketing.[61]

An analogy can be drawn between two people who build an interpersonal relationship and the type of relationship that marketers try to build between the company or its products and the consumer. Like personal relationships between individuals who are willing to do favours for each other, relationship marketers

www.bbb.org

Relationship marketing:
Marketing programs aimed at creating strong, lasting relationships with a core group of customers by making them feel a personal connection to the business.

WE DON'T JUST PUT CHOCOLATE ON THE PILLOW.
WE REMEMBER WHICH PILLOW TO PUT UNDER THE CHOCOLATE.

Imagine a hotel that offers 10 types of pillows, and remembers the one
you prefer. That's the kind of personal attention that makes staying at The Benjamin
so comfortable. In a classic building restored to its 1927 grandeur, this new
hotel offers you the perfect marriage of elegance and intimacy.

For conducting business, each spacious room or suite is equipped with all of
the state-of-the-art amenities that today's busy executive needs. And for pleasure,
An American Place restaurant beckons, as does a relaxing treatment from the
Woodstock Spa—both the perfect precursors to a night of restful comfort.

For reservations and information, call your travel counselor or 1-888-4-BENJAMIN.

INTRODUCING

THE BENJAMIN
AN EXECUTIVE SUITE HOTEL

125 East 50th Street, New York, New York 10022 ♦ 212.320.8002 ♦ Fax: 212.465.3697 ♦ www.thebenjamin.com
Manhattan East Suite Hotels

EXHIBIT 15-2

AD PROMOTING A FIRM'S CONSUMER
RELATIONSHIP PROGRAM

Courtesy of Manhattan East Suite Hotels.

offer loyal customers special services, discounts, increased communications, and attention beyond the core product or service, *without* expecting an immediate payback (see Exhibit 15-2). However, they are hoping that, over time, they will reap the advantages of sustained and increasing transactions with a core group of loyal customers. Jaguar, for example, two years before opening its South Coast Jaguar dealership in the midst of the biggest luxury car market in the United States (Orange County, California), started underwriting fund-raising events for local charities and targeting about 500 leading philanthropists and business executives who live in the area. According to the head of the South Coast project for Jaguar, the marketing opportunity was seen as follows:[62] "It's not about bricks and mortar, or even about cars. It's about the overall experience. These are people who can afford to buy all the luxury goods they want. What we have set out to do is to create a retail experience that they cannot buy—one that shows them how important they are. Everything else will flow from that."

Although a relationship marketing strategy may use direct marketing, sales promotion, and general advertising, the emphasis is on long-term commitment to the individual customer. Advances in technology like UPC-scanning equipment and relational databases make it simpler to track customers, thus influencing the trend toward relationship marketing. Indeed, Wal-Mart's database is second in size only to that of the U.S. government.[63] A recent study suggests that relationship marketing programs are more likely to succeed if the product or service is one that buyers consider to be high-involvement because of its association with financial, social, or physical risk.[64]

Relationship marketing programs have been used in a wide variety of product and service categories. Many companies call their relationship programs a club, and some even charge a fee to join. Membership in a club may serve as a means to convey to customers the notions of permanence and exclusivity inherent in a committed relationship. Additionally, those firms that charge a fee (such as the American Express Platinum card) increase customers' investment in the relationship that may, in turn, lead to greater commitment to the relationship and increased usage loyalty.

Airlines and major hotel chains, in particular, use relationship marketing techniques by awarding points to frequent customers that can be used to obtain additional goods or services from the company. This kind of point system may act as an exit barrier because starting a new relationship would mean giving up the potential future value of the points and starting over with a new service provider. Moreover, companies have recently been broadening the scope of such relationship programs.

Best Buy Canada, which owns Future Shop and Best Buy stores, is stepping up its services to its best customers to differentiate itself from Wal-Mart and other competitors. Best Buy plans to tailor each outlet to its most profitable consumers. The retailer surveys more than 200 000 customers each year and has found that there are distinct segments among its customers; it plans to provide special services to the best customers. For example, some stores would target the family woman by offering personal shopping assistants, more educational computer games for her children, and photo services that are prominently displayed. The company also plans to have a "geek squad"—a 24-hour computer support group—that would travel in "geekmobiles" to customers' homes to set up electronic equipment for a fee.[65]

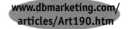

Ultimately, it is to a firm's advantage to develop long-term relationships with its existing customers because it is easier and less expensive to make an additional sale to an existing customer than to make a new sale to a new consumer.[66] This is why, for example, Lands' End tells consumers that if they are not 100 percent satisfied with their purchase, they can return it at any time, for any reason.[67] However, the effort involved in developing and maintaining a customer relationship must be weighed against the expected long-term benefits. Marketers must determine the lifetime value of a customer to ensure that the costs of obtaining, servicing, and communicating with the customer do not exceed the potential profits.[68] Recent research also suggests not only that a consumer's participation in a relationship marketing program is based on past and present experiences but that it also incorporates expected future use and expected future satisfaction with the program.[69] Figure 15-9 portrays some of the characteristics of the relationship between the firm and the customer within the spirit of relationship marketing.

www.dbmarketing.com/
articles/Art190.htm

Why is relationship marketing so important? Research shows that consumers today are less loyal than in the past, owing to six major forces: (1) abundance of choice, (2) availability of information, (3) sense of entitlement (consumers repeatedly ask "What have you done for me lately?"), (4) commoditization (most products and services appear to be similar—nothing stands out), (5) insecurity (consumer financial problems reduce loyalty), and (6) shortage of time (not enough time to be loyal). These six forces result in consumer defections, complaints, cynicism, reduced affiliation, greater price sensitivity, and litigiousness.[70] Consequently, relationship programs that can retain customers are a vital part of a company's marketing program.

FIGURE 15-9   Characteristics of Relationship Marketing

The firm provides
- Products/services
- Individualized attention
- Continuous information
- Price offers
- Customer services
- Extras and perks, etc.

Trust and promises

The customer provides
- Repeat purchase
- Increased loyalty
- Goodwill
- Positive word of mouth
- Lower costs for the firm, etc.

Source: In part, this portrayal was inspired by Mary Long, Leon Schiffman, and Elaine Sherman, "Understanding the Relationships in Consumer Marketing Relationship Programs: A Content Analysis," in *Proceedings of the World Marketing Congress* VII-II, eds. K. Grant and Walker (Melbourne, Australia: Academy of Marketing Science, 1995), 10/27–10/26.

PURCHASE, POST-PURCHASE PROCESSES, AND MARKETING STRATEGY

The outputs of a consumer's decision-making process are of great interest to marketers, whose primary goals are to influence those outputs. Let us look at some ways in which the concepts and ideas discussed in this chapter could enable a marketer to attract and maintain buyers:

Encourage trial: One of the outputs of consumer decision making is trial. Of course, marketers always hope that consumers will move from trial to purchase, but trial is in itself a desirable output for a marketer. Companies can encourage trial through samples, in-store demonstrations, coupons, test usage, and so on.

Encourage purchase and repeat purchase: Marketers can encourage customers to buy a product through better payment options, "buy now, pay later" deals and other means. Repeat purchase is encouraged by reward programs (e.g., every nth item free). Increasing switching costs or making the costs of finding and evaluating other brands less attractive can also lead to repeat purchases. For example, magazines lower the price of reordering (e.g., they offer long-term subscriptions and automatic renewals).This makes the option of searching for better magazines or better prices for the same magazine more expensive (in terms of switching costs). Lawn-care companies do the same by offering renewals in the fall for the next year.

Increase brand loyalty: Marketers have to attempt to get consumers to go beyond repeat purchase to brand commitment and brand loyalty. Although reward programs create repeat purchase, they do not always lead to brand loyalty. Companies can increase brand loyalty through good customer relationship management, increased customer satisfaction, and good customer service.

Make efforts to increase customer satisfaction and decrease dissatisfaction: One way of creating loyal customers is to make sure they are satisfied. Making realistic product claims and delivering on the promised product quality and other attributes would help increase customer satisfaction. However, it is equally important for marketers to make sure that customers come to them to express their dissatisfaction with the product and that any such customer complaints are taken care of immediately. A customer who feels that his or her complaint was handled well is likely to have greater loyalty to the brand.

Have you heard about the American Girl? You may have, if you have a preteen relative. The dolls are extremely popular among preteen girls and have become almost a craze among this age group. How did American Girl dolls achieve this status? Besides an extremely innovative marketing strategy that included high price (around US$140), American Girl has an entire culture surrounding the dolls (they have sisters, a school, a dog, designer clothes, and so on) and an attractive website portal. The company also provides excellent—in fact, exceptional—customer service that leads to high levels of customer satisfaction.

Wendy Walters gives an example of the quality of customer service that American Girl offers. A Canadian living in Toronto, she bought her nine-year-old daughter one of these dolls. A little later, when her daughter was playing with the authentic-looking period book bag that came with the doll, a strap broke. Crying, the girl picked up the phone and called 1-800-American Girl. After conferring with Walters about the problem, the customer service representative spoke to her daughter who explained why she was dissatisfied with the bag. One week later, a new one arrived, compliments of American Girl. Walters had to pay only a few dollars for postage. Needless to say, the company has an extremely satisfied customer who will spread the word.[71]

Create symbolic meanings for your products: Another way to make customers satisfied with your product or service is to help them develop their own memories and symbolic meanings for the product. If such meanings already exist, marketers can use them effectively to market their products. For example, Tim Hortons runs ads that emphasize that Tim's is a part of Canada and symbolizes Canada when someone is travelling abroad.

Determine whether consumers choose a brand first or a store first and market accordingly: One of the first outputs of consumer decision making is the choice of either a store or a brand. In other words, having recognized a problem, gathered information, and evaluated alternatives, consumers need to decide on a brand or a store. Of course, sometimes these decisions are made concurrently. Marketers have to determine whether consumers choose a store first or a brand first and change their marketing programs accordingly. For example, as discussed earlier, if consumers choose a store first, then in-store promotion, incentives for store personnel for pushing your product, and good co-op advertising programs become important.

Develop a good customer relationship management strategy: As we saw above, making sure that customers remain loyal to your brand requires that you develop a good long-term relationship with them. This should go beyond the encouragement of repeat purchase to development of a program that offers something of value to the customer. Special services, more attention than what is necessary or expected, increased and regular communication, and other initiatives would help in the development of good customer relationship.

Part of making sure that your customer relationship program works also involves ensuring that your employees are well trained to provide customer satisfaction and to deal with customer complaints and with the unexpected. This requires a good internal marketing program and rewards for employees who excel in customer service.

WestJet, one of Canada's top marketers, holds annual birthday parties for its 1600 employees and gives out "Best of WestJet" awards to employees who deliver on WestJet's values of great customer care. The company makes sure that its employees know what is expected of them by promoting the company's values internally. The company also has a program that lets customers nominate employees who made them smile. Every year, there are two draws for customers who nominate employees; the prizes are, of course, free WestJet flights. Last year, WestJet received more than 2000 nominations from customers.[72]

SUMMARY

- The outcome phase of the consumer decision-making model includes the actual purchase (or trial) and post-purchase evaluation.

- The order of choice between store and product might vary. Sometimes consumers choose the store first and then the product; sometimes they choose the brand first and then the store. The order has implications for marketers.

- The process of gift exchange is an important part of consumer behaviour. Various gift-giving and gift-receiving relationships are captured by the following five specific categories in the gifting classification scheme: (1) inter-group gifting (a group gives a gift to another group); (2) inter-category gifting (an individual gives a gift to a group or a group gives a gift to an individual); (3) intra-group gifting (a group gives a gift to itself or its members); (4) interpersonal gifting (an individual gives a gift to another individual); and (5) intra-personal gifting (a gift to oneself).

- Consumer purchase decisions are influenced to a great extent by outlet factors, such as the retail environment, outlet layout, and in-store promotions.

- Many consumer purchase decisions are made in the store.

- Consumer behaviour also includes the pleasure and satisfaction derived from possessing or collecting "things." The outputs of consumption are changes in feelings, moods, or attitudes; reinforcement of life styles; an enhanced sense of self; satisfaction of a consumer-related need; belonging to groups; and expressing and entertaining oneself.

- Some possessions serve to assist consumers in their effort to create personal meaning and to maintain a sense of the past.

- Post-purchase evaluation of purchases can lead to post-purchase dissonance, customer satisfaction or dissatisfaction, and brand loyalty.

- Customer satisfaction results when the actual performance exceeds the expected performance; dis-

satisfaction results when the actual performance is below the expected.

- Dissatisfaction can lead to negative word-of-mouth communication; it can be controlled by developing realistic expectations, giving customers ways to complain, and resolving their complaints effectively.

- Relationship marketing affects consumers' decisions and their consumption satisfaction. Firms establish relationship marketing programs (sometimes called loyalty programs) to foster usage loyalty and a commitment to their products and services.

- At its heart, relationship marketing is all about building trust between the firm and its customers, and keeping promises made to consumers. Therefore, the emphasis in relationship marketing is almost always on developing long-term bonds with customers by making them feel special and by providing them with personalized services.

DISCUSSION QUESTIONS

1. How can a marketer of very light, very powerful laptop computers use its knowledge of customers' expectations in designing a marketing strategy?

2. How do consumers reduce post-purchase dissonance? How can marketers provide positive reinforcement to consumers after the purchase to reduce their dissonance?

3. What factors influence a retail store's image? How can a marketer upgrade the image of a retail store?

4. Why are both attitudinal and behavioural measures important in measuring brand loyalty?

5. What leads to customer satisfaction or dissatisfaction? What are some measures that a marketer can take to reduce the chances of customer dissatisfaction?

6. Define relationship marketing. What are some steps that a firm, such as a clothing store, can take to develop good long-term relationships with its customers?

7. What are the five different types of gift-giving situations? Give one example from your own gift giving of each of the above.

CRITICAL THINKING QUESTIONS

1. Think about the last few purchases that you made. Can you think of one where you chose the store first and one where you chose the brand first? What factors affected your decision to choose the store (or the brand) first?

2. Think about products that you buy as self-gifts (or intra-personal gifts). What do they have in common? What can a marketer do to increase the chance of a product becoming a self-gift?

3. Assume that you are in charge of the customer service department of an airline. What steps would you take to reduce customer dissatisfaction and increase customer satisfaction during peak travel times?

4. For which of the following products is post-purchase dissonance most likely? How would you go about reducing the chances of such dissonance?

(a) an exercise machine
(b) the Swiffer
(c) an electronic organizer
(d) a digital camera
(e) new brand of laundry detergent
(f) an undergraduate program (or choice of a university)

INTERNET EXERCISES

1. Visit the websites of two car manufacturers and two banks. What measures do they seem to be taking to get feedback (especially complaints) from consumers?

2. Assume you have the money to buy a brand new car priced under $25 000. Visit the website of two independent firms in the industry (e.g., Autonet, AutoTrader, or Carguide) and find out the brands available in your area in this price range. Reduce the alternatives to three. How long did this process take you? How would you rate the experience?

3. Visit the websites of two clothing retailers and look at their efforts to develop a relationship with customers. Which retailer is doing a better job? Why?

4. Visit the website of your university. Is the university taking any measures to develop a relationship with its current and past students? What do you think of its efforts at relationship marketing?

KEY TERMS

Brand loyalty   *(p. 507)*
Consumption process   *(p. 505)*
Gifting behaviour   *(p. 501)*
Inter-category gifting   *(p. 502)*
Interpersonal gifting   *(p. 502)*

Intra-group gifting   *(p. 502)*
Intra-personal gifting   *(p. 502)*
Post-purchase cognitive
  dissonance   *(p. 511)*
Purchase behaviour   *(p. 494)*

Relationship marketing   *(p. 513)*
Self-gifts   *(p. 501)*

CASE 15-1: A REALLY BIG ZIPPO

Since it introduced its first lighter in 1932, the name Zippo has been synonymous with reliable cigarette lighters. Indeed, the company's standard flip-top windproof lighter has achieved cult collector status. Now the company has a new product, known as the Zippo Multi-Purpose Lighter. It is 20 centimetres (eight inches) long, comes with a black or silver barrel, has a window to show how much fuel is left, and is childproof, and the flame is adjustable. The product can be used for lighting a barbecue grill or candles, or to start a fire in a fire-place. The black-barrel version has a list price of $14.95, whereas the deluxe version, in silver, is $19.95 (and comes with a pouch and gift box).

A number of other manufacturers offer products that perform the same function; many are disposable and selling in stores like Kmart for under $5. However, as it does with its Zippo cigarette lighters, Zippo guarantees to fix its refillable Multi-Purpose Lighter if it should ever break; that is, it offers a lifetime guarantee.

QUESTION

1. Considering the discussion of "gifting" in this chapter, do you think that the Zippo Multi-Purpose Lighter is likely to be a commercial success?

Source: Cara B. DiPasquale, "Zippo: Rebel Has New Cause," *Advertising Age,* July 15, 2002, 3, 40.

NOTES

1. Steven Buckler, "Funny Farm," *Marketing Magazine*, February 16, 2004, 16.

2. Emily Booth, "Getting Inside a Shopper's Mind," *Marketing* (U.K.), June 3, 1999, 33.

3. Robert A. Peterson, Sridhar Balasubramanian, and Bart J. Bronnenberg, "Exploring the Implications of the Internet for Consumer Marketing," *Journal of the Academy of Marketing Sciences,* 25, 1997, 329–346.

4. Julie Baker, Dhruv Grewal, and A. Parasuraman, "The Influence of Store Environment on Quality Inferences and Store Image," *Journal of the Academy of Marketing Science*, 22, 4, 1994, 328–339.

5. As this book goes to print, Target, the U.S. department chain, was attempting to buy Zellers, the low-priced chain that is owned by Hudson's Bay.

6. Joseph W. Alba, Susan M. Broniarczyk, Terence A. Shimp, and Joesl E. Urbany, "The Influence of Prior Beliefs, Frequency Cues, and Magnitude Cues on Consumers Perceptions of Comparative Price Data," *Journal of Consumer Research*, 21, September 1994, 219–235.

7. Susan M. Broniarczyk at al., "Consumers Perceptions of the Assortment Carried in a Grocery Category: The Impact of Item Reduction," *Journal of Marketing Research*, 35, May 1998, 166–176.

8. Frank H. Alpert and Michael A. Kamins, "An Empirical Investigation of Consumer Memory, Attitude and Perceptions Toward Pioneer and Follower Brands," *Journal of Marketing*, 59, October 1995, 34–45.

9. Gary F. McKinnon, J. Patrick Kelly, and E. Doyle Robinson, "Sales Effects of Point-of-Purchase In-Store Signing," *Journal of Retailing*, 1981, 49–63.

10. Gerald J. Gorn, Amitava Chattopadhyay, Tracey Yi, and Darren W. Dahl, "Effects of Color as an Executional Cue in Advertising: They're in the Shade," *Management Science,* 43 (10), 1387–1400.

11. Michelle Warren, "Caution! Floss Ahead," *Marketing Magazine*, April 5–12, 2004, 4.

12. Ronald Milliman, "The Influence of Background Music on the Behaviour of Restaurant Patrons," *Journal of Marketing*, Summer 1982, 178–185. Also see Richard Yalch and Eric Spangenberg, "Effects of Store Music on Shopping Behaviour," *Journal of Consumer Marketing*, Spring, 1990, 55–63.

13. Eric Spangenberg, Ayn E. Crowley, and Pamela W. Henderson, "Improving the Store Environment: Do Olfactory Cues Affect Evaluation and Behaviour?" *Journal of Marketing*, April 1996, 67–80.

14. *The 1995 POPAI Consumer Buying Habits Study,* Point of Purchase Institute, Washington, D.C., 1995.

15. Ibid.

16. Ibid.

17. Deborah Y. Cohn and Leon G. Schiffman, "Gifting: A Taxonomy of Private Realm Giver and Recipient Relationships," Working Paper, City University of New York, Baruch College, 1996, 2.

18. Russell W. Belk and Gregory S. Coon, "Gift Giving as Agapic Love: An Alternative to the Exchange Paradigm Based on Dating Experiences," *Journal of Consumer Research,* 20, December 1993, 393–417.

19. "More Consumers Buy Gifts for Themselves Than to Give as Gifts; 'Gift Market' Is a Misnomer, Since Most Consumers Buy Gift Products for Personal Consumption," *Business Wire,* April 17, 2000, 1.

20. Michael Laroche, Gad Saad, Elizabeth Browne, Mark Cleveland, and Chankon Kim, "Determinants of In-Store Information Search Strategies Pertaining to a Christmas Gift Purchase," *Reveue canadienne des sciences de l'administration*, 17, 1, 2000, 1–19.

21. Julie A. Ruth, Cele C. Otnes, and Frédéric F. Brunel, "Gift Receipt and the Reformulation of Interpersonal Relationships," *Journal of Consumer Research,* 25, March 1999, 385–402.

22. Cele Otnes, Tina M. Lowrey, and Young Chan Kim, "Gift Selection for Easy and Difficult Recipients: A Social Roles Interpretation," *Journal of Consumer Research,* 20, September 1993, 229–244.

23. John F. Sherry, "Reflections on Giftware and Giftcare: Whither Consumer Research?" in *Gift Giving: An Interdisciplinary Anthology,* eds. Cele

Otnes and Richard F. Beltramini (Bowling Green, KY: Popular Press, 1996), 220.

24 Stephen J. Gould and Claudia E. Weil, "Gift-Giving and Gender Self-Concepts," *Gender Role,* 24, 1991, 617–637.

25 Cynthia Webster and Linda Nottingham, "Gender Differences in the Motivations for Gift Giving," in *2000 AMA Educators' Proceedings,* 11, eds. Gregory T. Gundlach and Patrick E. Murphy (Chicago: American Marketing Association, 2000), 272.

26 David B. Wooten, "Qualitative Steps toward an Expanded Model of Anxiety in Gift-Giving," *Journal of Consumer Research,* 27, 1, June 2000, 84–95.

27 Constance Hill and Celia T. Romm, "The Role of Mothers as Gift Givers: A Comparison across Three Cultures," in *Advances in Consumer Research,* 23, eds. Kim P. Corfman and John G. Lynch, Jr., 21–27.

28 For a really interesting article on self-gifts, see John F. Sherry, Jr., Mary Ann McGrath, and Sidney J. Levy, "Monadic Gifting: Anatomy of Gifts Given to the Self," in *Contemporary Marketing and Consumer Behavior,* ed. John F. Sherry, Jr. (Thousand Oaks, CA: Sage, 1995), 399–432.

29 David Glen Mick and Mitchelle DeMoss, "To Me from Me: A Descriptive Phenomenology of Self-Gifts," in *Advances in Consumer Research,* ed., Goldberg, Gorn, and Pollay, 677–682; and Shay Sayre and David Horne, "I Shop, Therefore I Am: The Role of Possessions for Self-Definition," in *Advances in Consumer Research,* 23, eds. Kim P. Corfman and John G. Lynch, Jr., (Provo, UT: Association for Consumer Research, 1996), 323–328.

30 Cynthia Crossen, "'Merry Christmas to Moi,' Shoppers Say," *Wall Street Journal,* December 11, 1997, B1, B10.

31 Kim K. R. McKeage, Marsha L. Richins, and Kathleen Debevec, "Self-Gifts and the Manifestation of Material Values," in *Advances in Consumer Research,* 20, eds. Leigh McAlister and Michael L. Rothschild (Provo, UT: Association for Consumer Research, 1993), 359–364.

32 Kathleen M. Rassuli and Gilbert D. Harrell, "A New Perspective on Choice," in *Advances in Consumer Research,* eds. Goldberg, Gorn, and Pollay, 737–744.

33 For an interesting article on "consumption practices," see Douglas B. Holt, "How Consumers Consume: A Typology of Consumer Practices," *Journal of Consumer Research,* 22, June 1995, 1–16.

34 James M. Perry, "Mike Weaver Proves That Everything Can Be a Collection," *Wall Street Journal,* August 16, 1995, 1.

35 Kent Grayson and David Shulman, "Indexicality and the Verification of Irreplaceable Possessions: A Semiotic Analysis," *Journal of Consumer Research,* 27, 1, 17–30.

36 Mary M. Long and Leon G. Schiffman, "Swatch Fever: An Allegory for Understanding the Paradox of Collecting," *Psychology and Marketing,* 14, August 1997, 495–509.

37 "Nicholas Hayek Sees Affinities in Making Movies and Watches, David Evans Finds Swatch Head Stages Timely Job Switch," *South China Morning Post* (Hong Kong), April 3, 2000, 10.

38 Russell W. Belk, "The Role of Possessions in Constructing and Maintaining a Sense of Past," in *Advances in Consumer Research,* eds. Goldberg, Gorn, and Pollay, 669–676.

39 Stacey Menzel Baker and Patricia F. Kennedy, "Death by Nostalgia: A Diagnosis of Context-Specific Cases," in *Advances in Consumer Research,* 21, eds. Chris T. Allen and Deborah Roedder John (Provo, UT: Association for Consumer Research, 1994), 169–174.

40 Andy Wright, "Oh, the Stuff We Collect Series: XPRESS," *St. Petersburg Times,* August 30, 1999, 3D.

41 The Smithsonian Institute, **http://kids.si.edu/collecting**.

42 Linda L. Price, Eric J. Arnould, and Carolyn Folkman Curasi, "Older Consumers' Disposition of Special Possessions," *Journal of Consumer Research,* 27, September 2001, 2, 179–201.

43 Robert L. Oliver, "Whence Brand Loyalty?" *Journal of Marketing,* 63, 1999, 33–44.

44 Dinae Crispell and Kathleen Brandenburg, "What's in a Brand," *American Demographics,* May 1993, 28.

45 Arjun Chaudhuri and Morris B. Holbrook, "The Chain of Effects From Brand Trust and Brand Affect to Brand Performance: The Role of Brand Loyalty," *Journal of Marketing,* April 2001, 81–93.

46 Alan S. Dick and Kunal Basu, "Customer Loyalty: Toward an Integrated Conceptual Framework," *Journal of the Academy of Marketing Science,* 22, 2, 1994, 99–113.

47 Jean-Marc Léger, "The Fickle Beer Consumer," *Marketing Magazine,* May 10, 2004, 22.

48 Jaishankar Ganesh, Mark J. Arnold, and Kristy E. Reynolds, "Understanding the Customer Base of Service Providers: An Examination of the Differences Between Switchers and Stayers," *Journal of Marketing,* July 2000, 65–87.

49 Grahame R. Dowling and Mark Uncles, "Do Customer Loyalty Programs Really Work?" *Sloane Management Review,* Summer 1997, 71–82.

50 Michelle L. Roehm, Ellen Bolman Pullins, and Harper A. Roehm, Jr., "Designing Loyalty-Building

Programs for Packaged Goods Brands," *Journal of Marketing Research*, May 2002, 202–213.

51   Rebecca Bennett and Sharyn Rundle-Thiele, "A Comparison of Attitudinal Loyalty Measurement Approaches," *Journal of Brand Management*, January 2002, 193–209.

52   Ernest R. Cadotte, Robert B. Woodruff, and Roger L. Jenkins, "Expectations and Norms in Models of Consumer Satisfaction," *Journal of Marketing Research*, 24, August 1987, 305–314.

53   Kare Sandvik, Kjell Gronhaug, and Frank Lindberg, "Routes to Customer Retention: The Importance of Customer Satisfaction, Performance Quality, Brand Reputation and Customer Knowledge," in *AMA Winter Conference*, eds. Debbie Thorne LeClair and Michael Hartline (Chicago: American Marketing Association, 1997), 211–217.

54   Del Hawkins, Roger Best, and Kenneth Coney, *Consumer Behaviour: Building Marketing Strategy*, 9th ed., Irwin, 2004, 640–41.

55   S.P. Brown and R.F. Beltramini, "Consumer Complaining and Word-of-Mouth Activities," in *Advances in Consumer Research*, vol. 16, ed. T.K. Srull, p. 9–11.

56   Robert Bryce, "Here's a Course in Personal Finance 101, the Hard Way," *New York Times*, April 30, 1995, F11.

57   Susan M. Lloyd, "Toward Understanding Relationship Marketing from the Consumer's Perspective: What Relationships Are and Why Consumers Choose to Enter Them," in *2000 AMA Educators' Proceedings*, 11, eds. Gregory T. Gundlach and Patrick E. Murphy (Chicago: American Marketing Association, 2000), 12–20; Leonard L. Berry, "Relationship Marketing of Services—Growing Interest, Emerging Perspectives," *Journal of the Academy of Marketing Science* 23 (Fall 1995): 236–245; and Mary Jo Bitner, "Building Service Relationships: It's All About Promises," *Journal of the Academy of Marketing Science* 23 (Fall 1995): 246–251.

58   Mary Long, Leon Schiffman, and Elaine Sherman, "Understanding the Relationships in Consumer Marketing Relationship Programs: A Content Analysis," in *Proceedings of the World Marketing Congress VII-II*, eds. K. Grant and Walker (Melbourne, Australia: Academy of Marketing Science, 1995), 10/27–10/32.

59   Patricia A. Norberg, "Relationship Issues in Business-to-Consumer Markets," in *2001 AMA Educators' Proceedings*, 12, eds. Greg W. Marshall and Stephen J. Grove (Chicago: American Marketing Association, 2001), 381–390.

60   Marc E. Duncan, "The Internet and Relationship Marketing: A Framework for Application," in *2000 AMA Winter Educators' Conference*, 11, eds. John P. Workman and William D. Perreault (Chicago: American Marketing Association, 2000), 72–82.

61   Lauren Barack, "Pretty, Pretty, Please," *Business 2.0*, April 2000, 176–180.

62   John O'Dell, "Advertising and Marketing; Jaguar Is Talking Relationships; Luxury Car Maker Is Wooing South O.C.'s Elite Before New Dealership Is Built," *Los Angeles Times*, June 10, 1999, 1.

63   Emily Nelson, "Why Wal-Mart Sings, 'Yes, We Have Bananas,'" *Wall Street Journal*, October 6, 1998, B1, B4.

64   Mary Ellen Gordon and Kim McKeage, "Relationship Marketing Effectiveness: Differences between Women in New Zealand and the United States," in *1997 AMA Educators' Proceedings*, eds. William M. Pride and G. Tomas M. Hult (Chicago: American Marketing Association, 1997), 117–122.

65   Marina Strauss, "Best Buy Courting Its Best Customers," *Globe and Mail*, August 13, 2004, B3.

66   Jagdish N. Sheth and Atul Parvatiyar, "Relationship Marketing in Consumer Marketing: Antecedents and Consequences," *Journal of the Academy of Marketing Science*, 23, Fall 1995, 255–271.

67   Barbara B. Stern, "Advertising Intimacy: Relationship Marketing and the Services Consumer," *Journal of Advertising*, 26, Winter 1997, 7–19.

68   Robert F. Dwyer, "Customer Lifetime Valuation to Support Marketing Decision Making," *Journal of Direct Marketing*, 3, 1989, 8–15; Jonathan R. Copulsky and Michael J. Wolf, "Relationship Marketing: Positioning for the Future," *Journal of Business Strategy*, July–August 1990, 16–20; and Philip Kotler, "Marketing's New Paradigm: What's Really Happening Out There," *Planning Review*, September–October 1992, 50–52.

69   Katherine N. Lemon, Tiffany Barnett White, and Russell S. Winer, "Dynamic Customer Relationship Management; Incorporating Future Considerations into the Service Retention Decision," *Journal of Marketing*, 66, 1, January 2002, 1–14.

70   Steve Schriver, "Customer Loyalty: Going, Going...," *American Demographics*, September 1997, 20–23.

71   Wendy Walters, "Just an American Girl," *Marketing Magazine*, March 22, 2004, 9.

72   Lesley Young, "From the Inside Out," *Marketing Magazine*, April 19, 2004, 13–15.

CASE APPENDIX

CASE 1-1: REACHING THE GENEALOGICAL TOURIST

Have you ever tried to trace your ancestors or learn more about them? Enthusiasm for genealogy—the study of family descent or ancestry—has been growing in Canada. Unlike in the past, genealogical research is not limited to professional historians or genealogists. Today, there are many amateur genealogists who spend several hours tracing their ancestry; many of these consumers also travel to see the places their ancestors came from. This form of tourism—genealogical tourism—is a growing industry in many parts of the world.

Genealogical tourism is usually classified as a sub-segment of heritage tourism, which is itself one of the many forms of cultural tourism. Though most Canadians interested in tracing their roots travel to places like the United Kingdom, there are many who begin their search into their past by travelling within Canada to the parts of the country that their ancestors originally came from.

Newfoundland and Labrador is one Canadian province trying to raise its tourism revenue by increasing the number of genealogical tourists to the province. Tourism became a significant industry in Newfoundland only after the Trans-Canada Highway was finished in 1966. Since then, the province's tourism industry has grown significantly. This was helped by several events like the five-hundredth anniversary in 1997 of John Cabot's landing in the province, Soiree '99 (the fiftieth anniversary of Newfoundland joining Canada), and the thousandth anniversary, in 2000, of the arrival of the Vikings. Newfoundland and Labrador also has the potential to increase the number of genealogical tourists to Canada for various reasons: (1) Newfoundland and Labrador already emphasizes cultural tourism, (2) some of the top attractions for visitors to the province are its historic sites, (3) there are many expatriate Newfoundlanders, (4) there are more than 60 000 Canadians of Newfoundland descent in other provinces, and (5) the province has taken several steps to integrate various aspects of interest to the genealogical tourist. An example is the creation of The Rooms in St. John's, a state-of-the-art centre incorporating high curatorial and archival standards, which is built above a working archaeological site and which houses an art gallery, museum, and provincial archives.

A recent study found that the typical genealogical tourist is different from the usual visitor to the province. Statistics provided by the Canadian Tourism Corporation (1997) show that the typical non-resident Newfoundland and Labrador visitor

- is 45 to 54 years old (24 percent were in this age group; 16.5 percent were 55+);
- is likely to be from other parts of Canada (37 percent from Ontario, 25 percent from the Maritimes, 12 percent from western Canada, and 16.5 percent from the U.S.); and
- has a degree and an annual income of more than $60 000.

However, the typical *genealogical* tourist to the province

- is more than 60 years of age (64.6 percent), with another 27.1 percent being in their fifties
- is most likely to be from the United States (41.7 percent) or from Ontario (29.2 percent)
- is very likely to hold a bachelor's (31.9 percent) or higher degree (21.3 percent)
- is likely to be from middle- or upper-income groups: 35 percent earned $30 000–$59 999/year; another 35 percent earned $60 000–$89 999/year and 17.5 percent had earned more than $90 000 a year
- is an avid user of the internet: more than 85.4 percent had internet access at home (which is much higher than the Canadian average of 55 percent), and 71 percent of them went online at least once a day
- is comfortable shopping online; nearly 50 percent had made online purchases
- is comfortable using the internet for genealogical research (92 percent had already done so) and for making travel plans (47.6 percent)
- is married rather than widowed, separated, or single (77.2 percent of married

respondents had taken a genealogical trip versus 63.3 percent of unmarried respondents)

Men and women were equally likely to take a genealogical trip, most often with their partners. While in Newfoundland and Labrador, genealogical tourists were also interested in visiting relatives (77 percent), local communities (58.6 percent), and museums or heritage sites (53.4 percent).

The results of the above survey are in line with previous research on the cultural tourist segment. Cultural tourists are likely to be middle-aged or older, with higher than average income and education (Canadian Tourism Commission, 1997).

Questions:

1. Using the above information, segment the market for genealogical tourism to Newfoundland and Labrador. Specify the segmentation base that you would use and the actual segment that you would target.

2. Would the decision to engage in genealogical research or take a genealogical trip be best explained by an economic, passive, cognitive, or emotional view of consumer behaviour? Justify your answer.

3. Which internal and external factors listed in the simplified model of consumer behaviour described in Chapter 1 do you feel would have an impact on the decision to take a genealogical trip to Newfoundland and Labrador? How would these factors affect a consumer's decision in this case?

Sources: Case written by Mallika Das and Vanessa George. For more information, refer to Vanessa George, "Genealogical Tourism in Newfoundland and Labrador," unpublished B.B.A. Honours thesis, Mount Saint Vincent University, Halifax, N.S., 2003. Courtesy of Vanessa George; Canadian Tourism Commission, *Assessing the Markets: 1997 Newfoundland and Labrador Air Exit Survey,*" 1997. Courtesy of Canadian Tourism Commission.

CASE 1-2: PREPACKAGED SALADS: WHAT EXPLAINS THEIR POPULARITY?

Canadians are buying more and more prepackaged salads and pre-cut vegetables. Prepackaged salads and vegetables account for nearly 10 percent of the $5 billion worth of produce sold in Canada annually. Tom Chang, produce manager at Safeway in Vancouver feels that it is because of the convenience that these products offer. "People will look at a salad-to-go for home or for a picnic. They grab it and go," says Chang. "It's an instant world we live in and the bagged vegetables sell very well." Another produce manager agrees and adds that "people want to get in, get out, make their meals and get on with their lives."

There are other reasons for the increasing popularity of prepackaged vegetables. Consumers are getting older and more concerned about healthy eating. There are more two-income families who are pressed for time, and at the same time, there are more singles who want the convenience that this product offers.

Consumers are also looking for more variety in prepackaged vegetables. It cannot be just lettuce any more; more and more shoppers are looking for a variety of vegetables such as carrots, zucchini, cauliflower, and broccoli. Oriental mixes are also gaining in popularity.

But not all consumers are sold on prepackaged salads. As Dave Nemrava, store manager, Safeway, Burnaby, BC, notes, some cultural groups are reluctant to try them. "I have a very Italian clientele who don't eat anything unless it's made from scratch. That's the way the Italian people have always cooked," says Mr. Nemrava. Others find customers complaining about the high cost of prepackaged vegetables and their short shelf life.

Another factor that seems to affect the sales of prepackaged produce is the amount of shelf space given to it and the number of shelf facings that the products have. Some grocers consider five shelves with side-by-side displays to be the most effective.

What comes after prepackaged vegetables? Prepackaged fruits, of course! Some producers and grocery chains are already starting to experiment with fruits.

Questions:

1. Refer to the simplified model of consumer behaviour found in Chapter 1 and identify the key internal and external factors that seem to be driving the sales of prepackaged vegetables.

2. Do you see the sales of these products growing in the next few years? Why? What changes would the industry have

to make to increase the sales of prepackaged vegetables?

3. Which view of consumer decision making (economic, passive, cognitive or emotional) best explains the decision to buy prepackaged vegetables and salads?

4. Assume that you want to increase the sales of prepackaged vegetables to consumers who currently do not buy them. How would you identify the reasons that they do not buy these products? What research methodology would you use and why?

Source: David Kosub, "Salad Days Are Here Again," *Canadian Grocer*, Toronto, May 2003, Volume 117, Issue 4, 63–64.

CASE 2-1: MARKETING SHEEP'S MILK

Have you tried sheep's milk? Most Canadians are used to cow's milk and not milk from other animals. Stewart Cardiff wants to change that and get Canadians to drink sheep's milk.

Sheep's milk can be used to make delicious cheeses and yogourt. In the words of Stewart Cardiff, president of Shepherd Gourmet Dairy, a small cheese manufacturing firm in Tavistock, Ontario, "sheep's milk yogourt is rich like crème fraîche with a delightful yogourt tang." Stewart and his brother Robert raise the sheep on a 240-hectare farm in Brussels, Ontario; they have 1200 milking ewes.

Sheep dairying is widely practised in Europe, but there are very few such operations in North America, where it seems to be limited to small firms; the products (primarily cheese) are sold only by specialty firms such as Shepherd Gourmet and Vermont Cheese store. In Europe, several high-quality cheeses are made from sheep's milk—in fact, the well-known French blue cheese Roquefort is made totally from sheep's milk.

Shepherd Gourmet makes four products with sheep's milk—yogourt, Liptauer fresh cheese (which is called Liptoi by the firm), feta, and Romano Pecorino. Liptauer, a soft, mild, spreadable Hungarian cream cheese, contains only 16 percent fat (but 69 percent moisture) and has, says Cardiff, "an amazing taste to it...and is phenomenal on bagels."

Sheep's milk has several properties that should make it appealing to Canadians:

- It is naturally homogenized.
- It has much smaller fat globules and is therefore more digestible.
- It is slightly sweeter than cow's milk.
- It has a high milk-solid content, which makes it better suited to produce yogourt and cheese.
- It is far more nutritious than cow's milk. Sheep's milk has almost twice as much calcium as cow's milk and twice as much phosphorus, iron, and zinc. It contains more vitamin A, E, C, and B complex than cow's milk and is rich in other minerals and vitamins. It also contains 50 percent more protein than cow's milk (5.5 percent versus 3.7 percent in cow's milk).
- People are less likely to be allergic to sheep's milk than cow's milk. In fact, Julie Daniluk, a Toronto nutritionist who is lactose-intolerant, was so impressed by her first taste of sheep's milk yogourt and its low allergenicity that she wrote a paper on it. Daniluk says that besides the low allergenicity, the yogourt was "so rich and thick that (it tastes like) sheep's cream thawed out."

In spite of all its nutritional values, most Canadians would be uncomfortable drinking sheep's milk. Although there is a demand for sheep's milk cheese among Canadians from the Middle East and Europe, sheep's milk products (especially the milk), do not seem to have captured the hearts of mainstream Canada.

Questions:

1. What accounts for Canadians' lack of willingness to drink sheep's milk?

2. Using any three motivational concepts covered in Chapter 3, develop a strategy to market sheep's milk (and sheep's milk products) in Canada.

3. How would you teach Canadians about the qualities of sheep's milk and sheep's milk products? What learning theory would you use and why?

4. How can you change Canadians' attitude toward sheep's milk?

5. Develop an ad for sheep's milk and sheep's milk products using one of the following:

(a) learning concepts

(b) attitude change strategies

(c) motives

Source: All quotes in this case are from Judy Creighton, "You've Got to Taste It," *Halifax Mail-Star*, August 6, 2003, C8.

CASE 2-2: *CANADIAN IDOL*: YES. POLITICAL ELECTIONS: NO—GETTING YOUNG CANADIANS TO VOTE

Canadian politicians are facing a major problem—the country's young people do not seem to be interested in them at all. Millions of young Canadians voted in the recent *Canadian Idol* TV contest, but they are not turning up to vote at municipal, provincial or territorial, or federal elections. Although the turnout among other age groups has remained more or less consistent, the turnout among young Canadians (defined as people 18–25 years of age) has been consistently dropping, leading to an overall decline in voter turnout in the country. In the 2004 federal election, for example, only 38 percent of young Canadians voted, far below the average for other age groups. Age is considered to be the single largest indicator of a person's likelihood to vote.

Why is this a major issue? Strong democracies are built on the premise that the government represents the will of the people, and if people do not vote, governments lose their legitimacy. It is feared that over a period, this will lead to a system in which public policy will be shaped by the few who vote and will fail to meet the needs of the general population. The lower turnout among young people is not just a Canadian problem; the same trends have been observed in countries such as Great Britain and the U.S.

Why don't young Canadians vote? Several reasons for this voter apathy have been suggested:

1. Younger voters are not interested in politics and have very little knowledge of political issues or process.

2. Many of the issues debated during election campaigns—such as health care—have little relevance to young people.

3. To vote, a person has to go to the right polling station on the right day with the necessary documents (usually proof of identity and proof of residence within the polling area). Young people, with lower interest in the political process, are not willing to make the effort to find out where the polling station is and go there on election day.

4. Younger voters (like those from other age groups) are not convinced that elected politicians will listen to them. There is the general feeling that politicians will continue to do what they want regardless of who voted for them—in other words, there is a lack of trust in politicians and the political process.

5. Perhaps due to the above factors, younger voters, more than any other group, are not convinced that politics affects their day-to-day lives.

What can be done to solve the above problem? Some of the suggestions that have come forth are:

■ *Lower the voting age to 16:* Proponents of this idea argue that a habit like voting has to be developed early in life. Eryn Fitzgerald, 17, one of two Edmonton teenagers from the University of Alberta who have appealed a court decision denying their application to give voting privileges to 16- and 17-year-olds says, "If you don't start caring early, there is no light bulb that switches on when you turn 18."[1] Fitzgerald and Jairam Singh, her co-appellant, argue that since high school students are in social studies classes in which political issues are raised, allowing them to vote at 16 would help them link their voting decisions to what is happening in their world and convince them of the importance of voting. Furthermore, if you are allowed to work at 16, required to pay taxes on your earnings, and in some cases, allowed to marry, why can't 16- and 17-year-olds be allowed to vote?

Many other countries are considering lowering the voting age to 16 including Great Britain, Germany, Austria, and several states in the U.S. As shown in Table 1, voting ages around the world vary considerably.

[1]Bob Weber, "Vote? Not!" *Halifax Mail-Star*, October 2, 2003, A 16.

TABLE 1	Voting Age in Different Countries
Age	**Country**
15	Iran
16	Brazil, Cuba, Nicaragua
17	Indonesia, North Korea, Sudan
18	Canada, U.S., Britain, Australia, and European Union member countries (In Italy, the voting age for the Senate is 25)
20	Japan, South Korea, Taiwan, Cameroon, Tunisia
21	Central African Republic, Fiji, Gabon, Kuwait, Lebanon, Morocco, Pakistan, Singapore

Opponents of lowering the voting age to 16 argue that this will not solve the problem and point out that when the voting age was lowered from 21 to 18 in the 1960s, voting patterns or turnouts did not increase significantly. The fact that the percentage of first-time voters was the lowest among all age groups (22.4 percent), indicates that the novelty of voting does not seem to encourage younger voters to vote.

■ *Introduce online voting:* Young Canadians, who have grown up in the internet era, are probably less willing to accept the old-fashioned voting mechanisms that are still prevalent today. If the process is the issue, proponents of online voting argue, letting people vote online may solve the problem. This is probably even more likely in the case of younger Canadians because they spend a considerable amount of their time in front of the computer and are very comfortable with the technology.

■ *Reduce voter apathy by showing them the consequences of not voting:* If the reason for the lower turnout among young Canadians is their lack of conviction that their vote would make a difference, then one way to increase their participation in elections is by convincing them that if they do not vote, someone else will speak for them.

The last approach was the one used by Elections Ontario in the 2003 provincial election. Elections Ontario attempted a major campaign to increase voter turnout (especially among the young) through a two-pronged approach. The first step involved an informative campaign aimed at explaining the process—how to get registered, how to vote, and so on. This was followed by an "engage" campaign aimed at motivating voters by letting them know that if they don't vote, they lose their voice and someone else will speak for them.

Palmer Jarvis DDB, the company hired to develop the ads, tested its creative concepts in focus groups and found them to be effective. The ads showed young people at a restaurant or hair salon having their requests being interrupted by another person who basically "orders" for them. For example, in "Restaurant" a couple is interrupted as they are enquiring about the menu by another customer who orders a cheeseburger on a pita for the woman and says the man doesn't want anything. The ads closed with the tag line "When you don't vote, you let others speak for you."

The ad campaign was supported by print ads that had another person's mouth superimposed on a voter's face with the same tag line. One ad, which had an older person's mouth on a younger person's face, drew a lot of criticism from seniors' groups and even got the campaign some free publicity.

Was the campaign successful? Initial analysis indicates that although the actual overall turnout decreased (from 58.3 percent in 1999 to 57 percent in 2003), Elections Ontario was able to add 600 000 names to the registry. This was a significant achievement in itself, because a more complete voters' list helps to identify the total number of eligible voters. Moreover, everyone on the list receives a card telling them where to vote; it also serves as a reminder. Elections Ontario claims that the decreased turnout is due to a more complete voter registry and that previous percentages had been based on inaccurate calculations of the total number of eligible voters.[2]

[2] Dan Rath, "A Challenge Too Big for Marketing?" *Marketing Magazine*, October 27, 2003.

Questions:

1. What decision process would voters (especially younger voters) go through while making the decision to vote?

2. Would lowering the voting age work? Why and why not?

3. Would younger voters be more likely to vote if given the option of online voting? Why?

4. What motives was the Elections Ontario campaign appealing to? What stage in the decision process was it aimed at?

5. Why did the Elections Ontario campaign not succeed in increasing voter turnout among young adults?

6. Using the consumer behaviour principles that you have learned in the chapter on motivation, develop an ad that would appeal to young Canadians and make them vote.

7. What learning theory can be used to teach younger voters the importance of voting? Using the learning theory that you have chosen, develop an ad that would appeal to young voters.

8. What attitude change strategy would you use to change young Canadians' attitudes toward voting? Develop an ad that incorporates the attitude change strategy that you have chosen.

CASE 2-3: VAN HOUTTE COFFEE

Van Houtte Coffee Inc. is a Montreal-based company that specializes in producing and distributing coffee in Canada and the U.S. With total sales of $316 768 000 ($88.5 million of it in the U.S), Van Houtte (VH) is a major player in the coffee business, especially in Canada, where it holds 50 percent of the office-coffee market.

Founded in 1919 by Albert-Louis Van Houtte, a European immigrant, the company has grown significantly in the past few decades. The company went private in 1987; it has 1750 employees and every day con-

sumers buy or make more than 1.2 billion cups of Van Houtte coffee. It has four major lines: Gourmet, International, Flavoured and Organic/Socially Responsible Coffee. In each line, the company offers six or seven varieties. For example, its Gourmet line has two House Blends (light and dark), two Mocha Javas (light and dark), 100 percent Colombian, and Decaffeinated. Its newest addition, the Organic and Socially Responsible Coffees, which was introduced in 2002, offers seven varieties of organic coffee (100 percent Colombian, Peru, Frenchroast, Mexico, Mocha Java Light, Breakfast Blend, and Mexico Dark).

VH segments its markets in two ways—by type of coffee (as described above) and by type of distribution. The company distributes its coffee through retail stores, 68 franchised cafés in Quebec, hotels, restaurants, and institutions or the HRI market, and offices. The company is well known in Quebec because of its 68 cafés and the more than 500 Alimentation Couche-Tard outlets where its coffee is sold. However, outside Quebec, the brand is not well known, though the company has made inroads in western Canada.

Sixty-five percent of VH's total revenue comes from the office coffee market and the company holds 50 percent of the total market for office coffee in Canada. The company's success in the office-coffee market is based on the excellence of its products (both its coffee and its equipment), its customer service, and the efficiency of its sales force. In fact, its premise has been, in the words of CEO Mr. Monette, "Office coffee does not have to be bad!"[1] VH markets high-end gourmet coffee to offices and provides both traditional and single-cup coffee brewing machines to this market. Its Keurig and VOG coffee makers are made by its subsidiary, VKI Technologies, in collaboration with Malongo, a European company which is a leader in the industry.

The company used to sell its office coffee under the Selena and Red Carpet brand names, but has begun to use its Van Houtte brand name in this market. The move is one of the company's efforts to strengthen the brand identity for its products. Although the

[1] Shirley Won, "Van Houtte Brews Plan to Bolster Brand Name, Fend Off Competitors," *Globe and Mail*, July 3, 2004, B3

office-coffee market accounts for a significant part of its revenue, the company would like to see its overall sales outside Quebec—especially to the consumer market—increase. VH has taken several steps to achieve this goal:

- In 2002, it started selling a single-cup coffee brewer in the consumer market. Named "Keurig B100," this is a retail version of its single-cup Keuring brewer sold in the office market. The easy-to-use coffee maker fits under most kitchen cabinets and is built to serve single servings of coffee or tea. Consumers have to just put a K-cup coffee package (or a Bigelow tea package) in the machine and switch it on; within a minute, one hot cup of coffee is ready. The machine holds enough hot water to make eight single servings. Though the introductory price was $299, the regular retail price was set at $349; the price included a coffee machine and 50 free K-cup packages of coffee or tea, which the customer could get through the company's website.

- VH has started selling its brand through 112 Chevron convenience stores (with self-service coffee bars) and 225 Safeway supermarkets in British Columbia.

- VH hopes to open more of its cafes (which are modelled on Second Cup and Starbucks) in markets outside Quebec.

- As stated earlier, it has started using its Van Houtte brand name in its office market.

- VH has started selling its products through its website to let consumers buy the product in places where it is not available in retail outlets.

Coffee is the most popular hot drink in Canada. Consider the following statistics:

- 67 percent of adult Canadians drink coffee every day; they drink an average of three cups a day.

- 74 percent of all coffee drunk is roast and ground, 20 percent is instant and 6 percent is specialty.

- 69 percent of all coffee is drunk at home or in someone else's home; 13 percent of coffee is consumed at work or school, and 12 percent in restaurants or take-out locations.

- 57 percent of people between the ages of 18 and 24 drink coffee every week; for those who are 65 and over, the rate is 88 percent.

Questions:

1. How would you segment the consumer market for coffee? Which target market would you choose for Van Houtte and why?

2. If you were asked to develop a marketing strategy for VH, how would you motivate consumers to buy VH coffee (i.e, what motives would you appeal to)?

3. What personality or life-style concepts can be used to develop a strategy to reach final consumers for VH coffee?

4. Consumers already know—or have heard of—Van Houtte coffee through its presence in the office market. How can you teach consumers to buy it for home use?

5. Are consumers looking for different things when they buy coffee for home use (compared to office use)? What would the differences be?

6. Develop an ad for VH coffee (for the consumer market) using:

   motivational concepts

   learning theory/concepts

   personality or life style ideas

Sources: Shirley Won, "Van Houtte Brews Plan to Bolster Brand Name, Fend Off Competitors," *Globe and Mail*, July 3, 2004, B3. Reprinted with permission from *The Globe and Mail*; Van Houtt's 2003-04 annual report, **www.vanhoutte.com**; press releases provided on the company's website; and "Everything About Coffee," on the company's website.

CASE 3-1: CAN SALADS BE MADE SEXY?

Obesity is the disease du jour in Canada and the U.S. Several research studies have shown that nearly 50 percent of Canadians are overweight and one in five is obese. The obesity epidemic has reached the youth market too—Statistics Canada figures show that nearly 5 percent of teenagers are obese, and nearly 17 percent of boys and 10 percent of girls in the 12–19-year category are overweight. Similar results have been found in the under-12 age group.[1] How does all this affect food

[1]"Parent and Child Factors Associated with Obesity," *The Daily*, Statistics Canada, November 3, 2003.

marketers in the packaged goods and fast food (or Quick Service Industry as they are sometimes called)? Several firms in these industries have launched healthful initiatives. For example, Kraft Foods (Canada) started an "obesity initiative" with a four-prong attack on obesity—product initiatives (e.g., cap on the size of servings), better marketing practices (e.g., elimination of all in-school advertising), consumer information (e.g., better labelling practices) and advocacy (e.g., engaging schools and communities in healthy living initiatives). Kraft also has a "Healthy Living" section on its website, which provides information about obesity (e.g., body-mass calculators, calorie counters). McDonald's, which was recently involved in a class-action suit in the U.S. that claimed that its food had led to childhood obesity, has also been actively promoting its "Healthy Choices" menu options. In fact, the company's Canadian operation was the first to introduce the healthier alternatives, and it is spending $15–$20 million to promote these options. The company is also introducing more yogourt and vegetables in its Happy Meals options and dropping its super-size fries and drinks.

Why is McDonald's (or any other firm) interested in promoting healthful eating? There are several reasons: the companies are worried about possible lawsuits; they feel that healthy eating might be here to stay and hence that there might be a market; it is a good public relations move for them; and perhaps they recognize that it is better for them (in the long run) if their customers stay alive!

However, we as consumers, are not making things easier for food marketers or fast food chains. Consider the following:[2]

- Almost all Canadians eat at a fast-food restaurant at least once a month.

- 29 percent of Canadians eat at a fast-food outlet at least once a week.

- Younger Canadians (under 35) are more likely to eat fast food than others.

- 26 percent eat at McDonald's most often, 12 percent at Wendy's, and 10 percent at Subway.

- Only 6 percent of Canadians consider McDonald's offerings to be healthful;

45 percent consider it to be the least healthful choice.

- A few years ago, drive-throughs accounted for only 10 percent of McDonald's business, but now they account for nearly 60 percent of its business.

Furthermore, when fast food chains start offering more healthful options, Canadians did not seem to be excited. For example, McDonald's started offering salads in the late 1990s, but as one McDonald's executive said, "We couldn't give them away." The same problem arose with the McLean burger; even though consumers said it tasted like "sawdust in a bun," blind taste tests found that consumers liked its taste. Although salads have become more popular, many researchers think that these healthful product offerings by fast food outlets are bound to fail for two important reasons. To begin with, the typical fast food patron is not interested in these products (after all, if they cannot walk 10 steps into the restaurant to place their order for the food, can they really be interested in healthful food?); secondly, many consumers believe that healthful food has to taste bad. One researcher remarked, perhaps we "like fries not in spite of the fact that they're unhealthy, but because of it."[3]

Fast food chains have followed different strategies to promote their more healthful menu options. McDonald's has run an interesting campaign for its "Healthier Choices" menu. One ad shows two joggers, both tired-looking, and one asks the other how far they've run. The answer—"two blocks"—makes his face drop. Of course, McDonald's is there to help them in their healthful living initiatives with its "Healthy Choices" menu. Subway, on the other hand, uses a different strategy. Its "6 subs under 7 grams of fat" campaign and "Jerrad" ads use an "it's better for you" message.

Questions:

1. Why do consumers continue to choose unhealthful food such as fast food meals, especially fries, big burgers, and so on?

[2] Dave Scholz and Gilbert Paquette, "Jumping On-or-Off the Fat Bandwagon," *Marketing Magazine*, March 8, 2004.

[3] Lara Mills, "The Fat of the Land," *Marketing Magazine*, April 2, 2001, **http://www.marketingmag.ca/ magazine/current/commentary/ article.jsp?content=20010402_17070**.

2. Identify the cultural values that may be encouraging us to continue our love affair with "junk" food. What cultural values would work against the consumption of junk food by Canadians?

3. Using your knowledge of young adults, explain whether McDonald's' approach or Subway's would work in making these consumers move toward healthier choices.

4. Young men are the primary consumers of fast food. How would you make this group choose the healthier options (such as salads) in fast food?

5. Using concepts covered in the chapters on culture and subculture, develop an ad to attract the following groups to more healthful fast food offerings: young men (20–34), teenagers (13–19), young women (20–34), older adults (65+).

Sources: Sarah Dobson, "Executives Decry Lack of Innovation," *Marketing Magazine*, January 27, 2003; Jim McElgunn, "Soy Salads," *Marketing Magazine*, July 15, 2002; Lesley Young, "In the Fat Seat," *Marketing Magazine*, August 11, 2003; Karl Moore, "Demise of the Super Size," *Marketing Magazine*, June 7, 2004; Lesley Young, "Special K Walks Its Talk," *Marketing Magazine*, January 12, 2004; Lesley Young, "McDonald's Lightens Up Its Menu," *Marketing Magazine*, January 26, 2004.

CASE 3-2: MARKETING ORGANIC FOODS TO THE GENERAL PUBLIC

Organic foods have been increasing in popularity in Canada. A.C. Nielsen's Fresh Track surveys found that sales of organic fruits and vegetables increased by 8 percent in 2002 and reached annual sales volume of $33 million; industry experts expect sales figures to experience double-digit growth for the next few years.

Though these numbers are encouraging, there are reasons for organic farmers to worry. A.C. Nielsen figures indicate that only 28 percent of the Canadian population have ever bought organic produce. Even more worrisome to some researchers is the finding in the U.S. that while sales of organic foods are likely to grow in the near future, this growth would come from increased sales to current purchasers rather than an increase in the total number of organic food buyers. Only 3 percent of non-organic food buyers in the U.S. said they would buy organic food in the next six months. Clearly, if there is to be continued growth in the organic foods industry, it has to persuade current non-purchasers to start buying organic foods.

Who is the typical organic food purchaser? Let us look at some research done in British Columbia, which is one of the leaders in organic food sales in the country. A 2003 study showed that slightly more than 50 percent of BC residents had bought some organic food in the past 12 months. The Certified Organic Associations of British Columbia has done considerable research to identify current buyers of organic produce. Here are some of their findings:[1]

- Organic food buyers are slightly younger than non-organic food buyers; 38 percent of non-organic food buyers were under 44 years of age compared to 44 percent of light purchasers of organic food,[2] 48 percent of medium purchasers, and 51 percent of heavy purchasers.

- Organic food buyers are slightly more likely to have some university education.

- Organic food buyers are slightly more likely to belong to higher income groups.

- Among organic food buyers, heavy users are more likely to be single, while medium and light users are likely to be from family households.

- Men and women are equally likely to buy organic foods.

- Light users of organic foods are more likely to buy these foods because they think organic foods taste better; medium and heavy users are more likely to buy organic foods for health reasons ("it's better for you").

- Better taste is also mentioned more often by people who buy organic meats, poultry, and eggs than those buying organic fruits and vegetables.

[1] COABC Market Survey, September 18, 2003, **www.coabc.ca**.

[2] Respondents were classified as "light" purchasers of organic foods if organic foods constituted 1–9 percent of their grocery purchases, "medium" purchasers if 10–24 percent of grocery purchases were organic, and "heavy" if 25 percent or more of their grocery purchases were organic.

- Medium to heavy users of organic foods are more likely than light or non-users to say they do not watch TV news.

- Organic food buyers seem to prefer CBC radio; nearly 20 percent said CBC was the radio station they listened to the most.

Why don't Canadians buy organic foods? The main reason stated by non-buyers was price, with 54 percent giving high price as a reason for not buying organic foods. A significant percentage of non-buyers (19 percent) had no particular reason; 9 percent thought there were no differences between organic and non-organic foods, and 7 percent did not trust that foods labelled "organic" were really organic in nature. Another 6 percent were just not interested and thought "regular" food was fine. Another study found that non-buyers consider organic food to be for hippies and to be limited to tofu and brown rice.[3] As noted by a major organic foods retailer in BC, many non-buyers are unaware of the benefits of organic foods—better taste, promotion of environmental responsibility and sustainability, and lack of pesticides.

Grocers like organic foods because they provide higher margins. However, many grocery stores have only a limited selection of organic foods. There are stores that specialize in organic foods, such as Planet Organic (with stores in Edmonton, Calgary, Victorian and Port Coquitlam) and Whole Foods (in Toronto).

Questions:

1. What cultural values promote the popularity of organic foods? Which ones would work against Canadians buying organic foods?

2. Would you use an opinion leader to promote organic foods? If so, who would it be?

3. From the information provided, which VALS segment would you consider to be the most likely purchasers of organic foods? Who would be possible buyers of organic foods?

4. From the information provided, how would you create positive attitudes toward organic foods among non-

buyers? Which attitude change strategy would you use and why?

5. How would you change consumers' perception of organic foods (as being for hippies and being different from "regular" food)?

6. Consumers seem to consider organic foods to be too expensive and, perhaps, not worth the extra cost. How can you change this negative image?

7. Using your answers to the questions above, develop a strategy to market organic foods to consumers who do not currently buy these foods.

CASE 3-3: SELLING THE TRADES

Would you like an occupation that would give you a six-figure salary? One that does not involve an expensive college or university education that would leave you with a huge loan? Well, perhaps you should have considered a skilled trade rather than a community college or university education.

Most industry and government studies find that Canada is facing a shortage of skilled workers, and this shortage is only going to increase with time as the aging trade workers start retiring. For example, the Government of Ontario has identified 12 trades were a shortage of workers exists currently—trades such as refrigeration and air conditioning mechanics, construction boilermakers, and general carpenters. Other trades such as heavy manufacturing, oil and gas, and construction have had shortages for some time. This shortage can have a significant impact on all Canadians; not having enough plumbers to fix a leaking pipe or carpenters to build homes can make it difficult and expensive for everyone. Moreover, this can also lead to Canadian firms losing out to foreign competitors with a better pool of skilled workers.

What is surprising is that this is happening at a time when university and community college graduates are having a hard time finding suitable jobs. Given the advantages that an education in trades can offer, one would expect young Canadians to opt for the trades in greater number. Consider the following:

- The hourly starting wages for students or apprentices in the trades range from $15

[3] Eve Lazarus, "Planet Organic Plots Suburban Push," *Marketing Magazine*, March 8, 2004.

to $25; so you can not only complete the training without a student loan, but can probably have some savings before you complete your training.

- Experienced tradespeople (e.g., electricians, toolmakers) make around $35 an hour or up to $72 000 if they are employed full-time.

- An apprentice program, which takes three or four years to complete, offers the trainee the chance to earn good wages for 44 to 46 weeks a year; this has to be followed by 6 to 8 weeks of classroom education.

- Trades offer people the chance to work with their hands and produce something tangible—that can be a rewarding experience.

- Trades also offer people the opportunity to become their own bosses since it is easy for them to set up their own businesses.

- The predicted vacancy rates in most trades is significant; for example, the Automotive Parts Manufacturers Association predicts a 42 percent vacancy rate in skilled trades by 2007.

Why, then, are Canadians reluctant to enter the trades? Studies reveal that most high school students plan to go to a university or community college rather than a trade school. In fact, a survey by Human Resources Development Canada showed that only 6 percent of high school students were planning to attend a trade school, and 44 percent would not consider a job in the skilled trades. There are several reasons for the low enrolment in trade schools.

Statistics Canada found that high school students consider skilled trades to be "usually high paying" (58 percent agreed with the statement), to be able to "provide long-term secure jobs" (56 percent agreed), and to provide "excellent benefits" (51 percent agreed), but to be "not exciting jobs" (23 percent agreed) and to "require manual labour" (61 percent agreed). Other factors also seem to play a part in reducing the attractiveness of a trade school education or apprenticeship:

- High schools have been emphasizing academic programs more; this has led to students having less exposure to trades. In 1966, about 20 percent of the credits obtained by a typical Ontario high school graduate were in technical subjects; by 1990, this had dropped to 5 percent and is even lower now.

- Each province has its own apprenticeship system, standards, and certifications, making a unified appeal difficult; this also makes it more difficult for trade school graduates to move across Canada.

- In the case of apprentice programs, students have to make a four-year commitment at an age when they are not ready to do so.

- Completion rates in apprenticeship programs are very low. For example, although there were more than 200 000 people registered in apprenticeship programs in 2001, only 18 260 received completion certificates. And the completion rates in some apprenticeship programs (e.g., construction) have been falling since 1995.

However, some researchers feel that the real reason the trades do not attract young Canadians has to do with their image. An economist with the Conference Board of Canada said, "We're going to need a seismic cultural and value shift within society.... There is a bias against this type of education, especially in parents' minds."[1] Mr. Williams, chair of the Apprenticeship and Industry Training Board in Alberta, agrees: "The trades have suffered something of an image problem for many, many years....[2] Parents are something of a stumbling block... Most want their children to go to university."[3] Guidance counsellors also feel that many parents view trades as being inferior and less prestigious than white-collar or professional occupations. This might be partly the result of better marketing efforts by universities, but is probably reflective of the value our culture places on different occupations. Whereas parents in some European countries may feel it is something to celebrate when their teenaged son or daughter decides to embark on a trade-school education, most middle- or upper-class Canadian parents would be a little disappointed to hear the same. This view is reinforced by

[1] Katherine Harding, "Trading Spaces," *Globe and Mail*, August 27, 2003, C2.
[2] Ibid., C1
[3] Ibid., C2

teachers and guidance counsellors who imply that non-academic courses are meant for students who aren't "bright."

Skills Canada Ontario, a non-profit organization involved in getting more Canadian youth to choose skilled trades, has tried to combat the negative image of the trades by running ads that featured young trades people driving luxury cars. The campaign was aired first in the Kitchener-Waterloo area and aimed to show that the trades are "cool" by showing good-looking young people who chose skilled trades as being successful.

Questions:

1. What cultural values work against the choice of skilled trades as an occupation by young Canadians? What would work in their favour?

2. Besides parents, who are the other major influencers in a teenager's decision to choose an occupation?

3. Do you agree with the approach taken by Skills Canada Ontario? Why or why not?

4. Who would be reference group members for high school students? Who would be opinion leaders?

5. What attitude change strategy would you suggest to change the attitudes of young Canadians and their parents toward the trades as an occupation?

6. Develop an ad for attracting Canadian teenagers toward the trades. Use one or more concepts learned in this text about:

    attitudes and changing attitudes

    learning

    motivation

    cultural values

    reference groups

    opinion leadership

7. Develop an ad aimed at parents of Canadian teenagers toward the trades. Use one or more concepts learned in this text about:

    attitudes and changing attitudes

    learning

    motivation

    cultural values

Sources: Katherine Harding, "Trading Spaces," *Globe and Mail*, August 27, 2003, C1–2; Ross Marowits, "Building a Trade," *Halifax Chronicle-Herald*, September 11, 2003, A14; Wallace Immen, "Keep the Trades on Track," *Globe and Mail*, January 21, 2004, C1,C2, C8.

CASE 4-1: REACHING THE DEAF AND HEARING-IMPAIRED[1]

Nearly 10 percent of Canadians—or nearly three million people—having some degree of hearing loss and could benefit from the use of a hearing aid. Yet, only 20 percent of these people actually buy a hearing aid. Some organizations say that the actual number of Canadians with some hearing loss is much higher—the Canadian Hearing Society's 2001 survey puts the number of Canadians with hearing loss at 25 percent.

Close to 90 percent of people with hearing loss have what is called sensorineural hearing loss, or hearing loss due to damage to the inner ear or the hearing nerve in the brain (refer to Exhibit 1 for more details). Contrary to what most people think, hearing loss is not restricted to older people; nearly half of the Canadians affected by hearing loss are under 65 years of age. According to the Canadian Hearing Society (CHS), nearly 80 percent of Canadians have worked with someone, or have a friend or relative, who is hearing-impaired. The average age of those experiencing hearing loss is 51; nearly 25 percent of Canadians suffering from hearing loss are under 40, and 70 percent are under 60.

Hearing loss affects a person's life significantly. For example, a hearing-impaired person is often left out of conversations and hence may avoid company. This loneliness can lead to depression. To compound the problem, people with normal hearing may be uncomfortable with a person who has difficulty hearing. In fact, surveys by CHS have found that one in eight Canadians actively avoids dealing with people who have hearing loss, primarily because they don't know how to talk to them. Yet, unlike in the case of vision problems, people are reluctant to seek help or get a hearing aid. Nearly one in six Canadians say they would rather live with

[1] This case is based on information from the following sources: Canadian Hearing Society, **www.chs.ca**; Hearing Loss Web, **www.hearinglossweb.com**; and Mark Ross, "Why People Won't Wear Hearing Aids," http://www.hearinglossweb.com/Technology/HearingAids/no_wear.htm.

hearing loss than wear a hearing aid. Most people with hearing loss deny that a problem exists and blame their inability to hear (and hence communicate effectively) on others (e.g., "people mumble"). Why are people so reluctant to seek help to correct the loss of one of the five basic human senses?

Audiologists and others working with the hearing-impaired, offer several explanations:[2] (1) people associate deafness with old age and, given the North American emphasis on youth, are reluctant to admit that they suffer from hearing loss; (2) hearing loss is associated with loss of mental faculty—after all, we talk of being "deaf and dumb"; (3) hearing loss is often very gradual; this makes it difficult for the person involved to realize that he or she has a problem, that is, is suffering from hearing loss; (4) some people hesitate to wear hearing aids for cosmetic reasons; unlike glasses, hearing aids have always been considered ugly and something to be hidden; (5) hearing aids are visible statements of a person's disability, and being recognized as having a disability is hard for most of us; (6) in older people, there is a reluctance to try something new; hearing aids represent new technology, and some older consumers are afraid of handling a miniature, sophisticated device; (7) hearing aids often do not solve the problem totally—hearing aids are often not fitted well and can lead to "whistling" in your ear; they distort your own voice and do not function very effectively when there is a lot of "cross-talk" or noise; and (8) they are expensive—$800 to $2000 (although this is covered at least partly by some provincial health care plans). While all of the above contribute to consumers' unwillingness to buy hearing aids, many researchers feel that the primary issues are the stigma associated with the product (i.e., perceptions that being deaf also means that you are not as sharp mentally), the perception that it is a disease of the old (84 percent of Canadians believe that hearing loss is a natural part of aging), and the unwillingness to admit that one has a disability. Further, the slow, gradual, nature of hearing loss makes it difficult for people to recognize that they have a problem.

Unfortunately, marketers have helped perpetuate the problem in some ways. Most makers of hearing aids stress the fact that their product is small and "no one would know that you are wearing one," indirectly conveying the message that hearing loss is something to be hidden. Even audiologists and other professionals help perpetuate the stereotypes by prescribing smaller hearing aids that can be "hidden" rather than larger, behind-the-ear products, even when a patient would be better served by the larger model.

Among people less than 65 years of age, men are more likely to suffer from hearing loss; the gender difference decreases over the age of 65, but even then, men are more likely than women to experience hearing loss. Furthermore, men are more likely to resist admitting that they have a problem or to start using a hearing aid. Often, they go to see an audiologist only because their partner or other family members complain about them turning up the volume on the television.

Questions:

1. How can you trigger problem recognition in those suffering from hearing loss?

2. What type of a decision (routinized, limited, or extended problem solving) situation is the choice of a hearing aid?

3. Canadians seem to have negative attitudes toward using a hearing aid. How would you try to change these negative attitudes? What attitude change strategy would you recommend and why?

4. What motives underlie a consumer's decision to buy a hearing aid? What motives would prevent a consumer from buying a hearing aid?

5. What role do personality and self-concept play in this decision?

6. How can you teach consumers that they have to check their hearing and use hearing aids if necessary? Which learning theory or concept would you use and why?

7. Develop an ad to make consumers change their perceptions of hearing aids and people wearing them using:

   attitude change strategies

   motivational concepts

   personality and self-concept

   learning theories

8. Develop an ad to trigger problem recognition among people suffering from hearing loss.

[2] Adapted from Mark Ross, "Why People Won't Wear Hearing Aids," http://www.hearinglossweb.com/Technology/HearingAids/no_wear.htm.

EXHIBIT 1:   HEARING LOSS: CAUSES, SOLUTIONS, AND DIAGNOSIS[3]

Why Can't You Hear Well?

Hearing loss or deafness (i.e., the decrease in the perception and understanding of sound), can range from mild to profound. Whereas people with normal hearing can hear sounds in the 0–25 decibel (dB) range, those with mild hearing loss can hear only in the 26–45 dB range. Those with moderate hearing loss hear sounds in the 46-65 dB range, those with severe hearing loss can hear sounds only in the 66–85 dB range, and those with profound hearing loss can hear sounds only above 85 dB.

Hearing loss can be of two types—conductive hearing loss and sensorineural hearing loss. *Conductive hearing loss* occurs when sound is not properly conducted or passed through the ear canal or there are problems with the ear drum or the middle ear. The common causes for this condition are

- blockages in the ear (e.g., ear wax or a foreign object),
- perforations to the ear drum, middle ear infections, and
- injuries to the small bones in the middle ear.

Conductive hearing loss can usually be reversed by surgery. *Sensorineural hearing loss* (which is the cause of hearing loss in nearly 90 percent of the cases), is due to damages to the inner ear or cochlea or the hearing nerve in the brain. Common causes for sensorineural hearing loss are

- excessive noise,
- viral or bacterial infections,
- side effects of some medications, and
- tumours or other diseases such as Ménière's disease.

Unlike conductive hearing loss, sensorineural hearing loss is generally permanent, and hearing aids would be required to help the person to hear better.

Hearing Aids

There are four basic types of hearing aids: behind the ear (BTE), in the ear (ITE), in the canal (ITC), and completely in the canal (CIC). These are shown below:[4]

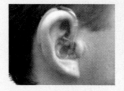 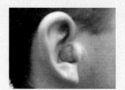 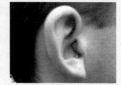

BTE   *ITE*   *ITC*   *CIC*

As can be seen from the above pictures, CICs are invisible, and BTEs are the most visible of hearing aids.

Hearing aids can be classified into three types according to the type of sound processing that they employ. *Analogue hearing aids* are the most basic type of hearing aids; they are linear in nature—that is, they just amplify all sounds equally. So if you want to hear softer sounds better, you just need to turn up the volume in your hearing aid manually. They need

[3] American Academy of Audiology and Canadian Academy of Audiology (Consumer information sections); Mark Ross, "Why People Won't Wear Hearing Aids," **http://www.hearinglossweb.com/Technology/ HearingAids/no_wear.htm**.

[4] Used with the permission of the American Academy of Audiology, **www.audiology.org**.

to be sent to the manufacturer for corrections. *Programmable with analogue signal processing* hearing aids use analogue technology but can be programmed digitally for non-linear sound signal processing (i.e., softer sounds can be amplified more and loud ones can be amplified less). Hearing aids that are *programmable with digital signal processing* are the latest in audiology technology. Since these use digital sound processing, they are capable of doing several million calculations on the sounds that they receive and can be programmed to respond (or amplify) different sounds to different levels. In other words, they can be programmed to amplify human speech sound more than other noises.

How can you tell if you have hearing loss? While only a trained audiologist can tell you if you are suffering from hearing loss, here are a list of questions that you can ask yourself to see if you need to visit an audiologist:

Do you experience any of the following problems?[5]

- difficulty hearing over the telephone?
- difficulty following the conversation when two or more people are talking at the same time?
- people complaining that you turn the TV volume up too high?
- difficulty in understanding conversations without straining?
- trouble hearing in noisy surroundings?
- having to ask people to repeat themselves?
- feeling people are mumbling (or not speaking clearly)?
- often misunderstanding what others are saying and replying inappropriately?
- difficulty understanding the speech of women and children?
- other people getting annoyed because you misunderstand what they say?

[5] Adapted from Canadian Academy of Audiology; **http://www.canadianaudiology.ca/consumer-information/you_and_your_hearing_loss.html**.

CASE 4-2: WET TOILET PAPER?

What's new in the highly competitive world of toilet paper (or bathroom tissues as it is called in the industry)? Moist bathroom tissues—not the "baby wipes" that you might be familiar with, but moist bathroom tissues meant for the entire family.

Moist bathroom tissues were first test marketed in the U.S. in the late 1970s by Proctor and Gamble, the consumer products giant.[1] The product, called "Certain" was not one of P&G's success stories. Introduced in a two-roll version, in trial markets in the Southern U.S., the product failed to capture the hearts and minds of the typical American consumer. There were several reasons for its failure—the first test-marketed versions were not of high quality, the perfume used in the product was irritating to some consumers, the price was considered too high by some consumers, the product

[1] David L. Loudon and Albert J. Della Bitta, *Consumer Behaviour*, Second Edition, McGraw-Hill, 1984, Case 4-6: "Certain."

required consumers to change their bathroom tissue dispenser (to hold the moist tissue), and perhaps the biggest reason—Americans were just not ready for wet toilet paper. There were also fears that the product might clog their toilet. The company reintroduced an improved version of the product a few years later; again, it failed to capture enough market share and was dropped. The product never went beyond the test-marketing stage, though the company spent considerable funds on promotion.

The bathroom tissue market is a huge—$700 million in 2003—and competitive one, dominated by two large multinational companies: P&G (Charmin) and Kimberly-Clark (Cottonelle, Scott, and White Swan in the U.S.). In Canada, the main contenders are P&G with its Charmin brand, Scott Paper which markets Cottonelle, Scott, Purex, Soft and Pure, Capri, and White Swan brands; and Irving, which owns Majesta and Royale (which acquired P&G in 2001). (Cottonelle is owned by Kimberly Clark in the U.S., owing to the merger of K-C and Scott Paper in 1995, but in Canada, it is still owned by Scott Paper, which is a subsidiary of Kruger.) Cottonelle is the leading brand in eastern Canada, and Scott Paper's other brand—Purex—is the industry leader in the western provinces.

In 2001, Kimberly-Clark (K-C) entered the market with its version of moist bathroom tissue—Cottonelle Fresh Rollwipes. According to the company, this is the first real innovation in the bathroom tissue category in 100 years. The product was introduced in the southeastern and northeastern United States (nearly half of the country), and was to be phased in to the rest of the country in stages. Unlike P&G's attempt to replace dry toilet paper with moistened ones, K-C seems to be trying to introduce its version as a supplement to dry toilet papers. The dispenser solves some of the problems that the earlier product faced: it snaps on to an existing toilet roll dispenser and has an easy-to-use format. It also lets consumers use their regular bathroom tissue by providing a spindle for it at the bottom. The product is also alcohol-free, flushable, biodegradable, and sewer-and-septic safe. It was introduced in a four-roll pack with a dispenser for US$8.99; refills of four-packs cost US$3.99.

The company spent over $100 million to develop the roll and the dispenser, and it holds over 30 patents on it. The launch cost K-C $40 million and the company expected the product category sales to reach $500 million in a few years. Its own research had found that consumers would accept the moist bathroom tissue as a complement to dry toilet paper as it was easy and convenient and provided superior cleaning and freshness. In fact, its research indicated that 63 percent of consumers already use some form of wet cleaning after using the toilet and one in four used moist cleansing every day. K-C introduced the product with a television blitz, which was supported by print and internet advertising. The television ad showed several people swimming, biking, or walking with close-ups of their behinds; the ad ended with the announcer stating, "Introducing Cottonelle Fresh Rollwipes. Together with dry toilet paper, these new pre-moistened wipes on a roll leave you feeling cleaner and fresher.... Cottonelle Fresh Rollwipes.... What it means to feel clean." The ad ended with the slogan " sometimes wetter is better."

Not to be outdone, P&G also introduced its version of moist wipes: Charmin Fresh Mates Rolls at a lower price: $2.49–$2.99 for a dispenser and a sample roll. Interestingly, this product was launched the same day as Cottonelle Fresh Rollwipes and in the same areas. Although P&G did not say what it spent on the development and marketing of Charmin Fresh Mates Rolls, industry insiders think that the company would have spent considerable amounts on the new product's launch. P&G's ads were less direct than K-C's. They featured a bear and duck, with the duck emphasizing the importance of being fresh; then the bear gets the picture and goes behind a tree with Charmin Fresh Mates.

The results were similar to those in the seventies. Both products failed, and while K-C still continues to sell Cottonelle Fresh Rollwipes in some areas, P&G has dropped the Fresh Mates Rolls. Both companies have the same products in a tub version similar to baby wipes. Industry analysts offered several explanations for the new product's failure including high price, poor marketing including ads that did not convey the product's key message effectively, the nature of the product itself (bathroom tissues are not easy products to talk about!) and consumers' resistance to the idea.

Scott Paper which owns the Cottonelle brand in Canada is yet to introduce moist bathroom tissue to this market though it carries them in the tub format.

Questions:

1. What type of an innovation is moist bathroom tissue? What factors would lead to the quick adoption of this innovation? What would work against this product? (Refer to Chapter 13, Figure 13-12).

2. Why do you feel consumers are so reluctant to try moist bathroom tissues? What cultural values are in favour of this product? What values are against this product? Would this product succeed in another culture?

3. Do you like the ads run by K-C and P&G? Why/why not?

4. What type of a decision making situation does moist toilet paper represent (i.e, is it a routinized, limited or extensive problem-solving situation)?

5. Obviously, consumers are satisfied with their current choices in terms of bathroom tissue. How can you trigger problem recognition in this instance?

6. Would you use an opinion leader for promoting this product? Why/why not? If you would use an opinion leader, who would it be?

7. How can you change consumer attitudes toward this product? What attitude change strategy would you suggest?

8. Which learning theory would be appropriate to use in this situation? Why?

9. Develop an ad for promoting this product that incorporates your answers to the above questions.

Sources: "First Major Toilet Paper Innovation in Over 100 Years" **emailwire.com/news/hou457.shtml**; Linda Kwong, "Kimberly-Clark Corporation Announces Cottonelle Fresh Rollwipes, America's First Dispersible Pre-Moistened Wipe on a Roll," **http://investor. kimberly-clark.com/news/20010116-35431.cfm?t=n;** Rob Walker, "Ad Report Card: Cottonelle's Bizarre End Run" **http://slate.msn.com/?id=2061246;** Emily Nelson, "The Tissue That Tanked: Marketing Miscues Hobble a Much-Hyped Toilet Paper Product," *Wall Street Journal*, Classroom edition, September 2002; "Wet Toilet Paper Products Hit Bottom." The Associated Press, September 2, 2003.

glossary

Abrasive advertising: Advertising that is unpleasant or annoying.

Absolute threshold: The lowest level at which an individual can experience a sensation.

Acculturation: The process of learning a new or foreign culture.

Activation: Relating new data to old ones to make the new material more meaningful.

Actual self-image: How consumers in fact see themselves.

Adopter categories: A classification scheme that shows where a consumer stands in relation to other consumers in terms of time (or when the consumer adopts a new product).

Adoption process: A micro process that focuses on the stages through which an individual consumer passes when deciding to accept or reject a new product.

Advertising resonance: Wordplay, often used to create a double meaning, used in combination with a relevant picture.

Advertising wear-out: The reduction in attention and retention caused by overexposure to advertisements.

Affective involvement: Involvement at an emotional level in products.

Age subculture: Age subgroup of the population.

Approach object: An object that the consumer is directed toward.

Attitude: A learned predisposition to behave in a consistently favourable or unfavourable way with respect to a given object.

Attitude-toward-behaviour model: A model that proposes that a consumer's attitude toward a specific behaviour is a function of how strongly he or she believes that the action will lead to a specific (favourable or unfavourable) outcome.

Attitude-toward-object model: A model that proposes that a consumer's attitude toward a product or brand is a function of the presence of certain attributes and the consumer's evaluation of these attributes.

Attribution theory: A theory concerned with how people assign causality to events and form or alter their attitudes as an outcome of those attributions.

Attribution toward others: Consumers' perception that another person is responsible for either positive or negative product performance.

Audience profile: Psycho-demographic profile of the readers, viewers, or listeners of a medium.

Autonomic decisions: Family purchase decisions in which the final decision is made by either spouse individually.

Avoidance object: An object that the consumer is directed away from.

Baby boomers: Persons born between 1946 and 1964.

Behavioural learning theory: A theory that states that learning has happened when observable responses to external stimuli occur in a predictable way.

Benefit segmentation: Segmenting consumers according to the benefits of the product or service that is meaningful to them.

Brand community: A group of consumers whose social bonds are based on their interest in and usage of a brand.

Brand loyalty: Consistent preference and/or purchase of the same brand in a specific product/service category.

Brand personification: The ascription of specific personality-type traits or characteristics to brands.

Broad categorizers: People who make their choices from a wide range of alternatives.

Celebrity credibility: The audience's perception of both the celebrity's expertise and trustworthiness.

Central route to persuasion: The reaching of highly involved consumers through ads that focus on cognitive learning.

Class consciousness: An individual's sense of belonging to or identification with others of the same social class.

Classical conditioning: Conditioned learning or learning that occurs through the pairing of stimuli.

Closure: The need to complete incomplete patterns.

Cognitive age: An individual's perceived age (usually 10 to 15 years younger than his or her chronological age.

Cognitive dissonance theory: The discomfort or dissonance that consumers experience as a result of conflicting information.

Cognitive involvement: Involvement at a rational level in products that are seen as major purchases.

Cognitive learning: Learning based on mental activity or processing of information.

Cognitive theories of personality: A school of personality theories that see individual personality differences as differences in cognitive process, i.e., in how consumers process and react to information.

Communication: The transmission of a message from a sender to a receiver via a medium (or channel) of transmission.

Comparative advertising: Advertising that explicitly names or identifies a competitor for the purpose of claiming overall superiority or superiority on one or more attributes.

Compensatory decision rules: Decision rules in which consumers evaluate each brand in terms of each relevant attribute and then select the brand with the highest weighted score.

Composite variable indexes: The systematic combining of a number of socio-economic factors to form one overall measure of social-class standing.

Comprehension: The grasping of the intended message of an advertisement.

Concentrated marketing: Targeting just one segment with a unique marketing mix.

Conditioned learning: Learning that results when a stimulus is paired with another stimulus and draws the same response as that stimulus.

Conditioned stimuli: Stimuli or objects that are linked to a previously known and liked stimulus (i.e., unconditioned stimuli) to elicit the same response.

Conjunctive decision rule: A non-compensatory decision rule in which minimum criteria are established and brands that do not meet these minimum cutoffs are eliminated from further consideration.

Consumer-action group: A group that is dedicated to helping consumers make the right purchase decisions, use products and services, and improve the quality of their lives.

Consumer behaviour: The behaviour that consumers display in searching for, purchasing, using, evaluating, and disposing of products and services that they expect will satisfy their needs.

Consumer decision making: Two distinct but interlocking stages: the process (recognition of problem, pre-purchase search, and evaluation of alternatives) and its outcomes (purchase and post-purchase processes). Both stages are influenced by factors internal and external to the consumer.

Consumer decision rules or heuristics: Procedures used by consumers to facilitate brand (or other consumption-related) choices.

Consumer ethnocentrism: A consumer's predisposition to accept or reject foreign-made products.

Consumer fieldwork: Observational research by anthropologists of the behaviour of a small sample of people from a particular society.

Consumer imagery: The enduring perceptions or images of products, prices, and product quality that consumers develop using various stimuli.

Consumer innovativeness: The degree to which a consumer is receptive to new products, services, or practices.

Consumer innovators: People who are likely to be the first to try new products, services, or practices.

Consumer learning: The process by which individuals acquire the purchase and consumption knowledge and experience that they apply to future related behaviour.

Consumer materialism: A personality-like trait that distinguishes between individuals who regard possessions as essential to their identities and their lives and those for whom possessions are secondary.

Consumer profile: Psycho-demographic profile of the target market of a product or service.

Consumer research: Methodology used to study consumer behaviour.

Consumer socialization: The process by which children acquire the skills, knowledge, attitudes, and experiences necessary to function as consumers.

Consumption process: The input (consumption set and consuming style), process (using, possessing, collecting, and disposing), and output stages (feelings moods, attitudes, and behaviour) that follow the purchase decision.

Content analysis: A method for systematically analysing the content of verbal, written, and pictorial communication. Often used to study cultural values.

Continuous innovation: A new product that is an improved or modified version of an existing product; this is the least disruptive influence on consumer consumption patterns.

Controlled experiment: A causal research study in which some variables (independent variables) are manipulated in one group but not in another to ensure that any difference in the outcome (the dependent variable) is due to different treatments of the variable under study and not to extraneous factors.

Core values: Criteria or values that both affect and reflect the character of a society.

Counter-segmentation: Recombining two or more segments into a larger single segment that could be targeted with an individually tailored product or promotional campaign.

Cues: The stimuli that give direction to motives.

Culture: The sum total of learned beliefs, values, and customs that direct the consumer behaviour of members of a particular society.

Customer lifetime value (CLV): Profiles of customers drawn from internal data that show the net value of customers to the firm.

Customer satisfaction measurement: Quantitative or qualitative studies aimed at gauging customer satisfaction and its determinants.

Defence mechanisms: Methods of coping with the frustration that results when a person fails to achieve a goal.

Depth interview: A long (generally 30 minutes to an hour), unstructured interview between a respondent and a highly trained interviewer

Differential threshold, or j.n.d.: The minimal difference that can be detected between two similar stimuli.

Differentiated marketing: Targeting several segments with individual marketing mixes.

Diffusion of innovations: The framework for examining consumer acceptance of new products throughout the social system.

Diffusion process: A macro process concerned with the spread of a new product (an innovation) from its source to the consuming public.

Direct reference groups: Groups with which a person interacted on a direct basis, such as family and close friends.

Discontinuous innovation: A dramatically new product entry that requires the establishment of new consumption practices.

Disjunctive decision rule: A non-compensatory decision rule in which minimally acceptable cutoffs are set and any brand that meets or surpasses any cutoff is chosen.

Distributed learning: A learning schedule that is spread out to facilitate retention of the material.

Dynamically continuous innovation: A new product entry that is innovative enough to have some disruptive effects on established consumption practices.

Ego-defensive function: A component of the functional approach to attitude formation and change that suggests that consumers want to protect their self-concepts from inner feelings of doubt.

Elaboration likelihood model (ELM): A theory that suggests that a person's level of involvement during message processing is a critical factor in determining which route to persuasion is likely to be effective.

Emotional motives: Goals chosen according to personal or subjective criteria such as desire for social status.

Encoding: The process of choosing a word or visual image to represent a perceived object.

Enculturation: The process of learning one's own culture.

Enduring involvement: Involvement that is long-lasting; arises out of a sense of high personal relevance.

Evoked set: The set of brands that a consumer considers while making a choice.

Expected self-image: How consumers expect to see themselves at some specified future time.

Exploratory study: A small-scale study carried out to identify the critical issues that need to be examined in further detail.

Extended self: Consumers' use of possessions to confirm or extend their self-images.

Extensive problem solving: Consumer decision-making situations in which there are no established criteria for evaluating a product category or brands, or those in which the number of brands have not been narrowed to a small subset.

Extrinsic cues: Cues such as price or country of origin that are external to the product.

Family: Two or more persons related by blood, marriage, or adoption who live together.

Family branding: The marketing of an entire product line under the same brand name.

Family life cycle: Classification of families into distinct and significant stages.

Feedback: Verbal or non-verbal communication from the receiver of a message back to the sender.

Field observation: A cultural observation technique that observes behaviour that takes place in a natural environment (sometimes without the subject's knowledge).

Figure and ground: The organization of perceptions into background and dominant (or figure) relationships.

Focus group: A focused discussion of a product or any other subject of interest with a group of 8 to 10 respondents moderated by a trained researcher.

Foot-in-the-door technique: A theory of attitude change that suggests individuals form attitudes that are consistent with their own prior behaviour.

Formal communications source: A for-profit or not-for-profit organization that sends a message to the consumer.

Formal reference groups: Groups with formal membership structures and rules.

Gender subcultures: Subcultures based on gender or sex roles.

Generation X: People born between the years 1965 and 1977.

Generation Y: People born between the years 1977 and 1994.

Generic goals: Product categories or classes that a consumer seeks in order to fulfill his or her needs.

Geodemographic segmentation: A type of hybrid segmentation that uses geographic variables (e.g., postal codes or neighbourhoods) and demographic variables to segment markets.

Geographic segmentation: Dividing the market or consumers by location.

Gestalt psychology: The study of principles of how people organize or configure stimuli.

Gifting behaviour: The process of exchanging gifts between two or more individuals.

Goals: The sought-after results of motivated behaviour.

Grouping: The tendency to organize information into chunks or groups to facilitate memorization and recall.

Hedonic consumption: The need to obtain pleasure through the senses.

Husband-dominated decisions: Family purchase decisions in which the husband is the key decision maker.

Hybrid segmentation: Combining several segmentation variables to divide the market.

Ideal self-image: How consumers would like to see themselves.

Ideal social self-image: How consumers would like others to see them.

Identification influence: A type of reference group influence that occurs because we identify with, and have internalized, the group's values and behaviour.

Imagery: The ability of consumers to form mental pictures or images.

Impersonal communications: Communications through such mass media as television, newspapers, and magazines that are directed toward large audiences.

Index of Status Characteristics: A weighted measure of occupation, source of income, house type, and dwelling area.

Indirect reference groups: Groups with which a person does not come into face-to-face contact.

Inept set: Brands that the consumer is aware of but excludes from purchase consideration.

Inert set: Brands that the consumer is aware of but indifferent toward and hence does not consider while making a choice.

Informal communications source: Parents, friends, or other personal sources of communication.

Informal reference groups: Groups in which there are no official memberships or formal structures.

Informational influence: A type of reference group influence that occurs when a member of a reference group provides information that is used to make purchase decisions.

Innovation: A totally new product, service, idea or practice.

Institutional advertising: Advertising that is intended to promote a favourable company image rather than specific products.

Instrumental or operant conditioning: A theory which states that learning occurs through trial and error as a result of reinforcements received for specific behaviour.

Interactive communications: Impersonal or interpersonal communications that permit the audiences of communication messages to provide direct feedback.

Inter-category gifting: Gifts from an individual to a group or a group to an individual.

Interpersonal communications: Communications that occur directly between people by telephone, email, mail, or in person.

Interpersonal gifting: Gifts exchanged between individuals.

Interpretivism: A postmodernist approach to the study of consumer behaviour that focuses on the act of consuming rather than the act of buying.

Intra-group gifting: Gifts by a group to itself or its members.

Intra-personal gifting: Gifts given to ourselves.

Intrinsic cues: Physical characteristics of a product, such as size, colour, or flavour.

Involvement: The level of personal relevance that a consumer sees in a product.

Joint decisions: Family purchase decisions in which the final decision is made with equal involvement from both spouses.

Just noticeable difference (j.n.d.): The minimal difference that can be detected between two similar stimuli.

Knowledge function: A component of the functional approach to attitude formation and change that suggests that consumers have a strong need to know and understand the people and things with which they come into contact.

Latent motives: Motives that the consumer is either unaware of or unwilling to recognize.

Level of aspiration: New and higher order goals that individuals set for themselves.

Lexicographic decision rule: A non-compensatory rule in which attributes are first ranked in terms of importance, brands are compared on the most important attribute first, and the brand that scores the highest is chosen. The process is repeated if necessary.

Licensing: Affixing a well-known brand name to the products of other manufacturers.

Limited problem solving: Consumer decision-making situations in which basic criteria for product evaluation have been established, but fully established preferences about a select group of brands have not been set.

Long-term store: The retaining of processed information for extended periods of time.

Manifest motives: Motives that the consumer is aware of and willing to recognize.

Marketing concept: A consumer-oriented marketing philosophy that states that, to be successful, a company must determine the needs and wants of specific target markets and deliver the desired satisfaction better than the competition.

Marketing ethics: Designing marketing mixes and programs in such a way that negative consequences to consumers, employees, and society in general are avoided.

Marketing mix: The combination of product, price, promotion, and place (or distribution) that a company offers.

Market maven: A person whose influence stems from general knowledge and market expertise that lead to an early awareness of a wide range of new products and services.

Market segmentation: The process of dividing a market into distinct subsets of consumers with common needs or characteristics.

Maslow's hierarchy of needs: A theory of motivation which states that people move through five levels of needs—from physiological to self-actualization.

Massed learning: A learning schedule (or information presentation) that is compressed to facilitate fast learning.

Message framing: The designing of messages stress either the benefits to be gained by using the products or the benefits that will be lost if the product is not used.

Metaphor analysis: The use of one form of expression (e.g., pictures collages) to describe or represent feelings about a product or service.

Micromarketing: Highly regionalized marketing strategies that use promotional campaigns geared to local market needs.

Modelling: The process through which individuals learn behaviour by observing the behaviour of others and the consequences of such behaviour.

Motivation: The driving force within individuals that impels them to action

Motivational conflict: Conflict between two motives.

Motivational research: Qualitative research aimed at uncovering consumers' subconscious or hidden motivations.

Multi-attribute attitude models: Attitude models that examine the composition of consumer attitudes in terms of selected product attributes or beliefs.

Multiple selves: The different images that consumers have of themselves in response to different situations and different people that may cause them to react differently.

Multi-step flow of communication theory: A modification of the two-step theory, the multi-step theory views the interpersonal flow of communication as a multi-step process in which information flows both ways between opinion leaders and opinion receivers, and between opinion receivers and information receivers.

Narrow categorizers: People who limit their choices to a few safe alternatives.

Need for cognition: The personality trait that measures a person's craving for or enjoyment of thinking.

Need recognition: The realization by a consumer that there is a difference between his or her actual and desired states.

Negative motivation: A motive that drives a person away from an object.

Negative reinforcement: Outcomes that decrease the likelihood of a behaviour being repeated when the same stimuli are presented.

Neo-Freudian personality theories: A school of personality theory that stresses that social relationships are fundamental to the formation and development of personality.

Non-compensatory decision rules: Rules in which a positive evaluation of an attribute does not compensate for a negative evaluation of the same brand on another attribute.

Non-probability samples: Samples that are chosen by non-probability methods that lead to findings that may not be projectable to the entire population.

Normative influence: A type of influence that occurs when we conform to a group's norms or expectations in order to belong to that group.

Objective measures: Using selected demographic or socio-economic variables to measure a person's social class.

Objective price claims: Promoting a single discount level.

One-sided messages: Messages that state only the positive features or benefits of the product.

Operant or instrumental conditioning: A theory which states that learning occurs through trial and error as a result of reinforcements received for specific behaviour.

Opinion leader: The person in a word-of-mouth encounter who offers advice or information about a product or service.

Opinion leadership: The process by which one person (the opinion leader) informally influences the actions or attitudes of others, who may be opinion seekers or merely opinion recipients.

Opinion seekers: Individuals who actively seek information and advice about products from others.

Opponent process theory: A theory that states that an extreme positive (or negative) initial reaction will be followed by an extreme negative (or positive) reaction.

Optimum stimulation level: The level of stimulation that an individual considers to be ideal.

Order effect: The effect of the order of presentation of the ad; that is, whether it is placed first, last, or in the middle of a set of ads.

"Ought-to" self: Consists of traits or characteristics that an individual believes it is his or her duty or obligation to possess.

Participant-observer: A researcher who participates in a study without informing those who are being observed.

Perceived price: Consumers' perceptions of price as fair, high, or low.

Perceived quality: Consumers' perceptions of product quality.

Perceived risk: The uncertainty that consumers face when they cannot foresee the consequences of their purchase decisions.

Perception: The process by which an individual selects, organizes, and interprets stimuli into a meaningful and coherent picture of the world.

Perceptual blocking: The subconscious screening out of stimuli that are threatening or inconsistent with our needs, values, beliefs, or attributes.

Perceptual mapping: A technique used to determine how consumers perceive a company's products, either in relation to other products or in regard to key attributes.

Peripheral route to persuasion: The use of passive learning processes to reach consumers in a low-involvement situation.

Personality: Those inner psychological characteristics that both determine and reflect how a person responds to his or her environment.

Physiological needs: Innate or biogenic needs, such as the need for food.

Positioning: Developing a distinct image for the product or service in the mind of the consumer in order to differentiate the offering from those of competitors.

Positive motivation: A motive that drives a person toward an object.

Positive reinforcement: Outcomes that increase the likelihood of behaviour being repeated when the same stimuli are presented.

Positivism: A research approach that regards consumer behaviour as an applied science and focuses primarily on consumer decision making.

Post-purchase cognitive dissonance: The discomfort or dissonance that consumers experience after purchase about whether or not they made the right decision.

Prepotent need: The need or motive that serves as the triggering mechanism which moves a consumer to action.

Pre-purchase search: The stage in consumer decision making in which the consumer perceives a need and actively seeks out information about products that will help satisfy that need.

Price-quality relationship: Perceived relationship between the price of a product and its quality.

Primary data: Data collected specifically for the purposes of a particular research study.

Primary research: Original research aimed at collecting primary data.

Priming: The desire for more of a stimulus (or product) that occurs when a person is exposed to small amounts of it.

Probability samples: Samples in which respondents are chosen by some probability technique that leads to findings that are projectable to the entire population.

Product concept: The assumption that consumers will buy the product that offers them the highest quality, the best performance, and the most features.

Production concept: The assumption that consumers are mostly interested in product availability at low prices.

Product-specific goals: Specific brands that a consumer seeks in order to fulfill his or her needs.

Projective techniques: Motivational research methods designed to tap the underlying (and often unconscious) motives of individuals.

Psychoanalytic theory: A theory of personality built on the premise that unconscious needs or drives, especially sexual and other biological drives, are at the heart of human motivation.

Psychographic segmentation: Segmenting consumers on the basis of their activities, interests, and opinions.

Psychological (or psychogenic) needs: Acquired needs learned in response to our cultural environment.

Psychological noise: Barriers to message reception such as competing advertising messages or distracting thoughts.

Psychological reactance: Motivational arousal due to a threat to behavioural freedom.

Psychological segmentation: Segmenting the market by means of intrinsic or inner qualities (e.g., motivation, personality) of consumers.

Publicity: Messages that appear in space or time usually reserved for editorial messages, usually through public relations efforts by the firm.

Purchase behaviour: The outcome of a consumer's decision-making process, including brand, store, and payment option choices.

Purchase pal: An information source who accompanies a consumer on shopping trips; may or may not be an opinion leader.

Qualitative research: Research methods (interviews, focus groups, projective techniques, etc.) that are more subjective and that try to explain the act of consumption and hidden motivations for consumption.

Quantitative research: Research methods (surveys, observation, and experiments) that are empirical and descriptive, and that describe consumer behaviour, explain the effects of marketing inputs on consumer behaviour, or predict consumer behaviour.

Racio-ethnic subcultures: Subcultures based on race (genetically imparted physiognomical features such as colour of skin) and/or ethnicity (which includes race, origin or ancestry, language, and religion).

Rational motives: Goals chosen according to totally objective criteria, such as quantity or price.

Reasoning: The highest form of cognitive learning, which involves creative thinking.

Recall tests: Unaided recall tests in which consumers are asked if they have read a specific magazine (or watched a specific television show) and can remember any ads from it.

Recognition test: Aided recall test in which consumers are shown an ad and asked if they remember seeing it and remember its key points.

Reference group: A person or group that serves as a point of comparison (or reference) for an individual in forming either general or specific values, attitudes, or a specific guide for behaviour.

Reference price: The price that a consumer uses as a basis for comparison in judging another price.

Regional subcultures: Groups that identify with the regional or geographical areas in which they live.

Reinforcement: A positive or negative outcome that influences the likelihood that a behaviour will be repeated in response to the same cue or stimulus.

Relationship marketing: Marketing programs aimed at creating strong, lasting relationships with a core group of customers by making them feel a personal connection to the business.

Reliability: The degree to which a measurement instrument is consistent in what it measures.

Religious subcultures: People who are followers of a particular religion (e.g., Christianity, Judaism, Islam, Hinduism).

Repositioning: Attempting to change the image that consumers have of a product.

Reputational measures: Using selected community informants to make judgments about which social class other members of the community belong to.

Response: How individuals react to a drive or cue.

Retrieval: The process by which we recover information from long-term storage.

Ritual: A type of symbolic activity consisting of a series of steps (multiple behaviours) that take place in a fixed sequence and are repeated over time.

Ritualistic behaviour: Any behaviour that is made into a ritual.

Rokeach Value Survey: A self-administered inventory consisting of 18 terminal values (or personal goals) and 18 instrumental values (or ways of reaching personal goals).

Rote learning: Learning of concepts or ideas through simple repetition.

Routinized-response behaviour: Decision-making situations in which consumers have experience with the product category and a well-established set of criteria with which to evaluate brands they are considering.

Schema: The whole package of associations brought to mind when a cue is activated.

Secondary data: Data collected for purposes other than problems under study.

Secondary research: Research aimed at locating secondary data.

Selective perception: The conscious and subconscious screening out of stimuli by consumers through selective exposure, selective attention, perceptual defence, and perceptual blocking.

Self-gifts: Gifts to ourselves.

Self-perception theory: A theory which suggests that consumers develop attitudes by reflecting on their own behaviour.

Selling concept: The assumption that a marketer's primary goal should be to sell the product(s) that it has unilaterally decided to produce.

Sensation: The immediate and direct response of the sensory organs to stimuli.

Sensory adaptation: Getting used to certain sensations or becoming accommodated to a certain level of stimulation.

Sensory receptors: The human organs (the eyes, ears, nose, mouth, and skin) that receive sensory inputs.

Sensory store: The storing of sensory input for a few seconds in memory.

Sex role: The traits that are attributed to males and females.

Shaping: The reinforcement of pre-purchase behaviour to lead the consumers slowly toward making a purchase.

Shopping group: Two or more people who shop together, whether for food, for clothing, or simply to pass the time.

Short-term store or working memory: The processing of information and its short-term storage.

Single-variable index: A measure of social class that uses just one socio-economic variable.

Situational involvement: Short-term involvement in a product or purchase of low personal relevance.

Sleeper effect: The tendency of communications to lose the impact of source credibility over time.

Social class: The division of members of a society into a hierarchy of distinct status classes, so that members of each class have the same relative status and members of all other classes have either more or less status.

Social comparison theory: A social-psychological concept which states that individuals compare their own material possessions with those owned by others in order to determine their relative social standing.

Socialization of family members: A process of imparting to children the basic values and modes of behaviour consistent with the culture.

Social self-image: How consumers feel others see them.

Social status: The amount of status the members of that class have in comparison with members of other social classes.

Societal marketing concept: A philosophy of marketing which requires that all marketers adhere to principles of social responsibility in the marketing of their goods and services.

Socio-cultural segmentation: Using group and cultural variables to segment consumers.

Socio-economic Status Score: A measure using three basic socio-economic variables: occupation, family income, and educational attainment.

Source credibility: The apparent honesty and objectivity of the source of communication.

Stages in the adoption process: The process by which an individual moves from product awareness to interest, evaluation, trial, and finally, adoption.

Stimulus discrimination: The ability to differentiate (or discriminate between) similar stimuli.

Stimulus generalization: Making the same response to similar stimuli.

Subcultural interaction: The interaction between the various subcultural memberships of consumers and its impact on their behaviour.

Subculture: A distinct cultural group that exists as an identifiable segment within a larger, more complex society.

Subjective measures: Asking people to estimate their own social-class position.

Subliminal perception: Unconscious awareness of weak stimuli.

Surrogate buyers: Professional buyers who help buyers purchase products; often, they act as opinion leaders.

Surrogate indicators: Attributes that are used as indicators of another attribute.

Symbol: Anything that stands for something else.

Symbolic group: A group that a person identifies with by adopting its values, attitudes, and behaviour despite knowing that he or she cannot belong to that group.

Targeting: The selection of one or more segments to focus on with a distinct marketing mix.

Tensile price claims: Promoting a range of price discounts for an entire product line, department, or store.

Theory of reasoned action: A comprehensive theory of the interrelationship among attitudes, intentions, and behaviour.

Traditional family life cycle: A progression of stages through which many families pass, starting with bachelorhood, moving on to marriage, then to family growth (with the birth of children), to family contraction, and ending with the dissolution of the basic unit.

Trait theory: A theory of personality that focuses on the measurement of specific psychological characteristics.

Tri-component model: An attitude model consisting of three parts: a cognitive (knowledge) part, an affective (feeling) part, and a conative (behavioural) part.

Two-sided messages: Messages that state the positive and some negative features or benefits of the product.

Two-step flow of communication theory: A theory that portrays opinion leaders as direct receivers of information from impersonal mass-media sources who in turn transmit (and interpret) this information to the masses.

Unconditioned stimuli: Stimuli that consumers already know and like.

Utilitarian function: A component of the functional approach to attitude formation and change which suggests that consumers hold certain attitudes partly because of the brand.

Validity: The degree to which a measurement instrument accurately measures what it claims to measure.

Value-expressive function: A component of the functional approach to attitude formation and change that suggests that attitudes express consumers' general values, life styles, and outlook.

Verbalizers: Consumers who prefer written or verbal information.

Viral marketing: Encouraging consumers to spread a marketing message to others; can lead to exponential growth in message exposure.

Virtual groups: Groups that exist by virtue of using the internet as the medium of communication.

Visualizers: Consumers who prefer visual information.

Weber's law: A law that states that the j.n.d. between two stimuli depends on the intensity of the first stimulus.

Wife-dominated decisions: Family purchase decisions in which the wife is the key decision maker.

Word-of-mouth communications: Informal conversations about a product or service.

Company Index

Note: Italicized page numbers indicate figures/tables.

A

AB Electrolux, 451
Abercrombie & Fitch, 327
A.C. Nielsen, 531
Accenthealth.com, 417
ACDelco, 218
Acer, 490
A.C.Nielsen Research, 49
ActiveBuddy, 417
Acuvue, 220, 221
Aeroplan, 205
Air Canada, 15–16, 66, 193, 213
Alimentation Couche-Tard, 528
Allure, 377
AM 1320, 336
AM 1470, 336
Amazon.com, 214, 231
America Online, 378, 427
American Academy of Audiology, *536*
American Audiology Association, 534
American Demographics, *285*
American Express, 11, 164, 249, 514
American Girl, 516
American Girl magazine, 387
Anheuser-Busch, 232
Apple Computer, 145, 260
Apprenticeship and Industry Training
    Board, 533
ARCthe.hotel, 72
Arm & Hammer, 164, 166
Aston Marin, 343
Automotive Parts Manufacturers
    Association, 533
Avon Products, 249, 339, 377

B

Baby Gap, 52
*Balian's Outdoor and Nature
    PhotoWorld*, 422
Banana Repubic, 52
The Bay, 219, 497, 498
Bayer, 107
B.C. Dairy Foundation, 253, 265, 266
Beiersdorf Canada, 433
Bell ExpressVu, 154
Bell Mobility, 254
Benetton, 161
Best Buy Canada, 514
Better Homes and Gardens, 387
Big Fat Inc., 424
bigplanet.com, 378
Blockbuster Video, 313, 428
BMW, 114, 226, 306, 329, 343, 355, 461
BOSE, 429
Boston Consulting Group, 355
Boston Pizza, 394

Boy's Life, 387
Brewers Association of Canada, 144
Brown Forman, 117
Buckley's, 206
Budweiser, 359
Burger King, 216
Business Depot, 497
Business Development Bank of
    Canada, 34
Business Society, 371
Buy.com, 231

C

Cadillac Fairview, 472
Campbell Soup Company, 56, 188, 309,
    486
Campbell's of Canada, 250
Canada Post, 33
Canada Tourism, 243
Canadian Academy of Audiology, *536*,
    537
Canadian Airlines, 15
Canadian Audiology Association, 534
Canadian Bankers Association, 27, 49, 51
Canadian Beef Information Centre, 244
Canadian Cattlemen's Association
    (CCA), 244
Canadian Corporate Newsnet, 34
Canadian Dental Association, 175
Canadian Deposit Insurance Corporation
    (CDIC), 135
Canadian Geographic, 128, *129*, 252
Canadian Hearing Society, 534
Canadian Imperial Bank of
    Commerce, 233
Canadian Inter@ctive Reid Report, 475
Canadian Living, 285
Canadian Tire, 323, 372
Canadian Tourism Commission
    (CTC), 265, 269, 523, 524
Cartier, 343
Catelli, 393, 394
Cavendish Farms, 493, 494
CBC, 532
CBCA: Canadian Business and Current
    Affairs, 34
Celestial Seasonings, Inc., 117, 118, 218,
    220
Certified General Accountants of
    Canada, 371
Certified Organic Associations of British
    Columbia, 531
Chanel, 343
charityguide.org, 297
charitynavigator.org, 297
Chevrolet, 418

Chevron, 529
childfree.net, 406
Chronicle-Herald, 67
CIA, 33
Cirque du Soleil, 249
Claritas, 63, 129, 130
Clorox, 217
COABC Market Survey, *531*
Coastal Forest and Lumber
    Association, 198
Coca-Cola Company, 86, 90, 119, 150,
    195, 245, 464
Coke Canada, 464
Colgate-Palmolive, 98, 165, 166
Comedy Central, 434
Compaq, 490, 497
Competition Bureau, 255
CompuServe, 441
Conference Board of Canada, 34, 533
Conservative Party, 66
Consumer Panel of Canada, 34
Consumer Reports, 96, 248, 267, 432, 467,
    469, 470
Cosmopolitan, 377
Cossette Communication-Marketing, 494
countrycollector.com, 507
CTV, 411
Customatix.com, 473

D

Daffy's, 424
Dell Computer, 16, 197, 466, 495
Delta Hotels, 193
Details, 377
Diesel, 246
Dieticians of Canada, 249
Digital Ad Network, 173
Discovery Channel, 173
Disney. *See* Walt Disney Co.
Dodge, 200
Dove, 236
DragonSurf.com, 378
Duke Energy Corporation, 63
Duncan Hines, 90
Duracell, 199
Dynamism.com, 495, 496
Dyson, 451

E

E-Lab LLC, 304
eBay, 46, 495
Eddie Bauer, 63, 129
Elections Ontario, 527
emode.com, 127
Enduron, 427
Environics Group, 63, 130–131, *133*, 281,
    299, 328

Name Index

Note: Italicized page numbers indicate figures/tables.

Subject Index

Note: Italicized page numbers indicate figures/tables; key terms and the pages on which they are defined are indicated in bold.